Computers Today

Computers Today

Donald H. Sanders
Educational Consultant

McGraw-Hill Book Company
New York St. Louis San Francisco Auckland Bogotá Hamburg
Johannesburg London Madrid Mexico Montreal New Delhi
Panama Paris São Paulo Singapore Sydney Tokyo Toronto

COMPUTERS TODAY

5 6 7 8 9 0 K G P K G P 8 9 8 7 6 5 4 3

ISBN 0-07-054681-9

This book was set in Times Roman by York Graphic Services, Inc.
The editors were James E. Vastyan, Barbara Brooks, and Edwin Hanson;
the designer was Merrill Haber;
the production supervisor was Dennis J. Conroy.
The drawings were done by Fine Line Illustrations, Inc.
Kingsport Press, Inc., was printer and binder.

Photo research was performed by Inge King.

Library of Congress Cataloging in Publication Data

Sanders, Donald H.
    Computers today.

    Includes index.
    1. Electronic data processing.   2. Computers.
I. Title.
QA76.S289   1983   001.64   82-4626
ISBN 0-07-054681-9

About the Author

DONALD H. SANDERS is the author of six books about computers—their uses and their impact—spanning 20 years. His books have been widely used by training programs in industry and government as well as by colleges and universities.

After receiving degrees from Texas A & M University and the University of Arkansas, Dr. Sanders was a professor at the University of Texas at Arlington, at Memphis State University, and at Texas Christian University.

In addition to his books, Dr. Sanders has contributed articles to journals such as *Data Management, Automation, Banking, Journal of Small Business Management, Journal of Retailing,* and *Advanced Management Journal.* He has also encouraged his graduate students to contribute computer-related articles to national periodicals, and over 70 of these articles have been published. Dr. Sanders is chairperson of the ''Computers and Data Processing'' Subject Examination Committee, CLEP Program, College Entrance Examination Board, Princeton, N. J.

Contents in Brief

Contents

module 1 Background
Computers Today: What They Are and What They Do **1**

module 2 Hardware
Computer Hardware Systems   105

5

module 3 Programming
Computer Software Concepts   315

module 4 Systems

Information Systems Concepts 459

module 5 Social Impact

Computers and Society 549

Preface

At the time this jingle was being sung on radio in the mid-1970s, most computers were controlled by organizations. Only a few microcomputers existed, and people generally used machines with "little rubber feet" for their personal needs. The situation has changed more today than anyone could have imagined 10 years ago. Millions of personal computers are now available, and computer usage will explode in the years ahead.

Ogden's "Law" says that "The sooner you fall behind, the more time you have to catch up." Anyone (meaning any of today's students) who falls behind in learning about computers may spend plenty of time—perhaps a lifetime—trying to catch up. An essential outcome of education in the next decade must be computer literacy. Computer literacy is "knowing" computers. It's knowing what they are, what they can and cannot do, how they are put to work, and how their use can affect society. It's vital, of course, to continue to educate the many thousands of people who will become computer specialists. And this book certainly contains the information required to introduce these future specialists to the subject of computers and data processing. But computer literacy is now needed by *all* students so that they will not be intimidated by daily life, but will instead feel a sense of belonging in a computer-rich society.

The Purpose of Computers Today

This is the sixth in a series of computer data processing books that I've written. Several of these titles have appeared in multiple editions and have been translated into German, French, and Spanish versions. And hundreds of thousands of copies have been used in college courses and industry/government training programs. Drawing on two decades of experience, I've designed *Computers Today* for use in an introductory one-term course in computer data processing. No data processing or mathematical background is required or assumed.

Computers Today is an ambitious title for a book because it suggests a breadth of contemporary computer/data processing information not found in other texts. Some introductory books focus only on the constructs of a particular programming language. Some maintain this specific language focus, but also introduce program development concepts. Some place the emphasis on computing equipment and then show how this equipment may be programmed to solve problems. And some concentrate primarily on computer/data processing applications and the resulting social impact of these applications.

The purpose of *Computers Today*, however, is to acquaint readers with *all four* of the following related areas of knowledge required for computer literacy:

1. **Computers Themselves.** The organization, function, capabilities, and limitations of the equipment in modern computer systems of all sizes is presented.

2. **What Computers Do.** Common data processing uses or applications of computers in today's society are treated. The focus is generally on business data processing applications, but many of the selected applications are also processed by not-for-profit organizations such as governments, hospitals, and schools.

3. **How Computers Are Put to Work.** The techniques used in the analysis and design of information systems are explained, and the procedures that are used to prepare programs are outlined. Programs for a number of the common data processing applications that have

been identified earlier are then coded using the constructs of the BASIC programming language.

4. **The Social Impact of Computers at Work.** The ways in which people and organizations may be affected by present and future computer applications are presented.

Flexible Organization: Delivery of the Promise

Computers Today is specifically designed and organized to meet the needs of courses with different subject emphases and with different presentation sequences. This flexibility is possible because *Computers Today* is organized into five modules. The first Background Module presents an overview of *all four areas* of study mentioned above. The essence of the knowledge required for computer literacy is presented in the four chapters of this module. Chapter 1 introduces readers to computer hardware and stored program concepts. Chapter 2 presents an introduction to common data processing applications. A summary of the system analysis, design, and program preparation steps needed to put the computer to work processing applications is given in Chapter 3. And the social impact of computers on people and organizations is previewed in Chapter 4.

These first four chapters should be covered in sequence. As the detailed chart below shows, however, once these chapters have been completed, users of *Computers Today* can turn *immediately to any of the remaining modules* to meet whatever sequence and depth requirements are needed in a particular course.

As you can see, Modules 2 through 5 build on and add further detail to the topics first introduced in Chapters 1 through 4 of Module 1. Thus, a course can easily be structured so that Chapters 12 through 15 in the Programming Module immediately follow the completion of Chapter 4. Or, readers may be more motivated to study computer data processing if some time is spent on the Social Impact chapters (19 through 21) after Chapter 4 is completed. Of course, it's also logical to consider computing equipment in more detail (Chapters 5 through 11), and then move to the Systems Module (Chapters 16 through 18) prior to studying programming concepts. But you get the idea: *Computers Today* gives you the flexibility to choose the sequence that is best for your needs. It also permits you to vary the depth of the material covered in a one-term course. Although it's unlikely that you'll be able to cover all 21 chapters in a single term, you'll have the freedom to select those topics that are most appropriate for your needs.

One final note on organization: Some texts have promised modular flexibility in the past and have failed to deliver on this promise. This failure is common enough, in fact, to prompt one surprised reviewer of *Computers Today* to remark: "You know, when you finish Chapter 4 you *really can* go to any module!"

MODULE	CHAPTERS	MODULE NAME	PREREQUISITE MODULE
1 BACKGROUND	1–4	Computers Today: What They Are and What They Do	None
2 HARDWARE	5–11	Computer Hardware Systems	1
3 PROGRAMMING	12–15	Computer Software Concepts	1
4 SYSTEMS	16–18	Information System Concepts	1
5 SOCIAL IMPACT	19–21	Computers and Society	1

Programming Examples: Relief from the Unrelated

In addition to its workable modular flexibility, *Computers Today* incorporates another unique feature: *integrated programming examples*. This innovative approach introduces readers to the methodology and techniques of computer programming. The programming examples used in most texts involve a series of unrelated data processing applications at a number of separate businesses. Since readers are often unfamiliar with common business systems and with the interrelated nature of the outputs produced by those systems, these examples are often viewed as random and boring exercises. To counter this problem, a new business enterprise created by two college students is presented and discussed in the early chapters of *Computers Today*. The information needs of this new business—R-K Enterprises—are outlined in a number of applications examples in Chapter 2. (These examples include order entry/shipping/billing, sales compensation, sales analysis, inventory control, word processing, the preparation of mailing labels, and other topics.) An analysis and redesign of the student entrepreneurs' order entry/shipping/billing system is presented in Chapter 3. This theme of an "actual" business with realistic interrelated data processing needs is then carried to Chapters 12 through 14 in the Programming Module. Readers will see how the R-K Enterprises' applications presented in Chapter 2 are analyzed, flowcharted, and coded in the BASIC language. A progression of billing programs, beginning with simple examples and continuing on to more complex cases is discussed, charted, and coded. Multiple sales compensation programs and sales analysis programs are similarly handled, as are the inventory control and mailing label programs for R-K Enterprises. Creating a realistic enterprise that students can identify with, discussing a number of the most common applications that such a business must process, and then carrying these interrelated applications through the analysis, flowcharting, and BASIC coding steps is unique to *Computers Today*.

Other Features and Aids to Learning

Included among the numerous additional features and learning aids found in *Computers Today* are:

▌ Hundreds of *full-color* photographs, drawings, and illustrations are provided. Since these up-to-date pictures and diagrams often show computers in realistic environments, they are effective in visually conveying some of the excitement found in the use of computers today.

▌ A *vignette* that highlights some aspect of the contents of a chapter, and a *chapter outline* are used to open each chapter. Each vignette/outline is then followed by a *Looking Ahead* section that previews the chapter contents and lists the *Learning Objectives* for each chapter.

▌ *Feedback and Review* sections are presented in every chapter to reinforce reader understanding. A variety of formats are used in these sections.

▌ *Boxed inserts* are included in each chapter to provide applications, cases, and items of interest to support chapter material. These inserts are effective in stimulating discussions.

▌ A *Closer Look* reading to provide additional information follows each chapter. These readings also stimulate discussion and permit more in-depth coverage of selected topics.

▌ At the end of each chapter is a *Looking Back* section that summarizes the main points found in the chapter, a listing of chapter *Key Terms and Concepts* that includes the page number where the terms and concepts are first mentioned, a number of *questions for review and discussion*, and the *answers* to the Feedback and Review sections found in the chapter.

▌ Up-to-date chapters on CPU, data entry, secondary storage, and output concepts are followed in the Hardware Module by acclaimed chapters on the uses and characteristics of actual micros, minis, mainframes, and supercomputers, data communication and distributed data processing networks, and word processing and electronic mail/message systems.

▌ An overview of programming languages is presented in Chapter 13, and an R-K Enterprises' application is coded in several different languages. This gives readers an idea of language differences prior to being introduced to BASIC in Chapter 14.

▌ Topics that can often be intimidating to readers of introductory texts—e.g., system analysis, design, and implementation considerations and the concepts and functions of operating systems, data base management systems, and management information systems—are presented in a nonthreatening way in Chapters 15 through 18.

▌ The chapters in the Social Impact Module give readers a balanced presentation of the possible positive and negative effects that computer usage may have on the people and organizations in a society.

▌ A *Glossary* of the terms frequently found in the computer/data processing field is included at the back of the book.

Supplements for Computers Today

Several supplements have been prepared to make the *Computers Today* package a more complete teaching/learning tool. They include:

▌ *Inside Computers Today.* This student Study Guide is designed to provide extensive self-tests for each corresponding chapter in *Computers Today.* Each Study Guide chapter contains learning objectives; a chapter overview and summary; and varied self-test sections including key term matching, multiple choice, true or false, and completion exercises. Answers for all exercises are included in the Study Guide. *Inside Computers Today* is an instrument planned to reinforce and integrate text concepts. It is designed for success—no "tricky" questions have been included intentionally. Successfully completing the Study Guide exercises should increase the confidence of all levels of students. It is a straightforward, no-frills, self-testing implement written for students, not for teachers.

▌ *Instructor's Resource Kit.* The components of this Kit provide instructors with extensive support

materials for teaching a course with *Computers Today.* The following supplements are included:

1. *Instructor's Manual.* Beyond supplying resource material for each chapter of the text, this Manual contains FORTRAN, COBOL, and Pascal programs dealing with R-K Enterprises applications. (The logic of each program is analyzed in text Chapter 12.) These programs use the same input data and produce the same output results as the BASIC programs discussed in Chapter 14 of the text. Anyone wishing to consider an additional language or an alternative to BASIC will likely find the needed programs in this section. The manual also supplies transparency masters of selected text illustrations.

2. *Overhead Transparencies.* A set of 48 color transparencies serves as a visual classroom aid which can be used to further explain text concepts.

3. *Test Bank.* This set of more than 2000 questions covers the important ideas and definitions in *Computers Today.* The Test Bank contains, for each text chapter, two different quizzes—"A" and "B" sets—plus an extensive set of Additional Questions, which may be used as a separate test (Quiz C) or from which you may supplement the A and B Quiz items. No questions from the text or the Study Guide are repeated in the Test Bank. Finally, the Test Bank is available for use with the Examiner Test Generation System.

Acknowledgments

It's customary for authors to conclude a preface by acknowledging the contributions and suggestions received from numerous sources. This is particularly appropriate in the case of *Computers Today* because a full-color project of this scope just doesn't happen without the input of many people.

The authorities who responded to a preliminary questionnaire and helped shape the content and organization of *Computers Today*, and the professionals who reviewed the manuscript and made many helpful suggestions are acknowledged separately following this Preface.

Another word of thanks must go to the equipment manufacturers, publishers, and photo agencies who furnished materials, excerpts, and photographs for this text. Their individual contributions are acknowledged in the body of the book.

The final tribute and greatest appreciation, however, is reserved for these few: to Barbara Brooks, a super developmental editor whose creative ideas and craftsmanship are visible on almost every page; to Rob Fry, whose editorial skills seem to be limitless (now you know how Rob Brooks, an R-K Enterprises' partner, was named); to Mel Haber, Inge King, and Dennis Conroy, whose design, photo research, and production efforts were a pleasant surprise to a critical author; to Ed Hanson, Jim Vastyan, and Charles Stewart for their editorial support; to Anne Green for her artistic talents; to Gary D. Sanders, University of Illinois, and Craig Elders, Texas Christian University, for their program contributions and suggestions; and to Joyce Sanders for her suggestions and encouragement.

Donald H. Sanders

Acknowledgments

Ms. Felicia Abramowitz
Monroe Business Institute

Professor Charles Allen
Northeast Missouri State University

Mr. Robert Baker
Marconi Technical Center

Professor David Barton
University of Missouri

Professor William L. Bonney
Hudson Valley Community College

Professor Robert D. Brown, Jr.
University of Georgia

Professor Gilbert Chang
San Jose State University

Dr. Jon Clark
North Texas State University

Professor W. Cornette
Southwest Missouri State University

Professor Stephen L. Davies
Golden Gate University

Professor Mary C. Durkin
St. Petersburg Junior College

Professor E. Allen Eckhard
San Jose State University

Professor George Fowler
Texas A&M University

Clinton P. Fuelling
Ball State University

Professor Gary Green
University of Nebraska

Professor Alice Griswold
University of Dubuque

Professor Anthony Halaris
Iona College

Professor William Harrison
Oregon State University

Professor Hugh Juergans
University of Wisconsin

Professor Dorothy Landis
California State University

Professor Hollis Lattimer
Tarrant County Junior College

Professor Marilyn Moore
Indiana University

Professor Charles McNernay
Bergen Community College

Professor William O'Hare
Prince George's Community College

Professor Robert F. Palank
St. Louis Community College

Professor Opal Pelton
Nashville State Technical Institute

Mr. Don Proia
Harry Ells High School

Mr. Stephen Radin
College of Staten Island

Professor Steve Rados
Purdue University, Calumet Campus

Professor Eugene Rothswohl
University of San Diego

Professor Maria S. Rynn
Northern Virginia Community College

Professor Joseph Safer
Fresno City College

Professor Alfred St. Onge
Springfield Technical Community College

Professor William A. Shannon, Jr.
Miami Dade Community College

Professor Kathleen Short
Modesto Junior College

Professor Vincent Skudrna
Bernard M. Baruch College

Professor Donald M. Springer
  University of Portland

Professor Robert M. Stern
  Rochester Institute of Technology

Professor Richard Westfall
  Cabrillo College

Professor David C. Whitney
  San Francisco State University

Professor Gary Wicklund
  University of Iowa

Professor Judith Wilson
  University of Cincinnati

Mr. Robert Wright
  NCR Corporation

Computers Today

module 1 Background

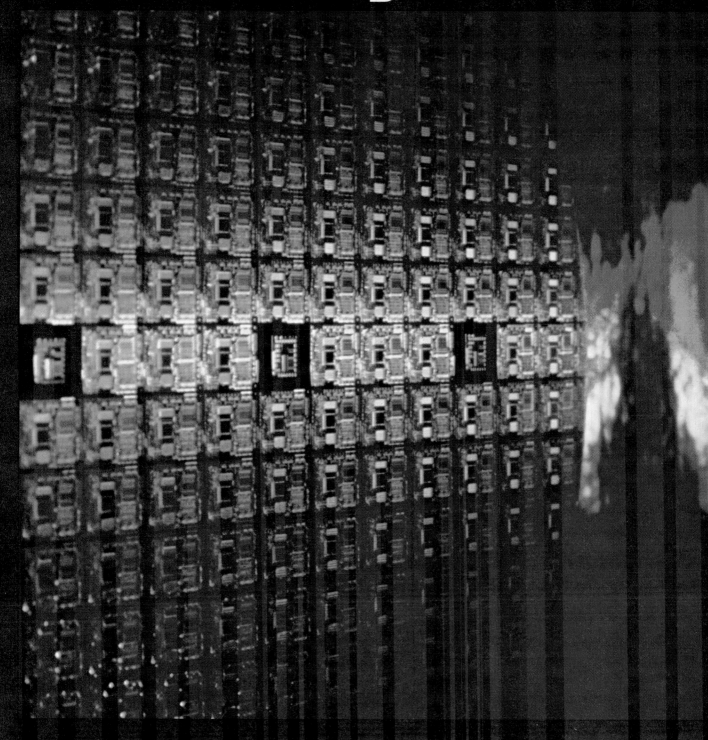

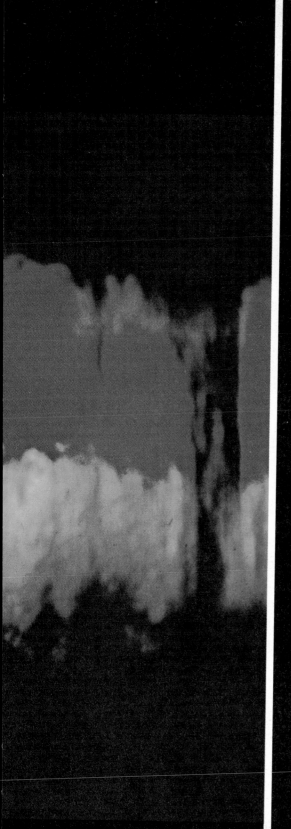

Computers Today
What They Are
and What They Do

To be an educated citizen today, you must be acquainted not only with computers themselves, but also with what computers do, how they are put to work, and the impact of their use on individuals and organizations in a society. An overview of all these topics is presented in the chapters of this Background Module. Each of the four remaining modules in the book will then consider one of these topics in greater detail.

The chapters included in this Background Module are:

1. Computer Concepts: An Introduction
2. Computers at Work: An Overview
3. Putting the Computer to Work: A Summary
4. The Impact of Computers at Work: A Preview

Just as yesterday's room-sized computers have been replaced by today's single chips, so will the multiple boards that make up a large computer today be replaced in the next decade by a single superchip. (Courtesy Intel Corporation)

chapter 1

Computer Concepts
An Introduction

NO ESCAPE

After months of reading, writing and talking about computers, it was time to take a vacation. I needed to get away, preferably to some remote part of the globe where a computer salesperson or the like had yet to plant the corporate banner in the sand, and the natives still thought that an apple was something you ate. Automation may be an enthralling subject, but enough was enough.

A friend suggested a fishing village on the northern coast of Massachusetts. I pictured lobster dinners; rocky beaches; craggy pipe-smoking "old salts" telling harrowing tales of storms on the North Sea. Not a mainframe or a mini in sight. We were on our way.

The first indication that escape might not be all that easy came as we were passing by Newport, R.I., where the America's Cup trials were in progress. I had visions of stopping off to admire some of the town's fabled old mansions and perhaps watch the racing. As we approached Newport, however, we picked up one of the local stations on the car radio. The announcer was interviewing a computer type who talked about the integral role computers play today in ocean racing. Scratch Newport from the itinerary.

In the fishing village we stopped at an inn that the travel guide described as quaint and charming. While checking in, I discovered the manager doing some paperwork in his office just off the lobby. The office had a big picture window looking out on the Atlantic and a fireplace. There was also something that looked suspiciously familiar sitting on the manager's desk. "Is that. . . ?" I asked apprehensively.

Airline passengers write their own plane tickets automatically at this one-stop travel center located at LaGuardia Airport in New York. The self-service ticketing and checking system is based on intelligent-terminal technology. (Courtesy Honeywell Information Systems)

"My new micro," he said in a New England accent as thick as clam chowder. "Makes life a lot easier."

I told him I was sure it did and fled to my room for the purpose of extracting a bottle of bourbon from my bag posthaste.

The following morning I picked up *The Boston Globe* to read about the Red Sox and found not one, not two, but three computer-related stories in the paper's business section. I chucked the newspaper and turned on the "Today" show, where a computer science professor was being interviewed. The professor had devised a program to pick the Miss America winner in advance. Last year he'd been right on the money. This year he liked Miss Oklahoma, I think it was. Bert Parks, where are you when we need you?

We went to the beach. The sun and sea were terrific. After two days I began to feel remotely human again. Then, on Monday a man I vaguely recognized said hello as my wife and I were shopping in one of the local stores. He and I had been classmates in college. He'd married twice, had four kids and owned his own business. "Software," he explained, looking very prosperous.

"That's great," I told him.

"Maybe we could have dinner," he suggested.

I lied and told him we had another appointment. My wife later said I had been rude. I told her she didn't understand me and turned on the U.S. Open tennis matches. Between games IBM ran an ad about a dairy farmer who was buying his first computer. "My cows will be tickled pink," he told the IBM salesman.

"Moooo," I said.

"What was that?" my wife asked from the bathroom.

"Nothing," I told her, and went back to watching the tennis.

—Laton McCartney, *output,* September 1980, p. 6. Reprinted with Permission of Output magazine. Copyright by Technical Publishing Company, a Dun & Bradstreet Company, 1980, All Rights Reserved.

In the preceding vignette, the editor of a computer magazine described his unsuccessful attempt to "get away" from the influence of computers. Perhaps this account has convinced you that you need to know more about such commonplace machines. But if you are not yet convinced, the following section begins with a short explanation of computer literacy and why you need it. A brief rundown of what you can expect to learn in this book follows. Chapter 1 then introduces you to the computer itself. We'll examine the elements that define it, discuss its speed and accuracy capabilities, and describe the functions and organization of its components. You'll see how a series of instructions stored in a computer can control these components as they execute a specific task. The final section describes differences in computer systems and the factors that can limit their use.

Thus, after studying this chapter, you should be able to:

▌ Understand your need for computer literacy

▌ Define the term "computer" and outline some of its speed and accuracy capabilities

▌ Outline the activities involved in data processing and the data processing operations that computers can perform

▌ Identify the hardware components in a basic computer system and describe the functions of each component

▌ Explain how a computer can accept and process data, and produce output results, by following the detailed set of instructions contained in a stored program

▌ Describe some ways in which computer systems may differ

▌ Discuss some limiting factors in the use of computers

▌ Understand and use the key terms and concepts listed at the end of this chapter

YOUR NEED FOR COMPUTER LITERACY

Just 30 years ago, the few computers in existence were enormous and expensive machines. They were often used for special scientific purposes and thus had little direct impact on the lives of most people. Only a handful of pioneers had first-hand knowledge of computer capabilities and limitations, and most people probably expected to live happy lives without ever using—or ever touching—the laboratory curiosities.

But how times have changed! Millions of computers, ranging from small, relatively inexpensive micro-sized units to supercomputers, now inhabit offices, factories, schools, homes, hospitals, government agencies, banks, and retail stores as well as laboratories. These computers, like automobiles and electricity, exert a daily influence on your life. You saw in the opening vignette that it's almost impossible to avoid reading, seeing, or hearing about computers, even on vacation. If you're still a skeptic, let's suppose that the following events occurred one day last week:

▌ *You made travel arrangements for a trip.* An efficient computer-controlled airline reservations system kept track of available seats and quickly recorded your reservation. Other computer-based systems were used to reserve a rental car and a hotel room.

▌ *You received some junk mail.* If computers weren't available to maintain mailing lists and print address labels, you would seldom receive this unwanted material.

▌ *You bought gasoline for your car with a credit card and then (alas) you received a traffic ticket.* Computers were used to control the refining process that produced the gasoline. Computers also make possible the processing of millions of daily credit card transactions. (A record of your credit history probably resides in one or more of the computer memory systems used by banks, retail stores, and other organizations.) Before approaching you the police officer who gave you the ticket may have radioed a request for a computer check to see if you were driving a stolen car. The ticket information was entered into your driving record in a state computer system and was later forwarded to your insurance company's computer center.

▌ *You went jogging.* Computer-controlled monitoring stations were checking the quality of the water in a nearby stream and the air you were breathing.

▌ *You went to a hospital for a physical examination.* If the exam was for insurance purposes, your medical history and the doctor's findings were forwarded to the insurance company where they were stored in a large computer "bank" of data. Unknown to you, some possibly sensitive private information may now be available to several other organizations.

▌ *You picked up your paycheck and went shopping with a friend.* If you work for an organization of much size, it's likely that a computer calculated the deductions and prepared the check. When the check is cashed, it's automatically processed by computers in the banking system. Electronic point-of-sale checkout stations, linked to store computers, read the codes printed on garment tags and product boxes, saved checkout time, and provided you and your friend with detailed and accurate sales slips.

In these few examples you never saw a computer. Yet their presence in your daily life cannot be denied or ignored. As you may have noticed, some examples appeared to offer benefits (your travel arrangements were made quickly and efficiently, your credit card was readily accepted, and your pay-

COMING TO TERMS WITH COMPUTER LITERACY

Just a few years ago literate people were people who could read and write, and literacy in the printed word was a major goal of education. But, just a few years hence, the term may often be associated with those who can speak and teach the language of computers. What is computer literacy, what are the reasons for the interest in it, and how can we become computer literate?

Computer Comfort

Beverly Hunter of the Human Resources Research Organization assigns a very general definition to computer literacy: it is "whatever a person needs to know and do with computers in order to function in our information-based society." Functioning comfortably with computers is the key element. In computer literacy, we're not talking about abstract knowledge of computers; rather, the term refers to a person's ability to use a computer.

Key figures in the computer literacy field suggest that being computer literate means we can use computers as a problem-solving tool for many aspects of life. David Moursund, Editor of *The Computing Teacher,* stresses that "computers are an everyday working tool like reading and writing." In other words, we should feel as free and easy using them as we do using books. Computer literacy, according to Moursund, includes an understanding of how computers aid problem-solving in any discipline.

To Arthur Luehrmann, President of a company called Computer Literacy, computer literacy is being able to "do computing," just as print literacy is being able to *do* reading and writing. He says the key question in deciding whether someone is computer literate is "whether that person can use computers to solve a problem."

Just how much about computers do we need to learn to be literate problem-solvers?

"People are computer literate when they can determine how to make the computer do what they want it to do," says Karen Billings, director of the Microcomputer Resource Center at Columbia Teachers College. Billings notes that someone teaching a course about computers requires more knowledge of them than a teacher who just wants to load and run a drill and practice program. To some people, computer literacy is the ability to write programs; to others, it is the ability to give effective instructions to a programmer.

—Carol Klitzner, "Coming to Terms with Computer Literacy," Reprinted with permission from *Personal Computing,* August 1981, p. 57. Copyright 1981, Hayden Publishing Company.

check was on time and accurate). But other examples had less desirable consequences (you resent being checked for auto theft, and you dislike the idea that the personal information you gave your doctor during a physical may wind up in the hands of strangers). However, the fact that a revolutionary invention like the computer can have both good and bad effects on individuals should not come as a surprise. After all, automobiles give us mobility and freedom, but they also kill us by the thousands.

Computer applications will expand greatly in the years ahead. There will be vast potential for widespread benefits as well as undesirable results. Educated citizens should not rely solely on computer specialists to prevent the possible dangers and bring about the positive potential. Rather, citizens should learn about computers so that they can better participate in the benefits, and so that they can insist that the designers of ill-conceived computer systems assume the responsibility for the effects these systems have on people. This need for **computer literacy** is a fact. It's also the purpose of this book.

What to Expect

Computers Today is an ambitious title for a book. It suggests a breadth of contemporary computer information that's usually not found in other texts. Many introductory books place an emphasis on computing equipment and how this equipment may be instructed to solve problems. Other texts focus on computer applications and the resulting social impact of these applications. But *the purpose of this book* is to acquaint you with *all four* of the following related areas of knowledge required for computer literacy:

1. ***Computers themselves.*** You should understand the organization, capabilities, and limitations of the various machines, or **hardware,** that make up a modern computer system.

2. ***What computers do.*** You should be familiar with some of the more common uses or **applications** of computers in today's society. The focus in this book will be primarily on business data processing applications.

3. ***How computers are put to work.*** You need to know the *analysis, design,* and *program preparation procedures* that must be carried out in order to produce written programs of instructions, or **software.** These programs are necessary to cause the hardware to function in a desired way to process applications.

4. ***The social impact of computers at work.*** Finally, you should be aware of how individuals and organizations may be affected by present and future computer applications.

How This Book Is Organized

To provide a well-rounded introduction to the field of data processing, *Computers Today* is organized into five modules. An overview of *all four areas* of knowledge mentioned above is presented in the four chapters of this Background Module. You should read Chapters 1 through 4 in sequence, but once you've completed them you can then turn immediately to *any of the other modules.* For example, you can go to the chapters in the Hardware Module for further information on computer hardware systems. Or you may save these chapters until later and go directly to the chapters in the Programming Module. Figure 1-1 shows the organization and flexibility of *Computers Today.* Before considering a later module, however, you need to know more about the computer itself.

INTRODUCING THE COMPUTER

Most people are aware that a computer is a machine that can perform arithmetic operations. But it's much more than just a fast arithmetic device. It's also a machine that can choose, copy, move, compare, and perform other non-

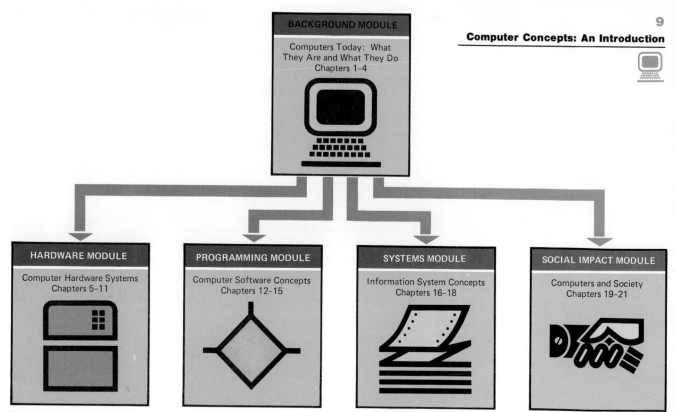

Figure 1-1 How *Computers Today* is organized. After reading the first four chapters, you will then have the background needed to permit you to go immediately to any of the other modules.

arithmetic operations on the many alphabetic, numeric, and other symbols that humans use to represent things. The computer manipulates these symbols in the desired way by following an "intellectual map" called a program. A **program,** then, is a detailed set of humanly prepared instructions that directs the computer to function in a specific way to produce a desired result. And a **computer** is a fast and accurate electronic symbol (or data) manipulating system that's designed and organized to automatically accept and store input data, process them, and produce output results under the direction of a detailed step-by-step stored program of instructions. In the following pages we'll examine the elements in this not-so-simple definition in more detail. At the same time, we'll cover some important computer and data processing concepts.

Computer Speed and Accuracy Capabilities

A computer works one step at a time. It can add and subtract numbers, compare letters to determine alphabetic sequence, and move and copy numbers and letters. There's certainly nothing profound in these operations.

Unit of time	Part of a Second	Interpretation
Millisecond (ms)	One-thousandth (1/1000)	A baseball pitched at a speed of 95 miles-per-hour (mph) would move less than 2 inches in a millisecond.
Microsecond (μs)	One-millionth (1/1,000,000)	A spaceship traveling toward the moon at 100,000 mph would move less than 2 inches in a microsecond.
Nanosecond (ns)	One-billionth (1/1,000,000,000)	There are as many nanoseconds in one second as there are seconds in 30 years, or as many nanoseconds in a minute as there are minutes in 1,100 centuries.
Picosecond (ps)	One-trillionth (1/1,000,000,000,000)	Electricity (and light) travels at 186,000 miles-per-second or about 1 foot in a nanosecond. In a picosecond, electricity would move less than 1/50th of an inch. A picosecond is to a second what a second is to 31,710 years.

Figure 1-2 The minuscule units used to measure computer speed.

What's significant is the computer's _speed_. This speed is measured in the units shown in Figure 1-2. The time required for computers to execute a basic operation—e.g., add—varies from a few **microseconds** for the smallest machines to 80 **nanoseconds** or less for the larger ones. Thus, the slowest computers can perform hundreds of thousands of additions in a second while the largest systems can complete several million additions in the same period.

The benefit of this speed capability is that we humans are freed from calculations to use our time more creatively. Our time dimension has been broadened. We can now often obtain information that could not have been produced at all a few years ago or that could have been prepared only after great human effort. John Kemeny, former President of Dartmouth College and an author of a popular language used to prepare computer programs, has noted that in 1945 it took many people a full year of working around the clock to complete certain calculations at the atomic laboratories at Los Alamos. The same calculations, Kemeny observes, could now be done in one afternoon by a single undergraduate student while sharing a computer's time with dozens of others. Of course, as you'll see in Chapter 2, some jobs are gathered into batches and are then processed by the computer only at scheduled times. When this approach is used, the delay required to accumulate the jobs for processing may seem excessive to impatient computer users.

In addition to being very fast, computers are also very _accurate._ It's estimated that you or I would make one error in every 500 to 1,000 operations with a calculator. But the circuits in a computer require no human intervention between processing operations and have no mechanical parts to wear and malfunction. Thus, these circuits can perform hundreds of thousands (or millions) of operations every second and can run errorless for hours and days at a time. Beyond this, computers also have built-in, self-checking capabilities that permit them to monitor the accuracy of their _internal_ operations. _If_ the input data entering the computer are correct and relevant, and *if* the program of processing instructions is reliable, *then* the computer can generally be expected to produce accurate output. The phrase **"garbage in–garbage out,"** or **GIGO,** is used often by people who work with computers. (GIGO is an example of an **acronym**—a term formed from the first letters of related words.) These people recognize that "computer errors" can usually be traced to incorrect input data or unreliable programs—and both are usually caused by human and not computer frailties.

Computer Symbol (Data) Manipulating Capability

The first computers were built to manipulate numbers in order to solve arithmetic problems. But as Figure 1-3 shows, we create, use, and manipulate many other symbols that represent facts in the world in which we live. Luckily for us, early computer experts soon made the important discovery that a ma-

Figure 1-3 A few of the symbols used by people to communicate facts and concepts.

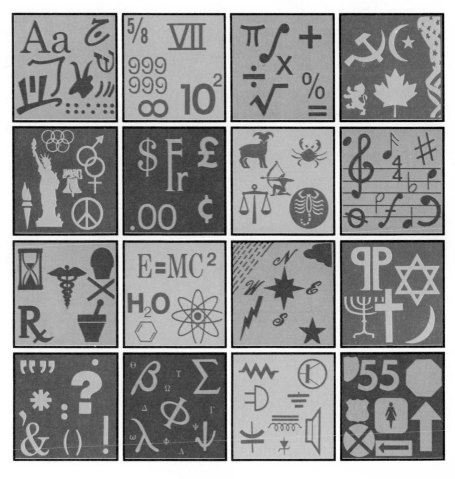

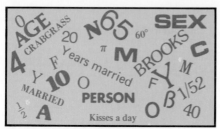

(a) Raw data input

Person	A	B	C
Age	10	65	20
Kisses a day	0	4	40
Sex	M	M	F
Married	N	Y	Y
Years married	0	40	1/52

(b) Selected data have been arranged (processed) in an ordered form to produce information

Figure 1-4 Processing converts raw data into information. All information consists of data, but not all data produce specific and meaningful information. The accumulation of additional data can often add new dimensions to existing information, but the interpretation of the information generally requires human judgment and may vary from person to person.

chine that can accept, store, and process numbers can also manipulate non-numerical symbols. Manipulating these familiar symbols is possible if an identifying code number is assigned to the symbol to be stored and processed. Thus, the letter A can be represented by a code, as can the letter B, the addition symbol (+), and so on. Of course, someone must give the computer instructions if it is to manipulate the coded and stored symbols in a desired way. Instructions are needed, for example, to put a stored list of names into an alphabetical sequence.

Data versus Information. The word "data" is the plural of datum, which means "fact." **Data,** then, are facts or the raw material of information. Data are represented by symbols, but they are *not* information except in a limited sense. As used here, information is data arranged in ordered and useful form. That is, **information** is relevant knowledge produced as output of data processing operations and acquired by people to enhance understanding and to achieve specific purposes. Figure 1-4 illustrates the distinction between data and information. You can see that information is the result of a transformation process. Figure 1-5 shows that just as raw materials are transformed into finished products by a manufacturing process, raw data are transformed into information by data processing.

Data Processing Activities. Data processing consists of gathering the raw data input, evaluating and bringing order to it, and placing it in proper perspective so that useful information will be produced. All data processing, whether done by hand or by the latest computer system, consists of three basic activities: capturing the input data, manipulating the data, and managing the output results.

Figure 1-5 Information is the result of a transformation process. Products produced by a manufacturing process (part a) have little utility until they are used; similarly, information produced by data processing (part b) is of little value unless it supports meaningful human decisions and actions.

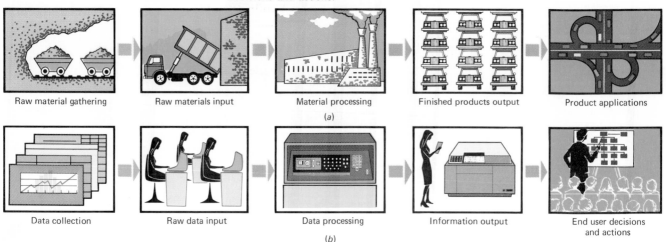

Raw material gathering	Raw materials input	Material processing	Finished products output	Product applications

(a)

Data collection	Raw data input	Data processing	Information output	End user decisions and actions

(b)

⊥ ▮ *Capturing the input data.* Data must be *originated* in some form and *verified* for accuracy prior to further processing. They may initially be recorded on paper **source documents** and then converted into a machine-usable form for processing, or they may be captured directly in a paperless machine-readable form.

⊥⊥ ▮ *Manipulating the data.* One or more of the following operations may then have to be performed on the gathered data:

(1) *Classifying.* Organizing items with like characteristics into groups or classes is called **classifying.** Data taken from a retail store's sales ticket, for example, may be classified by product sold, sales department, salesperson, or any other classification useful to store managers. Classifying is usually accomplished by assigning predetermined abbreviations or codes to the items being arranged. The three types of codes used are *numeric* (postal Zip codes used for geographic classification), *alphabetic* (persons A, B, and C in Figure 1-4), and **alphanumeric** (letters and numbers, like the identification codes used to classify General Motors trucks by type of engine, chassis, body, and assembly location).

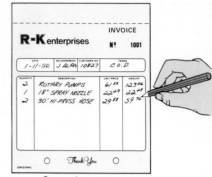

Source document

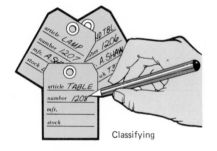

Classifying

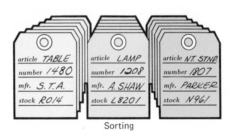

Sorting

Calculating

(2) *Sorting.* Usually, it's easier to work with data if they are arranged in a logical sequence. Examples include first to last, biggest to smallest, oldest to newest. Arranging classified data in such a sequence is called **sorting.** Retail sales tickets may be sorted by the name or number of the salesperson. Most often, numeric sorting is used in computer-based processing systems because it's usually faster than alphabetic sorting.

(3) *Calculating.* Arithmetic manipulation of the data is called **calculating.** In calculating a salesperson's pay, for example, the hours worked multiplied by the hourly wage rate gives the total earnings. Payroll deductions such as taxes are then calculated and subtracted from total earnings to arrive at the salesperson's take-home pay.

(4) *Summarizing.* Reducing masses of data to a more concise and usable form is called **summarizing.** For example, the general manager of a retail store is interested only in a summary of the total sales of each department. A summary report would give only total sales information. Department managers may want more detailed information, such as the total sales of each department broken down into sales by product type and by salesperson.

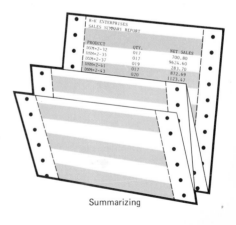

Summarizing

Storing and retrieving

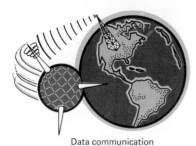

Data communication

 Managing the output results. Once data have been captured and manipulated, one or more of the following operations may be needed:

(1) *Storing and retrieving.* Retaining data for future reference is **storing**. Of course, facts should be stored only if the value of having them in the future exceeds the storage cost. Storage media such as paper (in sheet, punched card, or punched tape form), microfilm, or magnetizeable disks and tapes are generally used. Recovering stored data and/or information is the **retrieving** activity. Retrieval methods vary. One slow approach is for people to search file cabinets. A much faster method is to use electronic inquiry devices that are connected directly to a computer which, in turn, is connected directly to a mass-storage unit containing the data.

(2) *Communicating and reproducing.* Transferring data from one location or operation to another for use or for further processing is **data communication**—a process that continues until information, in a usable form, reaches the final user. Sometimes, of course, it's necessary to copy or duplicate data. This **reproduction** activity may be done by hand or by machine.

Processing by Computer. There's nothing new about the data processing steps just outlined. They've been performed down through the ages, first by hand, then by machine-assisted manual and electromechanical punched card methods, and now by computers. You can take a closer look at the evolution of data processing in the reading that follows this chapter. The four function categories which follow are all that a computer can perform, but they include most data processing steps.

Input/output operations. A computer can accept data (input) from and supply processed data (output) to a wide range of input/output devices. Such devices as keyboards and display screens make human/machine communicating possible. Multiple output documents may be reproduced by computer-controlled printers.

Calculation operations. The circuits in a computer are designed to permit addition, subtraction, multiplication, and division. Such operations, of course, make calculating possible.

Logic/comparison operations. The computer also has the ability to perform certain logic operations. For example, when two data items represented by the symbols A and B are compared, there are only three possible outcomes: (1) A is *equal to* B (A $=$ B); (2) A is *greater than* B (A $>$ B); or (3) A is *less than* B (A $<$ B). The computer is able to perform a simple comparison and then, depending on the result, follow a *predetermined branch,* or course of action, in the completion of that part of its work (see Figure 1-6). This comparison ability thus makes it possible to *classify* item A as having or not having the characteristic of B, to determine the sequence between A and B for *sorting* purposes, or to determine if A meets the selection criterion of B for *summarizing* purposes. This simple ability to compare is an important computer

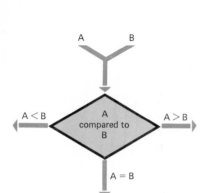

Figure 1-6 A computer can compare two items and then take an appropriate action branch depending on the outcome. By using combinations of these simple comparisons, the computer is able to perform sophisticated procedures and answer complicated questions.

property because more sophisticated questions can be answered by using combinations of comparison decisions.[1]

- *Storage and retrieval operations.* Both data and program instructions are stored internally in a computer. And once stored, both may be quickly called up, or retrieved, for use. The time required for data or instructions to be retrieved is measured in micro- or nanoseconds.

We might be tempted to say that the computer has made a "decision" by choosing between alternative courses of action. But it's more appropriate to say that the computer has *followed* the logic and decisions made earlier by the human *programmer* who has prepared the instructions that are being used.

Feedback and Review 1-1

So far, we've seen that a computer is a very fast and accurate machine. Computers can accept input data in the form of numeric and nonnumeric symbols, manipulate these data through a series of data processing activities, and manage the output results in order to produce useful information. Now is a good time to pause so that you can test and reinforce your understanding of these concepts. This "pause that reinforces" will occur from time to time in each chapter. The *crossword puzzle* used here is one of a variety of formats you'll see. You'll find the answers to each exercise at the end of the chapter. Fill in the puzzle form using the sentences and definitions found below.

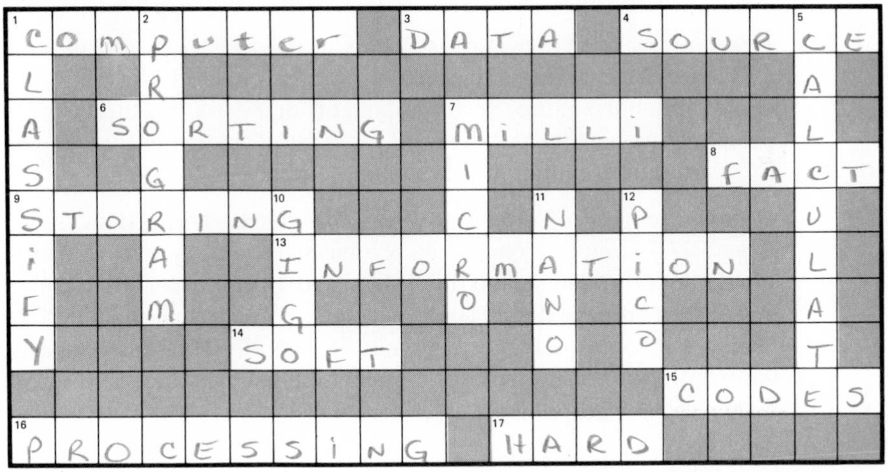

Across

1. A _______ is a fast and accurate electronic symbol (or data) manipulating system that will accept and store input data, process them, and produce output results under the direction of a stored program of instructions.

3. _______ are facts or informational raw materials represented by symbols.

4. Data may first be recorded on paper _______ documents and then converted into a machine-usable form for processing.

6. Arranging classified data in a predetermined sequence to facilitate processing is called _______.

7. A unit of time equal to one-thousandth of a second is a _______ -second.

8. The word "data" is the plural of datum, which means _______.

9. Retaining data for future reference is _______.

13. _______ is relevant knowledge produced as output of data processing operations and acquired by people to enhance understanding and to achieve specific purposes.

14. _______ -ware is the name given to the programs that have been written to cause computers to function in a desired way.

15. The three types of _______ used to classify data items are numeric, alphabetic, and alphanumeric.

16. The purpose of data _______ is to capture raw input data, evaluate and bring order to them, and place them in proper perspective so that useful information will be produced.

17. _______ -ware is the name given to the various machines that make up a computer system.

Down

1. To _______ is to organize data items with like characteristics into groups or classes.

2. A _______ is a detailed step-by-step set of instructions that cause a computer to function in a desired way.

5. To _______ is to perform arithmetic manipulations on data.

7. A _______ -second is one-millionth of a second.

10. _______ is an acronym that recognizes the fact that "computer errors" can usually be traced to incorrect input data or unreliable programs.

11. A _______ -second is one-billionth of a second.

12. A _______ -second is one-trillionth of a second.

[1] Let's assume, for example, that the data in a large listing have been organized in some logical order (alphabetically or in numerical sequence) on a computer-readable medium. The computer can be programmed to search for a specific data item by looking first at the middle item in the listing. If, as a result of a comparison, the desired item is alphabetically or numerically less than this middle item, the last half of the listing can be quickly eliminated. Thus, this one comparison has cut the search problem in half. An additional comparison using the middle item of the remaining half of the listing can now be made, and this search procedure can be continued until the desired item is either located or shown to be missing from the listing.

COMPUTER SYSTEM ORGANIZATION

Now that we've examined what computers do, let's look again at our computer definition: A computer is a fast and accurate symbol manipulating system that is organized to accept, store, and process data and produce output results under the direction of a stored program of instructions. This section explains why a computer is a system and how a computer system is organized.

The System Concept

The term "system" is used often and in different ways. For example, everyone is familiar with expressions such as "Professor Nastie has an impossible grading system," or "Marty has a system for betting on the horses." But for our purposes, a **system** is a group of integrated parts that have the common purpose of achieving some objective(s). The following characteristics are key:

1. *A group of parts.* A system has more than one element. A steel ball is not a system, but it might be part of a bearing assembly that could be combined with other components to produce an irrigation system.

2. *Integrated parts.* A logical relationship must exist between the parts of a system. Mechanical and electronic systems such as washing machines and video games have components that work together. And a personnel management system may consist of integrated procedures for recruiting, training, and evaluating employees.

3. *Common purpose of achieving some objective(s).* The system is designed to accomplish one or more objectives. All system elements should be controlled so that the system goal is achieved. Totally automated systems have tightly controlled operations; systems operated by people sometimes manage to get out of control. (Humans regularly lose control of those mechanical systems called cars and wind up in body shops or hospitals.)

A computer is a group of integrated parts that have the common purpose of performing the operations called for in the program being executed: It also is a system. Now any system may be comprised of smaller systems or subsystems. A **subsystem** is a smaller system contained within a larger one. Some of the component parts found in most computer systems—e.g., printers—are systems in their own right. And computers, in turn, may be considered subsystems in larger **supersystems** such as the air traffic control system used to monitor flights of the nation's aircraft.

Organization of Computer System Components

Figure 1-7 shows the basic organization of a computer system. Key elements in this system include input, processing, and output devices. Let's examine each component of the system in more detail.

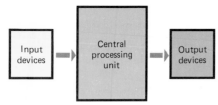

Figure 1-7 The basic organization of a computer system.

Input Devices. Look now at Figure 1-8. Computer systems use many devices for **input** purposes. Some allow direct human/machine communication. The keyboard of a workstation connected directly to—or **online** to—a computer is an example. Some require data to be recorded on an input medium such as paper or magnetizeable material. Devices that read data magnetically recorded on specially coated plastic tapes or flexible or *floppy* plastic disks are popular. Regardless of the type of device used, all are components for interpretation and communication between people and computer systems.

Central Processing Unit. The heart of any computer system is the **central processing unit** (CPU). As Figure 1-9 shows, three main sections are generally located within CPUs of all sizes.

▎ *The primary storage section.* The **primary storage section** is used for four purposes. Three of these relate to the data being processed (see Figure 1-9):

(1) Data are fed into an **input storage area** where they are held until ready to be processed.

(2) A **working storage space** that's like a sheet of scratch paper is used to hold the data being processed and the intermediate results of such processing.

(3) An **output storage area** holds the finished results of the processing operations until they can be released.

(4) In addition to these data-related purposes, the primary storage section also contains a **program storage area** that holds the processing instructions.

The separate areas used for these four general purposes are not fixed by built-in physical boundaries in the storage section. Rather, they can vary from one application to another. Thus, a specific physical space may be used to store input data in one application, output results in another, and processing instructions in a third. The programmer writing the application instructions (or "housekeeping" software prepared by other programmers) determines how the space will be used for each job.

In addition to the primary storage or **main memory** section, most computers also have **secondary** (sometimes called **auxiliary** or **external**) **storage** capabilities. As shown above the CPU in Figure 1-9, secondary storage devices are machines that are generally connected *online* to the CPU where they serve as reference libraries by accepting data directly from and returning data directly to the CPU without human intervention. Computer-usable data are also retained outside the CPU on paper and magnetizeable secondary storage media. However, these facts are frequently **offline,** that is, the CPU doesn't have direct and unassisted access to them (see Figure 1-9).

▎ *The arithmetic-logic section.* All calculations are performed and all comparisons (decisions) are made in the **arithmetic-logic section** of the

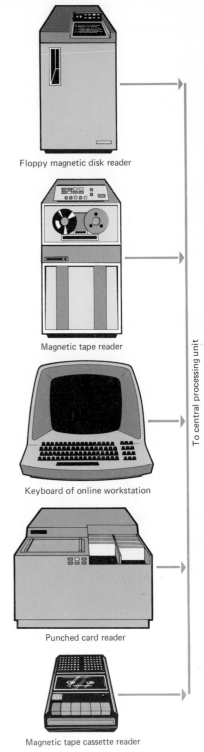

Examples of Input Devices

Floppy magnetic disk reader

Magnetic tape reader

Keyboard of online workstation

Punched card reader

Magnetic tape cassette reader

To central processing unit

Figure 1-8 Input devices.

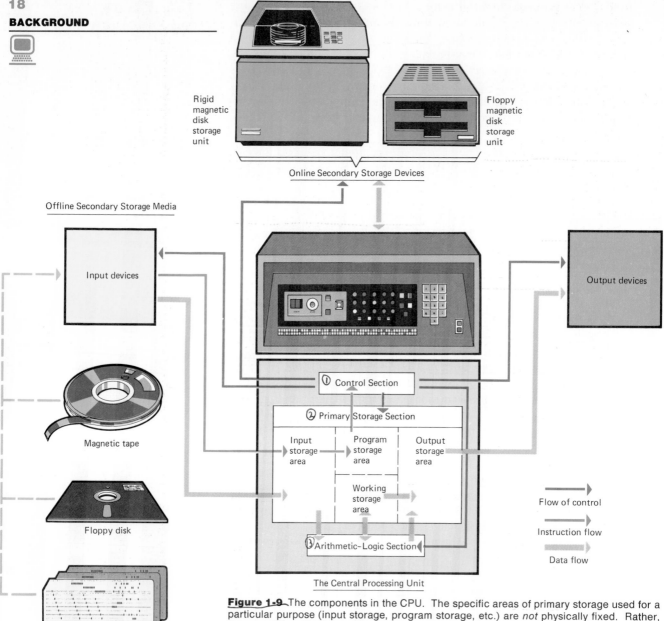

Rigid magnetic disk storage unit

Floppy magnetic disk storage unit

Online Secondary Storage Devices

Offline Secondary Storage Media

Input devices

Output devices

Magnetic tape

Floppy disk

Punch cards

① Control Section

② Primary Storage Section

Input storage area

Program storage area

Output storage area

Working storage area

③ Arithmetic–Logic Section

Flow of control

Instruction flow

Data flow

The Central Processing Unit

Figure 1-9 The components in the CPU. The specific areas of primary storage used for a particular purpose (input storage, program storage, etc.) are *not* physically fixed. Rather, they vary depending on the application program. The dashed lines in the storage section are used to indicate this boundary flexibility.

CPU (see Figure 1-9). Once data are fed into primary storage from input devices, they are held and transferred as needed to the arithmetic-logic section where processing takes place. No processing occurs in primary storage. Intermediate results generated in the arithmetic-logic unit are temporarily placed in a designated working storage area until needed at a later time. Data may thus move from primary storage to the arithmetic-logic unit and back again to storage many times before the processing is finished. Once completed, the final results are released to an output storage section and from there to an output device. The type and number of arithmetic and logic operations a computer can perform are determined by the engineering design of the CPU.

▍ *The control section.* How does the input device know when to feed data into storage? How does the arithmetic-logic section know what should be done with the data once they are received? And how is the output device able to obtain finished rather than intermediate results? It's by selecting, interpreting, and seeing to the execution of the program instructions that the **control section** of the CPU is able to maintain order and direct the operation of the entire system. Although it doesn't perform any actual processing on the data, the control unit acts as a central nervous system for the other components of the computer (see Figure 1-9). At the beginning of processing, the first program instruction is selected and fed into the control section from the program storage area. There it's interpreted, and from there signals are sent to other components to execute the necessary action(s). Other program instructions are then selected and executed in a sequential fashion until the processing is completed.

Output Devices. Like input units, **output devices** are instruments of interpretation and communication between humans and the computer system. As shown in Figure 1-10, the devices take output results from the CPU in machine-coded form and convert them into a form that can be used (*a*) by people (e.g., a printed report) or (*b*) as machine input in another processing cycle (e.g., magnetic tape).

All the input/output and secondary storage units shown in Figure 1-10 are sometimes called **peripheral devices** (or just *peripherals*). This terminology refers to the fact that although these devices are not a part of the CPU, they are often located near it.

▶ Feedback and Review 1-2

Now that you've seen how computer systems may be organized, try the *scrambled words* format below to test and reinforce your understanding of this section. Rearrange the letters to spell out the correct word for the space indicated in the corresponding sentence.

1. A group of integrated parts that have the common purpose of achieving some objective is a _____.

Ⓣ Ⓔ Ⓢ Ⓢ Ⓨ Ⓜ *System*

2. The heart of any computer system is the _____ processing unit.

Ⓣ Ⓛ Ⓝ Ⓒ Ⓐ Ⓔ Ⓡ *Central*

3. The _____ storage area of the primary storage section of a CPU is used to hold the intermediate results of data processing.

Ⓚ Ⓞ Ⓡ Ⓖ Ⓝ Ⓘ Ⓦ *working*

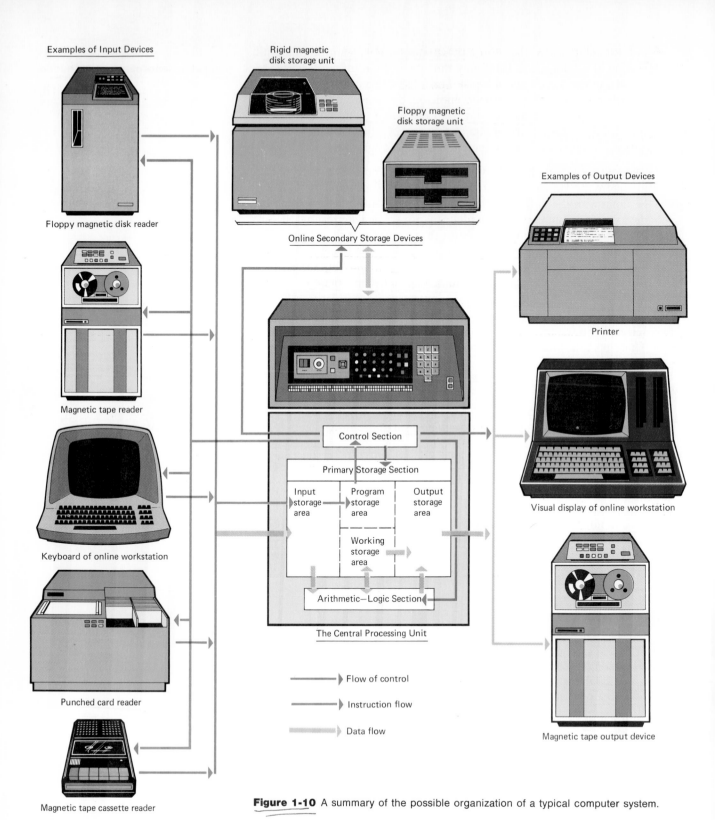

Examples of Input Devices

Floppy magnetic disk reader

Magnetic tape reader

Keyboard of online workstation

Punched card reader

Magnetic tape cassette reader

Rigid magnetic disk storage unit

Floppy magnetic disk storage unit

Online Secondary Storage Devices

Examples of Output Devices

Printer

Visual display of online workstation

Magnetic tape output device

Control Section

Primary Storage Section

Input storage area

Program storage area

Output storage area

Working storage area

Arithmetic—Logic Section

The Central Processing Unit

Flow of control

Instruction flow

Data flow

Figure 1-10 A summary of the possible organization of a typical computer system.

4. CPUs of all sizes have primary storage, arithmetic-logic, and _____ sections.

Ⓛ Ⓞ Ⓞ Ⓝ Ⓡ Ⓒ Ⓣ Control

5. The input, output, and working storage areas in the primary storage section of a CPU are used for data-related purposes, but the _____ storage area is used to hold instructions.

Ⓜ Ⓐ Ⓡ Ⓡ Ⓞ Ⓖ Ⓟ program

6. Input and _____ devices are combined with a CPU in a typical computer system.

Ⓤ Ⓤ Ⓣ Ⓣ Ⓞ Ⓟ output

7. Actual data processing operations are performed in the arithmetic-logic section, but not in the _____ storage section or the control section of a central processor.

Ⓡ Ⓡ Ⓨ Ⓘ Ⓟ Ⓐ Ⓜ primary

8. The control section of a computer _____, interprets, and sees to the execution of program instructions.

Ⓔ Ⓔ Ⓢ Ⓢ Ⓛ Ⓣ Ⓒ selects

9. In addition to a primary storage section, most computers also have secondary storage devices that are connected _____ to the CPU and are thus able to accept data directly from, and return data directly to, the CPU without human intervention.

Ⓝ Ⓞ Ⓔ Ⓛ Ⓝ Ⓘ online

10. The locations used to store input data, intermediate and output results, and program instructions in the CPU can _____ from one application to the next.

Ⓨ Ⓐ Ⓥ Ⓡ vary

THE STORED PROGRAM CONCEPT: AN EXAMPLE

The computer system components just described are able to accept data, process it, and produce output results *only* by following the detailed set of instructions contained in a stored program. Let's now see how such a program might be used to process an application. In our example, let's assume that it is time for Longhorn College to issue checks to the part-time student workers that it employs. Follow the process as shown in Figure 1-11 as you read the explanation here. Input data for each student are first entered on time sheets. As shown in Figure 1-11, these data are then transferred from the time sheets to a computer-readable input medium (in this case a floppy magnetic disk) by a keying operation. The first student to be paid is Rob Brooks.[2]

Processing the Payroll Application

The program required to process the student payroll has been entered into the Longhorn computer's CPU through an appropriate input device. The 11 steps in this program are now stored in a program storage area shown in Figure 1-11. Next, the computer operator places the floppy disk containing the payroll data in a disk reader. Then the operator sets the computer to the location in the program storage area that contains the first instruction and the processing starts.

---

[2]We'll run into Rob again in later chapters where we'll see that he is an entrepreneur with an appreciation for business data processing and a sponsor of the fine arts. He's also a part-time college groundskeeper—a vocation for which he's now being paid.

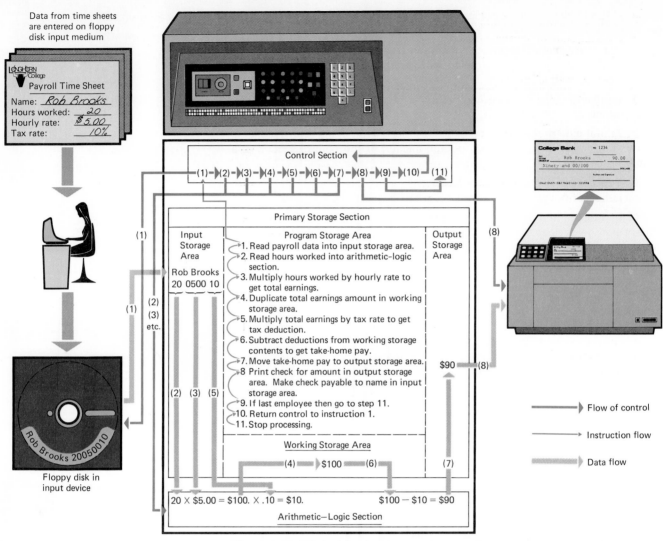

Data from time sheets
are entered on floppy
disk input medium

Payroll Time Sheet
Name: *Rob Brooks*
Hours worked: *20*
Hourly rate: *$5.00*
Tax rate: *10%*

Floppy disk in
input device

Control Section

(1)→(2)→(3)→(4)→(5)→(6)→(7)→(8)→(9)→(10) (11)

Primary Storage Section

Input Storage Area	Program Storage Area	Output Storage Area

Rob Brooks
20 0500 10

1. Read payroll data into input storage area.
2. Read hours worked into arithmetic-logic section.
3. Multiply hours worked by hourly rate to get total earnings.
4. Duplicate total earnings amount in working storage area.
5. Multiply total earnings by tax rate to get tax deduction.
6. Subtract deductions from working storage contents to get take-home pay.
7. Move take-home pay to output storage area.
8 Print check for amount in output storage area. Make check payable to name in input storage area.
9. If last employee then go to step 11.
10. Return control to instruction 1.
11. Stop processing.

Working Storage Area

(4)→ $100 (6)

$90 (8)

$20 X $5.00 = $100. X .10 = $10. $100 − $10 = $90

Arithmetic−Logic Section

College Bank   № 1234
Rob Brooks   90.00
Ninety and 00/100

→ Flow of control
→ Instruction flow
→ Data flow

Figure 1-11 Only by following the steps in a stored program is a computer able to accept and process data and produce output results. The program is held in primary storage, data to be processed are supplied to an input device, the computer is set to the location of the first program instruction, and the processing begins. The program steps are executed automatically and without human intervention. Unless directed by a specific instruction to do otherwise, the computer executes the program steps in sequence.

This initial control setting feeds the first program instruction ("Read payroll data into input storage area") into the control section of the CPU where it is interpreted. Control signals are then sent to the input device which executes the instruction and transfers Rob's payroll data to an input storage area of the CPU. (See the lines labeled 1 in Figure 1-11 for the interpretation and execution of this first step. Other program steps are similarly shown, but some lines have been omitted to simplify the figure.)

The control section automatically selects program instructions *in sequence* after the initial control setting unless specifically instructed to do otherwise. Thus, as soon as the first instruction has been dealt with, the control unit automatically begins interpreting the second step. This instruction directs the control unit to "Read hours worked into arithmetic-logic section." The control section is not concerned that Rob has worked 20 hours (the next student's hours may differ). It merely carries out program orders, and so places 20 hours in the arithmetic-logic section.

And so the processing continues in sequence: the 20-hour figure is multiplied by the $5 hourly rate to get Rob's total earnings of $100 (step 3); this total earnings figure is duplicated in the working storage area (step 4); the tax deduction is found by multiplying the $100 earnings by the 10 percent tax rate to get a $10 deduction (step 5); and this deduction is subtracted from the $100 total earnings figure that was temporarily stored in the working storage area to get Rob's take-home pay (step 6). After this take-home pay has been computed, the amount is transferred to the output storage area (step 7) and sent to a printer which is instructed to print Rob's check (step 8).

At this point in the program a **branchpoint** is reached and a decision must be made. Is Rob the last student to be paid? The computer follows an appropriate logic/comparison technique, which we'll discuss in the next chapter, to answer this question. If Rob is the last to be paid, then program control jumps to step 11 and the processing will stop. Since he is not the last student, however, program control moves to the next instruction in the sequence (step 10). This step directs the control section to reset itself to instruction 1 so the processing may be repeated for the next student. Thus, the same instructions will be executed over and over again until the repetitive payroll task is completed. As the data for the next student are read into the input storage area, they will erase and replace Rob's data just as recording music on a sound tape recorder erases any music that may have previously been stored on the tape.

This payroll example demonstrates most of the computer concepts and capabilities discussed in this chapter. To review:

- The various components of a computer system can manipulate and process data automatically and without human intervention by following the directions contained in a stored program of instructions.

- A computer has the built-in ability to obey different types of commands such as READ, PRINT, MULTIPLY, and MOVE. (Every computer is designed with a particular set or **repertoire** of these instruction types.)

- A computer follows the steps in a program in sequence until explicitly told to do otherwise.

- A change in the sequence of steps can result from the ability to follow different paths depending on the answer to a simple question.

As noted earlier, there's nothing difficult about these computer capabilities. What's impressive, however, is the speed with which computer operations are performed and the accuracy of the resulting output.

 **Feedback and Review 1-3**

Understanding the stored program concept is a basic part of the knowledge required for computer literacy. In the chapters of the Programming Module, we'll return to this important subject. For now, place a T or F in the space provided in the following *true-false* questions to test and reinforce your understanding of the concepts presented:

T **1.** It's only by following the steps in a stored program that computer hardware is able to accept and process data and produce output results.

T **2.** Both data and program instructions are entered into the CPU through an input device, and are stored in primary storage.

F **3.** Processing begins when the control unit is set to the last instruction stored in the program storage area.

F **4.** The control section interprets and then executes all processing instructions.

T **5.** The control section automatically selects program steps in sequence unless specifically instructed to do otherwise.

F **6.** All data processing is done in the control and arithmetic-logic sections of the CPU.

F **7.** The working storage area is used to accept output results and the program instructions that actually do the processing work.

T **8.** The computer can be programmed to consider simple questions and then follow different program paths depending on the answer.

F **9.** A computer can be programmed to return program control to an earlier step to repeat operations, but it cannot jump ahead and bypass steps in the sequence.

SOME COMPUTER SYSTEM DIFFERENCES

All computer systems of interest to us are similar in that they contain input, central processing, and output hardware components. They all perform basic machine operations under the direction of stored programs which can be quickly changed to permit the processing of a stream of different applications. Of course, when applications differ widely there's usually a need for different system resources to process them. In other words, the personal computer used in the home to play Space Invaders would hardly be used in a NASA mission control center to monitor an actual space shuttle launch.

Size Differences

Modern computers vary in physical size from those that fill rooms to those with CPUs the size of a dime. Generally, the larger the system the greater is

A

B

C

D

Figure 1-12 (*a*) A magnified print of a microcomputer chip. This chip is one of only three that make up Intel Corporation's Micromainframe™ computer system. The three-chip system is called a micromainframe because its processing performance exceeds that of several popular mainframe computers that were introduced a few years earlier. (Courtesy Intel Corporation) (*b*) The TRS-80 Model III shown here is a popular personal computer. All versions of this microcomputer have an input keyboard, a CPU, and an output display screen. This version also has two online secondary floppy disk storage units. (Courtesy Radio Shack Division, Tandy Corporation) (*c*) Another popular personal computer is the Apple. The Apple II and Apple III models shown here have CPUs housed in the cabinet with the keyboard and separate visual display screens. These systems also have separate output printers. (Courtesy of Apple Computer Inc.) (*d*) The IBM System/23 Datamaster computer system. The desktop unit shown features an input keyboard, the CPU, an output display screen, and two online secondary floppy disk storage units. An output printer is also included in this system designed for business applications. (Courtesy IBM Corporation)

the processing speed, storage capacity, and cost. Also, the larger systems are better equipped to handle a greater number of more powerful input and output devices.

Systems on the low end of the size scale are called microcomputers or minicomputers. **Microcomputers** (Figure 1-12) are the smallest general-purpose systems. But they may perform the same operations and use the same program instructions as much larger computers. **Minicomputers** (Figure 1-13) are also small general-purpose systems, but they are typically more powerful and more expensive than micros. In physical size, minis can vary from a desktop model to a unit the size of a small file cabinet.

Continuing up the size scale, **mainframe computers** (Figure 1-14) are systems that may offer faster processing speeds and greater storage capacity than a typical mini. A whole series of mainframe models ranging in size from small to very large are generally lumped together under a *family designation* by mainframe manufacturers. There's quite a bit of overlap possible in the cost, speed, and storage capacity of larger minis and smaller mainframes.

Finally come the **supercomputers** (Figure 1-15), designed to process complex scientific applications. These systems are the largest, fastest, and most expensive computers in the world. You'll find more information on computers in each size category in Chapter 9.

Architectural Differences

Most small and medium-sized computers follow the traditional design approach of using single control, primary storage, and arithmetic-logic sections

Figure 1-13 (*left*) Multiple terminals with keyboards and display screens and a printer are supported by this minicomputer. (Courtesy Wang Laboratories, Inc.) (*right*) The Eclipse C/150 system is a popular mid-sized minicomputer. (Reproduced by permission of Data General Corporation, Westboro, Mass.)

Figure 1-14 (*left*) A mainframe model from the Honeywell DPS8 family of computers. There are at least six different DPS8 processors in this mainframe family. (Courtesy Honeywell, Inc.) (*right*) One of several computers available in IBM's 4300 series of mainframes, this 4341 processor is considered to be a medium-sized mainframe model. (Courtesy IBM Corporation)

in the CPU. But there are several ways this design, or architecture, can be changed. For example, by adding additional control and arithmetic-logic sections (see Figure 1-16), several instructions can be processed at the same instant. Such a **multiprocessor** architecture makes it possible for the system to work *simultaneously* on several program segments. This design represents, in effect, a system with two or more central processors.

Figure 1-15 This Cray-1 supercomputer is one of the largest, fastest, and most expensive computers in existence. (Courtesy Fairchild Camera and Instrument Corporation)

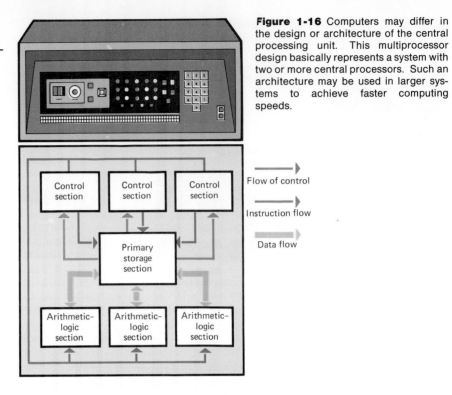

Figure 1-16 Computers may differ in the design or architecture of the central processing unit. This multiprocessor design basically represents a system with two or more central processors. Such an architecture may be used in larger systems to achieve faster computing speeds.

Flow of control

Instruction flow

Data flow

Figure 1-17 A large-scale mainframe, the IBM 3081 has two identical processors that share a large main memory and a system control unit. (Courtesy IBM Corporation)

Another variation from traditional design involves separating the arithmetic-logic section into several parts. While one part is performing addition other elements can, at the same time, be multiplying and making comparisons. Such variations from traditional design result in faster computing speeds and are used in some larger systems such as the IBM 3081 (Figure 1-17).

SOME COMPUTER LIMITATIONS

By now you know that computers are capable of processing data accurately and at very high speeds. Further, they have the important ability to compare data items and then perform alternative operations based on the results of the comparison. These easy-to-grasp capabilities make the computer one of the most powerful tools ever developed. But we've all read newspaper articles similar to the one about a woman who was billed $26,000 for a set of tires by a computer system, or the one that told how a man was treated for pneumonia and then charged by the hospital's computer system for the use of the delivery room and nursery. Such "computer failures" may be amusing, but in most cases the blame for the foul-up can be laid at the feet of people who failed to give proper attention to the following limitations: program reliability, logic clarity, and application suitability.

Programs Must Be Reliable

As a machine, the computer does what it's programmed to do and *nothing else*. This doesn't mean that it must be stupid. Clever programs can be written to direct the computer to store the results of previous decisions. Then, by using the branching ability designed into the program, the computer may be able to modify its behavior according to the success or failure of past decisions. But a seemingly flawless program that has operated without a problem for months can suddenly produce nonsense. Perhaps some rare combination of events has presented the system with a situation (*a*) for which there's *no* programmed course of action, or (*b*) where the course of action provided by the programmer contains an error that's just being discovered. Of course, a reliable program that's supplied with incorrect data may also produce nonsense.

Application Logic Must Be Understood

The computer can only process applications which can be expressed in a finite number of steps leading to a precisely defined goal. Each step must be specifically and clearly defined. If the steps in the problem solution cannot be precisely stated, the job cannot be done. The computer may not be of much help to people in areas where qualitative material, or evaluations, are important. The computer will not, for example, tell you how to "get rich quick" in the stock market, and it may not tell a sales manager if a new product will be successful. The market decision may be of a qualitative nature because sales volume data may rest on future social, political, technological, and economic events. However, the computer *can* let the manager know how the product will fare under *assumed* price, cost, and sales volume conditions.

Even if program steps are finite and understood, there are still some tasks whose execution could take millions of years, even on a giant computer. Joseph Weizenbaum, a computer scientist at MIT, has observed that a program could be written "to try every legal move in a certain chess situation; for each move try every possible response; for each response try its response; and so on until the computer has found a move which, if suitably pursued, would guarantee it a win. Such a program would surely be finite, but the length of time required by a computer to execute it would be unimaginably large. In principle, then, a computer could carry out such behavior: in fact, it cannot."[3]

Applications Must Be Suitable

Just because a computer can be programmed to do a job does not always mean that it should. Writing programs is a human task. It can be time-consuming and expensive. Thus, nonrecurring jobs are often not efficient areas for business data processing applications. Rather, as a general rule it's most economical to prepare business programs for large-volume, repetitive applications such as payrolls that will be used many times.[4]

[3]Joseph Weizenbaum, "The Last Dream," *Across the Board*, July 1977, p. 39. The term "combinatorial explosion" is given to this type of problem where a finite number of steps generates an impossibly large number of computer operations.
[4]As with most general rules, there are exceptions to this statement about business applications. We'll see some exceptions later on in the book. Also, in engineering and scientific computing, the importance of a nonrecurring task often warrants the necessary investment in programming time. An example might be the engineering planning and construction scheduling, by computer, of a single multimillion-dollar office building.

"I found myself fantasizing about it while I was on the beach in Hawaii..."

1. The use of computers has expanded so rapidly that their presence can no longer be denied or ignored. Soon, everyone will need to feel comfortable with these machines in order to function in a modern society. To be a computer-literate person, you need to know about computers themselves, the *hardware;* what they do, their *applications;* how they are applied through *software;* and the *social impact* of their use. Providing knowledge in these four areas is the purpose of this book.

2. A computer is a fast and accurate electronic symbol (data) manipulating system that's designed and organized to automatically accept and store input data, process them, and produce output results under the direction of a detailed stored program of instructions.

3. Computers perform at very high speeds. The time required to execute a basic operation such as addition is usually measured in *microseconds* (one-millionth of a second) for the smallest computers, and in *nanoseconds* (one-billionth of a second) for larger machines. The reliability of computer circuits enables them to run errorless for hours and days at a time. Computer "errors" can usually be traced to faulty programs or inaccurate input data—both generally caused by human and not computer frailties.

4. Computers can manipulate both numeric and nonnumeric symbols. *Data* are facts or informational raw materials represented by these symbols. *Information* is the relevant knowledge that results from the processing and arranging of data in an ordered and useful form.

5. *Data processing* consists of (*a*) capturing the raw input data; (*b*) manipulating it by using classifying, sorting, calculating, and summarizing techniques; and (*c*) storing, retrieving, communicating, and reproducing the output results of the manipulation.

6. These data processing activities are readily carried out by computers. A computer can accept input data from, and communicate processed output to, a large number of devices. The circuits in a computer are designed to facilitate calculating. Classifying, sorting, and summarizing are made possible by the computer's ability to perform simple comparisons and then, depending on the result, follow a predetermined course of action. And split-second storage and retrieval activities are possible through the use of primary and secondary storage devices.

7. A *system* is a group of integrated parts that have the common purpose of achieving some objective(s). Since a computer is made up of integrated components that work together to perform the steps called for in the program being executed, it is a system. A basic computer system is comprised of input and output devices and a central processing unit (CPU). CPUs of all sizes contain primary storage, arithmetic-logic, and control sections.

8. The space in the primary storage section is divided into four areas: input, where data are held for processing; working storage, where intermediate processing results are kept; output, where finished results are kept prior to release; and program storage, which holds the processing steps. In addition to primary storage components, most computers also have secondary storage devices. These devices are usually connected online to the CPU where they can accept data directly from, and return data directly to, the CPU without human intervention.

9. All calculations and comparisons are made in the arithmetic-logic section of the CPU. Engineering design determines the type and number of arithmetic and logic operations that can be performed. The control section of the CPU maintains order among the system components and selects, interprets, and sees to the execution of program steps. After an initial control setting, it automatically selects program instructions in sequence until specifically instructed to do otherwise.

10. Computers have the built-in ability to obey different types of instructions. Once problem-solving or job instructions are stored in a computer, the system can process data automatically and without human intervention until the problem is solved or the job is completed.

11. Computer systems differ in size and in design. Sizes vary from the smallest microcomputers to minis, mainframes, and supercomputers. And the architecture can vary from systems that use single arithmetic-logic and control sections to those that use multiple sections in order to work simultaneously on several program segments and thus speed up processing.

12. Computers have impressive capabilities, but they also have a few important limitations. Programs must be reliable, applications logic must be understood, and applications must be suitable.

KEY TERMS AND CONCEPTS

You should now be able to define and use the following terms and concepts (the numbers shown indicate the pages where the terms and concepts are first mentioned):

TOPICS FOR REVIEW AND DISCUSSION

1. If computer literacy was a rare skill 20 years ago, why do you need it today?

2. (*a*) What is a computer program? (*b*) Why can a computer program be described as an "intellectual map?"

3. (*a*) What is a computer? (*b*) What capabilities does a computer possess?

4. (*a*) Discuss the different views that people may have of computers as they are reflected in cartoons, magazines, newspapers, movies, television, and science fiction. (*b*) Discuss four ways that computers have affected your life.

5. Electricity can travel about one foot in a nanosecond. Does this fact place any upper limits on computer operating speed?

6. Discuss this statement: "If computers are so accurate, why is the phrase "garbage in–garbage out" associated with their use?"

7. (*a*) What are data? (*b*) What is information? (*c*) What's the difference between these two terms?

8. What additional facts could be supplied to transform the data item "102.2" into useful information?

9. (*a*) What is data processing? (*b*) Identify and explain the basic data processing activities.

10. In order to classify data, codes are assigned to the items being arranged. Light trucks are classified with an alphanumeric identification code by General Motors. A code for a particular vehicle is CCL247F153278. How might this code be interpreted and used for classification purposes?

11. Why is the computer's ability to make a simple comparison between two data items important?

12. (*a*) What is a system? (*b*) What three hardware components are required in a computer system?

13. "The primary storage section of the CPU is used for four purposes." What are these four purposes?

14. What's the difference between primary and secondary storage devices?

15. (*a*) What's the function of the arithmetic-logic section of the CPU? (*b*) What's the function of the control section?

16. What's the typical data flow pattern in a computer system?

17. What's the stored program concept and why is it important?

18. How may computers be classified according to size?

19. Discuss some limitations of computer usage.

ANSWERS TO FEEDBACK AND REVIEW SECTIONS

1-1

The solution to the crossword puzzle is shown at the right:

1-2

1. system
2. central
3. working
4. control
5. program
6. output
7. primary
8. selects
9. online
10. vary

1-3

1. T
2. T
3. F
4. F
5. T
6. F
7. F
8. T
9. F

Our Debt to the Past
The Evolution of Data Processing

It has taken thousands of years for data processing to evolve from the use of notches in sticks to the application of the latest computer system. In fact, written history really began when people started keeping records. Let's look now at the highlights of this historical path.

The First Record Keepers

For centuries, people lived on the earth without keeping records, but as social organizations such as tribes began to form, records became necessary. The complexities of tribal life required that more details be remembered. Methods of counting based on the biological fact that people have 10 fingers developed this way. However, the limited number of fingers combined with the need to remember more facts posed problems. For example, if a

shepherd was tending a large tribal flock and had a short memory, how could that shepherd keep control of the inventory? Problems bring solutions, and the shepherd's solution might have been to let a stone, a stick, a scratch on a rock, or a knot in a string represent each sheep in the flock.

As tribes grew into nations, trade and commerce developed. Stones and sticks no longer met the needs of early traders. By 3500 B.C., ancient Babylonian merchants were keeping records on clay tablets. An early manual calculating device was the *abacus*. Although it's over 2,000 years old, the abacus is still widely used. The abacus shown in Figure 1-A is the type used in the Orient since the thirteenth century.

The First Record-Keeping Machines

Manual record-keeping techniques continued to develop through the centuries, with such innovations as record audits (the Greeks) and banking systems and budgets (the Romans). Machines were introduced in Europe over 300 years ago to improve the performance of *single* data processing steps. In 1642, for example, the first mechanical calculating machine, pictured in Figure 1-B, was developed by Blaise Pascal, a brilliant young Frenchman. About 30 years later, Gottfried Leibniz, a German mathematician, improved upon Pascal's invention by producing a calculating machine which could add, subtract, multiply, divide, and extract roots. But in the 20 years following the Civil War, the main tools of data processing in the United States were pencils, pens, and rulers. Work sheets were used for classifying, calculating, and summarizing; journals for storing; and ledgers for storing and communicating.

Figure 1-A A thirteenth-century abacus. The abacus was first used by the ancient Babylonians to perform calculations. (Courtesy IBM Corporation)

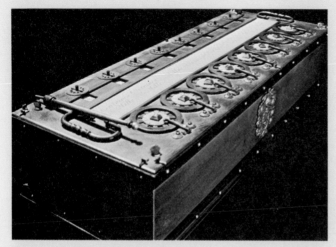

Figure 1-B Blaise Pascal developed the first mechanical adding machine in 1642. Pascal's device, called the Machine Arithmetique, was made up of interlocking gears that represented the numbers 0 through 9. (Courtesy IBM Corporation)

The volume of business and government records during this period was expanding rapidly, and, as you might expect, such complete reliance on manual methods resulted in information that was relatively inaccurate and often late. To the consternation of the Census Bureau, for example, the 1880 census was not finished until it was almost time to begin the 1890 count! Fortunately for the Bureau and for others with a need for improved data processing methods, a number of new machines were introduced at about this time. For example, the typewriter was introduced in the 1880s as a recording aid that improved legibility and doubled writing speeds. And machines that could calculate and print the results were produced around 1890. These devices *combined* calculating, summarizing, and recording steps, and produced a printed tape record suitable for storing data. The most important breakthrough at this time, however, was the development of electromechanical punched card equipment.

The Weaver, the Statistician, and Their Cards

The history of the punched card dates back to about the end of the American Revolution, when a French weaver named Joseph Marie Jacquard used them to control his looms. Although they continued as a means of process control, it was not until the use of manual methods resulted in the problem of completing the 1880 census count that cards began to be looked at as a medium for data processing. The inventor of modern punched card techniques was Dr. Herman Hollerith, a statistician. He was hired by the Census Bureau as a special agent to help find a solution to the census problem. In 1887, Hollerith developed his machine-readable card concept and designed a device known as the "census machine." Tabulating time with Hollerith's methods was only one-eighth of the time previously required, and so his techniques were adopted for use in the 1890 count. Although population had increased from 50 to 63 million in the decade after 1880, the 1890 count was completed in less than 3 years. (Of course, this would be considered intolerably slow by today's standards. The 1950 census, using punched card equipment, took about 2 years to produce; the 1980 census yielded figures in a few months.)

After the 1890 census, Hollerith converted his equipment to business use and set up freight statistics systems for two railroads. In 1896 he founded the Tabulating Machine Company to make and sell his invention. Later, this firm merged with others to form what is now known as International Business Machines Corporation (IBM).

Punched card processing is based on a simple idea: Input data are first recorded in a coded form by punching holes into cards. These cards are then fed into machines that perform processing steps. The early Hollerith cards measured 3 by 5 inches; different sizes are used today, and different coding schemes are employed. You'll find more information on modern cards and their codes in Chapter 6.

A number of electromechanical punched card machines were needed to perform the typical processing

Figure 1-C Steps in punched card data processing.

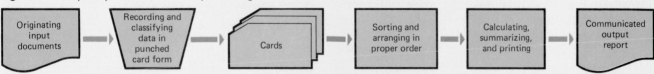

Figure 1-D The IBM Model 29 card punch. The card punch is still a popular data entry device that is used to prepare input for *computer* processing. (Courtesy IBM Corporation)

steps shown in Figure 1-C. After data were recorded in cards through the use of a keypunch or *card punch* machine (Figure 1-D), the cards were usually carried to sorters and collators. The job of the *sorter* was to put the cards in some desired order or sequence. The *collator* could perform several functions. One function (merging) was to combine two decks of sequenced cards into a single sequenced deck. Another function (matching) was to compare agreement between two sets of cards without combining them. After the cards were arranged in the desired order, they were then taken to a *calculator* that could perform the necessary arithmetic operations and then punch the results into the card that supplied the data or into a following card. An *accounting machine* or *tabulator* was then used to summarize data from the cards it received and to print the desired reports. Finally, a *reproducer* could be used to duplicate the data found in a large number of cards.

From this brief survey, it's obvious that punched card data processing was a significant improvement over the manual methods that went before. Gains in speed and accuracy were made. Punched card equipment proved effective in performing many of the individual steps necessary. But it was still necessary to have people handle trays of cards between each step. Separate machines had to be fed, started, and stopped. This need for human intervention between processing stages was a

major disadvantage. With the computer, of course, this disadvantage disappears: human intervention is not required between each step.

Computer Development

About 50 years before Hollerith's efforts, Charles Babbage, Lucasian Professor of Mathematics at Cambridge University in England, had proposed a machine, which he named the "analytical engine." Babbage was an eccentric and colorful individual who spent much of his life working in vain to build his machine. Babbage's dream—to many of his contemporaries it was "Babbage's folly"—would have incorporated a punched card input; a memory unit, or *store;* an arithmetic unit, or *mill;* automatic printout; sequential program control; and 20-place accuracy (see Figure 1-E). In short, Babbage had designed a machine that was a prototype computer and that was 100 years ahead of its time. After Babbage's death in 1871, little progress was made until 1937.

Beginning in 1937, Harvard professor Howard Aiken set out to build an automatic calculating machine that would combine established technology with Hollerith's punched cards. With the help of graduate students and IBM engineers, the project was completed in 1944. The completed device shown in Figure 1-F was known as the Mark I digital computer. Internal operations were controlled automatically with electromagnetic relays; arith-

Figure 1-E Babbage's analytical engine concept.

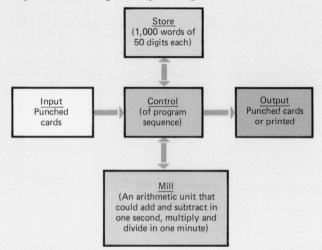

metic counters were mechanical. The Mark I was thus not an *electronic* computer but was rather an <u>*electromechanical*</u> one. In many respects the Mark I was the realization of Babbage's dream. Appropriately, this "medieval" machine is now on display at Harvard University.

The first prototype *electronic* computer was conceived in the winter of 1937–1938 by Dr. John Vincent Atanasoff, a professor of physics and mathematics at Iowa State College. After concluding that none of the calculating devices then available was adequate for his needs, Atanasoff decided to build his own machine. Using design concepts that crystalized in his mind late one winter night in a small roadside tavern in Illinois, Atanasoff teamed up with Clifford Berry, his graduate assistant, and began the task of building the first electronic computer. This computer was called the "Atanasoff-Berry computer" (ABC). The ABC used vacuum tubes (see Figure 1-G) for storage and arithmetic-logic functions.

During 1940 and 1941, Atanasoff and Berry met with John W. Mauchly and showed him their work. Mauchly, working at the Moore School of Electrical Engineering of the University of Pennsylvania, then began formulating his own ideas on how a general-purpose computer might be built. (The ABC was designed for the special purpose of solving systems of simultaneous equations.) Mauchly's ideas came to the attention of J. Presper Eckert, Jr., a graduate engineering student at the Moore School, and the team of Mauchly and Eckert was formed. This team

Figure 1-G The vacuum tubes used for arithmetic-logic and storage functions in an early computer. (Courtesy IBM Corporation)

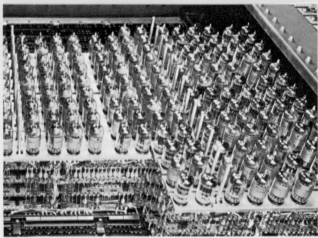

was responsible for the construction of ENIAC in the early 1940s.

ENIAC was the first electronic general-purpose computer to be put into full operation (Figure 1-H). It was funded by the U.S. Army, and was built as a secret wartime project at the Moore School (the Army was interested in the rapid preparation of artillery trajectory tables). Vacuum tubes (18,000 of them!) were also used in ENIAC. It could do 300 multiplications per second, making it 300 times faster than any other device of the day. Operating instructions for ENIAC were not stored internally; rather they were fed through externally located plugboards and switches. ENIAC was used by the Army until 1955 and was then placed in the Smithsonian Institution.

In the mid-1940s, in collaboration with H. H. Goldstine and A. W. Burks, John von Neumann, a mathematical genius and member of the Institute for Advanced Study in Princeton, New Jersey, wrote a paper in which he suggested that (1) *binary* numbering systems be used in building computers and (2) computer *instructions* as well as the *data* being manipulated could be stored internally in the machine. The origin of these ideas is disputed, but they became a basic part of the philosophy of computer design. The binary numbering system is represented by only 2 digits (0 and 1) rather than the 10 digits (0 to 9) of the familiar decimal system. Since electronic components are typically in one of two conditions ("on" or "off," conducting or not conducting), the binary concept facilitated computer equipment design.

Although these design concepts came too late to be incorporated in ENIAC, Mauchly, Eckert, and others at the Moore School set out to build a machine with stored-program capability. This machine—the EDVAC—was not completed until several years later. To the EDSAC, finished in 1949 at Cambridge University, must go the distinction of being the first *stored program electronic computer.*

One reason for the delay in EDVAC was that Eckert and Mauchly founded their own company in 1946 and began to work on the Universal Automatic Computer, or UNIVAC (Figure 1-I). In 1949, Remington Rand acquired the Eckert-Mauchly Computer Corporation, and in early 1951 the first UNIVAC-1 became operational at the Census Bureau. In 1963, it too was retired to the Smithsonian Institution—a historical relic after just 12 years!

Figure 1-H J. Presper Eckert, Jr., left foreground, and John Mauchly, center, are shown here with the ENIAC. Weighing 30 tons and occupying the space of a three-bedroom house (1,500 square feet), ENIAC could perform 300 multiplications per second. (Courtesy IBM Corporation)

Computers in Business

The first computer acquired for data processing and record keeping by a business organization was another UNIVAC-1, which was installed in 1954 at General Electric's Appliance Park in Louisville, Kentucky. The IBM 650 first saw service in Boston in late 1954. It was a comparatively inexpensive machine for that time and it was widely accepted. It gave IBM the leadership in computer production in 1955.

In the period from 1954 to 1959, many organizations acquired computers for data processing purposes, even though these *first-generation* machines had been designed for scientific uses. Managers generally considered the computer to be an accounting tool, and the first applications were designed to process routine tasks such as payrolls. The potential of the computer was frequently underestimated, and more than a few were acquired for no other reason than prestige.

But we shouldn't judge the early users of computers too harshly. They were pioneering in the use of a new tool; they had to staff their computer installations with a new breed of workers; and they initially had to cope with the necessity of preparing programs in a tedious machine language. In spite of these obstacles, the computer was found to be a fast, accurate, and untiring processor of mountains of paper.

The computers of the *second generation* were intro-

Figure 1-I UNIVAC I (Universal Automatic Computer) was the first commercially available computer (1951). (Courtesy Sperry Univac)

duced around 1959 to 1960 and were made smaller, faster, and with greater computing capacity. The vacuum tube, with its relatively short life, gave way to compact *solid state* components such as diodes and transistors. And the practice of writing applications programs in machine-oriented languages gave way to *higher-level languages* that are easier to understand. Unlike earlier computers, some second-generation machines were designed with nonscientific processing requirements in mind.

In 1964, IBM ushered in a *third-generation* of computing hardware when it announced its System/360 family of mainframe computers. During the 1970s, many manufacturers introduced new equipment lines. For example, IBM first announced its System/370 line and then later introduced newer mainframe models in a 4300 series. Dozens of new minicomputers were unveiled, and the microcomputer industry was created. Machines of all sizes continued the trend toward miniaturization of circuit components. Improvements in speed, cost, and storage capacity were realized. In Chapter 4 we'll look at some recent developments in computer technology.

The Computer Industry

In 1950, the developers of the first computers agreed that eight or 10 of these machines would satisfy the entire demand for such devices for years to come. We now know that this was a monumental forecasting blunder. By 1956, over 600 computer systems (worth about $350 million) had been installed. Today, the theme of a recent computer conference—"Computers . . . by the millions, for the millions"—characterizes the size and scope of the computer industry.

There are dozens of computer manufacturers. Many small firms specialize in assembling small scientific and/ or process-control machines, or produce the even smaller personal computers used by individuals. The growth of some of these microcomputer manufacturers has been phenomenal. One firm that began by assembling its product in a garage in the late 1970s was reporting sales of over $100 million just 3 years later.

Although the largest manufacturers also produce personal-sized computers, much of their effort in the past was devoted to supplying organizations with families of mainframe computers. Of the larger companies, most were initially business-machine manufacturers (IBM, Burroughs Corporation, Sperry UNIVAC, and NCR Corporation), or they manufactured electronic controls (Honeywell). Exceptions are Control Data Corporation and Digital Equipment Corporation which were founded to produce computers. The industry leader is IBM with annual revenues of well over $20 billion.

chapter 2

Computers at Work
An Overview

ERNA IN COMPUTERLAND

When Erna Morton, an 11-year-old sixth grader in southern California, fell on the school playground, she hit a bicycle rack and severely lacerated her jaw. Erna was rushed to the emergency room of a hospital in the San Diego suburb where she lives with her parents. She was x-rayed and treated by a plastic surgeon, and a dentist was brought in to determine if her jaw was dislocated. The two doctors disagreed, and a second dentist was brought in for consultation. Erna's jaw was not, after all, dislocated.

During the two-week period in which Erna was seeing doctors and having her jaw x-rayed, her mother made a count of the forms, bills, and checks that had to be filled out and processed. All in all, Mrs. Morton counted 81 documents that she personally processed. And that doesn't include the paperwork the accident generated for the school, Mrs. Morton's employer, the hospital, and so on.

For complex reasons, we seem to be becoming a society of paper pushers and form processors. Technologists claim that computers are the answer to lightening the crush of paper. Increasingly, machines will process insurance forms, pay medical and dental bills electronically, and store the receipts for later income tax filing (more forms!).

Do we want to use and trust machines to such an extent? It is beginning to look as if we no longer have a choice.

—Source of data: Laton McCartney, *output*, August 1981, p. 7.

Computers are as much involved today in the production of goods as they are in the production of services. The programmable controls shown here guide complex industrial operations such as material handling and process control—that is, manufacturing and refinery-type operations. (Courtesy General Electric)

Looking Ahead

Computers operate on data that have been organized into logical groupings. After learning how data are organized, you'll then see how computers can perform input/output, calculation, logic/comparison, and storage and retrieval operations on these data. As examples, you'll learn about applications that emphasize each type of operation. The examples selected are among the most common used in business. But many of the example applications are also used in nonprofit organizations such as schools, hospitals, and government agencies.

Thus, after studying this chapter, you should be able to:

▌ Describe how data are organized into logical groupings to facilitate computer processing

▌ Discuss the computer applications presented in this chapter

▌ Outline two ways in which files may be organized and processed

▌ Identify the applications that account for the greatest use of business computing resources

▌ Understand and use the key terms listed at the end of this chapter

ORGANIZING DATA FOR COMPUTER PROCESSING

All computers do is operate on data. They merely accept and process data and communicate results. They cannot directly carry out any physical activities. They cannot bend metal, for example, but they can supply the information needed to control metal-bending machines.

Normally, the data on which computers operate will be organized into logical groupings so that processing will be effective and output results will be useful. The smallest logical data entity is a **field,** which consists of a group of related characters that are treated as a single unit. Several fields were illustrated in the Longhorn College payroll example discussed in the last chapter. There was a name field (containing "Rob Brooks"), an hours-worked field, an hourly-pay-rate field, and a tax-rate-deduction field. During processing, the several data characters in each of these fields were dealt with collectively and as a single unit.

Fields are normally grouped together to form a record. **A record,** then, is a collection of related fields or data items[1] that are treated as a single unit. Thus, there would be a record made up of four fields for each of the student workers at Longhorn College. Records are then grouped to form a file. **A file** is a number of related records that are treated as a unit. The student payroll file at Longhorn College consists of the records of all student employees (see Figure 2-1). Finally, a **data base** is a collection of logically related data elements

---

[1]Some make the distinction that a field is a designated physical location for a data item on a storage medium while the data item itself represents whatever might be contained in the location. This may be a valid distinction, but the terms tend to be used interchangeably.

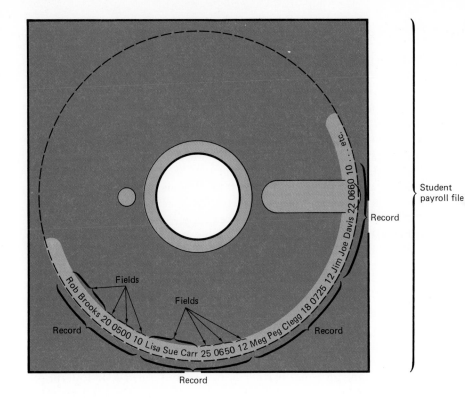

Fields

Record

Rob Brooks 20 0500 10 Lisa Sue Carr 25 0650 12 Meg Peg Clegg 18 0725 12 Jim Joe Davis 22 0660 10 . . . . etc.

Record

Record

Record

Fields

Record

Student payroll file

Figure 2-1 Longhorn College's student payroll file. The record for each student consists of four fields, and all student records make up this file. Thousands of records can be stored on this one small floppy disk. Files are also maintained on other media such as punched cards and magnetic tape. In a card file, each card may represent a record; in a magnetic tape file, a record is stored on a short length of the tape.

that may be structured in various ways to meet the multiple processing and retrieval needs of organizations and individuals. Figure 2-2 summarizes the data organization hierarchy used by computer-based processing systems.

WHAT COMPUTERS DO: AN INTRODUCTION TO APPLICATIONS

As you'll recall from the last chapter, the operations which computers perform on data are classified into four categories:

1. Input/output

2. Calculation

3. Logic/comparison

4. Storage and retrieval

Simply because computers can do these four types of operations, they are being put to work performing literally thousands of different tasks, or **applications.** Example applications that emphasize each of the four categories are presented in the following sections. Since most of these examples relate to one particular business, let's pause briefly here for some background information.

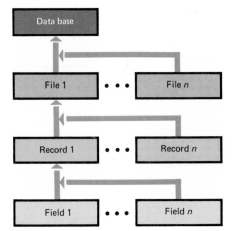

Data base

File 1 · · · File n

Record 1 · · · Record n

Field 1 · · · Field n

Figure 2-2 Data are normally organized into a hierarchy for computer processing. The field is the smallest entity to be processed as a single unit. Related fields are grouped to form records, and related records are combined to form files. The highest level in the data organization hierarchy is the data base, which is a collection of logically related data elements that may be structured in various ways and used for multiple purposes.

The initial product of R-K Enterprises.

R-K Enterprises

You know that Rob Brooks is a student and part-time groundskeeper at Longhorn College. But he's much more than that. He's also a founder and partner in R-K Enterprises. The idea for what was to become R-K Enterprises' first product came to Rob some months ago while he was reading a newspaper. The article that caught his eye told about a state legislator who, after fighting a losing battle with swarms of large mosquitos at a family picnic, had introduced a bill in the legislature to make the mosquito the official state bird.[2] Intrigued by this account, Rob decided to paint a picture of a "mosquito bird" and an appropriate slogan on one of his tee shirts to show his support for the lawmaker's bill. To his surprise, dozens of students tried to buy the shirt right off his back.

Realizing then that he had a marketable product, Rob made arrangements with a manufacturer for a supply of the shirts. It wasn't long before they became the latest fad. Demand spread far beyond the Longhorn campus. After hiring some fellow students to help sell the shirts, Rob began to think about further ways to exploit the mosquito bird fad. His friend, Kay Oss, is a music major, and so Rob asked her to write a song in support of the mosquito bird movement. When he heard Kay sing her song (accompanied by guitar and kazoo) he decided to market a record and a tape cassette of "The Mosquito Bird Song." Since Kay created these products and helped finance their introduction, she became an equal partner in the newly formed R-K Enterprises. The success of these products led to others that will be discussed in later chapters.

Any successful business must perform data processing tasks, and R-K Enterprises is no exception. Drawing on Rob's experience in a computer data processing course, the partners decided to use a computer to handle certain input/output, calculation, logic/comparison, and storage/retrieval operations. Let's now look at these applications and at other ways in which a computer can be used.

An Input/Output Application: The Mailing List

Computers are often used to print the names and addresses of prospective customers on gummed labels to ease the mailing of a large volume of promotional material. Since the partners use mailings to introduce and advertise their products, a mailing label application was developed right away. Input data for this application are contained in a file of prospect records. Each record has fields for the prospect's name, address, city, state, and Zip code.

The data needed to develop this file were gathered from the first orders received, from the letters and calls of prospective customers, and from responses to a few small newspaper ads. After these facts were captured, they

ED'S CULTURAL CENTER
822 PHILHARMONIC AVENUE
CRAMPS, TEXAS 77786

PIERRE'S RECORD SHOP
6453 ORLEANS STREET
BOOGIE, LOUISIANA 54321

ROCKY COLLEGE STORE
1563 BEETHOVEN DRIVE
ROCKTOWN, MARYLAND 20765

WYNN D. TOOTS, INC.
120 BROWNING STREET
GONG, CALIFORNIA 98765

---

[2]This is not entirely fiction. Such a bill was actually introduced by a fun-loving legislator in a southern state.

were logically organized on a machine-readable medium to create the master prospect file. Since then, the computer has been used periodically to add, delete, and change records through a **file maintenance** or **file updating** operation (see Figure 2-3).

To process this mailing list application and produce the gummed labels, the computer system follows the procedure shown in Figure 2-4. Let's assume that the input data in the prospect master file are stored on magnetic tape. This tape closely resembles the tape used in a sound tape recorder, but it's wider. The data are represented by tiny magnetically formed patterns that are invisible to our eyes.

The computer operator uses a magnetic tape input device to enter records on the prospect file tape into the primary storage section of the CPU. A tape record is read into the input storage area, the record fields are arranged in the desired format and moved to the output storage area, and the mailing label is then printed. If additional records are contained on the tape, program control will branch back to step 1 and the next record will be processed. After the last record has been printed, the processing will stop.

Computers are often used for such basic input/output purposes. And they are not only used by businesses. Political, religious, and charitable organizations solicit support and contributions with the help of computer-produced labels. Also, computer listings of personnel and products are sometimes extracted from personnel and product files for management purposes.

Figure 2-3 File maintenance is required to add new records and delete or make changes to existing records. A maintenance program stored in the computer can cause the system to (1) read additions, deletions, and changes to be made from one input device; (2) read the old master file records from another input device; (3) insert new records and delete or change existing records as needed; and (4) produce as output an updated master file.

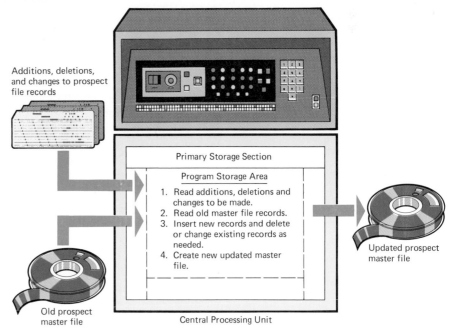

Additions, deletions, and changes to prospect file records

Primary Storage Section

Program Storage Area

1. Read additions, deletions and changes to be made.
2. Read old master file records.
3. Insert new records and delete or change existing records as needed.
4. Create new updated master file.

Updated prospect master file

Old prospect master file

Central Processing Unit

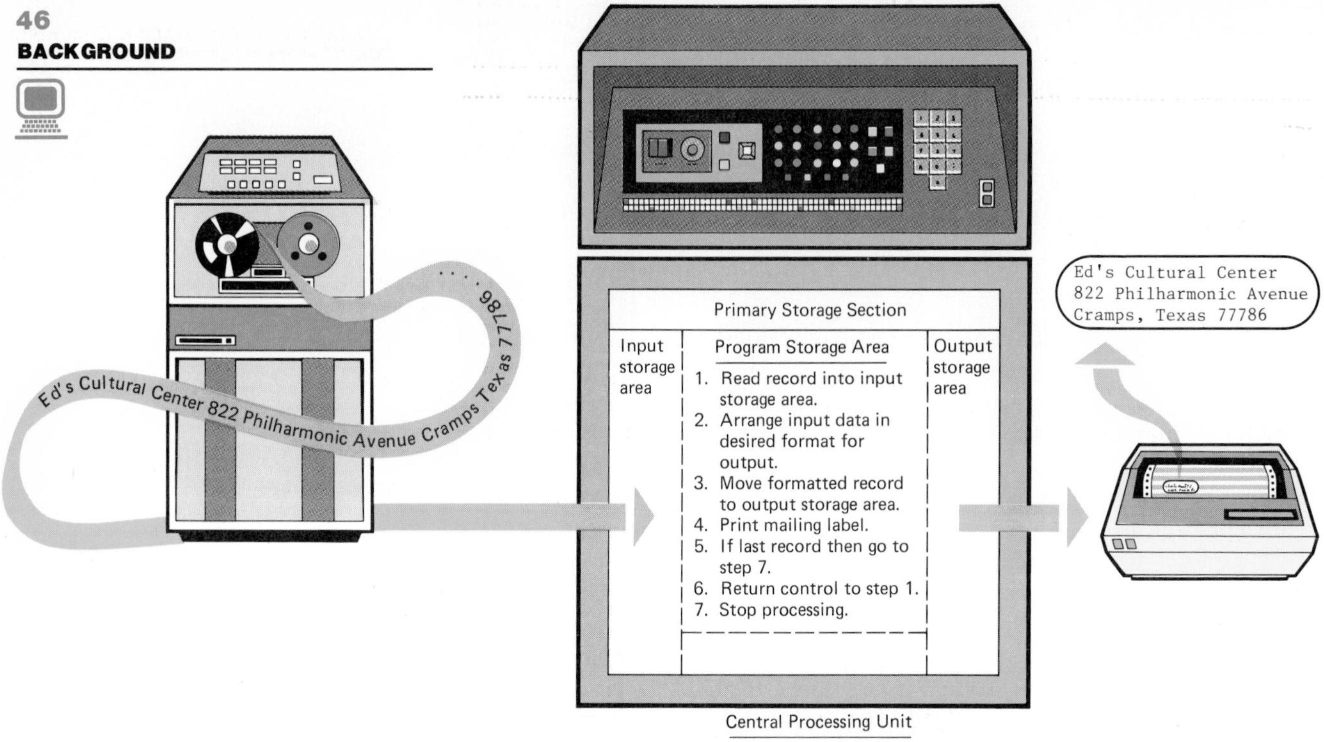

Figure 2-4 Using a computer to prepare mailing labels is an example of a basic input/ output application. The following steps are taken during the processing of this application: (1) A record from a prospect master file is read into the input storage area of the CPU under program control; (2) the record fields are arranged in the desired format; (3) the formatted record is moved to the output storage area in the CPU; and (4) the mailing label is printed. These steps are repeated until all input records have been processed.

Calculation Applications

You may have noticed that no calculation activities were performed in the mailing label example. Alphanumeric data were merely entered in one form and reproduced as output in another. But some calculations are usually needed in computer applications. For example, calculations were required during the preparation of the Longhorn College payroll application discussed in Chapter 1. They are also needed in a report that Rob and Kay use.

Sales Compensation Report. One of the partners' reports is a sales compensation document that shows the amount of sales and earnings for each salesperson during a 4-week period. The salespeople are paid a percentage of their total sales for the period. Figure 2-5 illustrates how this report can be prepared.

The input data are first transferred from the sales reporting forms to a machine-readable medium. Records are then entered (one at a time) into the input storage area of the CPU under program control. The first calculation involves adding the four weekly sales figures in a record to determine the *total sales amount* for the salesperson. The second computation consists of multiplying this total sales amount figure by a 10 percent commission rate to get the salesperson's *earnings* for the period. Finally, the salesperson's name, total sales amount, and earnings are printed on the output report. This report can then be used to evaluate salesperson performance and to prepare paychecks.

Updating Savings Account Records. Most of us have deposited and withdrawn money from a savings account at a bank, savings and loan, or other financial institution. Such transactions require calculations and are now usu-

Figure 2-5 In this application, calculations are required (1) to determine the total amount of sales made by each salesperson over a four-week period, and then (2) to determine the salesperson's earnings for the same period. The *nine* program steps required to process the input data and produce the output sales compensation report are shown in the program storage area of the CPU. The numbers in parentheses in this diagram refer to the program steps.

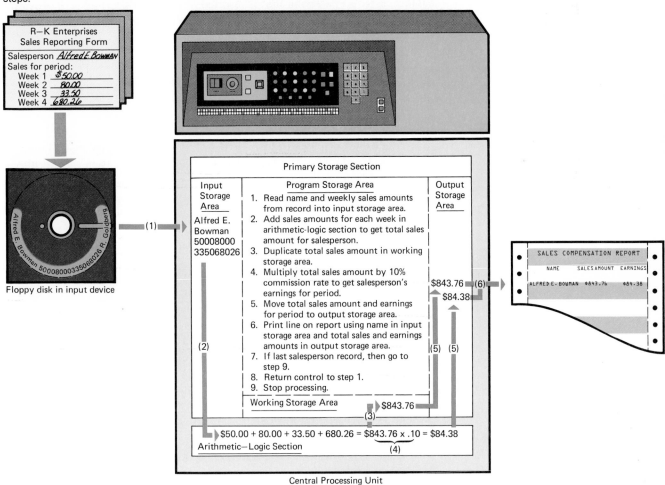

ally handled by computer systems. Let's assume that Rob has decided to deposit in his savings account the $90 paycheck he received from Longhorn College in Chapter 1. After filling out a deposit ticket, Rob presents the ticket, his savings account passbook, and his paycheck to a teller. The teller inserts the passbook into an online transaction terminal (see Figure 2-6) and keys in the transaction data in response to questions displayed on the terminal screen. The data are then sent to the input storage area of the CPU. In Rob's case, a transaction code "*D*" is entered. *D* indicates that a deposit is being made. However, the instructions in the program storage area of the CPU are also capable of handling withdrawal transactions.

After the input data have been entered, the computer then quickly retrieves Rob's savings account record from an online secondary storage device and adds the $90 deposit to his previous balance of $810. The account number, customer name, and new balance of $900 are then moved to the output storage area. From that location the updated record is used to (1) replace the old account record in online secondary storage, and (2) print an updated account balance in Rob's passbook that is inserted in the teller's terminal. This entire input/process/output operation takes only a few seconds.

Sequential and Direct-Access Processing

Implicit in the applications that we've now discussed is the fact that a file must be organized in some way to facilitate processing. File organization requires the use of some **record key** or unique identifying value that's found in every record in the file. The key value must be unique for each record; duplications would cause serious problems. In the sales compensation example, the record key was the salesperson's last name,[3] and in the savings account application, the record key was the customer's account number.

Sequential Processing. **A sequential file organization** consists of storing records one after another in a file in an ascending or descending order determined by the record key. The sales compensation application organizes the sales records by the salesperson's last name in an alphabetical sequence. Sequentially organized files that are processed by computer systems are typically kept on storage media such as magnetic tape, punched cards, and magnetic disks. **Sequential processing** (also called **batch** or **serial** processing) consists of reading and processing the first record in the file sequence, then the second record in the order, and so on. The processing of Rob's paycheck discussed in Chapter 1, and the mailing label and sales compensation applications described in this chapter are all examples of sequential processing. Another example is the preparation of the monthly bills that are sent to credit-card customers.

---

[3]In personnel files of much size where name duplications would be possible, the record key would likely be an employee identification number.

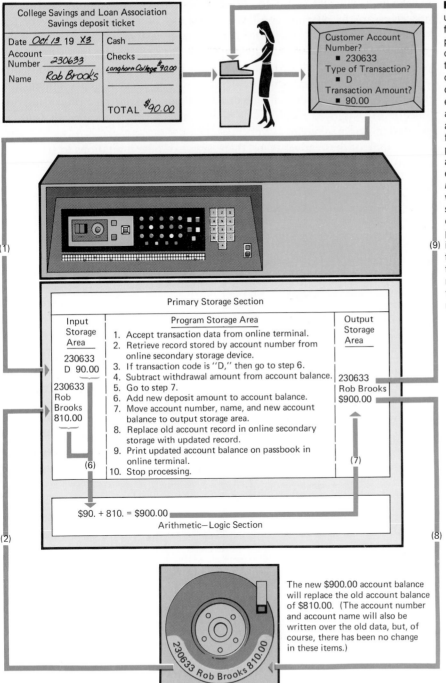

College Savings and Loan Association
Savings deposit ticket

Date *Oct. 13* 19 *X3*   Cash _____

Account
Number _*230633*_   Checks _____
                         Longhorn College $*90.00*

Name *Rob Brooks*

TOTAL $*90.00*

Customer Account
Number?
  ▪ 230633
Type of Transaction?
  ▪ D
Transaction Amount?
  ▪ 90.00

(1)

(2)

Primary Storage Section

Input Storage Area	Program Storage Area	Output Storage Area
230633 D 90.00	1. Accept transaction data from online terminal.	
	2. Retrieve record stored by account number from online secondary storage device.	
	3. If transaction code is "D," then go to step 6.	
	4. Subtract withdrawal amount from account balance.	230633
230633 Rob Brooks 810.00	5. Go to step 7.	Rob Brooks
	6. Add new deposit amount to account balance.	$900.00
	7. Move account number, name, and new account balance to output storage area.	
	8. Replace old account record in online secondary storage with updated record.	
	9. Print updated account balance on passbook in online terminal.	
(6)	10. Stop processing.	(7)

$90. + 810. = $900.00

Arithmetic—Logic Section

(8)

230633 Rob Brooks 810.00

The new $900.00 account balance will replace the old account balance of $810.00. (The account number and account name will also be written over the old data, but, of course, there has been no change in these items.)

Figure 2-6 A computer system may be used to update savings account balances by following the program steps outlined in the program storage area. Data from a deposit or withdrawal ticket are entered directly into the input storage area of the CPU from an online financial transaction terminal. The computer then quickly retrieves the customer's account record from an online secondary storage device and determines whether a deposit or withdrawal calculation is called for. If the transaction code is "D" (for deposit), program control branches to step 6 and the new deposit amount is added to the old account balance. If the transaction is *not* a deposit, then it is assumed here to be a withdrawal, and the transaction amount is subtracted from the old balance. After the computer has performed the necessary processing, the customer's updated record (9) is placed in online secondary storage and the updated account balance is printed on the customer's passbook by the online terminal. The entire transaction takes just a few seconds. (The figures in parentheses refer to effects of numbered program steps.)

Sequential processing is quite suitable for such applications because it's not necessary to prepare employee paychecks or customer bills every few hours. Rather, data on employee earnings and customer purchases are accumulated into batches of transactions (thus the name batch processing) and processed only at scheduled intervals. The processing delay that results presents no problems. And sequential processing is efficient and economical if there are a large number of file records to be updated during a processing run. Since most employee records will be updated during each payroll run, the processing cost per record is very low.

In spite of these advantages, there are also some limitations to sequential processing. As Figure 2-7 shows, when a sequential file is updated, the transac-

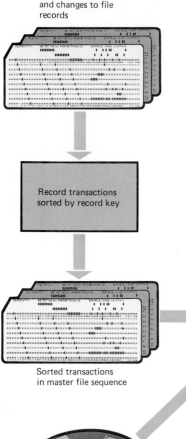

Additions deletions, and changes to file records

Record transactions sorted by record key

Sorted transactions in master file sequence

Old master file

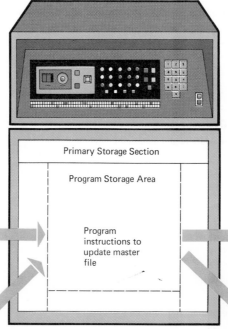

Primary Storage Section

Program Storage Area

Program instructions to update master file

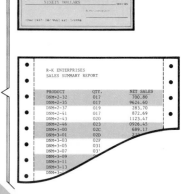

Payroll checks, bills, reports, etc.

Updated master file

Figure 2-7 The sequential file processing approach. Transactions affecting file records must be identified by a record key, and these transactions must be arranged into the same ascending or descending sequence as the master file before processing can begin. Transaction data and old master file records are then read into the CPU. The record key is used to match a new transaction with the appropriate old file record. The old record is updated by program instructions and a new file record is created and written on an output medium. Various documents such as checks, bills, and reports may also be prepared during the processing.

tions (additions, deletions, or changes) that affect the records in the old master file must first be sorted into the same sequence as the master file before processing can begin. A separate computer program written specifically to sort data into numeric or alphabetic sequence by comparing items to determine which is greater is typically used. And when processing a sequential file, records near the end of the file cannot be accessed until all preceding records in the sequence have been read into the CPU. Thus, if there's a need to update only a few records near the end of the file, these records cannot be retrieved until all earlier records have been read. Finally, for some applications the delay caused by accumulating the input data into batches prior to updating can be a serious problem. For example, if Rob needed to withdraw his recently deposited funds because of some emergency, he would be understandably upset if he were told that a 2-week wait would be required before the file could be updated to show if he did indeed have the needed funds on deposit.

Direct-Access Processing. Fortunately for all of us with bank accounts, processing alternatives exist to overcome sequential processing limitations. A **direct file organization** (also called a **random file organization**) consists of storing records in such a way that the computer can go directly to the key or identifying value of the record needed without having to search through a sequence of other records. The records in directly organized files must be kept in an online secondary storage device such as a rigid or flexible disk unit.

Direct-access processing (also called **online** or **random-access** processing) consists of directly locating and updating any record in a file without the need to read preceding file records. When a computer system is performing direct-access processing, it typically accepts input data from an online keyboard or from some other online data-collection or transaction-recording device. This was what was done in our savings account application. The record(s) being updated is then retrieved by the appropriate record key (Rob's savings account number in our example). The access to, and retrieval of, the record is quick and direct. It's located and retrieved in a fraction of a second, and it's obtained without the need for a sequential search of the file. Once the record has been updated, it's returned to the **direct-access storage device (DASD).**

In addition to quickly and directly updating records without the need to sort transactions, direct-access processing can also provide up-to-the-minute information in response to inquiries from *simultaneously usable* online stations (Figure 2-8). The speed of the system allows the CPU to switch from one using station to another and to do a part of each job in the allocated "time slice" until the work is completed. The speed is such that the user often has the illusion that no one else is using the CPU. Thus, a teller can quickly determine the exact balance in Rob's savings account at any instant. Also, any airline ticket agent can have immediate access to reservation system records to see if seats are currently available on particular flights. If a ticket is purchased for flight 205 to Boston, the agent can quickly update the appropriate record and reduce by one the number of available seats.

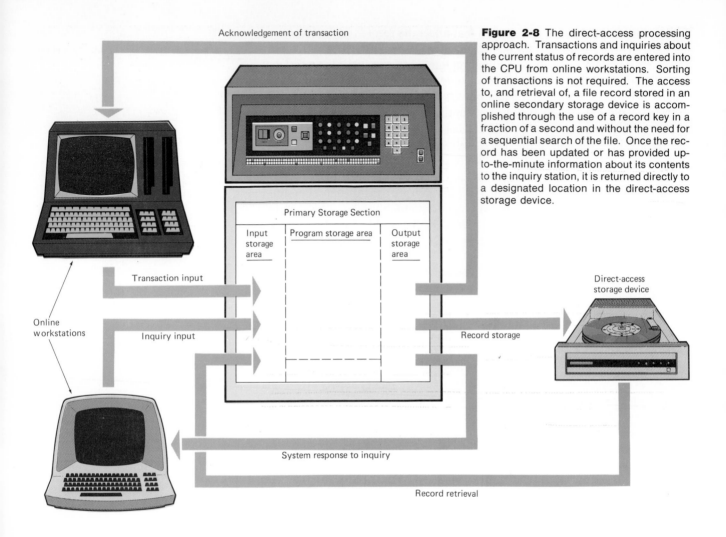

Acknowledgement of transaction

Figure 2-8 The direct-access processing approach. Transactions and inquiries about the current status of records are entered into the CPU from online workstations. Sorting of transactions is not required. The access to, and retrieval of, a file record stored in an online secondary storage device is accomplished through the use of a record key in a fraction of a second and without the need for a sequential search of the file. Once the record has been updated or has provided up-to-the-minute information about its contents to the inquiry station, it is returned directly to a designated location in the direct-access storage device.

Primary Storage Section

Input storage area

Program storage area

Output storage area

Direct-access storage device

Transaction input

Online workstations

Inquiry input

Record storage

System response to inquiry

Record retrieval

 **Feedback and Review 2-1**

In the preceding section you've seen how data may be organized for computer processing. You've seen how a computer can be used to process a mailing label application that emphasizes input/output operations. And you've looked at two applications that were used to illustrate the calculation operations performed by computers. In the first sales compensation application, the file of the partners' sales force was sequentially organized and sequentially processed. In the second application to update Rob's savings account record, a direct file organization approach was used and direct-access processing was employed. You can test your understanding of these concepts by using the following sentences and definitions to fill in the *crossword puzzle* form.

Across

1. Sequential processing is also called batch processing or _____ processing.

2. A _____ is a collection of related fields that are treated as a unit.

10. _____ file organization consists of storing records one after another in a file in an ascending or descending order determined by the record key.

11. When updating a sequential file, the transactions that affect the records in the old master file must first be _____ into the same sequence as the master file before processing can begin.

13. A _____ file organization consists of storing records in an online storage device in such a way that the computer can go directly to the key or identifying value of the record needed without having to search through a sequence of other records.

15. A _____ base is a collection of logically related data elements that can be used for multiple processing needs.

17. The first product of R-K Enterprises was a _____ shirt.

20. Computers cannot directly carry out any _____ activities. For example, they cannot bend metal, but they can supply the information needed to control metal-bending machines.

21. Computers are able to _____ and retrieve data.

22. Direct or _____ -access processing consists of directly locating and updating any file record without the need to read preceding file records.

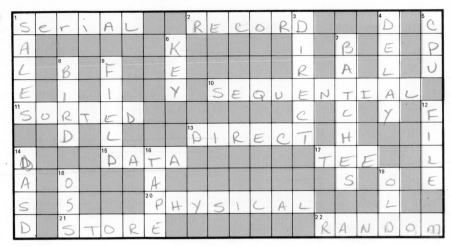

Down

1. One of the applications illustrating the calculating capabilities of a computer was a _____ compensation example.

3. When _____ -access processing is used, up-to-the-minute information about record contents can be provided to answer inquiries from operators of online stations.

4. The _____ caused by accumulating the input data into batches prior to file updating can be a problem when sequential processing is used.

5. A limitation of sequential processing is that records near the end of the file cannot be accessed until all preceding records have been read into the _____.

6. File organization requires the use of some record _____ or identifying value that's found in every record in the file.

7. In sequential processing, transactions are typically accumulated into _____ and processed only at scheduled intervals.

8. A tee shirt promoting the mosquito as the state _____ was the initial product of R-K Enterprises.

9. A _____ consists of a group of related characters that are treated as a single unit.

12. _____ maintenance is required to add new records and delete or make changes to the existing records in a file.

14. _____ is the acronym for direct-access storage device.

16. In the mailing label application, the prospect master file was stored on magnetic _____.

18. Rob's partner in R-K Enterprises is Kay _____.

19. A file update program can cause the system to read new record transactions from one input device, read the _____ master file records from another input device, change the existing records as needed, and produce an updated master file as output.

A Logic/Comparison Application

You saw in Chapter 1 that a computer system is able to perform logical operations by first comparing numbers, letters, or other symbols, and then by following a prescribed course of action determined by the result of the comparison. Although they've not been spelled out in detail, logical operations have been performed in several of our earlier applications programs. In the mailing label application, for example, step 5 in the program is "If last record, then go to step 7." The purpose of this step is to determine if the last prospect record has been processed. If the last record has not been processed, program control goes to the next step in the sequence and from there it branches back to the first program step and the next label is printed. If the last record has been processed, the computer is instructed to go to step 7 and stop the processing.

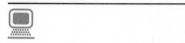

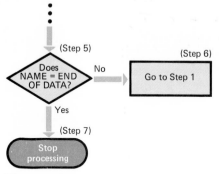

Figure 2-9

How does the computer know when the last valid record has been processed? One approach is to place a **dummy record** at the *end* of the prospect master file. In the record field reserved for the prospect's name, the contents in the last dummy record could be END OF DATA. The computer instruction in step 5 could then be revised to read: "If name = END OF DATA, then go to step 7." The computer will then compare each prospect name to "END OF DATA" and continue the processing until the dummy record is finally read after all valid data have been processed (see Figure 2-9).

The same approach could also be used in the program that processes the sales compensation report. Step 7 in that program (see Figure 2-5) reads: "If last salesperson record, then go to step 9." The salesperson's name in a dummy record at the end of the file could again be END OF DATA. Step 7 could then be revised to read: "If name = END OF DATA, then go to step 9." A comparison of each salesperson's name to "END OF DATA" will continue the processing until the dummy record is finally read.

Billing Application for R-K Enterprises. Rob followed a "cash-only" policy in his initial sales of mosquito bird tee shirts. But after R-K Enterprises was created and the sale of multiple mosquito bird products spread beyond the Longhorn College campus, it became profitable to accept orders from, and then make shipments to, selected customers without receiving immediate payment. This delayed payment policy made it necessary to design an *order entry, shipping,* and *billing system* for credit customers.

Orders from customers may result from the visits of salespersons, from telephone contacts, or from other sources. The **sales order** (or **customer order**) is the first document generated in the order entry process. Typically prepared

Figure 2-10 This illustration shows a system that may be used to accept and fill customer ▶ orders and prepare customer bills. An order from a customer is entered on a sales order form. The sales order data are then used to produce the shipping order which is used (a) to fill the order and (b) to supply the input data for the billing application. The input data are transferred to an input storage medium from where they are read under program control into the CPU during a billing run. The steps required to process R-K's bills are shown in the program storage area. The numbers in parentheses refer to the actions taken in response to numbered program steps. After reading in the input data (step 1), the program sets up the first logic/comparison operation (step 2). If the value of the quantity (Q) field in the input record is equal to −99.9, processing will stop. (This will occur when the last dummy record at the end of the file which has a quantity of −99.9 is read.) If Q is not −99.9, the program moves to the next step. To encourage large purchases, a 15 percent discount is given if the shipment quantity is equal to or greater than (>) 100 units. The dollar amount of the bill before any discount is applied is computed first by multiplying the units shipped times the unit price (step 3). This amount (A) is stored for future use in the working storage area (step 4). The computer next compares the value of Q to 100 (step 5). If Q is 100 units or more, as it is in our example transaction to Pierre's Record Shop, program control branches to step 8 and a 15 percent discount amount (D) is calculated and then duplicated in working storage (step 9). If Q is less than 100 units, the program moves to step 6 and no discount amount is applied. Once the discount amount is determined, it is subtracted from the total amount previously calculated to get the amount of the bill before a 6 percent sales tax is applied (step 10). Since this before-tax total will need to be preserved for later use, it is duplicated in a working storage area location (step 11). The amount of the sales tax (T) is then found by multiplying the before-tax total times the 6 percent tax rate (step 12). This value of T is also preserved in working storage (step 13). The next step is to add T to the before-tax total to get the total amount of the customer's bill (step 14). Finally, all the information that is needed to prepare the bill is moved to the output storage area of the CPU (step 15), and is then used to print the customer's bill in the desired format (step 16). The computer then resets itself to begin processing the next customer's bill (step 17).

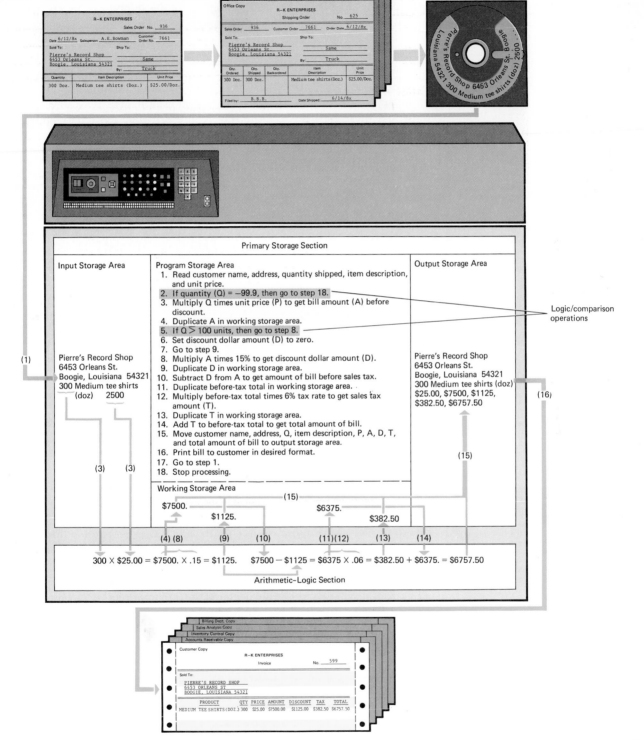

Floppy disk in input device

R–K ENTERPRISES
Sales Order No. 936

Date 6/12/8x Salesperson A.E.Bowman Customer Order No. 7661

Sold To:
Pierre's Record Shop
6453 Orleans St.
Boogie, Louisiana 54321

Ship To:
Same
By: Truck

Quantity	Item Description	Unit Price
300 Doz.	Medium tee shirts (Doz.)	$25.00/Doz.

Packing Copy
Filing Copy
Acknowledgment Copy
Office Copy

R–K ENTERPRISES
Shipping Order No. 625

Sales Order 936 Customer Order 7661 Order Date 6/12/8x

Sold To:
Pierre's Record Shop
6453 Orleans St.
Boogie, Louisiana 54321

Same
By: Truck

Qty. Ordered	Qty. Shipped	Qty. Backordered	Item Description	Unit Price
300 Doz.	300 Doz.		Medium tee shirts (Doz.)	$25.00/Doz.

Filed by: B.B.B. Date Shipped: 6/14/8x

Primary Storage Section

(1)

Input Storage Area

Pierre's Record Shop
6453 Orleans St.
Boogie, Louisiana 54321
300 Medium tee shirts
(doz)   2500

(3)   (3)

Program Storage Area
1. Read customer name, address, quantity shipped, item description, and unit price.
2. If quantity (Q) = −99.9, then go to step 18.
3. Multiply Q times unit price (P) to get bill amount (A) before discount.
4. Duplicate A in working storage area.
5. If Q > 100 units, then go to step 8.
6. Set discount dollar amount (D) to zero.
7. Go to step 9.
8. Multiply A times 15% to get discount dollar amount (D).
9. Duplicate D in working storage area.
10. Subtract D from A to get amount of bill before sales tax.
11. Duplicate before-tax total in working storage area.
12. Multiply before-tax total times 6% tax rate to get sales tax amount (T).
13. Duplicate T in working storage area.
14. Add T to before-tax total to get total amount of bill.
15. Move customer name, address, Q, item description, P, A, D, T, and total amount of bill to output storage area.
16. Print bill to customer in desired format.
17. Go to step 1.
18. Stop processing.

Output Storage Area

Pierre's Record Shop
6453 Orleans St.
Boogie, Louisiana 54321
300 Medium tee shirts (doz)
$25.00, $7500, $1125,
$382.50, $6757.50

Logic/comparison operations

(16)

(15)

Working Storage Area

(15)

$7500. $6375.
    $1125. $382.50

(4) (8)   (9)   (10)   (11)(12)   (13)   (14)

300 × $25.00 = $7500. × .15 = $1125. $7500 − $1125 = $6375 × .06 = $382.50 + $6375. = $6757.50

Arithmetic–Logic Section

Billing Dept. Copy
Sales Analysis Copy
Inventory Control Copy
Accounts Receivable Copy
Customer Copy

R–K ENTERPRISES
Invoice No. 599

Sold To:
PIERRE'S RECORD SHOP
6453 ORLEANS ST.
BOOGIE, LOUISIANA 54321

PRODUCT	QTY	PRICE	AMOUNT	DISCOUNT	TAX	TOTAL
MEDIUM TEE SHIRTS (DOZ.)	300	$25.00	$7500.00	$1125.00	$382.50	$6757.50

by a salesperson or an order clerk, this document provides the data needed to produce the **shipping order.** Multiple copies of the shipping order are generally made. One copy is needed by the employee(s) filling and shipping the order. Another copy may be sent to the customer to acknowledge receipt of the order. A third may be packed with the shipment. A fourth may be kept in the files.

After the order has been shipped, a **bill** or **invoice** must be prepared and sent to the customer. Bills must be sent out promptly to minimize the amount of money that a business has tied up in unpaid shipments. It's also very important that these bills be accurate: Overcharges irritate customers and undercharges can mean lost revenues. Because of this need for speed and accuracy, and because of the mountains of bills that many organizations must prepare each month, billing has long been a major computer application.

As shown in Figure 2-10, the data from the shipping order usually provide the input for the billing application. These data may be transferred to an input storage medium. From there they are read into the CPU under program control during a billing run. The steps required to process R-K Enterprises' bills are shown in the program storage area in Figure 2-10 and explained in detail. For our present purposes, it's not necessary to fully grasp all the program details presented in the CPU storage area and in the caption of Figure 2-10. But a careful study of this figure should give you some insights into several of the examples presented in the chapters of the Programming Module.

It is important here to point out that two logic/comparison operations are carried out in Figure 2-10. After step 1 in the program storage area of the CPU has been followed to read in the data from an input record, the *first* logic/comparison operation is set up by step 2. The value stored in the quantity-shipped field of the input record is compared to a value of -99.9. If the quantity (Q) is not -99.9, the processing continues in sequence. If Q is -99.9, program control will branch to step 18 and the processing will stop. A quantity of -99.9 dozen tee shirts will never be shipped, but such a value is used in a last dummy record at the end of the billing run to indicate that all valid data have been processed.

The second logic/comparison operation is accomplished in step 5. To encourage large purchases, Rob and Kay offer a 15 percent discount on shipments with a quantity equal to or greater than ($>$) 100 units. (Each unit is one-dozen tee shirts in our example.) In step 5, the computer is instructed to compare the value in the quantity-shipped field of the input record to 100. If the input value is 100 units or more (as it is in our example transaction to Pierre's Record Shop in Figure 2-10), program control branches to step 8 and a 15 percent discount amount is calculated. If the input quantity is less than 100 units, however, the program continues to step 6 which specifies that there should be no discount applied (see Figure 2-11).

The processing of the billing application continues in a step-by-step fashion in Figure 2-10 until all the needed information for the customer's bill has been prepared and moved to the output storage area of the CPU. From there the information is sent to a printer which prepares the customer's bill in the desired format. Program control then branches back to step 1 and processing begins on the next customer record.

Figure 2-11

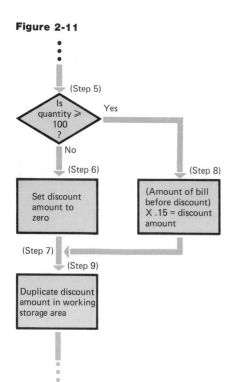

After Billing: Some Important Follow-Up Applications

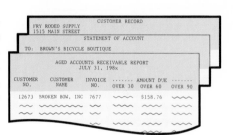

As we've just seen, it's a common business data processing practice to use the data found in the sales order to prepare the shipping order. The shipping order becomes the source of input data for the billing application. And it's common to use the data found in a customer bill as input to several other important business applications. As shown in Figure 2-10, multiple copies of the invoice are often prepared. Copies may then be forwarded to employees who are responsible for accounts receivable, inventory control, and sales analysis applications.

Accounts Receivable. A businesss that grants credit to its customers must maintain an **accounts receivable** (A/R) operation to keep track of the amounts owed by, and the payments received from, these customers (accounts). Thus, the primary *input* documents for the A/R application are customer invoices (showing amounts owed by customers) and payment vouchers (showing payments received from customers). The *output* results produced by the A/R application include:

1. Updated records of individual customers showing charges and payments for a period and the present amount owed

2. Monthly summary statements to remind customers of their debts

3. Management reports that give information about the amounts owed and the ages of the unpaid accounts.

The A/R application is obviously an important follow-up to the billing application. Accuracy of customer records and statements is required to avoid loss of revenue and/or customer irritation. And speed of processing is needed

CONTROLLING INVENTORY AT FIRESTONE

Early in 1980, managers at Firestone Tire & Rubber Company found themselves with $300 million in excess inventory. They lost no time in calling in A. T. Kearney Inc., a Chicago-based, computer-wise management consulting company.

Consultants from Kearney found two basic policies in place at Firestone: (1) Never lose a sale; and (2) produce tires at the lowest possible cost. Both policies are good

ones—up to a point. Both tend to drive up inventories because lowering unit costs means high-volume production runs and getting every sale means having a full range of tire sizes and types in every store and warehouse.

Following computer models developed by Kearney, Firestone changed some strategies. It showed its production managers how the higher unit costs on lower production

runs were more than offset by savings in inventory costs. In addition, Firestone decided to miss a few sales; several private-brand tires with higher inventory requirements (and lower profit margins) were dropped.

According to William M. McGrath, a Kearney vice-president, "Inventory management has come of age at Firestone."

—Source of data: *Wall Street Journal*, Aug. 15, 1980, p. 15.

since delays in preparing statements can result in slow collections and can tie up excessive amounts of capital in unpaid accounts.

Inventory Control. The **inventory control** application is a second important follow-up to the order entry/shipping/billing system. A business generally has two objectives in maintaining an inventory control operation. The first goal is to keep a low level of inventory on hand to minimize the amount of money invested and to reduce the costs associated with storing, handling, and insuring a large quantity of goods. The second goal is to maintain good customer relations by having the goods on hand when they are ordered. Unfortunately, these two goals are at cross-purposes. Stockouts and customer backorders can usually be avoided by carrying large inventories, but this is contradictory to the financial goal of minimizing carrying costs. The purpose of the inventory control application, then, is to give managers the information they need to strike a profitable balance between the two goals—i.e., to allow them to keep stock levels reasonably low while still giving good customer service.

The input documents for the inventory control application may include receiving reports (showing goods initially received or goods that customers have returned) and customer invoices (showing goods sold). The output results produced by the inventory control application include:

1. Updated records of individual inventory items

2. Management reports used to determine what items to reorder or discontinue, how much to reorder, and which items have experienced unusual changes in demand

In later chapters you'll see that an inventory control report is prepared for R-K Enterprises. This report (see Figure 2-12) shows the partners the quantities of each product on hand at the beginning of a period such as the first of the month, how many of each product were received and how many were sold during the period, and the quantities of each product that remain at the end of the period.

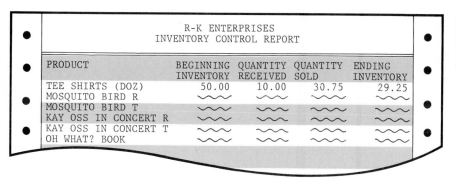

PRODUCT	BEGINNING INVENTORY	QUANTITY RECEIVED	QUANTITY SOLD	ENDING INVENTORY
TEE SHIRTS (DOZ)	50.00	10.00	30.75	29.25
MOSQUITO BIRD R				
MOSQUITO BIRD T				
KAY OSS IN CONCERT R				
KAY OSS IN CONCERT T				
OH WHAT? BOOK				

R-K ENTERPRISES
INVENTORY CONTROL REPORT

Figure 2-12 R-K's inventory control report. (The program that has been written to allow the computer system to prepare this report is discussed in Programming Module Chapter 12.)

```
                    R-K ENTERPRISES
              SALES REPORT FOR TEE SHIRTS (DOZ)

  PIERRE'S RECORD SHOP
  6453 ORLEANS ST.
  BOOGIE, LOUISIANA  54321

  QUANTITY   UNIT PRICE   NET AMOUNT   SALES TAX    TOTAL
    400        $25.00     $10,000.00    $600.00   $10,600.00

  ROCKY COLLEGE STORE
  1563 BEETHOVEN DRIVE
  ROCKTOWN, MARYLAND  20765

  QUANTITY   UNIT PRICE   NET AMOUNT   SALES TAX    TOTAL
    150        $25.00      $3750.00     $225.00    $3975.00

  WYNN D. TOOTS, INC.
  120 BROWNING STREET
  GONG, CALIFORNIA  98765

  QUANTITY   UNIT PRICE   NET AMOUNT   SALES TAX    TOTAL
     75        $25.00      $1875.00     $112.50    $1987.50
```
(a)

```
                   R-K ENTERPRISES
                 SALES SUMMARY REPORT

      PRODUCT             UNIT PRICE   QUANTITY   NET SALES
  TEE SHIRTS (DOZ)          $25.00
  MOSQUITO BIRD RECORD        6.00
  MOSQUITO BIRD TAPE          7.00
  KAY OSS IN CONCERT R        8.00
  KAY OSS IN CONCERT T        8.50
  OH WHAT? BOOK               9.95
```
(b)

Sales Analysis. The preparation of **sales analysis** reports is a *third* important follow-up activity to the order entry/shipping/billing system. The *input* documents that provide the sales analysis data include the customer invoices (showing who is buying, what they are buying, how much they are buying, where they are located, etc.) and the receiving slips (showing goods returned by customers). The *output* reports may provide information to answer questions such as: Who are our best customers? Which of our products are selling and which should we drop? Where are sales brisk and where are they lagging? Later on you'll see that two sales analysis reports help Rob and Kay manage their empire. One of these reports *classifies* the purchases made during a period by a named customer according to the type of product shipped (see Figure 2-13a). The other report *summarizes* the total sales for each product during the period (Figure 2-13b).

The computer's ability to perform the logic/comparison operations spelled out in a program makes it possible for it automatically to control its own operations during the repetitive processing of records in a file. This same logic/comparison ability makes it possible for a computer system to *sort* data into numeric or alphabetic sequence by comparing two items to determine which is greater. Finally, this logic/comparison ability enables the system to *classify* and *summarize* data and records to produce useful information.

Figure 2-13 In the sales report (a), customer purchases are *classified* by the particular type of product sold. (The program that produces this report is discussed in Programming Module Chapter 12.) Sales of all R-K Enterprises products are *summarized* in a periodic report (b). By comparing this report with those of earlier periods, Rob and Kay may be able to spot unusual sales patterns and then take appropriate action. (The program that makes this report possible is discussed in Programming Module Chapter 12.)

A Storage and Retrieval Application: Word Processing

So far, you've learned about the ability of a computer system to store huge quantities of data in a direct-access storage device and to directly retrieve and update any of the thousands of stored records in a fraction of a second. (You do remember the online system used by Rob's savings and loan association to process savings account records, don't you?) And we've already seen how such direct-access systems can be used by airlines and other organizations to provide up-to-the-minute information in response to inquiries from online workstations. Thus, we need not spend much more time here on additional storage and retrieval applications.

The Personnel Department for the City of Chicago uses a word processing system linked to a data base to produce personnel documents and letters of notification to employees. The system processes 75,000 personnel file transactions per year, and allows file enquiries to be made from 9 terminals distributed throughout the Personnel Department. (Photo reprinted by permission of Nixdorf Computer Corporation, Burlington, Mass.)

However, the recent rapid growth in word processing applications in many of the nation's offices is too important to ignore. **Word processing** is the use of computers to create, view, edit, store, retrieve, and print text material. Preparing the written communications that flow out of offices is time consuming and expensive. Furthermore, office productivity gains have lagged far behind the gains achieved in other business areas. Thus, thousands of word processing systems have recently been installed to improve office efficiency by helping employees create and produce letters, reports, and other paperwork.

For example, routine letters may be prepared by accounts-receivable employees and sent to customers to remind them when their accounts are past due. Of course, these letters could be preprinted, but such form letters are often ignored. To personalize each letter, and to create an original copy for each customer, a word processing system can be used. Let's assume that Kay and Rob want to use such a system to send out collection letters to their slow-paying accounts. The first requirement would be to create a series of collection letters using the keyboard of a word processing workstation (see Figure 2-14). The first letter in the series could be a pleasant reminder that the account is past due. If no response is received to this message, the partners could follow it up with a second sober letter and then, if necessary, with a third notification that the account is being turned over to a bill collection agency. The second requirement would then be to store these three letters in an online secondary storage device as shown in Figure 2-14. For call-up purposes, each letter is given a number in our example.

After a letter has been created and stored, it can be retrieved on demand by the operator of a word processing station. With a few keystrokes, the operator can notify the word processing program in the CPU that a particular stored document is needed. The program then locates the needed text and duplicates it in the primary storage section. The operator then keys in the name and address of the person to whom the letter should be sent, and these facts are also read into primary storage. Finally, under program control the name of the recipient of the letter is inserted into the text at appropriate places to "personalize" the message, and the letter is automatically printed. Figure 2-14 gives the program details of this text storage and retrieval application. The efficiency and productivity of office workers can obviously be enhanced by the use of word processing systems.

The Most Common Business Applications

You've now seen just a few of the thousands of computer system applications that exist. We classified these few examples rather arbitrarily according to one of the functions that they performed: input/output, calculation, logic/comparison, and storage/retrieval. But you can see, too, that in most applications the computer system will execute more than one of these functions.

Although our selected applications are limited, they are not random. Rather, our selection includes the applications that account for the greatest use of business computing resources. Figure 2-15 shows that a typical business

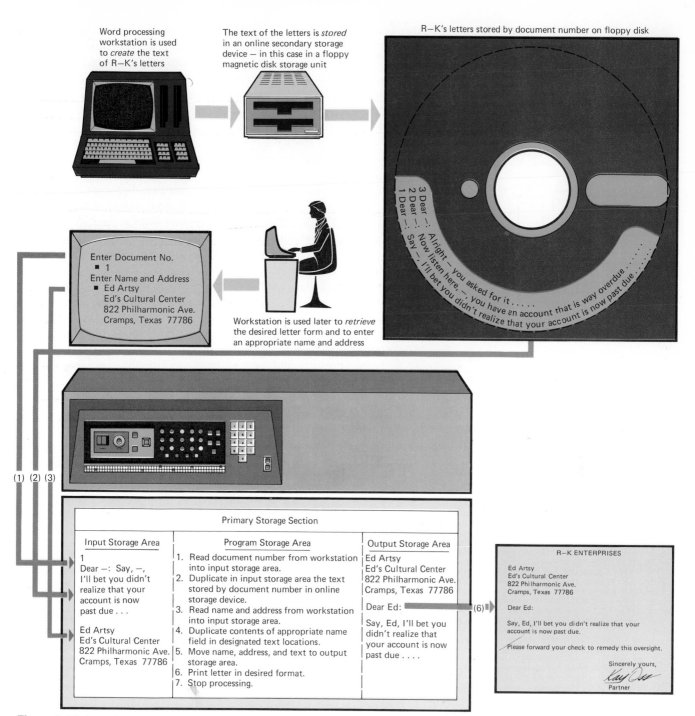

Word processing workstation is used to *create* the text of R–K's letters

The text of the letters is *stored* in an online secondary storage device — in this case in a floppy magnetic disk storage unit

R–K's letters stored by document number on floppy disk

3 Dear —:
2 Dear —:
1 Dear —:

Alright — you asked for it . . . .
Now listen here, — you have an account that is way overdue . . . .
Say —, I'll bet you didn't realize that your account is now past due . . . . .

Enter Document No.
■ 1
Enter Name and Address
■ Ed Artsy
   Ed's Cultural Center
   822 Philharmonic Ave.
   Cramps, Texas 77786

Workstation is used later to *retrieve* the desired letter form and to enter an appropriate name and address

(1) (2) (3)

Primary Storage Section

Input Storage Area	Program Storage Area	Output Storage Area
1 Dear —: Say, —, I'll bet you didn't realize that your account is now past due . . . Ed Artsy Ed's Cultural Center 822 Philharmonic Ave. Cramps, Texas 77786	1. Read document number from workstation into input storage area. 2. Duplicate in input storage area the text stored by document number in online storage device. 3. Read name and address from workstation into input storage area. 4. Duplicate contents of appropriate name field in designated text locations. 5. Move name, address, and text to output storage area. 6. Print letter in desired format. 7. Stop processing.	Ed Artsy Ed's Cultural Center 822 Philharmonic Ave. Cramps, Texas 77786 Dear Ed: Say, Ed, I'll bet you didn't realize that your account is now past due . . . .

(6)

R–K ENTERPRISES

Ed Artsy
Ed's Cultural Center
822 Philharmonic Ave.
Cramps, Texas 77786

Dear Ed:

Say, Ed, I'll bet you didn't realize that your account is now past due.

Please forward your check to remedy this oversight.

Sincerely yours,

Partner

Figure 2-14 A word processing system. Here the text is created at a workstation and stored in an online floppy disk device. When a specific letter is needed, the operator keys in the document number, which is read into the input storage area (see step 1 in the program storage area of the CPU). The program then duplicates the stored text in the input storage area (program step 2). Thus, although the text has been retrieved from online storage, it has not been erased. (Reading data *from* a magnetizeable storage medium such as a disk does not destroy the original data; entering data *into* a disk storage location, however, does erase the previous contents of the location.) Once the letter has been retrieved, the program reads from the workstation the name and address of the person to whom the letter should be sent (step 3). The letter is then "personalized" by inserting an appropriate name field into the text at designated places (step 4). After the name, address, and text message have been moved to output storage (step 5), the letter is printed (step 6), signed by Rob or Kay, and mailed to the customer.

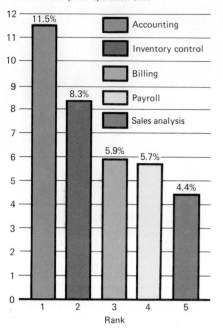

Percent of computer operation time

Average computer operation
time = 81.5 hours per week

Figure 2-15 The five application areas that represent the greatest use of business computing resources. Nearly 36 percent of a computer's operation time each week is spent on applications in these five areas. (Adapted from G. A. Champine, "Perspectives on Business Data Processing," *Computer,* November 1980, p. 86)

computer operates an average of 81.5 hours each week. Over 9 hours or 11.5 percent of that time is spent on processing accounting applications. We've already discussed one of these tasks—updating accounts receivable records and preparing summary statements to remind customers of their debts. Another accounting application is the **accounts payable** (A/P) application that keeps track of debts owed to suppliers for goods and services. One of its goals is to make sure that the discounts given for prompt payment are not lost. (A 2 percent discount is often given if a bill is paid within 10 days of receipt.) It may not be desirable to pay bills too early, however, because the organization would lose the use of the money for several days. Thus, an A/P system is designed to verify the accuracy of incoming bills, to make sure that discounts are not lost, and to issue payment checks toward the end of the discount period.

Figure 2-15 also shows that *inventory control, billing, payroll,* and *sales analysis* applications are among the most common in business. You saw how billing, accounts receivable, inventory control, and sales analysis applications were tied together earlier. You also saw examples of a payroll application in Chapter 1 and a report that computed sales compensation early in this chapter. Several billing, inventory control, sales analysis, and sales compensation computer programs for R-K Enterprises will be discussed in later chapters.

The other applications that have been presented are also quite common. Businesses such as savings associations, airlines, hotels, and car rental agencies use direct-access processing and have up-to-the-minute information available to answer inquiries from online stations. And a survey of businesses already using or considering small computer systems showed that about 40 percent were interested in word processing capability, and more than 20 percent were present or potential users of mailing list applications.[4]

And remember, business firms are not the only ones that process popular commercial applications. Nonprofit organizations such as schools, hospitals, and government agencies also produce payrolls, control inventories, prepare mailing labels, pay bills, and handle word processing.

Feedback and Review 2-2

As you now know, computers are easily able to perform logic/comparison and storage/retrieval operations. The R-K billing application was used to illustrate logic/comparison operations, and the word processing application showed the storage/retrieval capabilities of computers. The examples in Chapters 1 and 2 represent the most common business applications, and they account for the greatest use of business computing resources. You can test your understanding of the concepts that have just been presented by answering the following questions. Place the letter of the best response in the space provided.

_____ 1. A computer can determine when the last valid record in a file has been processed by comparing the contents of a designated field in each record to the contents of the same field in a dummy record placed

[4]See Karen E. Rosenfeld, "Small Users Value Maintenance, Ease of Use," *Computerworld,* Aug. 25, 1980, Special Report section, p. 3.

a) at the beginning of a file.
b) in the middle of a file.
c) at the end of a file.
d) at the end of the middle record.

_B_ **2.** In an order entry, shipping, and billing system,

a) the sales order is the last document to be produced.
b) the sales order provides the data needed to produce the shipping order.
c) only a single copy of the shipping order is usually needed.
d) the invoice generally provides the input data needed for the sales order.

_D_ **3.** The data found in a customer invoice are commonly used as input in the preparation of

a) accounts receivable statements.
b) inventory control reports.
c) sales analysis reports.
d) all the above.

_D_ **4.** In an accounts receivable application,

a) there's no reason to avoid delays in preparing statements.
b) the goal is to tie up excessive amounts of capital in unpaid accounts.
c) payments received from customers can be ignored.
d) management reports showing the ages of unpaid accounts are often produced.

_B_ **5.** In an inventory control application,

a) an objective is to keep a high level of inventory on hand.
b) an objective is to maintain good customer relations by having the goods on hand when they are ordered.
c) there's generally no conflict in the goals that are pursued.
d) management reports are useless since the inventory is constantly changing.

_C_ **6.** The use of computers for word processing

a) has increased the expense of written communications in all cases.
b) has caused a decline in office productivity.
c) is an application that makes use of the computer's ability to create, store, retrieve, and print text material.
d) requires that written communications be rigid and depersonalized.

_A_ **7.** Which of the following is not one of the most common business computer applications?

a) accounts postponable
b) billing
c) inventory control
d) sales analysis

Looking Back

1. All that computers do is operate on data, and these data are organized into logical groupings. The smallest data entity is a *field* consisting of related characters that are treated as a unit. Fields are grouped together to form *records,* and related records are then grouped to produce a *file.* A collection of logically related elements may then be organized into a *data base.*

2. Computers are able to perform operations on data that can be classified into input/output, calculation, logic/comparison, and storage/retrieval categories. Example *applications* emphasizing each of these types of operations have been presented in this chapter.

3. The preparation of mailing labels for R-K Enterprises was the application used to emphasize basic input/output operations. A file of prospective customers was created and maintained on a machine-readable medium. Under program control, a customer record was read into the CPU. The record fields were arranged in the desired format, and the mailing label was then printed.

4. Two example applications were used to illustrate the calculation operations performed by computers. The first was the preparation of a sales compensation report for Rob and Kay, and the second was the updating of Rob's savings account record. In the first application, the file of the sales force was organized sequentially using the salesperson's last name as the *record key.* In the second application, a direct file organization approach was used with the savings account number being the record key. File organization requires the use of some key or identifying value that is unique and is found in every record in the file.

5. If records are stored in an ascending or descending order determined by the record key, then a *sequential file organization* approach is being used. Sequential files are typically stored on such media as magnetic tape, punched cards, and magnetic disks. *Sequential (batch) processing* consists of reading and processing the first record in the file sequence, then the second record in the order, and so on. Such processing is suitable for applications such as payroll and customer billing, but when a sequential file is updated, the transactions that affect the records in the old master file must first be sorted into the same sequence as the master file before processing can begin. Also, it's not possible to quickly access a particular record in a file until all preceding records have been read into the CPU.

6. When a *direct file organization* approach is used, the computer can go directly to a key of the record needed without having to search through a sequence of other records. Directly organized files must be stored in an on-line secondary storage device such as a magnetic disk unit. When *direct-access (random-access* or *online) processing* is used, the desired record is retrieved in a fraction of a second and without the need for a sequential search of the file. Such processing can provide up-to-the-minute information in response to inquiries from online stations.

7. The billing application for R-K Enterprises was used to illustrate the logic/comparison operations performed by computers. After an order from a customer was entered on a sales order form, the sales data were then used to produce the shipping order. This shipping order, in turn, supplied the input data for the billing application. Under program control, the input data were read into the CPU a record at a time. In our example, a logic/comparison operation was used to recognize the appearance of a final *dummy record* and to thus determine when the processing should stop. After processing a record, the output information was used to print the customer invoice. Multiple copies of customer invoices are often prepared. In addition to the customer's copy, other copies are forwarded to those responsible for accounts receivable, inventory control, and sales analysis applications.

8. A word processing application was used to illustrate the storage/retrieval capabilities of computers. A series of collection letters was created and stored on a magnetic disk. Once stored, the desired letter can be retrieved on demand by the operator of a word processing station. Such an application can greatly improve the productivity of office workers.

9. The greatest uses of business computing resources are represented by accounts receivable, accounts payable, inventory control, billing, payroll, and sales analysis applications. All these applications were discussed at length in this chapter. Direct-access processing, word processing, and mailing list applications are also among the most common of business applications which we have also considered. Programs for many of these applications will be prepared in later chapters.

KEY TERMS AND CONCEPTS

You should be able to define and use the following terms and concepts (the numbers shown indicate the pages where the terms and concepts are first mentioned):

field 42	sequential (batch or serial)	sales/customer order 54
record 42	processing 48	shipping order 56
file 42	direct (random) file organization 51	bill/invoice 56
data base 42	direct-access (online or random-	accounts receivable (A/R) 57
applications 43	access) processing 51	inventory control 58
file maintenance/file updating 45	direct-access storage device (DASD)	sales analysis 59
record key 48	51	word processing 60
sequential file organization 48	dummy record 54	accounts payable (A/P) 62

TOPICS FOR REVIEW AND DISCUSSION

1. "When computers operate on data, the data will normally be organized into logical groupings so that processing will be effective and output results will be useful." Identify these logical groupings and discuss the relationship that exists between them.

2. Computers are able to perform operations on data that can be classified into four categories. What are they?

3. After a master file has been created, why is it necessary to periodically perform file maintenance or file updating?

4. (*a*) How was a computer used to prepare the mailing labels for R-K Enterprises? (*b*) Have you received any mail recently that made use of computer-prepared labels? (*c*) Have you·received any that didn't?

5. (*a*) How was a computer used to prepare a sales compensation report for Rob and Kay? (*b*) To update Rob's savings account record?

6. "A file must be organized in some way to facilitate processing." Identify, define, and discuss two ways in which files may be organized.

7. (*a*) What is sequential processing? (*b*) What are the strengths and limitations of this processing approach?

8. (*a*) What is direct-access processing? (*b*) What are the strengths and limitations of this processing approach?

9. How may a "dummy" record be used to indicate to a computer that the last valid record has been processed?

10. (*a*) How was a computer used to prepare bills for R-K Enterprises? (*b*) Discuss the flow of data from the time they are entered on the sales order form until they appear on the customer's invoice.

11. Identify and discuss the important business data processing applications that use input data taken from customer invoices.

12. (*a*) How was a computer used in the R-K word processing application? (*b*) Have you received any letters recently that were produced by a computer? (*c*) What was your reaction to these letters?

13. What applications account for the greatest use of business computing resources?

14. What is the purpose of an accounts payable application?

ANSWERS TO FEEDBACK AND REVIEW SECTIONS

S	E	R	I	A	L		R	E	C	O	R	D			D		C
A						K					I		B		E		P
L		B		F		E					R		A		L		U
E		I		I		Y		S	E	Q	U	E	N	T	I	A	L
S	O	R	T	E	D						C		C		Y		F
		D		L			D	I	R	E	C	T	H				I
D			D	A	T	A					T	E	E				L
A		O			A					S		O				E
S		S			P	H	Y	S	I	C	A	L		L		
D		S	T	O	R	E					R	A	N	D	O	M

2-2

1. C
2. B
3. D
4. D
5. B
6. C
7. A

Travel Agents On Hold

Travel agents sell over half the seats on U.S. airlines—about $15 billion annually. And they sell over $7 billion in other travel services as well. But only in the last few years has this big business been able to use the computer to streamline operations.

Until the late 1970s, when agents first tied into the airlines' reservation systems, employees spent as much as 44 percent of work time on clerical duties. A typical situation existed at West Penn American Automobile Association Travel Agency in Pittsburgh. Agents were spending hours leafing through the Official Airline Guides, waiting out busy telephone lines to make reservations, and then writing tickets by hand. In 1978, West Penn got their first terminals and tied into United Airlines' system. Agent productivity soared as the terminals reduced waiting time and printed tickets automatically. In 1979, the agency's sales rose 60 percent because it could take on new business it had formerly had to turn away. But things could be even better for the travel service business.

Agents would be delighted to have a single computerized reservation system that would connect them to each airline's network. Such a universal system would enable them to print tickets and itineraries and to balance accounts instantly and automatically. Such a system is easily feasible, but it doesn't exist and doesn't appear imminent. The reason? The airlines themselves, led by giants American and United, offer agents access to their own systems and refuse to cooperate in a single network. Agents are obviously more likely to book flights on United if their agency is hooked into United's Apollo reservations systems. The same situation applies to those agencies who subscribe to American's Sabre system.

The airlines also face outside competition: International Telephone and Telegraph and American Express have entered the competition with their own reservation systems. ITT's MARSPLUS system has six carriers on board: Eastern, Northwest, Piedmont, Hughes Airwest, Ozark, and international carrier TWA. MARSPLUS has picked up a number of smaller agencies since neither United nor American will offer its system to agencies that generate less than $1 million in annual ticket sales. But ITT charges its subscribers almost twice as much in monthly fees as do the airlines.

The American Society of Travel Agents (ASTA) is currently supporting the ITT system because it is closer than the others to a universal network. However, according to C. A. Moore of ASTA's automation committee, nothing is restricting the airlines from hooking all their systems together, but because of the competition in the business, "It's just not going to happen quickly."

—Source of data: "Computer Rescue for Travel Agents," *Business Week*, Apr. 7, 1980, pp. 81–82.

Figure 2-A Computer hookups have helped productivity in travel agencies take off, but a single, unified reservation system does not yet exist. (George Hall/Woodfin Camp & Associates)

chapter 3

Putting the Computer to Work
A Summary

REMAKING THE WORLD

Computers rival the invention of writing as one of the most profound innovations in human history and are "remaking the world at a phenomenal rate," according to noted astronomer and author Dr. Carl Sagan.

"We're in the throes of another mighty technological revolution, and the people who are alive today are the first ones to be a part of that revolution," Sagan said during a recent graduation address at Coleman College, a small southern California school specializing in undergraduate computing instruction.

Sagan, a Cornell University astronomy professor who is probably best known to the general public for his Pulitzer Prize-winning book *The Dragons of Eden* and for his recent *Cosmos* television series, credited computing with providing "a whole new way of looking at the world."

But at the same time, he warned, computers have also become the object of widespread public "anxiety," especially among the older generation, which has generally had much less exposure to high technology than many of today's schoolchildren.

"A lot of people are very concerned that this enormously powerful new technology is soon going to take over the world and run their lives," Sagan told a 96-member Coleman College graduating class that included his son Jeremy.

The Computer Gallery at Sesame Place is one of a growing number of facilities where children of all ages can take some time to get friendly with the computer. Computer summer camps are springing up all over the country. Sessions on programming, computer games, graphics, and robotics are replacing more traditional camp pasttimes such as nature hikes and water sports. One basic philosophy lies behind the popularity of the computer summer camp: the pressing need for computer literacy and the desire among children to learn as much as they can about computers. (*Gary E. Miller,* © *1980, Children's Television Workshop*)

To relieve the public's deep-seated misgivings about computers and assure the world that high technology is "fundamentally nice," systems personnel have an obligation to do much more than just put their equipment to work," Sagan said.

They must also explain to an uneasy world how their hardware operates, he added.

Systems personnel wield an "enormous amount of power" over the nontechnical majority of the population and thus have a responsibility to make sure that "computing technology is always applied humanely," the astronomer said. . . .

Sagan characterized the computer industry's recent pace of technological innovation as "simply phenomenal" and "astonishing," and he predicted at least another 10 years of continued rapid developments. . . .

This "absolutely stunning" pace of past and expected technological development means that systems personnel face the threat of professional obsolescence unless they constantly renew their knowledge of their chosen field, the astronomer said.

—Jeffry Beeler, *Computerworld*, Mar. 30, 1981, p. 37. Copyright 1981 by CW Communications, Inc., Framingham, Mass.

As Carl Sagan recognizes, it's *people* who put the computer to work to perform useful tasks. People in an organization must work together to complete
a step-by-step system study process that will first identify and then develop
needed informational improvements. Each of the steps in this process is outlined in this chapter.

Thus, after studying this chapter, you should be able to:

▌ Discuss why people are motivated to introduce new computer-based
systems or to modify existing ones

▌ Outline the steps in the system study process

▌ Explain the purpose of system analysis and system design

▌ Identify the uses of a system flowchart

▌ Understand the purpose of programming analysis, program preparation, and program implementation and maintenance

▌ Define and use the key terms listed at the end of this chapter

THE DATA PROCESSING SYSTEM:
INTRODUCTION AND REVIEW

Pick up a recent issue of your favorite magazine or newspaper.[1] Chances are
good that you'll quickly flip to one or more articles describing the work done by
computers. Without too much effort you could locate articles that take opposite views of computer output. Let's take a look at some headlines.[2]

One might imply that the computer had *human* characteristics:

Smart Machines Learn to See, Talk, Listen, Even "Think" for Us

Another might suggest that the computer was *subhuman:*

Computer Payments to Donald Duck Confound Managers

And a third might depict the computer as an *inhuman* instrument:

Computer Error Gets the Blame for Killing 1500 Research Mice

Now the facts described in all these articles are accurate. But the one fact
that is often slighted is a very important fact: computer *hardware* is just one
element in a broader data processing system. In Chapter 1 we described a
system as a group of integrated elements that have the common purpose of
achieving some goal(s). Other essential elements in a computer-based data
processing system include the necessary *input data,* the processing *procedures*
designed to convert the input data into the desired output, and the various
computer programs that allow the hardware to accept the input data and follow
the procedures.

---

[1] Now don't do it just yet. You have to finish reading this chapter!
[2] Adapted from *Smithsonian,* March 1980, p. 48; *Infosystems,* January 1979, p. 30; and Ft. Worth *Star-
Telegram,* March 31, 1980, p. 7.

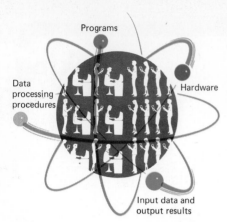

Programs

Data processing procedures

Hardware

Input data and output results

Figure 3-1 All elements of a business computer system revolve around the people in the system. Some of these people are specialists in data processing. But many other nonspecialists provide the input data needed, make suggestions for appropriate data processing procedures, and use the output results.

But something is still missing, and that something is people. The central and most important element in any computer-based system is *people* (Figure 3-1). It's people who put the computer to work. In businesses, it's people working together who determine processing needs, provide input data, design processing procedures, select hardware, write computer programs, and use processed output. Some of these people are data processing specialists. But contributions from nonspecialists such as clerks, secretaries, and supervisors who enter the data and use the output are equally essential to the creation of a successful system. When people create a clever system, the popular press often gives undue credit to the machine that processes the data. And when people produce a flawed effort, the machine may get unreasonable blame for the results.

Why are people in business motivated to introduce new computer-based systems or to modify existing ones? Generally speaking, they seek system changes in order to deal with the changing operating conditions that they face. Adding to or changing a system might result from changes inside or outside the organization. For example:

1. New government regulations change the accounting for employee pension plans.

2. Top managers can decide to acquire or merge with another organization.

3. A billing department manager wants to reduce the recent increase in billing errors.

4. A data processing specialist is convinced that new or existing data can be used in a more creative way to produce better information in a particular area of the business.

Whatever the motivation, new business computer systems are not overnight creations. Computer hardware will not by some miracle automatically begin to produce output results that will satisfy changing conditions. Rather, people—information users and data processing specialists—must work together to complete a series of steps in a system study.

THE STEPS IN A SYSTEM STUDY

A **system study** is a step-by-step process used to identify and then develop specific improvements in an organization's information system(s). The steps or stages in the system study process are outlined in Figure 3-2 and briefly summarized below. Later chapters in the Programming and Systems Modules will discuss all these steps in greater detail.

The first step in the system study is to clearly *identify the particular problem* to be solved or the tasks to be accomplished. Managers, departmental employees, and data processing personnel jointly participate in determining the problem and setting system goals.

The second step involves *system analysis*. After the problem has been identified, a study team works closely together to *gather* and then *analyze* data about current data processing operations.

The third stage is *system design*. After analyzing the procedures currently being followed, the people in the study team must then cooperate in the design of any new systems or applications that may be required to satisfy the need.

As a part of the system design phase, people must settle on the most feasible design alternative to achieve the study goals. And they must prepare new design specifications that include the output desired, the input data needed, and the processing procedures required to convert the input data into the output results.

The fourth step is *programming analysis*. The new system or application specifications may be turned over to one or more programmers. These specifications are then broken down into the specific input/output, calculating, logic/comparison, and storage/retrieval operations required to satisfy the need.

The fifth step is *program preparation*. At this stage, one or more programmers translate or code the required operations into a language and form acceptable to the computer hardware.

The sixth stage involves the *implementation* and *maintenance* of the system or application. People must first make sure that the coded program(s) is checked for errors and tested prior to being used on a routine basis. After programs appear to be running properly and producing correct results, the changeover to the new approach is made. The cooperation of the many people who may be involved in the preparation of input data and the use of output results is needed at this time if the new approach is to be successfully implemented. Finally, implemented systems and programs are usually subject to continual change and must therefore be maintained. This modification and improvement must be a cooperative effort between those served by the system or program and those responsible for maintaining it.

Figure 3-2 A summary of the system study process. This process must be people-oriented for a successful system or application to be created. And it should be a joint effort between those served by the system or application and those who create it. As this figure shows, computer hardware, by itself, cannot solve a single problem. (Photos courtesy Western Electric; Honeywell, Inc.; TRW, Inc.; General Electric Information Systems Company; Edith G. Haun/Stock, Boston; and Control Data Corporation)

Step 1: Defining the Need

To create a new system and/or improve or modify an existing one, people first have to recognize that a problem or need exists. As you've just seen, this problem or need may result from changing operating conditions. Managers, employees of departments that are affected by changing conditions, and data processing personnel often participate in requirements sessions until the problem has been defined and specific study goals have been outlined. These goals should then be put in writing and approved by all concerned.

Courtesy Honeywell, Inc.

Step 2: System Analysis

After users and specialists have identified the need for specific changes, a *study team* gathers and then analyzes data about current data processing operations. The people in this study team are often selected for the offsetting talents they can bring to the job. At least one member usually represents (and has a knowledge of the information needs of) the business sectors affected by the study. Another is a **systems analyst**—an information specialist who is knowledgeable about the technical aspects of analyzing, designing, and implementing computer-based processing systems. And a third may be an auditor who can see to it that proper controls are built into a new system.

Data Collection. The team's first job is to *gather data* about current data processing operations. These facts must be accurate, up-to-date, and sufficiently complete, for they will become the input to later study stages. Gathering such data can be difficult because a system may cut across several departments and involve many people using dozens of documents. Furthermore, *accurate* written statements outlining exactly what is done are usually missing. Procedure descriptions often exist, but they tend not to reflect the most current methods. Thus, a number of data-gathering tools and techniques must often be employed. Among these are questionnaires, interviews and observations, and system flowcharts.

Flowchart Preparation. A system flowchart is a diagram that shows a broad overview of the data flow and sequence of operations in a system. The emphasis is placed on input documents and output reports. Only limited detail is furnished about how a workstation or machine converts the input data into the desired output. Standard symbols are used in all flowcharts to clearly record and communicate information. The basic symbols representing input/output and processing are shown in Figure 3-3*a*. Although the input/output (I/O) symbol may be used to show any type of media or device, it's often replaced in system charts by other symbols whose shape suggests the particular medium or device being used (Figure 3-3*b*). Additional symbols are shown in Figure 3-3*c*.

Preparing flowcharts can help the study team gather data on current operations. Beginning with source-document inputs, each operation step is

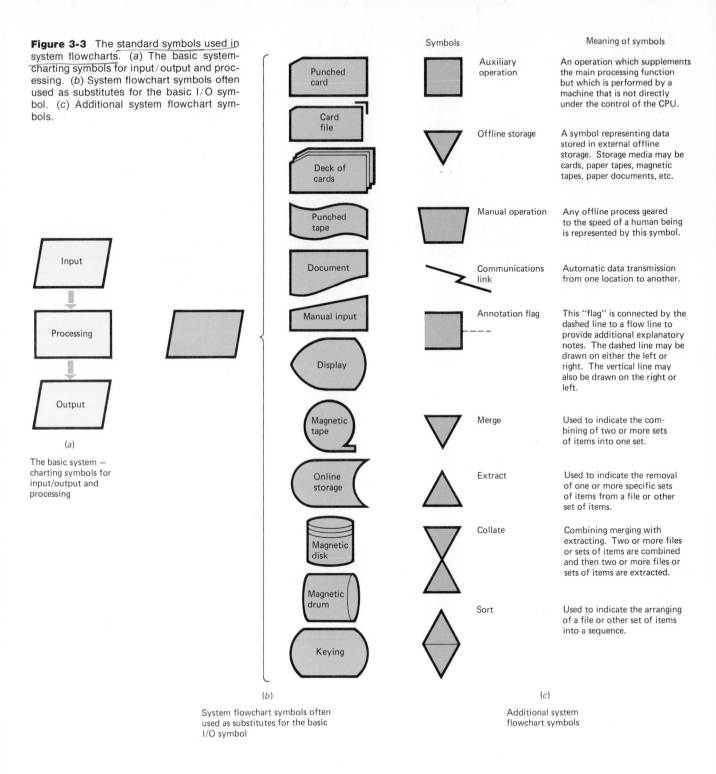

Figure 3-3 The standard symbols used in system flowcharts. (a) The basic system-charting symbols for input/output and processing. (b) System flowchart symbols often used as substitutes for the basic I/O symbol. (c) Additional system flowchart symbols.

(a)

Input

Processing

Output

The basic system — charting symbols for input/output and processing

(b)

Punched card

Card file

Deck of cards

Punched tape

Document

Manual input

Display

Magnetic tape

Online storage

Magnetic disk

Magnetic drum

Keying

System flowchart symbols often used as substitutes for the basic I/O symbol

(c)

Additional system flowchart symbols

Symbols		Meaning of symbols
	Auxiliary operation	An operation which supplements the main processing function but which is performed by a machine that is not directly under the control of the CPU.
	Offline storage	A symbol representing data stored in external offline storage. Storage media may be cards, paper tapes, magnetic tapes, paper documents, etc.
	Manual operation	Any offline process geared to the speed of a human being is represented by this symbol.
	Communications link	Automatic data transmission from one location to another.
	Annotation flag	This "flag" is connected by the dashed line to a flow line to provide additional explanatory notes. The dashed line may be drawn on either the left or right. The vertical line may also be drawn on the right or left.
	Merge	Used to indicate the combining of two or more sets of items into one set.
	Extract	Used to indicate the removal of one or more specific sets of items from a file or other set of items.
	Collate	Combining merging with extracting. Two or more files or sets of items are combined and then two or more files or sets of items are extracted.
	Sort	Used to indicate the arranging of a file or other set of items into a sequence.

charted, using the proper symbols. Files and equipment being used are identified, the processing sequence is described, the departments involved are located, and the output results are shown. For example, R-K Enterprises' current order entry/shipping/billing system described in Chapter 2 and shown in Figure 2-10 can be charted as shown in Figure 3-4. Notice that the arrows connecting the symbols show the direction of data flow. The main flow is usually charted from top to bottom and from left to right. Notes within the symbol further explain what's being done.

Analyzing the Findings. After the data about current operations have been gathered, the team members must then analyze their findings. **System analysis** is the study of existing operations to learn what they accomplish, why they work as they do, and what role (if any) they may have in future processing activities. In analyzing the current system, it's necessary to identify the essential data and procedures required for a new approach. It's also necessary to pinpoint current weaknesses and problems so that they will not be carried over to the new system. As part of this process, the system flowchart can be a helpful analysis tool.

Figure 3-4 As you saw in Chapter 2, R-K Enterprises' order-entry/shipping/billing system begins in the sales department when an order from a customer is entered on a sales order form. The sales order data are then used to produce the shipping order which, in turn, is used to fill the order, acknowledge the order to the customer, and provide the input data for the billing department. Data from the shipping order are keyed onto an input storage medium from where they are read under program control into the CPU during a billing run. The multiple invoice copies resulting from the billing run are then sent to the indicated destinations.

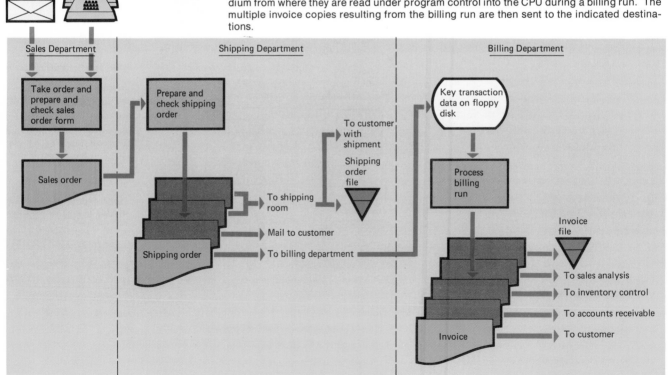

Step 3: System Design

System design is the process of creating alternative solutions to satisfy the study goals, evaluating the choices, and then drawing up the specifications for the chosen alternative. Design begins after the people in the study team have analyzed the current procedures. Since many factors have a bearing on the design process, it can be a complex and challenging task. For example, the design team must consider the personnel and financial resources of the business, the different procedures that can often be used to carry out a single business operation, and the many equipment alternatives that are available to perform a given data processing job. Also, the team must consider what effects changes made in one application or department will have on related applications. A proposed improvement in a billing system, for example, might require a redesign of accounts receivable and inventory control procedures.

To illustrate the system design challenge, let's assume that R-K Enterprises grows very fast.[3] When they started their partnership, Rob and Kay knew their credit customers. They were not worried about receiving payment for shipments. Their current system shown in Figure 3-4 has worked well. But let's assume now that too many shipments are being made to newer customers who are proving to be poor credit risks. Also, the increased business volume has caused a delay in the preparation of customer statements and inventory control reports.

After analyzing the current system and studying the flowchart in Figure 3-4, the R-K study team designed the alternative system shown in Figure 3-5. (The design changes are shown in white in Figure 3-5.) To deal with the lack of

Figure 3-5 A possible redesign of R-K's current order-entry/shipping/billing system shown in Figure 3-4 to provide better control over shipments being made to poor credit risks, and to improve the timeliness of customer statements and inventory control reports.

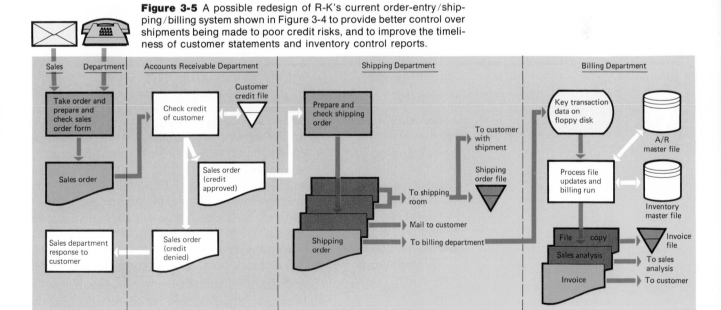

[3]Alas, as you'll see in the Programming Module, this is a false assumption.

WHY THE COMPUTER NEEDS SOFTWARE

A car can't run without fuel and a computer can't run without software. You can plug the computer in—and it will warm up—but it won't do any useful work without software to tell it to.

Software is a set of instructions that tell the computer what to do. Packaged software—programs that can be purchased and which are written, tested and modified for specific configurations of computer equipment—comes in two major types, systems software and applications software.

Systems software packages coordinate the computer system. They support the running of other programs (other software); communicate with peripheral devices (printers, card readers, disk devices); support the development of other types of software (custom programs designed in house); monitor the use of the machine's resources and manage storage space efficiently. Basic system software is available from hardware manufacturers as well as from software vendors. Because of its technical complexity, systems software is rarely developed in house.

Systems software is what you need to make the computer run. Applications software is what you need to make the computer do useful work. Applications software packages can be divided into two major categories—general purpose and specific purpose.

Traditionally, applications packages were limited to the general purpose functions of general ledger, general accounting and payroll because these applications were the reason why a company acquired a computer. Because there is such a great demand for these functions, packaged software supporting them is available on every kind of computer hardware.

However, the software industry has expanded to serve many specific markets. Specific purpose applications are related to operations in specialized areas, such as banking, hospital administration, insurance, publishing, manufacturing, science and engineering. In fact, many software companies are starting to offer computer systems to go along with their software as turnkey systems for specific industry needs. Development of specific purpose application packages has expanded along with the increased use of the computer in non-financial operations.

Most recently the development of software packages has been spurred on by the need for specific applications by the small business market which could never afford a computer before. Today the doctor, lawyer, real estate agency, advertising agency, local insurance agency and many other small businesses can purchase software to serve their specific needs.

—"Software: What Top Management Needs to Know," Reprinted from Forbes Magazine, Sept. 28, 1981. Prepared by Infosystems.

control over shipments being made to poor credit risks, the team has proposed that the sales order be sent to the accounts receivable (A/R) department as shown in Figure 3-5. After a credit check, the sales order is either approved or denied and then routed to the appropriate department. Although this design alternative provides better control over shipments, it also increases the time and cost required to fill a customer's order. In judging alternatives, system designers must constantly make such tradeoffs. No system alternative can be the best in every category. One with better control and greater accuracy may also be one that's more expensive and/or requires more processing time.

To improve the system for customer statements and inventory control reports in our example, the team has proposed that the A/R and inventory master files be stored in an online secondary storage device, and that a computer program be prepared to update these files at the same time the customer bills are being prepared (see Figure 3-5). This alternative involves tradeoffs:

Possible Benefits	Possible Costs
Faster statement preparation	Preparing at least one new
Faster bill collection	computer program
Better inventory control	Purchasing new system hardware
Reduced manual processing of copies	

It's the job of the designers to decide whether the benefits and possible savings expected from a design alternative outweigh the costs. (And, of course, it's up to Rob and Kay to approve design changes.)

After the team members have settled on the approach they consider best to meet the study goals, they must then prepare new design specifications. These specifications include the output desired, the input data needed, and the processing procedures required to convert input data into output results.

Step 4: Programming Analysis

After top managers give their approval, the design specifications provide the input for the programming analysis phase of the system study process. **Programming analysis** is the process of breaking down the design specifications into the specific input/output, calculation, logic/comparison, and storage/retrieval operations required to satisfy the study goals. One or more programmers will perform this important task. Analysis tools such as program flowcharts may be used at this time. The **program flowchart** evolves from the system flowchart: It's a detailed diagram showing how individual processing steps will be performed within the computer to convert the input data into the desired output. Chapter 12 deals with this process in detail.

Courtesy General Electric Information Systems Company

Step 5: Program Preparation

The detailed input/output, calculation, logic/comparison, and storage/retrieval operations identified during the programming analysis stage provide the input for program preparation. One or more programmers convert the required operations into a program (or programs) of instructions written in a language and form acceptable to the computer hardware. Further details on this activity appear in Chapters 13 and 14 in the Programming Module.

Step 6: Implementation and Maintenance

After the program(s) has been written, it must be checked for errors and tested before it can be used on a routine basis. When the program(s) appears to be running properly and producing valid results, the changeover to the new system is made. During this changeover period, the people who prepare input data and use output results must cooperate with the data processing specialists if the new system is to be successful. Resistance to change has been the cause of many system implementation difficulties. Such resistance may be reduced when a people-oriented system study approach is followed, a topic which will be considered again in the Systems Module.

Courtesy Control Data Corporation.

Finally, systems and programs that have been successfully implemented are usually subject to continual change. Just as R-K's system might need to be modified and improved to meet changing conditions, so, too, must other systems continually be maintained. A first-class maintenance effort requires the cooperation of those people served by the system/program, and those responsible for maintaining it. Of course, the need for a major change could trigger a new system study effort.

Feedback and Review 3-1

You've seen in this short overview that computer hardware, by itself, doesn't solve a single business problem. It's people—both data processing specialists and operating department members—who put the computer to work. Hardware is merely one or more boxes of electronic parts. By working together during all phases of a system study, however, people can transform these boxes into an exciting tool whose use is limited only by human ingenuity and imagination.

To test your understanding of these concepts, fill in the crossword puzzle form with the appropriate words needed to complete the following sentences and definitions.

Across

1. In a computer-based data processing system, computer hardware is just one of a _____ of integrated elements that have the common purpose of achieving some goal(s).

3. A system _____ is a step-by-step process to identify and then develop specific informational improvements in an organization.

5. A system flow- _____ is a diagram that shows a broad overview of the data flow and sequence of operations in a system.

8. Step number _____ in the system study process is the system analysis stage.

10. A systems _____ is an information specialist who is knowledgeable about the technical aspects of analyzing, designing, and implementing computer-based processing systems.

12. Step number _____ in the system study involves programming analysis.

13. The people on a system study _____ are often selected for the offsetting talents they can bring to the job.

14. In evaluating alternatives, system designers must constantly make tradeoffs because no alternative can be the _____ in every category of interest.

17. System difficulties can occur when people who prepare input data and use output results resist the use of new approaches. But this resistance may be _____ when a people-oriented system study approach is used.

18. Step number _____ in the system study involves program preparation.

19. A system flowchart can be a helpful analysis _____.

20. The same basic flowcharting symbol is used to represent both _____ and output.

Down

1. The first job of the system study team during the system analysis stage is to _____ data about current processing operations.

2. The central and most important element in any computer-based system is _____.

3. Information users and data processing specialists must work together to complete a series of steps in a _____ study.

4. One element in a computer-based processing system is the input _____.

6. The _____ flowchart is a detailed diagram showing how each processing step will be performed within the computer.

7. In evaluating possible processing alternatives, system designers must constantly make _____ -offs.

9. Step number _____ in the system study is to define the problem or need.

11. Standard _____ are used in all flowcharts to clearly record and communicate information.

13. Step number _____ in the system study is the system design stage.

15. System design can be a challenging _____ because there are many factors that have a bearing on the design process.

16. Step number _____ in the system study process is to implement and then maintain the new approach.

1. Computer hardware is just one element in a broader data processing system that also includes input data, processing procedures, computer programs, and people.

2. The central and most important element in any computer-based system is people. It's people who put the computer to work. Some of these people are data processing specialists. But the contributions of many others in the organization who enter the data and use the output are essential to create and maintain a successful data processing system.

3. People are often motivated to introduce computer-based systems in order to deal with the changing operating conditions they face. Before a computer can be put to work, however, system users and data processing specialists must work together to complete a *system study*. The system study is a step-by-step process used to identify and develop specific informational improvements in an organization.

4. The first step in this study process is to define the problem or need. Next, a study team gathers and then analyzes data about current operations in a *system analysis* stage. A *system flowchart* is a diagram that shows a broad overview of the data flow and sequence of operations in a system. Such a flowchart is one of many data-gathering and analysis tools that may be used.

5. After the team has analyzed current procedures, the third step in the study approach is to design any new systems or applications that may be needed to satisfy the study goals. *System design* can be a challenging task because of the many factors that have a bearing on the design process. In evaluating design alternatives, system designers must constantly make trade-offs. Higher processing costs, for example, may accompany design changes that offer the benefits of better control and greater accuracy.

6. The specifications prepared during system design provide the input to the *programming analysis* stage—the fourth step in the system study process. The specific input/output, calculation, logic/comparison, and storage/retrieval operations required to satisfy the design specifications are established at this time.

7. These specific operations are then converted into one or more computer programs in the fifth stage, *program preparation.* The programs are written in a language and form acceptable to the computer hardware.

8. The final step in the study approach is to *implement and maintain* the new program(s) and procedures. Programs must be checked for errors and tested before they are put to routine use. After implementation, they must be maintained to meet changing conditions.

KEY TERMS AND CONCEPTS

You should now be able to define and use the following terms and concepts (the numbers shown indicate the pages where the terms and concepts are first mentioned):

TOPICS FOR REVIEW AND DISCUSSION

1. (*a*) Identify five elements found in any computer-based data processing system. (*b*) Which of these elements plays a central role in the development and operation of such a system?

2. "The computer is usually at fault when a ridiculous bill is sent to a customer." Discuss this statement.

3. Why are people motivated to introduce new computer-based systems or to modify existing ones?

4. (*a*) What is a system study? (*b*) What is the first step in such a study?

5. "Since systems users may resist change, data processing specialists should be in charge of all phases of a system study." Discuss this statement.

6. "The people on a system study team are often selected for the offsetting talents they can bring to the job." Discuss the talents that may be needed.

7. (*a*) What is a system flowchart? (*b*) For what purpose is it used?

8. Explain the difference between system analysis and system design.

9. (*a*) What questions might the study team consider during the system analysis stage? (*b*) During the system design stage?

10. "System design can be challenging because there are many considerations that have a bearing on the design process." What are three such considerations?

11. "No alternative system design can be the best in every category." Discuss this statement.

12. (*a*) What is programming analysis? (*b*) What is a program flowchart?

13. (*a*) What is the purpose of the program preparation stage? (*b*) Of the implementation and maintenance stage?

ANSWERS TO FEEDBACK AND REVIEW SECTION

3-1

```
G R O U P   S T U D Y   C H A R T       P
A       E   Y   A   T                   R
T W O   O   S   T   R                   O
H   N   P   T   A N A L Y S T           G
E   E   L   E   D     Y   F O U R       R
R     T E A M   E     M                 A
    H           B E S T                 M
  S R E D U C E D     O   A
F I V E           T O O L S
  X E   I N P U T     S   K
```

Managing Information

The Commission on Federal Paperwork has proposed a broad-based approach to managing data-information management resources. This is the total application of systems, methods, techniques and controls to the management of a very special but costly resource . . . information.

Data provides a basis from which information is derived and for quantitative analysis; information assembled by compiling, manipulating and massaging data provides a qualitative basis for decision-making.

Management resources have often been described as the three M's—manpower, money and materials. Information can be considered a fourth resource because it has the attributes of a physical resource:

- It has value like money, raw materials or manpower.
- It has characteristics which make it measurable in terms of use, life and effect on other resources.
- It can be valued in terms of collecting, storing, retrieving.
- It can be budgeted and controlled.
- It can be related in terms of cost and use value to management objectives.

Why Manage Information?

One of the major problems confronting government, industry and the public today is the constantly accelerating demand for data and information. New technologies provide for rapid manipulation and massive storage of data, but it is the individual who must generate data in the first place and who, consequently, uses it.

The insatiable appetite for data and information is whetted by three major stimuli: specific legislative and regulatory requirements, legal needs and administrative determinations. The latter factor can be tagged as a major cause of the paperwork explosion. The first two are not without blame, however, as witness the efforts of such bodies as the Commission on Federal Paperwork to identify and reduce the paperwork burden imposed by government.

Modern technology has aided in opening the floodgates of information. In most cases, technology does not question the value of information flowing through the conduits and pipelines, but is concerned with moving more information and moving it faster. Who questions the need? Information resources management is the best way.

There are three important compelling reasons for a total management approach to information. The first is to eliminate waste. Second is to insure information availability. Third is to detect imposed burdens. Paperwork can be evidence of work performed, often a symptom of unnecessary work; paperwork is the tip of the iceberg.

Information resources management is applicable to any organization generating, acquiring and using information. The concept is applicable to both government and industry.

Critical and highly-specialized information requirements do not exclude specialty recording areas from a total information management approach. To the contrary, these requirements reinforce the need for this approach. There are many specialty areas where the data/information are subject to unique generating and using requirements. For example, nuclear quality assurance records, medical records, aerospace records, product liability records and, without exception, the data and information in these systems have exceptionally high value as resources.

Information resources management fits the technology to the need, not the product to the technology. Requirements are carefully measured before the system is designed and the design is completed before the techniques and hardware are selected.

—Edward N. Johnson, "What Are We Managing and Why?" *Information Manager*, December 1978, pp. 8–9. Reprinted with permission of the publisher.

chapter 4

The Impact of Computers at Work

A Preview

BUT CAN WE PUT WHEELS ON IT?

Today's hardware, software and systems are the Model Ts of the computing field and promise to have as profound a social and technological impact as Henry Ford's landmark auto, according to U.S. Navy Capt. Grace M. Hopper.

Just as the old Model T spawned a revolution in assembly line production methods and prefigured developments ranging from suburbia to the interstate highway system, so current computing technology heralds innovations that will powerfully alter the course of future civilization, Hopper said.

Within the next few years, existing CPUs will gradually give way to a new breed of vastly more sophisticated mainframes that promise to play a key role in addressing many of the world's most pressing social and economic ills, Hopper said. . . .

Although today's hardware and software are possibly the forerunners of a brave new technological world, they also raise troubling questions about the computing field's near- and long-term future.

—Jeffry Beeler, *Computerworld*, Feb. 16, 1981, p. 35. Copyright 1981 by CW Communications/Inc., Framingham, Mass.

Computer-controlled robots can sense the need for a specified task and can then take the actions necessary to perform the task. In the auto manufacturing and supply industries alone, it's expected that tens of thousands of jobs will be eliminated by robots during the 1980s. (© Dick Durrance II/Woodfin Camp & Associates)

Looking Ahead

Grace Hopper is right: Computer technology and computer usage are making an impact on people and organizations throughout our society. In this chapter, we'll first look at some of the advances in computer technology that are causing significant social change. We'll then discuss some of the positive and negative effects that computer-driven change is having on people and organizations.

Thus, after studying this chapter, you should be able to:

▌ Explain the advances in computer technology that are contributing to an information revolution

▌ Discuss the impact that computer usage may have on the people who live in a modern society

▌ Describe the impact that computer usage may have on the organizations that function in such a society

▌ Understand and use the key terms listed at the end of this chapter

THE TECHNOLOGICAL UNDERPINNINGS

You've seen a few examples of what computers can do in Chapter 2. But it's not enough just to be familiar with a few specific applications. As Grace Hopper pointed out at the beginning of this chapter, you should also be aware of the broad impact that computer usage is having on society right now.

In the eighteenth century, the development of the steam engine encouraged the use of large-scale factory production facilities as replacements for cottage industries, or home manufacturing units. An *industrial revolution* followed this harnessing of steam power. In the past few years, developments in computer technology have acquired a force and significance comparable to that of the steam engine. And our society is now in the throes of an **information revolution** that has been brought on by these advances in computer technology. The steam-powered industrial revolution removed many tedious tasks from human muscles, produced huge gains in productivity, and brought significant social and economic changes to the world. Today's computer-powered information revolution is removing burdens of drudgery from human brains, producing further gains in productivity, and bringing about significant changes in employment, competition, and social attitudes.

You'll find a brief outline of the impact that computer usage may have on individuals and organizations later in this chapter. Further discussion is left to the chapters in the Social Impact Module. Before examining these computer-usage effects, however, we should first pause and consider the cause. That is, we should consider the technological developments that underlie the information revolution. Let's begin with the rapid advances which are occurring in computer *hardware, software*, and *information systems technology*.

Hardware Development Factors	1950	1960	1970	1975	1980's
Size factor — Number of circuits per cubic foot	1,000	100,000	10 million	1 billion	Many billions
Speed factor — Time to execute an instruction in the central processor	300 microseconds	5 microseconds	80 nanoseconds	25 nanoseconds	5 nanoseconds or less
Cost factors — Cost (in cents) to process 1 million basic computer instructions	2,800	100	2	.1	Less than .01
Cost (in cents) to provide storage for one binary number in the central processor	261	85	5	.1	Less than .01
Storage capacity factors — Primary storage capacity (in characters) of the central processor	20,000	120,000	1 million	10 million	Much greater than 10 million
Characters of secondary online storage		20 million	Over 100 billion	Virtually unlimited	Virtually unlimited
Reliability factor — Mean (average) time between failures of some central processors	Hours	Tens of hours	Hundreds of hours	Thousands of hours	Years

Figure 4-1 A summary of hardware advances.

Hardware Advances

Figure 4-1 summarizes the gains that have been made in computer hardware. As you can see, there have been dramatic reductions in computer *size*. A number of separate electronic components such as transistors and diodes are combined to form computer circuits. Thousands of these circuits are now integrated and packaged on a single **silicon chip** (Figure 4-2) that measures perhaps a quarter of an inch square. Since the average number of chip components has doubled each year since 1965, it's now possible through such **large-scale integration** (LSI) to squeeze billions of circuits into a cubic foot of space. Nor is there any end in sight to these size reductions. Just as yesterday's room-sized computers have been replaced by today's single LSI chips, so will the multiple boards that make up a large computer today be replaced in the next decade by a single *superchip*. Through the use of **very large-scale integration** (VLSI) techniques, tomorrow's circuits will be hundreds of times more compact than those in use now.

Figure 4-2 A silicon chip rests on a dime with plenty of room to spare. (Reprinted with permission from Motorola, Inc.)

Editor's note: Imagine that it's 1990 and you've been asked to take a look at the effects of computer usage over the decade of the 1980s. The following predictions (see accompanying tables) are made from that perspective.

The Information Revolution of the mid-1980's changed the course of history. Only now, in 1990, can we fully comprehend its significance.

The emergence of microelectronics in the 1970's set the stage for the massive advance of electronic communications and processing resources. Through superscale computers, microelectronics created a host of new scientific and analytical applications.

The table shown here indicates the winners and losers of the Information Revolution. The mail service, teachers, secretaries, clerks, auditors, salesmen, and local retailers are among those occupations now performed by computers. Technical and analytical specialists, writers, artists, producers, directors, large financial institutions, and large retailers have become the pieces of our intricate information network.

Winners	Reasons
Financial institutions	More fee-based consumer and business services
Programming industry	Proliferation of new packaged programs
Larger universities	Programmed education opportunities
Insurance industry	Lower life, health, and property claims costs
Electronics industry	Greatly expanded markets
Communications utilities	Greater dependence on telecommunications
Computer services	Extensions into the home
Larger retailers	Leverage through electronic promotion techniques
Utilities	Better control over demand
Advertising agencies	More value-added services
Federal public administration	More direct reach to public, more interstate activities
Smaller creative entertainers	Released from domination by large TV networks
Smaller specialty retailers	Bigger reach at a lower cost

As the size of computers has been reduced, their operating *speed* has increased (see Figure 4-1). In part, this is because size reduction means shorter distances for electric pulses to travel. Figure 4-1 also shows some of the incredible *cost* reductions associated with computer usage. If automobile costs and technological developments had matched the trends in computer hardware over the last 15 years, you would now be able to buy a self-steering car for $20 that could attain speeds up to 500 miles per hour and could travel the entire length of California on 1 gallon of gas. The cost as well as the size of many basic computer components will continue to decline in the future while their speed increases. Cheaper, smaller, and more powerful computers will cause significant social change. Marvelous tools and gadgets will be built, and communications facilities and leisure activities will be affected. But employment

Losers	Reasons
Airlines	Less business travel
Petroleum companies	Less commuting and shopping travel
TV networks	Other packaged programming sources
Paper	Office use displaced by electronic communications
Postal Service	Siphoned away by EFT and electronic mail
Commercial construction	Lower demand for centralized facilities
Publishing	Competition from electronic sources
Smaller, general-purpose retailers	Competition with in-home shopping
Transportation manufacturers	Fewer commuting vehicles
State and local public administration	Proximity to "markets" less important
Wholesalers	Bypassed by direct communications systems
Credit agencies	Competition from large financial institutions
Bigger cities	Less commercial and commuter tax revenue
Gambling resorts	In-home alternatives

The Information Revolution has made our world smaller, has coordinated our efforts. History can now record the cooperation of a smoothly running system.

—*Creative Computing,* p. 145, November 1979. Used by permission of *Creative Computing,* P.O. Box 789-M, Morristown, N.J.

disturbances and organizational stress may also occur.

Finally, Figure 4-1 gives you an idea of what has happened to computer *storage capacity* and *reliability* in the last few decades. The storage capacity of both primary and online secondary storage units has increased thousands of times over the years. And the early computers that used to break down every few hours have been replaced by processors that can run for thousands of hours without failure. Some modern processors have self-diagnostic circuitry built within them to monitor hardware operations and pinpoint the cause of any failure that may occur. Self-repairing computers have even been designed for the unmanned space missions that last many years (Figure 4-3). These computers have built-in spare parts that can automatically take over the tasks of any original components that fail during the mission.

BACKGROUND

Figure 4-3 A view of Saturn and two of its moons, Tethys (above) and Dione, as seen by the Voyager 1 spacecraft. The shadows of Saturn's three bright rings and Tethys are cast onto the cloud tops above the planet. The computers in Voyager 1 that permit such photos to be made must be designed to function for many years. (Courtesy National Aeronautics and Space Administration)

Software Advances

Significant gains have also been made in the development of computer software. In the early 1950s, computer programmers had to write their problem-solving program instructions in the special machine code numbers that computer circuits can recognize (e.g., the number 21 might mean "add"). These strings of numbers were tedious to prepare, and they often contained errors. Special **programming languages** were then developed to permit the programmer to write instructions in a form easier for humans to understand. For example, a language might permit the word ADD or the plus (+) symbol to be used in place of the number 21. Unfortunately, the computer's circuitry only recognizes the number 21 as the instruction to add.

How, then, can the machine execute instructions if they are in a language it cannot understand? Just as an American and a German can communicate if one of them uses a translating dictionary, so too can the programmer and computer communicate if a separate translation program is employed. A **translation program** is one that transforms the instructions prepared by people using a convenient language into the machine language codes required by computers. Almost all problem-solving programs prepared today are first written in languages preferred by people and are then translated by special software or hardware into the equivalent machine codes. (The translating process will be discussed in detail in Chapter 13 of the Programming Module.) The impact that computers are having on society today is due in no small measure to this easing of human-machine communication.

Another factor that's contributing to increased computer usage is the greater availability of applications programs. An **application program** is one that has been written to control the processing of a particular task. Although many applications programs must be prepared for unique jobs, there are thousands of widely used applications for which generalized programs may be written. Computer users may now obtain **applications packages** (or **packaged programs**) for these widely used applications from equipment manufacturers and independent software firms. These packages can help smaller organizations convert to computer usage. Packaged programs for personal entertainment and other home uses may also be found at thousands of retail computer stores (Figure 4-4).

A third factor that has helped increase computer productivity and has thus contributed to a greater use of computers in society is the use of operating system programs. An **operating system** (OS) is an organized collection of software that controls the overall operation of a computer. The OS was initially a set of programs designed to help computer operators perform such "housekeeping" tasks as erasing the contents of CPU storage locations after the completion of a job and then loading the next program into the program storage area from an input device. Since the computer could do these tasks quickly, both human and machine time was saved. The objective of a current OS is still to operate the computer with a minimum of idle time during the processing of jobs, but the OS software is now much more complex. A further discussion of the functions of a modern OS will be presented in the Programming Module in Chapter 15.

Figure 4-4 A few of the packaged programs for home and business applications that are available for use with Apple personal computers. (Courtesy Apple Computer Inc.)

Advances in Information Systems

Information is needed to organize vacation activities, plan meals, make intelligent purchases, vote for a candidate, select a factory location, pick an investment, and study for a test. In short, information is power: It's needed every day by decision makers—all of us—both in our private lives and in our occupations. Information that is accurate, timely, and complete should improve the quality of our decisions. If our information does not possess these characteristics, however, the quality of our decisions may suffer.

Information systems have existed in organizations for centuries. But these traditional systems often supplied information that was inaccurate, out of date, or incomplete. Historians tell us, for example, that if the data that were available in bits and pieces at scattered points had been assembled in a timely manner in the early days of December 1941, the United States would have been prepared for the Japanese attack on Pearl Harbor. It's not surprising, then, that newer computer-based concepts have been designed and developed to improve information system performance. These new concepts may be characterized as being quicker responding and broader in scope than traditional systems.

Many **quick-response systems** have been developed to increase the timeliness and availability of information. You've seen examples of how savings associations, airlines, and other organizations use direct-access processing techniques to provide up-to-the-minute information to inquiry stations. These stations may be near the CPU, or there may be a **distributed network** of stations located at many distant points. Some quick-response systems are also taking a *broader data-base approach* to provide information that's more complete and relevant. In this approach, the system is designed around a collection of logically related data elements (the data base) that is maintained in a direct-access storage device. Data elements are introduced into the system only once and are then available as needed to all users of the data base. With the proper software to select and process the necessary data elements, a decision maker at an online terminal can use the data-base system to search and query file contents in order to extract answers to nonrecurring and unplanned questions that are not covered by regular reports. Further discussions about quick-response and data-base systems are presented in the Hardware and Systems Modules. As you'll see in the next sections, their use can have an impact on individuals as well as on the organizations that use them.

THE IMPACT OF COMPUTERS ON PEOPLE

The technological advances just presented have made the computer one of the most powerful forces in society today. They've made it possible for computer usage to spread into homes and organizations of all sizes. No one can doubt that the use of computers has had a strong impact on many people. But the computer is the driving force behind an information revolution, and as in any revolution some innocent people may be harmed. Let's briefly outline here some of the positive and negative effects that computer usage may have on individuals. (Chapter 19 in the Social Impact Module deals with this topic in greater detail.)

Positive Implications

People may benefit from computers in many ways. Among the benefits are the following:

Figure 4-5 Job prospects in computer-related fields will remain plentiful for years. (Courtesy Control Data Corporation)

1. *New job opportunities.* Hundreds of thousands of new jobs have been created in such areas as programming, computer operations, and information systems management (Figure 4-5). Current demand for persons qualified for these jobs far exceeds the current supply.

2. ***Greater job satisfaction.*** Scientists and engineers can tackle interesting problems that they could not have considered without computer help. And lawyers, teachers, clerical workers, and others can turn over repetitive and boring tasks to computer processing and then concentrate on the more challenging aspects of their work.

3. ***Use by businesses.*** The use of computers by businesses to avoid waste and improve efficiency may result in lower product prices and/or better service to individuals. In addition, the computer-controlled **robots** shown at the beginning of this chapter, along with other automated tools, can precisely carry out the dreary, dirty, and dangerous tasks that cause worker discontent. The net result of using these machines may be to improve the quality of the products assembled and sold to customers. Finally, computer-controlled products built by commercial firms can contribute to improved personal safety and can provide aid to the handicapped. For example, computer-controlled aircraft braking systems improve passenger safety. And to aid the sightless, computer-controlled reading machines are available that will read printed material and produce the corresponding speech sounds (Figure 4-6).

4. ***Use by public organizations.*** Avoiding waste and improving efficiency in government agencies, school districts, and hospital units can also result in better service and a reduced tax burden for citizens. Without computers, for example, the Social Security Administration could not keep up with the payment of benefits to widows, orphans, and retired

Figure 4-6 This interior view of a reading machine shows a computer-controlled camera eye which is able to scan printed or typed material. The scanner's output is automatically converted to computer signals which in turn may be converted to full-word English speech by the reading machine. (Courtesy Kurzweil Computer Products)

persons. The quality of education can be improved by the use of computer-assisted instruction techniques. And better personal health may result from a hospital's use of computers to provide better control of laboratory tests. Better control over pharmacy services is also possible (Figure 4-7).

5. *Use in the home.* Hundreds of thousands of microcomputers have been acquired for home use (Figure 4-8). Such personal systems are used for entertainment and hobby purposes, for educational uses, for family financial applications, and for countless other tasks. The benefits of personal computing are limited only by human ingenuity and imagination.

Potential Problems

In spite of the countless benefits that people receive from computer usage, such usage can also lead to potential dangers and problems. Some of these problem areas are:

1. *The threat of unemployment.* The greater efficiency made possible by computer usage can result in job obsolescence and displacement for some workers. For example, the computer-controlled robots pictured earlier can sense the need for a specified task, and can then take the actions necessary to perform the task. In the auto manufacturing and supply industries alone, it's expected that tens of thousands of jobs will be eliminated by robots during the 1980s.

Figure 4-7 Computer systems in pharmacies can be used to check a patient's medical profile against possible reactions to any ingredients in a new prescription or to determine the possibility of dangerous interactions between the ingredients in old prescriptions and those in the new prescription. (Courtesy Honeywell Inc.)

Figure 4-8 Personal computers such as this TRS-80 Color Computer model are now used in countless homes. (Courtesy Radio Shack Division, Tandy Corporation)

2. *The use of questionable data processing practices.* Input data about individuals are routinely captured by many organizations and entered into computer-processed files. In some cases, these facts have been compiled by those who have no valid reason to gather them. In other cases, inaccurate and incomplete data about people have been placed in computer-system files. Finally, human errors in preparing input data and in designing and preparing programs have resulted in system miscalculations that have harmed people.

3. *The trend toward depersonalization.* In most computer-based systems, the record key used to identify a person is a number—e.g., a social security, student, employee, or credit customer number. As people have come into contact with more computer systems, they have been identified by more numerical codes. Although many understand that being treated as a number results in efficient computer processing, they would prefer that systems be designed so that they are treated as persons rather than numbers.

4. *The systems security issue.* The lack of control over data security in a computer system has resulted in the destruction of an individual's records in some cases. The lack of control has also led to the accidental or intentional disclosure to unauthorized persons of confidential information of a very personal nature. Clever individuals have had no difficulty in the past in breaking through the security provisions of online computer systems in order to gain direct access to this confidential information.

5. *The privacy issue.* Lack of control over data storage, retrieval, and communication has led to abuses of a person's legitimate **right to privacy**—i.e., the right to keep private (or have kept on a confidential basis) those facts, beliefs, and feelings which one does not wish to publicly reveal. In at least one state, the records of patients hospitalized for psychiatric treatment were sent to the Department of Mental Health—and were then made available to insurance companies, police departments, the motor vehicle department, and all other licensing agencies.

THE IMPACT OF COMPUTERS ON ORGANIZATIONS

After noting that "The world is too much with us, late and soon," William Wordsworth took a stroll along a sandy beach to calm his ruffled sensibilities. What he could not know was that tiny silicon chips made from the sand he was walking on would cause feverish activity in the world of future generations. These chips have dropped into our midst like small stones into a lake, but they are causing waves rather than ripples! And the waves caused by computers are having both positive and negative effects on the organizations that use them. A few of these effects are outlined below. (Chapter 20 in the Social Impact Module provides further information on these effects.)

Positive Implications

We've seen that organizations may benefit from computers. Those benefits include the following:

1. ***Better planning and decision making.*** **Planning** is deciding in advance on a future course of action. Computer-based information systems that are quicker-responding and broader in scope than those previously available can have a positive impact on the planning and decision making that occurs in a business or nonprofit organization. Planning can be improved with the help of information systems that quickly notify managers of problems and opportunities. These same systems can then be used by managers to evaluate many alternative solutions and to then implement the final choice. Many of these systems cross national boundaries to link together the units of multinational organizations.

2. ***Better control of resources.*** **Control** is a follow-up to planning. It's the check on performance to see if planned goals are being achieved. Computer systems can be used to measure actual performance levels, compare these levels against planned standards, and then carry out preprogrammed decisions. For example, in an inventory control application the program can determine the current inventory level of a basic item, compare this level against a minimum acceptable quantity, and then produce an output reorder message when the quantity drops below the desired level.

3. ***Greater efficiency of operations.*** You've seen how greater efficiency may benefit individuals. But greater efficiency resulting from computer usage also benefits organizations. Banks and other financial institutions have improved their operating efficiency by using computers for the electronic transfer of money on a national and international scale. And supermarkets and other retailing outlets use automated checkout stations to improve efficiency (Figure 4-9). These stations read the special codes and symbols attached to products and then transmit the coded data to a computer. The computer looks up prices, possibly updates inventory and sales records, and then forwards prices and description information back to the stations. Computer systems are also used to save energy and improve the efficiency of heating and cooling offices, factories, hospitals, and schools (Figure 4-10). Without a strong commitment to improve efficiency through computer usage, many businesses will be unable in the future to successfully compete with foreign firms in national and world markets.

Figure 4-9 An automated checkout station in a supermarket. (Courtesy Norand Corporation)

Potential Problems

The following brief listing identifies some of the challenges that computer-using organizations may face:

1. *The problems in information system design.* The design of new computer-based information systems can be a very complex and challenging task. In some cases, past designs have produced disappointing internal results and a bad public image for the sponsoring organizations.

2. *The system security issue.* The failure to secure the information systems being used has threatened organizations as well as individuals. Assets have been stolen from organizations through system manipulation. Secrets have been copied and sold to competitors. And systems penetrators have repeatedly broken through the existing security controls of direct-access systems to gain access to sensitive information.

3. *The challenge to organizational structure.* When new computer systems are introduced, work groups in an organization may be created, disbanded, or realigned. Existing departments may be added to or eliminated. Such changes can lead to employee resistance and organizational stress.

4. *The concentration of power issue.* Organizations with limited computing resources may have difficulty competing against organizations with much greater sophistication in the use of computers for planning and decision making. And businesses that fail to introduce computer-controlled tools to improve their productivity may fall victim to more efficient competitors.

Figure 4-10 An operator at the control panel of an energy control system. Designed to control electrical energy consumption in small- to medium-sized commercial buildings, this system may be programmed to turn building equipment on and off at regular preset times. It's able to store energy data and adjust itself for daylight savings time, holidays, and vacation periods. It's also able to prompt the operator during programming and to diagnose its own problem if there is a malfunction. (Courtesy Honeywell Inc.)

Feedback and Review 4-1

The preceding pages have provided you with a basic understanding of the technological advances that underlie the information revolution and the effects these developments can have on individuals and organizations. The scrambled words format used below will test and reinforce your understanding of these topics. Rearrange the letters to spell out the correct word for the space indicated in the sentence.

1. An industrial revolution began in the eighteenth century with the harnessing of _____ power, and society is now in the throes of an information revolution that has been brought on by advances in computer technology.   Ⓜ Ⓣ Ⓢ Ⓔ Ⓐ

2. Thousands of computer circuits are now integrated and packaged on tiny chips of _____ .   Ⓛ Ⓘ Ⓞ Ⓝ Ⓢ Ⓘ Ⓒ

3. It's expected that the large computer of today may be replaced by a _____ superchip in the next decade.   Ⓝ Ⓘ Ⓢ Ⓔ Ⓛ Ⓖ

Ⓞ Ⓢ Ⓔ Ⓒ Ⓓ

4. A translation program is one that transforms the instructions prepared by people using a convenient programming language into the machine language _____ required by computers.

Ⓖ Ⓐ Ⓔ Ⓒ Ⓚ Ⓟ Ⓐ Ⓓ

5. Computer users may now obtain thousands of generalized _____ programs for widely used applications from equipment vendors and independent software firms.

Ⓣ Ⓡ Ⓐ Ⓞ Ⓘ Ⓔ Ⓟ Ⓖ Ⓝ

6. An _____ system is a collection of software that controls the overall operation of a computer.

Ⓒ Ⓤ Ⓘ Ⓚ Ⓠ

7. A system using direct-access processing techniques is an example of a _____ -response system.

Ⓐ Ⓣ Ⓓ Ⓐ   Ⓐ Ⓑ Ⓔ Ⓢ

8. Some information systems are taking a broader _____ - _____ approach to provide information that's more complete and relevant.

Ⓑ Ⓞ Ⓡ Ⓣ Ⓞ Ⓢ

9. Computer-controlled _____ and other automated tools can be used to improve the quality of the products assembled and sold to individuals.

Ⓡ Ⓟ Ⓨ Ⓐ Ⓘ Ⓥ Ⓒ

10. Lack of control over data storage, retrieval, and communication has led to abuses of a person's legitimate right to _____ .

A RECAP OF THIS BACKGROUND MODULE

You've come a long way in just four chapters. In Chapter 1, you were introduced to the computer itself. You saw that it's a very fast and accurate machine with the ability to handle input/output, calculation, logic/comparison, and storage/retrieval operations. You saw the types of hardware components that are organized to make up a working computer system. You saw how a detailed set of instructions could be stored within the CPU to cause it to accept input data and produce the desired output results. And you saw that computer systems can differ widely in size and design and that they are subject to certain limitations.

In Chapter 2, you gained a better understanding of what computers actually do. You saw how data are organized for computer processing, and many examples showed you how computer systems process the most common business applications.

In Chapter 3, you saw that a computer is but one element in a broader data processing system. It's only through the efforts of people that a computer is able to do anything at all. By working together to complete a series of steps in a system study, business system users and data processing specialists are able to put the computer to work doing useful tasks.

Finally, in this chapter you've learned that what computers do can have a profound impact on the people and organizations in a society. Because you've learned all this, you're not restricted now to following all the remaining chapters in sequence. Instead, with the background you now have, you can turn immediately to the first chapter of *any* of the remaining four modules in this book (Figure 4-11). Each of these remaining modules builds on what you've already learned.

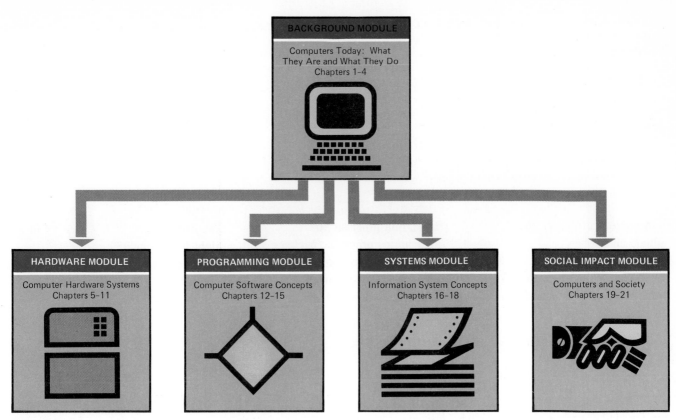

Figure 4-11 How *Computers Today* is organized. You are now ready to turn to the first chapter of any of the four remaining modules.

1. It's not enough just to be familiar with hardware, software, and applications concepts. You should also be aware of the impact that computer usage is having on society today. The rapid advances occurring in computer hardware, software, and information systems technology underlie the *information revolution* that's now under way.

2. There have been dramatic reductions in the size and cost of computer components and equally impressive gains in the speed, storage capacity, and reliability of these same components. In the software area, advances have occurred in the development of *programming languages* and *translation programs.* Thousands of *applications packages* are now readily available. And *operating system programs* have helped increase computer system productivity. Finally, information systems that are quicker responding and broader in scope have been designed to give decision makers information that is timely and complete.

3. These hardware, software, and systems advances have made the computer one of the most powerful forces in society. Computer usage has spread into homes and into organizational units of all sizes. As the last few pages of this chapter indicate, the impact of this spread of computer usage has both positive and negative effects for individuals and organizations.

KEY TERMS AND CONCEPTS

You should now be able to define and use the following terms and concepts (the numbers shown indicate the pages where the terms and concepts are first mentioned):

information revolution 86	**translation program** 90	**robots** 93
silicon chip 87	**applications program /package** 91	**right to privacy** 95
large-scale integration (LSI) 87	**operating system (OS)** 91	**planning** 96
very large-scale integration (VLSI) 87	**quick-response system** 92	**control** 96
programming languages 90	**distributed network** 92	

TOPICS FOR REVIEW AND DISCUSSION

1. "Society is now in the throes of an information revolution that has been brought on by advances in computer technology." Discuss the advances in (*a*) hardware, (*b*) software, and (*c*) information systems that underlie this information revolution.

2. (*a*) Discuss four ways that individuals may benefit from computer usage. (*b*) Identify four ways in which computer usage may have negative effects on people.

3. (*a*) Identify two ways that organizations may benefit from computer usage. (*b*) Discuss two challenges that computer-using organizations may face.

4. On the night of the 1980 presidential election, computer-aided projections based on models of "key precincts" were used by television announcers to declare President Reagan the winner. Only 1 percent of the vote had actually been counted, and the polls were still open in the western states. (In fact, Jimmy Carter made his television concession speech before the polls had closed on the West Coast.) How do you view this use of computers?

ANSWERS TO FEEDBACK AND REVIEW SECTION

4-1

1. steam
2. silicon
3. single
4. codes
5. packaged
6. operating
7. quick
8. data-base
9. robots
10. privacy

A Closer Look

You're fully aware by now that computer systems cannot operate without people. And computers would not exist without the contributions of thousands of people spanning hundreds of years. The Rogue's Gallery on these pages spotlights just a few of these people and briefly describes their contributions.

Charles Babbage (1791–1871) A man with a vision far ahead of his time, Babbage proposed a machine, the "difference engine," which was fundamentally a mechanical computer, in 1833. Had the technology of the day matched Babbage's genius, he could actually have built the first computer 150 years ago! (The Bettmann Archive, Inc.)

Blaise Pascal (1623–1662) Pascal developed the first mechanical calculator in 1642, at the age of 19. His machine could perform addition and subtraction calculations. (The Granger Collection)

Gottfried Wilhelm von Leibniz (1646–1716) Fifty years after Pascal created his mechanical calculator, von Leibniz built a machine which performed multiplication and division as well as addition and subtraction. (The Granger Collection)

Ada Augusta Byron, Countess of Lovelace (1815–1852) Daughter of the English poet, Lord Byron, Lovelace corrected errors in Babbage's work, suggested binary coding rather than the decimal system used by Babbage, and wrote descriptions of his plans for using a punched card system for input, output, and programming. (The Granger Collection)

Herman Hollerith (1860–1929) Hollerith developed modern punched card techniques for data processing. In 1896, he founded the Tabulating Machine Company, one of four firms which later joined together to form IBM. (Courtesy IBM)

John Atanasoff Between 1935 and 1942, Atanasoff developed the first automatic electronic digital computer prototype. (Photos courtesy Iowa State University Information Service)

John von Neumann (1903–1957) Von Neumann's concept of the stored program, now a basic part of all computer design, allowed the computer to execute instructions at its internal rate of speed rather than the much slower methods previously used. (United Press International Photo)

J. Presper Eckert (left) **and John W. Mauchly** (fifth from left) Shown here with other ENIAC officials, Eckert served as chief engineer and Mauchly as consulting engineer in developing the first operational electronic computer. Eckert and Mauchly formed their own computer company in 1947 and completed the UNIVAC in 1951. (University of Pennsylvania Archives)

Grace M. Hopper A pioneer in the field of ▶ computer languages, Hopper played an important role in the development of COBOL (COmmon Business Oriented Language). (United Press International Photo)

Howard H. Aiken Between 1937 and 1944, Aiken built an automatic calculating machine that combined established technology with the punched cards of Hollerith. In many respects this device, known as the Mark I, was the realization of Babbage's dream. (Wide World Photos)

John Bardeen, William Shockley, and Walter H. Brattain (left to right) The replacement of vacuum tubes by transistors for housing computer memory developed from the work of these men at Bell Telephone Laboratories. In 1956 they received the Nobel Prize in Physics "for their research on semi-conductors and the discovery of the transistor effect." (The Bettmann Archive, Inc.)

John G. Kemeny Twenty years ago, John Kemeny, now president emeritus of Dartmouth College, was aware of the impact that computers would have on our society. He was equally aware that few students were prepared to deal with the computers that would one day become part of their lives. Because existing computer languages were too complicated for students to master in a short time, Kemeny and Dartmouth Professor Thomas Kurtz developed the BASIC language in 1963–1964. (Courtesy Dartmouth College News Service)

Thomas J. Watson, Sr. Joining a company called C-T-R in 1914, Watson became its president in 1924 and changed its name to International Business Machines Corporation. Over the next 30 years Watson developed IBM into a powerful organization that controlled virtually all of the market for punched card equipment. But Watson did not see much of the future for computers in the late 1940s. (Courtesy IBM)

Thomas J. Watson, Jr. One who did not share his father's opinion about the computer's future was the younger Watson. When IBM's punched card equipment was displaced at the Census Bureau in the early 1950s by a UNIVAC-1 computer, his views prevailed and IBM quickly became a dominant force in computers. (Courtesy IBM)

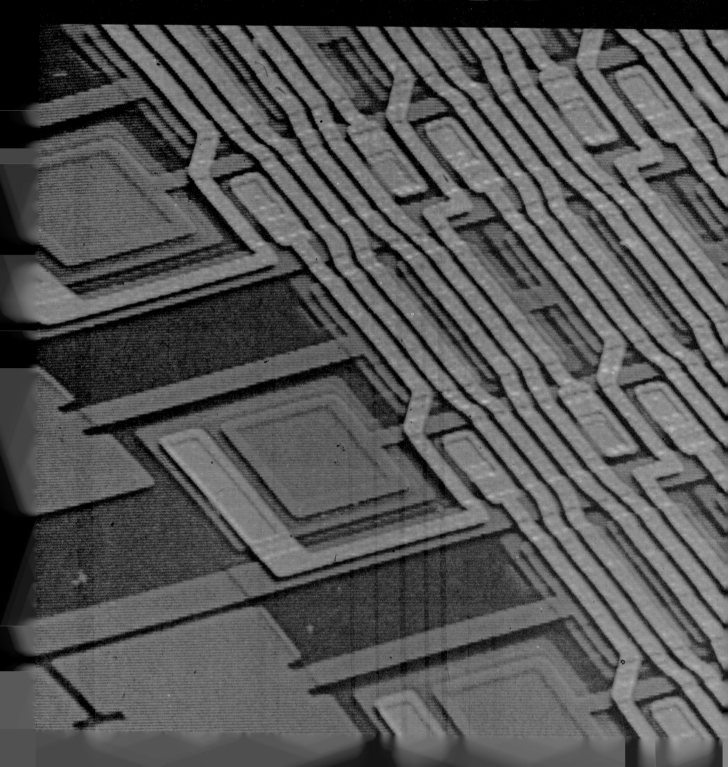

Computer Hardware Systems

In the Background Module you were introduced to the computer itself. You saw that the key elements in the basic organization of a computer system include input, central processing, and output devices.

The purpose of this module is to examine these hardware devices in greater detail and to consider some other related topics. The chapters included in this Hardware Module are:

5. Central Processor Concepts, Codes, and Components
6. Computer Data Entry
7. Computer Secondary Storage
8. Computer Output
9. Micros, Minis, Mainframes, and "Monsters"
10. Data Communication and Distributed Data Processing Networks
11. Word Processing and Electronic Mail/Message Systems

The Josephson junction is a superconducting switch that's at least 10 times faster than any other known device. To achieve this speed, a Josephson chip must be enclosed in a jacket of liquid helium so that it will be cooled to within a few degrees of absolute zero. (Bill Pierce from Rainbow)

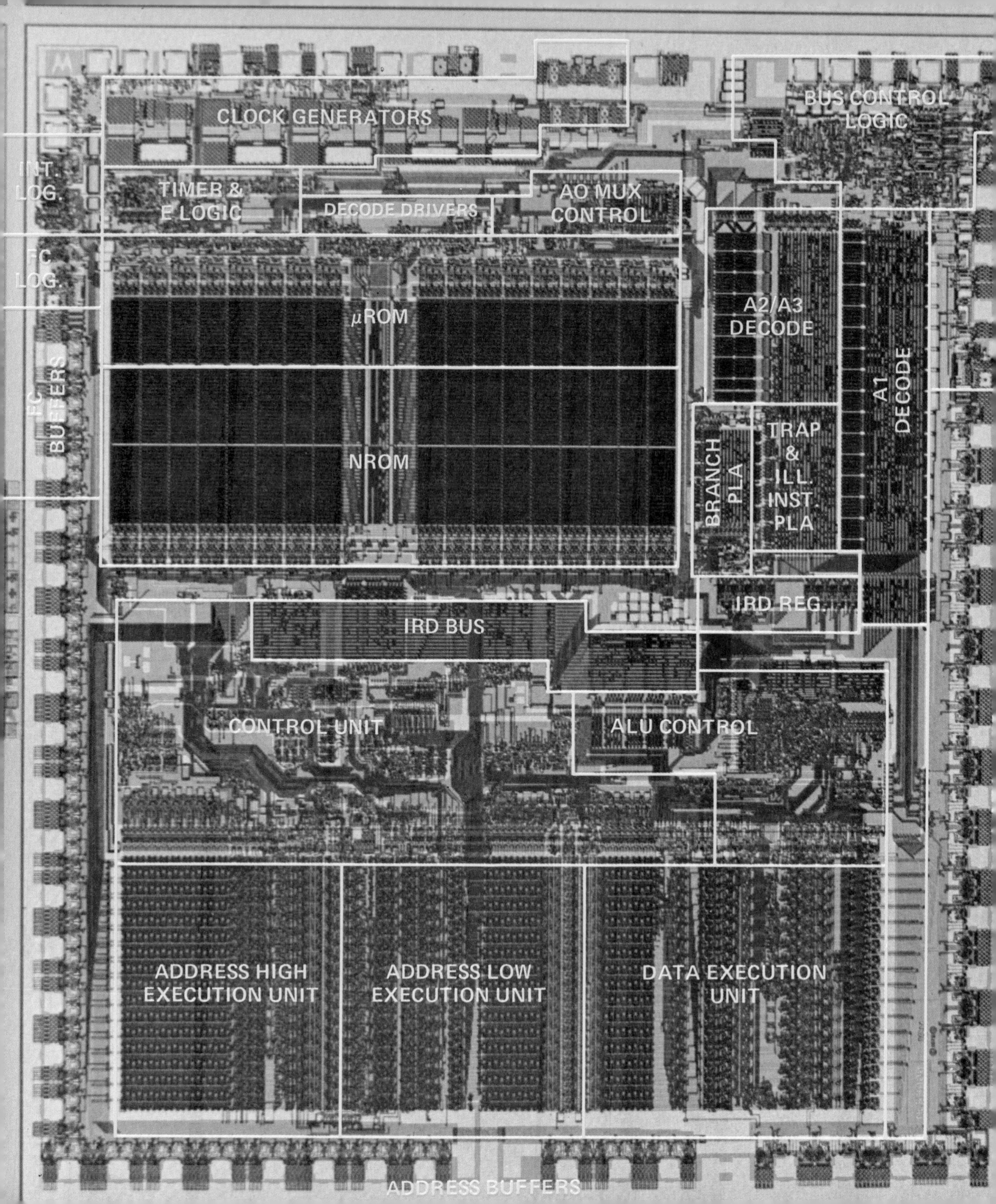

CLOCK GENERATORS

BUS CONTROL LOGIC

INT. LOG.

FC LOG.

EC BUFFERS

TIMER & E LOGIC

DECODE DRIVERS

AO MUX CONTROL

A2/A3 DECODE

A1 DECODE

µROM

NROM

BRANCH PLA

TRAP & ILL. INST. PLA

IRD REG.

IRD BUS

CONTROL UNIT

ALU CONTROL

ADDRESS HIGH EXECUTION UNIT

ADDRESS LOW EXECUTION UNIT

DATA EXECUTION UNIT

ADDRESS BUFFERS

chapter 5

Central Processor Concepts, Codes, and Components

DIGITAL VERSUS ANALOG

Calculating and computing devices come in two forms, digital and analog. Essentially, digital devices count and analog devices measure.

The abacus is a simple digital calculator. The positions of the beads directly represent numbers. Assuming the system doesn't malfunction (and the user is part of the system), the abacus will invariably give the same answer to the same problem.

The automobile speedometer is a simple analog calculator. It models speed with voltage. A small generator turned by the car's drive shaft produces a voltage that is proportional to the shaft rotation rate. The speedometer is just a voltmeter calibrated in miles per hour. Because of errors in adjustment, calibration, and reading, speedometers are often in error by two or three miles per hour. All analog computers are subject to such systematic errors.

Despite their inherent inaccuracy, analog computers were once important. Before the proliferation of electronic digital computers, analog machines offered one advantage: speed. Like a speedometer, many analog computers generate their readout almost instantaneously. Complex analog computers can quickly solve problems that require millions of operations when calculating by digital computer.

—Robert Schadewald, "Devices That Count," *Technology Illustrated*, October/November 1981, p. 37. Copyright 1981 Robert J. Schadewald.

Schematic of a microprocessor chip. This 16-bit machine rivals the power of many minicomputers. (Reprinted with permission from Motorola, Inc.)

Looking Ahead

Since the heart of any computer hardware system is the central processor, this first chapter in the Hardware Module focuses on the central processing unit. After looking first at how processors are classified, we will then examine the primary storage section of the CPU. You'll see how storage locations are identified and used and how their storage capacity can vary. Then, you'll see how data are coded in storage, and you'll study the types of components used in the primary storage section. Finally, you'll learn how stored instructions are executed by the arithmetic-logic and control sections of a CPU.

Thus, after studying this chapter, you should be able to:

▌ Outline how computers are classified

▌ Explain how storage locations are identified and then used during processing

▌ Discuss the capacity of storage locations

▌ Understand how data are coded in storage

▌ Identify the types of storage components used in a CPU

▌ Describe the operations of the arithmetic-logic and control sections in a CPU

▌ Understand and use the key terms and concepts listed at the end of this chapter

A digital processor, such as the scoreboard pictured here, directly counts discrete values—in this case the time left to play and the scores for each team. (Terry Wacher/Photo Researchers)

HOW COMPUTERS ARE CLASSIFIED

The word "computer" was defined and used many times in the Background Module. And in every case, we used the word to refer to a particular type of general-purpose system. While we'll continue to focus our attention almost solely on such general systems, you should also know about other, more specialized types of computers.

Digital, Analog, and Hybrid Computers

Computers are classified by the type of data they are designed to process. Data may be obtained either as a result of *counting* or through the use of some *measuring* instrument. Data that are obtained by counting are called **discrete data.** Examples of discrete data are the total number of students in a classroom or the total amount of an invoice. Data that must be obtained through measurement are called **continuous data.** Examples of continuous data are the speed of an automobile as measured by a speedometer, or the temperature of a patient as measured by a thermometer.

A **digital computer** is a counting device that operates on discrete data. It operates by directly counting numbers (or digits) that represent numerals, letters, or other special symbols. Just as digital watches directly count off the seconds and minutes in an hour, digital processors also count discrete values to achieve the desired output results.

In contrast to digital processors, however, there are also **analog machines** that do not compute directly with numbers. Rather, they deal with variables that are measured along a continuous scale and are recorded to some predetermined degree of accuracy. Temperature, for example, may be measured to the nearest tenth of a degree on the Celsius scale, voltage may be measured to the nearest hundredth of a volt, and pressure may be measured to the nearest "pounds per square inch" value. A service station gasoline pump may contain an analog processor. This processor converts the flow of pumped fuel into two measurements—the price of the delivered gas to the nearest penny, and the quantity of fuel to the nearest tenth or hundredth of a gallon or liter. Analog computing systems are frequently used to control processes such as those found in an oil refinery where flow and temperature measurements are important.

Analog computers may be accurate to within 0.1 percent of the correct value. But digital computers can obtain whatever degree of accuracy is required simply by calculating additional places to the right of the decimal point. To illustrate, anyone who has worked arithmetic problems dealing with circles knows that pi (π) has a value of 3.1416. Actually, however, the true value is 3.14159 . . . . . (this number could go on for pages). In fact, a digital computer once worked the value of pi out to 500,000 decimal places. Now that's more accuracy than most of us care to consider!

Desirable features of analog and digital machines are sometimes combined to create a **hybrid** computing system. In a hospital intensive-care unit, for example, analog devices may measure a patient's heart function, temperature, and other vital signs. These measurements may then be converted into numbers and supplied to a digital component in the system. This component is used to monitor the patient's vital signs and to send an immediate signal to a nurse's station if any abnormal readings are detected.

Analog and hybrid processors obviously perform important specialized tasks. But the overwhelming majority of all computers used for business and scientific applications are digital devices.

Special-Purpose and General-Purpose Digital Computers

Digital computers are made for both special and general uses. As the name suggests, a **special-purpose computer** is one that's designed to perform only one specific task. The program of instructions is wired into or permanently stored in such a machine. Although it lacks versatility, it does its single task quickly and efficiently. Special-purpose processors designed just to solve complex navigational problems are installed aboard U.S. atomic submarines. And microcomputers are routinely dedicated to such tasks as monitoring and controlling household appliances and automobile fuel and ignition systems.

Analog computers, such as used in this postal scale, convert the weight of a package into the cost of postage needed for mailing. (Dick Durrance/Woodfin Camp & Associates)

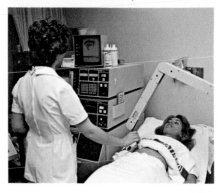

Hybrid computing systems combine the features of digital and analog machines. (Russ Kinne/Photo Researchers)

A **general-purpose computer** is one that can store different programs and can thus be used in countless applications. You've seen that by using different instructions such a machine can process a payroll one minute and a billing application the next. New programs can be written, and old programs can be changed or dropped. The versatility of a general-purpose system is limited only by the human imagination. And so, unless otherwise noted, all our future discussions of "computers" will be about general-purpose digital systems. Let's now become better acquainted with the primary storage, arithmetic-logic, and control sections found in the central processors of such systems.

PRIMARY STORAGE CONCEPTS

You learned in Chapter 1 that primary storage is used for four purposes. Data are fed into an *input storage* area. A *working storage* space is used to hold intermediate processing results. An *output storage* area holds the final processing results. And a *program storage* area contains the processing instructions. You also saw that the separate locations used for these four purposes don't have built-in physical boundaries. Rather, a specific storage location can be used to hold input data in one application and output results or program instructions in another. Now let's take a closer look at these storage locations.

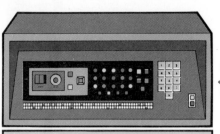

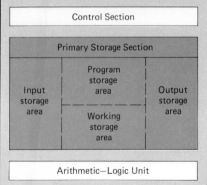

Storage Locations and Addresses

An analogy between primary storage and post office mailboxes is often used. In your local post office, each mailbox is identified by a specific number. Each box can hold different items. A letter containing instructions on how to tune an engine may have been placed in the box yesterday, and an electric bill for $46.18 may be put there today. Instructions are stored one day and data the next. The contents change, but the box and its number remain the same. A post office may have many such boxes that differ only in their identification numbers.

The primary storage section of a computer also has many small storage areas. Each one is assigned an **address**—a built-in and unique number that identifies the location. Like a mailbox, a storage location can hold either a data item or an instruction, and its identifying number remains the same regardless of its contents.

Comparing storage locations with mailboxes is convenient, but *this analogy breaks down in several important ways.* For one thing, a mailbox can hold several different messages at once while an address location only holds one item at a time. Another difference is that when a new item is placed in a mailbox the previous contents remain undisturbed. But when new data are stored in an address location the previous contents are erased and replaced. Finally, when the contents of a mailbox are retrieved the box is emptied. But when a computer system needs an item in a storage location, it merely reads and then duplicates the item elsewhere; it does not remove the item from its original location.

There are 4,096 storage locations in the primary storage sections of some small computers. The addresses in such a computer are numbered from 0000 to 4,095. Thus, one unique address is designated 0017. There's an important difference between the address number and the contents of the address. Suppose that $90 is the data item stored in address 0017. If the programmer wants that amount printed, she will *not* instruct the computer to print $90. Rather, the machine will be ordered to Print 0017, and it will interpret this instruction to mean that it should *print the contents of address 0017.* Just as you can locate friends in a strange city if you know that their home address is 4009 Sarita Drive, so too can the computer locate the desired data item if it knows the location number.

Use of Storage Locations

To get a general idea of how storage locations are used, let's take another look at the Longhorn College payroll application discussed in Chapter 1. You'll recall that input data for each part-time student employee are first entered on time sheets and are then transferred to a computer-readable floppy magnetic disk. The first input record was for Rob Brooks. The processing of this application was shown in Figure 1-11, page 22. But that figure showed the stored program concept in only the most general way. It made no reference to addressable storage locations.

Figure 5-1 presents a more realistic version of the CPU shown in Figure 1-11 because it does illustrate the use of storage addresses. The program steps shown in Figure 5-1 are identical in purpose to those discussed in Chapter 1. These instructions have been read into addresses 04 through 14[1] in the primary storage section of Figure 5-1. This choice of addresses for the *program storage* area is arbitrary; any space in primary storage could have been used.[2] Let's now trace through the program steps shown in Figure 5-1 to see how storage locations are used to prepare Rob's paycheck. (The circled address numbers shown in the figure indicate how the computer responds to the instruction stored in that address. Some flow lines have been omitted to simplify the figure.)

After the computer operator has loaded the payroll data in a disk reader and has set the computer to the first instruction in address 04, the processing starts. The first instruction (04) is fed into the control section of the CPU where it's interpreted. Control signals are sent to the disk reader which executes the instruction and transfers a record to the *input storage* area identified in the

---

[1]Leading zeros—e.g., 0004 or 0014—in the address numbers have been deleted here to simplify the figure. And the 18 addresses used—00 to 17—are a much smaller number than actually exist in the primary storage area but are enough to illustrate the concept.

[2]Programmers who write applications instructions in higher-level languages do not worry about address selection. Prewritten, specialized programs provided by computer manufacturers are generally used to assign storage locations to the different possible purposes.

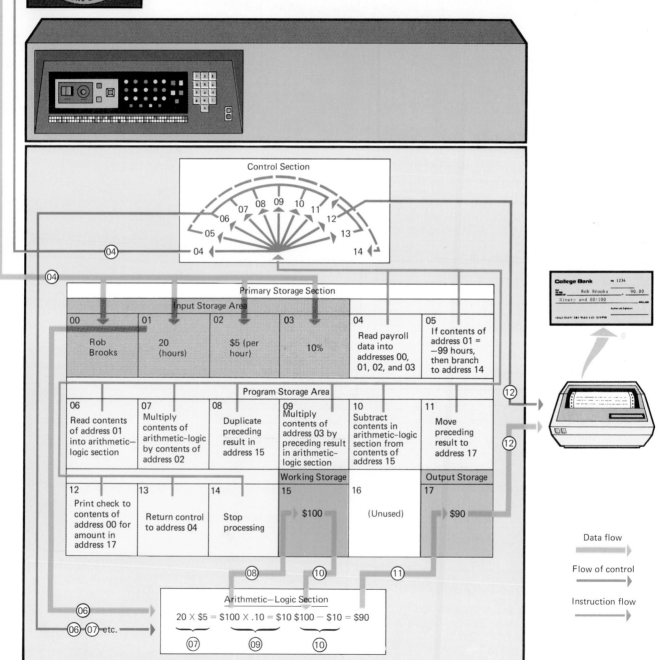

Figure 5-1 This figure illustrates the use of storage locations. The application is the Longhorn College student payroll example discussed in Chapter 1 and illustrated earlier in Figure 1-11. The areas used for input storage (addresses 00 through 03), program storage (addresses 04 through 14), working storage (address 15), and output storage (address 17) are shown. The selection of specific addresses to use for these purposes was arbitrary. The circled numbers in this figure refer to address numbers in the program storage area. The actions taken by the system in response to specific program steps are indicated by the circled numbers.

instruction. Thus, Rob's payroll data are read into addresses 00, 01, 02, and 03.[3] The data could easily have been assigned to other unused addresses, and so this is also an arbitrary choice.

As you know, the control unit will interpret the instructions automatically and in sequence after the initial control setting until directed to do otherwise. Thus, after the instruction in address 04 has been executed, the control unit begins to interpret the instruction in address 05. This instruction sets up a type of logic/comparison operation discussed in Chapter 2. It requires that the contents of address 01 be compared to a value of −99 hours. This value of −99 hours is placed in a last dummy record at the end of the payroll run to indicate that all valid data have been processed. If the contents do not equal −99 hours, the processing continues in sequence. If, on the other hand, the quantity in the hours-worked field does equal −99, program control will branch to address 14 and processing will stop. Since Rob has worked 20 hours, program control moves on to address 06. This instruction tells the control unit that the contents of address 01 are to be copied into the arithmetic-logic section, and so 20 hours is duplicated there.

By now you should be able to trace through the remaining program steps in Figure 5-1. The 20-hour figure in the arithmetic-logic section is multiplied by the $5 hourly rate stored in address 02 to get total earnings (instruction in address 07). This total earnings figure is copied (instruction, 08) in address 15, which is the *working storage* area.[4] The amount of the tax deduction is computed (instruction, 09) and subtracted from the total earnings figure that was temporarily stored in the working storage area (instruction, 10) to get Rob's $90 take-home pay. This $90 is then moved to address 17 which is the *output storage* area.[5] From there, the amount is sent to a printer which is directed to print Rob's check (instruction, 12). Finally, the control unit is directed to reset itself to address 04 (instruction, 13), and the processing is repeated for the next student.

When the payroll data for the next student are entered into addresses 00 through 03, they will erase Rob's data. This example thus illustrates a basic characteristic of computer storage: Entering data *into* a storage location is **destructive** of previous contents, but retrieving data *from* a location is **nondestructive.** Various terms are associated with entering new data into storage, and with retrieving existing data from storage. The act of *entering* new data into storage is called *read in, read into,* or *write.* The act of *retrieving* existing data from storage is called *read out, read from,* or simply *read.*

---

[3]As you'll see in the next section, the capacity of storage locations can vary. A few additional storage locations would probably be needed to hold all our input data. This would be no problem for the computer, but it would add unnecessary detail to our example.

[4]Why address 15 instead of 16 or some other unused location? Again, the choice is arbitrary.

[5]You guessed it: Any unused location would have been acceptable.

Address numbers

| 0015 | 0016 | 0017 |

| x | x | B | R | O | O | K | S | x | x | x | x | x | $ | 9 | 0 | x | x | x | x | x | x | x | x |

◄────── Word ──────►◄────── Word ──────►◄────── Word ──────►

(a) Fixed-length words of eight characters each,
occupying three address locations

Address numbers

0101 0102 0103 0104 0105 0106

| B | R | O | O | K | S |

A word of six characters
occupies six address locations

Address numbers

0111 0112 0113

| $ | 9 | 0 |

A word of three
characters occupies
three address locations

(b) Variable-length words of varying lengths

Figure 5-2 Fixed word-length storage compared with variable word-length storage. Each approach has distinct advantages. (*a*) Fixed-length words of eight characters each, occupying three address locations. (*b*) Variable-length words of varying lengths.

Capacity of Storage Locations

We've not yet considered the storage capacity of *each address.* All we've seen is that an address holds a specific data or program element. Actually, the storage capacity of an address is *built into* the computer. Over the years, computer manufacturers have used several different design approaches to partition the primary storage section into addresses.

One approach is to design the primary storage section to store a *fixed number of characters* in each numbered address location. These characters are then treated as a single entity or **word.** Thus, BROOKS might be treated as a single data word, and MULTIPLY might be a single instruction word. Machines built to store a fixed number of characters in each address are said to be **word addressable,** and they employ a **fixed word-length storage** approach.[6]

The primary storage section can also be organized so that *each* numbered address can only store a *single character* (8, B, $). Machines designed in this way are said to be **character addressable.** Thus, a sequence of characters such as BROOKS would require six storage addresses while $90 would occupy three addresses. Character-addressable machines are said to employ a **variable word-length storage** approach. Figure 5-2 summarizes the difference between the fixed-length and variable-length storage approaches.

Each of these ways of organizing the primary storage section has advantages and limitations. For example, variable word-length processors generally

---

[6]The number of characters that can be stored in each address varies depending on the make of computer. One modern design (the Control Data Corporation Cyber 170) can hold 10 alphanumeric characters in each address. Other machines have fixed word-lengths of two, four, six, and eight characters.

make the most efficient use of the available storage space, since a character can be placed in every storage cell. But if the storage capacity in each address of a fixed word-length processor is eight characters, and if many data words containing only two or three characters are placed in each address, then many of the storage cells cannot be used. On the other hand, fixed word-length machines have faster calculating capabilities. Such a machine can add two data words in a single operation. If the fixed-length word is eight characters, two eight-digit numbers can be added in a single operation. With a character-addressable processor, however, only one digit in each number is added during a single machine operation, and eight steps would thus be needed to complete the calculation.

Some of the largest and most powerful modern computers use *only* a fixed word-length storage approach. These giant processors are used primarily for scientific calculations and need the faster calculating capability of the fixed word-length design. Most currently used microcomputers, on the other hand, are variable word-length machines that operate *only* on one character at a time during processing. In between these two size extremes are the dozens of existing minicomputer and mainframe models that have built-in flexibility.

Most of today's business and scientific processing is handled by these flexible machines that can be operated as *either* variable *or* fixed word-length computers. Available program instructions permit these models to operate on either single characters or fixed-length words.

Let's first look at how a flexible computer operates as a variable word-length machine. Each address in this type of computer holds one alphanumeric character. Each character is represented in a storage location by a string of binary numbers (0s and 1s) that are treated as a unit. This unit or set of *bi*nary digi*ts*, or **bits,** is called a **byte.** Since a byte usually represents a single alphanumeric character, a flexible computer is often said to be **byte address-able.** By using an appropriate set of instructions, a programmer working with such a machine can retrieve a stored data item by identifying the address of the first character in the data word and by then indicating the number of address locations to be included in the word (see Figure 5-3). Since variable-length data words are common in business, instructions of this type are frequently used for business applications.

But bytes representing characters can also be grouped together in a flexible computer and operated on as a unit. Let's assume that a scientific application calling for numerous calculations is to be processed. To achieve faster calculating speeds, programmers can choose other available instructions that will cause the computer to automatically retrieve, manipulate, and store as a single unit a fixed word of 4 bytes. Or, they may choose to group 8 bytes into a single unit and have the machine function in this fixed-word format. Figure 5-4 illustrates the word arrangements possible with many of today's computers.

Figure 5-4 Word formats permitted with many byte-addressable computers.

Address 0186 is used to identify the word HELP! Retrieval begins with "H"

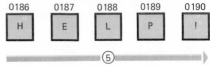

Computer retrieval path

Figure 5-3 A variable-length word in a byte-addressable computer is identified by the address number of the *first* character in the word. The number of characters included in the word must also be specified in a program instruction.

1 byte = 1 coded alphanumeric character

(a) *Variable word format: a variable number of bytes make up a word*

2 bytes
(This is the only fixed word format available with many minicomputers)

4 bytes
(This is the standard word size used by many mainframe models)

8 bytes
(This is a "doubleword" size used by many mainframe models)

(b) *Fixed word formats permitted*

Feedback and Review 5-1

Thus far in this chapter, you've seen (*a*) how computers are classified, (*b*) how primary storage locations are identified by address numbers, (*c*) how these addressable storage locations are used during processing, and (*d*) how the storage capacity of an address varies depending on the built-in design of the computer. To test and reinforce your understanding of this material, fill in the crossword puzzle with the words needed to complete the sentences and definitions found below.

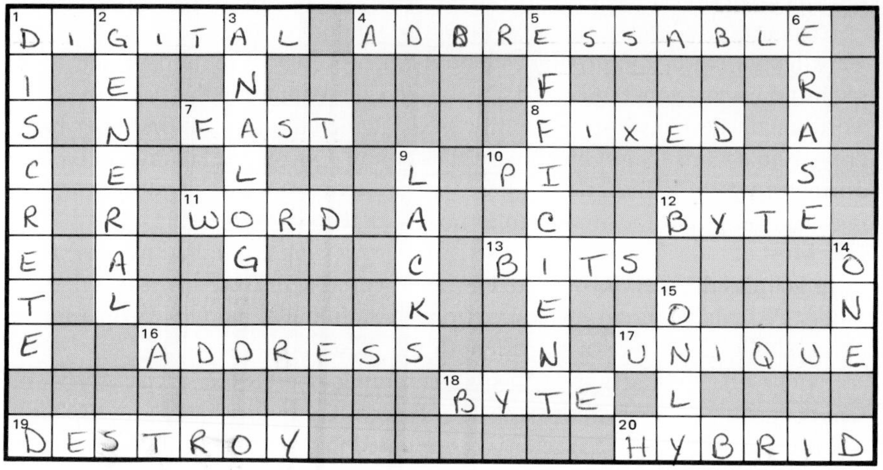

Across

1. A ______ computer is a device that operates by directly counting numbers.

2. Computers designed to store only a single character in each numbered address are said to be character-______.

7. Fixed word-length processors are ______ calculators, but they may not make the most efficient use of storage space.

8. Word-addressable computers employ a ______ word-length storage approach.

10. A digital computer has worked the value of ______ out to 500,000 decimal places.

11. A computer ______ is a group of characters that are treated as a single entity.

12. A string of binary digits treated as a unit is called a ______.

13. A group of binary digits, or ______ is used to represent a character in primary storage.

16. An ______ is a built-in number that identifies a location in storage.

17. Each address in storage must have a ______ number.

18. A ______-addressable computer can store one alphanumeric character in each numbered storage location.

19. Writing data *into* a computer storage location will ______ the previous contents, but reading data *from* a location is nondestructive.

20. A ______ computer system is one that combines desirable features taken from analog and digital machines.

Down

1. Data that are obtained by counting are called ______ data.

2. A ______-purpose computer is one that can store different programs.

3. ______ computers do not compute directly with numbers; rather, they measure continuously variable physical magnitudes.

5. An advantage of variable word-length computers is that they make ______ use of the available primary storage space.

6. Storing new data in an address location will ______ the previous contents.

9. A special-purpose computer performs only one specific task and thus ______ versatility.

14. An address location holds only ______ data item at a time.

15. Some of the largest and most powerful modern computers use ______ a fixed word-length storage approach.

CODING DATA IN STORAGE

Although the capacity of their storage locations can vary, every computer stores numbers, letters, and other characters in a coded form. As you saw in the last section, every character in storage is represented by a string of 0s and 1s—the only digits found in the binary numbering system. Let's see how it's possible to use just two digits to represent any character.

The Binary Numbering System

There's nothing mysterious about numbering systems. The first ones used an *additive* approach. That is, they consisted of symbols such as I for 1, II for 2, III for 3, etc. Each symbol represented the *same value* regardless of its position in the number. Since arithmetic is difficult when such systems are used, *positional* numbering systems were developed as the centuries passed. In a positional system, there are only a few symbols, and these symbols represent different values depending on the position they occupy in the number. For example, 5 equals the Roman numeral V, but 51 does not equal VI because the meaning of 5 has changed with the change in its position. The actual number of symbols used in a positional system depends on its *base*. The familiar decimal system has a base of 10, and it thus has 10 symbols (0 to 9). The *highest* numerical symbol always has a value of *one less* than the base.

Any number can be represented by arranging symbols in various positions. You know that in the decimal system the successive positions to the left of the decimal point represent units, tens, hundreds, thousands, etc. But you may not have given much thought to the fact that *each position represents a specific power of the base.* For example, the decimal number 1,684 (written $1,684_{10}$) represents:[7]

$$\underbrace{(1 \times 10^3)}_{1000} + \underbrace{(6 \times 10^2)}_{600} + \underbrace{(8 \times 10^1)}_{80} + \underbrace{(4 \times 10^0)}_{4}. \leftarrow \text{decimal point}$$
$$= 1,684$$

The principles that apply to the decimal system apply in *any other* positional system. An *octal* numbering system, for example, is one with a base of 8. In such a system, the possible symbols are 0 to 7 (8 and 9 don't exist in this case). Since each position in the octal number 463 (written 463_8) represents a power of the base, the decimal equivalent of 463_8 is:

$$\underbrace{(4 \times 8^2)}_{256} + \underbrace{(6 \times 8^1)}_{48} + \underbrace{(3 \times 8^0)}_{3}. \leftarrow \text{octal point}$$
$$= 307_{10} \text{ the decimal equivalent}$$

Similarly, the **binary numbering system** is one with a base of 2. The possible symbols, therefore, are just 0 and 1. Again, each position in a binary number represents a power of the base. Thus, the decimal equivalent of the binary number 1001 (written 1001_2) is:

$$\underbrace{(1 \times 2^3)}_{8} + \underbrace{(0 \times 2^2)}_{0} + \underbrace{(0 \times 2^1)}_{0} + \underbrace{(1 \times 2^0)}_{1}. \leftarrow \text{binary point}$$
$$= 9_{10} \text{ the decimal equivalent}$$

"By God, Cecily, she's a genius—she's already mastered the binary system!"

8 - Octal
16 - hexadecimal

---

[7]Just in case you've forgotten, n^0 is, by definition, 1. That is, any number raised to the zero power equals 1.

And the decimal number 202 is represented in binary as:

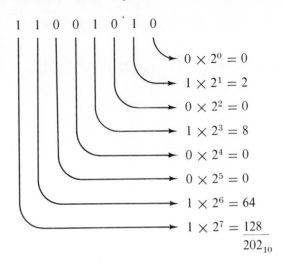

$$1 \quad 1 \quad 0 \quad 0 \quad 1 \quad 0 \quad 1 \quad 0$$

$$0 \times 2^0 = 0$$
$$1 \times 2^1 = 2$$
$$0 \times 2^2 = 0$$
$$1 \times 2^3 = 8$$
$$0 \times 2^4 = 0$$
$$0 \times 2^5 = 0$$
$$1 \times 2^6 = 64$$
$$1 \times 2^7 = \underline{128}$$
$$202_{10}$$

or:

Binary number	1	1	0	0	1	0	1	0
Power of base	2^7	2^6	2^5	2^4	2^3	2^2	2^1	2^0
Decimal equivalent	128	64	32	16	8	4	2	1

As you can see, the use of a smaller base may require more positions to represent a given value ($1001_2 = 9_{10}$). In spite of this fact, however, all but the very first computers have been designed to use binary numbers. Why the rush to binary? *One* reason is that computer circuits only have to handle 2 binary digits (bits) rather than 10. Design is simplified, cost is reduced, and reliability is improved. A *second* reason that computers use the binary system is that electronic components, by their very nature, operate in a binary mode. A switch is either open (0 state) or closed (1 state); a transistor is either not conducting (0) or is conducting (1). *Finally*, the binary system is used because everything that can be done with a base of 10 can also be done in binary.

On

Off

$$1 \quad 1 \quad 0 \quad 0 \quad 1 \quad 0 \quad 1 \quad 0 = 202_{10}$$

Computer Codes

Up to now we've been discussing true or "pure" binary numbers. But most computers use a *coded* version of true binary to represent decimal numbers. Although many coding schemes have been developed over the years, the most popular of these use a **binary coded decimal (BCD) approach.**

The BCD Approach. With BCD, it's possible to convert *each* decimal number into its binary equivalent rather than convert the entire decimal value into a pure binary form. The BCD equivalent of each possible decimal symbol is shown in Figure 5-5. Since 8 and 9 require 4 bits, *all* decimal digits are represented in BCD by 4 bits. You've just seen that 202_{10} is equal to 11001010_2 in a pure binary form. Converting 202_{10} into BCD, however, produces the following result:

$$202_{10} \text{ in BCD} = \underbrace{0010}_{2}\ \underbrace{0000}_{0}\ \underbrace{0010}_{2}\quad \text{or}\quad 001000000010$$

When 4 bits are used, there are only 16 possible configurations (2^4). As you saw in Figure 5-5, the first 10 of these combinations are used to represent decimal digits. The other six arrangements (1010, 1011, 1100, 1101, 1110, and 1111) have decimal values from 10 to 15. These arrangements *aren't used* in BCD coding. That is, 1111 doesn't represent 15_{10} in BCD. Instead, the proper BCD code for 15_{10} is 0001/0101.

Six-Bit BCD Code. Instead of using 4 bits with only 16 possible characters, computer designers commonly use 6 or 8 bits to represent characters in alphanumeric versions of BCD. In the **6-bit code,** the four BCD *numeric* place positions (1, 2, 4, and 8) are retained, but two additional *zone* positions are included (Figure 5-6). With 6 bits, it's possible to represent 64 different characters (2^6). This is a sufficient number to code the decimal digits (10), capital letters (26), and other special characters and punctuation marks (28). Figure 5-7 shows you how a few of the 64 possible characters are represented in a standard 6-bit BCD code.

Eight-Bit Codes. Since 64 possible bit combinations isn't sufficient to provide decimal numbers (10), lower-case letters (26), capital letters (26), and a large number of other characters (28+), designers have extended the 6-bit BCD code to 8 bits. With 8 bits, it's possible to provide 256 different arrangements (2^8). In addition to the four numeric place positions, there are four rather than two zone bit positions in an **8-bit code** (Figure 5-8). Each 8-bit unit used to code data is called a byte.[8]

Place Value

Decimal Digit	8	4	2	1
0	0	0	0	0
1	0	0	0	1
2	0	0	1	0
3	0	0	1	1
4	0	1	0	0
5	0	1	0	1
6	0	1	1	0
7	0	1	1	1
8	1	0	0	0
9	1	0	0	1

Figure 5-5 BCD numeric bit configurations and their decimal equivalent.

Zone bits		Numeric bits			
B	A	8	4	2	1

Figure 5-6 Format for 6-bit BCD code.

Figure 5-7 The coding used to represent selected characters in a standard 6-bit code.

Character	Standard BCD interchange code
0	00 1010
1	00 0001
2	00 0010
3	00 0011
4	00 0100
5	00 0101
6	00 0110
7	00 0111
A	11 0001
B	11 0010
C	11 0011
D	11 0100
E	11 0101

Zone bits				Numeric bits			
Z	Z	Z	Z	8	4	2	1

Figure 5-8 Format for 8-bit BCD codes.

[8]One alphabetic or two numeric characters can be represented in storage by one 8-bit byte.

Character	Extended BCD interchange code (EBCDIC)	ASCII
0	1111 0000	0101 0000
1	1111 0001	0101 0001
2	1111 0010	0101 0010
3	1111 0011	0101 0011
4	1111 0100	0101 0100
5	1111 0101	0101 0101
6	1111 0110	0101 0110
7	1111 0111	0101 0111
A	1100 0001	1010 0001
B	1100 0010	1010 0010
C	1100 0011	1010 0011
D	1100 0100	1010 0100
E	1100 0101	1010 0101

Figure 5-9 The coding used to represent selected characters in two popular 8-bit codes.

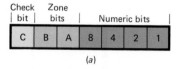

(a)

(b)

Figure 5-10 (a) Format of 6-bit BCD code with check bit included. (b) Format of 8-bit codes with check bit included.

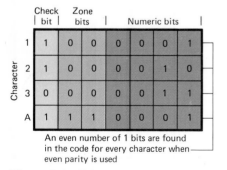

An even number of 1 bits are found in the code for every character when even parity is used

Figure 5-11 Using the check bit to make sure that every character has an even number of 1 bits. This is an example of the use of an even-parity format. Other computers are also designed to have the check bit produce an odd-parity format.

There are two popular 8-bit codes in common use. One is the Extended Binary Coded Decimal Interchange Code (**EBCDIC**). Developed by IBM, this code is used in most IBM models and in many machines produced by other manufacturers. The other 8-bit code is the American Standard Code for Information Interchange (**ASCII**). This code is popular in data communications, is used almost exclusively to represent data internally in microcomputers, and is frequently found in the larger machines produced by some vendors. Figure 5-9 shows how selected characters are represented in these 8-bit codes. The main difference is in the selection of bit patterns to use in the zone positions.

Detecting Code Errors. Computers are very reliable, but they're not infallible. If just one bit in a string of 6 or 8 bits is lost during data input, processing, or output operations, an incorrect character code will be created. Such an error can be caused by dust particles on storage media, by improper humidity levels near the computer, or by many other factors.

Fortunately, however, computer designers have developed a method for detecting such errors by adding an extra *check bit* or *parity bit* to each 6 or 8-bit character represented in storage. Thus, as you can see in Figure 5-10, a total of 7 or 9 bits will actually be stored. The designers of a particular computer model may then use the check bit to make sure that every valid character code will *always* have an *even* number of 1 bits. The 6-bit coding used to represent selected characters was presented earlier in Figure 5-6. Several of these characters have been reproduced in Figure 5-11. You'll notice that if the *basic code* for a character such as 1, 2, or A requires an odd number of 1 bits, an additional 1 bit is added in the check-bit location so that there will always be an *even* number of such bits. This is an example of an **even-parity** format, but other computers use the check bit to produce an **odd parity.** Since every valid character in a computer that uses even parity must always have an even number of 1 bits, circuits for **parity checking** are built into the computer to constantly monitor the data moving through the system. The computer operator is notified if a bit is lost and a parity error is detected. Of course, parity checking will only detect coding errors. It cannot signal the fact that incorrect data have been entered into the system if the data are properly coded.

Feedback and Review 5-2

You've seen in this section that computers store numbers, letters, and other characters in a coded form that's related to the binary numbering system. You've also seen that several different coding formats are used in modern computers. To test and reinforce your understanding of the material in this section, place a T or F in the space provided in the following true-false questions:

___F___ **1.** The first numbering systems used a positional approach.

___T___ **2.** In a positional numbering system, the highest numerical symbol always has a value of one less than the base.

_T_ **3.** Each position to the left of the decimal point in the decimal numbering system represents a specific power of the base of 10.

_F_ **4.** The possible symbols in the binary numbering system are 0 to 9.

_T_ **5.** The decimal equivalent of the true binary value of 110010_2 is 50_{10}.

_T_ **6.** The decimal value of 16_{10} is represented in pure binary as 100000_2.

_F_ **7.** The decimal value of 16_{10} is represented in 4-bit BCD as 00010101.

_T_ **8.** Alphanumeric versions of BCD commonly use 6 or 8 bits to represent characters.

_F_ **9.** A 6-bit alphanumeric code can represent 128 different characters.

_F_ **10.** There are four 8-bit codes in current use.

_T_ **11.** Each 8-bit unit used to code data is called a byte.

_F_ **12.** Eight-bit codes are limited to representing 128 different characters.

_T_ **13.** An extra check (or parity) bit is added to each 6- or 8-bit character represented in storage so that it will be possible to detect coding errors that may occur.

_T_ **14.** If a computer uses an odd-parity format to detect errors in character codes, then every valid character code will always have an odd number of 1 bits.

STORAGE COMPONENTS IN THE CPU

Many types of primary storage devices have been used over the years. The first general-purpose electronic computer built in the 1940s (the ENIAC) used vacuum tubes. These tubes were relatively large and each was able to hold only a single bit. Storage capacity was thus tiny by present standards. The most popular computer in the mid-1950s (the IBM 350) used a rotating drum coated with a magnetizeable material as the primary storage instrument. Thin films of magnetizeable material were later placed on flat surfaces and on small lengths of wire by manufacturers such as Burroughs and NCR. During the 15 years between 1960 and 1975, however, the dominant approach was to use tiny rings or *cores* of magnetizeable material in the primary storage section. And since thousands of existing computers still use **magnetic core storage,** a brief historical review of this fading technology follows.

Magnetic Core Storage: An Historical Review

Several tiny wires were threaded through each doughnut-shaped core. If a sufficiently strong electric current passed through these wires, the core was magnetized by the magnetic field created by the current. In Figure 5-12, the current flow from left to right caused the core to be magnetized in a counter-clockwise (0-bit) direction. Since the core permanently retained its magnetic state in the absence of current, it was a **nonvolatile** storage medium. However,

"0"

Current is applied; the core is magnetized

Core remains magnetized after current stops; storage is thus nonvolatile

"1"

Current is reversed; the core reverses its magnetic state

Figure 5-12 Magnetizing a core to represent a bit.

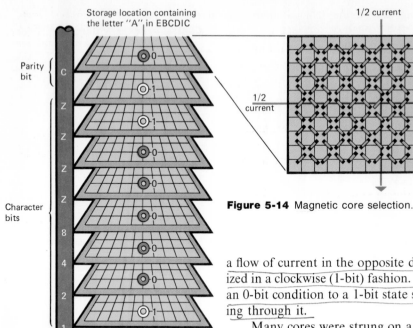

Storage location containing
the letter "A" in EBCDIC

Parity
bit

Character
bits

Figure 5-13 The letter A represented in core storage. The EBCDIC 8-bit code and an odd-parity format is used.

1/2 current

1/2
current

Figure 5-14 Magnetic core selection.

a flow of current in the opposite direction caused the core to become magnetized in a clockwise (1-bit) fashion. Thus, a core could be quickly changed from an 0-bit condition to a 1-bit state simply by reversing the flow of current passing through it.

Many cores were strung on a screen of wires to form a **core plane.** These planes, resembling small square tennis rackets, were than arranged vertically to represent data, as shown in Figure 5-13. You'll notice that nine planes were needed to code 8-bit bytes and provide for a parity check.

A simple technique made it possible to select and properly magnetize a few cores so that a desired character could be *placed into* storage. The imaginary core plane shown in Figure 5-14 shows how one bit in a character was selected. (The other bits in the character were similarly chosen in the other planes.) To make selection possible, two wires passed through each core at right angles. By sending only *half* the necessary current through each of two wires, only the core at the intersection of the wires was affected. All other cores in the plane either received no current at all, or they received only half the amount needed to magnetize.[9]

Magnetic cores have been popular for primary storage because they are safe, durable, and reasonably fast. However, the cost required to fabricate core planes and produce their associated circuitry is primarily responsible for their waning popularity.

[9]With a character now placed into storage, how did the computer *retrieve* it? For retrieval, a third *sense wire* was threaded diagonally through each core in a plane. The computer tested or read out the magnetic state of a core by again sending electric pulses through the two wires used in the data input operation. The direction of this current was such that it caused a 0 to be written at that core position. If the core was magnetized in a 1-bit state, the writing of a 0 abruptly *flipped* its magnetic condition. This changing magnetic field induced a current into the sense wire, and told the computer that the core contained a 1 bit. If *no reaction* was sensed, the computer then knew that the core was magnetized in the 0 state. But wait a minute! If all cores storing a character were changed to a 0 state as a result of the retrieval, didn't this destroy the character in its original location? The answer was yes, but only momentarily. Fortunately, a fourth *inhibit* wire was used to restore the cores containing 1 bits to their original state. The processor next tried to write back 1s in every core read an instant earlier. If the core was originally a 1, it was restored. If it was a 0, a pulse of current was sent through the inhibit wire in the plane to cancel out the attempt to write a 1.

Semiconductor Storage

Semiconductor storage elements are tiny integrated circuits. Both the storage cell circuits and the support circuitry needed for data writing and reading are packaged on chips of silicon. There are several semiconductor storage technologies currently in use. It's not necessary to consider the physics of these different approaches in any detail. It's enough just to mention that faster and more expensive *bipolar semiconductor* chips are often used in the arithmetic-logic and certain other sections of the CPU, while slower and less expensive chips that employ *metal-oxide semiconductor* (*MOS*) technology are usually used in the primary storage section.

The storage cell circuits in some semiconductor chips contain (1) a transistor that acts in much the same way as a mechanical on-off light switch, and (2) a capacitor that's capable of storing an electrical charge. Depending on the switching action of the transistor, the capacitor either contains no charge (0 bit) or does hold a charge (1 bit). Figure 5-15 shows how 64 bits might be arranged in a section of a chip. To locate a particular cell for writing or reading, row and column addresses (in binary) are needed. The storage location of the shaded cell in Figure 5-15 is the row numbered 0011 (3) and the column numbered 0101 (5). Since the charge on the capacitor tends to "leak off," provision is made to periodically "regenerate" or refresh the storage charge. Unlike a magnetic core, then, this semiconductor approach provides **volatile** or **dynamic storage.** That is, the data stored are lost in the event of a power failure. For this reason, a backup **uninterruptible power system (UPS)** is often found at larger computer installations.

Semiconductor memory chips have found their way into the newer models of most manufacturers for several good reasons:

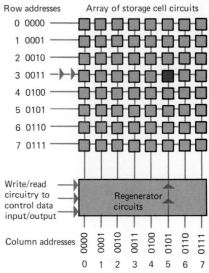

Figure 5-15 Semiconductor storage concepts.

1. *Economic factors.* For the last decade, the number of bits that can be stored on a chip has quadrupled every 3 years. During the same period, the cost per bit of storage has been cut in half every 3 years. There seems to be no end in sight to these cost reductions. The symbol **K** is often used when the storage capacity of chips is discussed. One K represents 2^{10} or 1,024 units. Today, a single chip is likely to store 64K, or 65,536 bits. But as you can see in Figure 5-16, these chips will soon be replaced in many systems by others that will each store 256K (262,144) bits, and the cost per bit will drop once again. It's then anticipated that the trend will continue with the development of first a megabit (or 1.048-million-bit) chip and then a 4-megabit chip.

2. *Compact size.* Semiconductor chips require much less than half the space needed by core storage devices of similar capacity.

3. *Faster performance.* Semiconductor devices are capable of faster performance than core storage units. Their more compact size contributes to this faster speed. However, the fastest core memories will outperform some of the slowest storage chips.

Figure 5-16 The number of bits that can be stored on a silicon chip has quadrupled every 3 years, and the cost per bit of storage has been cut in half every 3 years. This trend in semiconductor storage is expected to continue. (Adapted from George A. Champine, "Back-End Technology Trends," *Computer,* February 1980, p. 52)

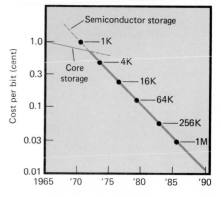

Future Primary Storage Components

Scientists in the United States, Japan, and Europe are now working on a primary storage approach that promises to be much more compact and much faster than anything in current use. The key element in this approach is the **Josephson junction**—named for British Nobel Prize winner Brian Josephson. This junction is simply a superconducting switch that can change from a 1-bit to a 0-bit state at least 10 times faster than any other known device. To achieve this speed, however, Josephson junction circuits must be wrapped in a jacket containing liquid helium so that they will be cooled to within a few degrees of absolute zero (more than 400 degrees below zero on the Fahrenheit scale). At that temperature, barriers that would ordinarily restrain the flow of electricity lose their resistive ability. Physicists are predicting that when this technology is available for commercial use in the early 1990s, a computer with 25 to 50 times the computing power of IBM's largest current model can be packaged in a space smaller than a basketball.

Specialized Storage Elements in the CPU

You know that every CPU has a primary storage section that holds the active program(s) and data being processed. In addition to this *general-purpose* storage section, however, many CPUs also have built-in *specialized* storage elements that are used for specific processing and control purposes (Figure 5-17).

One element used during *processing* operations is a **high-speed buffer** (or **cache**) memory that's both faster and more expensive per character stored than

temporary storage area

Figure 5-17 In addition to the primary storage section, many central processors also contain specialized storage elements that are used for processing and control purposes.

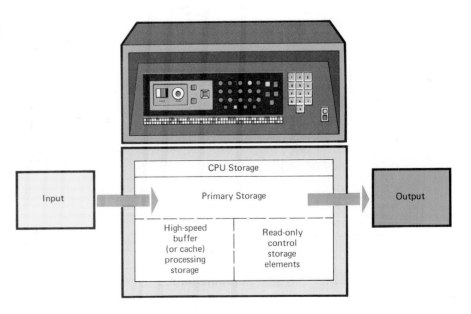

primary storage. This high-speed element is used as a "scratch pad" to temporarily store data and instructions that are likely to be retrieved many times during processing. Processing speed can thus be improved. Data may be transferred automatically between the buffer and primary storage so that the buffer is usually invisible to the application programmer.

Other specialized storage elements found in many CPUs are used for *control* purposes. The most basic computer functions are carried out by wired circuits. Additional circuits may then be used to combine these very basic functions into somewhat higher-level operations (e.g., to subtract values, move data, etc.). But it's also possible to perform these same higher-level operations with a series of special programs. These programs—called **microprograms** because they deal with low-level machine functions—are thus essentially substitutes for additional hardware. Microprograms are typically held in the CPU in special control storage elements.

Primary storage components are sometimes referred to as random access memory **(RAM)** chips because a programmer can randomly select and use any of the locations in a chip to directly store and retrieve data and instructions. But a microprogram will usually be held in one or more read-only memory **(ROM)** chips. That is, the microprogram control instructions that cause the machine to perform certain operations can be repeatedly read from a ROM chip as needed, but the chip will not accept any input data or instructions from computer users. ROM chips are supplied by computer manufacturers as part of the computer system and they can't be changed or altered by users. It's possible, however, for a user to "customize" a system by choosing the machine functions that will be performed by microprograms. For example, critical or lengthy operations that have been slowly carried out by software can be converted into microprograms and fused into a programmable read-only memory **(PROM)** chip. Once they are in a hardware form, these tasks can usually be executed in a fraction of the time previously required.

PROM chips are supplied by computer manufacturers and custom ROM vendors. Once operations have been written into a PROM chip, they are permanent and cannot be altered. There are other control chips available, however, that can be erased and reprogrammed. Since these erasable and programmable read-only memory **(EPROM)** chips may need to be removed from the CPU and exposed for some time to ultraviolet light before they can accept new contents, they are hardly suitable for use by application programmers. Regardless of the type of ROM chip used, they all serve to increase the efficiency of a CPU by controlling the performance of a few specialized tasks. A generalized CPU can be made to meet the unique needs of different users merely by changing microprograms.

Feedback and Review 5-3

To test and reinforce your understanding of the types of storage components found in a central processor, *match* the letter of the appropriate key term to the definition or concept to which it belongs. (Place the correct letter in the space provided.)

a) K
b) nonvolatile
c) nine
d) microprograms
e) Josephson junction
f) transistors
g) bipolar
h) magnetic cores
i) four
j) volatile
k) high-speed buffer
l) vacuum tubes
m) ROM chip

__l__ **1.** The type of primary storage device used in the 1940s by the ENIAC computer.

__h__ **2.** The dominant primary storage device between 1960 and 1975.

__b__ **3.** A _____ storage medium retains its magnetic state in the absence of electrical power.

__j__ **4.** A _____ or dynamic storage medium loses the data stored in the event of a power failure.

__c__ **5.** The number of planes needed in a core storage unit to code 8-bit bytes and provide for a parity check.

__g__ **6.** A type of very fast semiconductor storage chip.

__f__ **7.** The storage cell circuits in some semiconductor storage chips contain capacitors and _____ .

__a__ **8.** A symbol used to represent 2^{10} or 1,024 units.

__i__ **9.** During the last decade, the number of bits that can be stored on a chip has increased _____ times every 3 years.

__e__ **10.** The _____ is a superconducting switch that may be found in future primary storage components.

__K__ **11.** A specialized storage element found in the CPU and used during processing operations as a "scratch pad."

__d__ **12.** Special programs dealing with very low-level machine functions that can be substituted for additional hardware circuits.

__m__ **13.** A specialized read-only storage device used for control purposes that cannot be changed or altered by users.

EXECUTING STORED INSTRUCTIONS: THE ARITHMETIC-LOGIC AND CONTROL FUNCTIONS

Up to now, we've concentrated almost exclusively on the storage function of the CPU. It's logical to spend so much time on this function because the data that people are interested in must be stored in a coded form before they can be processed. But you know that to process data every computer must have components to perform the arithmetic-logic and general control functions. Let's now take a quick look at these components.

The Arithmetic-Logic Section

You'll recall that the arithmetic-logic section is where the actual data processing occurs. All calculations are made and all comparisons take place in this section (also called the arithmetic-logic unit or **ALU**). To see how an ALU operates on data, let's look once again at the Longhorn College payroll application presented earlier in the chapter. We won't need all the program instructions from the payroll application to demonstrate ALU operation. The ones from Figure 5-1 that we *will* need are reproduced in Figure 5-18a. These instructions are written so that we can understand them, but they cannot be interpreted in this form by the computer. A version of these same instructions that *would* permit machine interpretation is shown in Figure 5-18b.

The instruction in address 06—CLA 01—calls for the computer to first CLear the ALU of all previously stored data and then Add (store) the contents of address 01 to that section. Both the ALU and the control section have special-purpose storage locations called **registers.** The number of registers varies among computers as does the data-flow pattern. In Longhorn College's computer, the contents of address 01 are entered into an ALU register known as the **accumulator.** Thus, as Figure 5-19 illustrates, Rob's 20 hours worked—

Figure 5-18 (a) Five of the program steps needed to prepare the Longhorn College payroll application illustrated in Figure 5-1. (b) The five program steps presented in Figure 5-1 in a form the computer can interpret.

06	07	08	09	10
Read contents of address 01 into arithmetic–logic section	Multiply contents of arithmetic–logic section by contents of address 02	Duplicate preceding result in address 15	Multiply contents of address 03 by preceding result in arithmetic–logic section	Subtract contents in arithmetic–logic section from contents of address 15

(a)

06	07	08	09	10
CLA 01	MUL 02	STO 15	MUL 03	SUB 15

(b)

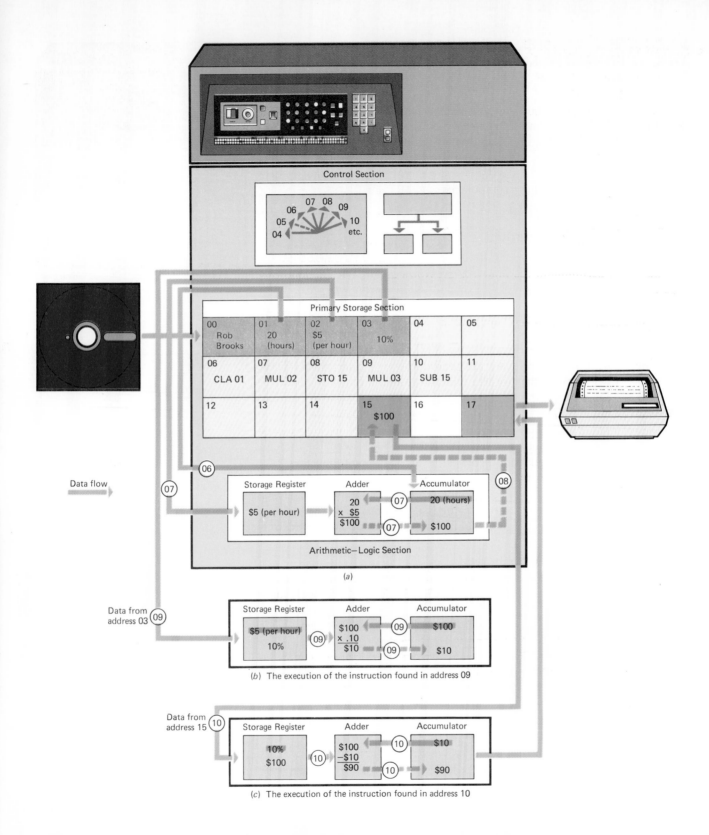

Control Section

Primary Storage Section

00 Rob Brooks	01 20 (hours)	02 $5 (per hour)	03 10%	04	05
06 CLA 01	07 MUL 02	08 STO 15	09 MUL 03	10 SUB 15	11
12	13	14	15 $100	16	17

Data flow

Storage Register	Adder	Accumulator
$5 (per hour)	20 x $5 $100	20 (hours) $100

Arithmetic—Logic Section

(a)

Data from address 03

Storage Register	Adder	Accumulator
$5 (per hour) 10%	$100 x .10 $10	$100 $10

(b) The execution of the instruction found in address 09

Data from address 15

Storage Register	Adder	Accumulator
10% $100	$100 −$10 $90	$10 $90

(c) The execution of the instruction found in address 10

◀ **Figure 5-19** (*a*) The operation of an arithmetic-logic section in a CPU. Every arithmetic-logic section uses special storage locations or registers. In this example, two such registers—the accumulator and storage register—are used to hold the data items being processed. All arithmetic functions are handled by the adder. The adder is also used in logic operations involving comparisons. By subtracting one value from another, the adder can tell if the first value is equal to, less than, or greater than the second value. The circled address numbers in the data flow lines indicate how the computer responds to the instructions stored in those addresses. (*b*) The execution of the instruction found in address 09. (*c*) The execution of the instruction found in address 10.

129

Central Processor Concepts, Codes, and Components

the contents of address 01—are now held in both address 01 and in the accumulator. (Once again, the circled address numbers shown in the figure indicate how the computer responds to the instruction stored in that address.)

The next instruction in address 07 is MUL 02. This is interpreted to mean that the contents of address 02 ($5 per hour) are to be <u>MUL</u>tiplied by the contents in the accumulator (20 hours) to get Rob's gross pay. The following steps are carried out in the execution of this instruction (see Figure 5-19*a*):

▌ The contents of address 02 are read into a *storage register* in the ALU.

▌ The data that are now in the accumulator (20 hours) and the storage register ($5 per hour) are copied in the **adder**—the arithmetic element in the ALU that also performs subtractions, multiplications, and divisions on binary digits.

▌ The multiplication is executed in the adder and the $100 result is *entered into the accumulator*. As you know, the act of writing the $100 result into the accumulator erases the 20 hours that was previously stored in that register.

After executing the instruction in address 07, the computer moves to the one in address 08. This instruction—STO 15—tells the machine to *STO*re the *contents of the accumulator* in address 15. Entering the $100 amount into address 15 is destructive to any previous data that might be there, but the read-out from the accumulator is nondestructive.

Figures 5-19*b* and 5-19*c* show how the ALU will execute the instructions found in addresses 09 and 10. In Figure 5-19*b*, the MUL 03 instruction in address 09 causes the data from address 03 (10 percent) to be entered into the storage register, thereby destroying the previous contents of $5 per hour. The contents of the accumulator ($100) and the storage register (10 percent) are now multiplied in the adder. The $10 result is entered back into the accumulator, thereby erasing the $100 amount. Figure 5-19*c* shows what happens when the instruction in address 10—SUB 15—is executed. The data stored in address 15 ($100) are read into the storage register and you know what this does to the 10 percent figure that was there. The adder then *SUB*tracts the $10 in the accumulator from this $100 amount in the storage register to get Rob's $90 take-home pay, which is entered back into the accumulator. From there, the $90 amount is first read into address 17 and then printed on Rob's paycheck.

By tracing through the operations of an ALU, you've seen that every arithmetic step requires two numbers and produces a result. Multiplication, for example, uses a multiplicand and a multiplier to get a product. Although *every* ALU must be able to manage the two data words and the result, different processing and storage techniques are used in different models.

In addition to arithmetic functions, the ALU also handles logic operations. You've seen that logic operations usually involve comparisons. The adder in the ALU is generally used to compare two numbers by subtracting one from the other. The sign (negative or positive) and the value of the difference tell the processor that the first number is equal to, less than, or greater than the second number. Branches are provided in the program for the computer to follow, depending on the result of such a comparison. Alphabetic data may also be compared according to an assigned order sequence. Some processors have a *comparer* in the ALU. Data from an accumulator and a storage register may be examined by the comparer to yield the logic decision.

The Control Section

The control section of the CPU selects and interprets program instructions and then sees that they are executed. The ALU responds to commands coming from the control section. You've just seen that a basic instruction that can be interpreted by a computer generally has at least two parts. The first part is the *operation* or *command* that is to be followed (MUL, STO, SUB, etc.). The second part is the *address* which locates the data or instructions to be manipulated. The basic components contained in the control section of Longhorn College's computer (shown once again in Figure 5-20) are the *instruction register, sequence register, address register,* and *decoder.*

Let's follow an instruction from the Longhorn payroll application through the control section to see how it's handled. We'll assume that the CLA 01 instruction in address 06 has just been executed and that 20 hours is stored in the accumulator of the ALU. The following steps are then carried out (the circled letters in the lines in Figure 5-20 correspond to these steps):

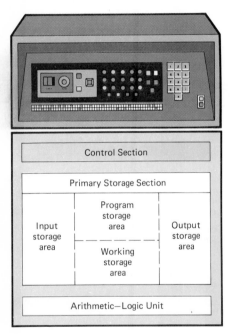

(a) The instruction in address 07 (MUL 02) is selected by the **sequence register** and read into the **instruction register** in the control section. [We'll have more to say about the sequence register in step (*e*) below.]

(b) The operation part (MUL) and the address part (02) of the instruction are separated. The operation is sent to the **decoder,** where it is *interpreted.* The computer is designed to respond to a number of commands, and it now knows that it's to multiply.

(c) The address part of the instruction is sent to the **address register.**

(d) The signal is sent to enter the contents of address 02 into the ALU. The command to multiply also goes to the ALU where the instruction is *executed.*

(e) The processing began when the sequence register was set to address 04, the location of the first program instruction. As each earlier in-

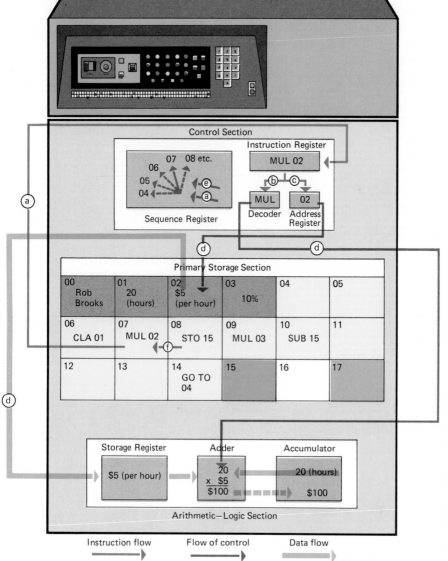

Figure 5-20 The operation of a control section in a CPU. An instruction to be executed is selected by a sequence register and read into an instruction register. The function to be performed is sent to a decoder where it is interpreted. The location of the data or other instruction to be manipulated is sent to an address register. A signal may then be sent to the ALU to execute the specified function using the contents of the specified address. These steps occur as each program instruction is considered. The circled letters in the lines refer to the steps discussed in the text.

struction was executed, the sequence register automatically moved to the next instruction in the processing sequence. Now as the multiplication in address 07 is being executed, the sequence register is again automatically moved to address 08. Note, however, that when the sequence register gets to address 14, it encounters an instruction that reads GO TO 04. This instruction alters the advance of the sequence register and resets it to address 04.

(f) The instruction in address 08 moves into the instruction register, and the above steps are repeated.

There are two cycles or phases that occur as each program instruction is considered. Step (*d*) is the **execution cycle.** The other steps comprise the **instruction cycle.** Most computers are *synchronous* machines. That is, the steps mentioned above are synchronized by an electronic clock that emits millions of regularly spaced electrical pulses each second. Commands are interpreted and then executed at proper intervals, and the intervals are timed by a specific number of these pulses. Although the operations of the ALU and the control unit may seem cumbersome, large systems can perform millions of these operations in a second.

Feedback and Review 5-4

The following multiple-choice review questions will test and reinforce your understanding of the operation of the arithmetic-logic and control sections of a CPU:

_b_ **1.** Both the ALU and the control section have special-purpose storage locations called

    a) adders.
    b) registers.
    c) accumulators.
    d) decoders.

_d_ **2.** The adder in the ALU is used

    a) only for addition.
    b) for arithmetic functions but never for logic operations.
    c) to store the results of addition, but it cannot store other arithmetic results.
    d) to perform all arithmetic functions.

_a_ **3.** The act of reading new data into a register

    a) erases the previous contents of the register.
    b) is nondestructive to existing contents.
    c) is possible only when the register is an accumulator.
    d) is possible only when the register is an accumulator or instruction register.

_c_ **4.** Although different computers use different processing techniques, the ALU in every computer must be able to

    a) select and interpret instructions.
    b) advance the sequence register.
    c) manage two data words and the result.
    d) control the decoder.

__b__ **5.** A basic instruction that can be interpreted by a computer generally has

    a) a decoder and an accumulator.
    b) an operation and an address.
    c) an instruction register and an address register.
    d) none of the above.

__a__ **6.** "An instruction is selected by the _____ register, read into the _____ register, and interpreted by the _____." The terms to complete this sentence are:

    a) sequence, instruction, decoder.
    b) instruction, address, decoder.
    c) decoder, address, accumulator.
    d) address, storage, accumulator.

__d__ **7.** The two cycles or phases that occur as each program instruction is considered are:
    a) synchronous and clocking.
    b) clocking and execution.
    c) pulsating and clocking.
    d) instruction and execution.

Looking Back

1. Computers are classified by the type of data they are designed to process. A *digital computer* is one that directly counts discrete values, while an *analog* computer measures continuously variable physical magnitudes that are analogous to the numbers being considered. Most computers are digital devices that are designed for special or general use. The emphasis in this book is on general-purpose digital systems.

2. Storage locations in the primary storage section of a CPU are identified by *address numbers*. These locations are able to hold either data or program instructions. When the contents of an address are needed by a program, the machine must be given the address number so that it can locate the desired item. The act of retrieving existing data or instructions from an address is nondestructive, but entering new contents into an address will erase the previous contents.

3. The storage capacity of an address is built into a computer. Some computers can only store a *fixed number of characters* in each numbered address location. They then treat these characters as a single entity or *word*. Such systems are said to be *word addressable,* and they use a *fixed word-length storage* approach. Other computers can only store a *single character* in each address location. These machines are said to be *character addressable,* and they employ a *variable word-length storage* approach. There are advantages and limitations to each of these approaches. Many of today's computers have been built with the flexibility to operate on either single characters or fixed-length words. Such systems are said to be *byte addressable.*

4. Every computer stores numbers, letters, and other characters in a coded form. Each character is represented by a coded string of binary digits (*bits*) that are treated as a unit. Binary numbers (0s and 1s) are used to simplify computer design. A 4-bit *binary coded decimal* (BCD) coding system can be used to represent decimal numbers, but 6- or 8-bit codes are used to represent characters in *alphanumeric versions* of BCD. Since the 64 possible characters permitted by the standard 6-bit BCD format isn't enough for many business applications, the 8-bit format is generally used. Each 8-bit unit used to code data is called a *byte.* The two popular 8-bit codes are *EBCDIC* and *ASCII.*

5. To detect any code errors that may occur, an extra *check bit* or *parity bit* is added to each 6- or 8-bit character represented in storage. The check bit is used to make sure that every valid character in a computer that uses even parity will always have an even number of 1 bits. Parity checking circuits in the computer can then notify the computer operator if a bit is lost.

6. Many types of primary storage devices have been used. Between 1960 and 1975, the dominant storage medium was *magnetic cores.* In recent years, however, *semiconductor storage chips* have found their way into most models because of economic and performance factors. And future storage devices using *Josephson junction* technology promise to be much more compact and much faster than anything in current use.

7. In addition to the primary storage section, many CPUs also have built-in specialized storage elements that are used for specific processing and control purposes. A *high-speed buffer* or *cache* memory may be used to improve processing speed. And special *microprograms* that deal with very low-level machine functions may be held in read-only memory (*ROM*) chips. Microprogram instructions are repeatedly called on to control the CPU as it performs certain basic operations.

8. The arithmetic-logic section does the actual processing under program control. During the execution cycle, stored data may be moved to registers in the *ALU.* From there they are manipulated by *adder* circuits to yield a result that may be stored in a *register* (e.g., the *accumulator*) or transferred to some other storage location. The adder may also be used to compare values for logic purposes.

9. The control section selects, interprets, and sees to the execution of program instructions in their proper sequence. Several basic registers are required to perform the control function.

KEY TERMS AND CONCEPTS

You should now be able to define and use the following terms and concepts (the numbers shown indicate the pages where the terms and concepts are first mentioned):

discrete data 108
continuous data 108
digital computer 108
analog computer 109
hybrid computer 109
special-purpose computer 109
general-purpose computer 110
address 110
destructive read-in (or write) 113
nondestructive read-out 113
word 114
word-addressable computer 114
fixed word-length storage 114
character-addressable computer 114
variable word-length storage 114
bit 115
byte 115
byte-addressable computer 115
binary numbering system 117

the binary coded decimal (BCD) approach 118
6-bit BCD code 119
8-bit BCD code 119
EBCDIC 120
ASCII 120
even parity 120
odd parity 120
parity checking 120
magnetic core storage 121
nonvolatile storage 121
core plane 122
semiconductor storage 123
volatile (or dynamic) storage 123
uninterruptible power system (UPS) 123
K 123
Josephson junction 124
high-speed buffer (or cache) storage 125

microprogram 125
RAM (random access memory) chip 125
ROM (read-only memory) chip 125
PROM (programmable read-only memory) chip 125
EPROM (erasable and programmable read-only memory) chip 126
ALU 127
register 127
accumulator 127
adder 129
sequence register 130
instruction register 130
decoder 130
address register 130
execution cycle 132
instruction cycle 132

TOPICS FOR REVIEW AND DISCUSSION

1. (*a*) What's a digital computer? (*b*) An analog computer? (*c*) A hybrid computer?

2. How does a special-purpose computer differ from a general-purpose machine?

3. (*a*) How is an addressable storage location similar to a post office box? (*b*) How do storage locations differ from mailboxes?

4. Discuss how storage locations are used during the processing of an application.

5. Discuss this statement: "Over the years, computer manufacturers have used several different design approaches to partition the primary storage section into addresses."

6. (*a*) Distinguish between word-addressable and character-addressable computers. (*b*) What is an advantage of each of these computer types?

7. (*a*) What is a byte-addressable computer? (*b*) How does it achieve its flexibility?

8. (*a*) What is the difference between an additive and a positional numbering system? (*b*) Give examples of both types of numbering systems.

9. Identify two principles that apply to any positional numbering system.

10. Why have computers been designed to use the binary numbering system?

11. (*a*) What is the decimal equivalent of 1101011_2? (*b*) Of 11010_2?

12. (*a*) What is 150_{10} in 4-bit BCD code? (*b*) What is 75_{10} in BCD?

13. Why has the standard 6-bit BCD code been extended to 8 bits?

14. Identify and discuss the two popular 8-bit codes.

15. How can a computer detect whether a bit in a character code is lost during processing?

16. (*a*) What types of primary storage devices have been used in the past? (*b*) What is the dominant primary storage technology at the present time? (*c*) What technology may emerge in the future?

17. Why are semiconductor chips popular as storage devices?

18. (*a*) Identify the specialized storage elements that may be found in a CPU. (*b*) How may these elements be used?

19. Discuss the operation of the arithmetic-logic section in a CPU.

20. Discuss the operation of the control section in a CPU.

ANSWERS TO FEEDBACK AND REVIEW SECTIONS

5-1
The solution to the crossword puzzle is shown below:

¹D	I	²G	I	T	³A	L		⁴A	D	D	R	⁵E	S	S	A	B	L	⁶E

(crossword grid)

```
D I G I T A L     A D D R E S S A B L E
I   E     N           F             R
S   N   F A S T       F I X E D     A
C   E     L       L   P I           S
R   R   W O R D   A   C       B Y T E
E   A     G       C   B I T S       O
T   L             K   E     O       N
E     A D D R E S S   N   U N I Q U E
              B Y T E   L
D E S T R O Y           H Y B R I D
```

5-2	5-3	5-4
1. F	1. l	1. b
2. T	2. h	2. d
3. T	3. b	3. a
4. F	4. j	4. c
5. T	5. c	5. b
6. T	6. g	6. a
7. F	7. f	7. d
8. T	8. a	
9. F	9. i	
10. F	10. e	
11. T	11. k	
12. F	12. d	
13. T	13. m	
14. T		

Chips for the Making

They're everywhere! In cars, color television sets, and microwave ovens. They bleep out at you from electronic toys, telephone lines, and automatic tellers at the bank. And they're multiplying. What *are* they? Called integrated circuits—or computer chips—these tiny bits of silicon have brought computing power out of science labs into everyday life. These minute chips, smaller than your fingernail, have caused a change comparable to, maybe even greater than, the invention of the telephone, airplane, and automobile.

Early Computing

The first general-use computers developed in the early 1940s were massive machines housed in huge buildings with carefully controlled air temperatures and filtering systems. They depended on thousands of vacuum tubes and miles of electrical wiring for their computing abilities. Toward the end of the decade, transistors were developed using semiconductors (substances that allow electricity to flow through them). This development reduced the size of computers. The transistors were wired on to circuit boards, several of which could process binary information when hooked together. In the 1950s these transistors became much smaller.

The Integrated Circuit

It wasn't until 1971, however, that computers became small enough for use outside large corporations, colleges, and government offices. M. E. Hoff, a Stanford University graduate backed by the Intel Corporation, invented an integrated circuit with over 2000 transistors on a small sliver of silicon. Integrated-circuit technology mushroomed and today's streamlined chip carries more transistors, is even tinier, and has as much computing power as

the first-generation computers. And, while the early computers cost millions of dollars to construct, today's chips can be purchased with a child's allowance.

How a Chip Is Made

Chips are designed by engineers much as buildings are designed by architects. Depending on the chip's function, an engineer may take years to complete a complex design. Drawings can be handcrafted on a drafting table or drawn on a computer (Figure 5-A). Once completed, the design is miniaturized on a "photomask"—which resembles a photographic negative (Figure 5-B). The design is repeated dozens of times over a small piece of film. The photomask is then used to transfer the design to a silicon wafer, several inches wide and sliced from a long tube-like silicon crystal, made from purified sand. While silicon and germanium are qualified semiconductors, sili-

Figure 5-A Diagrams for layers of chips. (Dan McCoy from Rainbow)

Figure 5-B Transferring the design to a photomask. (Dan McCoy from Rainbow)

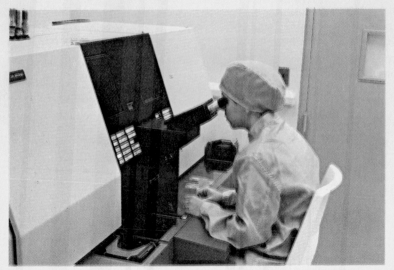

Figure 5-C This machine prints integrated circuit patterns on the wafers from which semiconductor devices are made. (Courtesy Perkin-Elmer Corp.)

con is inexpensive, abundant, and almost always used for making chips. The design is imprinted on the wafer by a chemical etching process with photosensitive emulsion applied to the silicon that is then exposed to ultraviolet light. An acid bath is used to wash away any unexposed areas. This process can be repeated as many as twelve times, creating successive layers of electrical circuitry on the chip (Figure 5-C).

Although the design layers have been etched on the wafer, the chips must also include different electrical characteristics to control the flow of electricity. Through a process called "doping," impurities are embedded into the silicon with boron, arsenic, or phosphorus. Doping changes the atomic configuration of the silicon by removing or adding an electron. This results in a positive or negative charge. The transistor effect is created when, for example, two negative areas surround a positive one. Chips can also be doped by a process called ion implantation in which molecules of boron are shot into the silicon with 100,000 volts of electricity. Scientists are currently working on laser technology to embed the impurities.

Once the chips have been doped, they're heated for hours in large furnaces while the impurities slowly sink into the various layers of circuitry. Testing begins after the chips are removed from the heat and separated from the other chips on the wafer with a diamond saw. Usually, less than half the chips from a wafer survive the manufacturing process and are usable (Figure 5-D).

Methods and manufacturing time vary depending on the complexity of design. A chip used in a microwave oven may have only a few layers of circuitry. State-of-the-art chips used in personal computers are much more intricate. Microprocessor chips, the heart of a personal computer, are the most complex chips manufactured today. Most of the steps involved in this process take place in "clean rooms" with air filters to remove the smallest particles of dust and dirt that might contaminate the chips. Employees wear sterilized white jump suits ("bunny suits") for the same reason.

Once the chips have passed testing, they are packaged with protective casings of ceramic, plastic, or metal

Figure 5-D Circuit patterns printed on silicon wafers form the tiny chips that are the hearts of electronic devices. (Courtesy Perkin-Elmer Corp.)

with gold or aluminum soldering. The packaging protects the chips and also provides electrodes for hooking up their circuits to the outside world. A lengthy manufacturing process is now done and the chips are available for a variety of tasks.

From "Chips for the Making," appearing in the January 1982 issue of *Popular Computing* magazine. Copyright 1982 Popular Computing, Inc. Used with permission of Popular Computing, Inc.

chapter 6

Computer Data Entry

THE DISPROPORTIONATE COST OF DATA ENTRY

Computers have always processed data far faster than it has been possible to get data into and out of them. The progress in data entry techniques and equipment has been modest in comparison with the phenomenal gains in the rates at which data can be processed within the computer. The US Department of Commerce's Institute for Computer Sciences & Technology estimates that the costs of data entry represent from 30 to 50 percent of the DP budget. The Institute considers these costs "disproportionately high" and "describes them as the largest single cost factor in many data processing activities."

The irony of these disproportionate costs stems from data entry's seemingly superfluous role of recapturing already accumulated data. Classic data entry involves several steps: transcribing source documents; creating machine-readable transactions from each document; rejecting and repairing any transactions which may be incomplete or inaccurate; processing the edited transactions, rejecting any with logical errors; and repeating the aforementioned steps until all transactions have been properly entered.

Most of the efforts to combat increasing costs are aimed at the concept itself. Data entry has been attacked for a long time and still is being attacked by a desire on the part of its detractors to eliminate it altogether.

—Wayne L. Rhodes, Jr., "The Disproportionate Cost of Data Entry," *Infosystems*, October 1980, p. 70. Reprinted with permission.

Advanced point-of-sale terminals, such as the programmable system shown here, are helping to lower the cost of data entry in retail operations. (Courtesy IBM Corporation)

Looking Ahead

The purpose of Chapter 6 is to give you an overview of the input media and devices used to enter data into computer processing systems. In the first section, you'll see how data entry techniques are affected by the type of processing being done. Data entry costs, the importance of input accuracy, and some methods used to detect input errors are also considered. Next, you'll learn about the input media and devices that are used in sequential (batch) processing applications. Then, in the last section, you'll read about the data entry devices that are used in direct-access (online) processing applications.

Thus, after studying this chapter, you should be able to:

▌ Describe the data entry approaches used in sequential and direct-access processing

▌ Recognize the importance of input accuracy and of the need to detect input errors

▌ Discuss the characteristics of sequential processing media such as punched cards, magnetic tape, and floppy disks, and describe the input devices used with these media

▌ Summarize the uses of magnetic ink and optical character-reading devices in sequential processing applications

▌ Outline the characteristics and applications of the several types of data entry devices used in direct-access processing

▌ Understand and use the key terms and concepts listed at the end of this chapter

DATA ENTRY: SOME BASIC CONCEPTS

You'll remember from Chapter 1 that the information that people need to support their decisions and actions is produced by a series of data processing activities. The first of these activities is to capture the raw input data. In computer data processing, these facts must either be originated in a machine-readable form or they must be converted into such a form before they can be entered into the computer. Once in the CPU, of course, they are manipulated and managed to produce the desired information. Much of this chapter deals with the media and devices used to enter data into computer systems. But before we look at media and devices, let's briefly consider some important concepts associated with the data entry function.

Sources of Input Data

The input data used by an organization are obtained from internal and external sources. The *internal* sources are the people and departments in an organization that produce the facts that must be processed. You've seen in Chapters 2 and 3, for example, that the data contained on the invoices produced by the billing department in an organization are used to provide the input for the organization's sales analysis, inventory control, and accounts-receivable reports.

②*External* sources of input data include individuals and groups located outside the organization. These sources include customers, suppliers, and competitors. The input data for the sales order, for example, must come from a customer. Business publications, trade associations, and government agencies are good sources of environmental statistics such as per capita income and consumer spending that can be used for planning purposes.

Data Entry Approaches

You saw in Chapter 2 that files are organized and then processed by the use of ① *sequential (batch)* or ② *direct-access (on-line)* techniques. Sequential processing, you'll recall, consists of reading and processing the first record in the file sequence, then the second record in the order, and so on. Direct-access processing, on the other hand, consists of directly locating and updating any record in the file without the need to search through a lengthy sequence of other records. The type of processing that is employed in a particular application has an important bearing on the data entry approach that is used.

Data Entry for Sequential Processing. In a sequential processing application, the raw data to be processed are typically captured on *source documents* such as sales tickets, customer invoices, and payroll time sheets. Data can be recorded directly in a machine-readable form at the source of the transaction through the use of devices such as the imprinters that enter credit card data on sales tickets. Or, the data on the documents may be entered on input media such as punched cards, magnetic tape, or floppy disks by data entry operators. Since customer statements, employee paychecks, and many types of reports need not be prepared on an hourly or daily basis, the invoice, payroll, and other data are accumulated into batches, sorted into the proper processing sequence, and then processed only at scheduled intervals. Data were entered into batch processing applications in several ways in Chapter 2. Figure 6-1 illustrates some common data entry approaches used in sequential processing applications. A section on the direct data entry devices used for sequential processing is presented later in the chapter.

A large amount of input data is usually prepared and processed in batch applications. Many organizations have one or more data entry departments that are responsible for the preparation of this mass of data. In some organizations, a single data entry group is located near the computer room. The data recorded on the input medium are then easily loaded into a nearby input device. In other organizations, data entry personnel may be found in outlying offices. In this case, the data may be loaded into an input device at a **remote batch station** at the outlying office and sent to the CPU over telephone lines or

Have low cost help and if time not import. -- this is best

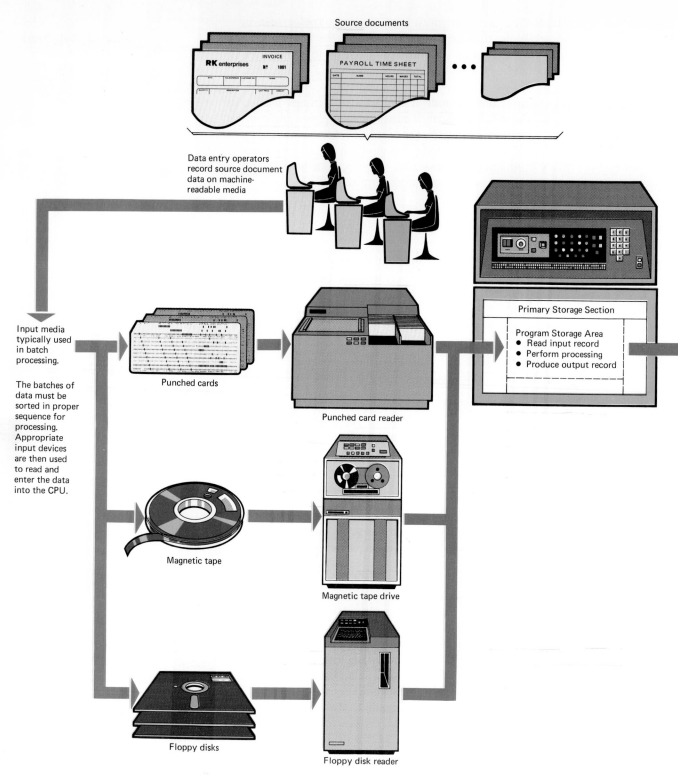

Source documents

RK enterprises   INVOICE   N° 1001

PAYROLL TIME SHEET

Data entry operators
record source document
data on machine-
readable media

Input media
typically used
in batch
processing.

The batches of
data must be
sorted in proper
sequence for
processing.
Appropriate
input devices
are then used
to read and
enter the data
into the CPU.

Punched cards

Punched card reader

Magnetic tape

Magnetic tape drive

Floppy disks

Floppy disk reader

Primary Storage Section

Program Storage Area
• Read input record
• Perform processing
• Produce output record

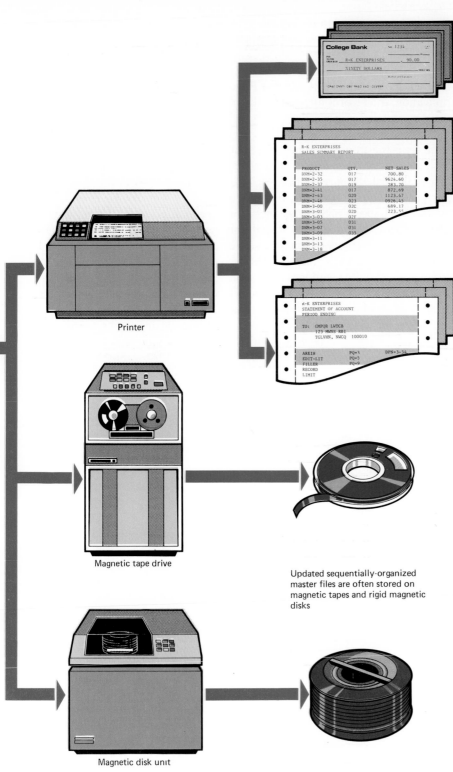

Updated sequentially-organized
master files are often stored on
magnetic tapes and rigid magnetic
disks

Figure 6-1 Data entry in sequential processing applications. Transaction data affecting many of the records and files of an
organization are captured on source documents. Data entry operators may then record these facts on a suitable input medium.
Batches of transaction data are periodically
arranged in the same sequence as the master file and are then read into the CPU for
processing. As shown here, the result of
batch processing is to create updated records in master files and produce various
documents such as payroll checks, customer statements, and management reports.

*by CRT
connected
to mainframe*

other data communication channels. As soon as the processing has been completed, the results can be transmitted back to the remote job entry station and printed at that location.

Data Entry for Direct-Access Processing. In a direct-access processing application, the records affected by the introduction of new input data are kept in a direct-access storage device (DASD). Input facts are entered from the keyboard of an online data entry device or from some other online instrument at the time the transaction occurs. Source documents may not be used. Because data entry often occurs at the transaction-origination point, online data entry is also called **source data entry,** and direct-access processing is sometimes referred to as **transaction-oriented processing.**

In direct-access processing, the file record(s) affected by the input data is quickly retrieved from the DASD without the need for a sequential file search. After the new transaction data have been processed, the updated record is returned to the DASD. Since DASD records are constantly being updated, system users at online stations can enter inquiries and receive up-to-the-minute reports about the current status of these records. Online processing eliminates the need to accumulate and then sort batches of transactions into a master file sequence prior to processing. However, online processing may require the use of relatively expensive hardware and software resources, and it is not as efficient as batch processing for some applications.

One example of data being entered in an online processing application was presented in Chapter 2 when Rob Brooks made a deposit to his savings account. Another example of online data entry in a factory setting is shown in Figure 6-2. Let's assume that a manufacturer receives an order from a customer to build 100 engine braces. These braces are made out of strips of steel that are cut to length, shaped, drilled, and painted. After the job has been authorized, a shop order is prepared and the identical order data are entered into a work-in-process file in a DASD. A job control number is used to identify the order in the DASD. A copy of the shop order is sent to a shop supervisor and the job is scheduled.

When production begins, and as each activity is completed, data collecting stations located on the shop floor are used by workers to *interact* with a computer program in order to update the job record in the DASD. Messages may be flashed under program control to a screen at the data collection station to guide the worker through the data entry activity. You'll notice in our example in Figure 6-2 that in the first message the worker is asked to enter an employee number and the job control number. The job control number is used to retrieve the job record from the DASD. A **menu** of possible activities related to the particular job is the next message displayed on the station screen. The worker need only key in the correct activity number (the completion of a job task in our example). The program then reads the job record and displays another menu of the different operations required to finish the job. (A different menu would have been displayed if a different activity number had been entered.) In our example, the worker has indicated that the steel for the engine braces has now been cut to length and bent into the proper shape. As a check

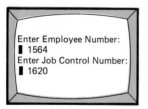

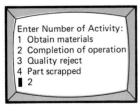

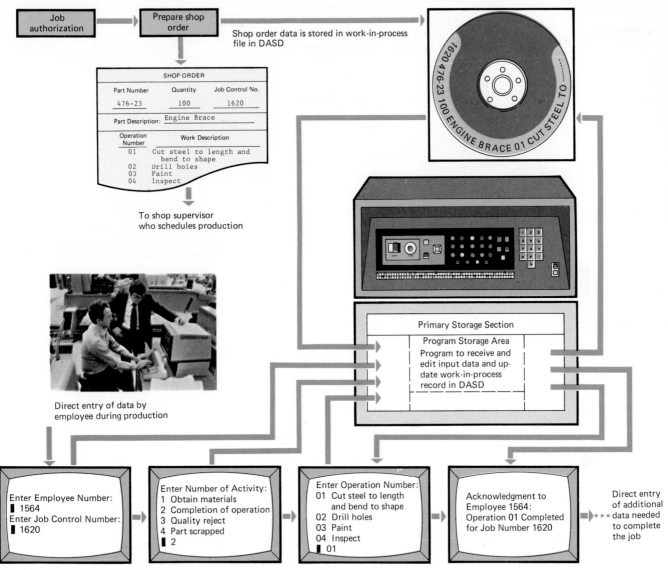

Figure 6-2 Data entry in a direct-access processing application used by manufacturing firms. The initial production order data are entered on a shop order and are stored in a work-in-process file in a DASD. When production begins, data collection stations on the plant floor are used by workers to update the job record in the work-in-process file. The production status of each job is tracked, and each job record is directly updated by workers when an activity has been completed. (Photo courtesy Raytheon)

on the accuracy of the data received, the program sends an acknowledgment message to the worker who then has a chance to correct any errors. The same **interactive data entry** procedure is followed as additional tasks are completed.

Such a system permits an up-to-the-minute account of the production status of each job in the work-in-process file. It can also be used to assign labor and material costs to each job. Managers can thus use the information produced by such a system to plan and control work flow, and to analyze how efficiently people and machines are being utilized.

Costs of Data Entry

You've probably noticed that data entry often involves copying facts that have originally been captured on source documents. The transactions on these documents are converted into a machine-readable form and checked for accuracy. Such transcribing activities are expensive since they may require the efforts of many data entry operators. As you saw in the vignette used to open this chapter, one estimate—made by the U.S. Commerce Department's Institute for Computer Sciences & Technology—put the cost of data entry at 30 to 50 percent of the entire data processing budget of a typical computer-using business.

Some progress has been made in controlling data entry costs by capturing data at the transaction source. You've just seen that data from a shop floor can be entered directly into a computer-based manufacturing system. Since task-completion documents are not used, the need to transcribe facts from such documents is eliminated. However, the progress that has been made in controlling data entry costs is quite modest when compared with the gains made in reducing the costs of processing within the CPU. Thus, as you'll see in later sections of this chapter, developing new direct data entry approaches that eliminate the need to recopy transaction data is a top priority of managers today.

Importance of Input Accuracy

People have a greater effect on the quality of output of a data processing system than do the data processing machines. This is true because it's people who prepare the input data for the machines and thus determine the output quality. You've seen that if reliable programs are used, processors, storage units, and output devices can generally be expected to produce predictable results. But these results will be correct only if the input prepared by people is accurate. The term GIGO (*garbage in—garbage out*), introduced in Chapter 1, emphasizes this fact and indirectly points out the important role people must play in a computer system.

People can introduce data errors into a computer system in at least two ways. One way is to record data incorrectly on source documents. Suppose a customer orders an item with a code number of 6783, and the sales order is written to ship product number 6873. If this transposition error is not caught in time, the wrong item will be shipped and an unhappy customer may be billed for an unwanted product. Errors with similar consequences can also be introduced when data entry operators make keying mistakes while copying accurate source document data on an input medium, or when employees strike the wrong keys at an online transaction-recording station.

It's important to catch these errors as early as possible. The Institute of Computer Sciences & Technology of the U.S. Commerce Department estimates that an error detected at the time of data entry can be corrected at a cost of about 10 cents per character in error. Mistakes that are not found until after they are entered into a file, however, may cost $2.00 or more per character to correct. Of course, if errors cause people to ship the wrong product or if they cause other inappropriate actions, the possible costs can be much greater.

Detecting Errors in Data Entry

Input data are normally checked for errors before they are used in a processing application. The goal of an error-checking system is control. That is, the goal is to make sure that all transactions are identified, that these transactions are accurately recorded at the right time, and that all recorded transactions are then entered into the system.[1] A few of the possible error-detecting procedures are:

▌ *Accounting for prenumbered source documents.* A missing number in a batch of consecutively numbered source documents signals a missing form.

▌ *Using control totals.* After knowledgeable people have inspected and edited source documents, a **control total** can be prepared for each batch that is to be entered into the system. For example, the total number of items shipped to all customers can be computed for a batch of shipping orders before the orders are recorded on an input medium. The same total can then be obtained from the input medium to see if the figures match. This procedure allows people to detect the presence of one or more transcription errors.

▌ *Using programmed tests.* Instructions can be written in applications programs to check on the reasonableness of data as they enter the processing operation. The number of such checks is limited only by the programmer's imagination. In the manufacturing example shown in Figure 6-2, for example, **edit checks** can be made to ensure that workers don't enter letters in numeric data spaces, don't use inactive job control numbers, or don't indicate that engine braces have been painted *before* the steel has been cut or the holes have been drilled. **Range checks** can also be written to ensure that numbers fall within an acceptable range of values. If a worker in Figure 6-2 entered an operation number of 14 for a job that only has 4 acceptable operations, a range check would cause an error message to be displayed on the screen of the data collection

---

[1]Most organizations must try to strike a balance between input accuracy and cost control. From a control standpoint, an ideal system would catch every error. But such a system (assuming it could be built) would be slow and expensive. The total costs of operating this "errorless" system might easily top the costs required to operate a less-accurate system and then correct at a later time the few errors that managed to slip through.

MAKE WAY FOR ELECTRONIC KEYS

A small Minneapolis company, Data-Key Inc., is making plastic keys with integrated circuits embedded in them. DataKey's first target market is sophisticated security systems for computers. The system is relatively inexpensive—$5 for each key and $50 for the electronic receptacle—and offers a more secure alternative to the easily foiled passwords now used to control access to security systems. In addition, by storing segments of the computer program on the key, computer makers aim to block the pirating of their expensive software.

William F. Flies, the founder and president of DataKey, sees an even bigger potential for the keys in hotel room security. Electronic door lock systems for hotels require each lock to be wired into a computer at the front desk. The DataKey system is less expensive because it can alter lock codes when a hotel room is va-

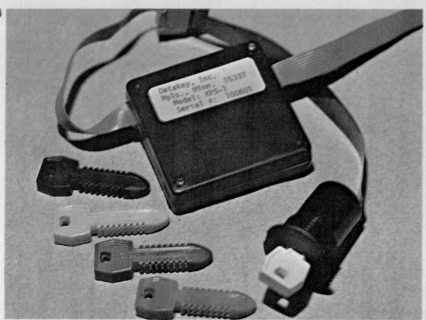

cated without the need to communicate with the computer, thus eliminating costly wiring.

Because the key can hold more customer data than any conventional credit card, car rental agencies are also evaluating the key as a way to speed rentals.

station. Finally, programmed **limit checks** can be used to verify that input data don't exceed reasonable upper or lower values. Such a check can catch inexcusable errors such as the one that resulted in a high school student receiving a Utah tax refund check for $800,014.39 when the correct amount should have been $14.39.

 ## Feedback and Review 6-1

You've seen in this section that input data are obtained from internal and external sources. You've also been reminded that the approaches used to enter these data into a computer system can differ depending on whether an application is to be processed by sequential or direct-access methods. Finally, you've learned that data entry costs can be high, that input accuracy is vital, and that error-detecting procedures are normally used to catch mistakes before they are entered into a file. To test and reinforce your understanding of these data entry concepts, place a T or F in the space provided in the following true-false questions:

_T_ **1.** The first activity in data processing is to capture the raw input data.

_F_ **2.** An internal source of input data is the purchasing department located within a customer's organization.

_T_ **3.** The Census Bureau in Washington is an external source of input data for many organizations.

_F_ **4.** In a sequential processing application, the data to be processed are typically captured by using online terminals.

_F_ **5.** Source documents are never used with direct-access processing applications.

_T_ **6.** A telephone line may be used to communicate data from a remote batch station to a CPU.

_T_ **7.** In a direct-processing application, a DASD is used to store the records that are to be updated.

_T_ **8.** Manufacturing companies can keep track of their work in process by installing online data collection stations on the shop floor and allowing workers to directly update job records.

_T_ **9.** When data are entered directly into a CPU from an online data collection station, the application program will generally contain instructions to ensure that the data entered are reasonable.

_F_ **10.** Greater progress has been made in controlling data costs than in reducing the costs of processing within the CPU.

_F_ **11.** Computers are primarily responsible for the quality of the output of an application.

_F_ **12.** In a batch processing application, if the source documents are accurate, then the data entering the computer must also be accurate.

_F_ **13.** It's better to let errors enter files so that they can all be corrected at once.

_T_ **14.** A control total can be used to detect transcription errors.

_T_ **15.** Edit checks, range checks, and limit checks can be written in applications programs to test the reasonableness of data entering the CPU.

INPUT MEDIA AND DEVICES FOR SEQUENTIAL PROCESSING

It's now time to examine the input media and devices that are used in batch processing. You've already encountered several examples in this book of the use of such media and devices. In Chapter 2, the use of punched cards and magnetic tape was illustrated. For example, in the R-K Enterprises' mailing list application, data were stored on magnetic tape and read into the CPU by a magnetic tape device. And in Chapter 1, you'll recall, the Longhorn College payroll data were entered on a floppy disk input medium and read into the CPU by an appropriate disk device.

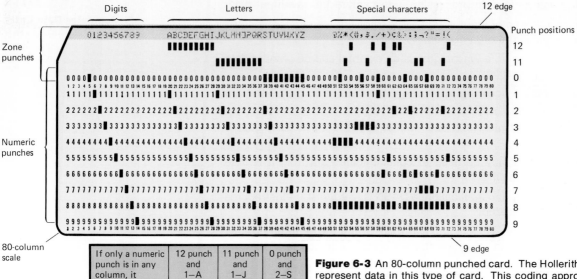

Figure 6-3 An 80-column punched card. The Hollerith Code is used to represent data in this type of card. This coding approach was named after Herman Hollerith, a statistician who developed modern punched card techniques in the late 1800s. Corners of punched cards are often trimmed to help maintain proper positioning during processing.

If only a numeric punch is in any column, it represents whatever number is punched out.	12 punch and	11 punch and	0 punch and
	1—A	1—J	2—S
	2—B	2—K	3—T
	3—C	3—L	4—U
	4—D	4—M	5—V
	5—E	5—N	6—W
	6—F	6—O	7—X
	7—G	7—P	8—Y
	8—H	8—Q	9—Z
	9—I	9—R	

Punched Cards

Punched cards are an old and familiar medium.[2] The demise of cards as a viable input medium has been predicted for some time, but *billions* of them are still made and used each year. There are two types of punched cards. One has 80 columns and the other has 96 columns.

The 80-Column Card. The **80-column card,** shown in Figure 6-3, is divided from left to right into 80 consecutively numbered vertical *columns.* Each column, in turn, has 12 horizontal positions, or *rows.* Each column can represent one data character. Columns 5 through 14 in Figure 6-3 show the *numeric* characters. You'll notice that only a single hole is punched in each column to represent a digit.

When a *letter* is recorded in a column, *two* holes must be punched. A **Hollerith Code** is used to represent data in 80-column cards. Along the top of the card are three *zone* punching positions—the 0 row and the blank area at the top of the card which is divided into punching positions 11 and 12. A logical combination of zone and numeric punches is required to represent letters in the Hollerith Code. For example, letters A through I are coded by using a 12-zone punch and numeric punches 1 through 9. *Special characters* are coded by using one, two, or three holes.

[2] An historical account of the development of punched card data processing is included in the "Closer Look" reading following Chapter 1, pages 35–36.

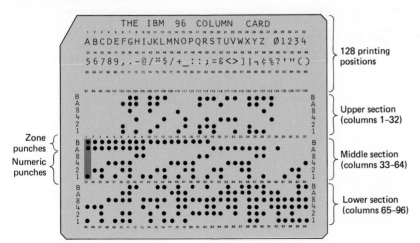

Figure 6-4 A 96-column card using 6-bit BCD coding to represent data.

The 96-Column Card. The **96-column card** shown in Figure 6-4 is only one-third the size of the more popular 80-column card. The 96 columns are separated into three 32-column sections or tiers. The upper third of the card is a print area.

In addition to having round rather than rectangular holes, the 96-column card also differs from the 80-column card in the coding method used. Each of the 96 columns has six punch positions. These are divided into B and A zone positions and 8, 4, 2, and 1 numeric positions. In the standard 6-bit BCD code discussed in Chapter 5, the letter A was represented by 11 0001. In column 33 of Figure 6-4, the letter A is represented by this same code. The presence of a hole in a punch position indicates a 1 bit. You can examine Figure 6-4 to see the 6-bit BCD coding used to represent other characters.

How Cards Are Used. Card columns are laid out in consecutive groups called **fields** for specific purposes. Fields are carefully planned by the designers of the application and may be of any width from 1 to 80 (or 96) columns.[3] Figure 6-5 shows how cards and fields can be used in a sales analysis application.

As you know, customer invoices provide input data for sales analysis reports. In Figure 6-5, the data from an invoice are punched into cards. The cards are divided into several fields. The first card shows the descriptive data at the top of the invoice and the data on the first line of the body of the invoice. You'll notice that the *item amount* field is seven columns wide. The maximum amount that can be recorded in this field is $99,999.99. (Columns are not used to punch the dollar sign, comma, and decimal point.) After the first card has been punched, columns 18 through 56, which contain information about the customer and the invoice, can be automatically duplicated in the following

---

[3]Judgment and compromises are required in determining field width. For example, a 15-column customer name field would be fine in most cases—until a sale is made to Agamemnon Southwesterfield. Then, Agamemnon's name must be abbreviated in some arbitrary way to fit into the field.

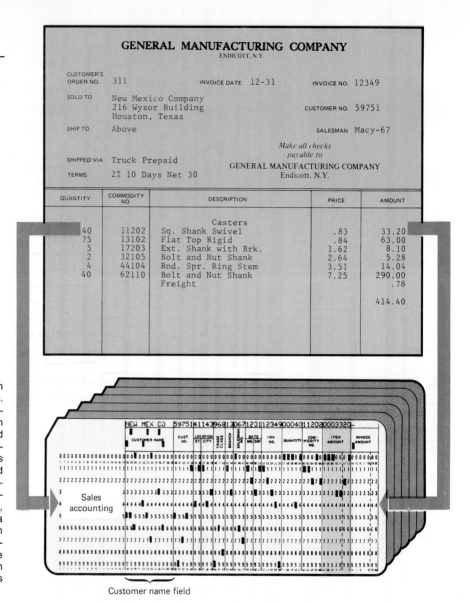

Figure 6-5 Punched cards can be used in the preparation of sales analysis reports. Data from customer invoice source documents are punched into designated areas in cards. Application designers have divided the cards into these areas or fields for particular sales analysis purposes. These fields provide *reference* data (customer name and number and invoice date and number), *classification* data (location of sale, trade classification, sales branch, salesperson number, and product number), and *quantitative* data used in calculation (quantity sold and item amount). Six detail cards are needed to record the sale of the six items described on the invoice. After the invoice data have been captured on cards, sales analysis reports are prepared.

cards by the card punch machine. The data in columns 57 through 73 are punched separately for each item sold. The total invoice amount would perhaps be punched in columns 74 through 80 in the last card. When the data from invoices have been captured, several sales analysis reports for a specified time period may be prepared. These reports can tell managers which items are selling, who is buying, which sales branches and salespersons are meeting their quotas, and so on.

Punched Card Equipment. Figure 6-6 shows how cards can be used to prepare one type of sales analysis report. You'll notice that several kinds of punched card machines are needed to provide input to the CPU.

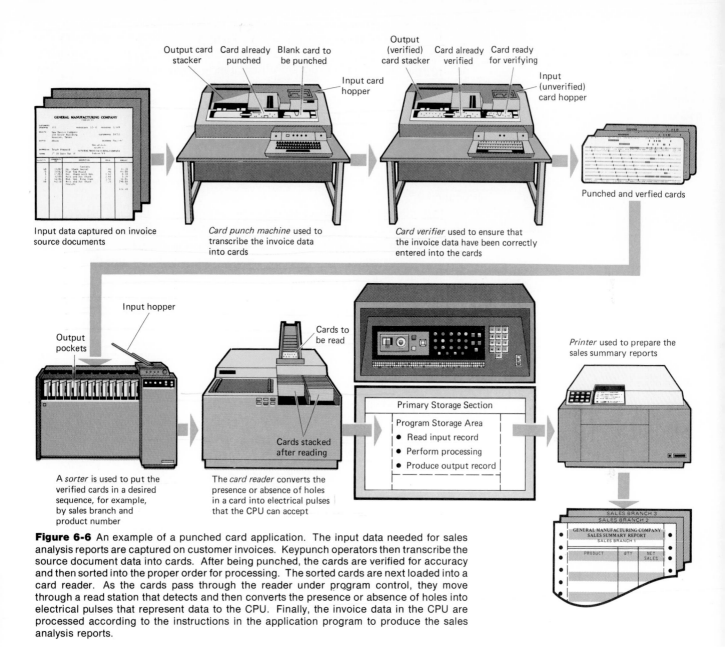

Figure 6-6 An example of a punched card application. The input data needed for sales analysis reports are captured on customer invoices. Keypunch operators then transcribe the source document data into cards. After being punched, the cards are verified for accuracy and then sorted into the proper order for processing. The sorted cards are next loaded into a card reader. As the cards pass through the reader under program control, they move through a read station that detects and then converts the presence or absence of holes into electrical pulses that represent data to the CPU. Finally, the invoice data in the CPU are processed according to the instructions in the application program to produce the sales analysis reports.

Card punch (or **keypunch**) machines are used to transcribe the invoice data into cards. The keyboard is similar to the one on a typewriter. When a data entry operator depresses a key, the correct combination of holes is produced in a card. The machine automatically feeds and positions the blank cards to be punched.

After punching, the next step is ensuring that the invoice data have been correctly entered into the cards. A machine called a **verifier** is used for this purpose. The cards are loaded into the verifier and an operator rekeys the invoice data. The verifier senses the facts being keyed and compares them with the data punched in the cards. If a mismatch occurs, the operator is notified to take corrective action.[4] From this discussion, you can see why data entry can be expensive.

The third card machine shown in Figure 6-6 is a **sorter.** Its job is to put the verified cards in some desired order or sequence. In our example in Figure 6-6, the output report is a sales summary for each sales branch showing the amount of each product that has been sold. Thus, for this report the sorter might first put the cards into a sales branch sequence (branch 1, branch 2, etc.) Then, within each sales branch, the cards might be sorted into a product number sequence.[5]

After the cards have been sorted in the correct order, they are placed in the input hopper of a **card reader.** From this hopper, the cards are individually fed to a read station under the control of the program in the CPU. Either photo-electric cells or metal brushes at the read station will detect and then convert the presence or absence of holes in a card into coded electrical pulses that the CPU can accept (see Figure 6-7). The speed with which a card reader supplies input data to a CPU is relatively slow when compared with the speed of most other batch processing input devices. Once the invoice data enter the CPU, they are processed according to the instructions in the program to produce the output reports.

Advantages and Limitations of Card Input. The following *advantages* are possible when punched card data entry is used:

▎ Cards are standardized and can thus be used to enter data into different hardware systems.

▎ Each card contains the data on a particular transaction. Records in a card file can be updated simply by inserting, removing, or replacing individual cards.

▎ Cards are humanly readable and are easy to handle. It's easy to write on cards and send them through the mail.

▎ Cards are an old and reliable medium. To the surprise of many, they remain a viable means of entering moderate amounts of data into computer systems.

There are, however, *limitations* to the use of punched card data entry:

▎ The term **data density** refers to the number of characters that can be stored in a given physical space. Even when all columns are punched,

---

[4]Punching and verifying are combined in a *verifying punch* machine. The first keying enters the data into a storage section in the machine. A rekeying of the same data is then compared to the stored data. If the data match, a card is punched. If there's a mismatch, the operator makes a correction and the card is then prepared.

[5]If each product is identified by a five-digit number in columns 62–66 (see Figure 6-5), the operator would set the sorter to column 66 and pass all the cards in the deck through the machine. The cards would then be retrieved from the pockets, the sorter would be set to column 65, and another pass would be made. This continues until the deck is sorted by column 62, the leftmost column in the field. The deck is then in a product number sequence.

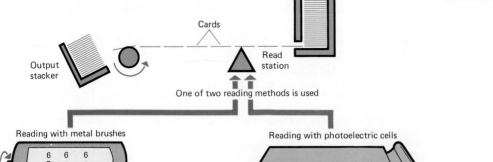

Input hopper

Cards

Read station

Output stacker

One of two reading methods is used

Reading with metal brushes

6 6 6
8 8
5 5 5
4 4 4
3 3 3
2 2 2
1 1 1
0 0 0

Reading with photoelectric cells

Light source

Card

Photoelectric cells

Pulses to the CPU

Pulses to the CPU

When a brush is riding on the card, the paper acts as an insulator and prevents current flow. When a hole appears under a brush, contact is made with the roller and an electrical pulse is sent to the CPU

As a card moves by a light source, the holes in the card permit the light to pass through and strike photoelectric cells which then send electrical pulses to the CPU

Figure 6-7 A specific card reader will use either metal brushes or photoelectric cells (but not both) to send electrical pulses representing data to the CPU. Card readers operate at speeds ranging from 100 to 2,000 cards per minute. A machine reading 2,000 80-column cards per minute could enter 2,667 characters into the CPU every second. This may seem fast, but it is actually slow when compared with the speed of other input devices used in batch processing.

the data density of a card is quite low. (Many more characters can be typed on the card with a typewriter than can be punched into it.) In most applications, however, not all columns will be punched and data density is thus further reduced.

▎ Because of this low density, card files are bulky. They are also slow to process since a lot of paper must be moved to gain access to the punched data.

▎ Cards can be misplaced or separated from their proper file deck. And as everyone knows, they can't be folded, stapled, or mutilated. A bent or warped card can jam equipment and further slow the processing.

▎ Cards must be sorted and processed in a designated order, and they can't be erased and used to enter new data.

Punched Paper Tape — military uses it

Small paper tape attachments are sometimes found on the typewriter-like terminals that are used to prepare source documents or other messages. The input data and output information being produced by the terminal can be

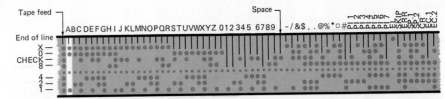

Figure 6-8 The eight-channel paper tape code. The 6-bit BCD code format discussed in Chapter 5 is used to represent data. In addition to the six channels used for coding purposes, there is also a "check" channel and an "end of line" channel. The check channel is used to perform the parity checking function mentioned in Chapter 5. In this case, you'll notice that an odd-parity format is used. When the basic character code requires an even number of holes (1 bits), an additional hole is then punched in the check channel so that all valid characters will have an odd number of holes in each column. Some provision must be made with a continuous-length medium such as paper tape to indicate to the computer when the end of a record has been reached. A hole is punched in the end of line channel in a paper tape to perform this function.

punched into a paper tape and then later entered into a computer by a *paper tape reader*. Data are recorded on the tape by punching round holes into it. The tape is laid out in columns (frames) and rows (channels). A character is coded by a punch or combination of punches in a column. There are 10 columns in an inch of tape, so there can be 10 characters in that space.

Figure 6-8 shows how data are coded on **punched paper tape.** The tape has eight channels. The bottom four represent the 8, 4, 2, and 1 numeric bit positions used in BCD coding. (The holes between channels 4 and 8 are sprocket holes used to feed the tape through the punching/reading machines and are not part of the code.) The zone channels are labeled X and 0. The 6-bit BCD code discussed in Chapter 5 is used to represent data. The presence of a hole represents a 1 bit. Thus, the letter A is represented once again in Figure 6-8 as 11 0001.

Paper tape provides greater data density than punched cards. There's no wasted space when records are short. Also, paper tape is cheaper than cards, and paper tape equipment is less expensive than comparable card machines. However, tape accuracy is harder to verify than card accuracy, and errors that are detected aren't as easy to correct. It's also harder to delete or add records to tapes (splicing is often necessary). Like cards, paper tapes are easily torn and mutilated.

Magnetic Tape

The **transfer rate** of an input medium is the speed with which data can be copied from the medium to CPU storage. Since **magnetic tape** has a much faster transfer rate than cards or paper tape,[6] it's a preferred medium for high-speed, large-volume batch processing applications.

[6]The transfer rate for reels of magnetic tape depends on such factors as (*a*) the data density of the magnetized characters on the tape surface (which varies from about 200 to 6,250 characters per inch), and (*b*) the speed of the tape movement (which varies from about 75 to 200 inches per second). Thus, the slowest transfer rate is about 15,000 characters per second (200 characters/inch times 75 inches), and the fastest transfer rate is about 1,250,000 characters per second (6,250 characters/inch times 200 inches). Since the *fastest* card reader can read less than 3,000 characters/second, you can see the input speed advantage enjoyed by magnetic tape.

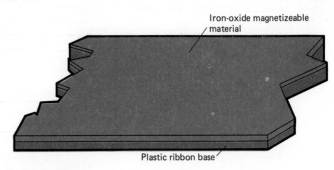

Iron-oxide magnetizeable material

Plastic ribbon base

(a) The tape in large reels is used in mainframe computer systems. This tape is usually ½ inch wide and 2,400 feet long. (Lengths of 300, 600, and 1,200 feet are also available.) The iron-oxide coating is applied to one side of the plastic ribbon base.

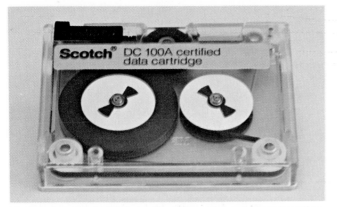

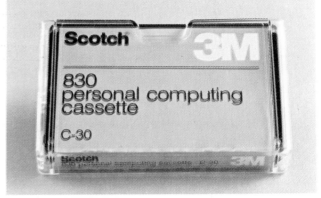

(b) Magnetic tape cartridges are used in minicomputers and data entry stations. This tape is ¼ inch wide and varies from 140 to 450 feet in length.

(c) Magnetic tape cassettes are used in microcomputers and data entry stations. This tape is either 150 or 300 feet long.

Figure 6-9 The magnetic tape input medium is packaged in different ways. (a) The tape in large reels is used in mainframe computer systems. This tape is usually $\frac{1}{2}$ inch wide and 2,400 feet long. (Lengths of 300, 600, and 1,200 feet are also available.) The iron-oxide coating is applied to one side of the plastic ribbon base. (b) Magnetic tape cartridges are used in minicomputers and data entry stations. This tape is $\frac{1}{4}$ inch wide and varies from 140 to 450 feet in length. (c) Magnetic tape cassettes are used in microcomputers and data entry stations. This tape is either 150 or 300 feet long. (Photos courtesy of 3M)

You'll notice in Figure 6-9 that the tape itself may be in a large **reel** or a small **cartridge** or **cassette.** However packaged, the tape is similar to the kind used in a sound tape recorder. It's a plastic ribbon coated on one side with an iron-oxide material that can be magnetized. Tiny invisible spots representing data are recorded by electromagnetic pulses on the iron-oxide side of the tape, just as sound waves form magnetic patterns on the tape of a sound recorder. Both the data and the sound can be played back many times. Like recorder tape, computer tape can be erased and reused indefinitely. Old data on a tape are automatically erased as new data are recorded in the same location.

Data Entry Approaches. Data are entered on magnetic tape in several ways. In one approach, data are entered into cards and are then transcribed on magnetic tape by a card-to-tape computer run. Or, the data used to update a tape file may be written on the tape by the computer during a processing run. Much of the time, however, the following data entry devices are used to record source document data directly on the tape:

1. *Single-station key-to-tape devices.* Many of these **key-to-tape devices** were installed in the late 1960s and early 1970s. They enable an operator to key data directly onto a tape. Keyed data are verified by first writing a record stored on tape into a storage section of the machine. The data are then reentered from the source document and a comparison is made to detect errors. Different-size tape is used with different machines. Data recorded in cartridges or cassettes may need to be copied onto larger reels prior to computer entry.

2. *Multistation key-to-tape devices.* In this approach, there are several keyboards connected to one or more magnetic tape units by a central controlling device. This controller consolidates the data coming from the keyboards.

3. *Multistation key-to-disk-to-tape devices.* As you can see in Figure 6-10, operators also key source document data into this type of system. A minicomputer is used to control the input coming from the keystations. As data are keyed and displayed at the stations, the types of programmed checks mentioned earlier may be made to ensure that the data are reasonable. Data that pass the programmed tests are temporarily stored on a rigid magnetic disk. Frequently used data fields can also be stored on a disk and called up by an operator to eliminate unnecessary keying. For example, the names and addresses of customers can be stored on a disk by their account number. The operator keying data from customer invoices can then call up this information merely by entering the customer number. After all source documents for a particular processing job have been keyed, the minicomputer program transfers the data on the disk to a magnetic tape for later computer processing. **Key-to-disk-to-tape systems** have replaced many of the earlier key-to-tape devices.

Data Representation on Magnetic Tape. Magnetic tape is divided into vertical columns (or *frames*) and horizontal rows (called *channels* or *tracks*). A **seven-track magnetic tape** format was used to represent data in earlier magnetic tape systems (see Figure 6-11). You'll notice that the track designations are like those used with 96-column cards and with paper tape. A 6-bit BCD code format with B and A zone positions and 8, 4, 2, and 1 numeric bit positions was used. The letter A, once again, was represented by a code of 11 0001. Magnetized spots on the tape indicate the presence of 1 bits, while the absence of such spots represent 0 bits. You'll also notice in Figure 6-11 that the seventh track was used for parity checking. Here an even parity code was used.

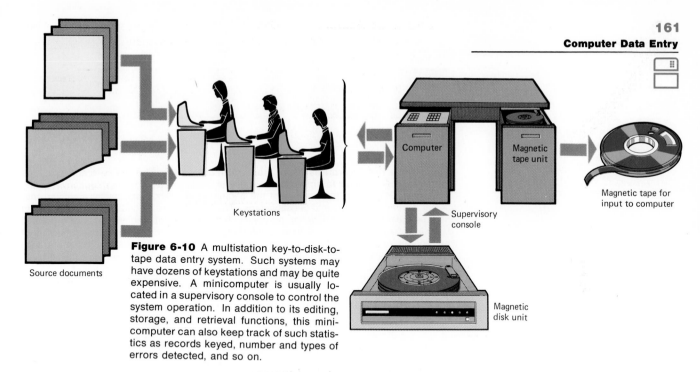

Figure 6-10 A multistation key-to-disk-to-tape data entry system. Such systems may have dozens of keystations and may be quite expensive. A minicomputer is usually located in a supervisory console to control the system operation. In addition to its editing, storage, and retrieval functions, this minicomputer can also keep track of such statistics as records keyed, number and types of errors detected, and so on.

An *extended* 8-bit BCD version of the older 6-bit BCD code is now used in most magnetic tape systems. Like the older coding arrangement, this **nine-track magnetic tape** format has four tracks for the 8, 4, 2, and 1 numeric bit positions, and a fifth track for a parity bit. However, as you saw in Chapter 5, the 8-bit BCD code has four rather than two zone positions. These additional zone tracks make it possible to extend the code to include more characters. Figure 6-12 shows a few characters coded in a nine-track arrangement. This arrangement has a peculiar appearance because the most frequently used tracks are grouped near the center of the tape. In Chapter 5, the letter A was shown to be represented by a code of 1100 0001 in the 8-bit EBCDIC format.

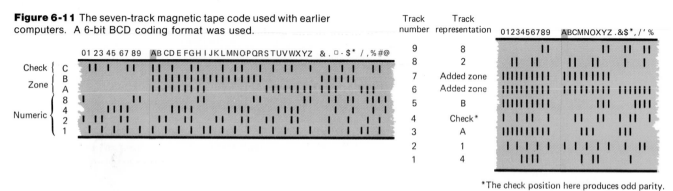

Figure 6-11 The seven-track magnetic tape code used with earlier computers. A 6-bit BCD coding format was used.

*The check position here produces odd parity.

Figure 6-12 A nine-track tape code used with many modern computers. An 8-bit EBCDIC format is used in this example.

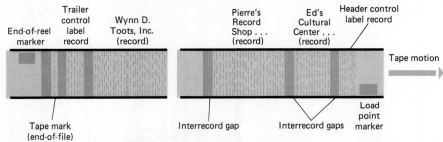

Figure 6-13 R-K Enterprises' file of prospective customers. The first several feet of tape are unrecorded to allow for threading on the equipment. A reflective marker known as the *load point* indicates to the equipment the beginning of usable tape, while a similar *end-of-reel* marker signals the end of usable tape. The markers are placed on opposite edges of the tape for machine identification purposes. Between the load-point marker and the first data record is a *header control label*, which identifies the tape contents, gives the number of the program to be used when the tape is processed, and supplies other control information that helps to prevent an important tape from accidently being erased. Following the last data record in a file is a *trailer control label*, which may contain a count of the number of records in a file. A comparison between the number of records processed and the number in the file may be made to determine that all have been accounted for. The end of a file may be signaled by a special one-character record. This special character is called a *tape mark*.

have to be at correct speed to record

You'll notice in Figure 6-12 that this is the code used to represent A in our example. You can also see that an odd-parity code is used in this example.

Since magnetic tape is a continuous-length medium, how can different file records be identified on a tape? The answer is that records may be separated by blank spaces on the tape called **interrecord gaps.** These gaps are automatically created when data are written on the tape. When record data are read from a moving tape into the CPU, the movement will stop when a gap is reached. The tape remains motionless until the record has been processed and then moves again to enter the next record into the computer. This procedure is repeated until the file has been processed. You'll recall from Chapter 2 that R-K Enterprises' file of prospective customers was maintained on magnetic tape. The records in this file were used to provide the input data needed to print mailing labels. Figure 6-13 shows how this prospect file could be represented on tape. Of course, tape records can be of varying lengths. If a tape contains a large number of very short records, and if each record is separated by an interrecord gap, then more than half of the tape could be blank and there would be a constant interruption in tape movement. To avoid this inefficient situation, several short records can be combined into a tape **block** (see Figure 6-14).

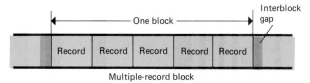

Multiple-record block

Figure 6-14 Several short records are commonly combined into a block and read into the CPU as a single unit to save tape space and speed data input. The program of instructions in the CPU separates the records within a block for processing.

Figure 6-15 A bank of tape drives in a large installation. (Courtesy Radio Shack Division, Tandy Corporation)

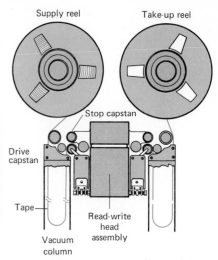

Figure 6-16 The movement of the tape during processing is from the supply reel to the take-up reel. Tapes may move at speeds up to 200 inches per second, and they achieve this rate in a few milliseconds. Several methods are used to prevent tape damage from sudden bursts of speed. One such method is to use vacuum columns to hold slack tape.

Magnetic Tape Equipment. Before the data on a magnetic tape can be processed by a computer, the tape must be placed in a machine called a **tape drive** or **tape transport** (see Figure 6-15). This machine can either read data from a tape into the CPU or it can write the information being produced by the computer onto a tape. Reading data from a tape into the CPU does not destroy the tape data, but writing data from the CPU onto a tape erases previous tape contents.

You can see in Figure 6-16 that the tape on a reel moves through a tape drive in much the same way that a film moves through a movie projector. The tape movement during processing is from the supply reel past a read/write head assembly to the take-up reel. There's a **read/write head** in the tape drive for each tape track. As you can see in Figure 6-17, each head is a small electromagnet with tiny gaps between the poles.

There are usually several tape drives used in an installation. In most applications, a tape is either read or written in a single pass. Therefore, if Rob and Kay want to update their file of prospective customers, they may have one unit reading in the old master file, another feeding in update transactions, and a third writing the updated master file. If the update program is kept on tape, a fourth drive will be needed to enter the processing instructions.

Advantages and Limitations of Magnetic Tape Input. The following *advantages* are possible with magnetic tape data entry:

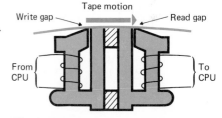

Figure 6-17 A read/write head. There are nine read/write heads in a nine-track tape drive. When a tape is being read, the magnetized patterns on the tape induce pulses of current in the read coils and these pulses are transmitted as data into the CPU. In the writing operation, electrical pulses flow through the write coils at the appropriate tracks causing the iron-oxide coating of the tape to be magnetized in the proper pattern.

▌ *Unlimited length of records.* The fixed size of punched cards tends to limit record length, but any number of characters can be placed in a magnetic tape record. Sequentially organized files can be as long as necessary.

▌ *High data density.* A typical 10½-inch reel of magnetic tape is 2,400 feet long and is able to hold 800, 1,600, or 6,250 characters in each *inch* of this length. (The actual number of characters per inch depends on the tape drive used.) Thus, if 6,250 characters are held in each inch of tape, and if the tape is 28,800 inches long (2,400 feet times 12 inches), then the maximum capacity of the tape is 180 million characters. It would take over 2 million punched cards to record an equivalent amount of data. That's a stack of cards a quarter of a mile high!

▌ *Low cost and ease of handling.* A 10½-inch reel of tape costs less than $20. This is much less than the hundreds of thousands (and even millions) of cards that it can replace. An additional cost benefit is that tape can be erased and reused many times. Since the reel is compact and weighs less than 3 pounds, it obviously takes up much less storage space and is much easier to handle than the equivalent number of cards.

▌ *Rapid transfer rate.* Neither cards nor punched tape can compare with magnetic tape in the speed with which data can be copied into (or received from) the CPU. A tape drive can enter data into the CPU hundreds of times faster than the fastest card reader.

But there are *limitations* to the use of magnetic tape for data entry. Included among these are:

▌ *Lack of direct access to records.* Magnetic tape is a batch processing medium. The entire tape must be read and processed to update the sequentially organized records in the file. If frequent access to file records is needed on a rapid and random basis, then the file should not be stored on magnetic tape. Too much operator time would be required to load and unload tapes, and too much machine time would be wasted in reading records that aren't needed.

▌ *Need for machine interpretation.* Since the magnetized spots on a tape can't been seen by people, a printing run must be made if the accuracy of tape data is questioned.

▌ *Environmental problems.* Specks of dust and uncontrolled humidity or temperature levels can cause tape-reading errors. Tapes and reel containers must be carefully labeled and controlled so that an important file is not erased by mistake.

Floppy Disks

In the early 1970s, IBM announced its 3740 data entry system (see Figure 6-18). This system allows source document data to be keyed directly onto a floppy magnetic disk. The **floppy disk** (also called a **diskette**) gets its name from the fact that it is made out of a flexible plastic material (see Figure 6-19). This plastic base is coated with an iron-oxide recording substance that's similar

Figure 6-18 The IBM 3740 data entry system. Source document data are keyed directly onto the floppy magnetic disk. (Courtesy of IBM)

to the material applied to the plastic ribbon of a magnetic tape. Data are recorded as tiny invisible magnetic spots on this coating. Each data entry disk is 8 inches in diameter and is packaged in a protective paper or plastic envelope from which it is never removed. The contents of 3,000 punched cards can be recorded on a single disk.

A **key-to-diskette** data entry station records the keyed data directly onto a floppy disk. The disk is loaded in this station in its protective envelope. As the disk is rotated inside the envelope, a read-write head assembly accesses the disk surface through a slot in the jacket to record the data. A small display screen shows the data being entered and helps the operator perform data editing and verification functions.

Once the data have been recorded, a **floppy disk reader** can be used to enter the data into the CPU. Again, the disk is loaded and rotated inside its envelope. Tiny electromagnetic heads in the disk reader access the data through the slot in the jacket.

Just like magnetic tape, a diskette is inexpensive and can be erased and reused many times. The erasable feature makes it easy to make changes and corrections during data entry. When compared with punched cards, the floppy disk offers a much faster transfer rate and much greater data density.

In addition to being an input medium for sequential processing, the floppy disk has also become the predominant online secondary storage medium used with microcomputers and with some of the data entry devices used for direct-access processing. In many cases, the storage disk is a scaled-down $5\frac{1}{4}$-inch version of the original 8-inch floppy.

Figure 6-19 An 8-inch floppy disk (or diskette) packaged in a protective envelope. (Courtesy of IBM)

Direct Data Entry Devices for Sequential Processing

The sequential processing media that we've now studied have one thing in common: Data from source documents are keyed on these media in a machine-acceptable form by operators of data entry machines. Although some improvements have been made in these input media and devices, you've seen that the transcribing activities carried out by data entry operators are still expensive and time consuming. To eliminate the need to recopy transaction data, several devices have been built to read the characters printed on the source documents and to then convert these facts *directly* into computer-usable input. Let's now examine some of these character readers that are used in high-volume sequential processing applications.

Magnetic Ink Character Readers. Magnetic ink character recognition **(MICR)** is widely used by banks to process the tremendous volume of checks being written each day. The sample check in Figure 6-20 is precoded along the bottom with the bank's identification number and with the depositor's account number. These numbers and other special symbols are printed with a special ink that contains magnetizeable particles of iron oxide. Employees at the first bank to receive the check after it has been written use the same ink to encode the amount in the lower right corner. The check can then be processed by machines as a punched card is processed.

Checks are accumulated into batches and placed in the input hopper of a **reader-sorter unit** (see Figure 6-21). As they enter the reading unit, the checks pass through a magnetic field which causes the particles in the ink to become magnetized. Read heads are then able to interpret the characters as the checks pass through the reading unit. The data being read can be entered directly into a CPU, or they can be transferred to magnetic tape for later processing. As up to 2,600 checks pass through the machine each minute, they are also sorted into pockets according to their identification code numbers. Several sortings may be required to move a check from (1) the initial bank receiving the check to, perhaps, (2) a Federal Reserve Bank, to (3) the depositor's bank, to (4) the depositor's account.

There are several *advantages* associated with the use of MICR:

| Checks may be roughly handled, folded, smeared, and stamped, but they can still be read with a high degree of accuracy.

| Processing is speeded because checks can be fed directly into the input device.

| People can easily read the magnetic ink characters.

The main *limitation* of MICR is that only the 10 digits and 4 special characters needed for bank processing are used. No alphabetic characters are available.

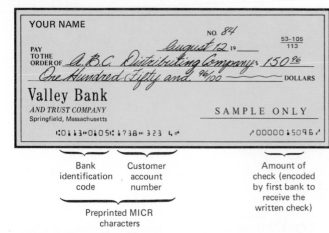

Bank identification code | Customer account number | Amount of check (encoded by first bank to receive the written check)

Preprinted MICR characters

Figure 6-20 A sample check encoded with MICR characters. These characters are printed with a special ink that contains particles of magnetizeable material.

Figure 6-21 MICR reader-sorter unit. (Courtesy Burroughs Corporation)

Optical Character Readers. Unlike MICR, **optical character recognition (OCR)** (see Figure 6-22) techniques permit the direct reading of any printed character (not just 14). No special ink is required. This OCR flexibility makes it possible for organizations to eliminate or reduce the input keying bottleneck. **Optical character readers** are designed to interpret *handmade marks and characters, machine-printed characters,* and special *bar codes.*

You've probably taken tests and marked your answers to questions on a special test-scoring sheet (Figure 6-23a). Your answer sheet was then scanned by an *optical mark reader* that was used to grade the test. Optical scanners can also read certain handmade letters and numbers, but these characters must usually be precisely written (Figure 6-23b). The automatic reading of handwritten script is still some years in the future. (Your penmanship is undoubtedly beautiful, but mine presents a formidable challenge to the equipment designers.)

Figure 6-24 shows an optical reading system that's capable of scanning handmade characters. This system also has the flexibility to read entire pages of machine-printed alphanumeric symbols. These symbols are often printed in the standard type font shown in Figure 6-25. Most optical character readers of this type scan the printed matter with a photoelectric device that recognizes characters by the absorption or reflectance of light on the document (characters to be read are nonreflective). Reflected light patterns are converted into electrical pulses and then transmitted to recognition logic circuits. There they are compared with the characters the machine has been programmed to recognize. If a suitable comparison is made, the data may be recorded for input into the CPU. If a mismatch occurs, the document may be rejected.

Such readers are used in many large-volume processing applications. For example, the computer-printed bills sent to customers by many public utilities, credit card companies, and other businesses are prepared with characters that

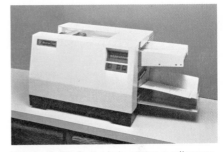

Figure 6-22 Optical character reading systems range in size from the compact machine shown here to large systems which are linked to minicomputers. The system pictured is self-contained because it houses a programmable microprocessor. (Courtesy National Computer Systems)

Figure 6-23 Machine-readable handmade marks and characters.

1   2   3   4   5   6
7   8   9   10   11   12

(a) A portion of a completed test-scoring sheet

Correct and readable | Incorrect and probably unreadable

(b) Handprinted numeric characters

167

Figure 6-24 An optical page reading system. Several thousand machine-printed characters, and up to 1,200 handprinted characters, can be read each second by this type of data entry system. (Courtesy Recognition Equipment, Inc.)

Programmed controller directs input operation

Pages containing character patterns such as these are placed in an input hopper

ABCDEFGHIJKLMNOPQRSTUVWXYZ
1234567890:;∫=⌐?"$%|&'{}*+

Figure 6-25 This standard type font (designated OCR-A) is currently used in about three-fourths of the applications that rely on optical character reading for data entry.

can be read by optical scanners. When customers make their monthly payments, they are instructed to return the bill or a remittance stub with their checks. These documents are then entered directly into optical readers to update accounts-receivable records. Little or no human keying is needed. Other large-volume applications of scanners include the reading of Zip codes by the U.S. Postal Service, the reading of passenger tickets and freight bills by airlines, and the processing of social security forms and motor vehicle registrations by governments.

In addition to marks and alphanumeric characters, optical readers can also recognize data coded in the form of light and dark bars. First used by railroads in the 1960s for the automatic tracking of freight cars, **bar codes** are most commonly used today to identify merchandise in retail stores. For example, manufacturers print a **Universal Product Code (UPC)** on most items sold in grocery stores. The next time you spring out of bed at 6 A.M. to have a hearty breakfast before your eight o'clock class, you might find that your cereal box has a code similar to the one shown in Figure 6-26. When bar-coded items are received at a merchant's automated checkout stand, they are read by hand-held "wands" or they are pulled across a fixed scanning window (see Figure 6-27). As items are scanned, the bars are decoded and the data are transmitted to a computer that looks up the price, possibly updates inventory and sales records, and forwards price and description information back to the check stand. Besides using OCR readers at check stands, store personnel can also use

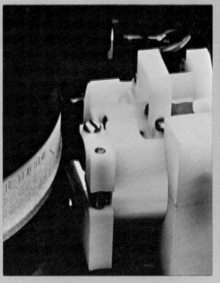

After moving beneath a reading system, the character data are transmitted to integrated circuit chips for recognition. The data may then be recorded on magnetic tape.

As each document is processed, a high-speed ink-jet printer capable of spraying 106,000 droplets of ink per second may be used to imprint a control code on the document.

Documents may then be directed to output pockets.

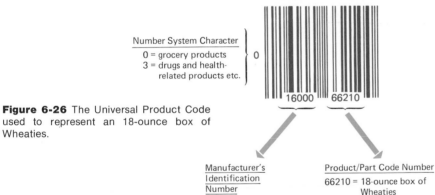

Number System Character
0 = grocery products
3 = drugs and health-
related products etc.

0

16000   66210

Figure 6-26 The Universal Product Code used to represent an 18-ounce box of Wheaties.

Manufacturer's
Identification
Number
16000 = General Mills
21000 = Kraft Foods, etc.

Product/Part Code Number
66210 = 18-ounce box of
Wheaties
67670 = 10-ounce box of
Buc Wheats etc.

Figure 6-27 Supermarket scanning. UPC bar-coded products may be pulled across a fixed scanning window at an automated checkout stand. (Courtesy of IBM)

wands attached to portable recording devices to replenish the store's inventory (see Figure 6-28). When an item must be restocked, the wand is used to read the item's bar code that's fastened on the shelf where the item is displayed. This reading accurately enters the item description into the recorder. The quantity needed is then keyed into the recorder. The recorder may later be connected by telecommunications lines to a warehouse computer system to complete the reordering procedure.

169

Figure 6-28 Portable recording devices are used to restock store inventory. (Courtesy MSI Data Corporation)

Medium	Input Device Used	Typical Data Entry Speed Ranges (CPS)
Punched card	Card reader	150–2,667
Paper tape	Tape reader	50–1,800
Magnetic tape	Tape drive	15,000–1,250,000
Floppy disk	Disk reader	12,500–60,000
Magnetic ink	MICR reader	700–3,200
Paper documents	OCR reader	100–3,600

Figure 6-29 A summary of the input speeds obtained with the media and devices used in sequential processing.

The primary *advantage* of OCR is that it eliminates some of the duplication of human effort required to get data into the computer. This reduction in effort can improve data accuracy and can increase the timeliness of the information processed. However, *difficulties* in using OCR equipment may be encountered when documents to be read are poorly typed or have strikeovers or erasures. Also, form design and ink specifications may become more critical than is the case when people key the data from the forms. Finally, many optical readers are not economically feasible unless the daily volume of transactions is relatively high.

Many organizations find that most of their processing needs are being met quite satisfactorily through the use of the data entry media and devices that we've now examined. After all, Figure 6-29 shows that these media and devices can provide a wide range of possible input speeds. And sequential processing is acceptable—perhaps even preferable—for the types of applications these organizations process. But we've also seen that there are other applications where quick and direct access to file records is needed. In the remainder of this chapter, we'll look at the data entry devices that are used for direct-access processing.

 **Feedback and Review 6-2**

You've now learned that input data for sequential processing may be keyed from source documents onto such media as punched cards, punched paper tape, magnetic tape, and floppy disks. You've also seen that MICR and OCR devices can be used to read the characters printed on the source documents and to then convert these facts directly into computer-usable input. To test and reinforce your understanding of these input media and devices, match the letter of the appropriate term to the definition or concept to which it belongs. (Place the correct letter in the space provided.)

_c_ **1.** The 80-column punched card has three _____ punching positions that are used in combination with numeric punches to represent letters and special characters.

_l_ **2.** The name of the code used to represent data in an 80-column punched card.

_i_ **3.** The type of code used to represent data in 96-column cards, punched cards, punched paper tape, and seven-track magnetic tape.

_d_ **4.** A designated area of consecutive columns in a punched card that is used for specific purposes.

_m_ **5.** Either photoelectric cells or _____ are used by card readers to convert the data in a punched card into a form that the CPU can accept.

_j_ **6.** A term that refers to the number of characters that can be stored in a given physical space.

_b_ **7.** The _____ of an input medium is the speed with which data can be copied from the medium to CPU storage.

_a_ **8.** A preferred medium for high-speed, large-volume batch processing applications.

_k_ **9.** The type of magnetizeable material used to coat magnetic tapes and floppy disks.

_n_ **10.** Used in key-to-disk-to-tape data entry systems to control the input coming from the keystations.

_e_ **11.** The type of code used to represent data on a nine-track magnetic tape.

_h_ **12.** Used to separate records on a magnetic tape file.

_o_ **13.** Several short records on a magnetic tape are commonly combined into a _____ and read into the CPU as a single unit.

_f_ **14.** Small electromagnets that are used to enter data into, and receive output from, magnetic tapes and floppy disks.

_p_ **15.** A popular online secondary storage medium for small computers as well as an input medium for sequential processing.

_r_ **16.** A direct data entry device designed for use in financial institutions.

_q_ **17.** Devices designed to interpret handmade marks, machine-printed characters, and bar codes.

_g_ **18.** A code used to identify merchandise in retail stores.

a) magnetic tape
b) transfer rate
c) zone
d) field
e) 8-bit BCD code
f) read-write heads
g) Universal Product Code
h) interrecord gap
i) 6-bit BCD code
j) data density
k) iron-oxide
l) Hollerith
m) metal brushes
n) minicomputer
o) block
p) floppy disk
q) optical character reader
r) MICR reader-sorter

DATA ENTRY DEVICES FOR DIRECT-ACCESS PROCESSING

You've already encountered several types of online data-entry stations in this book. In Chapter 2, an online financial transaction terminal was used to update Rob Brooks' savings account, and a word processing station was used to key in a name and address, retrieve a stored text, and produce a "personalized" letter. And earlier in this chapter, an online data collection station in a factory was used to keep track of the production status of each job in a work-in-process file.

The devices used in these and other online processing applications have the following characteristics:

▌ They are able to enter data directly into the CPU; data recording media are not required.

▌ They are generally located at or near the data source, and this can be far away from the CPU.

▌ They create a direct interactive relationship between people and computers.

▌ They handle economically a lower and/or more irregular volume of input data.

Online devices are being installed at such a rapid rate that their annual sales are expected to grow from $1.6 billion to $7 billion during the 1980s. Let's now take a closer look at some of these devices.

Teleprinter Terminals

A **teleprinter terminal** has a typewriter-like keyboard for data entry and a built-in printer to record what has been typed (see Figure 6-30a). The terminal can also receive and print output information from the CPU. Some of the earliest teleprinter terminals were designed to communicate telegraph messages. Other early stations were essentially electric typewriters that had been adapted for use in a direct-access processing environment. Many of these older

Figure 6-30 (*left*) A teleprinter terminal used in a direct-access processing environment. (Courtesy Teletype Corporation) (*right*) A portable teleprinter may be used by people on the move to enter data into and receive output from distant computer systems. (Courtesy Texas Instruments)

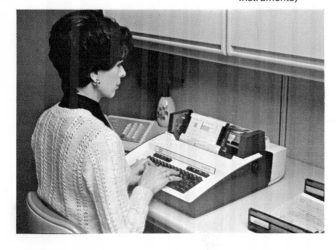

terminals are still in operation. In addition, hundreds of small portable teleprinters are being used today by salespeople, managers, newspaper reporters, engineers, and others on the move.

Portable Data Entry Terminals

The portable teleprinter, in effect, lets these people take a computer with them wherever they go (see Figure 6-30b). For example, a salesperson can attach the terminal to a customer's telephone, dial in to a company computer system, key in questions about the availability of stock, and receive immediate confirmation on the terminal printer that if the customer places an order it can be filled. If a sale is then made, the sales order can be keyed directly into the system from the customer's office. Similarly, a manager can carry a terminal along on a business trip and keep up with office work during airport layovers or hotel stays. And a reporter can type and file a story into a computer system from a remote location.

Some other portable terminals are battery-powered, weigh less than 2 pounds, and are small enough to fit in the palm of your hand. These terminals have small keyboards and are used to send data to a computer, but they often have little or no ability to receive information from the CPU. Such devices are often used by salespeople as electronic order books (see Figure 6-31). For example, a route salesperson calling on retailers can carry a terminal through a customer's store. When items are found to be in short supply, the salesperson can key in the product number and quantity needed into the terminal. (Or, as we've seen, bar codes may be read by a penlike optical reading wand that may be attached to the terminal.) Semiconductor storage chips are then generally used to hold the data that have been entered in the terminal. Every few hours, or at the end of the day, the salesperson can attach the terminal to a telephone and send the order(s) in to a company computer system. In 1980, about $250 million was spent on all types of portable terminals. By 1990, this market is expected to be 12 times larger, with the sales figure placed at $3 billion.

Figure 6-31 A portable bar-code reader. (Courtesy Norand Corporation)

Point-of-Sale Terminals

You've seen that **point-of-sale (POS) terminals** equipped with optical scanners that read UPC symbols are replacing cash registers in supermarkets. Similar equipment is also being used at the checkout counters of other retail stores. Hand-held wands are used by clerks in department stores to speed up the checkout process. By passing the wand across a special tag attached to the merchandise, the clerk reads the item description and price into the terminal. Under computer control, the terminal may display the scanned data and then print an itemized sales receipt that shows the total amount of the purchase including taxes. If a credit card is used to complete the transaction, the wand can read and enter the numbers on the credit card into the computer to update the customer's credit account. Transaction data can also be used to update inventory records and provide sales analysis information to managers.

Figure 6-32 An automated teller machine that handles routine financial transactions at any hour of the day or night. (Courtesy Honeywell Inc.)

Figure 6-33 Visual display terminals are the most popular input devices used today in direct-access processing applications. (Courtesy Hewlett-Packard Company)

Financial Transaction Terminals

In addition to the online teller terminals used to handle customer deposits and withdrawals, there are also several other types of **financial transaction terminals** in common use. Some of these devices are used in the electronic transfer of funds. One such **electronic funds transfer (EFT)** station is the **automated teller machine** (or **ATM**) shown in Figure 6-32.

An ATM is an *unattended* device that's located on or off the financial institution's premises to receive and dispense cash and to handle routine financial transactions 24 hours a day. To use an ATM, you insert your plastic "currency" or "debit" card into the machine. Your account number and credit limit are magnetically encoded on a strip of tape on the back of the card. The terminal reads and then transmits the tape data to a CPU which activates your account. By following instructions displayed on a screen, and by pushing a few keys, you then direct the computer to carry out the desired transaction(s). However, a possible technological alternative to the use of ATMs is being developed in Europe. Instead of using a magnetic strip (or stripe), the card is made with a built-in microcomputer chip. This chip can store a considerable amount of information. Data representing a specific amount of cash can be encoded in the chips before the cards are issued to customers. As the cards are used to make purchases, bits of the stored data are destroyed by special electronic registers used by merchants. These electronic registers are not connected to a CPU. In effect, customers gradually "cash in their chips" and use up their electronic money. These "smart cards" are also able to keep a stored record of more than 100 purchases. Look for competition between ATM/magnetic stripe technology and smart cards in the future.

An ATM isn't the only type of EFT station that's connected directly to financial computers. Other terminals owned by financial institutions are located at the checkout counters of stores, hotels, hospitals, and so on. These EFT stations are used to verify that a customer's check or credit card transaction will be honored. They can also be used to electronically transfer funds from a shopper's account to a merchant's account. A Touch-Tone telephone can also become an EFT terminal. A depositor can call up a bank computer, enter data through the telephone buttons, and transfer funds from his or her account to the account of a creditor.

Visual Display Terminals

The most popular input devices used today in direct-access processing applications are **visual display terminals** (see Figure 6-33). A terminal keyboard is used to enter data into a CPU, and a **cathode ray tube (CRT)** that looks like a television picture tube is used to display the input data and receive messages and processed information from the computer. Many low-cost display terminals are strictly *alphanumeric* devices and are only used to enter and retrieve letters, numbers, and special characters. Other display terminal systems possess *graphic* as well as alphanumeric capabilities. Let's look at a few of the ways that these devices are used.

Alphanumeric Display Applications. You've already seen how alphanumeric display stations are used by shop employees to update production records, by word processing operators to create "personalized" letters, and by tellers to update savings account records. In each of these applications, the terminal operator carried on an interactive "conversation" with the computer program by supplying data in response to displayed questions and instructions. In the factory application, the employee merely keyed in the correct response number from a menu of displayed responses. In office applications, the user sometimes uses a **light pen** attached to the terminal, rather than the terminal keyboard, to choose a displayed response or to request further information (see Figure 6-34). The light pen is a photocell placed in a small tube. When the user moves the pen over the screen, the pen is able to detect the light coming from a limited field of view. The light from the CRT causes the photocell to respond when the pen is pointed directly at a lighted area. These electrical response are transmitted to the computer, which is able to determine that part of the displayed item which is triggering the photocell response.

Since alphanumeric display stations can provide a window into a computer's data base, they are commonly used to provide quick response to operator inquiries. The status of a customer's credit, the availability of airline seats, hotel rooms, or inventory items, the addresses and telephone numbers of college students—these and many other facts are kept current in online files and are instantly available for display when an inquiry message is entered. The keyboard can then be used to update these files to reflect any transaction that's made at a display station. For example, an airline ticket agent can reduce by one the number of seats available on a flight when a ticket is sold.

Alphanumeric display stations are also being used by programmers to prepare and/or maintain computer programs. Pencils and coding sheets are giving way to these **programming workstations.** New program instructions are entered at the keyboard. A special program in the computer interacts with the

Figure 6-34 A light pen attached to the display station may be used to choose a displayed response or to request further information. (Courtesy of IBM)

Figure 6-35 A designer develops a circuit board layout using automated drafting tools. (Courtesy Teletype Corporation)

programmer to edit the programmer's efforts and to detect any errors that may have been made in the syntax of a programming language. A constantly changing menu of admissible instructions may be displayed during program preparation to guide the programmer. The use of these workstations has improved programmer productivity.

Graphical Display Applications. Several years ago, designers and architects made preliminary sketches to get an idea down on paper. As the idea was developed, additional drawings were made. And when the final design or plan was finished, further detailed drawings were prepared. Much of this drawing-preparation time can now be saved by instruments that enable computers to directly receive human graphic input (see Figure 6-35).

One such instrument is the light pen. The user "draws" directly on the screen with the pen. By using the pen and a keypad attached to the terminal, the user can select different colors and line thicknesses, can reduce or enlarge drawings, and can add or erase lines. Another instrument is the **input tablet,**[7] which comes in different sizes. A tablet is a worksurface that typically contains hundreds of copper lines that form a grid. This grid is connected to a computer. Each copper line receives electrical impulses. A special pen or stylus attached to the tablet is sensitive to these impulses and is used to form the drawings. However, the pen does not mark directly on the tablet. Instead, a designer, architect, or other user draws on a piece of paper placed on the tablet. The tablet grid then senses the exact position of the stylus as it is moved and transmits this information to the CPU.

The developing sketch may be displayed on the CRT. But there's a difference between the drawing and the display. Poorly sketched lines are displayed as straight; poor lettering is replaced by neat printing; and poorly formed corners become mathematically precise. Changes and modifications in the drawing can be quickly made. For example, a line can be "erased" from, or shifted on, the display unit with a movement of the stylus. Once the initial sketching is finished and satisfactorily displayed on the CRT, the computer may then be instructed to analyze the design and report on certain characteristics. For example, the computer might be asked to work out the acoustical characteristics of a theater design, or evaluate the flight characteristics of an aircraft design. The user may then modify the sketch on the basis of the computer analysis. This interactive graphics capability helps people save valuable time for more creative work.

Computer graphics are currently being used in the design of ships, highways, aircraft, electronic circuits, and buildings (see Figure 6-36).[8] They are also being used to present business financial and operating data in graphical form so that managers can spot trends and relationships and can then make

Figure 6-36 A 3-D structural design of a building as the designer would see it on a color terminal. (Courtesy Computervision Corporation)

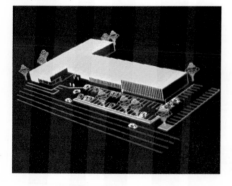

---

[7]A *digitizer* is an input instrument that is similar in function to the input tablet. It has a small reading device that can be used to trace over the lines in drawings, X-ray images, or other graphic representations. The digitizer then sends precise numeric descriptions of these lines or images to a CPU for analysis and processing.

[8]In one interesting application, architects use display stations to prepare sketches of a proposed building. The computer is then instructed to draw a whole series of sketches, each from a slightly different angle. These sketches are then assembled into an animated film. When the film is shown to clients, it gives them the impression that they are walking through the proposed building!

faster and better decisions. Pages of computer printouts detailing the perform-ance of product lines and sales divisions can be replaced by a few colorful charts, graphs, and maps. These visual presentations are first created on the CRT screen through human-machine interaction. They can then be copied onto paper by various printing devices, or they can be photographed from the screen. This business management use of computer graphics is expected to outpace other uses in the 1980s.

Intelligent Terminals

There are more than 500 terminal models currently being offered by more than 150 manufacturers. Most of these models can be classified into the teleprinter, visual display, and special-purpose categories that we've now used. In an attempt to classify the bewildering range of products that do exist, how-ever, the computer industry has also divided these offerings into dumb, smart, and intelligent categories.

A simple, low-cost teleprinter or alphanumeric display device is generally classified as a **dumb terminal.** These units have keyboards for input, a means of communicating with a CPU, and a printer or screen to receive output. **Smart terminals** have additional features. They usually contain a microprocessor and some internal storage. They have data editing capability and the ability to consolidate input data prior to sending them to the CPU. However, smart terminals cannot be programmed by users.

keyboard. + printer no storage

Intelligent terminals combine terminal hardware with built-in microcom-puters that can be programmed by users. Being programmable, they can be used in many ways. Small data processing jobs can be handled by the terminal without the need to interact with a larger CPU. Online secondary floppy disk storage devices are often used during the processing of these small jobs. Pro-grammed error-detection tests can also be stored in the terminal to check on the validity of input data. The input data being edited may be entered at the intelligent terminal, or they may be entered at dumb terminals that are linked to the intelligent station. After the data have been collected and edited, they can be stored for later transmission to a larger computer. Many of the termi-nals discussed in this section are smart or intelligent devices. And since it now costs very little to add microcomputer components to a terminal, most future terminals will have smart or intelligent features to help make data entry and retrieval easier for people.

storage

Voice Input Systems

Input devices, basically, do nothing more than convert human language into machine language. Why, then, doesn't someone invent a machine that will let a person talk to the computer in English? As a matter of fact, a few manufacturers have done just that (see Figure 6-37). A microphone or tele-phone is used to convert human speech into electrical signals. The signal pat-

Figure 6-37 Reliable computer speech recognition someday might be incorporated in telephones featuring hands-free dialing. This experimental, voice-controlled dialing system compares the user's spoken words to the stored patterns in its memory. (Courtesy Bell Laboratories)

terns are then transmitted to a computer where they are compared to a "dictionary" of patterns that have been previously placed in storage. When a close match is found, a word is "recognized" and the computer then produces the appropriate output.

Most voice recognition systems are **speaker-dependent.** That is, they can't be used until after the speaker has repeated a word several times to "train" the system to recognize his or her particular voice pattern. Recently, however, **speaker-independent** systems have been developed that can recognize words spoken by anyone. But no existing system can recognize an unlimited number of words spoken in a continuous stream. Vocabularies of all systems are very limited, users must speak distinctly, and they must pause between each word or each short phrase. In one experiment, the words "recognize speech" were interpreted as "wreck a nice beach" by the computer. And the words "half fast" were . . . well, you get the idea. Other problems in speech recognition are caused by speaker accents and dialects (people's voice prints are as unique as their fingerprints), and the fact that the meaning of words can vary depending on the context in which they are used.[9]

Although speech recognition is now in its infancy, it's likely to be used much more often in the future in situations where a person's hands are busy, where a worker's eyes must remain fixed on a display or measuring instrument, or where telephone input is desirable. Some current applications of voice recognition include:

▎ A "hand's busy" loading dock employee at a Ford Motor Company warehouse can pick up a package, read the package destination into a microphone, and then put the package on a conveyor belt. The system then moves the package to the correct storage location. A similar United Parcel system zips packages into the right trucks as workers read destinations aloud.

[9]Scientists from IBM have been working for nearly a decade on a word processing system that can take dictation. However, it's believed that a commercial product that can do this is still at least another decade away.

■ As Lockheed Aircraft Company assembly workers use hands and eyes to build components for the Trident missile system, they also use a microphone to enter inventory data into a computer system.

■ A state employee in Illinois gets clearance to make a long-distance phone call on the state's private lines by calling a computer and reciting his or her authorization number into the system. If the number is accepted, the computer then switches the employee to the next available long-distance line.

■ A shareholder in one of the 22 mutual funds managed by Fidelity Management & Research Company can dial a computer, supply a fund number, and get information about the current yield and value of the shares owned. If more information is needed, the shareholder can request human help.

Feedback and Review 6-3

As you've seen in this section, there are different types of data entry devices that can be used for direct-access processing. The following multiple-choice questions will help you test and reinforce your understanding of these devices. (Put the letter of the most-correct response in the space provided.)

_C_ **1.** Which of the following is *not* a characteristic of the data entry devices used in direct-access processing:

    a) They create a direct interaction between people and computers.
    b) They are economical even when input data volume is low or irregular.
    c) They require the use of data recording media.
    d) They are generally located at the data source.

_d_ **2.** Teleprinter terminals

    a) are all intelligent devices.
    b) are of very recent origin.
    c) cannot be portable.
    d) have keyboards, printers, and the ability to communicate with distant CPUs.

_C_ **3.** POS terminals

    a) are general-purpose devices capable of handling more applications than teleprinter terminals.
    b) are used only in supermarkets.
    c) may use optical scanners to read tags, bar codes, and credit cards.
    d) cannot be used in conjunction with financial transaction devices.

_b_ **4.** An automated teller machine

a) is operated by a skilled teller.
b) transmits data coded on a plastic card to a CPU.
c) can be used only during banking hours.
d) generally reads data from a microcomputer chip embedded in a plastic card.

_d_ **5.** A visual display terminal

a) is, by definition, a dumb terminal.
b) can possess either graphic or alphanumeric capabilities, but not both.
c) must be located at the site of the CPU.
d) is the most popular input device used today in direct-access processing.

_a_ **6.** A visual display terminal generally does *not* receive input data from

a) a felt-tip pen.
b) an input tablet.
c) a keyboard.
d) a light pen.

_d_ **7.** Computer graphic techniques

a have declined in popularity in recent years.
b) are currently being used in the design of airplanes and buildings, but they are of little use to business decision makers.
c) have increased the time required to complete final engineering drawings.
d) make it possible for a designer to make quick changes and modifications to preliminary drawings.

_b_ **8.** An intelligent terminal

a) has a microprocessor, but it can't be programmed by the user.
b) can be used for small data processing jobs without the need to interact with a larger CPU.
c) carries on a conversation in English with the user.
d) cannot be used to edit data originating at dumb terminals.

_c_ **9.** Voice input systems

a) must be speaker-dependent.
b) must be speaker-independent.
c) have limited vocabularies and can't accept words spoken in a continuous stream.
d) are able to take dictation and produce finished letters.

1. Input data must either be originated in a machine-readable form or they must be converted into such a form before they can be used by a CPU. Data used by organizations are obtained from both internal and external sources. The data entry approach followed in a given application is determined to a large extent by the processing method that's used. In a typical sequential processing application, the raw data are captured on source documents and are then copied at considerable expense onto cards, tape, or floppy disks by data entry operators. The transcribed data are accumulated into batches, sorted into a sequence, and then processed at scheduled intervals. In a direct-access processing application, however, the records affected by transactions are kept in a direct-access storage device (DASD). Input data are then entered from online terminals at (or near) the data source to immediately update the records in the DASD. An example of direct data entry in a manufacturing application was presented in this chapter.

2. The quality of output of a data processing system is more dependent on people than on machines. This is because people prepare the data input (and programs) for the machines. Mistakes entered on source documents or errors made during keying are not uncommon, and it's important to catch them as early as possible. Several error-detecting techniques are described in this chapter.

3. Punched cards, punched paper tape, magnetic tape, and floppy disks are input media used in sequential processing. Punched cards remain popular in spite of predictions to the contrary. These cards have either 80 or 96 columns. The 80-column card uses the Hollerith Code to represent data, while the 96-column card uses a 6-bit BCD code. Card columns are laid out in consecutive groups called fields for particular purposes. Reference, classification, and quantitative data pertaining to a particular transaction are then punched into appropriate card fields by a card punch operator. A verifier may be used to ensure that data have been correctly entered. The verified cards are fed into a sorter which puts them in a desired sequence. They are then placed in a card reader which converts the presence or absence of holes into electrical pulses that the CPU can accept. Cards are an old and reliable medium, but they have a very low data density. Card files are thus bulky and slow to process.

4. A 6-bit BCD code is also used to represent data on punched paper tape. Paper tape has greater data density than cards, but it's much easier to add or delete card records than paper tape records.

5. Data can be transferred from magnetic tape to CPU storage at a much faster rate than from cards or punched tape. This is due, in part, to the fact that the data density of magnetic tape is much greater than with cards or punched tape. Magnetic tape is packaged in reels, cartridges, or cassettes. Data are generally entered from source documents by single or multistation key-to-tape devices, or by multistation key-to-disk-to-tape systems. An 8-bit BCD code is generally used now to represent data on magnetic tape, but a 6-bit code was used in earlier tape devices. Interrecord gaps may be used to identify different tape records. Frequently, however, several records are combined into a block and read into the CPU as a single unit to save tape space and speed data input. A tape drive is used to read data from a magnetic tape into the CPU. In spite of its high data density, rapid transfer rate, and low cost, magnetic tape can't provide rapid and random access to file records, and it can't be read directly by people.

6. A key-to-diskette station is used to enter source document data on a floppy disk. A floppy disk reader is then used to enter the data into a CPU. Like magnetic tape, a disk is inexpensive and can be erased and reused many times. When compared to cards, the floppy disk offers a much faster transfer rate and much greater data density. The floppy disk is also the predominant online secondary storage medium used with microcomputers.

7. Magnetic ink and optical character readers have been developed to eliminate the need to recopy transaction data from source documents. Magnetic ink reader-sorter units are special-purpose devices used to process checks in the banking system. They only recognize the 14 characters needed for check processing. Optical character readers, on the other hand, can directly read handmade and machine-printed letters, numbers, and special characters, as well as bar codes and handmade marks. Such readers are often used in large-volume processing applications such as billing. They are also frequently used at point-of-sale stations to scan the items marked with the bars of the Universal Product Code.

8. Hundreds of thousands of new data entry devices used for direct-access processing are now being produced each year. The trend is to distribute these devices to data origination points. These locations can be far away from the CPU that processes the data. Online terminals create a direct interactive relationship between people and computers. Some of the earliest terminals were teleprinters, and these devices are still popular. Portable teleprinters are particularly useful to people who do a great deal of traveling. The use of other types of portable data entry devices is also expanding rapidly.

9. Point-of-sale (POS) and financial transaction terminals are special-purpose devices used by retail stores and financial institutions. POS terminals can reduce customer waiting time at checkout counters and can directly update the online files used in accounts receivable, inventory control, and sales analysis applications. Automated teller machines can handle routine financial transactions 24 hours a day. Other electronic funds transfer terminals can be used by stores and hotels to verify that a customer's check is good.

10. Visual display terminals are the most popular type of data entry devices used in direct-access processing applications. Some visual display units are only used to enter and retrieve alphanumeric characters, while others possess graphic as well as alphanumeric capabilities. Several alphanumeric and graphic uses of display terminals are discussed in the chapter. Keyboards, light pens, and input tablets are the data entry instruments that are used with visual display stations.

11. Unlike terminals classified as dumb or smart, intelligent terminals have built-in microcomputers that are user-programmable. These terminals are thus able to do small data processing jobs without having to interact with a larger CPU. They often use floppy disk devices for the online secondary storage of data and programs. Outlying dumb terminals may be linked to an intelligent station. The intelligent terminal can then accept input data from the outlying devices, use programmed error-detection tests to check on the validity of the data being received, and then store the data for later transmission to a larger CPU.

12. Voice input systems have been implemented to convert human speech into electrical signals that a computer can recognize. Although speech recognition technology is in its infancy, and many problems remain to be solved, it's now being used in a number of interesting ways.

KEY TERMS AND CONCEPTS

You should now be able to define and use the following terms and concepts (the numbers shown indicate the pages where the terms and concepts are first mentioned):

remote batch station 143
source data entry 146
transaction-oriented processing 146
menu 146
interactive data entry 147
control total 149
edit checks 149
range checks 149
limit checks 150
punched cards 152
80-column cards 152
Hollerith Code 152
96-column cards 153
fields 153
card punch (keypunch) 155
verifier 155
sorter 156
card reader 156
data density 156
punched paper tape 158
transfer rate 158

magnetic tape 158
reel 159
cartridge 159
cassette 159
key-to-tape devices 160
key-to-disk-to-tape systems 160
seven-track magnetic tape 160
nine-track magnetic tape 161
interrecord gap 162
block 162
tape drive or tape transport 163
read/write head 163
floppy disk (diskette) 164
key-to-diskette device 165
floppy disk reader 165
magnetic ink character recognition (MICR) 166
reader-sorter unit 166
optical character recognition (OCR) 167
optical character reader 167

bar codes 168
Universal Product Code (UPC) 168
teleprinter terminal 172
point-of-sale (POS) terminal 173
financial transaction terminal 174
electronic funds transfer (EFT) 174
automated teller machine (ATM) 174
visual display terminal 174
cathode ray tube (CRT) 174
light pen 175
programming workstation 175
input tablet 176
computer graphics 176
dumb terminals 177
smart terminals 177
intelligent terminals 177
speaker-dependent voice input system 178
speaker-independent voice input system 178

TOPICS FOR REVIEW AND DISCUSSION

1. Identify and discuss the sources of the input data used by organizations that you know about, belong to, and/or work for.

2. (*a*) Describe the data entry approach that is typically used in a batch processing application. (*b*) Describe the approach used in direct-access processing.

3. What advantages are there to capturing data at the transaction source?

4. "People have a greater effect on the quality of output of a data processing system than do the data processing machines." Discuss this statement.

5. (*a*) How are data errors introduced into a computer system? (*b*) Why is it important to catch these errors as early as possible?

6. How can errors be detected in input data?

7. Explain the different methods used to code data in 80-column and 96-column punched cards.

8. Describe how punched cards and punched card equipment can be used in a data processing application.

9. Discuss the advantages and limitations of punched cards.

10. How does punched paper tape differ from punched cards?

11. (*a*) How is magnetic tape packaged? (*b*) How are data entered on magnetic tape? (*c*) How are data represented on tape?

12. (*a*) How can different file records be represented on a magnetic tape? (*b*) Why are short records commonly combined into a block?

13. Discuss the advantages and limitations of magnetic tape?

14. (*a*) How are data recorded on a floppy disk? (*b*) How are floppy disks similar to magnetic tape? (*c*) How are they different?

15. MICR and OCR devices are similar in that both types of machines convert source document data directly into computer-usable input. How do these machines differ?

16. (*a*) What is the Universal Product Code? (*b*) How is it used?

17. Discuss the general characteristics of the data entry devices used for direct-access processing.

18. (*a*) What is a teleprinter terminal? (*b*) How may teleprinters be used?

19. (*a*) What's the purpose of a POS terminal? (*b*) Of transaction recording stations?

20. (*a*) What is a visual display terminal? (*b*) How may visual display units be used? (*c*) How may data be entered at such terminals?

21. (*a*) What is an intelligent terminal? (*b*) How may intelligent terminals be used?

22. "Voice input systems may be speaker-dependent or speaker-independent." How do these systems differ?

ANSWERS TO FEEDBACK AND REVIEW SECTIONS

5-1	5-2	5-3
1. T	1. c	1. C
2. F	2. l	2. D
3. T	3. i	3. C
4. F	4. d	4. B
5. F	5. m	5. D
6. T	6. j	6. A
7. T	7. b	7. D
8. T	8. a	8. B
9. T	9. k	9. C
10. F	10. n	
11. F	11. e	
12. F	12. h	
13. F	13. o	
14. T	14. f	
15. T	15. p	
	16. r	
	17. q	
	18. g	

Data Entry Operators
You and Me

She was somewhat impatient, but the man in front of her finished his transaction with dispatch. Nilda Estrada stepped up to the Automated Teller Machine in the Citicorp branch at 8th Avenue and 15th Street on Manhattan's lower West Side. Four days remained until Christmas, and Nilda was withdrawing money for a brief trip to Florida to spend the holiday with her parents. After she slipped her card into the slot and punched in her account number and personal code number, she looked at the long line of people snaking around the velvet ropes. They were waiting an average of a half hour to conduct their business with a teller in the traditional manner of doing banking business.

Nilda punched in the figures to withdraw $500 from her savings account—or so she thought. A message flashed on the screen that her balance was $3,205.46 and that her request for a $5,000 withdrawal could not be approved. She had punched in the wrong information and had to recode her request. The central computer, located in the bank's headquarters at 53d Street and Lexington Avenue, approved her request, and 10 packs of $50 each in varying denominations dropped into the drawer along with a slip confirming the withdrawal. The screen flashed a thank you and a happy holiday message. Nilda smiled and was on her way.

At just about the same time, Nilda's brother, Javier, an engineer by training and now a sales representative for a large oil drilling supply company in Houston, Texas, connected his small, typewriter-like computer terminal into a phone line in a customer's office. Javier typed in his code number, the code number for a sales transaction, and in seconds received confirmation of an order of 3,000 feet of plastic pipe to be delivered to his customer on January 7. Javier's terminal is now the equivalent of an old-fashioned sales pad. He thanked his customer, got on an airport bus, and headed for Miami to spend the holidays with his parents and sister.

In the years to come, as data entry stations become more user-friendly, each of us will be increasingly our own data entry operators. And with the development of better voice input systems, Javier may not even need to carry his terminal in his briefcase. He will be able to dial the computer and give his order to the computer vocally.

I am a data entry operator also. I typed this brief story on a TRS-80 Model III computer keyboard and checked it on the screen. I had misspelled Nilda's name, made three typos, and left out a comma. After correcting my mistakes on the screen (No Liquid Paper corrections for me!), I pressed a key and the line printer produced a hard copy of what you are reading.

Have you spoken to a computer today?

An automated teller machine that handles routine financial transactions at any hour of the day or night. (Courtesy IBM)

chapter 7

Computer Secondary Storage

WHAT'S THE DIFFERENCE BETWEEN A CALCULATOR AND A COMPUTER?

In one sense, a computer is a glorified calculator—that is, it performs basic arithmetic calculations. Of course, the computer is vastly faster than a calculator, and it can perform many steps on the data entered.

Perhaps the most important difference between the two instruments is not the speed of operation or the complexity of the problems solved: the crucial difference is the computer's ability to store enormous amounts of information. A calculator can store only a few results at a time; a large mainframe computer can store literally millions of calculations or other bits of information.

Most information is stored not in the CPU's primary storage section, but in what is called secondary storage. Secondary storage doesn't hold the program steps that are guiding the computer at a given instant in time—that is the function of primary storage. Secondary storage devices hold the enormous amounts of information that must be processed in order to solve a complex problem or that must be available to the CPU for large processing applications.

You can carry a small electronic calculator with you wherever you go. You can't carry around a large computer. But large, stationary computers, such as those at the Bureau of the Census in Washington, can store many facts about each and every one of the more than 200 million citizens of the United States. Perhaps an apt analogy would be to say that computers, like big houses, have very large closets.

Optical disk technology, which has made the home videodisk popular, is proving to be an excellent storage method for increasing computer memory capacity. (Photo courtesy of 3M)

Looking Ahead

The purpose of Chapter 7 is to examine the secondary storage media and devices that are available today. You'll see in the first section that a series of different storage elements are found in most computer systems. These elements form a storage hierarchy, and are usually selected for different tasks on the basis of retrieval speed, storage capacity, and storage cost. Files that are sequentially organized and processed are likely to be stored on the low-cost, high-capacity sequential-access secondary storage media that you'll read about in the second section. However, if quick access to any stored record is needed at any time, the direct-access secondary storage media and devices that you'll read about in the third section must be used.

Thus, after studying this chapter you should be able to:

▌ Identify the elements in the storage hierarchy and discuss the factors to be considered in storage selection

▌ Summarize the characteristics of the secondary media used to store data that are sequentially organized and processed

▌ Outline the characteristics of the secondary media and devices that can provide quick and direct access to stored records

▌ Understand and use the key terms and concepts listed at the end of this chapter

THE STORAGE HIERARCHY: AN OVERVIEW

By now you know that all computers must be able to store and retrieve data. In the case of some small personal systems, only a few thousand characters may need to be retained. But large systems need access to billions of characters stored in a computer-readable form. Computer specialists often refer to the fact that most computer systems have a **storage hierarchy.** That means that a series of different storage elements are found in all but the smallest computer systems. These different elements are likely to be ranked according to the following criteria:

1. *Retrieval speed.* The **access time** of a storage element is the time it takes to locate and retrieve stored data in response to a program instruction. A fast access time is preferred.

2. *Storage capacity.* An element's ability to store the amount of data needed now and in the future must be considered. A large capacity is desired.

3. *Cost per bit of capacity.* An obvious goal is to minimize this cost.

Elements in the Storage Hierarchy

Figure 7-1 gives you a general idea of how different storage elements meet these three criteria. At the top of the storage hierarchy pyramid are the *primary storage* components found in the CPU. The principal element is the primary storage section which was discussed in Chapter 5 along with other specialized processing and control storage elements that may be found in the CPU. The semiconductor storage chips commonly used in the CPU have the fastest access times. Relative to other available storage elements, however, chips have the smallest storage capacity and the highest cost per bit of capacity.

Secondary (or **auxiliary**) **storage** elements supplement primary storage in most computer systems. Included in the secondary storage classification, and located below primary storage in the hierarchy of Figure 7-1, are *direct-access storage devices* (DASD). The data retained in these secondary storage units are *online* and are available to the CPU at all times. Compared with primary storage, the storage capacity of a DASD is larger and the cost per bit stored is lower. Although the access time of a DASD may be only a few milliseconds, primary storage speed is thousands of times faster. Different DASDs provide different levels of cost and performances, as you'll see later in this chapter.

At the base of the storage hierarchy is another type of secondary storage. The data retained on **sequential-access storage media** are periodically accessed and updated by the sequential processing techniques discussed in earlier chapters. These stored data are *offline* from the CPU except when loaded on an input device. The storage capacity of these media is virtually unlimited, and the storage cost is very low. But before the CPU can gain access to a particular record, a computer operator must locate the sequential file and load it on an input device. The CPU must then read all preceding records until the desired one is found. This procedure alone takes several minutes.

Storage Selection

If a single storage element were superior in all three criteria—speed, capacity, and cost—there would be no need for a storage hierarchy. Since this isn't the case, computer system designers must study each application to be processed and then choose the best storage approach for the job. That is, the way the data are organized and processed determines the approach they select. If a file can be organized sequentially, and if records require only periodic updating, then the lowest-cost option is likely to be the use of a sequential-access secondary storage medium. On the other hand, if quick access to any file record may be needed at any time, direct-access processing is required, and a DASD must be used.

In selecting a DASD, designers must usually make compromises between performance and cost. For example, in specialized scientific applications where processing speed is paramount and cost is secondary, the system selected

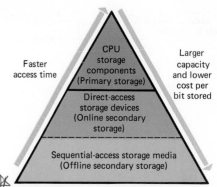

Figure 7-1 The storage hierarchy pyramid. A faster access time is obtained by moving up the pyramid. A larger storage capacity and a lower cost per bit stored are the results of moving down the pyramid. Thus, CPU storage components generally have the *fastest* access times, the *smallest* storage capacity, and the *highest* cost per bit stored. The *primary storage* of a computer system consists of the components in the CPU. Supplementing primary storage is the *secondary* (or *auxiliary*) *storage* of a computer system. This broader classification includes all the online direct-access storage devices and all the offline sequential-access storage media that hold data in a computer-readable form.

may have a large primary storage section linked to a very fast DASD. In business applications, a slower DASD with larger capacity may be picked over a faster and more expensive device that has less capacity.

Figure 7-2 summarizes the storage hierarchy options open to designers. Let's look now at the available secondary storage media and devices in more detail.

SEQUENTIAL-ACCESS SECONDARY (AUXILIARY) STORAGE

Punched paper media, magnetic tape, and portable magnetic disks are used to store data that are sequentially organized and accessed. You'll remember from Chapter 2 that the records in a sequentially organized file are stored one after the other in an ascending or descending order determined by the record key. To access records, the computer starts with the first one in the sequence. This record is read and is either processed or passed over. The second record is then accessed, followed by the third, and so on.

Punched Paper Media Storage

In addition to being used for data entry, *punched cards* and *punched paper tape* also provide offline secondary storage of data. Data are represented by holes punched in card and tape columns. Once the holes have been punched, of course, the data are as permanent as the media. An example in Chapter 6 showed how data from invoices can be captured on punched cards. These cards can then be stored until needed later to produce sales analysis and inventory control reports.

The number of characters that can be stored in a given physical space is low for both cards and paper tape. Card and paper tape files are thus bulky, and the paper media are easily torn and mutilated. However, the storage capacity of punched paper media is virtually unlimited, and the cost per bit stored is low.

Magnetic Tape Storage — most popular now

Magnetic tape is a popular storage medium for large files that are sequentially accessed and processed. Thousands of reels of stored data are maintained in the magnetic tape libraries of large computer systems (see Figure 7-3). On a considerably smaller scale, you've seen how R-K Enterprises' mailing label file is stored on magnetic tape.

Data are stored as tiny invisible magnetized spots on an iron-oxide material that coats one side of the plastic tape. The stored facts can be read many times. They will remain for years or until erased by the recording of new data. Magnetic tape has a high data density (over 6,000 characters can be stored on

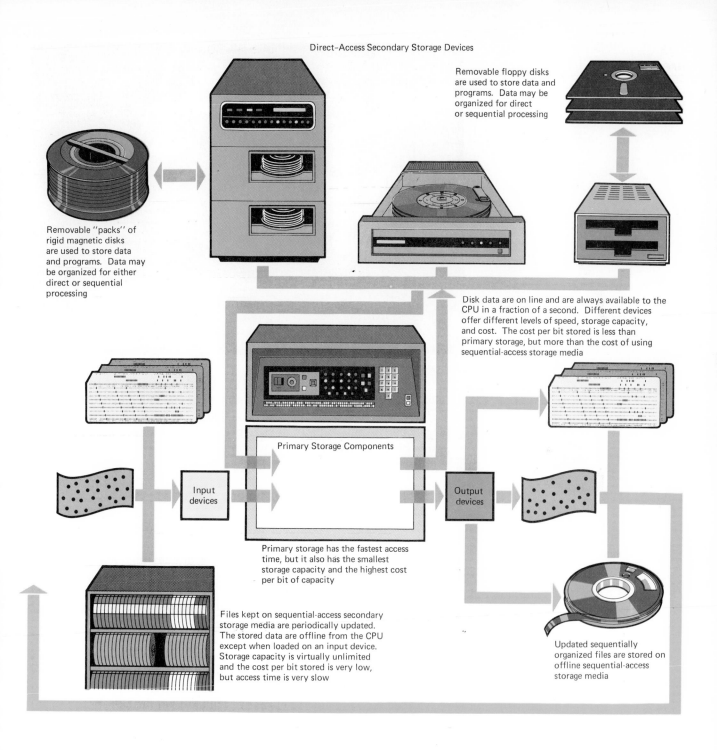

Direct–Access Secondary Storage Devices

Removable floppy disks are used to store data and programs. Data may be organized for direct or sequential processing

Removable "packs" of rigid magnetic disks are used to store data and programs. Data may be organized for either direct or sequential processing

Disk data are on line and are always available to the CPU in a fraction of a second. Different devices offer different levels of speed, storage capacity, and cost. The cost per bit stored is less than primary storage, but more than the cost of using sequential-access storage media

Primary Storage Components

Input devices

Output devices

Primary storage has the fastest access time, but it also has the smallest storage capacity and the highest cost per bit of capacity

Files kept on sequential-access secondary storage media are periodically updated. The stored data are offline from the CPU except when loaded on an input device. Storage capacity is virtually unlimited and the cost per bit stored is very low, but access time is very slow

Updated sequentially organized files are stored on offline sequential-access storage media

Figure 7-2 A summary of some of the options in the storage hierarchy. Compromises between speed, capacity, and record accessibility are generally required in the interest of economy.

191

Figure 7-3 Large computer systems make use of extensive tape libraries, which contain thousands and thousands of reels of stored information and may occupy entire rooms in an organization. (Courtesy AT&T)

an inch of tape). Thus, it's possible to store over 100 million characters on a single 10½-inch reel of tape that costs less than $20. The cost per bit stored is obviously microscopic. But it can take several minutes to gain access to a tape record between processing cycles.

Disk Storage for Sequential Access - most popular

A magnetic disk is a metal or plastic platter that resembles a grooveless phonograph record. As you saw in Chapter 6, data can be recorded and stored on the surface of a floppy disk in the form of tiny invisible magnetic spots. These and other portable magnetic disks can be used to provide sequential-access secondary storage in much the same way that magnetic tape is used. But as the following analogy shows, magnetic disks are not limited to storing records that must be organized and retrieved according to sequence.

Let's assume that you have both a sound tape player and a record player. Let's also suppose that 10 songs are recorded on your favorite tape, and your favorite record has seven pieces of music. Now what must you do if you only want to listen to (or access) the sixth song on the tape and the fourth song on the record? To get to the sixth tape song, you must put the tape on the player and wait until the tape used to record the first five songs has moved through the player. Although your player may "fast forward" the tape quickly past the first five pieces, there is still a delay of several seconds. To get to the fourth song on the record, you can follow either of two approaches. You can place the record on the player, position the pickup arm at the beginning of the first song, and wait until the arm has passed over the first three pieces. (Following the stored sequence in this way is logically similar to accessing the music on a tape.) Or, you can *directly* move the pickup arm across the record to the groove where the fourth song begins.

Like the songs on a sound tape, the data records organized on a magnetic tape must be retrieved according to the storage sequence. And like the music on a record, the data recorded on a magnetic disk can also be accessed in sequence if they have been organized in a way that supports such retrieval. When the data records on a disk are sequentially accessed to support batch processing applications, the direct-access capability of the disk really isn't used. The first record may be directly retrieved, but all others are then read in sequence as if they were stored on a magnetic tape.

The facts stored on a disk can be read many times. They will remain indefinitely or until the disk surface is erased and reused. The storage capacity of a floppy disk varies depending on its size and on other factors that we'll consider later. Well over a million characters can be stored on a diskette that costs less than $10. The cost per bit stored is thus very low. In addition to plastic floppies, other types of disks used in sequential processing applications are made of thin metal plates coated with a magnetizeable material. These rigid disks can usually also be removed from their disk storage devices (see Figure 7-4). They come in different sizes and are packaged in various ways. Many disk devices use one- or two-disk **cartridges,** or **packs** of three or more disks mounted on a single shaft. The storage capacity of single cartridges usually varies from about 5 million to 28 million characters. For a single disk

Figure 7-4 Portable packs of rigid magnetic storage disks are shown here resting on multiple disk storage devices. (Courtesy Honeywell Inc.)

pack, the storage capacity usually ranges from about 30 million to 300 million characters. A disk pack equal in storage capacity to a reel of magnetic tape may be about 25 times more expensive. However, the cost per bit stored is still modest.

DIRECT-ACCESS SECONDARY STORAGE

access randomly

Even though records stored on magnetic disks are often sequentially organized and processed like tape records, the popularity of disk storage devices is largely due to their direct-access capabilities. Let's now consider disk and other direct-access secondary storage devices in more detail.

Disk Storage for Direct Access

Magnetic disks are the most popular medium for direct-access secondary storage. All magnetic disks are round platters coated with a magnetizeable recording material, but their similarities end there. As the following listing

Figure 7-5 Rigid disks are packaged in a number of ways. There are three sizes of disk packs shown here in front of two types of disk cartridges. (Courtesy Memorex)

Figure 7-6 Winchester was the code name used by IBM during the development of this technology. The story is told that IBM designers originally planned to use dual disk drives to introduce the new concepts. Each drive was to have a storage capacity of 30 million characters. The product was thus expected to be a "30-30." Since that was the caliber of a famous rifle, the new product was nicknamed "Winchester." The dual-drive plans were later dropped, but the name stuck. There's no extra charge for this bit of computing trivia. Many other vendors now make Winchester disk drives. For example, the drive pictured here houses two 5¼-inch rigid disks. Data can be written and stored on all four disk surfaces. Occupying the space of a mini floppy disk unit, this drive is able to store over 6 million bytes of data. (Courtesy Texas Instruments)

shows, they come in different sizes. They can be portable or permanently mounted in their storage devices (called **disk drives**). And they can be made of rigid metal or flexible plastic. (See Figure 7-5.)

Types of Magnetic Disks. Here are some of the possible options:

1. Very large disks made of a thin metal. These disks are used in some larger computer systems, and are mounted permanently in their cabinets.

2. Medium-sized (14-inch) metal disks permanently housed in sealed, contamination-free containers. These disks are used in all but the smallest computer systems. Their containers are usually not removed from the disk drive. High-capacity systems using these sealed housings are said to employ **Winchester technology** (see Figure 7-6).

3. Other medium-sized metal disks packaged in removable cartridges or disk packs (discussed a few paragraphs earlier). These are also used in all but the smallest systems. Multiple disk storage devices, each capable of holding one or more cartridges or packs, may be connected to a CPU.

4. Small (8-inch) and mini-sized (5¼-inch) rigid disks permanently housed in Winchester disk devices. These are used in mini- and microcomputer systems.

not removable

5. Small (8-inch) and mini-sized (5¼-inch) portable floppy (flexible) disks individually packaged in protective envelopes (see Figure 7-7). In addition to their data entry uses, these diskettes are currently the most popular online secondary storage medium used in microcomputer and intelligent terminal systems.

removable

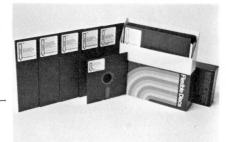

Figure 7-7 Floppy disks come in 8-inch and 5¼-inch sizes. (Courtesy Memorex)

Figure 7-8 The user of this TRS-80 Model II microcomputer can gain access to the information stored on the selected 8-inch floppy disk by inserting it into the disk drive that's located to the right of the display screen. (Courtesy Radio Shack Division, Tandy Corporation)

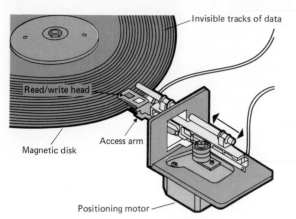

Figure 7-9 Data are stored on invisible tracks on the surface of a disk. There are from 35 to 77 tracks on a floppy disk surface, and from about 200 to over 800 on hard-disk surfaces. Both the top and bottom of a hard disk are generally used for data storage, but only one surface of a floppy disk may be used. One or more read/write heads are assigned to each storage surface to record and retrieve data. These heads are fastened to access arms or actuators which are moved in and out over the spinning disk surfaces by positioning motors. The heads can thus be quickly located over any track to read or write data.

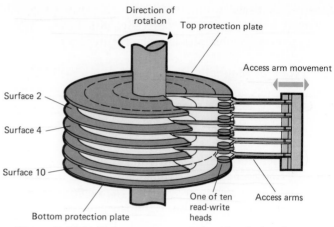

Figure 7-10 Multiple access arms and read/write heads are used with disk packs. The arms move in and out in unison among the individual disks. Two heads are frequently mounted on each arm to access two surfaces. In this example, the heads on the top arm access the bottom of the top disk and the top of the second disk. Data aren't stored on the top surface of the top disk or the bottom surface of the bottom disk because these surfaces are easily scratched. In this illustration, the pack has ten recording and two protective surfaces.

Storing Data on Magnetic Disks. Music is stored on a phonograph record in a continuous groove that spirals into the center of the record. But there are no grooves on a magnetic disk. Instead, data are stored on all disks in a number of invisible concentric circles called **tracks**. These tracks, like the rings in a tree, begin at the outer edge of the disk and continue toward the center without ever touching (see Figure 7-9). Each track has a designated number.

A motor rotates the disk at a constant and rapid speed.[1] Data are recorded on the tracks of a spinning disk surface and read from the surface by one or more *read/write heads*. If a floppy disk is used, the head is in contact with the disk. If hard disks are used, the heads "fly" on a cushion of air a few micro-inches (or millionths of an inch) above the surface. When multiple disks are packaged together, a number of **access arms** and read/write heads are used (see Figures 7-10 and 7-11). Data are written as tiny magnetic spots on the disk surface. A 1-spot is magnetized in one direction, a 0-spot in another. Eight-bit BCD codes are generally used to represent data. The writing of new data on a disk erases data previously stored at the location. The new magnetic spots remain indefinitely or until they too are erased at a future time. Reading of recorded data is accomplished as the magnetized spots pass under a read head and induce electrical pulses in it.

The more disk surfaces a particular system has, the greater its storage capacity will be. But the storage capacity of a disk system also depends on the

[1]The rotational speed of floppies is usually between 300 and 400 revolutions per minute (rpm). Hard disks rotate from 2,400 to 4,700 rpm, with 3,600 being a common speed.

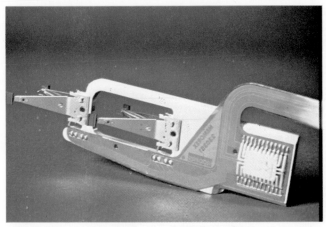

Figure 7-11 (*left*) A head-arm assembly used in a hard-disk drive. (*right*) One of the four thin-film read/write heads on the arm assembly shown next to a needle's eye for perspective. (Courtesy Memorex)

bits per inch of track and the **tracks per inch of surface.** That is, the storage capacity depends on the number of bits that can be stored on an inch of track, and the number of tracks that can be placed on an inch of surface (see Figure 7-12). A constant goal of disk-drive designers is to increase the data density of a disk surface by increasing the number of tracks. To accomplish this goal, it's necessary to reduce the distance between the read/write head and the disk surface so that smaller magnetized spots can be precisely written and then retrieved. But as designers gradually found ways to reduce this distance and improve the data density, they ran into a problem. As Figure 7-13 shows, they

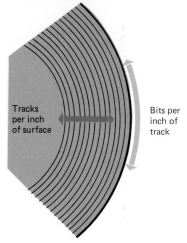

Tracks per inch of surface

Bits per inch of track

Figure 7-13 Data density can be improved and storage capacity can be increased by reducing the flying height of read/write heads over disk surfaces. Each reduction in height allows an increase in bits per inch of track and tracks per inch of surface. The reason Winchester technology was developed to control the disk environment is obvious in this illustration. A smoke particle 250 millionths of an inch in diameter can't begin to fit in the space between head and disk. And a human hair looks like Pike's Peak to the flying head. The head flies 20 millionths of an inch above the disk at speeds of over 100 miles per hour. That's comparable to an airplane flying 600 miles per hour around the circumference of a lake at an altitude of $\frac{1}{4}$ inch.

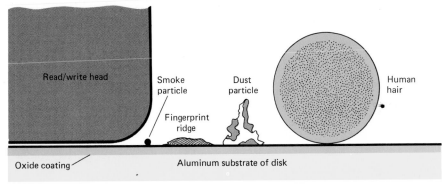

Read/write head

Smoke particle

Dust particle

Fingerprint ridge

Human hair

Oxide coating

Aluminum substrate of disk

Figure 7-12 Factors determining the storage capacity of a magnetic disk system include bits per inch of track, and tracks per inch of surface. Many hard-disk systems can store well over 6,000 bits on an inch of track and have over 400 tracks on an inch of disk surface. Such high data density permits a minisized (5¼-inch) Winchester disk device to store over 6 megabytes (a *megabyte* is a million bytes or characters). Eight-inch Winchester systems can store over 40 megabytes, and over 100 megabytes can be held on a 14-inch system with a single platter. The 14-inch disks packaged in removable cartridges and packs usually have a lower data density than Winchester disks. Floppy disk systems come in either single- or double-density versions and record on one or both surfaces of a diskette. Thus, the capacity of a single-density, single-sided 5¼-inch diskette may only be a little over 100 kilobytes (a *kilobyte* is a thousand bytes or characters), while the capacity of a double-density, dual-sided 8-inch diskette may be almost 2 megabytes.

197

moved the read/write head so close to the disk surface that a human hair or a dust particle on the disk loomed like a mountain in the path of the flying head. The resulting collision caused the head to bounce up and then **crash** on the far side of the particle. This often damaged the head, the disk, and the data. Winchester technology was developed to reduce this problem. Sealing the disks in contamination-free containers reduced head crashes, permitted smaller distances between head and disk, and increased disk storage capacity.

Accessing Data on Magnetic Disks. Just as the pickup arm of a record player can move directly to the location of a specific song without playing other music, so, too, can an access arm move a read/write head directly to the track that contains the desired data without reading other tracks. Before this direct access can be accomplished, however, the program instructions that control the disk drive must specify the **disk address** of the desired data. This disk address information specifies the track number, surface number, and so on to enable the access mechanism to pinpoint the exact location of the data.

Disk-drive manufacturers use either the *cylinder method* or the *sector method* to organize and physically store disk data. Figure 7-14 shows the cylinder approach. Access arms move in unison in and out of the disk pack. Thus, if the read/write head that serves the top recording surface is positioned over the twentieth track, each of the heads on the arms that serve other surfaces are similarly positioned over the same track. All the twentieth tracks together comprise the twentieth **cylinder** of the disks. If there are 200 or more tracks on a single hard-disk surface, there are also 200 or more cylinders in a multiple stack of the disks. Before a disk drive can access a cylinder record, a computer program must provide the record's disk address. This address supplies the cylinder number, the surface number, and the record number. Thus, a desired record might be on cylinder (track) 20, on surface 1, in record location 5. If a large number of related records are typically processed in sequence after record

Figure 7-14 When data are organized by cylinders, the cylinder number, surface number, and record number are needed to access the stored data. All tracks with the same number in a disk pack form a cylinder with the same number. Each invisible cylinder passes vertically through the pack.

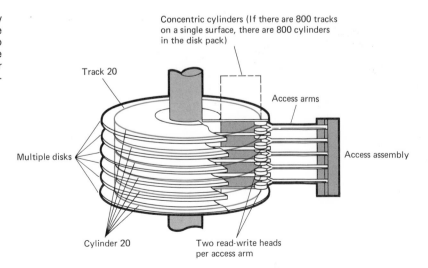

5, they can be organized to follow record 5 on this same track and surface and can then be continued on the same track of other surfaces in the cylinder. In one revolution of the disk the data on track 20 of surface 1 is read. In the next revolution, control is instantly switched to the read/write head over surface 2 and a full track of data can be read in a single revolution. This procedure can continue down the cylinder without any delays caused by the movement of access arms.

The sector approach to organizing disk data is used with single disks (including floppies) as well as with cartridges or packs of multiple disks. As shown in Figure 7-15, a disk surface is divided into pie-shaped segments or **sectors.** (The number of sectors varies with the disk system used.) Each sector holds a specific number of characters and records. Before a record can be accessed, a computer program must again give the disk drive the record's address. This disk address specifies the track number, the surface number, and the sector number of the record. One or more read/write heads are then moved to the proper track, the head over the specified surface is activated, and data are read from the designated sector as it spins under the head.

The access time for data stored on a disk is basically determined by:

1. The **seek time**—the time required to position a head over the proper track.

2. The **search** (or **latency**) **time**—the time required to spin the needed data under the head.

The average access time for most hard-disk storage systems is usually between 10 and 100 milliseconds.[2] For floppy disk systems, the average time usually ranges from 100 to 600 milliseconds.[3] Most disk drives have a single read/write head for each disk surface. But some of the faster hard-disk systems either have a *fixed-head* for *each* track of a surface, or they use *multiple heads* on each movable access arm to service a number of adjacent tracks. A **fixed-head-per-track device** has *no* seek time delay, and multiple heads reduce the average length of horizontal movement of the access arms and thus decrease the seek time. Of course, these faster systems are more expensive than the single-head-per-arm devices.

Once the data have been accessed, they are copied from the disk to the CPU. The transfer rate depends on the density of the stored data and the rotational speed of the disk. For floppy systems, the maximum transfer rate is typically between 30,000 and 150,000 characters per second. For hard-disk systems, the maximum rate usually ranges between 400,000 and 2 million characters per second.

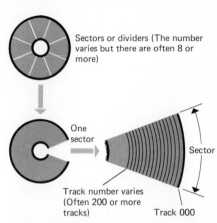

Figure 7-15 When data are organized by sectors, the track number, surface number, and sector number are needed to access the stored data. The outside track is generally numbered 000 (or 00 in the case of floppies). The inside track on a disk with 800 tracks is numbered 799.

[2]Technically speaking, disk drives have *direct* but not *random* access to records. Random access refers to a storage device in which the access time is independent of the physical location of the data. Since the disk access time does vary with the data location, it's more correct to say that disks provide direct access. This distinction is not always observed, however, and disk drives are sometimes referred to as random access units.

[3]Floppy disks rotate much more slowly than hard disks and so their search time is much longer. A floppy can't turn too fast or centrifugal force will bend it out of shape and damage the stored data. A rigid metal disk doesn't have this problem.

Advantages and Limitations of Magnetic Disks. When compared to magnetic tape, disks have the following *advantages:*

▌ Disk records can be stored sequentially and processed like magnetic tape records, or they can be stored for direct-access processing.

▌ Online disk records can be accessed and updated in a few milliseconds. No sorting of transactions is necessary.

▌ A single input transaction can be used to simultaneously update the online disk records of several related files.

But disks also have *limitations* when compared to magnetic tape:

▌ Sequential processing using disks may be slower and less efficient than when tapes are used.

▌ A disk pack equal in storage capacity to a reel of magnetic tape may be about 25 times more expensive. On a cost-per-bit basis, the cost of disks is low. But the cost of magnetic tape is even less.

▌ When a tape file is updated, the old master tape remains unchanged and available in case of system malfunctions. When the records in a disk file are updated, however, the old records may be erased when the new records are written on the disk. Special backup procedures are thus required to protect disk records from malfunctions.

▌ People have broken through security provisions and gained access to sensitive online disk files from remote terminals. These files have been manipulated and destroyed. It's easier to maintain the security of tape files.

"Watch where you walk in here, Howard—they dropped a storage chip and you may destroy the entire literature of the 18th century!"

Magnetic Drum Storage

A **magnetic drum** is a cylinder that has an outer surface plated with a metallic magnetizable film. A motor rotates the drum on its axis at a constant and rapid rate. Data are recorded on the rotating drum and read from the drum by read/write heads, which are positioned a fraction of an inch from the drum surface. The writing of new data on the drum erases data previously stored at the location. The magnetic spots written on the drum surface remain indefinitely or until they too are erased. The drum rotates several thousand times each minute to produce a relatively fast access time.

Magnetic drums were an early means of primary storage. They were then used for online secondary storage when fast response was more important than large capacity. For example, they were used to store mathematical tables, data, or program segments that were frequently needed during processing operations. Since drums are permanently mounted and can't be be replaced like disks, and since their storage capacity is relatively low, they are seldom used today.

Mass Storage Devices *— combined tape + disk*

Wouldn't it be nice to combine the magnetic tape advantages of low cost and high storage capacity with the advantages of direct record accessibility? This is essentially the objective of mass storage devices. The storage medium may be considered to be a length of flexible plastic material upon which short strips of magnetic tape have been mounted. These strips are then placed in cartridges, and the cartridges are loaded into a storage device that is online to the CPU. **Mass storage devices** employ the same techniques used to read and write data on magnetic tape.

An example of such a device is the IBM 3850 Mass Storage System (see Figure 7-16). Honeycomb storage compartments are used in this system to hold the data cartridges. It requires several seconds for this device to locate the cartridge specified by an instruction from the CPU. Once the cartridge has been located and placed in a position to be read, several more seconds are needed to transfer the data to a magnetic disk and then to the CPU. A 10-second access time is thus common. That's fast compared to the time it would take to locate, load, and read a reel of magnetic tape. But it's an eternity compared to many other devices in the storage hierarchy. Of course, as you've probably anticipated, a mass storage device has a huge storage capacity and a very small cost per bit stored. Over 400,000 books the size of this one can be stored in the IBM 3850.

Magnetic Bubble Chips and Charge Coupled Devices

Magnetic Bubble Storage. **Magnetic bubble storage** devices were introduced in quantity in the late 1970s. At that time, some researchers expected that this technology was likely to eventually replace many magnetic disk systems. One reason for this optimism was that since bubble units are made with solid-state electronic chips and have no moving parts, they should be much more reliable than units with spinning disks that use mechanical components. Bubble devices have so far failed to live up to these optimistic expectations. Disk storage costs fell much faster than expected while bubble storage costs remained higher than predicted.

This isn't the first time that promising technology has failed to live up to expectations. Long-time observers of the computer hardware scene know that at any given time researchers are working on several new approaches that could replace the technology that's currently number 1. But these researchers are not shooting at a stationary target. Advances are usually also being made in the dominant technology. And before the potential of a new approach can be realized, it's possible that some other method will break through and make both the new approach and the dominant technology obsolete.

Some bubble-chip makers haven't given up, however, and large numbers of bubble chips are now being used in specialized areas rather than as a replacement for disks (see Figure 7-17). Portable terminals use bubble devices to store data until they can be transmitted to a larger system. And bubble chips are also being used in machine tools, robots, and military computers.

Figure 7-16 (*top*) The IBM 3850 mass storage system. (*bottom*) Honeycomb storage compartments are used in this system to hold data cartridges. (Courtesy of IBM)

Figure 7-17 Magnetic bubble chip. (Courtesy Intel Corporation)

For our purpose, a magnetic bubble can be thought of as a tiny positively charged island in a sea of negatively charged film. The presence of a bubble is analogous to the presence of a hole in a punched paper tape column. (The absence of a bubble, of course, is analogous to the absence of a hole.) Data are represented in bubble storage by the presence or absence of bubbles just as they are represented in punched tape form by the presence or absence of holes. Although we've seen in Chapter 5 that some electronic chips have volatile storage, bubble chips retain their stored data in the absence of power.

Figure 7-18 shows how information is stored in a single small bubble chip. When data are placed into storage, bubble sites from the minor loops are transferred to the major loop, carried past a *write* station, and then returned to the minor loops. When data are retrieved from storage, the correct bubbles are transferred, at a signal, from the minor loops into the major loop, which carries them past the *read* station. The retrieval time, of course, varies with the location of the needed bubbles in the minor loop "pipelines." Since the stored data bits are only available as they come around to the transfer sites in a bit-by-bit stream, a bubble chip is sometimes called a **serial-access memory.**

The Charge Coupled Device (CCD). There are several similarities between a bubble storage device and a **charge coupled device.** Both are referred to as serial-access memories. Both circulate the stored data in closed pipelines. Both use the charges in a storage crystal to represent data. And both are fabricated on semiconductor chips and are thus completely electronic. However, the CCD is faster than bubbles, is very compact, and may be inexpensive to produce in the future. Unfortunately, however, CCD storage is volatile. The future of CCD systems is uncertain.

Figure 7-18 Magnetic bubble storage. The access time depends on the position of the desired bubbles in the minor loops. The bubbles move around the minor loops in a serial fashion. If a needed bubble has just passed a transfer site, there will be a delay until the bubble can loop back again to the site.

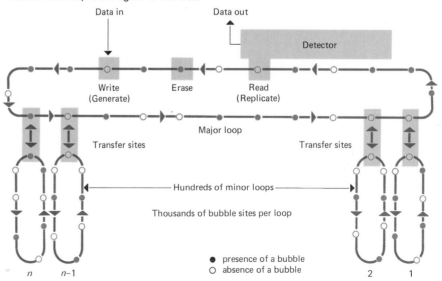

LASER TECHNOLOGY CAN STORE GIGABITS

In technical circles, laser optical recording is the focus of much attention because of its high-density storage capability—a single optical disk can store as much information as a set of encyclopedias; and the labs of RCA Corp. and North American Philips have demonstrated disks that can store as much data as 25 tape reels or floppy disks (magnetic media commonly used to store computer data). Theodore Maiman, the laser's inventor, notes that in some research labs, optical storage with densities of a gigabit (1 billion bits) of information per square centimeter has been achieved. "This is fantastic storage density—hundreds, if not thousands, of times greater than we can get using magnetic techniques," he observes.

Why are scientists developing such minuscule data-storage systems? Answers Maiman: "As we ask the computer to automate more and more things, each of these things requires more [of the computer's] memory. The computer needs access to more information in order to accomplish each new task."

—"Lasers and Computers: A Bright Future," *output,* July 1981, p. 57. Reprinted with Permission of *Output* magazine. Copyright by Technical Publishing Company. A Dun & Bradstreet Company 1981. All rights reserved.

Optical Disk Technology — toward future

You're probably aware that **optical disks** are now used by consumer electronics companies to record movies, concerts, football games, and other audio/visual presentations for playback on television sets. These grooveless "videodisks" are created by **laser recording systems.**[4] A beam of laser light is used to burn tiny holes (or pits) into a thin coating of metal or other material deposited on a spinning disk. Visible only under a powerful microscope, these holes are used to represent images and sounds. Of course, they can't be erased and the disk can't be reused. At a later time, a less-powerful laser light beam in a videodisk player is used to read the hole patterns, convert these patterns into audio/visual signals, and transmit the signals to a television set.[5]

The same technology that's used to record and play back sound and images can also be used to store and retrieve data. The storage density of optical disks is enormous, the storage cost is extremely low, and the access time is relatively fast. Laboratory systems with the potential to store on a single disk the contents of a library of several thousand volumes have already been demonstrated. Permanent archives now stored on microfilm and magnetic tape may in the future be placed on optical disks. One small inexpensive disk will be able to replace 25 reels of magnetic tape. And disk players will be able to access any data on this disk in a few milliseconds.

[4]Not all videodisk systems use laser optical technology. The RCA SelectaVision system has grooved disks that are stamped out much like phonograph records.

[5]In the Magnavision system, for example, variations in the length of holes modulate the laser beam to produce a video signal.

Across

1. A series of different storage elements are found in most computer systems. These different elements are called the storage _____.

3. The _____ time of a storage element is the time it takes to locate and retrieve stored data in response to a program instruction.

8. A beam of _____ light is used to record and retrieve data on optical disks.

10. Data retained in a DASD are _____ to the CPU, but the data stored on sequential-access storage media are offline except when loaded on an input device.

12. The _____ or latency time is the time required to spin the needed data under a read/write head in a disk drive.

13. A _____ disk is a portable storage medium that is packaged in a protective envelope.

14. In studying applications and choosing storage approaches to use, system designers must usually make _____ -offs between access time, storage capacity, cost, and record accessibility.

16. In some magnetic disk storage systems, a disk surface is divided into pie-shaped segments called _____.

17. Data stored on disks can be accessed in either a sequential or _____ way.

18. The _____ storage of a computer system includes all the online DASDs and all the offline sequential-access storage media that hold data in a computer-readable form.

19. A magnetic _____ chip is a serial-access memory that is used in portable terminals and robots.

Down

2. A dust particle on a magnetic disk can cause a flying head to bounce up and then _____ on the disk surface.

4. Disk drive manufacturers use either the _____ method or the sector method to organize and physically store disk data.

5. Portable magnetic disk cartridges and packs can be used to _____ data online or offline.

Feedback and Review 7-1

You now know that most computer systems have a storage hierarchy. At the top of this hierarchy are the primary storage components found in the CPU. Supplementing primary storage is the secondary storage of a computer system. This broad classification includes the offline sequential-access storage media and the online direct-access storage media and devices presented in this chapter. To test and reinforce your understanding of the chapter material, fill in the crossword puzzle form presented below.

¹H	I	²E	R	A	R	²C	H	Y		³A	⁴C	C	E	⁵S	S		⁶C		⁷W
		R									Y			T			C		I
⁸L	A	S	E	R		A		⁹C		L				O			D		N
						S		¹⁰O	N	L	I	N	E		R				C
		¹¹T				H		S				N		¹²S	E	A	R	C	H
¹³F	L	O	P	P	Y			¹⁴T	R	A	D	E		E					E
L		R								E		N				¹⁵S		S
Y		N				¹⁶S	E	C	T	O	R	S		¹⁷D	I	R	E	C	T
														E		E		E
¹⁸S	E	C	O	N	D	A	R	Y		¹⁹B	U	B	B	L	E		K		R

6. The acronym for a volatile serial-access storage chip is _____.

7. The generic name given to high-performance storage systems that use metal magnetic disks permanently housed in contamination-free containers is _____.

9. As online storage capacity increases, the _____ per bit stored tends to decrease.

11. Paper secondary storage media are easily _____ and mutilated.

12. Read/write heads are used to _____ data to and from magnetic media.

13. Read/write heads _____ on a cushion of air a few micro-inches above the surfaces of rigid magnetic disks.

15. The _____ time is the time required to position a head over the proper track on a magnetic disk.

1. Most computer systems have a storage hierarchy. The different components in the hierarchy are usually ranked according to their access time, storage capacity, and cost per bit of capacity. Primary storage generally has the fastest access time, the smallest storage capacity, and the highest cost per bit stored. Supplementing primary storage is the secondary storage of a computer system. This classification includes the online DASDs and the offline storage media that hold data in a computer-readable form.

2. Computer system designers must study each application to be processed and then select a storage approach to use. This approach is determined by the way the data are to be organized and processed. Sequentially organized files that require only periodic updating can be stored on an offline secondary storage medium. But if quick access to any file record may be needed at any time, a DASD must be used. In selecting an appropriate DASD, designers must usually make compromises between performance and cost.

3. Punched cards, punched paper tape, magnetic tape, and portable magnetic disks are used to store data that are sequentially organized and processed. Punched paper tape media can be used to store small files. They have a low data density, are bulky, and are slow to process. But the cost per bit stored is low. Magnetic tape is a popular storage medium for large sequentially organized files. "Mag" tape has such a high data density that over 100 million characters can be stored on a single reel. The cost to store the information in 100 books the size of this one is less than $20. Portable magnetic disks can also be used to store large sequential files. When the records in these files are stored and accessed in sequence, the direct-access capability of disks isn't being used. Rather, the records are read and processed as if they were stored on magnetic tape.

4. Even though magnetic disks can be used for sequential processing, their popularity is largely due to their direct-access capabilities. Disks come in different sizes, are either portable or permanently mounted in their disk drives, and are made of rigid metal or flexible plastic. There are scores of different disk storage systems available. These systems come in a wide price range, and provide an equally wide range of access times, storage capacities, and transfer rates.

5. Data are stored on the surface of all magnetic disks in a number of invisible concentric circles called tracks. Tiny magnetic spots representing data are recorded on, and read from, these tracks by one or more read/write heads. The storage capacity of a disk system depends on the data density of a disk surface, and the number of disk surfaces that are available. The data density is determined by the bits per inch of track and the number of tracks that can be placed on a surface. Winchester disk systems have very high densities.

6. Before a disk drive can directly access a needed record, it must receive program instructions that specify the disk address of the record. When the cylinder method is used to organize and physically store disk data, this address supplies the cylinder number, surface number, and record number. When the sector method is used, the disk address specifies the track number, surface number, and sector number of the record. A read/write head is then moved directly to the specified address to access the data. The access time is determined by the seek time needed to position the head over the proper track, and the search time needed to spin the needed data under the head.

7. The advantages of magnetic disk storage are that records can be processed sequentially or directly. Direct-access time is fast, and single transactions can be used to update the online disk records of several related files. However, sequential processing with disks may be slower than when magnetic tapes are used. A disk pack costs much more than a tape reel of equal storage capacity, and special backup procedures are required to protect disk records from malfunctions. Also, it's harder to secure disk files from unauthorized persons.

8. Other devices used for direct-access secondary storage include magnetic drums, mass storage systems utilizing short strips of magnetic tape placed in directly accessible cartridges, magnetic bubble chips, charge coupled devices, and optical disks. Each of these storage approaches has been briefly outlined in the chapter. Magnetic drums represent a fading technology and are seldom used today. Optical disks represent an emerging technology with strong potential. The use of magnetic bubble storage chips is expected to grow steadily in specialized applications. And the future of charge coupled devices is uncertain.

KEY TERMS AND CONCEPTS

You should now be able to define and use the following terms and concepts (the numbers shown indicate the pages where the terms and concepts are first mentioned):

storage hierarchy **188**
access time **188**
secondary (auxiliary) storage **189**
sequential-access storage media **189**
disk cartridge **193**
disk pack **193**
disk drive **195**
Winchester technology **195**
tracks **196**

access arm **196**
bits per inch of track **197**
tracks per inch of surface **197**
head crash **198**
disk address **198**
cylinder **198**
sector **199**
seek time **199**
search (latency) time **199**

fixed-head-per-track device **199**
magnetic drum **200**
mass storage device **201**
magnetic bubble storage **201**
serial-access memory **202**
charge coupled device (CCD) **202**
optical disk **203**
laser recording systems **203**

TOPICS FOR REVIEW AND DISCUSSION

1. "In a storage hierarchy, it's generally necessary to make compromises between retrieval speed on the one hand, and storage capacity and cost per character stored on the other." Explain this statement and give examples to support it.

2. What components make up the storage hierarchy of your school's computer system?

3. What storage elements are included in the secondary storage classification?

4. "The storage approach selected for a particular application is determined by the way the data are organized and processed." Discuss this statement.

5. (*a*) Identify the offline secondary media used to store sequentially organized files. (*b*) Discuss some of the characteristics of these media.

6. Identify and discuss the types of magnetic disks used for direct-access secondary storage.

7. (*a*) How are data stored on magnetic disks? (*b*) What factors determine the storage capacity of disks?

8. (*a*) What causes head crashes? (*b*) How can Winchester technology reduce the head crash problem?

9. (*a*) How can data stored on magnetic disks be accessed? (*b*) What determines the time required to access the needed data?

10. What are the advantages and limitations of magnetic disks?

11. What is the storage medium used in mass storage devices such as the IBM 3850?

12. What are the characteristics of magnetic bubble storage?

13. What are the potential storage benefits of optical disk technology?

ANSWERS TO FEEDBACK AND REVIEW SECTION

7-1

¹H	I	E	R	A	²R	C	H	Y		³A	⁴C	C	E	S	⁵S		⁶C		⁷W
					R						Y				T		C		I
⁸L	A	S	E	R		A		⁹C			L				O		D		N
						S		¹⁰O	N	L	I	N	E		R				C
		¹¹T				H		S			N			¹²S	E	A	R	C	H
¹³F	L	O	P	P	Y			¹⁴T	R	A	D	E		E					E
L		R									E			N			¹⁵S		S
Y		N			¹⁶S	E	C	T	O	R	S		¹⁷D	I	R	E	C	T	
														E			E		E
¹⁸S	E	C	O	N	D	A	R	Y		¹⁹B	U	B	B	L	E		K		R

207

Improving the Memories of Micros

Although micros are slower machines than their larger cousins, speed has not really been a problem in most business applications with the desktop computers. The biggest drawback has been in the storage limitations of the small processors.

Interestingly enough, limits on the number of files a microcomputer can store have been set by software choices. Microsoft BASIC, the high-level programming language used most widely in microcomputers, can access a maximum of 32,000 different records. In contrast, Digi-

Figure 7-A IBM introduced its Personal Computer with a powerful accounting software package which contributed to the speedup in improvements in micro storage capabilities. (Courtesy IBM Corporation)

tal Research's CP/M, which is used in many business applications, has the capability of addressing 8 million characters—if hard-disk storage is available.

In addition to improvements in languages and more efficient programs, hard-disk storage can greatly increase the applications possible with microcomputers. Millions of characters can be stored on hard disks. Such technology can be expensive, however. The hard disk for Radio Shack's TRS-80 Model II sells for around $5,000.

What amounts to almost daily upgrading of micro storage devices and systems software makes the fixed limits for business use almost impossible to pin down. With IBM's entry into the personal computer market via its Personal Computer (Figure 7-A), the race for improved memory capacity has speeded up even more. Commodore's 8050 disk drive triples the capacity of a floppy disk; Apple's DOS 3.3 operating software increases the capacity of a $5\frac{1}{4}$-inch disk by nearly one third.

Business applications software will continue to increase in efficiency and versatility. That leaves only the issue of a micro's speed in handling multiple-user applications as a real limit on its business use. And systems for

Figure 7-B The disk drive pictured here combines Winchester technology with flexible disk capacity in one unit. The Winchester component has a 4.6 million byte storage capacity—enough to satisfy even the busiest microcomputer user. (Courtesy of Hewlett-Packard)

linking micros together efficiently are in the works today. What will be left to differentiate micros from minis when both their speeds and their storage capacities match looks like just one small item: their price tags.

—Source of data: Steve Ditlea, "Practical Limits of Small Computers for Business," *Popular Computing*, January 1982, pp. 36–37.

chapter 8

Computer Output

GETTING IT OUT OF THE COMPUTER

According to a joke making the rounds among computer specialists, a computer programmed for evaluating interplanetary space travel was once asked to assess the chances for success of a proposed manned-space vehicle completing a round-trip voyage between Earth and Venus.

The interrogation, which required several hours to program into the computer, took place, so the story goes, deep within the bowels of the Pentagon and was carried out in the presence of some of the nation's top military advisers. At the completion of the arduous programming procedure the programmer, along with the visiting VIPs, sat back and waited expectantly for the computer's decision. Within seconds the computer responded, "Yes."

The programmer, unsatisfied with such a response to a series of complex and multilayered questions, impatiently retorted, "Yes, what?" to which the computer meekly replied, "Yes, sir!"

—From *Smithsonian*, March 1980, by Richard M. Restak, M.D.

Important trends and relationships are easily highlighted by processing data through graphics systems and charting the results on a desktop plotter, as shown here. (Courtesy of Computer Sciences Corporation)

Looking Ahead

Our main topics in this chapter are more "down-to-earth" than the subject considered in the opening vignette. That is, our interests here are on the media and devices used to receive output information from computer systems. After explaining the importance of computer output, the first section gives you an outline of the various types of computer output. Detailed descriptions of these media and devices then follow: punched paper and magnetic media; devices to print or film output; and devices to display information, prepare computer graphics, and generate voice responses.

Thus, after studying this chapter you should be able to:

▌ Understand why computer output is needed

▌ Discuss the types of computer output that may be produced

▌ Explain why computer output is entered on punched paper and magnetic media

▌ Describe the devices used to prepare printed and filmed output

▌ Summarize the characteristics of the devices used to display alphanumeric/graphic information and generate voice responses

▌ Understand and use the key terms and concepts listed at the end of this chapter

COMPUTER OUTPUT: SOME BASIC CONCEPTS

You'll recall that most of Chapter 6 dealt with input media and devices. Similarly, most of this chapter deals with the media and devices used to produce computer output. But just as it was necessary to pause at the beginning of Chapter 6 to discuss some basic data entry matters, so, too, is it necessary here to summarize some basic computer output concepts.

Why Computer Output Is Needed

Early in Chapter 1 you saw that computer data processing transforms input data into output information. This output information can give people the knowledge they need to improve their understanding of issues and achieve specific goals. For example, the output of personal computers is helping many people analyze investments, prepare tax returns, monitor home energy usage, and so on.

Besides being helpful to individuals who use it to achieve personal ends, computer output is also used by decision makers in most organizations. These people must perform certain tasks to achieve organizational goals. Although different goals are pursued, the basic tasks generally involve:

1. *Planning* for the future use of scarce human and capital resources. (Capital is money and the things money can buy.)

2. *Organizing* these resources into logical and efficient units.

3. *Controlling* these resources.

The success of any organization is determined by how well its people perform these three tasks. And how well these tasks are carried out often depends, in part, on the quality of the available computer output. This is true because each task involves decision making, and decision making must generally be supported by output information that is as accurate, timely, complete, concise, and relevant as possible. If the output information doesn't possess these characteristics, the quality of the decisions will probably suffer, and the organization (at best) will likely not achieve the success it might otherwise have had.

In summary, as Figure 8-1 shows, good output information in the hands of those who can effectively use it will support good decisions. Good decisions will lead to the effective performance of organizational tasks, and effective task performance will lead to success in reaching the organization's goals. Of course, decision makers must often use important information that's not produced by their organization's computer(s). But as Figure 8-1 suggests, computer output is now an important bonding agent that helps hold many organizations together.

Figure 8-1 The success of an organization may depend on its output information.

Types of Computer Output

You've seen in Chapter 6 that the processing method used in an application has an important bearing on computer input. Not surprisingly, the processing method also plays an important role in computer output.

Output from Sequential Processing. Computer output can be grouped into internal and external categories. **Internal output** is information that's intended for use solely within an organization. In sequential processing applications, this output can be in the form of updated files written on *punched paper or magnetic media.* As we've seen, the information in these files is typically reentered into the computer at a later date. When the purpose is to help decision makers in an organization perform their jobs, however, the internal output must be in a humanly readable form (see Figure 8-2). If the information is likely to be retained for some time, the output from the computer can be recorded directly on *microfilm.* In most cases, however, a *printed* report is prepared. Any format that meets the needs of the designated users is acceptable. For example, **detailed reports** that show the amount of a particular product that each customer has purchased might help salespeople and others make day-to-day operating decisions. However, decision makers at higher levels don't need (and probably won't use) reports that contain an excessive amount of detailed information. For these people, the output information should be presented in the form of summary reports and exception reports.

Figure 8-2 Printed reports can provide detailed and/or summarized information. They can also point out exceptions to expected results to alert managers to the need for decisions and/or actions. (Courtesy Versatec)

Figure 8-3 Output created by using graphic software packages makes mountains of data easier to understand. (Reprinted with permission from ISSCO, San Diego, California)

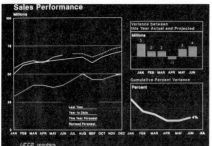

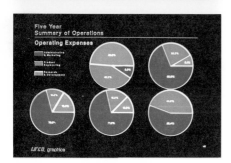

A summary report condenses and sifts the detailed data so that managers can spot patterns and trends and then take appropriate action. The same information printed in summary reports is also frequently presented in the form of **computer graphic output** (see Figure 8-3). It's thus often possible to further condense several pages of summary information into a few pictures.

Unlike detailed and summary reports that are prepared at regularly scheduled intervals, **exception reports** are usually triggered to supply computer output to managers only when operating data fall outside the normal limits specified in a program. The purpose of an exception report is to alert a manager to the need for decisions and/or actions. For example, such a report can be triggered to tell a manager when certain inventory items fall below a specified level, when a customer's charges reach a credit limit, or when sales of products fall outside the normal ranges. Exception reports save human time by permitting managers to concentrate their attentions on the important exceptions. Computer time and printer paper are also saved since there's no need to print lengthy reports that would merely show that most operating data fall within the normal limits.

External output is information that will be used outside the organization. In sequential processing applications, this output can be the invoices and statements sent to customers, the checks issued to employees and suppliers, or the income-tax withholding forms sent to the Internal Revenue Service. These and other output documents issued by the organization must often be prepared on designated forms. Colorful trademarks and other attractive symbols are often preprinted on many of these forms by the paper suppliers to present a favorable image of the organization.

Output from Direct-Access Processing. As you know from Chapter 6, online terminals are used in direct-access processing applications to create a direct interactive relationship between people and computers. People use terminals to enter data into computer systems and to request and receive information from the systems. When online teleprinters, point-of-sale terminals, or financial transaction terminals are used, a computer often responds with a *printed output* produced by the terminal. This output can be intended solely for the use of the members of an organization. For example, the output sent to a portable teleprinter in response to a salesperson's inquiry about the availability of parts can include part code numbers that a customer wouldn't understand.

But the printed response sent to a terminal may also be external output intended for the use of people outside the organization. Such a response, of course, should not include unidentified code numbers. For example, the itemized sales receipt printed by a point-of-sale terminal and given to a customer should furnish clearly worded item descriptions rather than item code numbers. It's important for online systems to be "user-friendly" to those who receive the computer output (see Figure 8-4).

Visual display terminals are the most popular devices used today to receive output during direct-access processing (see Figure 8-5). Output messages and processed information are displayed on the screen of a CRT. You saw in Chapter 6 how an alphanumeric display station on a shop floor was used to update production records. A shop employee carried on a "conversation" with the computer program by supplying data in response to the output messages shown on the screen. The employee merely keyed in the correct response

```
ONE-STOP SHOPPING AT
PATHMARK OF SHIRLEY 646

  PM-NAPKINS      .35 T
  ARMOUR LARD     .69
  NF BTH TISS     .31 T
  NF BTH TISS     .31 T
  LI DISH DET    1.65 T
  DOMINO SUGAR   1.29
  DANNON YOGUR    .79
  CHOCKFULLNUT   1.79
  EGGS-LARGE     1.05
  PM BUTTER      1.15
  AX SALT-FREE   1.09
  AX SALT-FREE   1.09
  DM ICE CREAM   2.49
  TAX DUE         .19
  TOTAL         14.24

  CSH TEND      20.00
  CHG DUE        5.76

  TAX PAID        .19
9/04/81 20:54      165
```

[handwritten: camera or printing device tied to it]

Figure 8-4 Cash register tapes have become user-friendly by itemizing purchases for the customer.

Figure 8-5 Visual display terminals create a direct, interactive relationship between people and computers. (Courtesy Hewlett-Packard)

215

number from a menu of displayed messages. Graphic display terminals can also be used to produce output in the form of graphs, maps, and drawings. Information displayed on CRT screens is often printed if permanent copies are needed.

As you know, word processing operators can prepare letters by calling up stored messages, adding appropriate text, and then printing the information shown on their screens. Although most displayed messages and information are intended for internal use, some screen output is used by people who aren't members of the organization. Automated teller machines, for example, often display instructions to help bank customers carry out transactions.

In addition to presenting output information from direct-access processing in a printed or visual display format, computer systems can also prepare *voice responses* to inquiries. Voice response techniques are routinely used to supply internal and external output information.

Let's now take a closer look at the media and devices mentioned in this section that are used to produce computer output.

PUNCHED PAPER AND MAGNETIC MEDIA OUTPUT

Punched cards, punched paper tape, magnetic tape, and portable magnetic disks are **triple-purpose media.** In addition to being used for *data entry* and *secondary storage* purposes, they also receive information *output* from the CPU. Sequentially processed files are kept on these media and are periodically updated. Figure 8-6 repeats an application you first met in Chapter 2. The records stored on an old master file are read into the CPU along with recent transaction data. Old file records are updated by the recent transactions, a new file record is created, and these updated records are written as output on punched paper or magnetic media. Various output documents such as detail and summary reports, invoices, and checks are usually printed at the same time. At a later date, the output information written on the new master file will be reentered into the computer and updated by subsequent transactions.

Since we've already considered punched paper and magnetic media and devices in connection with their data entry and secondary storage functions, we don't need to spend much more time on them here. The same *tape drives* and *disk drives* used to read the data on magnetic media into the CPU are also used to write output information on magnetic tapes and disks (see Figure 8-7). During input, read/write heads are used to read data into the CPU; during output, the heads are used to write information from the CPU.

When output is recorded on punched paper media, however, additional equipment is required. Blank cards or paper tape are loaded on machines that can punch holes. On command from the computer program, the blank media are moved to punch stations where processed information is received. The machines then automatically punch and verify the holes. Punched cards are moved to a stacker, and a take-up reel may be used to receive punched tape. Punched paper output speeds are very slow because of the electromechanical movement of the die punches. But card punches have proven useful in produc-

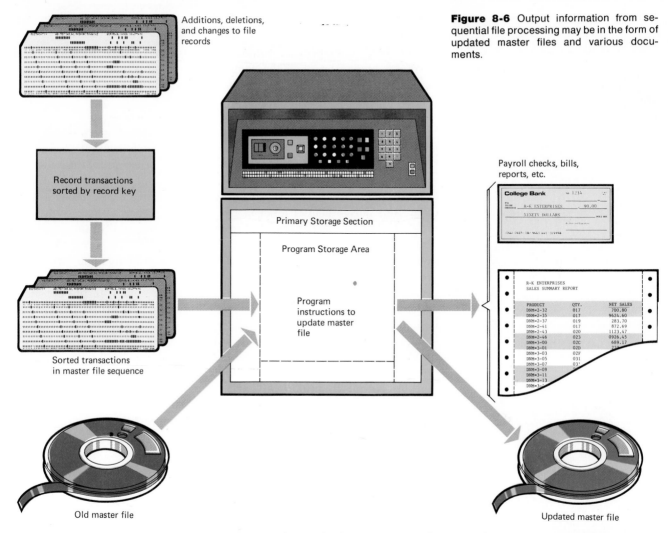

Additions, deletions, and changes to file records

Record transactions sorted by record key

Sorted transactions in master file sequence

Old master file

Primary Storage Section

Program Storage Area

Program instructions to update master file

Figure 8-6 Output information from sequential file processing may be in the form of updated master files and various documents.

Payroll checks, bills, reports, etc.

College Bank

Updated master file

ing documents that are later reentered into processing operations. An example of such a **turnaround application** is the billing approach still used by some organizations. Bills sent to customers are in the form of cards prepared as computer output. Appropriate data are punched into each card. When all or a part of the card is returned by the customer with the payment, the card supplies input data that requires no keypunching. Many organizations that formerly used this billing approach now find it more economical to print the bills with characters that can be read later by optical scanners.

PRINTED AND FILMED OUTPUT

When the output of sequential processing applications is to be used by people rather than reentered into computers, it's usually printed or filmed. Of course, as we've seen, printed output is also common in direct-access processing applications.

Figure 8-7 During output operations, tape drive read/write heads are used to write information from the CPU. (Photo reprinted by permission of Nixdorf Computer Corporation, Burlington, Mass.)

Printed Output

Printers are the primary output devices used to prepare permanent documents for human use, and the competition among printer manufacturers is fierce. The printers being produced today can generally be classified by how they print and by how fast they operate.

Character (or Serial) Printers. **Character (serial) printers** are one-character-at-a-time devices used with microcomputers, minicomputers, and tele-printer terminals for low-volume printing jobs. The techniques used to print characters vary widely. **Impact methods** use the familiar typewriter approach of pressing a typeface against paper and inked ribbon. Serial impact printers often use a **daisy-wheel** or a **dot-matrix** printing mechanism (see Figure 8-8).

In the daisy-wheel approach (Figure 8-9a), each "petal" of the wheel has a character embossed on it. A motor spins the wheel at a rapid rate. When the desired character spins to the correct position, a print hammer strikes it to produce the output. (Some printers substitute print "thimbles" or "cups" for print wheels, but their operation is essentially the same.) In the dot-matrix approach (Figure 8-9b), an arrangement of tiny hammers strike to produce the desired characters. Each hammer prints a small dot on the paper. Thus, the letter E would be formed as shown in Figure 8-9b.

Dot-matrix printers are usually faster than daisy-wheel devices and are often less expensive, but their print quality isn't as good. Thus, some organizations use dot-matrix printers for internal reports and daisy-wheel devices for the external output generated by word processing and other systems. All impact printers can produce multiple copies by using carbon paper or its equivalent.

There are also **nonimpact** character printers available that use thermal, electrostatic, chemical, and inkjet technologies. With the **inkjet** approach, for example, droplets of ink are electrically charged after leaving a nozzle (Figure 8-9c). The droplets are then guided to the proper position on the paper by electrically charged deflection plates. The print quality is good because the character is formed by dozens of tiny ink dots. If a droplet isn't needed for the particular character being formed, it's recycled back to the input jet. Of course, inkjet and other nonimpact printers can't produce multiple copies of a document in a single printing.

High-Speed Impact Line Printers. **High-speed line printers** use impact methods to produce *line-at-a-time* printed output. They typically use rapidly moving *chains* or *bands* of print characters or some form of a print *drum* to print lines of information on paper (see Figure 8-10). From 300 to over 2,000 lines can be printed each minute depending on the printer used. Figure 8-11a illustrates the concept of a **print chain.** The links in the chain are engraved character-printing slugs. The chain moves at a rapid speed past the printing positions. Hammers behind the paper are timed to force the paper against the proper print slugs. A **band printer** (Figure 8-11b) is similar in operation to a chain printer. But instead of using a print chain, a band printer has a rotating

Figure 8-8 Print elements for (*top*) daisy-wheel and (*bottom*) dot-matrix character printers. (Photos supplied by Dataproducts Corporation, Woodland Hills, Calif.)

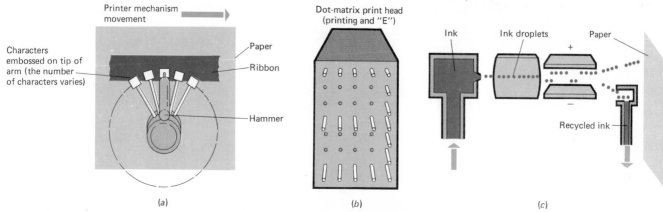

Figure 8-9 Some of the mechanisms used in character printers. (*a*) The daisy-wheel approach. Daisy print wheels are easily removed and replaced with wheels having different type fonts. The speed of a daisy-wheel printer is usually in the 25 to 60 characters-per-second (cps) range. (*b*) The dot-matrix approach. Dot-matrix printer speeds usually range between 30 and 350 cps. A 5-by-7 matrix is shown here, but other sizes are used. (*c*) The inkjet approach. Inkjet printer speeds are around 90 cps.

scalloped steel print band. Hammers force the paper against the proper print characters. Speeds of up to 2,000 lines per minute are also possible with band printers.

In the **drum printer,** raised characters extend the length of the drum (Figure 8-11*c*). There are as many bands of type as there are printing positions. Each band contains all the possible characters. The drum rotates rapidly, and

Figure 8-10 A scalloped steel print band (*left*) is used in a high-speed impact band printer (*middle*). The print drum (*right*) used in a high-speed drum printer. (Photos supplied by Dataproducts Corporation, Woodland Hills, Calif.)

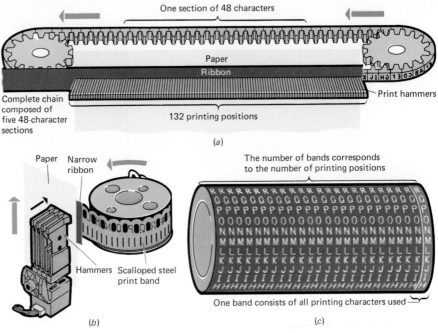

One section of 48 characters

Paper

Ribbon

Complete chain
composed of
five 48-character
sections

Print hammers

132 printing positions

(a)

Paper   Narrow
ribbon

The number of bands corresponds
to the number of printing positions

Hammers   Scalloped steel
print band

One band consists of all printing characters used

(b)   (c)

Figure 8-11 Some of the mechanisms used with impact line printers. (a) The print chain approach. Print hammers are located at each print position. Speeds of over 2,000 lines per minute are reached with chain printers. (b) The bank printer approach. Similar in operation to a chain printer, a band or belt printer uses a rotating scalloped steel print band rather than a print chain. The print bands can be removed and replaced with bands using different type fonts. Speeds of up to 2,000 lines per minute are possible. (c) The print drum approach. Print hammers are located opposite each print band. Speeds of over 2,000 lines per minute are possible with drum printers.

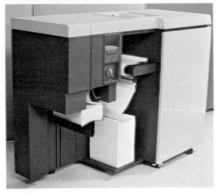

Figure 8-12 A high-speed laser page printer. (Courtesy of Hewlett-Packard)

one revolution is required to print each line. A fast-acting hammer opposite each band strikes the paper against the proper character as it passes. Thus, in one rotation, hammers of several positions may "fire" when the A row appears, several others may strike to imprint D's, etc. At the end of the rotation, the line has been printed.

High-Speed Nonimpact Page Printers. **High-speed page printers** are devices which can produce documents at speeds of over 20,000 lines per minute (see Figure 8-12). (That's fast enough to print this entire book in about one minute!) Electronics, xerography, lasers, and other technologies have made these high-volume systems possible. Each page produced on these printers is an original since there are no carbon copies. Although their six-figure cost will exceed the cost of many computer installations, these printers can be economical when hundreds of thousands of pages are printed each month. The costs of special report forms can also be reduced since these devices can print both the form layout and the form contents at the same time.

Filmed Output

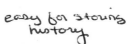

We've seen that some output documents such as invoices, accounts payable checks, and payroll checks are destined for external use. These documents must be prepared on paper. Other documents such as detailed reports are used internally, are examined briefly, and are then often filed away for possible future reference. The internal documents can be printed on paper or they can be prepared on film.

Computer-output-to-microfilm (COM) technology is used to record computer output information as microscopic filmed images. The information that can be printed on a page of paper can be reduced in size 48 or more times and recorded on a sheet or roll of microfilm. A 4-by-6-inch sheet of film is called a **microfiche.** (Fiche is a French word meaning "card," and is pronounced "fish" as in "fiche or cut byte.") A typical microfiche reproduces up to 270 page-sized images, but some ultrafiche systems can store 1,000 standard pages in the same space. Rolls of 16- and 35-millimeter film packaged in cartridges are also used.

The COM approach is shown in Figure 8-13. Output information may be read onto magnetic tape and then, in an offline operation, entered on film by a **microfilm recorder.** Or, the recorder may receive the information directly from the CPU. Most recorders project the characters of output information onto the screen of a CRT. A high-speed camera then takes a picture of the displayed information at speeds of up to 32,000 lines per minute. In some systems, the recorder processes the film from the camera; in other systems, a separate automated film developer is used. Film duplicators can make as many copies of the developed film as needed.

The information on the sheets or rolls of film is read by users from the screens of small desk-top **microfilm viewing stations.** In some COM systems, users must locate and then manually search through the film cartridge or card to find the needed information. In other COM systems, however, a **computer-assisted retrieval (CAR)** approach is used. Each microfilmed document is as-

easy for storing history

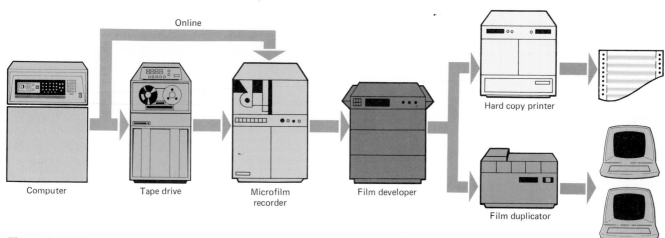

Figure 8-13 The computer-output-to-microfilm (COM) approach.

Online

Computer

Tape drive

Microfilm recorder

Film developer

Hard copy printer

Film duplicator

Microfilm viewing stations

signed an "address" that gives its cartridge or fiche drawer location. An index of document locations is stored in the memory of a small computer connected to the viewer stations. To retrieve a document, a user calls up this index, quickly locates the correct film magazine, and waits a few seconds for the viewing station to pick out the correct document from the thousands of pages that may be recorded on the film. If a paper copy of the document is needed, a reader-printer is used to provide full-size prints. This may be the first time the output information has been placed on paper (see Figure 8-14).

Banking and insurance companies, government agencies, public utilities, and many other types of organizations are regular users of COM. The *advantages of COM* are:

▋ *Relatively fast output.* A COM system can film information 10 to 20 times faster than a high-speed impact printer can print it. Thus, a single COM recorder can do the work of a dozen line printers.

▋ *Relatively low film costs.* The cost of the paper needed to print a 1,000-page, three-part report is about 30 times greater than the cost of the film needed to do the same job. Also, since a 1-ounce microfiche can hold the equivalent of 10 pounds of computer paper, the mailing and storage costs of filmed documents are much less than paper documents.

However, some possible *COM disadvantages* are:

▋ *Relatively high system costs.* A COM recorder is an expensive piece of equipment. To justify the cost, a high-volume workload is usually needed.

▋ *The limitations of film.* People who like to write notes on the margins of printed reports may feel uncomfortable when using a COM system. Also, the loss or misplacement of a few microfiche can create a significant gap in an organization's records.

DISPLAYED OUTPUT, COMPUTER GRAPHICS, AND VOICE RESPONSE

The output from direct-access processing usually comes from character printers or from terminals with visual display screens. Chapter 6 showed you that the keyboard on a visual display terminal is used to enter data into the CPU, and the screen is used to display output information. Computer-prepared voice responses are also used to reply to inquiries entered from online terminals.

Displayed Output and Computer Graphics

Alphanumeric Terminal Output. A majority of the visual terminals in use today are **alphanumeric display devices** that are used only to enter data and receive output in the form of letters, numbers, and special characters. The

Figure 8-14 A computer-assisted retrieval system. (Photo courtesy 3M Micrographic Products Division)

number of characters that can be shown at any one time varies among terminals. A frequently used display format consists of 24 lines with up to 80 characters on a line. A maximum of 1,920 characters can thus be displayed. Microcomputer terminals often have less capacity. For example, a 16-line-by-64-characters/line format is used in some popular systems. Some microcomputer systems will display only uppercase letters. A number of uses for alphanumeric display devices were discussed in Chapter 6. By providing a window into a computer's data base, a terminal can quickly display information in response to operator inquiries.

Graphic Terminal Output. A study made by a computer manufacturer indicates that people communicate with words at a rate of 1,200 per minute. When pictures are used, however, the rate of comprehension leaps. Maybe the old saying that one picture is worth a thousand words understated the true ratio! Graphs, charts, maps, and other visual presentations prepared from pages of statistical data are better able to capture and hold the interest of a user. Data showing the relationships, changes, and trends that are often buried in piles of alphanumeric reports can be highlighted with a few graphic presentations. Although a loss of precision may result when tabular information is presented in graphic form, this is usually not a problem.

You'll recall from Chapter 6 how **graphic display terminals** are used by designers, engineers, and architects to display preliminary sketches. Computers can be programmed to analyze the sketches and report on certain characteristics. Designers can then interact with their computers to produce finished drawings. A booming market for graphic terminals has also developed in business offices. Using alphanumeric data as input, managers can create colorful and informative pictures on the screens of their terminals. After design drawings or business graphic presentations have been displayed on a screen to a user's satisfaction, permanent copies can be prepared using the following graphics devices:

▍ *Printers.* A **dot-matrix printer/plotter** can produce effective pictures through its ability to generate 200 lines of tiny dots on an inch of paper. Nonimpact **electrostatic printer/plotters** using processes similar to photocopying are also available.

▍ *Plotters.* In addition to dot-matrix and electrostatic devices, plotters are also available that use pen or inkjet approaches. **Pen plotters** use either drum or flat-bed paper holders (see Figure 8-15). When a **drum device** is used, the paper is placed over a drum that rotates back and forth to produce an up-and-down motion. A carriage holding one or more pens is mounted horizontally across the drum, and the pen(s) can move along this carriage to produce motion across the paper. Under computer control, the carriage and drum movements act together to produce a pic-

Figure 8-15 The pen plotter shown here can be connected to a variety of computers to produce high-quality precision technical graphics. (Courtesy of Hewlett-Packard)

ture. When several pens are mounted on a carriage, each pen can be filled with a different ink color. Since each pen is program-selectable, the plotter has the ability to produce color pictures. When a **flat-bed** (table) **plotter** is used, the paper doesn't move and the pen-holding mechanism must provide all the motion. **Inkjet plotters** are able to produce large drawings containing many colors. The paper is again placed on a drum, and jets with different-colored ink are mounted on a carriage. The computer program controls the color and amount of ink placed on the paper.

Film Recorders. The screen of the CRT can be photographed with black and white or color film to produce prints and 35-millimeter slides. Videotape copies can also be made.

Voice Response

Just as a voice recognition system will allow you to talk to a computer, so, too, will a **voice response system** permit a computer to talk back to you (see Figure 8-16. In fact, a computer has probably "talked" to you many times. For example, when you try to call a telephone number that has been changed, a signal is sent to a telephone company computer. You then hear: "The number you have dialed has been changed to 9-2-6-2-5-6-3." The first part of this

Figure 8-16 An audio-response unit used in a voice response system. (Courtesy National Semiconductor)

response is a conventional recording, but the new number is given in the "voice" of the computer's audio-response unit. This voice may be choppy and unnatural, but it's easily understood.

Many other organizations use audio-response systems to respond to human inquiries that are transmitted over telephone lines to a central computer. All the sounds needed to process the possible inquiries are prerecorded on a storage medium. Each sound is given a code. When inquiries are received, the processor follows a set of rules to create a reply message in a coded form. This coded message is then transmitted to an audio-response device, which assembles the sounds in the proper sequence and transmits the audio message back to the station requesting the information.

Audio-response techniques, combined with briefcase-sized terminals, turn every telephone into a potential computer I/O device. A traveling engineer, for example, can check on a project's status by keying an inquiry directly into the home-office computer. A computer-compiled audio response then gives the engineer the necessary output information. Similarly, construction personnel can enter and receive labor, material, and equipment information.

Audio-response systems can be inexpensive. Many are available for use with personal microcomputers. Such a system is also used in Texas Instruments' Speak & Spell product to teach children to spell and pronounce over 200 basic words. A single integrated circuit chip costing a few dollars synthesizes the selected sounds that are used for audio response. Thus, the spoken word in machine-usable form is now very cheap—cheap enough, in fact, to be installed in your future microwave oven or washing machine if you want talking appliances.

 **Feedback and Review 8-1**

You've learned in this chapter that people in many organizations need computer output to carry out planning, organizing, and controlling functions. The output from sequential processing is usually written on punched paper or magnetic media, on microfilm, or on printer paper. Printed detail, summary, and/or exception reports are prepared for decision makers. Teleprinter terminals receive and print the output from direct-access processing in many applications. However, visual display terminals are the most popular devices used today to directly receive alphanumeric and/or graphic output. The use of computer graphics is growing rapidly. Graphic output can be reproduced by plotters and film recorders. Systems are also available to permit computers to send back voice responses to direct human inquiries.

To test and reinforce your understanding of the material in this chapter, rearrange the scrambled words to spell out the correct word for the space indicated in the following sentences:

1. Good output information in the hands of those who can effectively use it will support good decisions; good decisions will lead to the effective performance of tasks; and effective task performance will lead to success in reaching an organization's _____ . Ⓐ Ⓛ Ⓖ Ⓞ Ⓢ

2. _____ output is information that's intended for use solely within an organization, while external output is information that will be used outside the organization. Ⓣ Ⓔ Ⓘ Ⓝ Ⓡ Ⓛ Ⓝ Ⓐ

3. A _____ report condenses detailed data to help decision makers spot patterns and trends. Ⓜ Ⓐ Ⓡ Ⓨ Ⓢ Ⓤ Ⓜ

4. _____ reports are triggered to supply information only when operating data fall outside specified limits. Ⓒ Ⓔ Ⓔ Ⓧ Ⓞ Ⓝ Ⓟ Ⓣ Ⓘ

5. _____ output is used in both sequential and direct-access processing applications. Ⓣ Ⓓ Ⓟ Ⓡ Ⓔ Ⓘ Ⓝ

6. Punched cards, magnetic tape, and portable magnetic disks are _____ -purpose media. Ⓘ Ⓟ Ⓣ Ⓡ Ⓛ Ⓔ

7. _____ are the primary output devices used to prepare permanent documents for human use. Ⓘ Ⓔ Ⓟ Ⓡ Ⓡ Ⓢ Ⓝ Ⓣ

8. Unlike inkjet printers, daisy-wheel and dot-matrix printers are character-at-a-time devices that use _____ methods to produce printed characters. Ⓟ Ⓐ Ⓘ Ⓒ Ⓣ Ⓜ

9. High-speed impact line printers typically use rapidly moving chains or bands of print characters or some form of a print _____ to print lines of information on paper. Ⓓ Ⓤ Ⓜ Ⓡ

10. High-speed nonimpact _____ printers are fast enough to print this entire book in about one minute. Ⓐ Ⓟ Ⓔ Ⓖ

11. After COM technology is used to record computer output as microscopic filmed images, these images can be displayed on the screens of desk-top _____ stations. Ⓘ Ⓥ Ⓝ Ⓖ Ⓔ Ⓦ Ⓘ

12. Although a single microfilm recorder can do the work of a dozen line printers, and the cost of the film needed to record large documents is much less than the paper that would be required, a _____ -volume workload is usually needed to justify the cost of a recorder. Ⓗ Ⓗ Ⓘ Ⓖ

13. _____ plotters are computer graphics devices that use either drum or flat-bed paper holders. Ⓔ Ⓟ Ⓝ

14. Some organizations use _____-response systems that directly respond to human inquries that are transmitted to a central computer over telephone lines. Ⓘ Ⓒ Ⓥ Ⓞ Ⓔ

Looking Back

1. Computer output is vital for decision makers who must perform planning, organizing, and controlling functions in order to achieve goals. Output can be grouped into internal and external categories. Internal output is information that's intended for use within an organization, while external output is meant for outside use. In sequential processing applications, internal output can be written on punched paper or magnetic media, printed on paper, or recorded on microfilm. Different types of reports (detail, summary, exception) are printed or filmed to meet the needs of decision makers. Of course, sequential processing also generates invoices, checks, and other printed documents that are sent outside an organization.

2. Online terminals are used to request and receive output information during direct-access processing applications. Printed output is produced by teleprinter, point-of-sale, and financial transaction terminals. Depending on the application, this printed output is used by people both within and outside an organization. Internal and external output is also shown on the screens of visual display terminals during direct-access processing.

3. Punched cards, punched paper tape, magnetic tape, and portable magnetic disks are triple-purpose media. That is, they are used for data entry, secondary storage, and information output purposes. Updated records produced as output during the processing of sequentially organized files are written on these media. At a later time, this output will be reentered into computers and updated by the next batch of transactions.

4. Printers are the primary output devices used to prepare permanent documents for human use. Impact or nonimpact character-at-a-time printers are used for low-volume printing jobs. When impact mechanisms are used, a typeface strikes against paper and inked ribbon to create a character. Daisy-wheel and dot-matrix devices are examples of serial impact printers. Nonimpact printers use thermal, electrostatic, chemical, and inkjet technologies to produce their output. High-speed impact line printers typically use rapidly moving chains or bands of print characters, or some form of print drum, to print at speeds that can exceed 2,000 lines per minute. And even faster nonimpact page printers use xerography, lasers, and other technologies to produce output at speeds that can exceed 20,000 lines/minute.

5. Internal documents that are examined briefly and then filed away for possible future reference are sometimes recorded on film by a computer-output-to-microfilm process. Hundreds of page-size images can be recorded on a single 4-by-6-inch microfiche. Output information from the CPU can be sent directly to a microfilm recorder and entered on film, or the information can be written on magnetic tape and transmitted to the recorder at a later time. Once information has been placed on film, it can be recovered by people using desk-top viewing stations and manual search or computer-assisted retrieval techniques. Full-sized documents can be printed from the filmed images. A COM system is faster than a printing system, and film costs much less than an equivalent amount of paper. But a high-volume workload is a must to realize the significant savings that are possible.

6. Visual display terminals are used to receive alphanumeric and graphic output information. A majority of these terminals in use today are used only for alphanumeric purposes, but a booming market has now developed for terminals with graphic capabilities. In addition to displaying design drawings, graphic terminals are also used extensively by decision makers. The relationships, changes, and trends that often lie buried in piles of alphanumeric reports are being highlighted through the use of graphs, charts, maps, and other visual presentations. And when graphic presentations are displayed on a screen to a user's satisfaction, permanent copies can be prepared using printers, plotters, and film recorders.

7. Voice response systems permit computers to talk back to people. In many cases, such a system is used to respond directly to human inquiries that are transmitted to a central computer over telephone lines. The inquiries are usually keyed into the system from portable terminals attached to telephones. The output responses are then generated by the system and transmitted back over the telephone to users.

KEY TERMS AND CONCEPTS

You should now be able to define and use the following terms and concepts (the numbers shown indicate the pages where the terms and concepts are first mentioned):

internal output 213
detailed reports 213
summary report 214
computer graphic output 214
exception reports 214
external output 214
visual display 215
triple-purpose media 216
turnaround application 217
character (serial) printers 218
impact methods 218
daisy-wheel printer 218

dot-matrix printer 218
nonimpact printer 218
inkjet printer 218
high-speed line printers 218
print chain 218
band printer 218
drum printer 219
high-speed page printers 220
computer-output-to-microfilm (COM) 221
microfiche 221
microfilm recorder 221

microfilm viewing stations 221
computer-assisted retrieval (CAR) 221
alphanumeric display devices 222
graphic display terminals 224
dot-matrix printer/plotter 224
electrostatic printer/plotters 224
pen plotters 224
drum device 224
flat-bed plotter 225
inkjet plotters 225
voice response system 225

TOPICS FOR REVIEW AND DISCUSSION

1. (*a*) How can computer output benefit the users of personal computers? (*b*) Why is computer output likely to be needed by decision makers in most organizations?

2. (*a*) What's the difference between internal and external output? (*b*) What should a system designer consider when planning the type of output to be produced by a computer?

3. Identify and discuss the three types of output reports mentioned in this chapter.

4. (*a*) Identify four output devices used in sequential-processing applications. (*b*) Identify four output devices used in direct-access processing.

5. Why is computer output entered on punched paper and magnetic media?

6. (*a*) What is a "turnaround" application? (*b*) Have you ever been involved in such an application?

7. (*a*) What's an impact printer? (*b*) Identify and discuss two types of impact character printers. (*c*) Identify and discuss three types of impact line printers.

8. (*a*) What's a nonimpact printer? (*b*) Identify and discuss the inkjet approach to nonimpact printing.

9. (*a*) What type of internal documents are typically placed on microfilm? (*b*) How is computer output placed on microfilm? (*c*) How are microfilm images retrieved?

10. Identify and discuss the advantages and limitations of COM.

11. (*a*) What's the display format of a CRT screen available to you? (*b*) What's the maximum number of characters that can be displayed?

12. Why has the use of computer graphics become so popular in recent years?

13. How can pictures displayed on a screen be permanently preserved?

14. How are voice response systems used?

ANSWERS TO FEEDBACK AND REVIEW SECTION

8-1

1. goals
2. internal
3. summary
4. exception
5. printed
6. triple
7. printers
8. impact
9. drum
10. page
11. viewing
12. high
13. pen
14. voice

Using Computer Graphics in Business
From Numbers to Pictures to People

The use of computer graphics for business purposes has been neatly summed up by David Friend of Computer Pictures Corporation: "The underlying principle is this: Business runs on numbers. People run best on pictures. The job of an information graphics system is to turn numbers into usable pictures."

Business managers produce "products" in the form of decisions. Computer graphics help managers produce better decisions by helping them visualize relationships—contrasts, trends, comparisons—the stuff of which decisions are made. Computer graphics show relationships through pie charts, bar charts, graphs, three-dimensional or exploded images. Up until the early 1980s most business graphics were produced by large and medium-sized computers with sophisticated software. Now, however, software producers are delivering packages that will enable personal microcomputers to produce high-quality, high-resolution graphics for business use.

Coloring Board, a color graphics program for the Apple II, costs $60 and allows users to create, erase and change, store, and retrieve graphics employing both

Figure 8-A High-quality graphics from a microcomputer system. (Courtesy IBM)

Figure 8-B A fanciful graphic design produced by a sophisticated system. (Courtesy of Melvin L. Prueitt, Los Alamos National Laboratory, under contract to the Department of Energy)

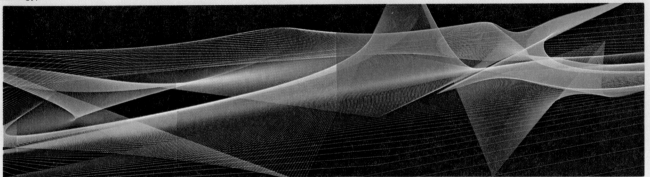

drawings and alphanumerics. Coloring Board offers six colors, automatic generation of arcs, circles, squares, rectangles, ellipses, triangles, and other shapes, as well as maps of the United States and the world.

With software like Coloring Board, users can ask their small business computers to produce, for example, brightly colored charts showing sales of a product by district, region, or state. Costs for producing that product can be broken down on a multicolored pie chart.

The old "send it to the art department" method of producing color graphics for decision-making help or for presentations has become archaic. Today's interactive computer graphics systems enable users to manipulate images on a CRT screen (soft copy) until they are ready to produce hard copy—for example, a 35 mm slide.

The old saw that "A picture is worth a thousand words" is in no danger of extinction from computer graphics.

—Sources of data: Alan Rockhold, "Computer Graphics as a Business Tool," *Infosystems,* November 1981, pp. 68–71; Stan Miastkowski and Rachael Wrege, "Computer Graphics," *Popular Computing,* December 1981, pp. 70–75.

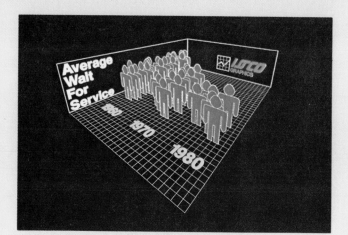

The sophisticated charts and maps on these pages provide a sampling of the possibilities computer graphics hold for the business user. (Reprinted with permission from ISSCO, San Diego, Calif.)

Far right, top: An abstract graphic design. (Courtesy of Melvin L. Prueitt, Los Alamos National Laboratory, under contract to the Department of Energy)

Far right, bottom: The Videoprint system turns computer-generated images into high-quality photographic prints. (Courtesy Image Resource Corporation)

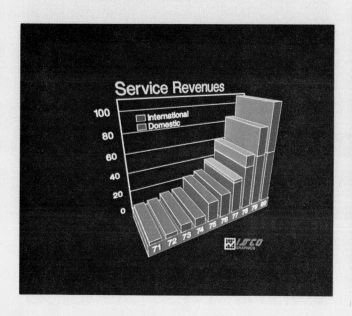

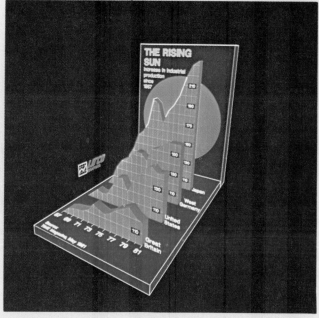

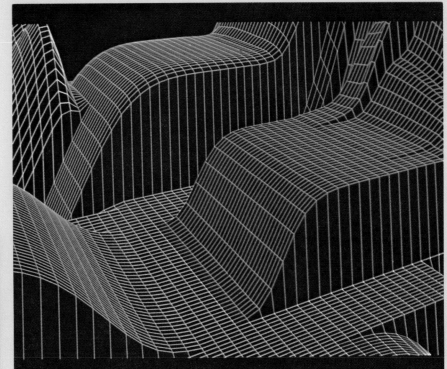

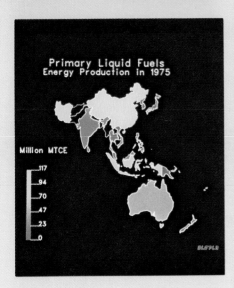

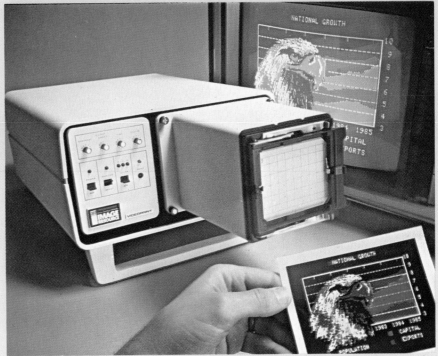

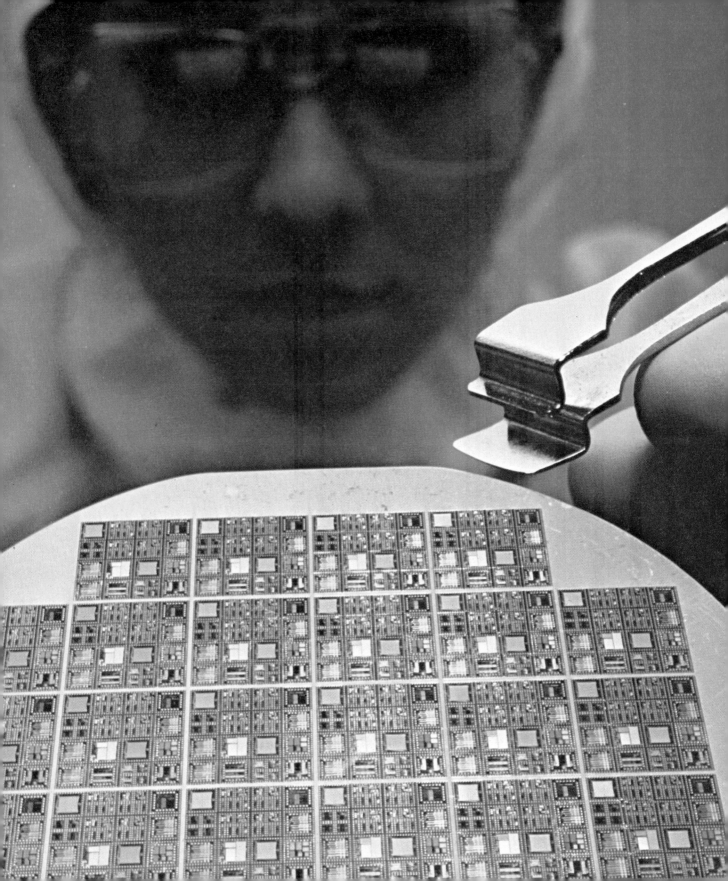

chapter 9

Micros, Minis, Mainframes, and "Monsters"

MICROPROCESSING POWER

To understand the whole microelectronic phenomenon and its potential consequences, you have to go back to 1969 when the concept of the microprocessor was introduced. That year a thirty-six-year-old electronics engineer named Victor D. Poor began work on a project that had long intrigued him. For years Poor had been involved with the development of special-purpose computers, machines developed for specific and often unique functions. . . . The computer architecture of the day dictated that each new machine boast as much new gadgetry as possible, and the computers coming off the drawing boards were invariably faster and more powerful than their predecessors. Poor felt that much of this effort was for show rather than progress. "People were putting too much into the machines simply for the sake of saying the specifications were improved," he asserts.

Working with another young engineer, Harry Pyle, Poor took an entirely different tack, reverting to the design concepts of the early days of computer development. By concentrating strictly on the bare bones of computer architecture—the computational and logic circuitry—Poor believed he could condense these vital machine innards to the limited confines of the silicon medium.

Poor himself now readily admits he had virtually no inkling of the tremendous potential of the microelectronics technology for which he had laid the foundations. "Mine was a very narrow point of view," he says. "I simply wanted to avoid having to build a processor from the ground up every time there was a dedicated [specialized] function to be performed."

—"Technology Update," *output,* February 1981, p. 26. Reprinted with Permission of Output magazine. Copyright by Technical Publishing Company, a Dun & Bradstreet Company 1981. All rights reserved.

Very high speed integrated circuit chips. (Courtesy Honeywell, Inc.)

Looking Ahead

Earlier chapters in this Hardware Module have given you a general introduction to the CPU and to I/O and storage media and devices. This chapter gives you more specific information about real computer systems. While it's difficult to classify computers purely on the basis of size and computing capabilities, they are arbitrarily grouped here into micro, mini, mainframe, and "monster," or supercomputer categories. There's a section in the chapter which describes each category in detail.

Thus, after studying this chapter, you should be able to:

▌ Explain what micros are and why they were developed, give examples of micros, discuss a few of their hardware/software characteristics, and list some ways they may be used.

▌ Give a definition of a minicomputer, tell why minis were developed, recall examples of minis, outline some of their hardware/software characteristics, and discuss some ways they may be used.

▌ Differentiate between a mainframe and a smaller computer, give examples of mainframe families, and point out some characteristics and uses of mainframe models.

▌ Outline the characteristics of supercomputers that make them different from other machines, and discuss the types of applications for which they are designed.

▌ Understand and use the key terms listed at the end of the chapter.

THE CLASSIFICATION DILEMMA

A fictitious CPU was illustrated in the Background Module and in Chapter 5 to give you an understanding of the capabilities, concepts, and components of a central processor. And specific examples were often missing in the introduction to input, secondary storage, and output media and devices presented in Chapters 6, 7, and 8. The characteristics we've attributed to our "make-believe" CPU are found in most modern computer systems, and these systems all use a varying number of the input, storage, and output devices that we've covered. But no matter how accurately these model computer systems describe reality, they are still make-believe systems. This chapter introduces you to some of the characteristics of real computer systems, ranging in size from the smallest to the largest. Before reading about these systems, though, you should be aware of an unavoidable problem.

The problem is how to *classify* the broad range of available machine sizes and capabilities. Many organizations have central-site computers and "smaller" systems in outlying branches. These systems can be assembled with a wide range of peripheral I/O devices and "add-on" CPU components. Similar variations are also available for the systems individuals buy for personal use. The result is that there's a great overlap in system size, cost, and performance. And computer technology is changing fast. Within a matter of months after a new computer model comes on the market, it's faced with two potential successors. One costs the same and has a much higher performance; the other has the same performance and costs much less. Thus, a recently introduced small system can outperform the large models of a few years ago, and a new microcomputer can do the work of an earlier minicomputer at a much lower cost. This rapid technological pace plays havoc with classification schemes. In fact, if you conducted a survey now among a dozen computer experts, asking each of them to tell you the difference, for example, between minicomputers and mainframe family models, you would likely get a dozen very different answers.

In the pages that follow, we'll classify computers as *micros, minis, mainframe family models,* and *supercomputers.* But you should know that the classifications used here (and anywhere else) are quite arbitrary. As Figure 9-1 indicates, the cost and performance capability of machines in different classifications are likely to overlap. For example, a powerful computer sold as a mini by its maker may have more processing capability (and cost more) than a machine sold as a small mainframe model.

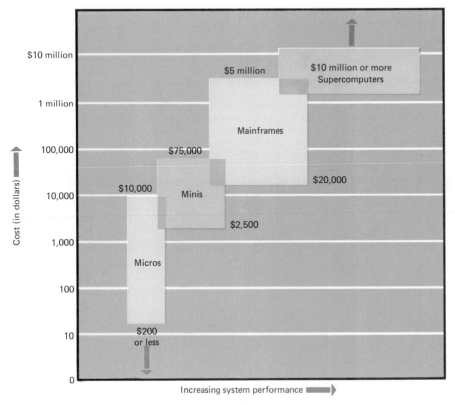

Figure 9-1 Computer systems may be classified into micro, mini, mainframe, and supercomputer ("monster") categories depending on size, cost, and system performance. Any such classification is arbitrary. Since categories overlap, the most powerful systems in one category may exceed the capabilities (and cost) of the least powerful systems in another.

MICROCOMPUTER SYSTEMS

A **microcomputer** is the smallest general-purpose processing system that can execute program instructions to perform a wide variety of tasks. A microcomputer system has all the functional elements found in any larger system. That is, it's organized to perform the input, storage, arithmetic-logic, control, and output functions. Although some complete microcomputer CPUs are packaged on a *single* silicon chip (Figure 9-2), most micro CPUs are larger and employ *several* chips. A **microprocessor chip,** for example, performs the arithmetic-logic and control functions (see Figure 9-3). Several *random-access memory (RAM) chips* are available for operator use as needed and are employed to handle the primary storage function. And additional *read-only memory (ROM) chips* may be used to permanently store preprogrammed data or instructions.

Most microcomputers are self-contained units which are light enough to be moved easily. They are designed to be used by one person at a time; that is, they are single-user-oriented. In addition to the CPU, the typical micro has an operator keyboard for input. Magnetic tape cassette players and/or floppy disk drives are used to enter data and programs and to receive processed output. Small magnetic tapes and floppy disks are used for offline secondary storage, and small rigid disk drives employing Winchester technology are available to provide a considerable amount of online secondary storage. A visual display screen and/or a character printer is used to prepare output in a humanly readable form.

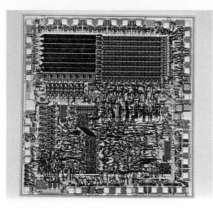

Figure 9-2 An 8-bit microcomputer, complete on one silicon chip. (Courtesy Intel Corporation)

Figure 9-3 (*left*) Zilog's Z80 microprocessor chips shown in various stages of production. Dozens of identical chips are formed by photographic and chemical processes on polished wafers of silicon like the one shown in the background. A diamond cutter is used to separate the chips. A tested chip is then externally wired and sealed in the packaged form shown in the foreground. (*right*) The size of a microprocessor chip can be seen relative to a small pearl ring. (Photos reproduced by permission of © 1980 Zilog, Inc. These photographs shall not be reproduced without the written consent of Zilog, Inc. Zilog and Z80 are trademarks of Zilog, Inc., with whom the publisher is not associated.)

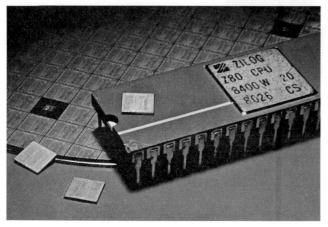

Why Micros Were Developed

You saw in the opening vignette that for several years prior to 1969, Victor Poor, a Datapoint Corporation electronics engineer, had been working on the design and development of special-purpose computers. Each time a custom-designed device was needed, Poor and other engineers started the design effort with a blank sheet of paper. Designing each processor from scratch seemed to Poor to be a big waste of time. Instead, he reasoned, if the basic arithmetic-logic and control elements of a computer could be placed on a single silicon chip, the chip could be mass produced and then programmed in different ways to perform the special jobs for which it would be used. So in 1969, Poor and Harry Pyle, another young Datapoint engineer, developed a model of a micro-processor chip. Since Datapoint Corporation used electronic components made by others to build finished computer systems for its customers, Poor took his "chip processor" model to two component manufacturers—Texas Instruments and Intel Corporation—in hopes they would manufacture the chip for Datapoint. No immediate decisions came from these meetings, but the component manufacturers were free to use the microprocessor chip concept at a later time.

And so it was that in the early 1970s, engineers at Intel built the first microprocessor chip for a Japanese maker of desk calculators. At the time, calculators were being built from specialized circuit chips that could perform only a single function. However, this first microprocessor chip could be pro-grammed to perform multiple specialized calculator functions. This chip—the Intel 4004—was very limited in the number of instructions it could execute, and it could manipulate only 4-bit "words" of data at one time.

But it wasn't long before the engineers at Intel and other companies pro-duced more powerful microprocessors that could operate on **8 bits.** This devel-opment, in turn, led to the introduction in 1974 of personal-sized micro systems for the hobbyist market. The first such personal computer was the ALTAIR 8800, which used an 8-bit Intel microprocessor and was originally offered in kit form at a price under $400. The lead article in the January 1975 issue of *Popular Electronics* featured this machine. That article introduced many peo-ple to the beginning of the micro explosion. Later in 1975, the first retail store devoted exclusively to selling and servicing personal microcomputers was opened in Santa Monica, California. There are now thousands of stores selling microcomputers from coast to coast. You can take a closer look at these com-puter retail outlets in the reading found at the end of this chapter. Millions of micro systems produced by dozens of manufacturers have been sold in the last few years, and scores of computer clubs have sprung up since 1975. (The Southern California Computer Club alone has a membership of over 20,000.)

Micro Uses and Applications

Like their larger counterparts, microcomputers are used in *organizations* for data processing and decision-making purposes. Unlike the larger machines found in organizations, however, micro systems are also used by millions of *individuals* for entertainment and other personal applications. And since symbols are manipulated in our society in countless ways, there's virtually no limit to the number of possible applications for an inexpensive, general-purpose symbol manipulator. The Microcomputer Gallery on pages 242 and 243 features a sampling of the varied micro models available and highlights just a few of their uses. Following is a more detailed list.

In your home, for example, a personal microcomputer could be used to:

▌ Entertain you with hundreds of challenging games, many of which have impressive graphic and sound features.

▌ Balance your budget and checkbook.

▌ Monitor your home's energy usage.

▌ Help you learn a new subject, e.g., a foreign language or auto repair techniques.

▌ Help you compose music.

▌ Produce better typed documents through the use of word processing programs.

▌ Analyze your investments and prepare your tax returns.

▌ Compute your installment payments.

▌ Control your household appliances and security devices.

▌ File for easy retrieval and reference such information as recipes, names and addresses, telephone numbers, and dates of birthdays and anniversaries.

▌ Control a device to allow severely handicapped persons to feed themselves even when they have no upper-limb response.

▌ Give you information from the data bases of a number of information retrieval networks. For example, you can call a local telephone number, connect your personal computer to information networks such as *CompuServe* or *The Source* at the other end of the telephone circuit, and access up-to-the-minute information from a wide variety of data banks. The latest news from the Associated Press and *The New York Times,* the most recent stock market quotations, recipes from *Better Homes and Gardens,* all kinds of game programs—these and countless other types of information are instantly available to you. You can also communicate with other network users through the network's *electronic mail* capability. Messages left for you by a distant friend can be displayed and printed on your micro, and your responses can be stored in the network for delivery to your friend's computer.

COMPUTERS IN THE CAR

As automobiles and society become increasingly computerized, car makers are taking a serious look at video screens for future models. Cathode-ray tubes, or CRTs—small TV-like screens—are expected to replace traditional dashboard instrument clusters in some models around the mid-1980s.

"This opens the whole door to using computer technology in your car," says Len Dietch, research and development vice president of Zenith Radio Corp. The Glenview, Ill., company, together with the auto makers, has developed a CRT for use in automobiles.

Computers for engine control systems are already under the hoods of Detroit's new cars, and once they are connected to dashboard CRTs, drivers would have personal computer terminals at the wheel.

The new CRTs would display information in color about travel speed, fuel levels and time of day. At the touch of a button, the screens would also become a trip computer displaying fuel economy data, the number of miles to an empty gasoline tank, elapsed time and map location.

CRTs also could show the results of a checklist of tests done regularly by a computer under the hood. Words flashed across the screen could advise the driver, for example, to add a quart of oil or tune the engine, or they might warn of low tire pressure.

With a programmable calendar, a CRT also could remind drivers of important dates, such as a spouse's birthday. The screens could add other features, too, like an engine tachometer, without the need for another gauge at additional cost and without taking more dashboard space. "When you consider all the other display technologies, this has the best attributes of all of them," says R. J. McMillin, engineering director for General Motors Corp.'s Delco Electronics division.

The technology had to be improved to win Detroit's consideration. Although cathode-ray tubes are used in aircraft and ships, they had to be made more compact for use in cars. So Zenith shortened the electron gun that creates the TV picture by spraying electrons against phosphors on a screen, causing them to glow. A new system was developed to brighten the picture on the screen so it could be read in sunlight.

But the technology is too expensive for today's models, says General Motors and Ford Motor Co. The units cost $65 to $85, depending on volume. That range, Zenith says, compares with $30 for the conventional instrument cluster of today's stripped-down economy car. The cost difference is much less, though, when compared with crowded instrument clusters of option-laden luxury cars, which also include digital displays.

GM's Mr. McMillin is among those who say CRTs could appear in some cars by mid-decade however. "People are becoming used to these features in their home" with home computers, he says, "and will soon want them in their automobiles."

A Microcomputer Gallery

Micros Used in Business

Included among the representative microcomputer systems frequently found in organizations (in alphabetical order) are Altos' ACS-8000 series, Cromemco's Z-2 line, Data General's microNOVA series, Hewlett-Packard's HP-85, North Star's Horizon models, Vector Graphic's MZ, and Wang's PCS-IIA.

This Hewlett-Packard microcomputer—the HP-85—comes complete with a keyboard, a small visual display screen, a small built-in printer, and a magnetic tape cassette unit. Online secondary floppy disk storage drives and large printers are available. An optional graphics plotter is shown here beside the HP-85 computer. The cost of the system pictured here is under $6,000. (Courtesy Hewlett-Packard)

The IBM System/23 is a small-business system that can have two computer workstations with shared file capability. Primary storage capacity ranges up to a maximum of 128K bytes. The price of the system shown is about $10,000. (Courtesy of IBM)

The Texas Instruments Business System 200 features a 64K byte main memory and optional Winchester mass storage capacity. (Courtesy Texas Instruments)

Data General's small-business system. (Reproduced by permission of Data General Corporation, Westboro, Mass.)

The cost of a basic Apple II computer system is under $1,400. Using the Apple, as demonstrated here, is child's play. (Courtesy Apple Computer, Inc.)

Micros for Personal Use

Among the representative micro systems most often selected by individuals for entertainment and personal use are Apple Computer's Apple II and Apple III, Atari's 400 and 800, Commodore's PET, CBM, and VIC lines, Heath's H-89, IBM's Personal Computer, Ohio Scientific's Challenger series, Radio Shack's TRS-80 models, and Texas Instruments' 99/4. The TRS-80 and Apple models account for over half of this market. In addition to these desk-top personal systems, hand-held computers are also available from Panasonic, Quasar, Radio Shack, and Sharp.

The IBM Personal Computer system costs around $5,000 and provides a powerful resource for the home as well as for business use. (Courtesy IBM)

Radio Shack's TRS-80, model II. The CPU is housed in the cabinet in front of the user with the keyboard, visual display, and built-in 8-inch floppy disk drive. The CPU has either 32K or 64K bytes of RAM storage. A dot matrix printer and three additional disk drives (each providing a half-million characters of online secondary storage) are also shown. The price of this configuration is about $8,000. (Courtesy Radio Shack Division, Tandy Corporation)

The 24-pound Osborne 1 microcomputer is completely portable and can even run on batteries if no electricity is available. Priced at $1,795, the Osborne has been called the "Volkswagen of computers." (Courtesy Osborne Computer Corporation)

Micro systems are used in *organizations* to:

▌ Compute payrolls; maintain student, patient, customer, or client records; pay debts and collect receipts; and process the other general accounting tasks that may be required.

▌ Control machine tools and other production equipment in an industrial environment. For example, a micro is used to control the angles produced by a metal-bending machine to very close tolerances.

▌ Control inventory levels of thousands of different items.

▌ Produce personalized letters, mailing labels, and other printed documents through the use of word processing software.

▌ Control water flow and power generation. To illustrate, a micro is used at the Jones Bluff hydroelectric project on the Alabama River by the Army Corps of Engineers to (1) place generators on or off the line by activating large circuit breakers, (2) lower and raise voltage output, and (3) control motors that open or close the dam gates to regulate water flow.

▌ Provide quick answers to "what if" questions. For example, a financial planning program called VisiCalc is used with micro systems to manipulate cost and sales figures to arrive at profit estimates. To plan for the introduction of a new product, a manager often wants to consider what will happen if different raw material prices, labor costs, and sales volume figures are assumed. The assumed figures are fed into a micro and VisiCalc can then manipulate them to project the effect that different values will have on profits. In order to use programs such as VisiCalc, thousands of managers in large companies have bought personal-sized micros and have installed them in their business offices.

▌ Make possible the rapid expansion in the use of computer-assisted instruction techniques in educational institutions of all sizes.

▌ Monitor air temperature, humidity, wetness of crop leaves, and other variables in order to alert crop growers to the need to apply fungicides. Apple growers, for example, can prevent the outbreak of apple scab fungus with this information.

▌ Control desk-top graphic display units that are used (to cite just a few examples) by (1) managers to analyze financial data, (2) engineers for stress analysis and interactive design, (3) clinical laboratory technicians to plot quality-control data, and (4) anthropologists to plot the length of bones of prehistoric humanoids.

This listing of micro applications could go on and on, but you get the idea: The actual and potential uses of micros in the home and in organizations can be as numerous and varied as human ingenuity and imagination will permit.

Some Characteristics of Typical Micros

Virtually all microcomputer CPUs use the byte-addressable storage approach discussed in Chapter 5. At this writing, most existing micro systems are built around a few popular microprocessor chips. These chips—Zilog's Z80, MOS Technology's 6502, Intel's 8080, and Motorola's 6809—can manipulate only a single 8-bit byte at a time. Since larger computers can often retrieve, manipulate, and store 2, 4, or even 8 bytes as a single unit, it's easy to understand why micros are relatively slow by comparison. However, 16-bit microprocessor chips with the flexibility to simultaneously move and manipulate two 8-bit bytes have improved the performance of newer microcomputers. And component makers such as Intel, Hewlett-Packard, and National Semiconductor have now designed 32-bit microprocessor chips that can manipulate 4 bytes at a time (Figure 9-4). These latest chips have the arithmetic-logic and control capabilities of mainframe processors. The Hewlett-Packard design squeezes 450,000 transistors onto a chip about the size of this capital letter "M."

Primary storage in a personal computer is usually at least 4,096 bytes (or 4K, where K equals 2^{10}, or 1,024 bytes). Most micros have from 8K to 64K of RAM capacity. Semiconductor storage is used, and additional RAM chips may usually be added to a basic CPU. System processing and control programs are often permanently stored in the CPU in ROM chips. A wide range of peripheral and "add-on" devices for microcomputers are available from many small vendors. However, a given micro system can't support the number of I/O devices that can be attached to a larger system. A system **interface bus** is a device that serves as the electrical interconnection between the CPU and the various peripherals. Many personal computer manufacturers have adopted the S-100 interface bus originally used in the ALTAIR computer as a standard. But assembling a micro system from components made by different vendors can still be a problem. The ASCII data representation code discussed in Chapter 5 is used in most microcomputers.

Applications programs for micros are usually written in a high-level programming language. The most popular microcomputer language is BASIC (the subject of Chapter 14). Some of the other high-level languages used are Pascal, FORTRAN, and COBOL. Some sophisticated operating-system programs of the type mentioned in Chapter 4 are available for use in micro systems that employ floppy disks for secondary storage. Users of micros also have access to packaged programs prepared by the hundreds of vendors who have entered this software market (Figure 9-5). These programs are often packaged in machine-readable form on tape cassettes, floppy disks, and plug-in ROM modules. Scores of entertainment and educational programs, for example, are available from mail-order vendors and retail computer stores.

MINICOMPUTER SYSTEMS

In spite of the fact that it's almost impossible to define a minicomputer anymore, a definition is needed here. Thus, a **minicomputer** is a small general-purpose machine ranging in price from about $2,500 to $75,000. It can vary in

Figure 9-4 A 32-bit microprocessor chip. (Courtesy Intel Corporation)

Figure 9-5 Packaged programs. (Courtesy Apple Computer, Inc.)

size from a small desk-top model to a unit about the size of a four-drawer file cabinet. To be more specific, while there's a considerable overlap between the most powerful micro systems and the low-end minicomputers in terms of cost and processing capability, the typical mini system will surpass a micro in its storage capacity, speed of arithmetic operations, and ability to support a greater variety of faster-operating peripheral devices. For example, the larger hard-disk units used for online secondary storage in some mini systems have a much greater capacity and are faster operating than the floppy devices used in most micro systems. Unlike a micro system that usually has a single-user orientation, mini systems can be designed to simultaneously handle the processing needs of multiple users. Thus, minis are usually found in organizational settings. They represent only a tiny fraction of the machines selected by individuals for personal computing needs.

Why Minis Were Developed

The development of micros in the early 1970s is a case of history repeating itself. A few years earlier, the first minis were also created for single specialized applications or for a few small general applications. The trend among established computer manufacturers in the early 1960s was to build larger and faster systems that could provide at a central location all the processing power needed by an entire organization. Although this approach served the needs of some organizations well, other organizations were either unable to afford the larger systems or they had specific and specialized applications that a large centralized machine did not process effectively.

A need existed for low-cost *mini*mal computers that could fill the gaps left by the bigger, faster centralized approach. Several innovators recognized this need and formed new firms in the 1960s to produce these minimal machines. The first processors called minicomputers were developed and built by Digital Equipment Corporation (DEC). DEC is now the largest producer of minis. Other major vendors include Hewlett-Packard, Data General, Wang Laboratories, Honeywell, IBM, Datapoint, Texas Instruments, Prime Computer, Tandem Computers, and Perkin-Elmer.

The early minis were used primarily for the processing of a single specialized application—e.g., to monitor instruments and test equipment in a laboratory or to control a machine tool or a flow process in a factory—or they were used to process a number of general applications in a small organization. Since the 1960s, however, minis have improved to such an extent that many are much faster and more powerful than earlier large central systems.

"It was delivered just last week and the antique dealers are hounding us for it already!"

Many Uses for Minis

Sales of minicomputers are currently growing at an annual rate of 35 percent. It's obvious, then, that organizations have found uses for them. We've already seen that minis are being used in specialized ways to control laboratory instruments and machine tools. Dedicated minicomputers are also used to control the data input received from multiple key-to-disk encoding stations (see Figure 6-10, page 161). And the Minicomputer Gallery on pages 248–249 shows minis being used in organizations for general data processing purposes.

Although pages could be filled with examples of minicomputer uses, perhaps one other very important type of application will be enough. In recent years many organizations have decided to establish **distributed data processing (DDP) networks.** Typically, in a DDP network, a larger central **host computer** communicates with, and exercises some control over **satellite,** or **node, processors.** A satellite may, in turn, act as a host to subordinate processors and/or terminals. The satellite processors are likely to be minicomputers that handle much of the data processing done locally in offices and on factory floors. Connected to these satellite minis may be other subordinate minis, intelligent terminals with microprocessors, and/or dumb terminals. And in addition to the dozens of minis that are used in some large DDP networks to process data, still more minis are used to control the flow of communications between network stations. We'll look at DDP networks in more detail in Chapter 10.

Some Characteristics of Typical Minis

As you can see from the photos in the Mini Gallery, primary and online secondary storage capacities increase as mini systems get larger. Multiple users can be served at once in all but the smallest systems, and organizations can elect to use faster and more powerful peripheral devices.

H.P.
Data general
honeywell
IBM
Tandum

Most of the popular lines of minis in use today employ the byte-addressable storage approach. A majority of the minis currently in service also are **16-bit machines.** Thus, most minis are able to simultaneously move and manipulate data words consisting of two 8-bit bytes. This ability, of course, gives minis an edge in speed over 8-bit micros in applications that require lots of calculations. As we've seen, however, 16- or 32-bit microprocessor chips are available, and so this advantage of current minis is likely to diminish. Of course, some newer minis are powerful 32-bit machines and are able to operate on 4 bytes at a time. The mini makers are not standing still! Some of the more advanced minis also achieve faster processing speeds by employing a special *high-speed buffer,* or *cache,* storage section in the CPU to temporarily store very active data and instructions during processing. Since the cache storage unit is faster than the primary storage section, the processing speed is increased.

Because minis have been around longer than micros, mini manufacturers have built up larger libraries of prepared software of interest to organizations. More high-level programming languages are likely to be available for minis than for micros, and mini operating-system and translation programs are likely to be more sophisticated.

MAINFRAME FAMILY MODELS

In the 1960s, when the emphasis was on building larger and faster central computers to handle all the processing needs of an organization, the word

A Minicomputer Gallery

A model in the Wang 2200 line. The price of the CPU starts at under $10,000, and systems with up to nine peripherals may be built. Multiple keyboard/CRT workstations can be supported. The hard-disk unit at the right of the desk has a storage capacity of 10 million characters. (Courtesy Wang Laboratories, Inc.) ▶

There are 10 minicomputer models in Honeywell's DPS6 line. There are four small models of the type shown here, four medium-sized models, and two in the "supermini" class. The four low-end systems are 16-bit machines. The midrange models are 16-bit systems that can be upgraded to 32-bit machines. And the two large models are 32-bit systems. Prices range from under $30,000 for the system shown, to over $200,000 for the largest model equipped with peripherals. (Courtesy Honeywell, Inc.) ▼

Data General Eclipse C/150. (Reproduced by permission of Data General Corporation, Westboro, Mass.)

This is a model in IBM's 8100 line of computer systems. Primary storage capacity ranges from 256K to 1 million bytes. A small 8100 system costs less than $40,000. (Courtesy of IBM)

Wang VS systems can support up to 32 workstations. Models with up to 512K bytes of primary storage and over 1 billion bytes of disk storage are available. Although the smallest VS systems start at under $50,000, the largest configurations exceed $75,000. (Courtesy Wang Laboratories, Inc.)

A Nixdorf 8870 General Business System with disk drives and printer. (Photo reprinted by permission of Nixdorf Computer Corporation, Burlington, Mass.)

Texas Instruments' DS990 model series of mid-range systems provides a series of peripherals, remote terminal capability, and communications equipment. (Courtesy Texas Instruments)

Digital Equipment Corporation's PDP-11/24 minicomputer is its lowest-priced PDP-11 model, with packaged systems starting at around $20,000. (Courtesy Digital Equipment Corporation)

mainframe was used to mean the same thing as "central processor" or "CPU." Although the word may still be used synonymously with central processor, it took on an added meaning in the 1970s in the literature of computers and data processing. By way of differentiation, a computer that is generally *more powerful* than a typical micro or mini is now often called a **mainframe.** Figure 9-1 showed you that such machines vary widely in cost and performance capability. And we've already seen that there's considerable overlap possible in the cost and performance of large minis and small mainframes. The historical development of computers discussed in the "Closer Look" Reading following Chapter 1 dealt primarily with mainframes.

Mainframe Uses and Applications

Until minis and micros came along, virtually everything that was done with computers was done on mainframes. There are tens of thousands of these computers in use today. Most medium-sized and larger organizations in the country with a history of computer usage have one or more of them. Banks, insurance companies, colleges and universities, hospitals, and local, state, and federal government agencies—these are just a few of the types of organizations that use mainframes to meet their needs. Blue Cross Insurance Company of Virginia, for example, uses a large mainframe for interactive claims processing. Over 200 terminals in hospitals and doctors' offices are used to enter medical claims into the computer. The system prompts users on how to enter claims, notifies them immediately of any errors, and tells them when to expect payment.

In addition to providing, at a central site, all the processing power that may be needed by an entire organization, a mainframe is also used as the central host computer in a distributed data processing network. The mainframe communicates with, and exercises some control over, smaller satellite processors.

A whole series of mainframe models ranging in size from small to very large are typically lumped together under a *family designation* by mainframe manufacturers. It's usually possible to run programs prepared for one machine on other models in the same family with little or no modification. This **compatibility** between family models makes it easy for users to move up to larger systems in the same family if they outgrow their smaller machines. However, it's usually not as easy to convert programs to a larger system in a different product line, a fact that helps maintain the stability of a mainframe manufacturer's customer base. Unlike micros and minis, which are usually purchased, mainframes are often rented or leased. The Mainframe Gallery on pages 251–253 showcases a few of these families of computers.

A representative mainframe family is the IBM System/370. There are about a dozen different models in this series. (Well over half of all the mainframes installed in the 1970s were System/370 machines.) The 370 line ranges in size from the *smallest* model 115; to *medium-sized* models 138, 148, and 158; to a *large* model 168; to a *very large* model 3033.

The smallest computer in the System/370 line is the Model 115. Primary storage capacity is 353K bytes. The time required by the processor to execute a basic operation (the cycle time) is 480 nanoseconds. (Courtesy of IBM)

A medium-sized mainframe, the 370/148 has a primary storage of up to 2 megabytes. Hundreds of millions of characters of disk storage are possible. The cycle time is 180 to 270 nanoseconds, depending on the operation. These systems sold for about $500,000. (Courtesy IBM Corporation)

A medium-sized mainframe, the Model 138 is able to support a larger number of peripherals than the smaller System/370 models. (Courtesy of IBM)

A medium-sized mainframe, the 370/158 has a primary storage that can vary from 512K bytes up to 6 million bytes. Hundreds of millions of characters can be stored in online disk drives, and dozens of other peripheral devices can be supported. The purchase price of a 158 was between $1 and $2 million. (Courtesy IBM Corporation)

Multiple processing units are included in a large-scale Model 168 installation. Over 8 million characters of primary storage are possible, and cycle time is 80 nanoseconds. Price of a basic 168 was originally over $4 million. (Courtesy of IBM)

The Model 3033 is the most powerful computer in the 370 family. It may also have multiple processors. Twelve million characters of primary storage are available, the cycle time is 57 nanoseconds, and the price was originally about $5 million. (Courtesy of IBM)

There are several versions of the IBM 4331 mainframe shown here. (A smaller 4321 model is also available.) The price of the least expensive 4331 processor with 1 megabyte of primary storage is about $80,000—about half the cost of an earlier 370/125 mainframe that offered only about half the processing performance. (Courtesy IBM Corporation)

There are also several versions of the IBM 4341 CPU pictured here. A 4341 model is available that will easily outperform earlier medium-sized 370/158 mainframes. The cost of a 370/158 CPU with 1 megabyte of primary storage was about $1.6 million. The cost of a more powerful 4341 with 2 megabytes of primary storage is about $400,000. (Courtesy IBM Corporation)

The 3081 is a very large mainframe. It can execute up to 10 million instructions per second and has a purchase price of nearly $4 million. Primary storage varies from 16 to 32 megabytes. The machine cycle time is only 26 nanoseconds. (Courtesy IBM Corporation)

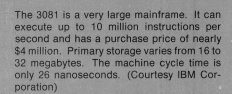

This small mainframe in NCR's 8000 series can support multiple peripherals such as terminals and printers. (Courtesy NCR, Dayton, Ohio)

A medium-sized NCR 8400 series mainframe, this processor has a primary storage of up to 1 million bytes. The machine cycle time is 112 nanoseconds, and prices start at under $100,000 for the CPU. (Courtesy NCR, Dayton, Ohio)

At the top of the NCR 8000 mainframe family are the processors in the 8600 series. Multiprocessors may be found in a single large cabinet, primary storage can vary from 4 to 16 megabytes, and high-speed buffer storage of up to 128K bytes is available. The purchase price of the largest 8600 CPU is nearly $2 million. (Courtesy NCR, Dayton, Ohio)

This Amdahl 580 is a large mainframe model. The CPU shown here has up to 32 megabytes of primary storage and two high-speed buffer storage units of 32K bytes each. Machines such as this model that will accept programs written for IBM mainframes without modification are often called plug-compatible mainframes. (Courtesy Amdahl Corporation)

Several small and medium-sized models in a newer IBM 4300 Series have been introduced. For example, the small 4331 is a more powerful and lower-priced processor than small System/370 models, and the 4341 has similar advantages over medium-sized 370 computers. And the first machine in what is speculated to be an "H series" family of more powerful mainframes has also been announced. This machine—the 3081—costs about as much as the Model 3033, but it offers twice the computing capability.

Another representative mainframe family with about a dozen models is NCR Corporation's 8000 Series, which has machines ranging in size from the *small* 8100 and 8200 models, to the *medium-sized* 8300 and 8400 mainframes, to the *large* 8500 and 8600 processors. Similar mainframe families are produced by UNIVAC Division of Sperry Rand Corporation (the 1100 Series and the 90 Series), Burroughs Corporation (the 700, 800, and 900 Series), Honeywell, Inc., (the Series 60 computers), and Control Data Corporation (the CYBER Series). Additional firms such as Amdahl Corporation, Magnuson Computer Systems, and National Advanced Systems make mainframes that accept programs written for, and directly compatible with, IBM family models.

Some Characteristics of Typical Mainframes

What was true of the other computer categories we've considered in this chapter remains true of mainframes: Primary and online secondary storage capacities increase as the systems get larger. Furthermore, in the larger mainframe models it's likely that one of the alternative computer-system architectures discussed in Chapter 1 (and shown in Figure 1-16, page 28) will be substituted for the **single-processor** or **uniprocessor** design approach used in smaller machines. For example, several arithmetic-logic and control units may be used in a large **multiprocessor** mainframe to process several tasks at the same instant in time. Also, high-speed cache storage sections are routinely used in larger mainframes. The result of such features, of course, is that larger mainframes can process applications faster than smaller computers.

Another characteristic that improves their performance is the fact that most mainframes are basically **32-bit machines** and can manipulate 4-byte words in a single machine cycle. And most mainframes also have instruction sets that give them the flexibility to automatically operate on 2 bytes (halfword) or 8 bytes (doubleword).

Mainframe vendors have *much larger* libraries of applications programs that may be of interest to organizations than do other computer manufacturers. Furthermore, most applications packages designed by software development firms in the past have been written for mainframe computers. All popular (and some not-so-popular) high-level programming languages are available for mainframes, and their operating-system programs are at a very high level of sophistication. Mainframe vendors can also provide customers with a high level of applications design support and maintenance service.

Figure 9-6 The central processing section of the CYBER 205 supercomputer. This CPU contains up to 4 million 64-bit *words* of primary storage. Storage components reserved for high-speed cache sections in smaller machines are used throughout the primary storage section. The CYBER 205 is capable of processing up to 50 million instructions per second. (Courtesy Control Data Corporation)

Figure 9-7 This CRAY-1 supercomputer is one of the largest, fastest, and most expensive computers in existence. (Courtesy Fairchild Camera and Instrument Corporation)

SUPERCOMPUTER SYSTEMS

As you've probably guessed, **supercomputers** are the largest, fastest, and most expensive computers made. Such "monsters" include Control Data's CYBER 205 (Figure 9-6), Burroughs' Scientific Processor, and Cray Research's CRAY-1 (Figure 9-7). Only a few of these monsters are produced each year because only a few organizations need (and can afford) their processing capabilities. The CRAY-1 is the current market leader, but less than 40 of these machines have been installed. In one recent year, CRAY-1 sales totaled—are you ready for this?—six systems! And Cray Research received about $50 million for these half-dozen machines.

Supercomputer Applications

Some of the CRAY-1s that have been delivered are making top-secret weapons-research calculations for the federal government at the Los Alamos Scientific Laboratory in New Mexico and at the Lawrence Livermore Laboratory in California. Another CRAY-1 is providing complex calculations for petroleum and engineering companies at a Kansas City data processing service. Still other CRAY-1s are working on weather-forecasting problems at the European Center for Medium Range Weather Forecasts in England and at the National Center for Atmospheric Research in Boulder, Colorado.

In weather forecasting and in research involving the earth's atmosphere, weather data supplied by a worldwide network of space satellites, airplanes, and ground stations are fed into supercomputers. These data are analyzed by a series of computer programs to arrive at forecasts. Although current programs certainly provide forecasts that are generally more accurate than unaided human guesses, there's still room for considerable improvement. It's not that scientists don't understand the principles involved well enough to be able to prepare programs that *could* provide much better forecasts. Rather, the problem is that even with the power of a CRAY-1 (100 million calculations per second), the thousands of variables involved cannot now be evaluated to the satisfaction of scientists in the time available for forecasting. (Nobody cares if a computer produces a storm warning 2 days after the storm has hit.) In short, the current forecast programs being run on supercomputers are crude models of what meteorologists would use if much more powerful computers were available. There is thus an incentive for supercomputer builders to make ever-larger machines. A CRAY-2 is under development, Fujitsu in Japan is working on two models, and ways are being developed by IBM and others to exploit the super-fast Josephson-junction technology discussed in Chapter 5.

Some Characteristics of Supercomputers

Since supercomputers are usually designed to process complex scientific applications, the computational speed of the system is most important. To maximize the speed of computations, each address location in the CRAY-1 holds 64 bits of information. Thus, in a single machine cycle, two 64-bit data words can be added together. The CRAY-1 **cycle time**—the time required to execute a basic operation—is only 12.5 nanoseconds (billionths of a second). This is about five times faster than the largest mainframes discussed in the last section, and those machines were "only" 32-bit systems. The entire primary storage section of the CRAY-1 makes exclusive use of the types of expensive components that are generally reserved *only* for a high-speed cache section in less powerful machines. This usage, combined with the large number of circuit chips required to process the large (64-bit) fixed-length words, makes the CRAY-1 very expensive. Prices start at $8 million.

 **Feedback and
Review 9-1**

You've learned about real computer systems ranging in size from the smallest micros to the largest supercomputers in this chapter. To test and reinforce your understanding of the material, answer the following true-false questions by placing a T or F in the space provided:

_____ **1.** A recently introduced microcomputer can often do the work of an earlier mini at a much lower cost.

_____ **2.** Computer experts agree on the definition of a minicomputer.

_____ **3.** The computer classifications used in this chapter are the standards of the computer industry.

T **4.** A minicomputer can have more processing capability than a mainframe model.

_____ **5.** A microcomputer can be placed on a single silicon chip.

_____ **6.** A microprocessor chip performs the arithmetic-logic and control functions of a microcomputer.

_____ **7.** ROM chips may be used in micros to permanently store program instructions.

F **8.** Most micros use rigid disk storage devices rather than floppy disk drives.

_____ **9.** Output from a micro is not available in humanly readable form.

_____ **10.** The idea for the microprocessor chip came from an engineer who grew tired of designing new arithmetic-logic and control elements each time a different special-purpose computer was built.

_____ **11.** The first microprocessor chip was made for Intel Corporation by a Japanese calculator firm.

_____ **12.** The first personal microcomputer was the Intellac, introduced in 1973.

_____ **13.** Most microcomputers in use today have 8-bit microprocessors, but 16-bit and 32-bit processor chips have been introduced.

_____ **14.** An interface bus is a device on a micro that serves as the electrical interconnection between the CPU and the various peripherals.

_____ **15.** Microcomputer usage is limited to less than 500 applications.

_____ **16.** Most minicomputers in service are 16-bit machines, but 32-bit minis are also common.

_____ **17.** Minicomputers can't use high-speed buffer storage components and are thus always slower than mainframe models.

T **18.** Minicomputers often serve as satellite processors to a larger central host computer.

_____ **19.** Mainframe models are typically given a family designation by their makers, and they can range in size from small to very large.

_____ **20.** Mainframes may have multiprocessor components that permit several tasks to be processed at the same instant in time.

_____ **21.** Most mainframes are 48-bit machines.

_____ **22.** The CRAY-1 is a micro that fits on a chip.

_____ **23.** Thousands of supercomputers are currently being built.

_____ **24.** Supercomputers are usually designed to process accounting applications.

_____ **25.** You thought you were never going to get to the end of this review section.

Looking Back

1. Technological changes are occurring so rapidly in the computer industry that it's now very difficult to classify the broad range of available machines on the basis of size and computing capabilities. We've made an attempt in this chapter to arbitrarily classify computers as micros, minis, mainframes, and supercomputers.

2. Developed in the 1970s, microcomputers are the smallest general-purpose symbol manipulators that can be programmed to process a wide variety of applications. A micro is built around a single microprocessor chip (which is usually an 8-bit device), uses RAM and ROM storage chips in the CPU, and is a single-user-oriented machine. Unlike larger systems that are used almost exclusively by people in organizations, micros are used by millions of people for entertainment and other personal applications. Representative micro systems and their uses have been discussed in the chapter. Micros range in price from $200 (or less) to about $10,000. Newer 16-bit micros have been introduced, and 32-bit microprocessor chips have been built.

3. A minicomputer is a small general-purpose machine ranging in price from about $2,500 to $75,000. There's considerable overlap between small minis and large micro systems. Minis were first developed in the 1960s to fill the gaps left by the bigger and faster central computers in an organization. In contrast to the current generation of micros, which are generally 8-bit processors, most minis are 16-bit machines. However, newer minis often have 32-bit processors. Representative small, medium-scale, and larger mini systems have been identified in the chapter. Minis have always been used for specialized control purposes and for general data processing applications. In recent years, however, organizations have also used thousands of minis as satellite processors in distributed data processing networks.

4. A mainframe computer is generally more powerful (and more expensive) than a mini, but again, considerable overlap may occur in these categories. Mainframes, ranging in size from small to very large, are typically lumped together under a family designation. Representative mainframe families have been identified in the chapter. Most mainframes are basically 32-bit machines and are designed to support almost every type of available peripheral device. Larger libraries of applications programs are available for mainframe computers than for smaller systems. Mainframes are used as central host computers in distributed systems, and they are used in thousands of other ways.

5. Supercomputers are the largest, fastest, and most expensive computing monsters in existence. They are few in number and are designed to process complex scientific applications.

You should now be able to define and use the following terms and concepts (the numbers shown indicate the pages where the terms and concepts are first mentioned):

microcomputer 238
microprocessor chip 238
8-bit machine 239
interface bus 245
minicomputer 245
distributed data processing (DDP)
    networks 247

host computer 247
satellite (or node) processors 247
16-bit machine 247
mainframe computer 250
compatibility 250
single processor (or uniprocessor)
    computer system 254

multiprocessor computer system 254
32-bit machine 254
supercomputer 255
cycle time 256

TOPICS FOR REVIEW AND DISCUSSION

1. Conduct a survey among five people in the computer/data processing field and ask them these two questions: (*a*) How would you differentiate between a microcomputer and a minicomputer? (*b*) How would you differentiate between a minicomputer and a small mainframe model? What were the results of your survey?

2. (*a*) What is a microcomputer? (*b*) Why was it developed? (*c*) What's the difference between a microcomputer and a microprocessor?

3. "Most microcomputers are stand-alone, single-user-oriented machines used by people at work and at play." Discuss this statement.

4. (*a*) Identify four ways to supply input data to a micro system. (*b*) Identify four ways that output may be received from a micro CPU. (You may want to review the I/O media and devices discussed in Chapters 6 and 8.)

5. How may micro systems be used (*a*) by individuals, and (*b*) by organizations?

6. Give four examples of representative (*a*) microcomputers, (*b*) minicomputers, and (*c*) mainframe computers.

7. Identify and discuss three characteristics of (*a*) microcomputers, (*b*) minicomputers, and (*c*) mainframe computers.

8. What's the most popular programming language used with micros?

9. (*a*) What is a minicomputer? (*b*) Why were minis developed? (*c*) How may minis be used?

10. (*a*) What is a mainframe computer? (*b*) How may mainframes be used?

11. "A large mainframe is generally software-compatible with the smaller computers in the same family." Explain this statement.

12. (*a*) What is a supercomputer? (*b*) How does a supercomputer differ from other machines? (*c*) How are supercomputers used?

ANSWERS TO FEEDBACK AND REVIEW SECTION

1. T	8. F	15. F	22. F
2. F	9. F	16. T	23. F
3. F	10. T	17. F	24. F
4. T	11. F	18. T	25. T
5. T	12. F	19. T	
6. T	13. T	20. T	
7. T	14. T	21. F	

Computer Stores

A few years ago, people laughed at the idea of selling computers over the counter. "Now it's the preferred way of doing business," according to Robert Rogers, director of retail sales development at Apple Computer Inc. Computer makers, trying to reach ever-broadening audiences with lower-priced machines, need new distribution channels.

For most computer makers, the shift to retailing is a drastic change. Traditionally, manufacturers sold through their own sales forces or through third-party systems houses. But for products selling for less than $5,000, such modes are simply too costly. John E. Schlacthenhauffen, vice-president of retail marketing at Xerox, laments that "the cost of marketing is becoming more than the cost of production. We need to find more cost-efficient distribution techniques." Three groups are expanding rapidly in the computer retail market—independent specialty chains, mass merchandisers, and computer manufacturers themselves.

The hottest segment is specialty chains, such as ComputerLand Corp. The San Leandro, California, based company operates more than 200 franchised units across the country, and is expanding its operations swiftly. ComputerLand has a growing crowd of competitors, including CompuShop, MicroAge, and Computer Store. Generally the strategy of these chains is to carry a broad range of goods from various manufacturers, price them competitively, emphasize software, and sell the expertise of store personnel.

Large mass retailers such as Sears, J. C. Penney, and Montgomery Ward, as well as several department store groups, are hoping to attract a large share of the volume market by concentrating on low-priced, compact machines that need little support or explanation. However, because the general home market has not really taken off,

These days, buying a computer can be easier than buying a car. All the models are under one roof at your local computer store. (Neal Slavin)

Sears is trying to get ahead of the pack by going after the first big group of customers—the small-business users. To reach these businesses and the work-at-home professional, Sears is locating its freestanding computer stores in the suburbs.

As for the manufacturers, Tandy Corp.'s Radio Shack Division—unique as both a general retailer and computer maker—started the race for customers with a commanding lead of more than 6,000 electronics stores. But companies with enormous resources such as IBM, Xerox, and Digital Equipment Corporation began opening stores to sell their own wares in the early 1980s. These stores have the strengths of comprehensive expertise and support systems. Their handicaps are that they are intimidating to inexperienced buyers and the variety of their inventory is limited. Several manufacturers carry only their own products.

As computer prices continue to fall, computer-retailing channels will likely split into two parts, much as stereo-equipment channels did. Department stores and consumer electronic stores will sell the low-cost popular equipment, while specialty stores will offer more sophisticated wares and service. Following the stereo model, a number of entrepreneurs have set up stores that will focus on selling software. Edward Cherlin, a computer industry analyst at Strategic Inc., notes that "you don't expect to buy stereo equipment and records at the same store."

Large mainframes and the supercomputers will, of course, continue to be sold through sales forces to their relatively few customers. Small computers, however, have already joined such products as dishwashers, television sets, and digital clocks on the shelves of America's retailers. And stores selling only computers and software are a new part of American business.

—Source of data: "Computer Stores," *Business Week*, September 28, 1981, pp. 76–82.

chapter 10

Data Communications and Distributed Data Processing Networks

THE WIRED CITY

Many of the largest corporations in the United States believe that a giant home information industry is taking shape. By 1990, these companies believe that the wired city—where communications grids will link every home with the information banks of computer centers—will no longer be the stuff of science fiction.

The ways in which people communicate, work, shop, and bank will all change drastically. People will perform these tasks without leaving home. Instead they will use the technology of home information retrieval systems, which have been given the generic label, *videotex*.

Life in "electronic cottages" will be comfortable, efficient, and center around the video screen and the home computer. People will do their shopping from video catalogs, pay all their bills electronically, send their work reports to the office via videotex channels, and call up the latest stock prices and sports news whenever they want them. At least some form of this wired society is with us today.

—Source of data: "Window on the World: The Home Information Revolution," *Business Week,* June 29, 1981, p. 74.

Optical fibers the size of a human hair transmit information via semiconductor lasers at the speed of light. Fiber optic technology promises to revolutionize communications. (Fred Ward/Black Star)

Looking Ahead

Data communications systems are an integral part of the "wired cities" and "electronic cottages" mentioned in the opening vignette. We'll focus on these systems that are vital to any modern society in Chapter 10. You'll see how data are transmitted and will learn about the transmission channels that are used and the organizations that provide these channels. Related issues involving the coordination and regulation of data communications follow, along with discussions of a number of specific processing systems that are supported by data communications. The final section describes examples of distributed data processing networks.

Thus, after studying this chapter you should be able to:

- Understand the current computing/communications setting.
- Describe the techniques and channels used to transmit data between distant locations.
- Identify the types of organizations that provide transmission channels and other services for businesses and individuals.
- Outline the components used to coordinate a complex computing/communications network.
- Give specific examples of systems supported by data communications.
- Present the characteristics of distributed data processing, and give examples of these types of networks.
- Understand and use the key terms and concepts listed at the end of this chapter.

THE COMPUTING/COMMUNICATIONS SETTING

You've become familiar with the term direct-access processing in many earlier chapters. This type of processing, as shown in Figure 10-1, generally involves online terminals located at or near the data sources, and these sources can be far away from the CPU. To cite just a few examples, teller and point-of-sale terminals are spotted in locations away from computers; airline, car rental, and hotel reservation systems have thousands of terminals located many miles from their CPUs; factory data entry stations may not be near a processor; and intelligent terminals and subordinate minicomputers may be great distances away from a central host computer. **Data communication** refers to the means and methods whereby data are transferred between ~~such~~ *two or more* processing locations. It makes possible the I/O operations that take place between remote online terminals and CPUs. It's the "glue" that permits a direct interactive bond between the people at these terminals and the central processing systems.

Figure 10-1 Transaction-oriented processing. (Photos courtesy Honeywell, Inc. and Norand Corporation)

Data Communications Background

There's nothing new about data communications. The ancient Greek runner carrying the message of victory on the plains of Marathon inspired a present-day athletic event. Pony Express riders carried messages and won the admiration of a nation in the brief period before they were replaced by telegraph service. For 30 years, telegraph companies enjoyed a monopoly on the use of electrical impulses to transmit data between distant stations. But in 1876, Alexander Graham Bell demonstrated that electrical signals could be used to transmit voice messages along telephone lines, and so a second data communications, or **telecommunications,** channel was established.

In the 75 years after the introduction of the telephone, a complex network of telecommunications systems was established to link locations throughout the world. The first linkage of computing and communication devices occurred in 1940 when Dr. George Stibitz used telegraph lines to send data from Dartmouth College in New Hampshire to a Bell Laboratories calculator in New York City. But it wasn't until the late 1950s that the computing/communications linkage began in earnest. Telegraph lines were used first to connect teleprinter terminals with computers, but telephone lines were quickly pressed into service. An early large-scale business application was the Sabre passenger reservation system developed in the late 1950s and early 1960s by American Airlines and IBM. Hundreds of scattered terminals were linked to a central processing center. Communications usage has grown steadily since then. Today, most of the larger minis and almost all of the medium- and large-scale mainframe systems are able to communicate with outlying terminals.

Twenty years ago computing capability was obtained from computer vendors, and communications service was supplied by telecommunications firms. The communications firms used computer-controlled message-switching devices to improve their services, and the computer vendors offered limited communications packages to sell data processing services. But it wasn't difficult to differentiate between the offerings of the two groups. Now that situation has changed: Many of the same electronic circuit chips are used in computing and communications devices. Computer vendors can offer a large package of communications services. And telecommunications suppliers can offer significant computing resources to those who use their offerings. Several new terms have been coined to reflect this merger of computing and communications technology. (The French use the word "telematique," the English use "telematics," and "compunications" has been suggested by a Harvard professor.) As more personal computers are attached to communications networks, and as more of the equipment in an organizational setting is linked together by the glue of data communications, the distinctions between computing and communications will become even more blurred.

DATA COMMUNICATIONS CONCEPTS

In a simple data communications system, terminals and other remote I/O devices are linked with one or more central processors to capture input data and receive output information. Equipment sometimes referred to as **interface elements** is used to bridge the different physical and operating environments that exist between I/O devices and central processors. And a variety of data transmission channels are available to carry data from one location to another. In the next few pages we'll concentrate on interface elements, data transmission channels, and related data communications concepts. You'll find detailed discussions of the I/O devices and central processors found in a data communications environment in Chapters 5 through 9 of this Hardware Module.

Data Transmission Techniques

You'll notice that interface elements called modems are shown at *each* end of the data transmission channels in Figure 10-2. **A modem** is a *mo*dulation-*dem*odulation device that converts the discrete stream of digital "on-off" electrical pulses used by computing equipment into the type of continuously variable analog wave patterns used to transmit the human voice. Since digital pulses cannot effectively travel any distance over a transmission network designed for voice communications, a modem is needed to *modulate* or convert the digital pulses into analog wave patterns when telephone lines are used to

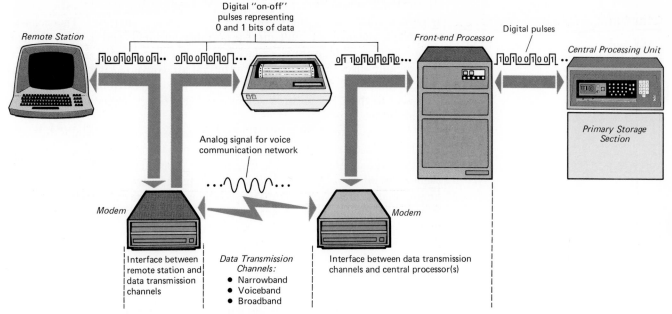

Digital "on-off"
pulses representing
0 and 1 bits of data

Remote Station

Front-end Processor   Digital pulses

Central Processing Unit

Analog signal for voice
communication network

Modem

Modem

| Interface between remote station and data transmission channels | *Data Transmission Channels:*
• Narrowband
• Voiceband
• Broadband | Interface between data transmission channels and central processor(s) |

Primary Storage Section

Figure 10-2 A simple data communications system typically links I/O devices at remote locations with one or more central processors. Interface elements such as modems and front-end processors are used to bridge and control the different data communications environments. Modems are used to permit the system to switch back and forth from computer digital data to analog signals that can be transmitted on voice communication lines. A front-end processor is a computer used to monitor and control the data transmission channels and the data being transmitted. In this system, data to be sent to a CPU are entered into a terminal through a keyboard. On command from the operator, the data in digital form are sent to a nearby modem to be converted into an analog signal. The converted data are then transmitted over telephone lines to another modem located near the CPU. This modem converts the analog signal back to a digital form. The data in digital form are then sent to a front-end processor which may check them for possible errors and then temporarily store them or route them to the CPU for immediate processing. The same route is followed when output information is sent from the CPU back to the remote location. The entire data communications activity is under the control of program instructions stored in communications processors and/or CPUs.

transmit data. For example, when data from a terminal are sent over telephone lines to a CPU, a modem is needed at the transmitting end to convert the digital pulses into analog signals. And another modem is needed at the receiving end to *demodulate* or recover the digital data from the transmitted signal. Of course, when output from the CPU is sent back to the remote site the process is reversed. The modem at the CPU location modulates the output, and the modem at the remote location demodulates the transmitted signal.

The I/O equipment shown at the remote station in Figure 10-2 is not likely to be moved, and so the modem is "hard-wired" directly to this equipment. But you'll recall from Chapter 6 that large numbers of portable terminals are now used by salespersons, managers, engineers, and others to communicate with distant CPUs. A special type of modem called an **acoustic coupler** is used in these situations to provide the necessary interface. The acoustic coupler is attached (or built into) a portable terminal, and a standard telephone handset is then usually placed in rubber cups located on the coupler. The digital pulses produced by the terminal are converted into audible tones that are picked up by the handset receiver. The signals from these tones are then sent to the CPU location where another modem converts them back to digital pulses.

The need to transmit large volumes of computer data over long distances has developed in a relatively short period of time. Organizations are currently making large investments to build communications networks designed for *all-digital transmission.* Such networks eliminate the need for modems because analog signals aren't used. Until these systems are more fully developed, however, the vast public network of telephone lines (and modems) will continue to handle much of the transmission workload.

Data Transmission Channels

Figure 10-2 indicates that the **data transmission channels** or "highways" used to carry data from one location to another are classified into narrowband, voiceband, and broadband categories. The wider the bandwidth of a channel, the more data it can transmit in a given period of time. *Telegraph lines,* for example, are **narrowband** channels, and their transmission rate is slow [from about 5 to 30 characters per second (cps)]. This is adequate to directly accept data being keyed into a terminal. Standard *telephone lines* are **voiceband** channels that have a wider bandwidth. They are able to speed up the transmission rate to over 1,000 cps. This is fast enough to accommodate the data being transmitted from a card reader to a CPU.

In many cases, a terminal operator at a remote location uses the regular dial-up telephone switching network, calls a number at the CPU location, and enters the data. When data volume is sufficient, however, it's often more economical for an organization to acquire a **dedicated** or **leased line(s)** which can be used for both voice and data purposes.

Different types of telephone and telegraph transmission circuits can also be selected to meet the needs of an organization. As Figure 10-3 shows, a **simplex** circuit permits data to flow in *only one* direction. A terminal connected to such a circuit is either a *send-only* or a *receive-only* device. Simplex circuits are seldom used because a return path is generally needed to send acknowledgment, control, or error signals. Thus, a **half-duplex** line that can *alternately* send and receive data, or a **full-duplex** connection that can *simultaneously* transmit and receive is usually used. A full-duplex line is faster since it avoids the delay that occurs in a half-duplex circuit each time the direction of transmission is changed.

Broadband channels are used when large data volumes must be transmitted at high speeds (over 100,000 cps is possible). Coaxial cables, microwave circuits, and communications satellites are commonly used to provide these

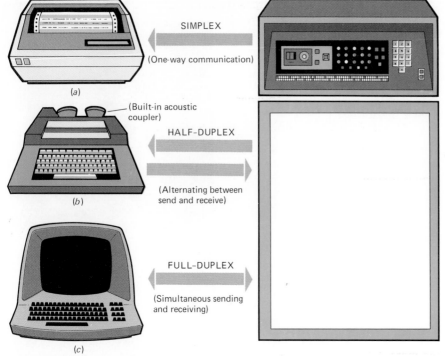

Figure 10-3 Data transmission circuits. (*a*) A simplex line permits communication in only one direction. That direction may be from the CPU to an I/O device as shown here, or it may be from a terminal to a CPU. (*b*) A half-duplex circuit permits data to be sent in both directions, but not at the same time. (*c*) A full-duplex connection does permit the simultaneous sending and receiving of data.

channels. **Coaxial cables** are groups of specially wrapped and insulated wire lines that are able to transmit data at high rates. **Microwave systems** use very high frequency radio signals to transmit data through space. When microwave facilities are used, the data may be transmitted along a ground route by repeater stations that are located, on the average, about 25 miles apart. The data signals are received, amplified, and retransmitted by each station along a route. Or, the data may be beamed to a **communications satellite** that acts as a reflector by accepting signals from one point on earth and returning the same signals to some other point on earth. The satellite appears from the earth to be a stationary target for the microwave signals because it's precisely positioned 22,300 miles above the equator with an orbit speed that matches the earth's rotation. Dozens of satellites are now in orbit to handle international and domestic data, voice, and video communications. Figure 10-4 lists some of these satellite systems.

Existing broadband channels are expensive and are generally used only by large organizations. However, it's expected that the rapidly maturing use of **fiber optic cables** and **laser technology** will soon permit huge amounts of data to be routinely transmitted at the speed of light through tiny threads of glass or

INTERNATIONAL

INTELSAT system. This International Telecommunications Satellite Consortium includes about 100 member nations on six continents. INTELSAT is headquartered in Washington D.C., which is also the home of the **Communications Satellite Corporation (COMSAT)**, an organization that was chartered by Congress in 1962 to be the United States representative to INTELSAT. COMSAT performs a management function for INTELSAT. Beginning with Early Bird in 1965, several generations of satellites have now been launched by INTELSAT, and these now form a global communications system that accounts for a major proportion of all long-distance international communications.

DOMESTIC

RCA Americom system. The first to offer domestic satellite service, RCA has several SATCOM satellites in orbit. Major transmitting/receiving stations are located in large cities from New York to California.

Western Union system. The first satellite in Western Union's Westar system was launched in 1974. Four second-generation "Advanced Westar" satellites are now planned. Western Union has major ground stations in several cities and, of course, a nationwide network of telegraph lines.

American Telephone & Telegraph system. AT&T currently leases several COMSTAR satellites from COMSAT. The system was recently given permission by the FCC to launch its own satellites.

Satellite Business Systems. SBS is likely to be a major force in future data communications. Developed by IBM, Aetna Life and Casualty Insurance Company, and COMSTAT at a cost of $400 million, SBS provides all-digital transmission services at very high speeds. SBS began operations in 1981 after a successful satellite launch late in 1980.

American Satellite Company. Jointly owned by Fairchild Industries and Continental Telephone Company, American Satellite provides high-speed, all-digital transmission services. It leases satellite capacity from Western Union, owns a 20 percent interest in the existing Westar system, and has contracted for 50 percent ownership of the Advanced Westar satellites.

Figure 10-4 Satellite data transmission systems. (Photo courtesy NASA)

plastic such as those shown at the beginning of this chapter. Teamed with a laser, a single glass fiber the size of a human hair may be used to transmit across the country in a single second all the characters in dozens of books of this size. Since thousands of these fibers can be packaged in a single cable, the future cost of broadband transmission capability should be within the reach of small organizations and individuals.

LASERS AND FIBER OPTICS: THE FUTURE OF DATA TRANSMISSION?

The semiconductor laser—about the size of a pinhead—is the world's smallest. But this tiny laser stands to revolutionize computer and voice communications through the young science of fiber optics. In fiber optics, semiconductor lasers transmit information in the form of light along hair-thin glass (optical) fibers at 186,000 miles per second (the speed of light), with no significant loss of intensity over very long distances.

Fiber optics speaks the same language as today's computers—namely, digital. Digital transmission is, in essence, a numerical Morse code that translates all information into two numbers—0 and 1. These numbers are represented by the on and off modes of the semiconductor laser, which flashes some 90 million times per second, with each flash representing a bit of information.

Even the time between these pulses can be utilized—with special multiplexing equipment. This equipment allows the simultaneous transmission or reception of multiple signals; that means computerized information, telephone conversations, and television shows can be transmitted along the same optical cable. The various signals are broken up at the transmitting end, coded, transmitted, and then reassembled at the receiving end—without missing a beat.

While experts agree that this type of transmission will, no doubt, be widely used in the future, there are still some technical difficulties to overcome. For instance, optical fibers don't currently allow complete switching or routing of light signals. As a result, at switching points, optical signals must be converted into electrical signals for routing and then back into light for further optical transmission.

Despite such glitches, however, fiber-optic transmission systems are already on the market, and their popularity is growing rapidly. Businesses are using the systems for in-house linkage of computers, and the federal government and telephone companies are investing heavily in the technology. Some major cities even have intracity fiber-optic lines; and the installations of at least three major trunk lines on the East, West, and Northwest coasts will be completed soon. Plans to span the oceans with undersea fiber-optic cables are also on the drawing boards—some experts believe this type of transoceanic communication will prove cheaper than satellite communication, and it will certainly open up more channels than the airways can provide.

—"Lasers and Computers: A Bright Future," *output,* July 1981, pp. 56–57. Reprinted with Permission of Output magazine. Copyright by Technical Publishing Company, a Dun & Bradstreet Company 1981. All rights reserved.

Data Communications Service Organizations

The data transmission channels that we've just examined are furnished by a number of data communications organizations. You're familiar, of course, with the large public telephone and telegraph networks offered for use by **common carriers** such as the Bell Telephone System companies, General Telephone and Electronics, and Western Union.

In addition to these common carriers that offer a broad range of facilities, there are also **specialized common carriers** whose public networks are restricted to a limited number of services. Included in the specialized carrier category are several of the satellite-using organizations listed in Figure 10-4 as well as:

> *MCI Communications Corporation.* MCI is a long-distance carrier that employs microwave circuits to serve business users. It offers dedicated leased lines that are arranged exclusively for data transmission. It also offers long-distance voice communications between selected cities.

▌*Southern Pacific Communications Company.* A subsidiary of the railroad company, the original SPC network followed the right-of-way of the tracks from San Francisco through Dallas. SPC now offers a nationwide private line service to 80 metropolitan areas. Microwave stations and broadband cables are used.

▌*ITT World Communications.* ITT Worldcom offers long-distance circuits between 88 cities in the United States. Services between the United States and other countries are also provided.

Another type of data communications service organization is the **value-added carrier.** This type of carrier offers specialized services, but it may not have its own transmission facilities. For example, GTE Telenet and Tymnet, Inc., both have computer networks that receive customer data coming in over telephone lines. These data are temporarily stored and organized into "packets" of characters. These packets are then computer-routed and transmitted at high speed over dedicated common carrier channels to Telenet and Tymnet offices near the final data destination. At these offices, data in the packets are reassembled into the complete message for transmission to the final destination. For the user of a value-added network, the transmission cost is frequently less than if the user had relied on less efficient means of directly utilizing common carrier channels. Telenet and Tymnet are sometimes referred to as **packet-switching networks.**

Finally, there are data communications organizations that provide services to *personal computer owners.* You may recall from Chapter 9 that microcomputer users can transmit and receive electronic mail messages and other data through the facilities of personal computing/communications networks. Plans to participate in what's expected to be a giant home information industry are now being made by many large firms. Thus, these networks, often referred to as **videotex systems,** are likely to experience explosive growth through the 1980s. Included among these network offerings are:

Videotex systems can bring telecommunications services into any home or business. (Courtesy The Source)

▌*The Source.* This is a network of Source Telecomputing Corporation, a subsidiary of *Reader's Digest.* Its Source Mail service allows an individual to use his or her personal computer to exchange messages with any other Source subscriber. Instant access to over 1,000 other information and communications services are available. A $100 one-time subscription fee is charged, and an hourly hookup rate is levied that varies according to the time of day. Transmission is over local telephone lines and the GTE Telenet and Tymnet value-added networks.

▌*CompuServe Information Service.* CompuServe is jointly owned by CompuServe, Inc., and H&R Block Inc., the income tax service firm. It's similar to The Source, offering an electronic mail system and access to dozens of large data bases. Subscriptions to the service are sold at Radio Shack stores, and subscribers hook into the network by using Radio Shack software. A variable hourly hookup fee is charged. Transmission is over local telephone lines and the Tymnet network.

You can take a closer look at some other representative videotex systems in the reading found at the end of this chapter.

Coordinating the Data Communications Environment

The simple data communications system shown in Figure 10-2 was typical of the types used in the late 1960s, and it's still appropriate for many organizations. But the data communications environment has changed rapidly since then. As Figure 10-5 indicates, much larger computing/communications networks are now in service, and the coordination required for efficient network use is complex. Such networks may have hundreds of terminals and many small processors located at dozens of dispersed sites. These sites, in turn, are linked by different transmission channels to larger host computers. The task of

Figure 10-5 A computing/communications network. The remote concentrators, message switchers, and front-end processors in such networks are typically micro- or minicomputers used for communications purposes.

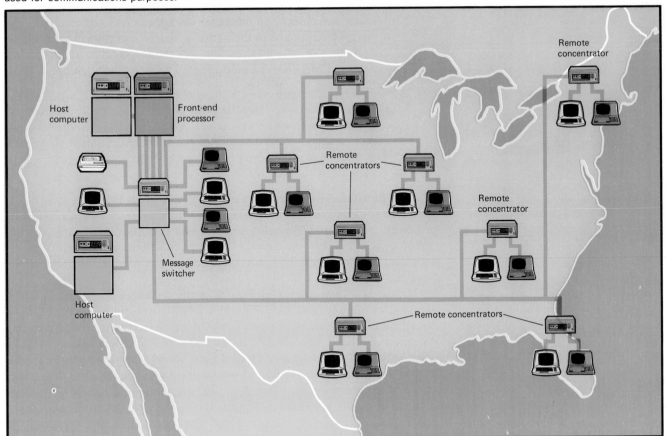

network designers is to select and coordinate the network components so that the necessary data are moved to the right place, at the right time, with a minimum of errors, and at the lowest possible cost.

Figure 10-5 shows that a number of **communications processors** (typically micro- or minicomputers) are used by network designers to achieve their goals. These processors are used for the following purposes:

1. *Remote concentration of messages.* The **remote concentrator** reduces transmission costs by receiving terminal input from many low-speed lines and then concentrating and transmitting a compressed and smooth stream of data on a higher-speed and more efficient transmission channel. Although faster communications channels are more expensive, they can do more work, and thus the cost per character transmitted may well be reduced. Devices called **multiplexors** also perform this concentration function. Multiplexors are less expensive than concentrators, but many are not programmable and thus don't have the flexibility of concentrators. However, microprocessor-equipped multiplexors have been introduced that perform much like concentrators.

2. *Message switching.* The **message switcher** receives and analyzes data messages from points in the network, determines the destination and the proper routing, and then forwards the messages to other network locations. If necessary, a message may be stored until an appropriate outgoing line is available.

3. *Front-end processing.* The **front-end processor** is usually located at a central computer site. Its purpose is to relieve a main computer—i.e., a **host computer**—of a number of the functions required to interact with and control the communications network.

The functions of communications processors differ from one network to another, and there may be an overlapping of functions. A message-switching processor, for example, may also function as a remote concentrator; a front-end processor may perform message-switching functions; and, in less complete networks, the host computer may perform most or all the functions of the front-end processor.

Up to now, we've been looking at communications situations in which data are transmitted between sites that are far apart. But in many organizations data are also transmitted between computers, terminals, word processing stations, and other devices that are all located within a compact area such as an office building or a campus. The communications system used to link these nearby devices together is referred to as a **local network** (or a *local-area network*). A local network is owned by the using organization. Transmission channels generally use coaxial or fiber optic cables and special interface units rather than telephone lines and modems. The transmission speed is very high, and terminals and computers made by different vendors can be integrated into a unified system. Two examples of the dozens of local networks used by organizations are:

▎*Ethernet*. Developed by Xerox, this network uses a coaxial cable for data transmission. Special integrated circuit chips called controllers are used to connect equipment to the cable, and small boxes called transceivers transmit and receive cable data at each workstation. Each station can exchange data with any other station or group of stations. Hundreds of thousands of characters can be transmitted each second.

▎*HYPERchannel*. A product of Network Systems Corporation, HYPERchannel can transmit millions of characters per second. It's often used to link large CPUs together.

Figure 10-6 A modern data communications network may use broadband satellite transmission channels to link the major East and West Coast offices of an organization. Various intracity data channels may include ground microwave stations, telephone and telegraph circuits, and the coaxial cables furnished by cable television companies. Within each major office, data may move over intrafacility local networks. Telephone and telegraph channels may be used to connect smaller offices to one or both of the major facilities.

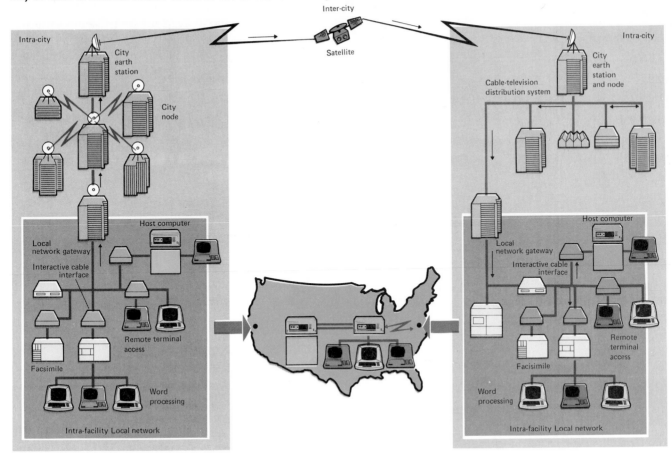

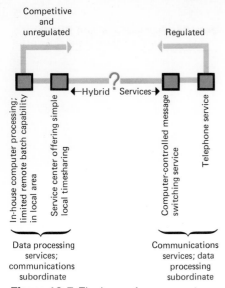

 at the top shows a diagram with the following labels:

Competitive and unregulated

Regulated

←Hybrid Services→

In-house computer processing; limited remote batch capability in local area

Service center offering simple local timesharing

Computer-controlled message switching service

Telephone service

Data processing services; communications subordinate

Communications services; data processing subordinate

Figure 10-7 The issue of government regulation in the data communications field has not been totally resolved.

In summary, then, a network designer must select and coordinate the communications elements that link far-flung sites with central locations. And within the central locations, the designer may also need to coordinate the intra-facility local network. Figure 10-6 illustrates a few of the possible options.

Regulation and Competition in Data Communications

We've seen that the technologies of computing and communications are converging. This fact is creating uncertainty about the governmental regulatory status of the many organizations that offer both computing and communications services. An *unregulated* legal status applies to organizations when their communications services are only incidental to their competitive computing services. And a *regulated* legal status generally applies to common carriers when data processing services are only incidental to their furnishing of communications channels. But between these defined areas are many "hybrid" organizations that offer significant services in both computing and communications. It's in this large middle area that the regulatory status has been unclear (Figure 10-7). The Federal Communications Commission (FCC) has held many hearings in the last decade to try to keep up with technological advances. These hearings have pitted rich and powerful organizations in the competitive computing industry against equally rich and powerful common carriers. Although the confrontations are likely to continue, the FCC has tended in recent years to rule in favor of a greater degree of unregulated competition in the data communications field.

ADDITIONAL SYSTEMS SUPPORTED BY DATA COMMUNICATIONS

You're already familiar with many direct-access processing applications supported by data communications. To cite one example, a teller at a branch bank may update online savings account records stored at a central computer site through the use of data communications facilities. Let's take a brief look at a few additional examples of important systems supported by telecommunications.

Real Time Processing Systems

The words "real time" have been defined in over 30 ways. However, the consensus is that a **real time processing system** is in a parallel time relationship with an ongoing activity and is producing information quickly enough to be useful in controlling this current live and dynamic activity. Thus, the words "real time" describe a direct-access or online processing system with severe time limitations. A real time system uses direct-access processing, but a direct-access system need not be operating in real time. The difference is that real time processing requires *immediate* transaction input from all input-originating terminals. Many stations are tied directly by high-speed telecommunications lines into one or more CPUs. Several stations can operate at the same time. Files are updated each minute and inquiries are answered by split-second access to up-to-the-minute records. But it's possible to have a direct-access system that combines immediate access to records for inquiry purposes with *periodic* (perhaps daily) transaction input and updating of records from a central collecting source. Such a direct-access system would meet many needs and would be simpler and less expensive than a real time system.

The reservation systems used by airlines, hotels, and car rental agencies are examples of real time systems that have been mentioned earlier. A few other examples of real time systems supported by telecommunications are:

- *Military systems.* A World Wide Military Command and Control System has been developed for U.S. military commanders from the President on down. The system links 35 large computers at 26 command posts around the world. And over a dozen computers at the North American Air Defense Command accept, store, and constantly update masses of data from worldwide radar installations. Every humanly produced object in earth orbit is tracked. If a rocket is launched, the computers quickly calculate its trajectory.

- *Air traffic control systems.* Millions of aircraft flights are tracked across the nation each year by air traffic controllers. These flights are monitored by computers as shown in Figure 10-8 and are switched to differ-

Figure 10-8 Air traffic control systems such as the one shown here are an example of real time processing systems supported by telecommunications. (Bohdan Hrynewych/Stock Boston)

ent control jurisdictions as they move across the continent. When a flight approaches Chicago's O'Hare International Airport, for example, a control system sends out special "beacon" signals. Answering signals from the aircraft give the plane's identity, altitude, and speed. These data are processed by computer and are instantly displayed on a controller's screen next to a "blip" of light that represents the plane. Over 100 aircraft can be tracked and controlled simultaneously by the system.

Timesharing and Remote Computing Service Systems

Timesharing is a general term used to describe a processing system with a number of independent, relatively low-speed, online, and simultaneously usable stations. Each station, of course, provides direct access to the CPU. The use of special programs allows the CPU to switch from one station to another and to do a part of each job in an allocated "time slice" until the work is completed. The speed is frequently (but not always) such that the user has the illusion that nobody else is using the computer.

A number of organizations sell timesharing and remote computing services to their customers. These organizations install terminals in customer offices and then use telecommunications channels to link the terminals to their central processors. A broad range of jobs may be processed, or the service organization may specialize in the needs of a particular group. In recent years, for example, the pharmacy operations in retail drugstores have been swamped with paperwork resulting from insurance billings and government legislation. Thousands of drugstores have thus turned to a number of timesharing services that supply total hardware, software, and communications packages geared to the needs of pharmacists. Other remote computing services (sometimes referred to as *service bureaus*) may accept a customer's input data over telecommunications lines, do custom batch processing for the customer, and then transmit the output information back to the customer's terminal.

Timesharing and remote computing service organizations generally offer a library of online applications programs to their clients who need only supply the input data and access the programs to obtain the desired information. Customers pay for the processing service in much the same way they pay for telephone service: There's an initial installation charge, there are certain basic monthly charges, and there are transaction charges (like long-distance calls) that vary according to usage. Some timesharing firms also sell applications programs to former customers who decide to acquire their own small hardware systems.

Electronic Mail/Message Systems

The ability to use telecommunications lines to send electronic messages between distant points obviously isn't limited to personal computer users. Organizations can use services such as Telemail provided by GTE Telenet, or On Tyme-II supplied by Tymnet, to send intracompany or intercompany messages. These messages may begin and end at communicating word processors or other I/O devices. Network computers are used to temporarily store and route the messages. We'll get into this subject in more detail in Chapter 11.

Banking Service Systems

Banks communicate with each other and send funds-transfer instructions over telecommunications networks. The Fed Wire transfer network, for example, is operated by the Federal Reserve System for use by member banks. Hundreds of member banks and the Federal Reserve banks are linked together. Dozens of computers and hundreds of terminals are used to handle over 25 million messages each year. Over $50 *trillion* is annually transmitted by Fed Wire. A cooperative funds-transfer network called BankWire also serves several hundred banks in the United States. And a cooperative international network called SWIFT (*S*ociety for *W*orldwide *I*nterbank *F*inancial *T*elecommunications) links banks in over 20 countries.

Bank-at-home systems also use telecommunications lines to permit people to interact with their individual banks. Personal computers or special input devices attached to television sets use telephone or two-way cable TV lines to access a bank computer. After a sign-on procedure has been followed, bank customers can:

- Display the current values of their checking and savings accounts, as shown in Figure 10-9.

- Display the balances owed on their mortgage, installment loan, and credit card accounts.

- Obtain information from a financial advisory service.

- Apply for loans.

- Display what they owe to creditors, and then enter the amounts they want the bank to pay on each bill.

Figure 10-9 Remote computing systems such as bank-at-home services permit people to use their personal computers to interact with their bank. (Jack Caspary/Woodfin Camp & Associates)

Data Base Retrieval Systems

In addition to The Source and CompuServe telecommunications networks that enable people to retrieve information from dozens of data bases, there are many other videotex systems that give people access to:

- Weather and traffic updates, article summaries from magazines, and news accounts from radio, United Press International, and Associated Press sources.

▌ Electronic shopping catalogs from retailers such as J. C. Penney and Sears, and electronic real estate listings from brokers.

▌ Classified advertising and community "bulletin-board" information.

Organizations also have telecommunications access to electronic libraries of information that are stored in central computers. These **data banks** tend to fall into statistical, bibliographic, and computational categories. *Statistical* data banks are compilations of numeric data. Included in this category are The Conference Board Data Base that provides information on capital spending and purchasing power for 20 different industries, and the Dow Jones News/Retrieval Service that gives current information on stock prices.

Bibliographic data banks contain text-based information abstracted from books, newspapers, magazines, and professional journals. Hundreds of these data banks are maintained by their producers. Most of the important ones are then indexed and stored on computers by a few large distributors. The distributors also provide the telecommunications links to their customers. Some of the largest information retrieval distributors are:

▌ *Lockheed Information Systems.* The Lockheed DIALOG system contains over 100 data bases in such fields as government, health, education, social and physical sciences, humanities, and business.

▌ *System Development Corporation.* SDC's search system has over 60 data bases, many of which are also found in the DIALOG system.

▌ *Bibliographic Retrieval Services.* BRS offers about 30 different data bases.

▌ *Mead Data Control.* Unlike the distributors above, Mead is both the producer and distributor of its LEXIS and NEXIS services. LEXIS is a vast library of legal information including federal and state codes and millions of court opinions. NEXIS, shown in Figure 10-10, is a computerized news research service.

▌ *New York Times Information Service.* Also a producer as well as distributor, the *Times* Information Bank abstracts many speciality and general-interest publications and over 20 news services.

Computational data banks allow users to manipulate raw data in order to produce economic models and forecasts. These data banks are prepared with data supplied by Standard & Poor's, Chase Econometric Associates, Data Resources, Inc., and others.

DISTRIBUTED DATA PROCESSING NETWORKS

A little earlier we used the word "timesharing" because it's commonly applied to multistation systems that make interleaved use of the time of a computer.

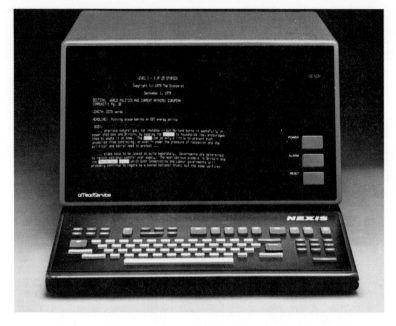

Figure 10-10 Subscribers to the NEXIS system enjoy access to a vast news research data base. (Courtesy Mead Data Central)

Figure 10-11 Twelve Florida counties supplement their mainframe capabilities by using DDP components to distribute the data processing function throughout a network of county departments. In this example, a terminal is located in Charlotte County's tax collector's office. Tax payments accepted over the counter are immediately entered into the system. Receipts and duplicate bills can be instantly generated on the printer. (Photo reprinted by permission of Nixdorf Computer Corporation, Burlington, Mass.)

We saw that a service organization can install terminals in the offices of many customers and then use telecommunications to link these terminals to its CPU. It's also quite possible for a single business to set up its own timesharing system using terminals linked to its own hardware. Timesharing isn't new. The relatively high cost of computer hardware in the 1960s spurred many organizations to establish a large central computer system and to then achieve economies of scale by sharing the time of that system among many users.

When one or two processors handle the workload of all outlying terminals, the word "timesharing" is probably still accurate. But as you know, it's possible now for an organization to buy many computers for the price of just one earlier large machine. And when *many* geographically dispersed or *distributed* independent computer systems are connected by a telecommunications network, and when messages, processing tasks, programs, data, and other resources are transmitted between cooperating processors and terminals, the timesharing term may no longer be broad enough.

Distributed data processing (DDP) network is the term often used today to describe this extension of timesharing. For our purposes, a DDP arrangement may be defined as one that places the needed data, along with the computing and communications resources necessary to process these data, at the end-user's location. Such an arrangement (Figure 10-11) may result in many computers and significant software resources being shared among dozens of users.

Examples of DDP Networks in Use

A distributed data processing network, like a timesharing system, may be intended for the use of a single organization, or it may be available for use by many organizations.

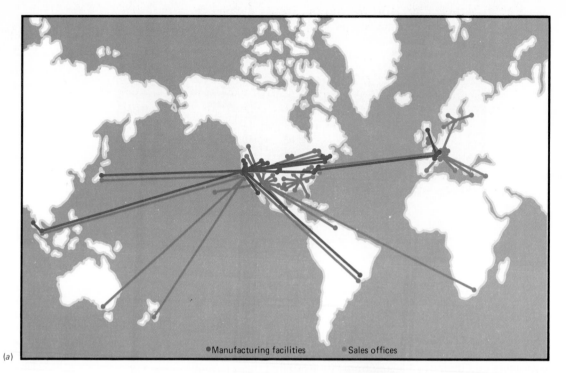

(a)

●Manufacturing facilities   ●Sales offices

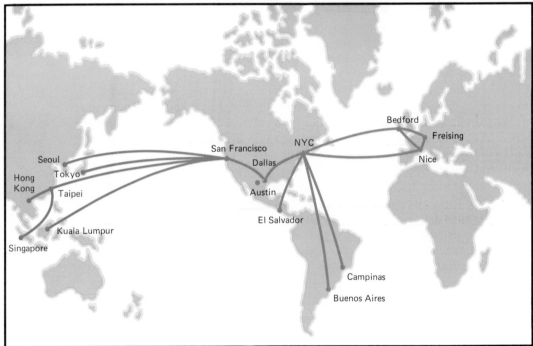

Bedford

Freising

San Francisco   NYC

Seoul   Dallas   Nice

Hong   Tokyo
Kong   Taipei   Austin

Kuala Lumpur   El Salvador

Singapore

Campinas

Buenos Aires

(b)

Figure 10-12 Single-organization DDP networks. (a) Hewlett-Packard Company's distributed data processing network. Hundreds of computers and terminals at over 100 manufacturing plants and sales offices are linked to corporate centers in Palo Alto, California and Geneva, Switzerland. (b) The worldwide network of Texas Instruments, Inc. Computers occupy different levels in the hierarchy of this DDP network.

Single-Organization DDP Networks. Some examples of private DDP networks have been developed by the following organizations:

■ *Hewlett-Packard Company.* Figure 10-12a shows the worldwide DDP network that Hewlett-Packard has developed for its internal business applications. Ten mainframes and 195 Hewlett-Packard minicomputers are scattered around the network to handle processing, data entry/ retrieval, and telecommunications work. About 2,500 visual display terminals are used. This network links manufacturing facilities and sales offices at over 100 sites to corporate offices in California and Switzerland. Although overall control of the network is maintained by the California center, division computers operate autonomously to process local jobs.

■ *Texas Instruments Incorporated.* Figure 10-12b shows the scope of TI's network. Over 7,000 terminals and hundreds of computers are now included in this expanding network. There are several computing levels in the network hierarchy. At the top of the hierarchy are five large mainframes located at the corporate information center in Dallas. Next in the hierarchy comes the medium-sized mainframes located at major sites around the world. A third level of TI minicomputers serves clusters of departmental terminals, and a fourth level of TI intelligent terminals serves individual employees.

■ *Bank of America.* The Bank of America in California has a network of over 50 minicomputers to support online inquiries from 6,000 teller terminals located in the 1,000 branch offices in the state.

■ *Otis Elevator Company.* One medium-sized mainframe, six minicomputers, and about 40 visual display terminals are used to link offices in Massachusetts, New Jersey, Illinois, Texas, and California with the corporate headquarters in Connecticut.

Multiple-Organization DDP Networks. A few examples of DDP networks that serve a number of organizations are:

■ *The ARPA Network.* Figure 10-13a shows the network of the Advanced Research Projects Agency of the U.S. Department of Defense. This net connects about 40 universities and research institutions throughout the United States and Europe with about 50 computers ranging in size from minis to supercomputers. A few of the schools included are Harvard, MIT, Carnegie-Mellon, Illinois, Utah, Stanford, UCLA, and USC.

■ *Travel reservation networks.* United Airlines' Apollo system, American Airlines' Sabre system, and the similar DDP nets of most other airlines obviously serve each sponsoring organization. But these and other reservation networks also serve thousands of other users. In the last few years, for example, about half the nation's 17,000 travel agencies have tied into these computerized travel reservation systems. Instead of

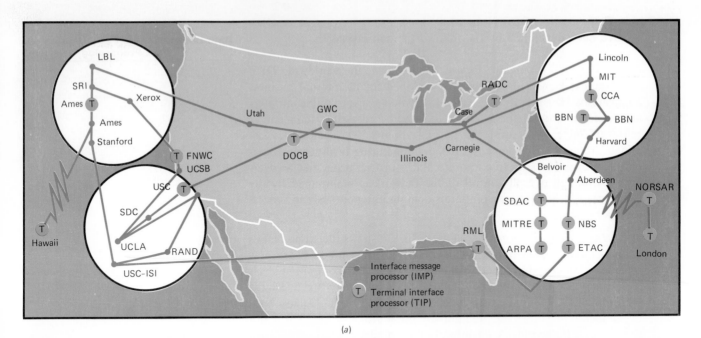

(a)

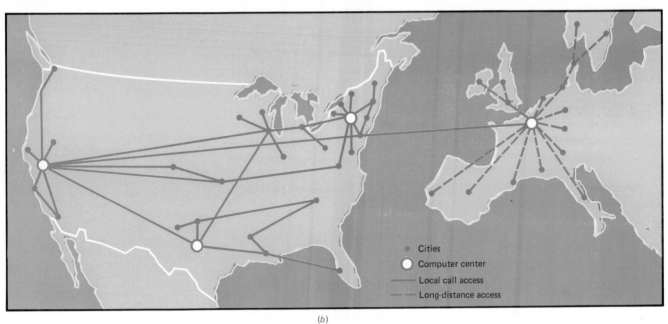

(b)

Figure 10-13 Multiple-organization DDP networks. (a) The DDP network of the Advanced Research Projects Agency of the Department of Defense. (b) The DDP network of Tymshare, Inc.

leafing through rate books and waiting out busy telephone lines, a travel agent can use a terminal to access flight schedules and rates. The availability of hotel rooms can also be determined. With a few keystrokes, an agent can immediately confirm air, car rental, and hotel arrangements. Tickets and itineraries can then be printed by the system.

▌ *The General Electric Network.* This net began as a timesharing service and has evolved into a system that uses over 100 computers to serve over 100,000 users in more than 20 countries.

▌ *Tymshare Network.* Similar in origin to the GE network, this system (Figure 10-13*b*) offers computing resources to customers in business, government, and education. It connects over 70 cities on two continents with 40 large-scale computers.

Network Configurations

Figure 10-14 shows some of the possible DDP network configurations which we'll now describe in detail.

The Star Network. In the star configuration (Figure 10-14*a*), a central host, or star computer(s) communicates with and controls a second level of satellite or node processors. These nodes, in turn, communicate with I/O terminals.

The Hierarchical Variation of the Star Network. In this arrangement (Figure 10-14*b*), the central host computer(s) are still linked to regional node processors. But these regional nodes may, in turn, act as hosts to subordinate small district processors. In addition to processing local applications, the small third-level processors in the hierarchy (usually minicomputers) may support local-level intelligent terminals and microcomputers that are also able to independently process small jobs. The higher-level computers in the hierarchy are used to manage large data bases and to serve the lower-level processors by executing jobs that require extensive computations. The Hewlett-Packard and Texas Instruments networks mentioned above are basically hierarchical variations of the star configuration. Most current networks, in fact, use the star arrangement or some hierarchical variation of it.

The Ring Network. This configuration (Figure 10-14*c*) is a "no-host" or ring arrangement of communicating equals. Each ring processor may have communicating subordinates, but within the ring there's no master computer. Few geographically dispersed ring networks now exist. However, this configuration is being used in local telecommunications networks such as Ethernet which links terminals and processors to a coaxial cable ring. It's possible, of course, to combine a ring structure at a local network site with a star structure for the entire DDP network.

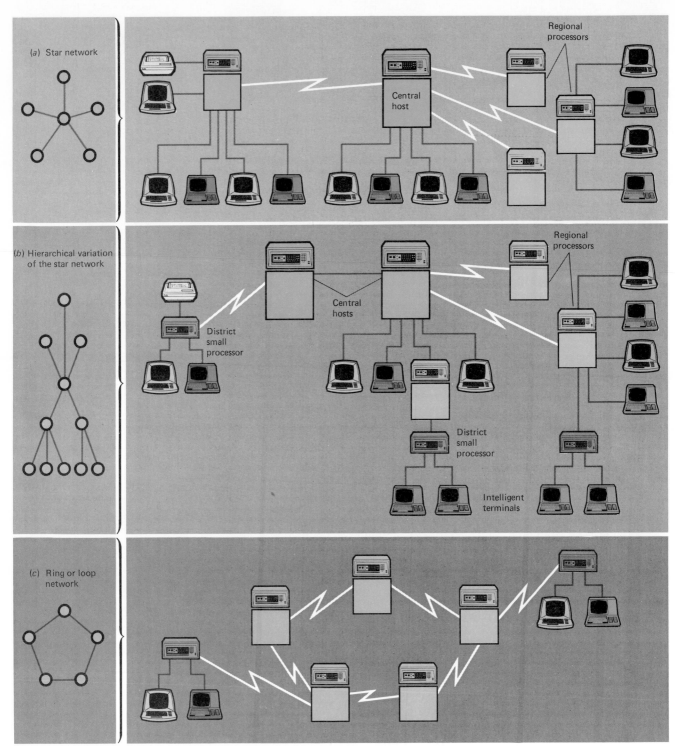

(a) Star network

Regional processors

Central host

(b) Hierarchical variation of the star network

Central hosts

Regional processors

District small processor

District small processor

Intelligent terminals

(c) Ring or loop network

Figure 10-14 Possible DDP network configurations. Countless variations of these themes are being implemented.

As you might expect, there are both advantages and disadvantages today to the sharing of computing resources through the use of DDP networks. Some of the advantages are:

- Sophisticated computers and a growing library of applications programs can be immediately available to end users whenever needed. Small local processors can often be used to quickly get local applications up and running, but large central systems are also available to do big number-crunching tasks.

- Skilled computer/communications specialists can be available to help network users develop their own specialized applications.

- The availability of multiple processors in the network permits peak-load sharing and provides backup facilities in the event of equipment failure.

- Users with access to nearby computers and data bases may be able to react more rapidly to new developments, and they may be able to interact with the other network resources to seek solutions to unusual problems.

- Telecommunication costs can be lower when much of the local processing is handled by on-site minis and micros rather than by distant central mainframes.

Unfortunately, however, some of the possible limitations to the use of DDP networks are:

- The reliability and cost of the telecommunications facilities used, and the cost and quality of the computing service received from other network sites may disappoint users in some cases.

- Security provisions for protecting the confidentiality and integrity of the user programs and data that are stored online and transmitted over network channels are generally ineffective today against a skilled person intent on penetrating the network.

- Today's DDP network environment is dynamic and turbulent, and the lack of adequate computing/communications standards has often made it difficult to merge the equipment produced by different vendors into a smoothly functioning entity.

Feedback and Review 10-1

This chapter has introduced you to a number of data communications concepts and DDP network examples. To test and reinforce your understanding of the material, use the following clues to fill in the crossword puzzle form presented below.

Across

1. _____ communication refers to the means and methods whereby data are transferred between processing locations.

2. A _____ is an interface device that converts the stream of "on-off" electrical pulses used by computing equipment into the type of analog wave patterns used to transmit the human voice over telephone lines.

5. Another name for the computing/communications networks that provide information retrieval services to personal computer users is _____ systems.

7. "Value-added" telecommunications carriers that receive customer data over telephone lines and then organize these data into groups for transmission over high-speed channels are sometimes referred to as _____ -switching networks.

8. A _____ -duplex transmission circuit is one that can simultaneously transmit and receive messages.

12. Data communications by means of electrical signals is also referred to as _____ -communications.

13. The companies that offer a broad range of telegraph and telephone services to the general public are referred to as _____ carriers.

14. _____ is the acronym for the government agency that has held hearings to determine the extent of regulation and competition that will be permitted in the telecommunications industry.

16. Customers often pay for timesharing services in much the same way they pay for _____ -distance telephone service.

17. _____ -band transmission channels use coaxial cables, microwave systems and satellites, and fiber optic cables to transmit large volumes of data at high speeds.

18. A standard telephone _____ is a voice-band channel that has a wider bandwidth and a faster transmission rate than a telegraph line.

19. In the _____ type of DDP network configuration, a central host computer communicates with and controls a second level of node processors.

20. _____ -sharing is a term used to describe a processing system with a number of independent, relatively low-speed, online, and simultaneously usable stations.

21. A communications _____ is precisely positioned in space and acts as a reflector by accepting signals from one point on earth and returning the same signals to other points on earth.

Down

1. Modems convert _____ "on-off" pulses into analog wave patterns.

2. _____ switchers are communications processors that receive and analyze data from points in a network, determine the destination and routing, and then forward the data to other network locations.

3. A _____ network is an extension of timesharing that employs many geographically dispersed computers and a telecommunications system to place data and computing resources at end-user locations.

4. _____ -wave transmission systems use radio signals to transmit data through space.

6. A specialized common carrier that offers long-distance circuits to 88 U.S. cities and to other countries is _____ World Communications.

9. A _____ network is used to transmit data between computers and I/O devices that are all located within a compact area such as an office building.

10. A _____ is taking place today between computing and communications technology.

11. Data _____ retrieval organizations tend to supply data that fall into statistical, bibliographic, and computational categories.

13. A coaxial or fiber optic _____ can be used to transmit data at high speeds.

15. _____ time processing systems are in a parallel time relationship with ongoing activities and are producing information quickly enough to be useful in controlling these current live and dynamic activities.

The completed crossword puzzle:

Across answers filled in: DATA, MODEM, VIDEOTEX, PACKET, FULL, TELE, COMMON, FCC, LONG, BROAD, LINE, STAR, TIME, SATELLITE

Down answers filled in: DIGITAL, MESSAGE, DISTRIBUTED, MICRO, ITT, FULL, LOCAL, MERGER, BASE, CABLE, REAL

1. Data communication refers to the means and methods whereby data are transferred between processing locations. There's nothing new about tele-communications. Telephones, for example, have been around for over 100 years. What's relatively recent, though, is the merging of computing and tele-communications technology.

2. When voice-grade telephone lines are used to transmit computer data, one modem must be used at the sending station to modulate the digital "on-off" pulses into the analog wave patterns used to transmit the human voice. And a second modem is needed at the receiving location to demodulate or recover the digital data from the transmitted signal. A special type of modem called an acoustic coupler is often used with portable terminals.

3. In addition to medium-speed telephone lines, narrowband telegraph chan-nels and high-speed broadband channels are also used to transmit data. The broadband channels use coaxial or fiber optic cables, and microwave/satel-lite systems. Transmitted data can move along simplex, half-duplex, or full-duplex lines depending on the needs of the user.

4. Most organizations offering telecommunications services can be classified into common carrier, specialized common carrier, or value-added carrier categories. Common carriers provide large public telephone and telegraph networks and a broad range of services. Specialized common carriers often use broadband facilities such as satellites to offer public networks that are restricted to a limited number of services. Value-added carriers generally use the telephone lines and transmission facilities of other carriers. Customer data are received, temporarily stored and organized into packets of charac-ters, and then routed over high-speed leased channels to their destinations. There are also service firms that offer computing/communications networks or videotex systems for home use.

5. Large computing/communications networks use a number of communica-tions processors to coordinate network components. Remote concentrators or multiplexors receive terminal input from low-speed lines and then concen-trate and transmit the data on higher-speed facilities. Message switchers receive data from points in the network, determine destination and proper routing, and then forward the data to other locations. And front-end proces-sors are used to relieve main computers of a number of the functions required to interact with and control the network.

6. Local networks are communications systems that are used to link the terminals, computers, word processing stations, and other devices located within a compact area. Transmission is generally over coaxial or fiber optic cables. These local networks must often be coordinated with the communi-cations elements that link geographically dispersed sites.

7. The convergence of computing and communications technologies has created uncertainty about the governmental regulatory status of many organi-zations that offer both computing and communications services. The Federal Communications Commission (FCC) has held numerous hearings in the last decade to try to determine which services should be competitive and which should be regulated. These hearings continue, but the FCC has tended to favor a greater degree of competition in recent years.

289

8. A real time processing system is in a parallel time relationship with an ongoing activity and is producing information quickly enough to be useful in controlling this current live activity. A real time system uses direct-access processing, but a direct-access system need not be operating under the severe time limitations of a real time system.

9. Timesharing is a general term used to describe the interleaved use of the time of a processor by a number of independent, online, simultaneously usable stations. A number of firms sell timesharing services to their customers.

10. In addition to supporting real time and timesharing systems, telecommunications has also made it possible to develop systems to transmit electronic mail, provide banking services, and retrieve information from numerous statistical, bibliographic, and computational data bases. Examples of all these applications are presented in the chapter.

11. A distributed data processing network consists of many geographically dispersed independent computer systems connected by a telecommunications network. It places the needed data, along with the computing/communications resources necessary to process these data, at the end-user's location. As examples in the chapter show, DDP networks may be intended for the use of a single organization, or they may be available for use by multiple organizations. The possible DDP network configurations include the star, a hierarchical variation of the star, and the ring arrangements. Several advantages and limitations to DDP networks are listed in the chapter.

KEY TERMS AND CONCEPTS

You should now be able to define and use the following terms and concepts (the numbers shown indicate the pages where the terms and concepts are first mentioned):

data communication 264	broadband channel 268	remote concentrator 274
telecommunications 265	coaxial cable 269	multiplexor 274
interface elements 266	microwave system 269	message switcher 274
modem 266	communications satellite 269	front-end processor 274
acoustic coupler 268	fiber optic cable/laser technology 269	host computer 274
data transmission channels 268	common carriers 271	local network 274
narrowband channel 268	specialized common carriers 271	regulation of telecommunications 276
voiceband channel 268	value-added carriers 272	real time processing system 276
dedicated (leased) lines 268	packet-switching networks 272	timesharing 278
simplex line 268	videotex system 272	bank-at-home systems 279
half-duplex circuit 268	communications processors 274	data base retrieval systems/data banks 279
full-duplex circuit 268		

TOPICS FOR REVIEW AND DISCUSSION

1. (*a*) What is data communication? (*b*) What can you tell a friend who is under the impression that data communications is a new phenomenon?

2. (*a*) Why are computing and communications technologies merging? (*b*) What are likely to be some of the effects of this merger?

3. What components are typically found in a simple data communications system?

4. (*a*) What's a modem and why is it needed? (*b*) What's an acoustic coupler?

5. Identify and discuss the three basic types of data transmission channels.

6. "A full-duplex line is faster since it avoids the delay that occurs in a half-duplex circuit." Explain this sentence.

7. (*a*) How are communications satellites used? (*b*) Identify four domestic satellite data transmission systems.

8. Identify, discuss, and give examples of three types of organizations that offer data communications services.

9. "A giant home information industry is being built around the development of videotex systems." Discuss this statement.

10. (*a*) Identify and indicate the purpose of the communications processors used to coordinate the operations of a data communications network. (*b*) What is a local network?

11. In your opinion, which computing/communications services should be regulated, and which should be open to unregulated competition?

12. (*a*) Explain this sentence: "A real time system uses direct-access processing, but a direct-access system need not be operating in real time." (*b*) Give some examples of a real time system.

13. (*a*) What is timesharing? (*b*) Give an example of the use of timesharing.

14. Identify three banking service systems that use telecommunications networks.

15. "The electronic libraries of information that are stored in central computers tend to fall into three categories." Identify these categories and give three examples of organizations that supply data bank information.

16. (*a*) What's a DDP network? (*b*) Give three examples of DDP networks used by single organizations. (*c*) Give three examples of DDP networks used by multiple organizations.

17. Identify and discuss the possible DDP network configurations.

18. (*a*) What are three possible advantages of DDP? (*b*) What are two possible limitations?

ANSWERS TO FEEDBACK AND REVIEW SECTION

10-1

¹D	A	T	A		²M	³O	D	E	⁴M		⁵V	I	⁶D	E	O	T	E	X
I					E		D		I				T
G					S		⁷P	A	C	K	E	T		⁸F	U	⁹L	L
I			¹⁰M		S			R							O		¹¹B
¹²T	E	L	E		A		¹³C	O	M	M	O	N		¹⁴F	C	C	A
A			R		G		A				¹⁵R		A		S
¹⁶L	O	N	G		E		¹⁷B	R	O	A	D		E		¹⁸L	I	N	E
			E				L				A
¹⁹S	T	A	R		²⁰T	I	M	E		²¹S	A	T	E	L	L	I	T	E

"What Will You Pay For From Videotex?"

The communications technology needed to put video-tex capability into American homes already exists. AT&T wants to use its telephone lines and switching equipment to provide videotex. Cable television companies plan to use their systems for videotex delivery. And the major television networks are able to provide teletext services—the use of television transmission to display printed information on television screens. However, the interactive capabilities of phone lines or cables seem to offer more to consumers. The technical side of providing videotex is not in question; what consumers want is.

Videotex in its interactive form will not be free to consumers. And just what services the public will pay for remains to be decided. At this time providing financial services, retailing services, and specialized information services seem ripest for videotex acceptance by the majority of American wage earners.

Financial Services

The first videotex systems are expected to be built around transaction processing. According to N. Richard Miller, vice-president of Diebold Group Inc., "Initially, we'll see banking and financial services such as commodity and stock trading, where the value added is sufficient to justify the price of the [videotex] service."

Large banks are moving aggressively to develop electronic banking-at-home. Paperless checking, automatic bill-paying, and record keeping are among the services the banks expect to supply. As banks pay higher interest rates on checking accounts, they will begin to charge more for checks—as much as 70¢ to $1 per check. Such charges will offset videotex fees (expected to run from $7 to $10 a month) and increase the attractiveness of electronic banking. In addition, many consumers are already accus-

Electronic banking services are expected to become more popular and to pave the way for other videotex services during the 1980s. (Jack Caspary/Woodfin Camp & Associates)

tomed to automated teller machines: they are primed for videotex transactions.

Retailing

Management Horizons, a market research firm, predicts that by 1990 20 percent of all retail sales will take place via videotex systems. Sears Roebuck, J.C. Penney Co., and Federated Department Stores have already conducted tests with electronic shopping catalogues.

Retailers expect shoppers to be able to view merchandise on their television screens and then to place their orders through their home computers.

Special Information Services

Videotex may prove a superior medium for such information as the classified ads provided by newspapers. Shoppers would be able to call to their screens only those homes, cars, etc. that fit their needs precisely. Pictures of both the interior and exterior of a house could be viewed.

Newspapers are anxious to join forces with cable companies to provide such information services, whereas AT&T hopes to develop its Yellow Pages into a videotex information system.

Other services will be developed, but they will have to offer consumers real financial and/or convenience advantages. Otherwise videotex would be a technology without a market.

—Source of data: "Window on the World: The Home Information Revolution," *Business Week*, June 29, 1981, pp. 74–83.

chapter 11

Word Processing and Electronic Mail/Message Systems

THE AUTOMATED OFFICE IS ON THE WAY

Remember in ninth-grade history reading about the Spaniards who spent years trekking through the Southwest in search of the lost city of gold? Well, there's a similar quest going on today in the information processing industry, with scores of manufacturers pursuing something called office automation, a concept that looms on the horizon like a mirage, at once tantalizingly close and elusive.

Simply defined, office automation is a convergence of a number of processing and communications technologies that will purportedly allow clerks, secretaries, and ultimately executives to function more efficiently and effectively—that is, they won't have to get up and walk over to a file cabinet to retrieve information or wait three days for someone from the mail room to drop off correspondence. These and other chores will be carried out electronically, as will more demanding functions like strategic planning, cash management, and portfolio analysis.

—Laton McCartney, editorial, *output,* July 1981, p. 6. Reprinted with Permission of Output magazine. Copyright by Technical Publishing Company, a Dun & Bradstreet Company 1981. All rights reserved.

Lightweight, portable terminals combined with other new technologies will broaden the concept of "the office" in the future. (Courtesy Hewlett-Packard)

Looking Ahead

Word processing and electronic mail/message systems are two of the basic building blocks for the automated office concept introduced in the opening vignette. Chapter 11 will give you a better understanding of these rapidly growing systems and how they will likely affect your future. You'll see how current problems in offices are causing organizations to turn to new technology and applications for the office environment. This technology often takes the form of word processing equipment and computing/communications devices needed to support the message distribution, document transmission, and computer conferencing functions of an electronic mail/message system. The chapter presents separate sections on word processing and electronic mail/message concepts and outlines a number of example applications.

Thus, after studying this chapter you should be able to:

▌ Explain why new office technology is needed and expected

▌ Discuss the historical and current developments in word processing systems, and identify the types of word processing systems in use today

▌ Outline some uses of word processing

▌ Understand why electronic mail/message systems have been developed in response to deficiencies in alternative message delivery systems

▌ Identify and discuss the functions performed by an electronic mail/message system

▌ Understand and use the key terms and concepts listed at the end of this chapter

TECHNOLOGY IN THE OFFICE: AN OVERVIEW

In addition to the term "office automation" used in the opening vignette, other phrases such as "office of the future" and "electronic office" have also been coined to describe the use of computing/communications technology to perform many office functions. We'll discuss some of the latest applications in office technology in this chapter. But before moving to these applications, let's pause briefly here to examine office functions and the status of the technology found in most offices today.

Office Functions and Problems

The functions performed in offices consist of the data processing activities you learned about in Chapter 1. In a traditionally organized office, data in the form of numerical symbols and/or text material are typically written or typed on source documents. These documents are then read, classified, and sorted. Calculations are performed on appropriate data, and facts may be summarized. Documents are often transmitted by mail between offices within an organization as well as between offices of separate businesses. The transmitted material generally takes the form of letters, memos, bills, purchase orders, and other documents that must be dealt with in an orderly way. Once the data have been manipulated and communicated, they frequently must be filed in a safe place, and they must be available for retrieval and reproduction when needed. Typewriters, desk calculators, file cabinets, and copying machines are among the traditional tools of office workers.

Although the necessary data processing work is accomplished in offices that follow these traditional methods, several problems have developed in recent years. A few of these problems are:

1. *Low productivity of office workers relative to other groups.* In the past decade, American farmers have invested about $50,000 per worker in equipment to increase the productivity of each worker about 185 percent. American industrial workers, aided by an investment of $35,000 per worker, have boosted productivity about 90 percent. But during the same period, office workers have been supported by equipment worth less than $3,000 on the average, and their productivity has increased by only 4 percent.

2. *Rising costs in the typical office.* The costs of preparing, mailing, storing, and duplicating documents have escalated in recent years. For example, IBM estimates that a typical one-page letter that has been dictated, typed, and corrected will cost a business over $6. Most of this cost is for labor. In the last decade the rate of growth in the number of office workers has exceeded the average rate of growth for the total workforce. And office labor costs have been rising 8 to 10 percent annually.

3. *Misfiling of documents.* People may be unable to locate records in large files because the records may have been stored under a number of different classification schemes.

4. *Personnel problems.* Monotonous job specialization can lead to boredom, frequent errors, high personnel turnover, and high training costs.

The Introduction of New Technology

Since a computer is a fast electronic symbol manipulating device, and since office work basically involves symbol manipulation, it's only natural that organizations have turned to computers and other technology for help. Widespread use of automated office technology has been predicted for at least the last 10 years, but progress has not yet lived up to these predictions. (This has led one observer to substitute the acronym OOF for office of the future!)

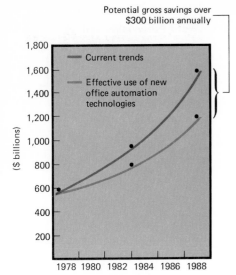

Potential gross savings over $300 billion annually

- Current trends
- Effective use of new office automation technologies

($ billions)

1,800
1,600
1,400
1,200
1,000
800
600
400
200

1978 1980 1982 1984 1986 1988

Figure 11-1 Projected direct cost of U.S. office-based white collar workers ($ in billions). Substantial savings are expected in the 1980s and beyond if new office technology is introduced and effectively used. (From Harvey L. Poppel, "The Automated Office Moves In," *Datamation*, Nov. 25, 1979, p. 76. Source: Extrapolations of historical employment and inflation trends; Booz, Allen productivity estimates.)

But things are beginning to change. Several factors are likely to lead to the introduction of new technology and applications in the office environments of many organizations in the next few years. Two of these factors are:

- The costs of electronic office equipment have been falling 30 percent per year. Executives are now more receptive to the idea of investing in new office technology in order to reduce rising labor costs and improve productivity. They're also encouraged by studies made by consulting organizations such as Booz, Allen & Hamilton, Inc., that project large potential savings through the effective use of new office technology (see Figure 11-1).

- Dozens of office equipment suppliers believe that the time is now ripe for the huge new automated office market they envision. They are working feverishly to develop new products.

In most organizations, the change from the traditional office setting to the electronic office environment is likely to evolve through several development stages. In the early stages, a limited amount of equipment is introduced to perform specific office tasks. But as users become more familiar with computing/communications equipment and technology, more functions are automated. Eventually, the "office" may become an integrated network of computing/communications systems that ties the entire organization together, as shown in Figure 11-2.

Figure 11-2 Paper may be scarce in the office of the future. Computing and communications equipment such as the word processor, printer, and microfiche stations shown here will help office workers to increase their efficiency and productivity. (Sepp Seitz/Woodfin Camp & Associates)

This office of the future is still in the future. Most organizations are in the early stages of development and are introducing equipment to perform the following specific tasks:

- *Word processing.* The efficient creation, editing, and printing of documents are supported by word processing equipment.

- *Message distribution.* Electronic mail/message systems accept messages addressed to one or more persons from a sending terminal and transmit the messages over communications channels to the terminal(s) of the recipient(s).

- *Document transmission and reproduction.* A special device scans documents, graphs, pictures, etc., at a sending location, and then transmits the data representing the scanned document over telecommunications lines to a similar machine at the receiving end that reproduces the document.

- *Computer conferencing.* People at different locations are using their workstations to attend conferences without ever leaving their offices.

The following pages discuss these applications in greater detail.

WORD PROCESSING

As used here, **word processing** describes the use of electronic equipment to create, view, edit, manipulate, transmit, store, retrieve, and print text material. Since you were first introduced to word processing (WP) concepts in Chapter 2, this topic isn't new to you. What you may not realize, however, is the speed with which WP equipment is now being introduced into offices. In dollar terms, sales are expected to quadruple to a $4 billion annual figure between 1981 and 1985.

Historical Perspective

The widespread use of WP devices began in 1964 when IBM announced the Magnetic Tape Selectric Typewriter (MTST). Frequently used form letters and paragraphs were typed once, and the text was recorded on magnetic tape. The MTST was then used to automatically prepare repetitive prerecorded letters or to compose letters and reports consisting of selected prerecorded paragraphs.

After the introduction of MTST, IBM and many other manufacturers brought out other devices that used magnetic cards, cassettes, and internal belts as the recording media. To justify the then-large investment in equipment, many early WP systems were installed in centralized facilities. Rigid procedures for logging-in, producing, and delivering text material were set up to maximize the use of expensive WP hardware. Secretaries were often assigned to the central facility to operate the WP devices. As you might guess, these early centralized WP systems were not always appreciated by users. Managers resisted losing secretaries with whom they had developed good working relationships, and secretaries resented the "factory" atmosphere and routine nature of their new assignments. Fortunately for everyone, dramatic reductions in the cost of WP equipment in recent years have reduced the economic need to set up centralized WP facilities. Decentralized WP stations are now affordable, and these stations need not be in constant use in order to justify their cost. The emphasis can now be placed on maximizing the effectiveness of people rather than on maximizing the use of equipment.

Word Processing Systems Today

In recent years, WP systems with keyboards for text input, visual display screens for text viewing and editing, floppy disks for text storage and retrieval, and various kinds of printers and data communications attachments for text output have been produced by dozens of vendors. If you think this description of a WP system sounds very much like the micro- and minicomputer systems discussed in Chapter 9, you're right.

A **dedicated word processor**—i.e., a device that's used exclusively for WP—is basically a disguised computer that perpetually runs a program to process text material. Thus, many dedicated word processors are spin-offs of small computers and intelligent terminals that have received a few hardware modifications and/or specialized software. And although they're not dedicated exclusively to the task, most micro- and mini-sized computers (as well as larger processors) can also be used as word processors simply by loading an appropriate WP program into the system. For example, popular microcomputer WP packages such as Electric Pencil, WordStar, Magic Wand, Scripsit, Easy Writer, and many others can be purchased from their suppliers in the form of floppy disks. Once a WP program diskette is loaded into a microcomputer system, the computer effectively becomes a word processor. (The author's microcomputer and a WP package were used to write this book.)

Word processing systems today generally fall into stand-alone, shared-logic, or shared-resource categories. A **stand-alone WP station,** as shown in Figure 11-3, is a small system that contains all the components needed to perform text processing. Electronic typewriters are sometimes considered to be low-level stand-alone systems. These devices can record and store a few pages of text in a small internal memory. Corrections can be made in the stored text before it's automatically printed in final form. A one- or two-line visual display provides a "thin window" into the internal memory of many electronic typewriters. A higher-level stand-alone WP system has the components mentioned at the beginning of this section and is able to display text over the entire surface of a CRT screen.

Figure 11-3 Word processing systems. (*above left*) The Wangriter is a dedicated, stand-alone system. (Courtesy Wang Laboratories, Inc.); (*above right*) The shared-logic system shown here is connected to a mainframe system. (Courtesy Nixdorf Computer Corporation); (*below right*) Shared resource systems combine the advantages of stand-alone systems with the larger capacity of a shared-logic system. (Courtesy Burroughs Corporation)

A **shared-logic WP system,** as shown in Figure 11-3, has a number of keyboard workstations that share the logic and storage sections of a single central computer. This computer is typically a minicomputer. Peripheral units such as printers are also shared by the workstations. Although it's economical to share system components among multiple workstations, a major disadvantage is that if the central computer fails, none of the workstations can be used.

The **shared-resource WP system,** as shown in Figure 11-3, also has multiple workstations, but each station has its own processor logic and storage sections. The failure of the computer at one station, of course, does not affect the processors at other workstations. Even though the stations can be individual stand-alone units, they share certain expensive resources such as printers and large-capacity disk drives.

Some Uses of Word Processing

A modern WP system is an amazingly flexible tool. As text is keyed into the system, it's displayed on the screen and can easily be recorded on a storage medium such as a floppy disk. Carriage returns are automatic and corrections are made easily. Sentences and paragraphs can be added, deleted, or moved around in the document or report being prepared. When the displayed text is correct, instructions about output format can be added. For example, the system can be instructed to automatically put headings and numbers on each page of a report, center headings on the page, and produce specified top, bottom, left, and right margins. Finally, the document or report can be printed at the local station, or it can be transmitted electronically to a word processor located at a distant point via data communications channels. Thus, letters and reports need not be mailed but can be printed for the first time on the receiving equipment. A printed copy may not be needed at the sending station since the text is available on an electronic file medium.

In addition, as we've seen, several prerecorded paragraphs can be called up from the dozens that are in storage and can then be assembled to prepare a quick response to a communication. An entire stored report can also be searched for specified words or phrases, and these characters can be deleted or replaced with other words or phrases. This **global search** feature can be used, for example, to substitute names in contracts, correct a word that's been misused or misspelled several times in a report, or substitute an abbreviation or acronym for a longer phrase.

A few examples of WP at work include:

- Continental Illinois Bank and Trust Company of Chicago has offices in Europe and New York. A proposal to a customer in Belgium can be prepared on the Brussels WP equipment and relayed to New York, where it's printed and studied. Changes may be made to the proposal in New York before it's sent to Chicago, and additional changes may be made in Chicago. Finally, the proposal can be forwarded back to Brussels, where it's printed and delivered to the customer. All this can be done in a single day.

- Reporters for a major national magazine use WP stations to compose and edit their articles. After photos for the articles are scanned by special input devices, the magazine pages are then prepared right on the WP display screens. Text and photos are arranged in an attractive layout. Any last-minute changes are made at the display screens. Broadband transmission channels are then used to send the magnetically stored edition of the magazine from the magazine's editorial offices to a printing company located hundreds of miles away. The printer's computerized system makes printing plates from the transmitted signals, and then uses these plates to print the magazine issue. The first time a paper copy of the magazine is prepared is when the printing press is finally used.

Figure 11-4 The use of a WP/OCR system.

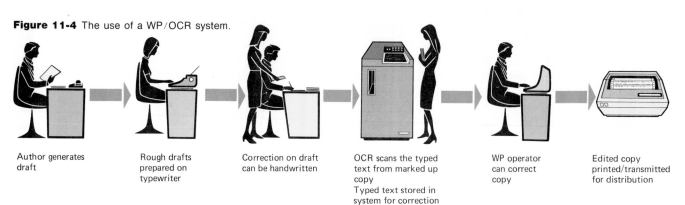

Author generates draft

Rough drafts prepared on typewriter

Correction on draft can be handwritten

OCR scans the typed text from marked up copy
Typed text stored in system for correction

WP operator can correct copy

Edited copy printed/transmitted for distribution

Some word processors are teamed with optical character readers so that existing office typewriters can "talk" directly to the WP equipment (see Figure 11-4). An original text draft is prepared at a typewriter. After the draft has been examined, the OCR reader scans this text and enters it into the WP system. The WP system is then used to edit, correct, and print or transmit the stored text. In such a WP/OCR system, every typewriter becomes an inexpensive wireless input terminal to the word processor(s).

ELECTRONIC MAIL/MESSAGE SYSTEMS

There's no general agreement on what is meant by the term "electronic mail." Some define it as any kind of message system that uses computer technology. We'll be a little more specific and say that an **electronic mail/message system (EMMS)** is one that can store and deliver, by electronic means, messages that would otherwise probably be forwarded through the postal service or sent verbally over telephone lines. As Figure 11-5 shows, the cost of sending a message over an EMMS has been steadily dropping, and this trend will likely continue.

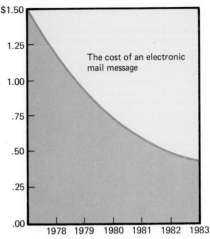

Figure 11-5 The cost of an EMMS message has been steadily dropping. (Source: The Yankee Group, Cambridge, Mass.)

Mailroom Drag and Telephone Tag

It's estimated that most large businesses in the United States will have advanced EMMSs up and running by 1985. Why this rapid movement to EMMS? One reason is the declining EMMS message costs mentioned earlier. But an EMMS can also overcome some of the limitations found in the message delivery systems provided by the postal service and telephone companies.

As you know, the postal service is relatively slow and messages are sometimes lost. The term "mailroom drag" describes the delays encountered in using this message delivery system. And using the telephone requires that (1) the message recipient can be located, and (2) the recipient is willing to be interrupted to take the call. Surprisingly enough, studies have shown that only about one in four calls made to people in organizations goes through on the first try. Three out of four times, then, people are either away from their phones or they are involved in activities where they don't want interruptions. In the cases when a call isn't completed, a frustrating game of **telephone tag** may then begin. Ms. Johnson leaves a message requesting that Mr. Burke return her call; Burke calls back to find that Johnson is in a meeting; Johnson tries again and learns that Burke has been called away from his desk. And so it goes—sometimes for days.

The EMMS concepts and examples that are discussed in the following sections have been developed in response to these shortcomings in the other message delivery systems. An EMMS can perform a number of functions. It can, for example, provide:

It is my heart-warm and world-embracing Christmas hope and aspiration that all of us—the high, the low, the rich, the poor, the admired, the despised, the loved, the hated, the civilized, the savage—may eventually be gathered together in a heaven of everlasting rest and peace and bliss—except the inventor of the telephone.
Mark Twain

303

✓ Message distribution services.

✓ Transmission of documents and pictures.

✓ Computerized conferences.

✓ Follow-up services.

Message Distribution Services

A keyed or spoken message is sent on the first try, and at any time of the day or night, to a *specified individual* who has a storage "mailbox" in the message system. (And it's just as easy for the sender to transmit a message to an identified *group of people* as it is to send it to a single person.) It's not necessary to locate the receiver(s) or interrupt him or her at a bad time. Rather, the receiver can periodically review stored messages at a time that *is* convenient. Stored voice messages can be received as reconstituted speech. And a visual display terminal or an **executive workstation** located in the office can be used to receive keyed messages (Figure 11-6). An executive workstation is a special terminal designed for the busy user who probably doesn't like to type. It includes special function keys, and may use touch screen menus and voice activation. In addition to the message distribution function, it can also be used to access data bases and information services, store appointments and address lists, and automatically dial specified telephone numbers.

After reviewing the messages, the receiver can fire off responses and other messages, and, *if necessary,* make a printed copy of the communication. The recipient can also receive and send messages at home during the evening, or during business trips, by using a portable terminal and a telephone. Beyond reducing interruptions, message distribution systems also provide *other benefits.* For example, people at remote sites no longer feel isolated because they

Figure 11-6 The Xerox 8010 Star is an executive workstation which is as easy to operate as an amusement park video game. The terminal features a simplified keyboard and a control mechanism called a "mouse," which is similar to a joystick and is shown here resting in front of the Star keyboard. (Courtesy Xerox Corporation)

can and do receive messages from headquarters as easily and quickly as do those who are located in the headquarters building. And people in different time zones can often communicate more easily since widely scattered offices may not be open at the same times. Another possible benefit is that EMMS messages tend to be brief and to the point, thus saving time.

Individuals and groups using the message system may be members of a single organization or they may belong to several different organizations. Many computer manufacturers—e.g., Wang Laboratories and Datapoint Corporation to name just two—offer message distribution systems to the users of their equipment. And, as you saw in Chapter 10, data communications service organizations such as GTE Telenet, Tymnet, The Source, and CompuServe provide facilities to support message distribution systems. A few examples of message distribution system users are:

▌ *Texas Instruments, Incorporated.* TI's DDP network discussed in Chapter 10 distributes more than 4 million messages each year. The average message is 600 to 800 characters in length, and goes to four destinations.

▌ *Hewlett-Packard Company.* Also described in Chapter 10, H-P's DDP network carries 25 million messages a year.

THE MIXED BLESSINGS OF AUTOMATION

As we move automation from the factory floor and the accounting department into the office, we are on new and slippery ground.

We are moving from the objective to the subjective, from productivity that can be measured in discrete units to that strange melange of human interaction and ambiguous communication that characterizes the office environment.

Pressed for results the tendency will be to do the do-able, to automate what we did manually in the past and then point to efficiencies that can be measured in people fired or not hired. The fact that we may be perpetuating management systems or work environments that are superfluous and wasteful may never be considered.

The office of our very near future may also add to a growing malaise in this country—lack of pride in work and the product of that work. Improperly implemented, our electronic gadgetry can form a technological barrier between the worker and the work—whether the individual is a secretary, manager, chief executive, or clerk.

It is also worth noting that Europeans are much more concerned about another facet of automation than we—the potential for the technological obsolescence of the individual and loss of jobs.

In the promised lotus land of the '70s, work took second place to "doing your own thing." In the '80s, work is regaining its status as a central activity of human life.

Studs Terkel, writing in his remarkable documentary *Working,* characterizes his book this way: "It is about a search . . . for daily meaning as well as daily bread, for recognition as well as cash, for astonishment rather than torpor, in short, for a sort of life rather than a Monday through Friday sort of dying."

To escape that kind of dying, to increase our productivity, to realize the potential that is implicit in this new electronic age, we must look afresh at all the time-honored ways of living and working in the office environment. We must devise new systems, new ways of implementing the technology that is developing around us.

Otherwise we will simply automate our mistakes, and, as the office environment disintegrates, we'll hear over and over again that weary refrain, "It wasn't my fault, it was the computer."

—John L. Kirkely, "The Office Merry-Go-Round," *Datamation,* February 1980, p. 43. Reprinted with permission of *Datamation*® magazine, ⓒ Copyright by Technical Publishing Company, A Division of Dun-Donnelley Publishing Corporation, A Dun & Bradstreet Company, 1978. All rights reserved.

Continental Illinois Bank and Trust Company of Chicago. About 2,000 employees are linked by this bank's EMMS, and electronic mail can be delivered around the world in seconds. A message is sent as soon as keying is completed. The next time the recipient (perhaps in Europe or the Far East) checks his or her mailbox, the message will be waiting. In fact, if the recipient's terminal has been left on, the message will be immediately printed or displayed.

University of Alaska. Students, professors, and staff members scattered around the state are able to freely exchange messages through the MAIL System that has been developed for the university's computer network.

Attorneys and their clients. Some lawyers and their clients communicate through a service called ELLA, an acronym for Electronic Legal Advice. To use this message system, a client dials a Tymnet phone number, gains access to the Tymnet network, keys in an account number and an access password, and then sends or receives messages. An attorney communicates with clients in the same way. After receiving a client's request, for example, the lawyer can draft a legal document and send it back to be printed at the client's terminal.

Transmission of Documents and Pictures

In this EMMS function, an original document can be placed in a sending **facsimile, or fax, machine** (see Figure 11-7). A communications link-up is then

Figure 11-7 This digital facsimile transceiver can transmit a one-page letter anywhere in the world in as little as 60 seconds. (Courtesy of 3M)

made with a receiving fax device at another location. As the sending machine scans the document, the receiving device reproduces the scanned image. Thus, when the transmission is completed, the receiving device has produced a duplicate, or "facsimile," of the original. The use of fax machines isn't new, but a great deal of emphasis is currently being placed on improving fax systems by increasing transmission speeds, by reducing transmission costs, and by integrating fax equipment into an automated office setting. A number of data communications service companies also provide fax transmission facilities. Satellite Business Systems, for example, offers high-speed fax services, and the Domestic Transmission Systems unit of ITT offers a Faxpak service for users. Faxpak rates permit users to send a page anywhere in the United States for a few cents.

Of course, copies of printed documents can also be sent electronically between intelligent copying machines or between communicating WP stations. In one case, for example, a Digital Equipment Corporation salesperson on the west coast sat down with a customer in front of a visual display. As sections of a proposed contract were displayed on the screen, changes were agreed on and then entered into the document stored in a WP station. After the contract had been revised, the communicating WP station forwarded it to a similar station at DEC's headquarters on the east coast. Corporate lawyers made a few alterations and then sent the contract back to the west coast. This contract was printed by the west coast WP station and signed by the salesperson and customer. The entire transaction was completed in less than one afternoon.

Computerized Conferences

A computer-based EMMS permits "conferences" to be held at the convenience of the participants. Since the conference dialog may be stored, it's *not* necessary for all participants to be online at their terminals *at the same time*. And, of course, it's also not necessary that they be physically present at the same place. Instead, a person can sit down at a terminal at a convenient time, call up any conversations she or he hasn't seen, make additional comments, respond to questions, etc., and then sign off. Several conference participants can "talk" at the same time. Once again, interruptions of other important work can be avoided. And a permanent history of all conference discussions can be recorded.

Infomedia Corporation of Palo Alto, California, offers two computer conferencing services called Planet and Notepad. To use these services, a group member dials a Tymnet local-access telephone number, couples the telephone to a terminal, and accesses a central computer file that's shared by all group members. Another computer conferencing network is the Electronic Information Exchange System sponsored by the New Jersey Institute of Technology. Subscribers are organized into groups devoted to specific topics such as technology for the handicapped. Many subscribers belong to more than one group, and they're encouraged to communicate with as many groups as they have time and interest for. Group members come from corporations, governments,

Teleconferencing services are expected to grow as their costs drop relative to the cost of travel. (Courtesy AT&T)

and nonprofit foundations. Access is generally through the GTE Telenet system.

The term **computer conferencing** refers to the types of EMMSs that we've just considered that permit people to participate at *different* times. An alternative to computer conferencing is **teleconferencing**—a term that refers to the electronic linking of geographically scattered people who are all participating at the *same* time. Facsimile devices, electronic blackboards that can cause chalk markings to be reproduced on distant TV monitors, the Picturephone Meeting Service supplied by AT&T—these and other technologies allow people to communicate over wide distances in real time. Of course, there are advantages in face-to-face meetings that teleconferencing can't replace. Facial expressions and "body langauge" can convey information that might be missed with teleconferencing. But time, energy, and money are saved when people don't have to travel long distances to conduct a meeting. Organizations using teleconferencing include:

▮ *Exxon Corporation*. If a problem had occurred a few years ago at a remote oil drilling site—e.g., in western Canada—a team of troubleshooting specialists would have been sent from Houston to Calgary to deal with the problem. Today, however, the Houston engineers and managers may "travel" to a Houston conference room to confer with people at Calgary on both a visual and audio basis. Instead of flying three engineers to Calgary in hopes that they can quickly resolve the problem, Exxon can assemble 20 Houston experts for a brainstorming session.

▮ *Holiday Inns*. This large chain offers a HI-Net electronic meeting service. Conference speakers go to a Cleveland Holiday Inn and other participants go to their local Holiday Inn facility. In one recent conference, 2,000 salespeople went to 33 Holiday Inn locations to participate in a convention.

Follow-up Services

In this EMMS function, the message system provides additional services to help the recipient take appropriate action after the message has been delivered. For example, the receiver may:

✓ Forward the message to others with or without further comments.

✓ Store the message in a "personal attention needed" electronic file.

✓ Store the message in a subordinate's electronic file with instructions for the subordinate to take the necessary action.

This chapter has introduced you to word processing and electronic mail/
message systems—two of the fastest-growing areas of computer usage today.
To test and reinforce your understanding of these dynamic forces in the office of
the future, answer the following multiple-choice questions by placing the letter of
the most nearly correct answer in the space provided.

___c___ **1.** The activities performed in most offices today

  a) are supported by an equipment investment of $50,000 per worker.
  b) are being performed with fewer and fewer total workers.
  c) consist of such data processing activities as originating-recording,
     classifying, sorting, calculating, summarizing, communicating,
     storing, and retrieving.
  d) would be impossible without WP and EMMS equipment.

___b___ **2.** Which of the following is not a problem in many of today's offices:

  a) low productivity of office workers relative to other groups.
  b) too many skilled office workers for the declining number of jobs
     available.
  c) escalation of costs.
  d) misfiling of documents.

___d___ **3.** Progress toward the "office of the future" has

  a) virtually stopped in recent years.
  b) been hampered by the rapidly increasing costs of electronic office
     equipment.
  c) been hampered by the lack of interest among equipment vendors
     in developing new products.
  d) not yet lived up to predictions.

___c___ **4.** Word processing

  a) usage has not grown much in recent years.
  b) devices have all used magnetic disks as a storage medium.
  c) devices were often installed in centralized facilities in the mid-
     1960s.
  d) systems were especially appreciated by secretaries right from the
     very beginning.

___a___ **5.** A modern WP system

  a) is basically a disguised computer that's programmed to do word
     processing.
  b) must be dedicated to performing only WP functions.
  c) cannot be implemented using micro- or minicomputer compo-
     nents.
  d) is always a shared-logic device.

d **6.** A shared-resource WP system

    a) has only a single station that contains all the components needed to perform text processing.
    b) has multiple stations that share the logic and storage sections of a single central computer.
    c) has only a one- or two-line visual display.
    d) has not been described by any of the above responses.

d **7.** Word processors can be used to

    a) relay text messages between communicating stations.
    b) prepare issues of magazines.
    c) accept input from an OCR reader.
    d) do all the above tasks.

a **8.** Electronic mail

    a) is a frequently used term that has no generally accepted definition.
    b) cannot be used to compete with the postal service.
    c) costs have been increasing in recent years.
    d) cannot be substituted for telephone messages.

d **9.** Which, if any, of the following functions cannot be performed by an EMMS:

    a) provide message distribution services.
    b) transmit copies of documents and pictures.
    c) provide computerized conference services.
    d) All the above functions can be performed by an EMMS.

b **10.** Messages sent over a message distribution system

    a) can be used by individuals but not by groups.
    b) can be periodically reviewed by the recipient at a convenient time.
    c) must be printed.
    d) tend to give a feeling of isolation to people at remote sites.

b **11.** A facsimile machine

    a) cannot be used in an EMMS.
    b) is needed at both the sending and receiving station.
    c) requires low-speed communication channels.
    not d) is the only device that can send copies of documents over telecommunications channels.

c **12.** Computer conferencing and teleconferencing

    a) are terms that mean the same thing.
    b) both require that people participate in conferences at the same time.
    c) are both used to link geographically scattered people.
    d) both permit people to participate at whatever times are convenient for them.

1. The functions performed in offices consist of such data processing activities as originating-recording, classifying, sorting, calculating, summarizing, communicating, storing, and retrieving. Traditional office tools and techniques are still often followed to perform these tasks. But rising costs, the relatively low productivity of office workers, and other problems are resulting in the introduction of new electronic technology into offices.

2. The change from the traditional office setting to an electronic office environment is likely to evolve through several development stages. Most organizations today are in the early stages of development and are introducing equipment to perform specific tasks such as word processing, message distribution, document transmission and reproduction, and computer conferencing.

3. Word processing is the rapidly growing use of electronic equipment to create, view, edit, manipulate, transmit, store, retrieve, and print text material. Word processors are basically computers that are programmed to process text material. Dedicated word processors perpetually run their WP programs, and small general-purpose computers can be temporarily converted into word processors merely by loading a WP program into storage.

4. Word processing systems can be classified into stand-alone, shared-logic, and shared-resource categories. A stand-alone WP station is a single unit that contains all the components needed to perform text processing. A shared-logic system has multiple keystations that share the logic and storage sections of a single central processor. A shared-resource system also has multiple stations, but each station has its own computer. These multiple stations simply share certain expensive resources such as printers and large-capacity disk drives. A number of examples of the uses of WP are presented in the chapter.

5. An electronic mail/message system is defined here to be one that can store and deliver, by electronic means, messages that would otherwise probably be forwarded through the postal service or sent verbally over telephone lines. The use of EMMS is growing rapidly, and this is partly due to postal service delays and the frustrations caused by "telephone tag."

6. An EMMS can provide electronic message distribution services, a means of transmitting copies of documents and pictures, computerized conference functions, and other services. A message distribution system allows messages to be sent at any time to specified individuals or groups. Recipients periodically review stored messages at convenient times. Interruptions are reduced, people may feel less isolated, and communication between time zones is facilitated. Many computer vendors and data communications services offer message distribution systems. Several examples of the uses of these sytems are presented in the chapter. The use of facsimile machines to transmit copies of documents and pictures, and a discussion of computer conferencing and teleconferencing are also presented. Computer conferencing and teleconferencing are both used to link people who are geographically separated, but computer conferencing permits people to participate at different times while teleconferencing requires participants to be online at the same time.

KEY TERMS AND CONCEPTS

You should now be able to define and use the following terms and concepts (the numbers shown indicate the pages where the terms and concepts are first mentioned):

word processing (WP) 299
dedicated word processor 300
stand-alone word processor 300
shared-logic WP system 301
shared-resource WP system 301

global search 302
electronic mail/message system
  (EMMS) 303
telephone tag 303
executive workstation 304

facsimile (fax) machine 306
computer conferencing 308
teleconferencing 308

TOPICS FOR REVIEW AND DISCUSSION

1. (*a*) What functions are performed in offices? (*b*) Identify and discuss the problems that have developed in recent years in offices that have followed traditional office practices.

2. Discuss two factors that are likely to lead to the introduction of new technology and applications in the offices of many organizations in the next few years.

3. "Most organizations today are in the early stages of developing an automated office and are now introducing equipment to perform a few specific tasks." What are these tasks?

4. (*a*) What is word processing? (*b*) How did it develop?

5. "A dedicated word processor is basically a disguised computer that perpetually runs a program to process text material." Discuss this statement.

6. Word processing systems today generally fall into three categories. Identify and discuss these categories.

7. Give three examples of how WP can be used.

8. (*a*) What's an EMMS? (*b*) What are the limitations of the alternatives to an EMMS?

9. (*a*) What are the benefits of an electronic message distribution system? (*b*) How are such systems used?

10. (*a*) How are fax machines used? (*b*) Can other devices perform the same function?

11. (*a*) What is computerized conferencing? (*b*) What is teleconferencing? (*c*) Give an example of each type of service.

ANSWERS TO FEEDBACK AND REVIEW SECTION

1. c	5. a	9. d
2. b	6. d	10. b
3. d	7. d	11. b
4. c	8. a	12. c

Voice Messaging Systems
Memos and Mailboxes of the Future

ECS Telecommunications is a small, privately held company based in Richardson, Texas. ECS was formed in 1978 by the inventor of the first electronic voice messaging system, Gordon Matthews.

ECS is now competing with two giants of the computer world, IBM and Wang, in the rapidly expanding market for voice messaging systems. According to the Yankee Group, a Boston consulting firm, the market for such systems could be worth $5 billion by 1985. And that is a market that did not exist before ECS sold its first system in 1980. With a year and a half lead time of selling its systems before Wang and IBM jumped into the fray, Matthews feels ECS has a commanding market lead—so much so that he took out a full-page advertisement in *The Wall Street Journal* welcoming IBM and Wang to the business. The ad depicted a jagged mountain with the letters ECS perched on top. The message read, "It's been lonely at the top." Matthews truly welcomed the competition: "When IBM entered the market, it legitimized us."

ECS's Voice Message System (VMS) functions somewhat like a mailbox. However, instead of holding a letter or a memo, it holds a recorded message. Caller's messages are converted into digital data—much like that stored on voice-synthesis memory chips. And messages can then be handled just as if the information had been generated on a word processing terminal. The same voice message can be sent to groups of people, for example.

Voice mailboxes eliminate (or at least reduce) many frustrations of telephone communications including:

- *Busy Signals.* It is estimated that only one out of four business calls goes through on the first try. ECS's large system handles 64 lines at a time and busy signals are rare.
- *"Telephone Tag."* This is the game of two busy people trying to reach each other. When one is in, the other is out. At 3M Company, the first purchaser of a VMS system, managers are saving a lot of time and feel their productivity is increased by handling their messages when it fits their schedules.
- *Wasted Time during Calls.* A NASA study found that a third of the average business phone call contains no pertinent exchange of information.
- *Costs.* ECS estimates that it costs between $5 and $7 to prepare and distribute a letter or memo. Voice mailbox messages cost about 10 cents each. If, however, a printed copy of a message is needed, the digital technology of a VMS allows a manager to give instructions for the voice message to be transcribed by a word processor.

Companies as diverse as American Express, Atlantic Richfield, Hercules, and Hoffman La Roche have tested the VMS, and employees are enthusiastic about it. A spokesperson for Hoffman La Roche, the pharmaceuticals firm, said the system had increased contact between people by 60 percent. "I don't think we could take this away from people now."

—Sources of data: "Voice Mail Arrives in the Office," *Business Week,* June 9, 1980, pp. 80–84; "Business Mail Goes Electronic," *High Technology,* January/February 1982, pp. 22–25.

module 3 Programming

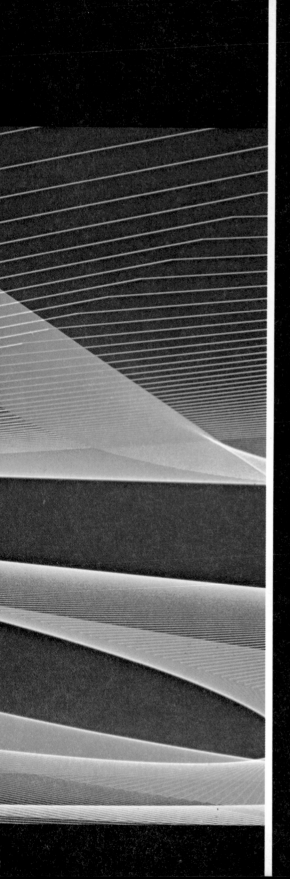

Computer Software Concepts

In the Background Module, you learned that computer hardware was just one element in a computer-based data processing system. The focus of this module is on the analysis and preparation of computer applications programs. And a brief outline of the functions of operating system programs is also included. The hardware components in a computer-based system are discussed in the preceding module, and the analysis and design of system procedures are treated in the following module. The chapters included in the Programming Module are:

Intricate, abstract patterns such as the one shown here are produced by complex computer programs. (Photo courtesy of Melvin L. Prueitt, Los Alamos National Laboratory)

chapter 12

Programming Analysis

THE MAPS OF PROGRAMMING

The earliest explorers in recorded history drew crude maps to help them find their way home and to guide others in later exploration. A map is a representation of a region of the earth or the heavens. As a verb, "to map" means to plan, to delineate, to arrange—especially in detail.

In this still-early phase of the computer age, programmers function somewhat like explorers as they seek to put computers to work solving problems. Data, from input to manipulation to output, must be ordered and traced. And programmers use a kind of map—complete with symbols and directions—to put computers to work. These maps are called flowcharts. In varying detail, flowcharts not only record the paths of data through computation but also serve as tools for finding effective and efficient paths. Flowcharts, the maps of programming, then, are used to solve problems and, like maps, to represent the road to goals.

Precise system flowcharts are valuable during the development of usable program charts. (Courtesy Informatics, Inc.)

Looking Ahead

This chapter is the first of three that deal with the analysis and preparation of computer applications programs. After a brief introduction to some program development concepts, you'll see here how problem specifications are broken down into the input/output, calculation, logic/comparison, and storage/retrieval steps that computers are able to perform. Program flowcharts are used to analyze and discuss the specifications for a series of applications problems—all of which were introduced in Chapter 2. (Solutions for all these problems are coded later in Chapter 14.) You'll also have the opportunity to prepare your own charts according to the specifications given in four Feedback and Review sections. The final pages of the chapter then give you a summary of the logic structures used in programs, and introduce you to two other programming analysis tools.

Thus, after studying this chapter, you should be able to:

▌ Define the programming process and have a general idea of how to develop a program

▌ Identify the basic symbols used in program flowcharts, and be able to construct a simple chart to meet a set of problem specifications

▌ Create the logic needed to process multiple records and understand the use of accumulators and counters

▌ Summarize the basic logic patterns used to solve problems

▌ Outline the benefits and limitations of flowcharts

▌ Identify and discuss alternative analysis tools that may be used to replace or supplement program flowcharts

▌ Understand and use the key terms and concepts listed at the end of this chapter

PROGRAM DEVELOPMENT: AN ORIENTATION

You'll recall from Chapter 3 that people must generally follow a series of steps before they can use computers to perform useful work. These steps are:

1. *Defining the need.* The particular problem(s) to be solved, or the tasks to be accomplished, must be clearly defined. In organizations, managers, employees, and data processing specialists often work together to identify the need and set goals. (cost-benefit requirements)

2. *System analysis.* Data pertaining to the problem(s) must be gathered and analyzed. In organizations, a study team comprised of information system users and one or more data processing specialists often collaborate to gather and analyze data about current data processing operations.

3. *System design.* The next step is to design any new systems or applications that are required to satisfy the need. Organizational study teams often prepare design specifications that include the output desired, the input data needed, and the general processing procedures required to convert input data into output results.

4. *Programming analysis.* Programmers must next break down the design specifications into the input/output, calculation, logic/comparison, and storage/retrieval operations required to satisfy the need.

5. *Program preparation.* The specific operations identified in step 4 must then be translated or coded by programmers into a language and form acceptable to the computer.

6. *Implementation and maintenance.* The coded program(s) must be checked for errors and tested prior to being used on a routine basis. Since the implemented program(s) are often subject to modification and improvement, they must therefore be maintained.

The **system analysis and design process** includes the *first three* of the six steps listed above. Further system analysis and design details are left to the chapters in the Systems Module. For our purposes in this module, **programming** is defined as the **process** of converting broad system specifications into usable machine instructions that produce desired results. But as Figure 12-1 shows, programming isn't just the program preparation or coding step. Rather, programming consists of the *last three* of the six listed steps. It's a challenging process that doesn't begin and end with the writing and/or keying of lines of code.

A Program Development Approach

Part of the challenge of programming is that different programmers can (and do) use different strategies to develop solutions for programming applications. However, certain questions must usually be considered by a programmer regardless of the **program development approach** used. The following checklist of these questions should be helpful to you as you develop your own programs:

1. *Have the problem specifications been spelled out clearly and completely?* A specification to "Write a program to prepare customer bills" is obviously inadequate. Before any significant progress can be made, the following type of revised specifications must be available:

> Write a program to print a number of customer bills, with each bill containing the customer's name, street address, city, state, Zip code, and net amount owed. The input data to be processed are customer name, street address, city, state, Zip code, quantity of a single product purchased, and unit price of the product.

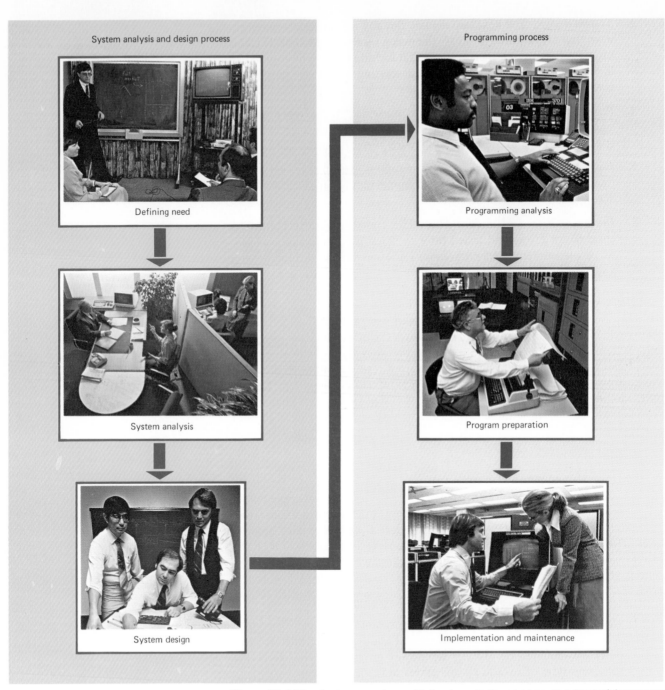

System analysis and design process

Defining need

System analysis

System design

Programming process

Programming analysis

Program preparation

Implementation and maintenance

Figure 12-1 The six steps people must follow in order to use computers for useful purposes may be classified into system analysis/design and programming stages. The chapters in this module deal with the three steps in the programming process. Details of system analysis/design are presented in the Systems Module. (Photos courtesy Western Electric; Honeywell, Inc.; TRW, Inc.; General Electric Information Systems Company; Edith G. Haun/Stock, Boston; and Control Data Corporation)

2. *Am I familiar with a solution method that will solve the problem?* An **algorithm** is a finite number of step-by-step directions that are sure to solve a particular type of problem. The algorithm to compute the acreage in a rectangular lot, for example, consists of the following steps: (*a*) Multiply the length (in feet) of the lot by the width (in feet) of the lot to get the square footage of the property, and (*b*) divide this square footage figure by 43,560—the number of square feet in an acre—to get the acreage of the property. In some cases, a programmer has personal knowledge of an algorithm or procedure that will solve the problem at hand. If this is the case, the problem solution may then be coded in a selected language; if this isn't the case, then the next question should be considered.

3 *Can I locate a solution method to solve the problem from other people or from books or journals?* Full or partial solutions to problem situations are often available. After all, the programmer who's given the task of writing a billing program today is certainly not the first one to have faced that problem. If other resources can provide the solution method, the necessary program may then be coded in a selected language. If a solution method is unavailable, then the next question must be considered.

4. *How can I develop an algorithm or procedure that will solve this problem?* This is the creative problem-solving question that often challenges programmers. An effective approach to follow in the programming analysis stage of program development is to *break down a large* (and seemingly unmanageable) *problem into a series of smaller and more understandable tasks* or subproblems. Each of the above questions in the checklist can then be applied to the individual subproblems. For example, the revised billing program specification listed in question 1 can be broken down into the following major tasks:

(a) Enter customer name, local address, city, state, Zip code, quantity purchased, and unit price into the CPU.
(b) Compute net amount owed by customer.
(c) Print customer name, local address, city, state, Zip code, and net amount owed.
(d) If there's another bill to process, branch program control back to **a.** Otherwise, continue to next task.
(e) Stop processing.

In many (perhaps most) cases, it will be desirable to break some of the initially identified tasks into still smaller units. For example, task **b** must be refined as follows:

(b) Compute net amount owed by customer.
(b1) Compute net amount owed by the formula $A = Q \times P$ (Where A is net amount, Q is quantity purchased, and P is unit price.)

The programming analysis stage continues until *every* small task or sub-problem has been reduced to the point that the programmer is confident he or she does have *a* solution method that will solve the task. Effective program coding can begin only after the programmer has this confidence. Note that it's not necessary that the first solution method be *the* best possible method. Improvements can often be added to functioning programs, and the best possible method may never be discovered.

A number of programming analysis tools are available to help the programmer break a problem down into smaller tasks in order to arrive at a solution method. One frequently used tool is the program flowchart.

PROGRAM FLOWCHARTS: SOME GENERAL CONCEPTS

Flowcharts have existed for years and have been used for many purposes. You'll recall from Chapter 3 that a *system flowchart* provides a broad overview of the processing operations that are to be accomplished, but it doesn't go into detail about how input data are to be used to produce output information. A **program flowchart,** on the other hand, *is* a detailed graphical representation of how steps are to be performed within the machine to produce the needed output. Thus, as Figure 12-2 shows, a program flowchart evolves from a system chart.

Levels of Program Flowcharts

There are no set standards on the amount of detail that should be provided in a program chart. The billing program outlined in Figures 12-2*b* and 12-2*c* could easily have been shown in a single chart. But as you've seen, it's often desirable in more complex situations to break major **program** segments or **modules** into still smaller and more manageable units. Figure 12-2*c* illustrates how a smaller chart can evolve from a higher-level chart. A chart that outlines the main segments of a program is called a **main-control, modular,** or **macro chart.** One that details the steps in a module is called a **micro chart.**

Symbols Used in Program Flowcharts

Only a few symbols are needed in program charting to indicate the necessary operations. These symbols, which have been adopted by the American National Standards Institute, are shown beside their descriptions, which follow. (Most of them have already been used in Figure 12-2.)

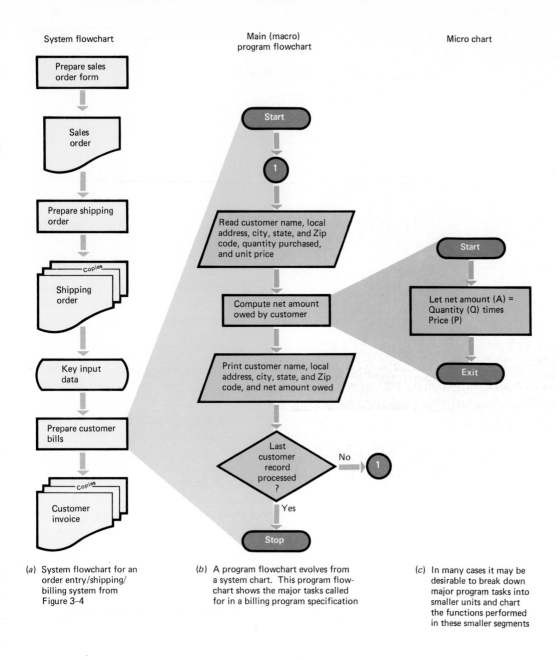

System flowchart

- Prepare sales order form
- Sales order
- Prepare shipping order
- Shipping order (Copies)
- Key input data
- Prepare customer bills
- Customer invoice (Copies)

Main (macro) program flowchart

- Start
- 1
- Read customer name, local address, city, state, and Zip code, quantity purchased, and unit price
- Compute net amount owed by customer
- Print customer name, local address, city, state, and Zip code, and net amount owed
- Last customer record processed ? — No → 1
- Yes
- Stop

Micro chart

- Start
- Let net amount (A) = Quantity (Q) times Price (P)
- Exit

(a) System flowchart for an order entry/shipping/ billing system from Figure 3-4

(b) A program flowchart evolves from a system chart. This program flow-chart shows the major tasks called for in a billing program specification

(c) In many cases it may be desirable to break down major program tasks into smaller units and chart the functions performed in these smaller segments

Figure 12-2 A program flowchart evolves from a system chart. In many cases, a main (or macro) program chart identifies the major tasks or modules to be performed, and then detailed micro charts are used to show the processing steps within specified modules. Thus, programmers may prepare one macro program chart and several micro charts during programming analysis.

Input/output

Input/Output. The basic **input/output symbol** used in system charts is also used in program charts to represent any I/O function. The special symbols designating cards, tapes, documents, etc., that are used in system charts are generally not used with program diagrams. In the program flowchart section of Figure 12-2, the same I/O symbol designates:

▌ The *input data* to be read into the CPU (customer name, address, quantity purchased, and product price).

▌ The *output information* to be printed on the customer's bill (customer name, address, and amount owed).

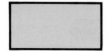

Processing

Processing. The rectangle used in system charts is again used in program charts to represent processing operations. Of course, the processing described in the rectangle of a program chart is only a small segment of a major processing step called for in a system chart. Arithmetic and data movement instructions are generally placed in these boxes. A **processing symbol** is shown in the micro chart in Figure 12-2c. The net amount of a customer's bill is computed by multiplying the quantity of a product purchased by the unit price of the product.

Terminal

Terminal. The **terminal symbol,** as the name suggests, represents the beginning (START) and the end (STOP) of a program. It may also be used to signal a program interruption point when information may enter or leave. For example, to detect certain errors in input data, the programmer may provide a special program branch ending in a terminal symbol labeled "HALT."

Decision

Decision. The I/O and processing symbols have two flow lines (one entry and one exit), while the terminal has a single entry or exit line. The diamond-shaped **decision symbol,** on the other hand, has one entrance and at least two exit paths or branches. This symbol indicates logic/comparison operations, and was used several times in Chapter 2. As shown in Chapter 2 and in the macro program chart in Figure 12-2b, exit paths are generally determined by a yes or no answer to some **conditional statement** written in the form of a question. In Figure 12-2b, the condition to be determined is whether or not the last customer record has been processed. As you'll recall from Chapter 2, a dummy record can be placed at the end of the customer file so that the computer program will know when the last valid record has been processed. So long as valid records remain, program control will exit from the conditional branch of the decision symbol labeled "NO." When the last valid record has been processed and the dummy record is then read, the "YES" branch is followed and processing stops.

Connector

Connector. A circular **connector symbol** labeled "1" is encountered in Figure 12-2b when program control exits from the decision symbol along the "NO" branch. This connector symbol is used when additional flow lines might cause confusion and reduce understanding. Two connectors with identical labels serve the same function as a long flow line. That is, they show an exit to some other chart section, or they indicate an entry from another part of the chart. How's it possible to determine if a connector is used as an entry or an exit point? It's very simple: If an arrow *enters but doesn't leave* a connector, it's an exit point and program control is transferred to the identically labeled connector that does have an outlet. Thus, in Figure 12-2b, the connector to the right of the decision symbol is an exit point, and program control loops back to the entry connector at the top of the chart when another record is to be processed.

Predefined Process. Programmers frequently find that certain kinds of processing operations are repeated in their programs. Instead of rewriting a module each time it's needed, the programmer can prepare it once and then integrate it into other programs as required. Libraries of these predefined processes, or **subroutines,** are often maintained to reduce the time and cost of programming. Thus, a single **predefined process symbol** replaces a number of operations that need not be detailed at that particular point in a chart. (Of course, a detailed micro flowchart of the subroutine should be available if needed.) In short, the subroutine is a commonly used module that receives input from the main-control program, performs its limited task, and then returns the output to the primary program.

Predefined process

Annotation. **Annotation flags** are used to add clarifying comments to other flowchart symbols. They can be drawn on either side of another symbol.

We'll use these flowchart symbols in the next section to analyze a number of program applications. Beginning with several very simple problem situations, we'll gradually develop these situations into more realistic examples. The problems that are charted in this chapter are coded in the BASIC programming language in Chapter 14.

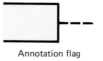

Annotation flag

PROGRAMMING ANALYSIS USING FLOWCHARTS

You learned in Chapter 2 that applications such as billing customers, paying employees, analyzing sales, controlling inventories, and preparing mailing labels account for the greatest use of business computing resources. Furthermore, many of these same applications are processed regularly by schools, hospitals, and government agencies. These, then, are the types of applications that we'll analyze and chart in this section. And all our applications will apply to a single organization—R-K Enterprises, which was introduced in Chapter 2.

Simple Input/Process/Output Charts

You know that programming analysis involves converting problem specifications into the I/O, calculation, logic/comparison, and storage/retrieval

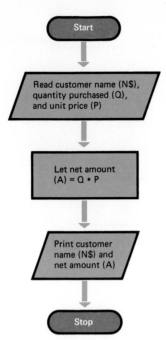

Start

Read customer name (N$),
quantity purchased (Q),
and unit price (P)

Let net amount
(A) = Q * P

Print customer
name (N$) and
net amount (A)

Stop

Figure 12-3 Program flowchart for problem 1: Simple Billing, Single Customer.

operations needed to solve the problem. (You also know, of course, that not every type of operation may be needed for every problem solution.) Let's now begin to analyze some problem specifications to see how the use of flowcharts can be of value.

Problem 1: Simple Billing, Single Customer. Let's assume that right after R-K's partners, Rob and Kay, decided to grant credit to selected customers of their mosquito bird tee shirts, they drew up the following specifications for a program to prepare customer bills:

▌ Input data to be processed are customer name, quantity of shirts purchased, and unit price of the shirts.

▌ The net amount owed by the customer should be computed.

▌ The printed output should be a bill giving the customer's name and net amount owed.

The flowchart shown in Figure 12-3 satisfies these specifications, and illustrates a simple input/process/output procedure. You'll notice that convenient abbreviations have been assigned by the programmer to identify the input data and the result of processing. The programmer has considerable freedom in selecting abbreviations, but, as we'll see in Chapter 14, the selections must conform to the rules of a programming language. As you saw earlier, the net amount owed by a customer is found by multiplying the quantity purchased times the unit price. In flowcharts and programs, the asterisk is generally used to indicate multiplication. Other operation symbols include + (addition), − (subtraction), and / (division).

Feedback and Review 12-1

Let's assume that the procedure charted in Figure 12-3 will give an accurate figure of the amount owed by out-of-state customers. Let's further suppose, however, that a sales tax of 6 percent of the net amount owed must be charged on bills sent to customers within the state. To test your understanding of the program development and flowcharting concepts you have just read, *prepare a program flowchart* for bills sent *within* the state. Your chart should reflect the following specifications:

▌ Input data to be processed are customer name, quantity of shirts purchased, and unit price of the shirts.

▌ The net amount owed by the customer should be computed.

▌ The sales tax amount should be computed using a tax rate of .06.

▌ The sales tax should be added to the net amount to get the total amount of the bill.

▌ The printed output should be a bill giving the customer's name, net amount owed, sales tax amount, and total amount owed.

You've probably already noticed what Kay and Rob quickly found out: Their initial billing program would compute one customer bill and then stop! After each bill was printed, the program would have to be reloaded into the computer before the next bill could be processed—hardly an efficient use of the partners' valuable time.

Problem 2: Simple Billing, Multiple Customers. In order to modify the program charted in Figure 12-3, the partners prepared the following revised specifications:

▌ Input data to be processed are customer name, local address, city, state, and Zip code, quantity of shirts purchased, and unit price of the shirts.

▌ The net amount owed by the customer should be computed.

▌ The printed output should be a bill for each customer giving the customer's name, local address, city, state, and Zip code, and net amount owed.

▌ The program should be able to process bills for any number of customers!

The flowchart shown in Figure 12-4 satisfies these requirements. The I/O operations and the net amount computation are similar to those shown in Figure 12-3. But this program is much more flexible: It can follow a controlled loop, repeat processing steps, and print any number of bills. A **loop** consists of a body made up of a sequence of instructions that can be executed repetitively, a test for exit condition, and a return provision. Without the ability to execute loops, computers would be little more than toys. The **body of the loop** in our example that makes repetition possible is found between the two connector symbols labeled "A." The repetitive processing of bills continues until the last valid bill has been printed and a "sentinel value" is encountered. This value is the quantity purchased amount of −99.9 that's shown in the decision symbol in Figure 12-4. It will appear in a last dummy record at the end of the customer file. A **sentinel value,** then, is simply some *arbitrary* data item that's placed at the end of a file to indicate that all valid data have been processed. (In our example, the sentinel could have been a unit price of −999.9 rather than a quantity value of −99.9.) Of course, the sentinel must have a value that *couldn't possibly occur* as a valid data item. A negative number consisting of a string of 9s is often used as the sentinel value because the 9s stand out and are generally understood to be artificial or "dummy record numbers."

In summary, then, as long as valid records are being processed, the answer to the **test for exit condition** shown in the decision symbol in Figure 12-4 will be "NO." The bill amount will then be calculated, the bill will be printed, and program control will loop back to read the next record to be processed. When all bills have been printed and the dummy record is read, the answer to the conditional statement is "YES." The exit path out of the loop is then followed

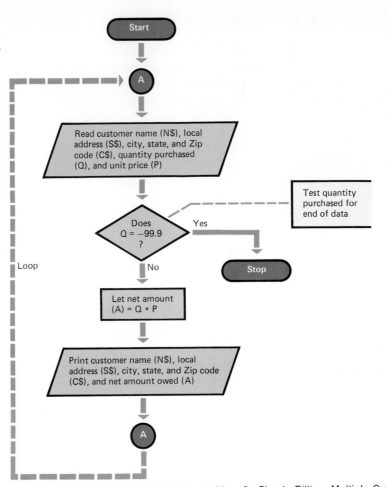

Figure 12-4 Program flowchart for problem 2: Simple Billing, Multiple Customers.

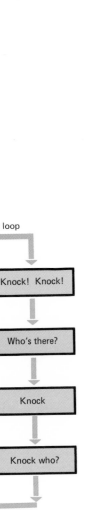

Figure 12-5 An irrelevant example of an endless loop. (From Stan Kelly-Bootle, *The Devil's DP Dictionary*, New York, McGraw-Hill Book Company, 1981. Used with the permission of the McGraw-Hill Book Company.)

and processing stops. Such an exit path must, of course, exist when loops are used. **Endless** or **infinite loops** (Figure 12-5) result from failure to provide an exit path and are a common and troublesome problem that programmers often run into.

Problem 3: Preparing Mailing Labels. You'll recall from Chapter 2 that Kay and Rob mail promotional material to the prospective customers on their mailing list. The following specifications were set up to prepare a program to print the names and addresses of these prospects on gummed labels:

▌ Input data to be processed are prospect name, local address, and city, state, and Zip code.

▌ The printed output should be a gummed label for each prospect giving the prospect's name, local address, city, state, and Zip code.

▎ The program should be able to process labels for any number of prospects.

Figure 12-6a shows a chart drawn to these specifications; Figure 12-6b shows the mailing label output. In this case, the dummy record inserted at the end of the prospect file has "END OF DATA" as the prospect's name. The exit path out of this loop will be followed only when the dummy record satisfies the exit condition test.

Problem 4: Sales Compensation, Single Commission Rate. You saw in Chapter 2 (and in Figure 2-5, page 47) that every four weeks Rob and Kay receive a sales compensation report that's used to evaluate salesperson performance and prepare paychecks. During the preparation of the sales compensation program, they drew up the following specifications for the report:

▎ The report should have headings indicating the name, sales amount, and earnings.

Figure 12-6 (a) Program flowchart for problem 3: Preparing Mailing Labels. (b) Mailing label output.

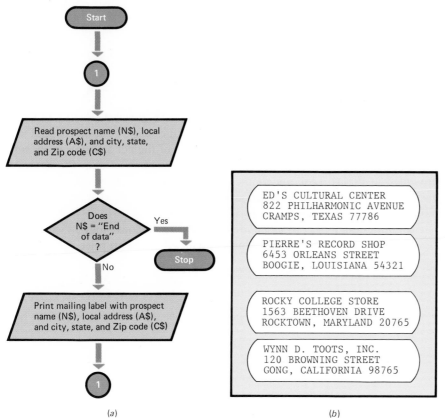

(a)   (b)

▎Input data to be processed are the name and weekly sales data for each salesperson.

▎The four-week total sales amount should be computed for each salesperson.

▎The total sales amount for each salesperson should be multiplied by a 10 percent commission rate to get the earnings of each salesperson.

▎Under the report headings should be printed the name, total sales amount, and earnings for each salesperson.

▎The program should be able to include any number of salespeople in the report.

The flowchart in Figure 12-7 meets these specifications. The report headings are printed first. The body of the loop that processes the data for each salesperson is then located between the connector symbols labeled "1." If the printing of the headings had been included in the loop, there would be a separate—and redundant—heading for each salesperson. The exit path out of the loop is followed after the computer reads a record—the last dummy record—that has a sales value of −99.9 for week number 1.

Feedback and Review 12-2

Let's assume once again that the billing procedure shown in Figure 12-4 will only produce accurate results for bills sent to out-of-state customers. And let's suppose once more that a sales tax of 6 percent of the net amount owed must be charged on bills sent to customers within the state. Using the concepts presented in Figure 12-4, *update the program flowchart you prepared in Feedback and Review 12-1* to meet these specifications:

▎Input data to be processed are customer name, local address, city, state, and Zip code, quantity of shirts purchased, and unit price of the shirts.

▎Compute the net amount owed by the customer.

▎Compute the sales tax amount using a tax rate of .06.

▎Add the sales tax to the net amount to get the total amount of the bill.

▎Print a bill for each customer giving the customer's name, local address, city, state, and Zip code, net amount owed, sales tax amount, and total amount owed.

▎The program should be able to process bills for any number of customers.

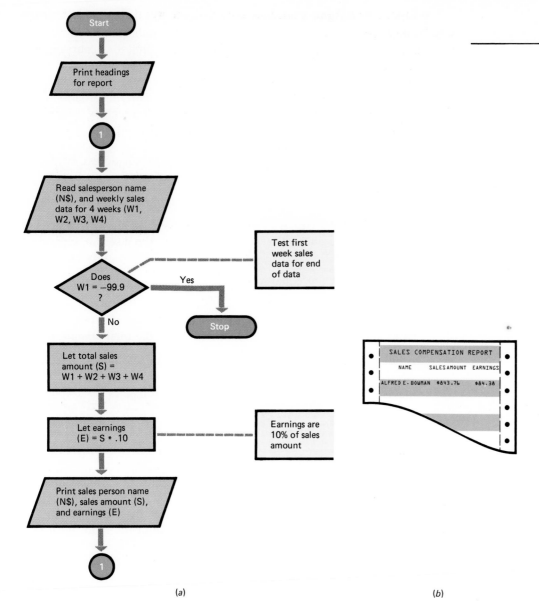

(a)   (b)

Figure 12-7 (a) Program flowchart for problem 4: Sales Compensation, Single Commission
Rate. (b) Sales compensation report from Figure 2-5.

Multiple-Decision Charts

It has been possible to chart each of the preceding problems using only a
single decision symbol. But the intricate logic needed to solve more complex
problems requires that *many* decision paths be available. The following problem gives an example of the use of multiple decisions. Later problems will also
use a series of logic decisions.

Problem 5: Simple Billing with Discount. We'll now add a second logic/comparison operation to the partners' billing application. (This operation was discussed briefly in Chapter 2.) Let's assume that to encourage large shipments, Kay and Rob decide to offer a 15 percent discount on purchases with a quantity equal to or greater than ($>$) 100 dozen tee shirts. Let's also assume that the customers who receive bills processed with this program must be charged a 6 percent sales tax on the amount owed after any discount is deducted. The following program specifications are drafted:

- Input data to be processed are customer name, local address, city, state, and Zip code, quantity purchased, and unit price.

- The amount owed before any discount should be computed.

- If quantity purchased is $>$ 100 (dozen tee shirts), allow a 15 percent discount on the amount owed. Otherwise, set the discount amount at zero.

- A sales tax amount equal to 6 percent of the amount owed should be computed after the discount is deducted.

- The sales tax amount should be added to the amount owed by the customer after the discount is deducted to get the total amount owed.

- A bill should be printed for each customer giving customer name, local address, city, state, and Zip code, quantity purchased, unit price, amount owed before discount, discount amount, sales tax owed, and total amount owed.

- The program should be able to process bills for any number of customers.

The flowchart for this program is shown in Figure 12-8. Since the first several steps are similar to those in Figure 12-4, we don't need to consider them here. The conditional statement in the second decision symbol—IS Q $>$ 100?—requires that the quantity purchased field of the input record be compared to 100. If the quantity is 100 (dozen) or more, a discount of 15 percent is computed. If the quantity is *less* than 100, a discount amount of zero is supplied. The last two processing symbols in the chart compute the sales tax and the total amount owed by the customer. Finally, a customer's bill is printed and program control branches back to read another customer record.

Feedback and Review 12-3

Here's your chance to update the sales compensation report program produced for problem 4 and charted in Figure 12-7. Let's suppose that Rob and Kay decided to pay salespeople a 12 percent commission if their total sales for a period are equal to or greater than $100. If total sales are less than $100, however, the

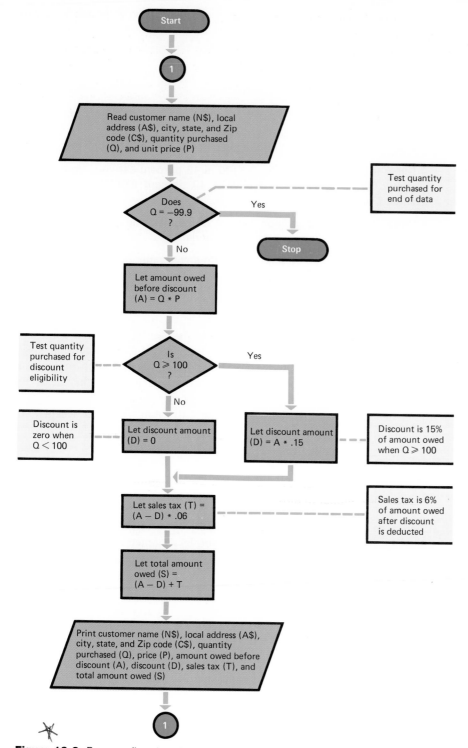

Figure 12-8 Program flowchart for problem 5: Simple Billing with Discount.

commission rate will remain at the 10 percent value used in problem 4. You should thus *prepare a revised sales compensation report flowchart* to meet these specifications:

▌ The report should have headings indicating the name, sales amount, and earnings.

▌ Input data to be processed are the name and weekly sales data for each salesperson.

▌ The 4-week total sales amount should be computed for each salesperson.

▌ If this total sales amount is $>$ $100, a 12 percent earnings commission should be computed. Otherwise, a 10 percent earnings commission should be calculated.

▌ Under the report headings should be printed the name, total sales amount, and earnings for each salesperson.

▌ The program should be able to include any number of salespeople in the report.

Charting the Use of Accumulators

Two sales analysis reports are used by the partners to manage their business. (These reports were discussed in Chapter 2 and presented in Figures 2-13a and b, page 59.) An important programming technique—the use of an accumulator—is used to prepare both these reports. **An accumulator** is a programmer-designated storage location in the CPU that's used to accept and store a *running total* of individual values as they become available during processing. The contents of the storage location *must* initially be set to zero. After this first step, each successive value placed in the accumulator is added to the value already there. Accumulators are used in the sales analysis reports to accumulate total sales figures.

Problem 6: Sales Report Classified By Type of Product. This report classifies the purchases made during a period by a named customer according to the type of product shipped. There are different reports for each of the products sold. The following specifications were used to prepare the report program:

▌ The product name should be entered and printed as part of the report heading.

▌ Input data to be processed should also include customer name, local address, city, state, and Zip code, quantity purchased, and unit price. The program should process any number of customers.

▌ The net amount purchased should be computed.

▌ A sales tax amount equal to 6 percent of the net amount purchased should be calculated.

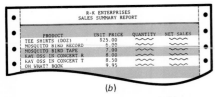

Sales reports (*a*) by product, and (*b*) a summary report of all products from Figure 2-13.

▌ The sales tax amount should be added to the net amount purchased to get the total sales amount for the customer.

▌ The total sales amounts for all customers should be accumulated to get a grand total amount of sales of the product.

▌ The name, local address, and city, state, and Zip code of each customer should be printed on the report.

▌ "QUANTITY," "UNIT PRICE," "NET AMOUNT," "SALES TAX," and "TOTAL" subheadings should be printed below the name and address of each customer.

▌ The quantity purchased, unit price, net amount, sales tax, and total amount figures for each customer should be printed below these subheadings.

▌ After all valid customer records have been processed, a "GRAND TOTAL" subheading and the accumulated grand total amount should be printed at the bottom of the report.

The chart in Figure 12-9 was produced to these specifications. You'll notice that the first operation is to set a grand total sales accumulator (G) to zero. The product name is then read, and a report heading is printed. As you'll see in the programming language used in Chapter 14, characters that are bounded by quotation marks in a printing operation are reproduced in exactly that way when a program is run. Thus, if the product name identified by P\$ is TEE SHIRTS (DOZ), the heading set up by our chart will be SALES REPORT FOR TEE SHIRTS (DOZ). (Of course, if P\$ is some other product, that product will be printed in the heading.)

The body of the loop to process the input data for each customer begins at the connector labeled 1. The input data from each customer record are read, the net amount purchased is computed, the sales tax is figured, and the total amount purchased is calculated. The next processing symbol then reads LET $G = G + S$, where G equals the value in the accumulator and S is the total purchases made by a customer. If the *first* customer's total purchases are \$500, then \$500 will be added to the initial value in the accumulator (0), and the new total of \$500 will now be stored in the accumulator. If the next customer's purchases are \$350, the total in the accumulator will then be \$850 (\$500 + \$350).

After the accumulator has been updated, the customer's name and address are printed. Several subheadings are printed below each name and address to highlight the output that's produced for each customer. After the last customer record is processed, the grand total of all purchases is stored in the accumulator. Once the exit condition has been met, a GRAND TOTAL subhead and the amount in the accumulator are printed.

Problem 7: Sales Summary Report. This report summarizes the sales of *all* products sold by the partners' business for a period. As you know, their first product was the mosquito bird tee shirt. You'll also recall from Chapter 2 that

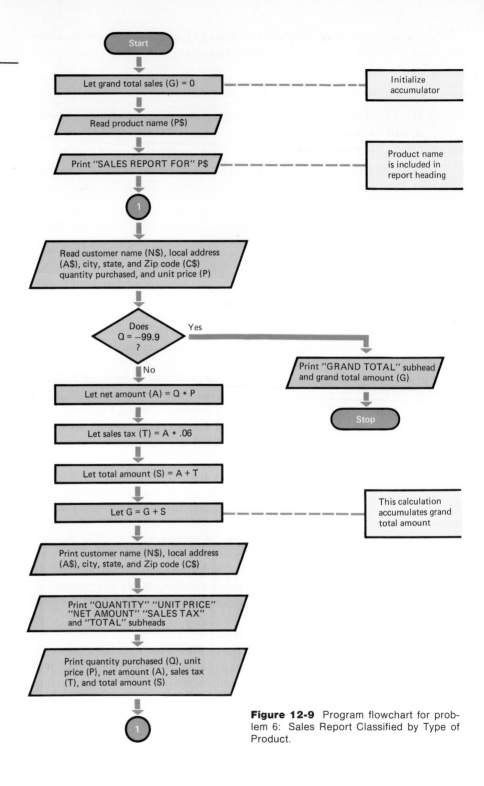

Figure 12-9 Program flowchart for problem 6: Sales Report Classified by Type of Product.

"The Mosquito Bird Song" is being sold as a record and a tape cassette. Capitalizing on her sudden fame as the creator of this song, Kay has also given a concert on campus. This concert was recorded by Rob and is now being offered as a "Kay Oss in Concert" record and tape cassette. To round out their product line, Rob has just published (over Kay's objections) a book of poems written by Ms. Fitt, his English teacher. Since these poems include such biggies as "Oh What Is the Meaning of Life?," "Oh What Is the Meaning of Truth?," and "Oh What Is the Meaning of Fast Food Franchises?," the book's title is *Oh What?*

The following specifications were used to prepare this summary report program:

▌ The report should be prepared with a "SALES SUMMARY REPORT" heading followed by a line of "PRODUCT," "UNIT PRICE," "QUANTITY," and "NET SALES" subheadings.

▌ Input data to be processed should include the name of each product, its quantity sold, and its unit price. The program should process all products sold.

▌ The net sales of each product should be computed.

▌ The total sales of all products should be accumulated.

▌ The product name, unit price, quantity sold, and net sales of each product should be printed on the report below the appropriate subheadings.

▌ After all products have been processed, a "TOTAL NET SALES" subheading and the accumulated total sales amount should be printed at the bottom of the report.

The chart used to prepare the summary report program is shown in Figure 12-10. Report headings are printed and the accumulator is set to zero. The body of the loop then begins with the reading of input data about a particular product. The net sales of this product are computed, and the amount is added to the total in the accumulator. The product name, unit price, quantity sold, and net sales amount are then printed, and the program loops back to read the data for the next product. When all products have been processed, the total of their sales is stored in the accumulator. Once the condition needed to exit the loop is met through the reading of a last dummy record, a "TOTAL NET SALES" subheading and the accumulated total sales are printed.

Feedback and Review 12-4

How would you feel about making some changes to the sales compensation report program chart that you worked on in Feedback and Review 12-3? (Don't tell me your answer, it might depress me.) Anyway, that's what we're going to do. Let's suppose this time that the program should meet these specifications:

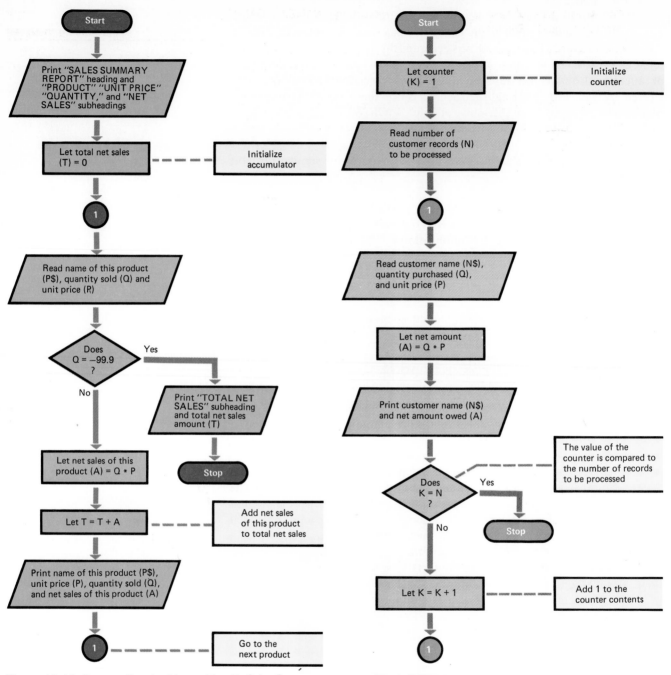

Figure 12-10 Program flowchart for problem 7: Sales Summary Report.

Figure 12-11 Program flowchart for problem 8: Simple Billing with a Counter.

▌ The report should have a heading line indicating "NAME," "SALES AMOUNT," and "EARNINGS."

▌ Input data to be processed are the name and weekly sales figures for each salesperson. The program should be able to include any number of salespeople.

▌ The 4-week total sales amount for each salesperson should be computed.

▌ The total sales amount for each salesperson should be multiplied by a 10 percent commission rate to get the earnings of each salesperson. (We'll not use multiple commission rates in this exercise.)

▌ The total sales for all salespersons should be accumulated.

▌ Under the report heading line should be printed the name, total sales amount, and earnings for each salesperson.

▌ After all salespeople have been processed, their total earnings should be computed by multiplying their accumulated total sales by .10.

▌ Print "TOTAL SALES" and "TOTAL EARNINGS" subheadings, and the amounts of total sales and total earnings for all salespersons at the bottom of the report.

Charting the Use of a Counter

You've now seen how accumulators may be used. Another important programming technique is the use of a counter. A **counter** is a special type of accumulator that's often used to record the number of times a loop has been processed. For example, if a programmer wants to process the procedure in a loop a fixed number of times, that number can be specified in the program. A counter can then be used to keep track of the number of passes through the loop. When the counter value reaches the predetermined number, an exit condition based on the value of the counter is satisfied, and an exit path out of the loop is followed.

Problem 8: Simple Billing With a Counter. The following specifications can serve to show how a counter is used to control a loop:

▌ Input data are the number of customer records to be processed, and the name, quantity purchased, and unit price data for each customer.

▌ The net amount owed by each customer should be computed.

▌ The printed output should be a bill for each customer giving the customer's name and net amount owed.

▌ Processing should stop after all customers have been billed.

The chart in Figure 12-11 shows how these specifications can be met. A counter is initialized (or initially set) at 1 in our example, and the number of records to be processed is entered. After the first customer record has been processed, a test for exit condition is made. The initial value of the counter (1) is compared to the number of records to be processed. Since the counter value does not yet equal this number of records, program control moves to the next operation. In this step, the counter is incremented (or added to) by a value of 1, and so the counter's value is now 2. When the last customer record has been processed, and when $K = N$, the exit path out of the loop will be followed without any need for a dummy record at the end of the file.

Additional Charting Examples

You'll be pleased to know that we are now down to the last two charts that analyze programs used in the partners' business. Since no major new programming or charting techniques are introduced in these two examples, we'll be able to move through them quickly.

Inventory control report from Figure 2-12.

Problem 9: Inventory Control Report. We discussed the purpose of an inventory control application in Chapter 2. And the format of the partners' inventory control report was shown in Figure 2-12, page 58. The essential specifications for this report are:

▌ Report headings are needed, and the input data consist of the name of each product and the beginning inventory, quantity received, and quantity sold figures for each product. Any number of products can be processed.

▌ The inventory available for sale during a period is found by adding the quantity received during the period to the inventory at the beginning of the period.

▌ The inventory at the end of the period is found by subtracting the quantity sold from the available inventory.

▌ The name of each product is printed on the report along with its beginning inventory, quantity received, quantity sold, and ending inventory.

Figure 12-12 shows the flowchart for this inventory control report. The body of the loop begins after the report headings shown back in Figure 2-12 are printed. Input data are entered, a test is made to see if all valid records have been processed, and the inventory available for sale is determined. The available inventory *should* be found by adding receipts (R) to the beginning inventory. If a data error shows quantity received to be less than zero (?), a provision is made to keep the available inventory equal to the beginning figure. The ending inventory *should* be found by subtracting sales from the quantity available. But if a data error shows quantity sold to be less than zero, no change is made to the available inventory. (Sales returns are treated as quantity received.) The output shown in the chart is then printed under the report headings.

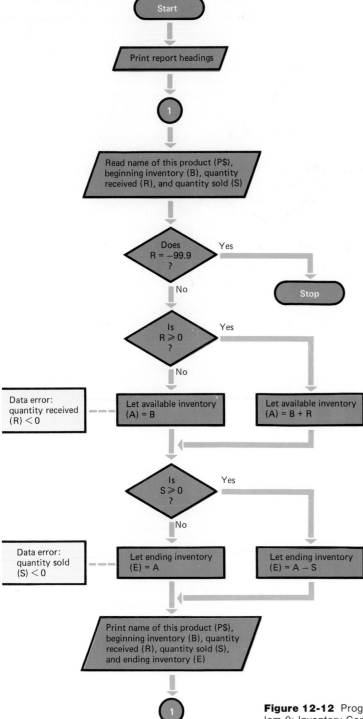

Figure 12-12 Program flowchart for problem 9: Inventory Control Report.

Problem 10: Final Billing Program. Many of the features of this final billing procedure were discussed earlier in problem 5. But a number of additional features have also been added. In this billing version, for example, the program must accommodate all possible products sold rather than just the single product processed in problem 5. The specifications for this billing procedure are:

▌ Input data include the names and addresses of multiple customers, and the quantity and price of the multiple products they've purchased.

▌ A heading line should be printed on each customer's bill. The total amount billed to all customers before and after discounts should be accumulated and printed after all bills have been prepared.

Figure 12-13 Program flowchart for problem 10: Final Billing Program.

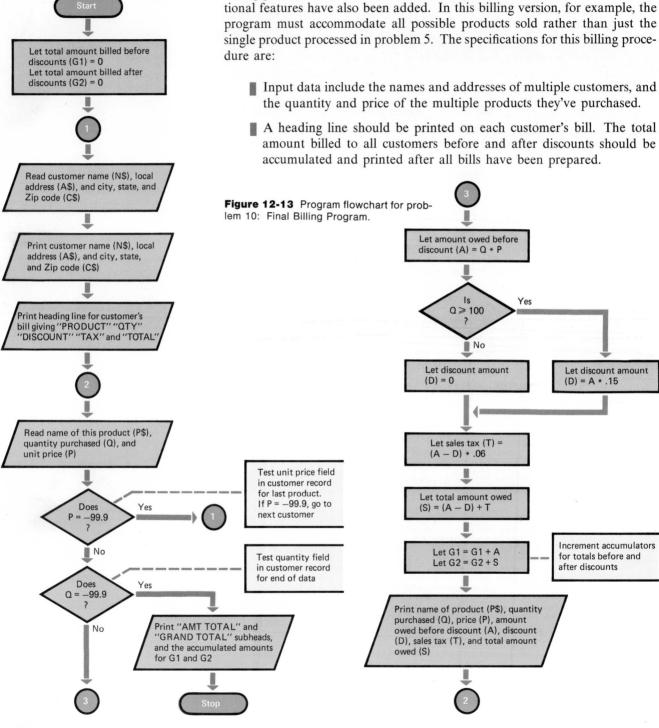

■ The amount owed before any discount should be computed for each product.

■ If the quantity purchased of a product is $>$ 100, a 15 percent discount is allowed. Otherwise, no discount is permitted.

■ A 6 percent sales tax should be computed after the discount is deducted, and this tax should be added to the after-discount amount to get the total amount owed for the product.

■ Each printed bill should give the customer's name and address. The name, quantity purchased, price, amount owed before discount, discount amount, sales tax, and total amount owed for *each product* should also be listed.

The chart in Figure 12-13 satisfies these conditions. Two accumulators are set up to total the amounts billed before and after discounts have been computed. The name and address of the first customer are then read and printed. A heading line for the customer's bill is also printed. The name, quantity, and price of the *first* product are entered next. The test in the first decision symbol is an end-of-record test designed to determine if *all* valid products in a customer's record have been processed. If they all *have* been processed, a dummy price field with a value of -99.9 at the end of the customer's record is encountered, and program control branches back to read and print the name of the next customer. Since none of the products purchased by the first customer have yet been processed, however, program control moves to the next decision symbol. This is an end-of-file test. When all valid data in the last customer's record have been processed, a dummy quantity field with a value of -99.9 is read, accumulated totals are printed, and processing stops.

But that operation comes later. Right now, we are processing the first product item bought by the first customer. Since the next several steps in the chart are identical to those explained in problem 5, we can skip them here. You'll notice, however, that the before and after discount amounts for the first product are added to the accumulators. The totals of all successive products will also be accumulated. The name of the first product and other pertinent facts are then printed on the first customer's bill. Program control now branches back to the connector labeled 2 and the next product is processed. This continues until the last product bought by the first customer has been accounted for. Then, as we've seen, the exit test condition for the first decision symbol will be met and processing will begin on the next customer's record.

A Summary of Logic Patterns

A number of different problems have now been analyzed and charted. As you examined the logic of these problems, you may have noticed that a few patterns were frequently repeated. What you probably didn't realize, however, is the rather surprising fact that *any* problem can be solved through the re-

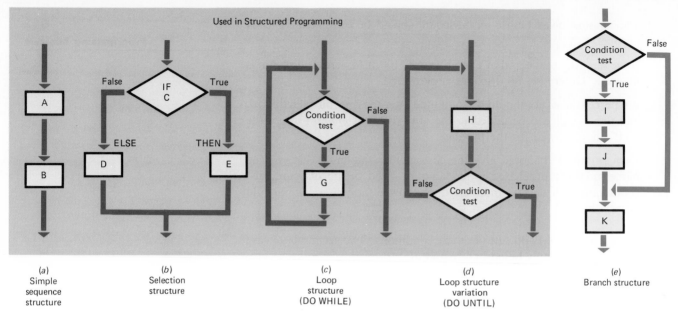

Used in Structured Programming

(a)
Simple
sequence
structure

(b)
Selection
structure

(c)
Loop
structure
(DO WHILE)

(d)
Loop structure
variation
(DO UNTIL)

(e)
Branch structure

Figure 12-14 Basic coding structures.

peated use of just a few basic logic structures. These patterns are shown in Figure 12-14. The **simple sequence structure** (Figure 12-14a) merely consists of one step followed by another. The **selection structure** (Figure 12-14b) requires a test for some condition followed by two alternative program control paths. As you know, the path selected depends on the results of the test. This pattern is sometimes referred to as an IF-THEN-ELSE structure. The **loop structure** involves doing one or more operations *while* a condition is *true* (Figure 12-14c). When the condition becomes false, the looping process is ended. If the condition is initially false, the operation(s) found in this DO WHILE structure aren't executed. A variation of this third basic pattern is one in which the operation(s) is (are) repeated *until* a condition is found to be true (Figure 12-14d) after which the exit path is followed. This variation is called a DO UNTIL structure.

These three basic logic structures are all that are necessary to prepare any program. Supporters of a programming approach built around the use of these three structures believe that the use of any additional patterns generally causes needless complexity and confusion. The **branch structure** shown in Figure 12-14e, for example, causes control to branch away from a sequence and GO TO operation K if the condition test is false. Adherents of the structured programming approach believe such a pattern is counterproductive. But it's included here since many programmers still use it today. A thesis of structured programming is that although the three basic patterns can be combined and/or "nested" in actual practice as shown in Figure 12-15, each pattern has a single entry and exit point, and each is readable from top to bottom. This inherent simplicity can lead to more understandable problem logic. Structured programming concepts have gained rapid acceptance. We'll discuss them in more detail in Chapter 13.

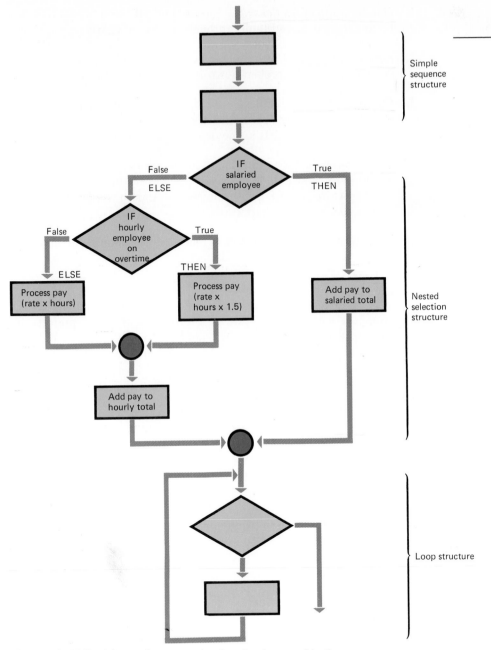

Figure 12-15 Partial payroll program showing structure combinations.

Benefits and Limitations of Flowcharts

The following benefits may be obtained when flowcharts are used during programming analysis:

1. *Quicker grasp of relationships.* Current and proposed procedures may be understood more rapidly through the use of charts.

2. *Effective analysis.* The flowchart becomes a model of a program or system that can be broken down into detailed parts for study.

3. *Effective synthesis.* Synthesis is the opposite of analysis; it's the combination of the various parts into a whole entity. Flowcharts may be used as working models in the design of new programs and systems.

4. *Communication.* Flowcharts aid in communicating the facts of a problem to those whose skills are needed in the solution. The old adage that "a picture is worth a thousand words" rings true when the picture happens to be a flowchart.

5. *Proper program documentation.* Program **documentation** involves collecting, organizing, storing, and otherwise maintaining a complete historical record of programs and the other documents associated with a system. Good documentation is needed for the following reasons: *(a)* Documented knowledge belongs to an organization and does not disappear with the departure of a programmer; *(b)* if projects are postponed, documented work will not have to be duplicated; and *(c)* if programs are modified in the future, the programmer will have a more understandable record of what was originally done. From what we've seen of the nature of flowcharts, it's obvious that they can provide valuable documentation support.

6. *Efficient coding.* The program flowchart acts as a guide or blueprint during the program preparation phase. Instructions coded in a programming language may be checked against the flowchart to help ensure that no steps are omitted.

A LITTLE-KNOWN CONTRIBUTION FROM GRACE M. HOPPER

Long recognized and honored for her pioneering work in compilers and programming languages, Captain Grace Murray Hopper was also present when one of the famous words of "computerese" was coined. In an interview with *Computerworld,* she reminisced about working on the Mark I computer at Harvard in the days following World War II.

"In 1945, while working in a World War I-vintage non-air-conditioned building on a hot, humid summer day, the computer stopped. We searched for the problem and found a failing relay—one of the big signal relays," she recalled.

"Inside, we found a moth that had been beaten to death. We pulled it out with tweezers and taped it to the log book," Hopper continued. "From then on, when the officer came in to ask if we were accomplishing anything, we told him we were 'debugging' the computer."

—Marguerite Zientara, "Capt. Grace M. Hopper and the Genesis of Programming Languages," *Computerworld,* Nov. 16, 1981, p. 50. Copyright 1981 by CW Communications, Inc., Framingham, Mass.

7. ***Orderly debugging and testing of programs.*** If the program fails to run to completion when submitted to the computer for execution, the flowchart may help in the "debugging" process. That is, it may help in detecting, locating, and removing mistakes.

In spite of their many obvious advantages, flowcharts have several *limitations:*

1. Complex and detailed charts are sometimes laborious to plan and draw, especially when a large number of decision paths are involved.

2. Although branches from a *single* decision symbol are easy to follow, the actions to be taken, given certain specified conditions, can be difficult to follow if there are *several* paths.

3. There are no standards determining the amount of detail that should be included in a chart.

OTHER PROGRAMMING ANALYSIS TOOLS

Because of such limitations, flowcharts may be replaced or supplemented by alternative analysis tools.

Decision Tables

A **decision table** can be a powerful tool for defining complex program logic. The basic table format is shown in Figure 12-16a. The table is divided into two main parts: The upper part contains the *conditions* and questions that are to be tested in reaching a decision, and the lower part describes the *actions* to be taken when a given set of conditions is present. The contents of the condition stub correspond to the conditions contained in the decision symbols of a flowchart, and the condition entries correspond to the paths leading out from decision symbols. Action statements corresponding to the statements located in nondecision symbols of a chart are listed in the action stub.

A decision table version of the inventory control report problem charted in Figure 12-12 is shown in Figure 12-16b. Each decision rule column is the equivalent of one path through the flowchart. Decision tables may thus be used in place of program flowcharts for the following reasons:

▌ Tables are easier to draw and change than charts, and they provide more compact documentation (a small table can replace several pages of charts).

▌ It's also easier to follow a particular path down one column than through several flowchart pages.

Table heading		Decision rules		
Condition	If			
	And stub	entries		
	And			
Action	Then			
	And stub	entries		
	And			

(a)

Inventory control report		Decision rule number				
		1	2	3	4	5
Condition	Quantity received = −99.9	N	N	N	N	Y
	Quantity received ≥ 0	Y	N	Y	N	
	Quantity sold ≥ 0	Y	N	N	Y	
Action	Let available inventory = B + R	X		X		
	Let available inventory = B		X		X	
	Let ending inventory = A − S	X			X	
	Let ending inventory = A		X	X		
	Print line on report	X	X	X	X	
	Read next record	X	X	X	X	
	Stop					X

(b)

Figure 12-16 (a) Decision table format. (b) Decision table for problem 9: Inventory Control Report.

```
Print report headings
Read first product record
DOWHILE there are more records
      IF quantity received ≥ 0
         THEN let available inventory = beginning inventory + receipts
      ELSE let available inventory = beginning inventory
      ENDIF
      IF quantity sold ≥ 0
         THEN let ending inventory = available inventory − sales
      ELSE let ending inventory = available inventory
      ENDIF
      Print line on report
      Read next record
ENDO (End of valid records)
Stop
```

Figure 12-17 Pseudocode for problem 9: Inventory Control Report.

But tables aren't as widely used as charts because:

▍ Charts are better able to express the total sequence of events needed to solve a problem.

▍ Charts are more familiar to, and are preferred by, many programmers.

Pseudocode

Another programming analysis tool is pseudocode. Since *pseudo* means "imitation" and *code* refers to instructions written in a programming language, **pseudocode** is a counterfeit and abbreviated version of actual computer instructions. These pseudoinstructions are phrases written in ordinary natural language (e.g., English, French, etc.). A pseudocode version of the inventory control report problem that we've now charted and put in a decision table format is shown in Figure 12-17.

As you can see, pseudocode is compact and is easy to revise. A few optional terms or "keywords" (shown in upper case letters) are generally used to identify basic logic structures. Computer professionals who use a structured programming approach in their work often prefer to use pseudocode in preparing a detailed plan for a program. However, there are no standard rules to follow in using pseudocode, and, of course, a graphic representation of program logic isn't available.

1. People must usually follow six steps in order to put computers to work. The first three (defining the need, gathering and analyzing data, and designing and preparing specifications to solve the problem) are included in the systems analysis and design process. The last three steps (programming analysis, program preparation, and program implementation and maintenance) are found in the programming process. Included among the questions that must be considered during program development are: (*a*) Are problem specifications clear and complete? (*b*) Is a solution method now known? (*c*) If not, can such a method be obtained from other sources? (*d*) If a solution method must be created, what approach should be used? Each of these questions is considered in this chapter.

2. A program flowchart is a detailed picture of how steps are to be performed within a CPU to produce the needed output. A single chart may be used to represent a problem solution, or the major program modules in a main-control chart can be drawn separately in a series of micro charts. The standardized symbols used in program flowcharts are introduced and explained in this chapter.

3. Ten problem situations dealing with such popular applications as billing customers, paying employees, analyzing sales, controlling inventories, and preparing mailing labels are analyzed and charted in this chapter. These same applications are coded in the BASIC language in Chapter 14. The specifications for each of the problems was presented, and a flowchart was drawn to meet these specifications. After examining a simple input/process/output chart, we moved to problem situations that required the flexibility made possible by the use of decisions and loops. Charts with multiple decision symbols were presented, and then the use of accumulators and counters were discussed.

4. Only a few logic structures were used in all our charting examples. In fact, the logic of all programs written for computers can be described using just the simple sequence, selection, and loop structures. A fourth branch structure is used by many programmers today, but some professionals believe that its use leads to needless complexity and confusion.

5. Flowcharts enhance communication and understanding, contribute to effective problem analysis and synthesis, provide good documentation, and are useful during program coding and debugging. However, complex and detailed charts can be hard to draw, and following the actions to be taken in specified situations can be difficult when many decision paths are available.

6. Other programming analysis tools such as decision tables and pseudocode are sometimes used to replace or supplement program flowcharts. A decision table is compact and is easy to draw and change. It's a powerful tool for defining complex program logic because a single table column can represent a maze of lines through several pages of flowcharts. Charts are more frequently used, however, because they are better able to express the total sequence of events needed to solve a problem. Pseudocode is a counterfeit and abbreviated version of actual computer instructions. It's compact and easy to change. But there are no standard rules governing its use.

KEY TERMS AND CONCEPTS

You should now be able to define and use the following terms and concepts (the numbers shown indicate the pages where the terms and concepts are first mentioned):

system analysis and design process 319
programming process 319
program development approach 319
algorithm 321
program flowchart 322
program modules 322
main-control (modular or macro) flowchart 322
micro flowchart 322
input/output symbol 324

processing symbol 324
terminal symbol 324
decision symbol 324
conditional statement 324
connector symbol 324
subroutines 325
predefined process symbol 325
annotation flag 325
loop 327
body of loop 327
sentinel value 327

test for exit condition 327
endless (infinite) loop 328
accumulator 334
counter 339
simple sequence structure 344
selection structure 344
loop structure 344
branch structure 344
documentation 346
decision table 347
pseudocode 348

TOPICS FOR REVIEW AND DISCUSSION

1. (a) What are the steps in the system analysis and design process? (b) What are the steps in the programming process?

2. "Although different programmers use different strategies to develop program solutions, certain questions must usually be considered regardless of the strategy used." Identify and discuss these questions.

3. In computer science, the term "stepwise refinement" is given to the process of breaking down a large problem into a series of smaller and more understandable tasks. How can the use of program flowcharts help in this process?

4. (a) What's the purpose of a program flowchart? (b) How does it differ from a system flowchart? (c) What symbols are used in program charts?

5. "A loop consists of a body, a test for exit condition, and a return provision." Discuss this statement.

6. (a) What's a sentinel value? (b) Why must the sentinel be a value that couldn't occur as a valid data item?

7. (a) What's an accumulator? (b) How is an accumulator initialized and then updated to compute a running total?

8. (a) What's a counter? (b) How can a counter be used to keep track of the number of times a loop has been executed?

9. Problem 10 is referred to as the "Final" Billing Program. Can you see any deficiencies in this program that might call for further modifications?

10. Using the chart for problem 5 in Figure 12-8, identify the simple sequence, selection, and loop structures in the program logic.

11. Discuss the benefits and limitations of flowcharts.

12. Why is proper documentation required?

13. What are the advantages and limitations of decision tables?

14. What is pseudocode?

15. Review the chart for problem 2 in Figure 12-4. How could you modify it so that the partners could interact with the program and supply the input data at the time of processing?

16. After reviewing the chart for problem 4 in Figure 12-7, how could you modify it so that Rob and Kay could interact with the program and supply the input data at the time of processing? Let's assume that the program should print instructions on how to enter the input data, and it should print a heading line for each salesperson showing "NAME," "SALES AMOUNT," and "EARNINGS." It should also print an "END OF DATA" message after each record has been processed to allow the partners to stop processing or to continue with another record.

17. After reviewing the chart for problem 8 in Figure 12-11, how could it be changed so that the total amount billed to each customer could be accumulated and then printed with a "TOTAL AMOUNT" subheading at the end of the billing run?

18. Let's assume that you need to prepare a program that will compute the number of acres in any number of rectangular lots. The program should interact with the user and request the length (in feet) and width (in feet) of each lot prior to computing its acreage and printing out the result. There are 43,560 square feet in an acre. After computing the acreage in a first lot, the program should then determine from the user if there are any additional lots to process. When the processing is completed, the program should print a "GOOD-BYE" message.

19. Now let's assume that Ms. Fitt, Rob's English teacher, has found a student guilty of chewing gum in class. The punishment is to write "I will not chew gum in class" 10 times. Prepare a flowchart for a program that will (*a*) accept any "naughty student" message, and (*b*) reproduce this message any designated number of times.

ANSWERS TO FEEDBACK AND REVIEW SECTIONS

Possible flowcharts for Feedback and Review sections 12-1 through 12-4 follow. Your versions may differ in some respects and still be correct.

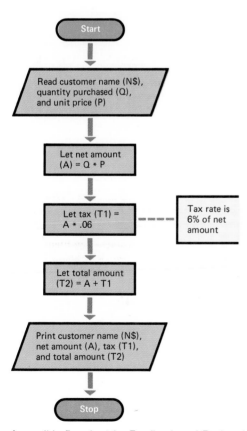

A possible flowchart for Feedback and Review 12-1.

A possible flowchart for Feedback and Review 12-2. (Note that the programmer has exercised his or her freedom to use some different abbreviations for input data and processing results.)

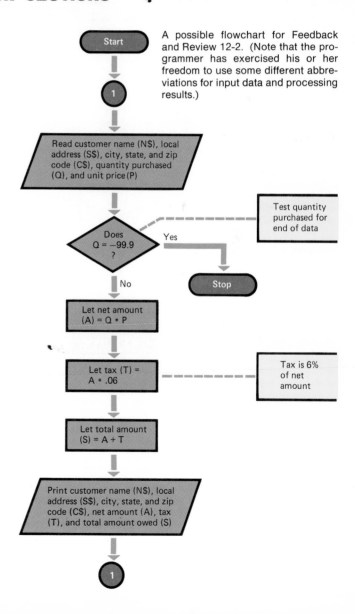

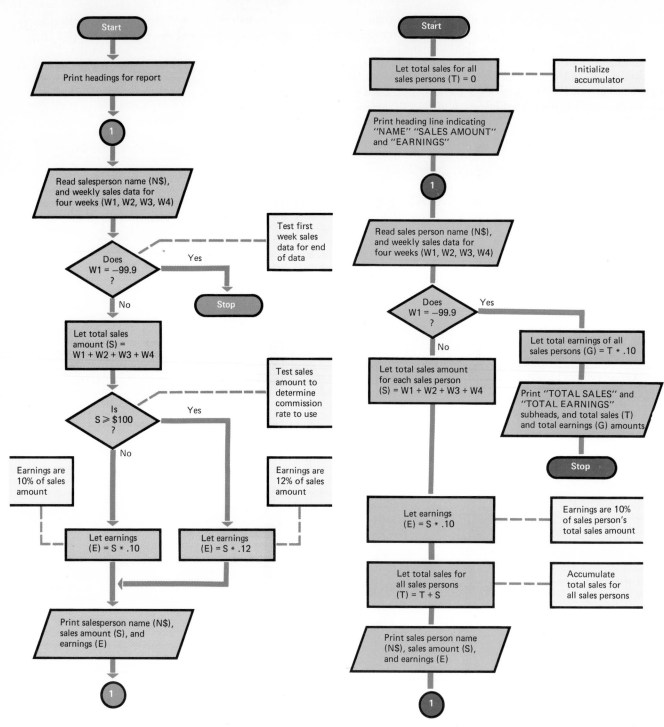

A possible program flowchart for Feedback and Review 12-3.

A possible program flowchart for Feedback and Review 12-4.

The Smash Hit of Software

Daniel Bricklin, 29, and Robert Frankston, 31, a team of new-wave composers, have penned a dynamite disc that has grossed an estimated $8 million. It is not a punk-rock smash, but an unmelodic magnetic number called VisiCalc, the bestselling microcomputer program for business uses. The featherweight sliver of plastic is about the size of a greeting card, but when it is placed in a computer, the machine comes alive. A computer without a program, or "software," is like a $3,000 stereo set without any records or tapes.

Three years ago, Bricklin, then a first-year Harvard Business School student, conceived VisiCalc while struggling with financial-planning problems on his calculator. He enlisted the aid of Frankston, a longtime friend and an expert programmer, to develop a new piece of computer software that would make juggling all those figures easier.

The partnership paid off. Since late 1979 nearly 100,000 copies of nine different versions of VisiCalc have been ordered at prices ranging from $100 to $300. It is far ahead of other business programs like Data Factory and General Ledger, and even outsells the programs for Star Cruiser, Dogfight and other arcade-like computer games.

VisiCalc translates simple commands typed on a keyboard into computer language that the machine then uses to solve problems. It enables a businessman, for example, to manipulate labyrinthine equations to calculate financial trends for his company. If he changes one figure, the machine can tell quickly how that affects the other numbers. A firm that gives its workers a 10% pay hike could estimate how that action would alter its costs, sales, profits, or dividends.

The computer program is being put to a wide range of uses. It helps Allerton Cushman Jr., a New York financial analyst, to project insurance-industry profits during the week and tote up his income taxes on the weekend. The Cabot Street Cinema Theatre in Beverly, Mass., bought VisiCalc to figure out which pattern of movie show times draws the best box-office receipts. An accounting firm in Las Vegas plans to use VisiCalc to tell its gambling-house clients how to position slot machines around the floor to ensure the biggest take. VisiCalc is obviously one composition that is in no danger of fading from the charts.

chapter 13

Preparing Computer Programs
An Overview

A COMMON LANGUAGE FOR COMPUTERS

Developing a single, standard programming language for all computers has long been regarded as impossible. In 1980, the Department of Defense presented Ada as its candidate for the common computer language. Behind the DOD's push was its finding that over 500 versions of a number of languages were being used on its computers.

Ada has a key advantage in its modularity: Programs can be broken into blocks or packages to make them easier to write, and they can then be easily reassembled. But Ada has a major drawback: It requires a larger variety of commands than do other high-level languages. Britain's Charles Hoare of Oxford has blasted Ada as trying to incorporate too many features in a single package. Such complexity, he argues, could result in the major failure of a space rocket or a nuclear warhead if Ada is the directing language.

IBM's John Backus, who led the FORTRAN design team some 20 years ago, holds that a standard language is not even desirable: "Standardization like this won't help because it takes a tremendous amount of retraining of programmers." Ronald F. Hudler at General Motors concurs: "We keep looking for a miracle [language], but we haven't found one. Ada isn't it."

It's impossible to predict whether Ada or another language will eventually become *the* language of all computers. And the widely used languages such as BASIC, FORTRAN, and COBOL are sure to be around for a long time to come.

—Source of data: "A Common Language For Computers," *Business Week*, Mar. 23, 1981, pp. 84b–84e; "Ada Under Fire," *Datamation*, Feb. 12, 1981, p. 94.

Preparing a program in the COBOL language. (Courtesy Radio Shack Division, Tandy Corporation)

Looking Ahead

In this second chapter dealing with the programming process, you'll learn about some of the issues that must be considered during the program preparation stage. The different categories of programming languages are then identified and discussed. Next, you'll be introduced to some of the major high-level languages used in program coding. And the implementation and maintenance of coded applications programs are presented in the final pages of this chapter.

Thus, after studying this chapter, you should be able to:

▌ Identify and discuss several of the issues that arise (and the options that are available) during program preparation

▌ Outline the characteristics of machine languages, assembly languages, and high-level languages

▌ Explain how instructions written in an assembly or high-level programming language can be translated into the machine language of a computer

▌ Describe some of the features and uses of a number of major high-level programming languages

▌ Summarize the steps that are taken during program implementation and maintenance

▌ Understand and use the key terms and concepts listed at the end of this chapter

PROGRAM PREPARATION: SOME ISSUES AND OPTIONS

After the programming analysis phase discussed in Chapter 12 has been completed, the second step in programming is to code the specific instructions needed to process an application into a language and form acceptable to a computer system. And the third step in the process is to then implement and maintain these coded instructions. The purpose of this chapter is to consider some of the issues and options that arise, and some of the concepts that apply, in preparing programs. The implementation and maintenance of applications programs are also discussed. The next chapter will show you in some detail how specific instructions are coded in a popular programming language.

Issues and Options in General

Preparing computer programs has historically been a painstaking art. It still is. There's little question about the objectives of those who write programs. They generally want to:

1. Create programs that serve user needs.

2. Reduce the time and money needed to develop and implement programs.

3. Produce programs with a minimum number of errors.

4. Produce programs that are easy to implement and maintain.

eparing Computer Programs

In trying to achieve one desirable goal, however, programmers in some cases are faced with undesirable tradeoffs. (Should we reduce development time at the risk of producing programs that are more error-prone and harder to maintain?) And in any case, programmers must usually deal with a number of issues involving methodology and the use of resources. Some examples of the questions to be considered are: Should we create a new program or should we buy a packaged program from a vendor? How should programming tasks be assigned? What program design methods should we use? One reason programming is still an art rather than an exact science is that reasonable people with essentially the same types of problems to solve have chosen different options when answering these and other questions.

In the next few pages we'll look at a few of the issues and options facing those who prepare programs. The field of **software engineering** has emerged in the last decade to address some of these issues by applying scientific principles to the development of computer programs. As a result, it's likely that professional programmers will follow a more scientific approach in dealing with programming issues in the years ahead.

The Make or Buy Issue

Perhaps the first issue to be considered is the "make or buy" question. Should a new program be created within an organization, or should an existing applications package be purchased from a supplier of such software? You'll recall from Chapter 4 that applications packages or **packaged programs** are programs written by outside vendors for widely used applications. There are over 8,000 software packages supplied by over 1,400 vendors. The multibillion dollar market for these products is growing rapidly. Generally speaking, the make or buy decision involves tradeoffs. The packaged program usually achieves the goals of lower cost (development costs are shared by many customers), faster implementation, and reduced risk of error (the package is available for testing). The in-house, custom-made program has the possible advantages of greater operating efficiency and the ability to more effectively satisfy the unique needs of users. These advantages are possible because in trying to appeal to many potential users the packaged program may sacrifice processing performance in areas important to a particular organization.

Whenever feasible, however, the use of an appropriate application package should always be considered as an alternative during program development. Some factors that should be examined in evaluating possible packages include:

▌ *Package quality*. A check of current users should be made to evaluate the suitability, ease of use, performance, and reliability of the software.

▌ *Vendor reputation*. The vendor should be financially strong, and should be able to provide the technical support needed to install, maintain, and update the package.

▌ *Documentation*. Adequate documentation should be available to meet the needs of those in the organization who must work with the package.

The Programmer Organization Issue

The output of a program preparation project should be an effective product at an economical price. Programmers are currently assigned to such program preparation projects in various ways. The following organizing options are often used:

Traditional hierarchical grouping. In this option, a programming manager assigns tasks to programmers, and exercises overall control over the project. But the manager does not normally participate in the actual coding. Rather, individual programmers code, test, and document the programs to which they are assigned. They may be shifted from project to project as the workload dictates.

Chief programmer teams. In the **chief programmer team** approach, each project is assigned to a team consisting of a senior-level *chief programmer*, a skilled *backup programmer,* and a *librarian*. Applications programmers and other specialists are added to this nucleus as needed. In many ways, this team is like a surgical team in a hospital. The chief programmer (surgeon) has responsibility for the project and is the key coder of the program(s) being prepared. The backup programmer (assisting doctor) is ready to take the chief programmer's place if necessary, and is expected to develop important elements of the program. Other team members (like nurses and an anesthesiologist) perform special tasks for the chief programmer. The librarian, for example, gathers and organizes the records and documents associated with the project. And applications programmers code modules that have been mapped out by the chief programmer.

"Egoless" programming teams. We've seen in the traditional approach that a programmer may often be responsible for coding and implementing an entire program. This close association with the program may serve to make it an extension of the programmer's ego. If errors are then discovered in the program (and they often are), the programmer may consider the discovery to be a personal attack. To avoid this situation, an **"egoless" programming team** is assigned to a project. Membership in the close-knit team seldom changes, and there's no designated chief. Assignments are determined in a democratic way with each member doing that part of the work for which he or she is best

"It says 'That last question was unworthy of you.'"

Most you project team share equally in programming

suited. During coding, team members check the work of each other to help locate and correct errors. The completed code is then not the responsibility of a single person but is rather the product of the entire team.

Each of these options for organizing programmers differs in significant ways from the others. There's no agreement on which approach is best. Some organizations are trying to develop other options for organizing programmers that combine some of the features of the three presented here.

The Issue of Program Construction Techniques

Different program construction techniques have been developed to help achieve the four goals listed at the beginning of this section. Again, different organizations often use a varying mix of the following program construction options:

The use of modular program design. You'll recall from Chapter 12 that a **main-control program** may be used to outline the major segments or *modules* needed to solve a problem. The main-control program specifies the order in which each module (or subroutine) in the program will be processed. When the **modular program design** technique is used, an instruction in the main-control program branches control to a subordinate module. When the specific processing operation performed by the module is completed, another branch instruction may transfer program control to another module or return it to the main-control program. Thus, the modules or subroutines are really programs within a program. Each module typically has only one entry point and only one exit point. Many programmers believe that modules should be limited in size to about 50 lines of code—the amount that can be placed on one page of printer output. Figure 13-1 summarizes the modular technique. Some of the advantages of using this construction option are:

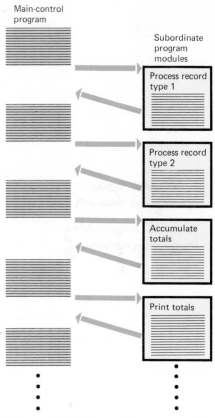

Figure 13-1 The modular programming option.

1. Complex programs may be divided into simpler and more manageable elements.

2. Simultaneous coding of modules by several programmers is possible.

3. A *library* of modules may be created, and these modules may be used in other programs as needed.

4. The location of program errors may be more easily traced to a particular module, and thus debugging and maintenance may be simplified.

5. Effective use can be made of tested subroutines prepared by equipment manufacturers and furnished to their customers. All these advantages help programmers realize their goals.

The use of basic coding structures. A clever programming "artist" can write programs containing a maze of branches to alter the sequence of processing operations. These programs may work at first. But since the artist may be the only one who understands the convoluted logic that was used, they can represent a nightmare for the person(s) responsible for their maintenance. To counter such artistic tendencies, many organizations specify that programmers stick to the use of the simple sequence, selection, and loop structures presented in Chapter 12. These organizations have found that when programs are so structured, and when modular techniques are used, programs can be read from top to bottom and are easier to understand. This greater clarity can help reduce (1) program errors, (2) the time spent in program testing, and (3) the time and effort spent on program maintenance.

FIRM SHARES TIPS ON STRUCTURED WALK-THROUGHS

Syntex Corp. has enjoyed great success in implementing *structured walk-throughs* in its everyday computing operations.

What were the secrets of Syntex's success? How did the company implement walk-throughs differently from most other users? And what formulas, if any, should would-be users follow to increase their chances of implementing walk-throughs successfully? Dorothy Deran, Syntex's research-information systems manager, suggested the following pointers:

- Avoid using walk-throughs as a tool for evaluating the performance and productivity of individual programmers. Remember that the sole purpose of conducting walk-throughs is to control the quality of a computing shop's main product—its programs. For walk-throughs to succeed, they have to gain their users' absolute confidence and acceptance. But how can they win such trust if programmers suspect the procedures are being used to measure their professional competence and thus might later be used against them?
- If you keep a log of all the programming errors your staff uncov-

ers during walk-throughs—a practice Deran recommends—make sure all entries remain strictly anonymous. Keeping an error log is a good way of measuring a walk-through's effectiveness. But when you're recording a mistake, make sure, you don't note the name of the individual who made it. Nothing will arouse a programmer's suspicion faster than an error log that names names.

- During walk-throughs, avoid using personal pronouns when referring to a mistake or to a person's work. Say "*this* error" not "*your* error"; "*this* program," not "*your* program." Remember that the subject of a faultfinding session should be a programmer's work, not the programmer himself.
- Refrain from criticizing a programmer's personal coding style. If a program contains bugs, can be shortened or otherwise needs to be clarified, by all means see that it gets corrected. But make sure all criticisms are based on genuine faults, and prevent walk-throughs from degenerating into mere squabbles over personal programming styles.
- For every bug uncovered during a

walk-through, require the finder to state the nature of the error and suggest a possible correction. Merely pointing out a mistake isn't enough.

- Don't apply walk-throughs selectively or preferentially. Once the techniques make their debut in a computing shop, no one in the department should be exempted from participation. Otherwise, staff members might get the mistaken impression that walk-throughs are intended only for individuals whose work can't be trusted.
- Don't allow walk-throughs to drag on indefinitely. An ideal length for most walk-throughs is an hour or less.
- Every walk-through team should designate one of its members as group chairman and grant that individual the authority to suspend any meeting that seems to be making little headway.

—Jeffry Beeler, "Firm Shares Tips on Structured Walk-Throughs," *Computerworld*, Sept. 1, 1980, p. 6. Copyright 1980 by CW Communications, Inc., Framingham, Mass.

The use of peer reviews. The technique of holding a **peer review** during program construction to detect software errors is called a **structured walk-through.** Each review is initiated by the programmer whose work is to be checked. Materials are handed out in advance of the review session, and the objectives of the session are outlined to participants. (Programmer managers are not invited.) The role of the participants is to detect errors, but no attempt is made during the session to correct any errors that are discovered. A walkthrough session will typically include three to five of the programmer's colleagues. (These colleagues will have their own work reviewed in other similar sessions.) During the session, the reviewee will walk through, step by step, the logic of the work. One participant will keep a record of any errors that are uncovered so that proper corrective action can be taken by the reviewee. The tone of the session should be relaxed, and there should be no personal attacks.

The possible advantages of the peer review technique are:

1. Fewer errors are likely to get through the development process.

2. Faster implementation, a reduction in development costs, and greater user satisfaction may then be possible.

3. Better program documentation may be obtained.

4. Later program maintenance efforts may be easier and less expensive.

5. Higher programmer morale may result from the spirit of cooperation that can exist.

These same advantages, of course, are possible when programmers are organized into the egoless programming teams described earlier.

The creation of a structured programming environment. The term **structured programming** has been compared to a snowman after a day in the warm sun—both may originally have been distinctly formed, but both are now rather vaguely defined. Originally, the term was defined to be the disciplined use of the three basic coding structures mentioned above. Care was taken to allow only one entrance and one exit from a structure and to minimize the use of branching instructions such as GO TO. Rules on indenting the coding structures written on coding sheets were also established to give a clearer picture of the coding logic. Since this original use of the term, however, a number of *other* techniques have also been added under the structured programming banner. Thus, many now expand the definition of structured programming to include the use of:

▌ A "top-down" approach to identifying a main function and then breaking it down into lower-level components for analysis and modular program design purposes.

▌ Structured walkthroughs.

▌ Chief programmer teams.

Combining these program construction and programmer organizing techniques into a disciplined structured programming environment can lead to improvements in programming efficiency and in software quality. But an organization must carefully weigh the possible benefits to be obtained from the use of structured programming techniques against its own needs and resources. To recklessly abandon traditional program preparation methods that may have yielded good results in a particular setting in favor of new techniques that may not live up to expectations (but may, instead, produce organizational shock) would, of course, be foolish.

PROGRAMMING LANGUAGE CLASSIFICATIONS

A language is a system of communication. **A programming language** consists of all the symbols, characters, and usage rules that permit people to communicate with computers. Every programming language must accept certain types of written instructions that will enable a computer system to perform a number of familiar operations. That is, every language must have instructions that fall into the following categories:

1. *Input/output instructions.* Required to permit communication between I/O devices and the central processor, these instructions provide details on the type of input or output operation to be performed and the storage locations to be used during the operation.

2. *Calculation instructions.* Instructions to permit addition, subtraction, multiplication, and division during processing are, of course, common in all programming languages.

3. *Logic/comparison instructions.* These instructions are used to *transfer program control,* and are needed in the selection and loop structures that are followed to prepare programs. During processing, two data items may be compared as a result of the execution of a logic instruction. As you know, program control can follow different paths depending on the outcome of a selection test (IF R > 0, THEN A, ELSE B). And a loop can be continued or terminated depending on the outcome of an exit condition test (does Q = −99.9?). In addition to the instructions in languages that set up tests or comparisons to effect the transfer of program control, there are also *unconditional* transfer instructions available that are not based on the outcome of comparisons.

4. *Storage/retrieval and movement instructions.* These instructions are used to store, retrieve, and move data during processing. Data may be copied from one storage location to another and retrieved as needed.

But even though all programming languages have an instruction set that permits these familiar operations to be performed, there's a marked difference to be found in the symbols, characters, and syntax of machine languages, assembly languages, and high-level languages.

Machine Languages

A computer's **machine language** consists of strings of binary numbers and is the only one the CPU directly "understands." An instruction prepared in any machine language will have at least two parts. The *first part* is the *command* or *operation,* and it tells the computer what function to perform. Every computer has an **operation code** or "op code" for each of its functions. The *second part* of the instruction is the **operand,** and it tells the computer where to find or store the data or other instructions that are to be manipulated. The number of operands in an instruction varies among computers. In a *single-operand* machine, the binary equivalent of "ADD 0184" could cause the value in address 0184 to be added to the value stored in a register in the arithmetic-logic unit. In a *two-operand* machine, the binary representation for "ADD 0184 8672" could cause the value in address 8672 to be added to the number in location 0184. The single-operand format is popular in microcomputers; the two-operand structure is likely to be available in most other machines.

By today's standards, early computers were intolerant. Programmers had to translate instructions directly into the machine-language form that computers understood. For example, the programmer writing the instruction to "ADD 0184" for an early IBM machine would have written:

$$00010000000000000000000000010111000$$

In addition to remembering the dozens of code numbers for the commands in the machine's instruction set, a programmer was also forced to keep track of the storage locations of data and instructions. The initial coding often took months, was therefore quite expensive, and often resulted in error. Checking instructions to locate errors was about as tedious as writing them initially. And if a program had to be modified at a later date, the work involved could take weeks to finish.

Assembly Languages   *lowest level used today*

To ease the programmer's burden, *mnemonic* operation codes and *symbolic* addresses were developed in the early 1950s. The word mnemonic (pronounced ne-mon'-ik) refers to a memory aid. One of the first steps in improving the program preparation process was to substitute letter symbols—mnemonics—for the numeric machine-language operation codes. Each computer now has a **mnemonic code,** although, of course, the actual symbols vary among makes and models. Figure 13-2 shows the mnemonic codes for a few of the commands used with IBM System/370 computers. (The complete instruction set has about 200 commands.) Machine language is *still*

Command name	Mnemonic (symbolic) operation code	Command name	Mnemonic (symbolic) operation code
Input/Output Commands		Compare Logical Character	CLC
Start I/O	SIO	Branch on Condition Register	BCR
Halt I/O	HIO	Branch on Condition	BC
Calculation Commands		Branch on Count	BCT
Add	A	*Storage/Retrieval and Movement Commands*	
Subtract	S	Load Register	LR
Multiply	M	Load	L
Divide	D	Move Characters	MVC
Logic/Comparison Commands		Move Numerics	MVN
Compare Register	CR	Store	ST
Compare	C	Store Character	STC

Figure 13-2 Partial instruction set for IBM System/370 computers.

used by the computer as it processes data, but **assembly language** software first translates the specified operation code symbol into its machine-language equivalent.

And this improvement set the stage for further advances. If the computer could translate convenient symbols into basic operations, why couldn't it also perform other clerical coding functions such as assigning storage addresses to data? **Symbolic addressing** is the practice of expressing an address *not* in terms of its absolute numerical location, but rather in terms of symbols convenient to the programmer.

In the early stages of symbolic addressing, the programmer assigned a symbolic name and an actual address to a data item. For example, the total value of merchandise purchased during a month by a department store customer might be assigned to address 0063 by the programmer and given the symbolic name TOTAL. The value of merchandise returned unused during the month might be assigned to address 2047 and given the symbolic name CREDIT. Then, for the remainder of the program, the programmer would refer to the *symbolic names rather than to the addresses* when such items were to be processed. Thus, an instruction might be written "S CREDIT, TOTAL" to subtract the value of returned goods from the total amount purchased to find the amount of the customer's monthly bill. The assembly language software might then translate the symbolic instruction into this machine-language string of bits:

$$
\underbrace{011111}_{\substack{\text{Mnemonic op code} \\ \text{(S)}}} \quad \underbrace{01111111111}_{\substack{2047 \\ \text{(CREDIT)}}} \quad \underbrace{000000111111}_{\substack{0063 \\ \text{(TOTAL)}}}
$$

Another improvement followed. The programmer turned the task of assigning and keeping track of instruction addresses over to the computer. The programmer merely told the machine the storage address number of the *first* program instruction, and the assembly language software then automatically stored all others in sequence from that point. So if another instruction was added to the program later, it was not necessary to modify the addresses of all instructions that followed the point of insertion (as would have to be done in the case of programs written in machine language). Instead, the processor automatically adjusted storage locations the next time the program ran.

Programmers no longer assign actual address numbers to symbolic data items as they did earlier. Now they merely specify where they want the first location in the program to be, and an assembly language program takes it from there, allocating locations for instructions and data.

This **assembly program,** or **assembler,** also enables the computer to convert the programmer's assembly language instructions into its own machine code. A program of instructions written by a programmer in an assembly language is called a **source program.** After this source program has been converted into machine code by an assembler, it's referred to as an **object program.** It's easier for programmers to write instructions in an assembly language than to prepare instructions in machine-language codes. But two computer runs may be required before source program instructions can be used to produce the desired output. These separate *assembly* and *production* runs are outlined and discussed in Figure 13-3.

Assembly languages have *advantages over machine languages.* They save time and reduce detail. Fewer errors are made, and those that are made are easier to find. And assembly programs are easier for people to modify than machine-language programs. But there are *limitations.* Coding in assembly language is still time consuming. And a big drawback of assembly languages is that they are *machine oriented.* That is, they are designed for the specific make and model of processor being used. Programs might have to be recoded if the organization acquires a different machine.

MACRO – instruction that generates several lower level instructions

High-Level Languages

The earlier assembly programs produced only one machine instruction for each source program instruction. To speed up coding, assembly programs were developed that could produce a *variable* amount of machine-language code for *each* source program instruction. In other words, a single **macro instruction** might produce *several* lines of machine-language code. For example, the programmer might write "READ FILE," and the translating software might then automatically provide a detailed series of previously prepared machine-language instructions which would copy a record into primary storage from the file of data being read by the input device. Thus, the programmer was relieved of the task of writing an instruction for every machine operation performed.

The development of mnemonic techniques and macro instructions led, in turn, to the development of **high-level languages** that are often oriented toward a particular class of processing problems. For example, a number of languages have been designed to process problems of a scientific-mathematic nature, and other languages have appeared that emphasize file processing applications.

Not machine dependent

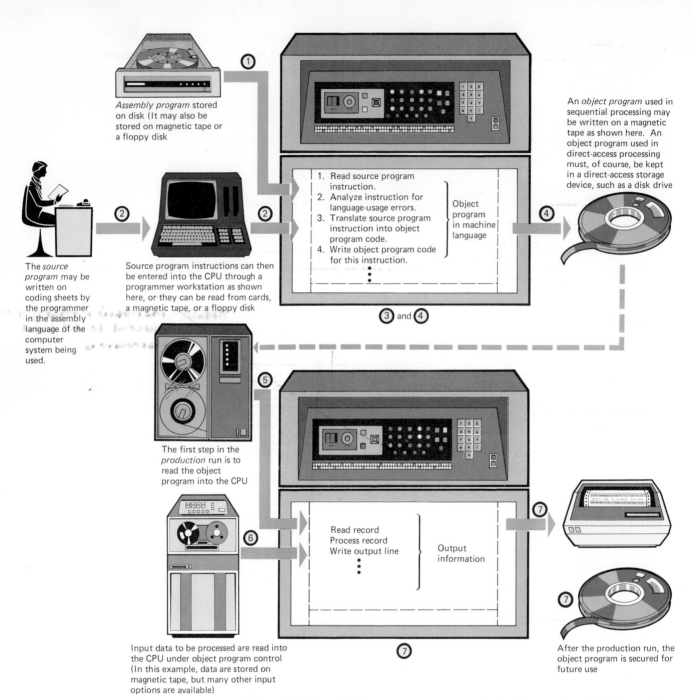

Assembly program stored on disk (It may also be stored on magnetic tape or a floppy disk

The source program may be written on coding sheets by the programmer in the assembly language of the computer system being used.

Source program instructions can then be entered into the CPU through a programmer workstation as shown here, or they can be read from cards, a magnetic tape, or a floppy disk

1. Read source program instruction.
2. Analyze instruction for language-usage errors.
3. Translate source program instruction into object program code.
4. Write object program code for this instruction.

Object program in machine language

③ and ④

An *object program* used in sequential processing may be written on a magnetic tape as shown here. An object program used in direct-access processing must, of course, be kept in a direct-access storage device, such as a disk drive

The first step in the *production* run is to read the object program into the CPU

Input data to be processed are read into the CPU under object program control (In this example, data are stored on magnetic tape, but many other input options are available)

Read record
Process record
Write output line

Output information

After the production run, the object program is secured for future use

Figure 13-3 Assembly language source program instructions are translated into machine-language code during the assembly run (steps 1–4). The machine-language object program is then used to process problem data during a production run (steps 5–7).

366

◄ Assembly Run

1. The *assembly program* is read into the computer, where it has complete control over the translating procedure. This program is generally supplied by the manufacturer of the machine. It's usually stored online on a disk or on secondary storage media such as a magnetic tape or a floppy disk.

2. The *source program* instructions are written by the programmer on coding sheets in the assembly language of the machine being used. These instructions can then be keyed into the CPU from a programmer workstation or they can be entered through the use of input media such as punched cards, a magnetic tape, or a floppy disk.

3. During the assembly run, the source program is treated as data and is read into the CPU, one instruction at a time, under the control of the assembly program.

4. The assembly program translates the source program into a machine-language *object program,* which may be stored online or recorded on a secondary storage medium as the output of the assembly run. It's important to remember that *during the assembly run no problem data are processed.* That is, the source program is *not* being executed. It's merely being converted into a form in which it can be executed by the CPU. If the assembly program is stored online, it remains available for use at any time. If it's stored on a secondary medium, it's filed until it's needed.

Production Run

5. The object program is read into the CPU during the first step in the *production run.* The frequently needed object programs used in direct-access processing are kept in an online storage device. The object programs used in sequential processing applications are usually stored on magnetic tape, cards, or floppy disks.

6. Input data, which may be recorded on a suitable input medium or entered from an online terminal, are read into the CPU under object program control.

7. The data are processed, information output may be produced, and the object program is secured for future use.

Unlike assembly programs, high-level language programs may be used with *different makes of computers* with little modification. Thus, reprogramming expense may be greatly reduced when new equipment is acquired. Other advantages of high-level languages are:

- They are easier to learn than assembly languages.

- They require less time to write.

- They provide better documentation.

- They are easier to maintain.

- A programmer skilled in writing programs in such a language is not restricted to using a single type of machine.

Compiler translation. Naturally, a source program written in a high-level language must also be translated into a machine-usable code. A translating program that can perform this operation is called a **compiler.** Compilers, like advanced assembly programs, may generate many lines of machine code for each source program statement. A *compiling run* is required before problem data can be processed. With the exception that a compiler program is substituted for an assembly program, the procedures are essentially the same as those shown in Figure 13-3. The production run follows the compiling run.

Interpreter translation. An alternative to using a compiler for high-level language translation is often employed with microcomputers. Instead of translating the source program and permanently saving the object code produced during a compiling run for future production use, the programmer merely loads the source program into the computer along with the data to be processed. A permanently hardwired **interpreter** program located inside the computer then converts each source program statement into machine-language form as it's needed during the processing of the data. No object code is saved for future use. The next time the instruction is used, it must once again be interpreted and translated into machine language. For example, during the repetitive processing of the steps in a loop, each instruction in the loop will have to be reinterpreted every time the loop is executed. The interpreter eliminates the need for a separate compiling run after each program change to add features or correct errors. But a previously compiled object program should obviously run much faster than one which has to be interpreted each step of the way during a production run.

MAJOR HIGH-LEVEL LANGUAGES USED IN PROGRAM CODING

Early work on high-level languages began in the 1950s. UNIVAC's Dr. Grace M. Hopper, for example, developed a compiler (named A-2) in 1952. Since then, many other high-level languages have been produced. A closer look at some of the people responsible for developing these languages is presented at the end of Chapter 3. Let's take a look now at a few of the most popular high-level languages.

BASIC

BASIC (Beginner's All-purpose Symbolic Instruction Code) is a popular interactive language that has wide appeal because it's easy to use. An **interactive language** permits direct communication between user and computer system during the preparation and use of programs. A problem-solver with little or no knowledge of computers or programming can learn to write BASIC programs at a remote terminal or microcomputer keyboard in a short period of time. Entering data is easy, and the problem-solver need not be confused about output formats because a usable format may be automatically provided. It's also easy to insert changes and additions into a BASIC program.

Because of its simplicity, BASIC was used in the first microcomputer to gain commercial success. It's now by far the most popular high-level language

```
10 REM *BILLING PROGRAM
20 REM *
30 REM *VARIABLE NAMES
40 REM * N$   NAME
50 REM * S$   ADDRESS
60 REM * C$   CITY AND STATE
70 REM * Q    QUANTITY PURCHASED
80 REM * P    UNIT PRICE
90 REM * A    NET AMOUNT
100 REM *
110 REM *READ NAME,ADDRESS,QUANTITY PURCHASED AND PRICE
120     READ N$,S$,C$,Q,P
130 REM *TEST QUANTITY FOR LAST INPUT
140     IF Q=-99.9 THEN 400
150 REM *COMPUTE NET AMOUNT
160     LET A = Q*P
170 REM *PRINT NAME,ADDRESS AND NET AMOUNT
180     PRINT N$
190     PRINT S$
200     PRINT C$
210     PRINT TAB(3);"NET = ";A
220     PRINT
230     PRINT
240     GO TO 120
260 REM *INPUT DATA
270     DATA "PIERRE'S RECORD SHOP"
280     DATA "6453 ORLEANS STREET"
290     DATA "BOOGIE,LOUISIANA 54321"
300     DATA  300.0,25.00
310     DATA "ROCKY COLLEGE STORE"
320     DATA "1563 BEETHOVEN DRIVE"
330     DATA "ROCKTOWN,MARYLAND 20765"
340     DATA  3.25,25.00
350     DATA "WYNN D.TOOTS,INC."
360     DATA "120 BROWNING STREET"
370     DATA "GONG,CALIFORNIA 98765"
380     DATA  2.00,25.00
390     DATA "L","L","L",-99.9,0.
400     END
```

Computer listing of the BASIC program

Figure 13-4 An example of a BASIC program. At the top of this figure is a computer listing of a simple billing program designed to process bills for multiple customers. (The flowchart for this program was shown in Chapter 12, Figure 12-4.) At the bottom of this figure is the output produced by the computer when the program is run. Each step of this example is discussed in the next chapter.

```
PIERRE'S RECORD SHOP
6453 ORLEANS STREET
BOOGIE,LOUISIANA 54321
   NET =    7500


ROCKY COLLEGE STORE
1563 BEETHOVEN DRIVE
ROCKTOWN,MARYLAND 20765
   NET =    81.2500


WYNN D.TOOTS,INC.
120 BROWNING STREET
GONG,CALIFORNIA 98765
   NET =      50
```

Output produced by the computer as the program is executed

```
C ...BILLING PROGRAM
      INTEGER ADDR1,ADDR2
      DIMENSION NAME(20),ADDR1(20),ADDR2(20)
C...READ NAME,ADDRESS,QUANTITY PURCHASED AND UNIT PRICE
   10 READ(5,70) NAME
      READ(5,70) ADDR1
      READ(5,70) ADDR2
      READ(5,75) QTY,PRICE
C ...TEST QTY FOR LAST CARD
      IF(QTY.EQ.-99.9) GO TO 20
C ... COMPUTE NET PRICE
      ANET = QTY*PRICE
C ...PRINT NAME,ADDRESS AND NET PRICE
      WRITE(6,80) NAME,ADDR1,ADDR2
      WRITE(6,85) ANET
      GO TO 10
   20 STOP
C ...FORMAT STATEMENTS
   70 FORMAT(20A4)
   75 FORMAT(2F10.2)
   80 FORMAT(//3(/3X,20A4))
   85 FORMAT(6X,6HNET = ,F10.2)
      END
```

Computer listing of the
FORTRAN Program

```
PIERRE'S RECORD SHOP
6453 ORLEANS STREET
BOOGIE,LOUISIANA 54321
   NET =     7500.00




ROCKY COLLEGE STORE
1563 BEETHOVEN DRIVE
ROCKTOWN,MARYLAND 20765
   NET =       81.25




WYNN D. TOOTS,INC.
120 BROWNING STREET
GONG,CALIFORNIA 98765
   NET =       50.00
```

Output produced by computer as
program is executed. The same
input data used in the BASIC
Program were punched on cards
and read into the computer under
program control.

Figure 13-5 A computer listing of the simple billing program written in the FORTRAN
language.

used in microcomputer systems. This fact makes it one of the most widely installed computer languages in the world. Interpreters are generally used in microcomputer systems to translate BASIC instructions into machine-language code. There are, however, some BASIC language compilers used with these systems. A number of recreational and educational programs are published in each issue of magazines such as *Byte, Creative Computing, Personal Computing,* and *Popular Computing* that cater to individual users of microcomputers, and these programs are usually documented in BASIC.

BASIC was developed between 1963 and 1964 at Dartmouth College under the direction of Professors John Kemeny and Thomas Kurtz. Their purpose was to produce a language that undergraduate students in all fields of study (1) would find easy to learn, and (2) would thus be encouraged to use on a regular basis. BASIC was a success at Dartmouth on both counts. The Dartmouth computer system used General Electric equipment, and BASIC was implemented on this equipment with the assistance of GE engineers. Recognizing the advantages of BASIC, GE then quickly made the language available for the use of their customers who were buying time on GE's commercial timesharing systems. And Hewlett-Packard and Digital Equipment Corporation offered early versions of BASIC to run on their timeshared computer systems.

By 1974, BASIC was available for most computers, and it's now offered by virtually all computer manufacturers. Although the original BASIC had a well-defined syntax, numerous extensions to the language were written in the decade after 1964. Little thought was given to making these extensions compatible with other versions of the language. And so it is today that "BASIC" is really a generic name for a group of dialects with many similar features. There's an American National Standards Institute **(ANSI) standard** for a minimal version of BASIC that was published in 1978. But this standard is so simple that it has been extended in virtually every available BASIC dialect.

Users of BASIC range from public school students to aerospace engineers to business managers. After studying the next chapter, you may also be included in this group because we'll be coding a number of applications in that chapter using the BASIC language. A BASIC version of a simple billing program designed to process bills for multiple customers is shown in Figure 13-4. This is the program for problem 2 that was discussed in Chapter 12 and charted in Figure 12-4, page 328.

FORTRAN

A FORTRAN program listing for this same simple billing problem is shown in Figure 13-5. When supplied with input cards containing the data shown in the BASIC program, this FORTRAN version will produce the same output, as you can see in Figure 13-5. We can trace the origin of **FORTRAN** (**FOR**mula **TRAN**slator) back to 1954 when an IBM-sponsored committee headed by John Backus began work on a scientific-mathematic language. The result of this effort was FORTRAN, which was introduced in 1957 for the IBM

704 computer. It's estimated that the cost of producing the 25,000 lines of detailed machine instructions that went into the first FORTRAN compiler was $2.5 million. FORTRAN is noted for the ease with which it can express mathematical equations. It has been widely accepted and has been revised a number of times. Several of its features were later incorporated into the first BASIC language.

The vast majority of all computers now in service—from small micros to the largest number-crunchers—can use FORTRAN. Compilers rather than interpreters are used. Because of its early widespread acceptance, work began in 1962 on FORTRAN standard languages. Two standards—a basic or minimal version of FORTRAN and a "full" or extended version—were approved by ANSI in 1966. FORTRAN thus has the distinction of being the first standardized language. The current FORTRAN standards were published by ANSI in 1978.

As you can see in Figure 13-5, a FORTRAN program consists of a series of *statements*. These statements supply input/output, calculation, logic/comparison, and other basic instructions to the computer. The words READ, WRITE, GO TO, and STOP in the statements mean exactly what you would expect. FORTRAN programs are executed sequentially until the sequence is altered by a transfer of control statement.

FORTRAN has the *advantage* of being a compact language that serves the needs of scientists and business statisticians very well. Huge libraries of engineering and scientific programs written in FORTRAN are available to scientists and engineers. The language is also widely used for business applications that don't require the manipulation of extensive data files. Because there are established FORTRAN standards, programs written for one computer are usually easily converted for use with another. *However*, it may be more difficult to trace program logic in FORTRAN code than in some other high-level languages. And FORTRAN is not as well suited for processing large business files as the next language we'll discuss, COBOL.

COBOL   *mainly for mainframes + business*

As its name indicates, **COBOL** (**CO**mmon **B**usiness **O**riented **L**anguage) was designed specifically for business-type data processing. And it's now the most widely used language for large business applications. The group that designed the language gathered at the Pentagon in Washington, D.C., in May 1959, with the official sanction of the U.S. Department of Defense. Members of the **CO**nference of **DA**ta **SY**stems **L**anguages (**CODASYL**) represented computer manufacturers, government agencies, user organizations, and universities. The CODASYL Short-Range Committee, which prepared the COBOL framework, consisted of representatives from federal government agencies and from computer manufacturers. From June to December 1959, this committee worked on the language specifications. Its final report was approved in January 1960, and the language specifications were published a few months later by the Government Printing Office.

Since 1961, COBOL compilers have been prepared for virtually all processors used in business data processing. They are even available now for use with small personal computers. Other CODASYL committees have continued to maintain, revise, and extend the initial specifications. An ANSI COBOL standard was first published in 1968, and a later version was approved in 1974. A new standard is scheduled to appear in the early 1980s.

Figure 13-6 shows a computer listing of a COBOL program. This program is a COBOL version of the BASIC and FORTRAN simple billing programs illustrated in Figures 13-4 and 13-5. If the same input data used in the earlier language examples are punched into cards and read into a computer under the control of this COBOL program, the output results will be essentially the same as you can see in Figure 13-6.

COBOL is structured much like this chapter. *Sentences* (analogous to statements in FORTRAN) direct the processor in performing the necessary operations. A varying number of sentences dealing with the same operation are grouped to form a *paragraph.* Related paragraphs may then be organized into a *section.* Sections are then grouped into a *division,* and *four divisions* complete the structural hierarchy of a COBOL program.

The *first* entry, line 1 in Figure 13-6, is IDENTIFICATION DIVISION— the first of the COBOL divisions. A required paragraph identifies the program, and additional optional paragraphs are included for documentation purposes. The *second* division, line 7, is the ENVIRONMENT DIVISION, which consists of two required sections that describe the specific hardware to use when the program is run. If the application is to be processed on different equipment, this division will have to be rewritten, but that usually presents no problem.

The DATA DIVISION (line 17 in Figure 13-6), the *third* of the four divisions, is divided into file and working storage sections. The purpose of this division is to present in detail a description and layout of:

▌ All the *input data* items in a record, and all the records in each file that's to be processed.

▌ All *storage locations* that are needed during processing to hold intermediate results and other independent values needed for processing.

▌ The format to be used for the *output* results.

The *last* COBOL division, the PROCEDURE DIVISION (line 52), contains the sentences and paragraphs that the computer follows in executing the program. In this division, input/output, calculation, logic/comparison, and storage/retrieval and movement operations are performed to solve the problem.

One *advantage* of COBOL is that it can be written in a quasi-English form that may employ commonly used business terms. Because of this fact, the logic of COBOL programs may often be followed more easily by the nonprogrammers in business. Thus, there may be less documentation required for COBOL programs. COBOL is better able to manipulate alphabetic characters than FORTRAN, and this is important in business processing where names, ad-

```
00001                    IDENTIFICATION DIVISION.                              BILLING
00002                    PROGRAM-ID.   BILLING PROGRAM.                        BILLING
00003                    AUTHOR.      CRAIG ELDERS.                            BILLING
00004                    REMARKS.      THIS PROGRAM PRODUCES A PRINTOUT CONTAINING:   BILLING
00005                                 NAME, ADDRESS, AND NET PRICE.            BILLING
00006                                                                          BILLING
00007                    ENVIRONMENT DIVISION.                                 BILLING
00008                    CONFIGURATION SECTION.                                BILLING
00009                    SOURCE-COMPUTER.    XEROX-SIGMA-9.                     BILLING
00010                    OBJECT-COMPUTER.    XEROX-SIGMA-9.                     BILLING
00011                                                                          BILLING
00012                    INPUT-OUTPUT SECTION.                                 BILLING
00013                    FILE-CONTROL.                                         BILLING
00014                        SELECT CARD-INPUT ASSIGN TO CARD-READER.         BILLING
00015                        SELECT PRINTOUT   ASSIGN TO PRINTER.             BILLING
00016                                                                          BILLING
00017                    DATA DIVISION.                                        BILLING
00018                    FILE SECTION.                                         BILLING
00019                    FD   CARD-INPUT                                       BILLING
00020                            RECORD CONTAINS 80 CHARACTERS                 BILLING
00021                            LABEL RECORD IS OMITTED                       BILLING
00022                            DATA RECORDS ARE CARD-NAME-ADDRESS-RECORD     BILLING
00023                                           CARD-QUANTITY-PRICE-RECORD.    BILLING
00024                    01   CARD-NAME-ADDRESS-RECORD.                        BILLING
00025                         05   CARD-NAME-ADDRESS          PICTURE X(30).   BILLING
00026                         05   FILLER                     PICTURE X(50).   BILLING
00027                                                                          BILLING
00028                    01   CARD-QUANTITY-PRICE-RECORD.                      BILLING
00029                         05   CARD-QUANTITY              PICTURE 999V99.  BILLING
00030                         05   CARD-PRICE                 PICTURE 999V99.  BILLING
00031                         05   FILLER                     PICTURE X(70).   BILLING
00032                                                                          BILLING
00033                    FD   PRINTOUT                                         BILLING
00034                            RECORD CONTAINS 132 CHARACTERS               BILLING
00035                            LABEL RECORD IS OMITTED                       BILLING
00036                            DATA RECORD IS PRINTER-RECORD.                BILLING
00037                    01   PRINTER-RECORD.                                  BILLING
00038                         05   FILLER                     PICTURE X(10).   BILLING
00039                         05   PRINT-AREA                 PICTURE X(30).   BILLING
00040                         05   FILLER                     PICTURE X(92).   BILLING
00041                                                                          BILLING
00042                    WORKING-STORAGE SECTION.                              BILLING
00043                    77   NET-COST                   PICTURE 99999V99.    BILLING
00044                    77   END-OF-DATA-FLAG           PIC X(3)  VALUE 'NO'. BILLING
00045                    77   MISSING-CARD-FLAG          PIC X(3)  VALUE 'NO'. BILLING
00046                    01   NET-COST-PRINT-LINE.                             BILLING
00047                         05   FILLER  VALUE SPACES       PICTURE X(10).   BILLING
00048                         05   FILLER   VALUE IS 'NET = ' PICTURE X(6).    BILLING
00049                         05   PRINT-NET-COST             PICTURE $$$,$$$.99.  BILLING
00050                         05   FILLER  VALUE SPACES       PICTURE X(106).  BILLING
00051                                                                          BILLING
00052                    PROCEDURE DIVISION.                                   BILLING
00053                    OPEN-UP-FILES.                                        BILLING
00054                        OPEN INPUT  CARD-INPUT.                          BILLING
00055                        OPEN OUTPUT PRINTOUT.                            BILLING
00056                                                                          BILLING
00057                        PERFORM READ-LOOP THRU READ-LOOP-EXIT            BILLING
00058                            UNTIL END-OF-DATA-FLAG = 'YES'.              BILLING
00059                                                                          BILLING
00060                        CLOSE CARD-INPUT.                                BILLING
00061                        CLOSE PRINTOUT.                                  BILLING
00062                        STOP RUN.                                        BILLING
00063                                                                          BILLING
```

```
00064                    READ-A-CARD.                                                    BILLING
00065                        READ CARD-INPUT                                             BILLING
00066                            AT END MOVE 'YES' TO END-OF-DATA-FLAG.                   BILLING
00067                                                                                     BILLING
00068                    READ-LOOP.                                                       BILLING
00069                        PERFORM READ-A-CARD.                                         BILLING
00070                        IF END-OF-DATA-FLAG = 'NO'                                   BILLING
00071                            MOVE ALL SPACES TO PRINTER-RECORD                        BILLING
00072                            MOVE CARD-NAME-ADDRESS TO PRINT-AREA                     BILLING
00073                            WRITE PRINTER-RECORD AFTER ADVANCING 2 LINES             BILLING
00074                            PERFORM READ-A-CARD                                      BILLING
00075                            IF END-OF-DATA-FLAG = 'NO'                               BILLING
00076                                MOVE CARD-NAME-ADDRESS TO PRINT-AREA                 BILLING
00077                                WRITE PRINTER-RECORD AFTER ADVANCING 1 LINES         BILLING
00078                                PERFORM READ-A-CARD                                  BILLING
00079                                IF END-OF-DATA-FLAG = 'NO'                           BILLING
00080                                    MOVE CARD-NAME-ADDRESS TO PRINT-AREA             BILLING
00081                                    WRITE PRINTER-RECORD AFTER ADVANCING 1 LINES     BILLING
00082                                    PERFORM READ-A-CARD                              BILLING
00083                                    IF END-OF-DATA-FLAG = 'NO'                       BILLING
00084                                        COMPUTE NET-COST =                           BILLING
00085                                            CARD-QUANTITY * CARD-PRICE               BILLING
00086                                        MOVE NET-COST TO PRINT-NET-COST              BILLING
00087                                        WRITE PRINTER-RECORD FROM                    BILLING
00088                                            NET-COST-PRINT-LINE AFTER ADVANCING      BILLING
00089                                            1 LINES .                                BILLING
00090                                    ELSE                                            BILLING
00091                                        MOVE 'YES' TO MISSING-CARD-FLAG              BILLING
00092                                ELSE                                                BILLING
00093                                    MOVE 'YES' TO MISSING-CARD-FLAG                 BILLING
00094                            ELSE                                                    BILLING
00095                                MOVE 'YES' TO MISSING-CARD-FLAG.                    BILLING
00096                                                                                     BILLING
00097                        IF MISSING-CARD-FLAG = 'YES'                                 BILLING
00098                            DISPLAY 'THERE ARE NOT ENOUGH DATA CARDS TO BE PROCESSED'BILLING
00099                                UPON PRINTER.                                        BILLING
00100                                                                                     BILLING
00101                    READ-LOOP-EXIT.                                                  BILLING
00102                        EXIT.                                                        BILLING
```

```
PIERRE'S RECORD SHOP
6453 ORLEANS STREET
BOOGIE, LOUISIANA 54321
NET = $7,500.00

ROCKY COLLEGE STORE
1563 BEETHOVEN DRIVE
ROCKTOWN, MARYLAND 20765
NET =     $81.25

WYNN D. TOOTS, INC.
120 BROWNING STREET
GONG, CALIFORNIA 98765
NET =     $50.00
```

Output produced by the
computer as the program
is executed

Figure 13-6 The computer listing of the simple billing program written in the COBOL language is numbered from 1 to 102. The four required divisions in any COBOL program are shown. The same input data used in the BASIC and FORTRAN examples were punched in cards and read into the computer under the control of this program. The output results are similar.

dresses, part descriptions, etc., are frequently reproduced. Also, a standard version exists; the language is relatively machine-independent; and it's maintained, updated, and supported by its users. Finally, there are large libraries of business applications packages available from vendors, and most of these packages have been written in COBOL. A *limitation* of COBOL, however, is that it's obviously not a compact language. It's not the easiest high-level language for most of us to learn, and it's not as well suited for complex mathematical computations as FORTRAN.

PL/I

We've seen that early languages such as FORTRAN and COBOL were written to solve *either* scientific or business data processing problems. But in the early 1960s, IBM and a committee of users of the IBM System/360 family of computers began development work on what was promoted as a "universal language." This **PL/I** language (Programming Language/I, where I stands for "one") was implemented in the mid-1960s to solve all types of business and scientific problems. As a scientific language, PL/I was designed to include some of the features of FORTRAN; however, COBOL-type file processing techniques are also used. An ANSI committee produced a PL/I standard in 1976. A "Subset G" of this full standard is also available for use with small computers.

Since it has features found in both FORTRAN and COBOL, PL/I is a flexible and sophisticated language. A portion of a PL/I program to average test grades is shown in Figure 13-7. Although this program was written on a general-purpose coding sheet, PL/I programs can be prepared in a rather free-form way. The basic element in PL/I is the *statement* which is concluded with a semicolon. Statements are combined into *procedures*. A procedure may represent an entire small program or a "building block" or module of a more complex program. Because of its modular structure, a novice programmer need only learn a small part of the language in order to prepare applications programs of a particular type. Also, modular procedure blocks and other features of the language support the use of structured programming concepts. And a PL/I compiler has built-in features—called *default options*—that can detect and correct common programming errors. But a *limitation* of PL/I is that it's more difficult to learn in its entirety than either FORTRAN or COBOL.

RPG

RPG (Report Program Generator) was introduced in the 1960s as a language that could readily duplicate the processing approach used with punched card equipment. Its use is still limited primarily to business applications processed on small business computers. As the name suggests, RPG is designed to generate the output reports resulting from the processing of such common

PUNCHING INSTRUCTIONS

| JOB | AVERAGE OF TEST SCORES | | WRITTEN AS: | | | | | | | | | | |
| BY | JOHN Q PROGRAMMER | DATE 1/26/99 | PUNCH AS: | | | | | | | | | | |

NOTES: PL/I

FIELD IDENTIFICATION

```
1   AVERAGE: PROCEDURE OPTIONS (MAIN);
2   DECLARE
3      N FIXED (2),
4      NAME CHARACTER (15),
5      SCORE FIXED (3),
6      TOTAL FIXED (4),
7      AVE FIXED (3),
8      SWT FIXED (1),
9      WORK FILE,
10     NWORK FILE PRINT;
11  TOTAL = 0;
12  N = 0;
13  SWT = 0;
14  OPEN FILE (WORK) INPUT, FILE (NWORK) OUTPUT;
15  READ: GET FILE (WORK) EDIT (NAME, SCORE) (X/
16  ON ENDFILE (WORK) GO TO OUTPUT;
17  IF SWT = 1 THEN GO TO CONTINU
```

Figure 13-7 A portion of a program written in PL/1.

business applications as accounts receivable and accounts payable. But RPG can also be used to periodically update accounts-receivable and accounts-payable files.

In spite of its file-updating capabilities, RPG is a *limited-purpose* language because object programs generated by the RPG compiler follow a basic processing cycle without deviation. The general form of this cycle is shown in Figure 13-8. Since the processing logic is built into the language and never varies, the RPG programmer is concerned only with *file description* and with specifications about *input, calculations,* and *output.* Very detailed coding sheets are used by programmers to write these specifications.

One *advantage* of RPG is that it's relatively easy to learn and use. Since program logic is fixed, there are fewer formal rules to remember than with many other languages. RPG is well suited for applications where large files are read, few calculations are performed, and output reports are created. It has been an important language of small business-oriented computers for years. Of course, the limited purpose for which it was designed is also a *disadvan-*

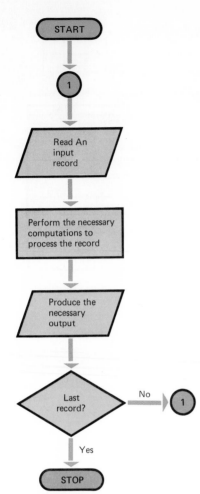

Figure 13-8 The processing logic built into the RPG language.

tage of the language: RPG has restricted mathematical capability and cannot be used for scientific applications. Finally, RPG is not a formally standardized language and so programs written for one processor may require modification before they will run on a different make of machine. However, the RPG versions produced by IBM have tended to become "de facto" standards.

ALGOL, Pascal, and Ada

ALGOL (ALGOorithmic Language) was introduced in 1958. It was designed by an international group of mathematicians, and developed by groups in Europe and the United States. John Backus of FORTRAN fame assisted in this development. As you might expect, ALGOL was intended for the use of those involved in scientific and mathematical projects. Several versions of the language have been created, and the current version is ALGOL 68. FORTRAN has generally been used instead of ALGOL in the United States, but ALGOL is very popular in Europe. Like PL/I, ALGOL is a block-structured or modular language that's well suited for use in a structured programming setting.

An offspring of ALGOL is **Pascal.** Named in honor of Blaise Pascal, a seventeenth-century French mathematician, philosopher, and inventor, this language was developed in the late 1960s and early 1970s by Professor Nicklaus Wirth at Switzerland's Federal Institute of Technology. Pascal was the first major language to be created after the concepts associated with structured programming became widely disseminated.

A Pascal version of a simple billing program similar to those presented earlier in other languages is shown in Figure 13-9. The output produced by this program when three input records are supplied is also shown. Like ALGOL, Pascal is block-structured. Programs are composed of *blocks* starting with BEGIN and terminating with END. Program *statements* proceed in a logical flow from start to finish. All variables are identified at the beginning of the program. The three basic logic structures are supported by statements in sequence separated by semicolons, IF . . . THEN . . .ELSE selection statements, and WHILE . . . DO loop statements.

Pascal can be used for both scientific and file processing applications. A growing number of college instructors are using it to teach programming to their computer science majors. And Pascal is now one of the major languages running on mini- and microcomputer systems. Professor Kenneth Bowles of the University of California at San Diego has pioneered the use of Pascal on small machines.

Another language in the ALGOL/Pascal lineage is **Ada,** which was mentioned in the opening vignette. This language is named in honor of Lord Byron's daughter Ada Augusta, the Countess of Lovelace. Ada worked with Charles Babbage on the concepts for an "Analytical Engine" in England during the first half of the nineteenth century. Because of her writings, she is considered by many to be the first "programmer."

```
(* BILLING PROGRAM
   VARIABLE NAMES:

   Q:   QUANTITY PURCHASED
   P:   UNIT PRICE
   A:   NET AMOUNT *)


PROGRAM PROGRAM1 (INPUT,OUTPUT);
VAR CH:CHAR; Q,P,A:REAL; I:INTEGER;
BEGIN
WHILE NOT EOF (INPUT) DO
BEGIN
FOR I:= 1 TO 3 DO
     BEGIN

        (*   READ AND WRITE NAME AND ADDRESS *)

        WHILE NOT EOLN DO
        BEGIN READ (CH);
        IF NOT EOF THEN WRITE (CH);
        END;
        IF NOT EOF (INPUT) THEN
            BEGIN READLN; WRITELN;
            END
     END;
     IF NOT EOF (INPUT) THEN
     BEGIN
                 (* READ QUANTITY AND PRICE *)
         READ (Q,P);
         A := Q * P;
         WRITE ('  NET = ',A);
         READLN;
         WRITELN;
         FOR I := 1 TO 2 DO WRITELN;
     END
END
END.
```

Computer listing of
the PASCAL program

```
PIERRE'S RECORD SHOP
6453 ORLEANS STREET
BOOGIE, LOUISIANA  54321
  NET =        7500


ROCKY COLLEGE STORE
1563 BEETHOVEN DRIVE
ROCKTOWN, MARYLAND  20765
  NET =        81.25


WYNN D. TOOTS, INC.
120 BROWNING STREET
GONG, CALIFORNIA  98765
  NET =          50
```

Output produced by the
computer as the program
is executed

Figure 13-9 A computer listing of the simple billing program written in the Pascal language.

The Ada language is sponsored by the U.S. Department of Defense (DOD) for use by the military services. In 1975, the DOD began a series of studies for the purpose of specifying and designing a new common language to be used by computer vendors and military programmers. The new language—Ada—was presented by the design team late in 1980. Critics called it unwieldy and inefficient, while supporters labeled it a breakthrough in software technology. It's still too early to know which view will prevail. Since the DOD will require military computers to have Ada capability, however, the language will endure. And announcements of powerful microcomputer chips supported by an Ada compiler have been made by Intel Corporation.

Other Languages

Dozens of other specialized languages have been developed. Among them are PILOT (Programmed Inquiry Learning Or Teaching) that's used to prepare educational programs. LISP (LISt Processing Language) and SNOBOL (StriNg Oriented SymBOlic Language) are used for nonnumeric applications. APL (A Programming Language) is used for scientific purposes, and APT (Automatically Programmed Tooling) is used in manufacturing applications.

The Programming Language Issue

As you've seen by now, many languages are available that will permit the programmer to write instructions to control the computer during the processing of an application. Which language should be used? Obviously, a selection must be made prior to program coding, but several factors may combine to make language selection difficult. Obtaining answers to the following questions will generally help in the selection process:

1. *Are company programmers familiar with the language?* In many cases, the language used is simply the one that's best known to the programmers. If a language is not familiar, can it be learned quickly? Is it easy to use?

2. *What's the nature of the application?* Does the language perform well in applications of this type?

3. *Does the language support structured programming concepts?* COBOL, PL/I, ALGOL, and Pascal are better able to support structured programming than BASIC or FORTRAN.

4. *Is satisfactory translating software available?* There's an important distinction between a language and a compiler. A language is a humanly convenient set of rules, conventions, and representations used to convey information from human to machine. A compiler is a trans-

lator written by one or more programmers. It's entirely possible that a good language, when used with an inefficient compiler, will yield unsatisfactory results.

5. *How often will the application be processed?* An assembly language program written by a clever programmer usually has a shorter production run time and takes less storage space than does a program of the same application written in a high-level language. If the job is run often enough, the value of the operating time saved may be more than enough to offset the cost of additional time spent in program preparation. For limited-life jobs, however, the faster the possible programming time is (with high-level languages), the more economical the approach.

6. *Will the program be changed frequently?* The ease of program modification varies with different languages. A high-level language is typically easier to modify than an assembly language.

7. *Is a hardware change anticipated during the life of the application?* Conversion of standardized high-level language programs is easier and faster. Machine-oriented programs may have to be completely rewritten.

8. *Is the language being supported, improved, and updated?* Are resources being committed to the support of the language? Will new computers continue to accept the language source programs? Who's sponsoring the language, and what's their committment to it?

PROGRAM IMPLEMENTATION AND MAINTENANCE

So far we've looked at some of the issues and options facing programmers during program preparation. We've also considered programming language categories and discussed several major high-level languages. All these topics occupy an important place in the program preparation stage. But this stage culminates with the actual writing (or coding) of the instructions needed to process an application into a language and form acceptable to a computer. **Program coding** is too important to be dismissed with a few paragraphs, and so Chapter 14 is devoted exclusively to writing instructions in the BASIC language. As you'll see, you must follow specific rules with respect to punctuation and statement structure.

Once a program has been written, the final step in the programming process is to see that it's implemented and then maintained. The time and effort required for these activities will often be determined by the options selected during the program preparation phase. For example:

- The use of tested applications packages may make it possible to bypass many implementation problems.

- The use of modular program design to divide complex programs into more manageable elements may make it easier to trace errors and to insert tested and proven subroutine modules into the program as needed.

- The use of basic coding structures can lead to programs that are easier to understand, and that are thus easier to test and maintain.

- The use of peer reviews can result in fewer errors, faster testing, better documentation, and easier maintenance.

Program Implementation

The first step in **program implementation** is to *debug* the program—i.e., to detect and correct errors that prevent the program from running. *Testing* the results produced by the program to see if they are correct is the next implementation step. And ensuring that a complete *documentation* package is available for the application is a third implementation step.

Debugging. There are days when things never seem to go quite right. Such days may be more common for programmers than for other mortals. *Bugs* are the clerical mistakes and errors that crop up in programs. These bugs or "glitches" (bugs have also been defined as "sons of glitches") just seem to occur even under the best of circumstances and even when matters are not being helped along by our natural human tendency to screw things up. It's unusual for complex programs to run to completion on the first attempt. In fact, the time spent in **debugging** and testing often equals or exceeds the time spent in program coding. Failure to provide for a possible program path, keying errors, mistakes in coding punctuation, transposed characters—these are but a few of the bugs that can thwart the programmer.

To reduce the number of clerical and logical errors, the programmer should carefully check the coding for accuracy prior to its entry into the computer. This **desk-checking** process should include an examination of program logic and program completeness. Furthermore, typical input data should be manually traced through the program processing paths to identify possible errors. In short, the programmer attempts to play the role of the computer.

After programs have been desk-checked for accuracy, an attempt is made to convert the source program into object-program form. Compiler programs and interpreters contain error-diagnostic features, which detect (and print messages about) mistakes caused by the incorrect application of the language used to prepare the source program. In many organizations, a programmer can sit at a programmer workstation and key in the program code from his or her coding sheets. The programmer can then call up an online compiler program to immediately convert the source code into object code. Next, a listing of the detected language-usage (or **syntax**) **errors** may be displayed on the screen of the workstation. The programmer may interact with program development software and use the editing features of the workstation to correct detected errors. When changes have been made in response to detected errors, a new compilation can be ordered. This process may continue until all detected syntax errors have been remedied.

You should realize, however, that compiler/interpreter diagnostic checks will *not* detect the presence of **logical errors** in a program. If an instruction should be "LET A = B*C" but has been coded "LET A = B+C," this error will not be noticed since no language rules have been broken. Thus, an "errorless" pass of the program through the compiler or interpreter *does not* mean that the program is perfected or that all bugs have been eliminated. But it usually does mean that the program is ready for testing.

Testing. A program to be tested has generally demonstrated that it will run and produce results. The purpose of **testing** is to determine whether the results are correct. The testing procedure involves using the program to process input test data that will produce known results. *The items developed for testing should include:*

- Typical data, which will test the generally used program paths.

- Unusual but valid data, which will test the program paths used to handle exceptions.

- Incorrect, incomplete, or inappropriate data, which will test the program error-handling capabilities.

A testing procedure that's often followed is to separately test different portions of a program. This helps to isolate detected errors to a particular program segment. The use of a modular programming approach, of course, eases this procedure. Another technique that's often used is to entrust much of the testing to someone other than the programmer who wrote the code. A fresh outlook is often helpful, and errors that are missed by a programmer who is "too familiar" with the code may be easily picked up by someone else.

If the program passes the tests, it may be released for use. It should be noted here, however, that errors may still remain. In complex programs there may be tens of thousands of different possible paths through the program. It simply isn't practical (and maybe not even possible) to trace through all these paths during testing. For example, the flowchart in Figure 13-10 looks rather simple, but the number of different possible paths is an astounding 10^{20}. If we could somehow check out one path per nanosecond, and if we had started our testing in the year 1, we would only be about half done today! This is why programs may suddenly produce nonsense months after they've been released for use. Some unique and unanticipated series of events has produced input or circumstances that turn up an error for the first time. The error was always there; it simply remained undetected. It's thus impossible to certify that very complex systems are error-free.

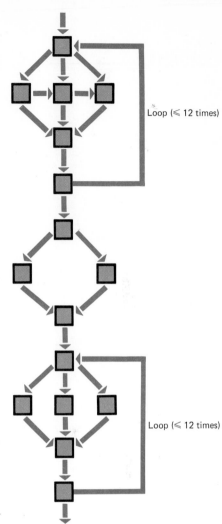

Loop ($\leq$ 12 times)

Loop ($\leq$ 12 times)

Figure 13-10 Errors can remain hidden in an obscure path in a program for years without even being detected. This is possible because complex programs contain billions of possible paths. In this simple-looking flowchart, for example, there are 10^{20} possible paths.

If the program does not pass a test, the programmer may do the following:

1. Call for a **trace program** run. The trace program prints out the status of registers after each operation. Errors may be discovered by noting register contents after each program step.

2. Call for a **storage dump** when the program "hangs up" during a test run. That is, obtain a printout of the contents of primary storage and registers at the time of the hangup. The programmer can then study this listing for possible clues to the cause of the programming error(s).

After the program appears to be running properly and producing correct results, there's frequently a transitionary cutover period during which the job application is processed both by the old method and the new program. The purpose of this period, of course, is to verify processing accuracy and completeness.

Documentation. **Documentation,** as we've seen, is the process of collecting, organizing, storing, and otherwise maintaining on paper (or on some relatively permanent medium) a complete record of *why* applications were developed, *what* functions they perform, *how* these functions are carried out, *who* the applications are to serve, and *how* they are to be used. Documentation is a most important—but often neglected—programming activity.

The *documentation package* for a program used in an organization should include:

1. *A definition of the problem.* Why was the program prepared? What were the objectives? Who requested the program and who approved it? Questions such as these should be answered.

2. *A description of the system.* The system or subsystem environment in which the program functions should be described (systems flowcharts should be included). Broad systems specifications outlining the scope of the problem, the form and type of input data to be used, and the form and type of output required should be clearly stated.

3. *A description of the program.* Program flowcharts, program listings, test data and test results, storage dumps, trace program printouts— these and other documents that describe the program and give a historical record of difficulties and/or changes should be available.

4. *A recitation of operator instructions.* Among the items covered should be computer switch settings, loading and unloading procedures, and starting, running, and terminating procedures.

5. *A description of program controls.* Controls may be incorporated in a program in a number of ways. For example, programmed controls may be used to check on the reasonableness and propriety of input data. A description of such controls should be a part of the documentation.

Program Maintenance

Changing business conditions, revised user needs, new laws—these and other factors require that production programs be continually *maintained* and modified. **Program maintenance** is an important duty of programmers and may involve all steps from problem definition through analysis, design, and program preparation. In some installations there are programmers who do nothing but maintain production programs. It generally takes less time for these programmers to make a change than it does to find the program location(s) where changes are needed.

When an organization first acquires a computer, much of the programming effort goes into the development of new applications. But as the number of installed programs in the organization grows, it's not unusual to find that more programming time is being spent on maintenance than on new development work. In fact, in many organizations well over half the total programming effort is spent on maintenance. And it's estimated that over the life cycle of a typical application, the maintenance and enhancement costs that are incurred may be two to four times larger than the initial development costs (see Figure 13-11).

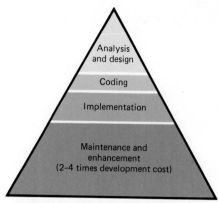

Figure 13-11 Cost pyramid of the program life cycle.

 **Feedback and Review 13-1**

You should now have an understanding of some of the decisions that must be made during program preparation. You should also be aware of some of the general characteristics of programming languages. And you should be able to outline the steps followed during the implementation and maintenance phase of the programming process. To test and reinforce your understanding of the material presented in this chapter, fill in the *crossword puzzle* form presented below.

Across

1. A computer's _____ language consists of strings of binary numbers and is the only one it directly understands.

2. One of the first high-level languages designed for scientific applications, and still one of the most popular, _____ was designed in the mid-1950s by an IBM-sponsored committee headed by John Backus.

5. The _____/I language was designed to solve all types of business and scientific problems. It includes features found in both FORTRAN and COBOL, and it facilitates the use of structured programming concepts.

7. The _____ division is the third of the four divisions required in a COBOL program. This division presents a detailed description of the input data to be processed, the working storage locations that are needed, and the format to be used for the output results.

9. After a program has demonstrated that it will run and produce results, the next step is to _____ it to see if the results are correct.

```
 1            2  3         4        5      6
[M][A][C][H][I][N][E]  [F][O][R][T][R][A][N] [P][L]  [S]
[O]                       [B]          [N]         [T]
 7  8                      9              10 11
[D][D][A][T][A]        [J][T][E][S][T]  [O][P]  [R]
                12        13               14
[U]   [D]      [C]     [P][E][E][R][I]   [R][A]  [U]
     15
[L]   [A][L][G][O][L]     [C]   [A]      [R][S]  [C]
    16
[E]   [B]      [B]     [T]   [C]   [E][G][C]   [T]
[ ]   [A]      [D]           [E]   [G]      [A]  [E]
 18           19          20      21
[A][S][S][E][M][B][L][Y]  [I]   [C][O][M][P][I][L][E][R]
[ ]   [I]      [U]        [N]                     [E]
 22                       23
[P][A][C][K][A][G][E][D]  [M][A][I][N][T][A][I][N][E][D]
```

385

10. The first part of a machine-language instruction is called the command or operation, and it tells the computer what function to perform. Every computer has an _____ code for each of its functions.

13. A _____ review is also called a structured walkthrough. The purpose of this review is to allow a programmer's colleagues to check his or her work in order to detect errors.

15. A block-structured scientific language that's very popular in Europe. Pascal is considered an offspring of this language.

18. _____ languages use mnemonic operation codes and symbolic addressing, and they are designed for a specific make and model of computer.

21. A program that translates the source code of a high-level language into the machine-language object code of a computer is called a _____. Unlike the object code produced by an interpreter, the object code produced by this program is saved for repetitive use.

22. Whenever feasible, the purchase of an appropriate _____ program should be considered as an alternative to the creation of an in-house custom-made program.

23. Changing conditions require that production programs be continually _____ and up-

dated. The effort spent on this activity can easily exceed the time spent on new program development.

Down

1. In a modular program, a main-control program specifies the order in which each _____ (or subroutine) in the program will be processed.

3. An assembler or compiler is used to translate a source program written in the language used by the programmer into a machine-language _____ program that the computer can understand.

4. An acronym for the organization that publishes programming language standards.

6. There can be little doubt about the existence of a _____ programming setting when programs are written using only a few basic logic structures, when program functions are broken down into lower-level components, and when peer reviews and chief programmer teams are used.

8. Named after Lord Byron's daughter, this recent language in the ALGOL/Pascal line is sponsored by the U.S. Department of Defense.

9. If a program fails to pass a test, the programmer can call for a _____ program run to check on the status of registers after each program operation.

11. The first major language to be created after structured programming concepts became widely disseminated, _____ is an offspring of ALGOL and is now running on many micro- and minicomputers.

12. Designed specifically for business-type data processing applications, _____ is a standardized language that requires the use of four divisions in every program. Programs can be written in a quasi-English form, and the language is suited to manipulating large files.

14. _____ is a nonstandard language used with small business computers to generate output reports. These reports result from the processing of common business applications.

16. The most popular language used with microcomputers and timeshared minicomputers, _____ is an easy-to-use high-level language that was originally developed at Dartmouth for the use of undergraduate students.

17. When a programmer is responsible for coding an entire program, the program may become an extension of the programmer's _____.

19. The inelegant term used to describe a clerical mistake or logical error that crops up in programs.

20. RPG is a language that uses built-_____ processing logic.

Looking Back

1. Programmers generally want to write programs that meet user needs, are produced on time and with a minimum cost, are accurate, and are easy to implement and maintain. In trying to achieve these goals, however, they must usually deal with a number of issues involving methodology and the use of resources. Included among these issues are: Should a new program be written or should an existing program package be purchased? How should programming tasks be assigned? What program design methods should be used? Which programming language(s) should be selected?

2. When compared with custom-made programs, packaged programs are generally less expensive and are likely to contain fewer errors. But the custom-made program can be designed to better fit the unique needs of users. The responsibility for preparing a program can be assigned to a programmer who codes and implements the task. Or a programming project can be assigned to a chief programmer or to egoless programming teams. Each of these options for organizing programmers differs from the others, and there's no agreement about which approach is best.

3. Different organizations also use different program construction techniques. Modular program design, the use of basic coding structures, the use of peer reviews, and the application of structured programming concepts—a mix of these and other techniques is often followed.

4. Assembly and/or high-level programming languages are selected for program coding. Most applications are coded in a high-level language. Before the source program instructions written in the programmer's language can be used by the computer, however, they must be translated into the machine-language object code that the computer understands. This machine language consists of strings of binary numbers. An assembly program (used with assembly languages) or a compiler or interpreter (used with high-level languages) is used to translate source programs into object programs.

5. An overview of some of the most popular high-level languages in use today is presented in this chapter. These languages include BASIC (an easy to use, general-purpose language), FORTRAN (a popular language for scientific-mathematic applications), COBOL (the most widely used language for large business applications), PL/I (a language suitable for both business and scientific applications), RPG (a limited-purpose language used to prepare business reports), ALGOL (a scientific-oriented language that's popular in Europe), Pascal (a general-purpose language that supports the structured programming approach), and Ada (a new language sponsored by the U.S. Department of Defense).

6. After a program has been coded, the final step in the programming process is to see that it's implemented and then maintained. Implementation consists of debugging the program, testing the results produced by the program to see if they are correct, and preparing a complete documentation package for the program. Maintenance consists of revising and updating production programs in light of changing conditions. Much of the programming effort in organizations with mature data processing operations is spent on maintenance.

KEY TERMS AND CONCEPTS

You should now be able to define and use the following terms and concepts (the numbers shown indicate the pages where the terms and concepts are first mentioned):

TOPICS FOR REVIEW AND DISCUSSION

1. "During program preparation, programmers must usually deal with a number of issues involving methodology and the use of resources." Discuss this statement and identify three of the possible issues.

2. What are the possible advantages and limitations of packaged programs?

3. Identify and discuss three ways that programmers can be assigned to program preparation projects.

4. (*a*) What is a modular program? (*b*) What advantages might there be to the use of modular programming techniques?

5. What advantages might there be in requiring that programmers use only simple sequence, selection, and loop structures in their programs?

6. (*a*) What's a peer review? (*b*) What advantages may there be to the use of this technique?

7. Identify the program preparation techniques that have often been included under the term "structured programming."

8. "Every programming language has instructions that fall into four categories." Identify and discuss these categories.

9. "An instruction prepared in any machine language has at least two parts." Identify these parts and discuss the function of each.

10. (*a*) How does an assembly language differ from a machine language? (*b*) How is an assembly language source program translated into a machine-language object program?

11. (*a*) What advantages do high-level languages have over assembly languages? (*b*) Discuss two approaches used to translate high-level languages into machine languages.

12. (*a*) What is BASIC? (*b*) Where did it originate? (*c*) How is it used today?

13. (*a*) What is FORTRAN? (*b*) How did it originate? (*c*) How is it used today?

14. (*a*) What is COBOL? (*b*) How did it originate? (*c*) How is it used today?

15. (*a*) What is PL/I? (*b*) What advantages does it possess?

16. (*a*) What is RPG? (*b*) How is it used? (*c*) Why is it a limited-purpose language?

17. Discuss the development and current use of (*a*) ALGOL, (*b*) Pascal, and (*c*) Ada.

18. What questions should be considered in determining the programming language to use in given situations?

19. What steps can be taken during debugging and testing to locate and remove program errors?

20. What should be included in a program documentation package?

21. Why is program maintenance needed?

ANSWERS TO FEEDBACK AND REVIEW SECTION

13-1
The solution to the crossword puzzle is shown at right.

Choosing Software for Business
Canned, Modular, or Custom?

You've decided to computerize your business. You know you're going to get a versatile personal computer, but what software should you get—canned software, modular software or custom software?

"Canned" software is prewritten, mass-market software usually available nationwide from computer stores and other sources. It's been developed by numerous software vendors for the usual business-accounting functions (general ledger, accounts receivable, accounts payable, payroll) and for specific applications such as CPA client write-up, legal time and billing, medical/dental billing, real estate management and job costing.

"Modular" software is a programming tool that enables persons with limited programming skills to develop useful computer programs with a minimum of effort. It includes financial planning and budgeting tools such as VisiCalc and Desktop Plan, information management and database management tools such as DB Master and Condor DBMS Series 20, file management and data-manipulation tools such as Prism and FMS-80, and language extensions and program generators such as Magsam and Pearl. Modular software represents a new generation of programming tools now available on personal computers.

"Custom" software is software programmed to your specifications by an experienced data processing person. The custom programmer is usually contracted to automate some or all of the highly-specialized business functions that must be performed. Custom programming is usually undertaken only when it has been determined that the necessary software does not exist.

Analyze for Complexity

The most important step in the software purchase decision-making process is to analyze in detail the functions you wish to computerize. The complete set of functions, once determined, is called "the application." The complexity and uniqueness of the application will probably be the single most important factor in determining whether canned, modular or custom software should be purchased.

Four Applications

Analysis of your business is the most important step to computerizing it. How complex is your application? How unique is it? If you can answer these two questions, you will be well on your way toward a solution.

There are four situations that arise which require different kinds of software solutions:

- The application is simple and common. Use canned software.
- The application is simple and unique. Use modular software and do it yourself.
- The application is fairly complex and unique. Use modular software and hire a competent programmer to use it.
- The application is very complex and unique. Hire a competent programmer to custom program for you.

—Darshan Singh Khalsa, "Custom vs. Canned Software: What Do You Need?" Reprinted with permission from *Personal Computing*, October 1981, pp. 124–126, and Copyright 1981, Hayden Publishing Company.

chapter 14

Programming in BASIC

ON ACQUIRING A NEW LANGUAGE

Infants begin to speak by mimicking the sounds made by their parents and other family members. In school, children begin the formal study of the laws of a language—its grammar (a discernible regularity of structure) and its syntax (arrangement into sentences). Still later, students may learn a second foreign language such as French, German, or Spanish.

You are about to begin to learn a new language. Compared with the one you speak and write, this new language is quite simple, containing only a few words. This new language is logical. The many irregular verbs and exceptions to rules brought about by the centuries of change in English have not cluttered up its structure.

This high-level programming language, BASIC, may not have the richness to produce Shakespeare's sonnets, but it does have its own elegant and purposeful simplicity. And it enables you to talk to computers, easily and quickly. BASIC is probably the easiest language you will ever learn.

While thousands of people have taught themselves to use BASIC, programming classes are a popular way to learn the language. (Courtesy AT&T)

Looking Ahead

The purpose of this chapter is to introduce you to BASIC—a popular programming language that makes it relatively easy for timesharing users and small computer owners to interact with their machines. In the first two sections of the chapter we'll discuss the BASIC programming environment and outline some necessities of the BASIC language. Ten example programs are then presented. All are based on the problems that we analyzed and flowcharted in Chapter 12. And, of course, all our program examples apply to R-K Enterprises.

Thus, after studying this chapter, you should be able to:

▌ Identify and discuss the general elements found in a BASIC statement

▌ Understand and use the types of BASIC statements discussed in the chapter to prepare programs

▌ Write programs that may incorporate input operations, calculations, decisions, loops, counters, accumulators, and output operations to achieve specified goals

▌ Understand and use the key terms listed at the end of the chapter

Figure 14-1 Learning the BASIC language has made interacting with the computer easier for countless users. (Courtesy AT&T)

THE BASIC PROGRAMMING ENVIRONMENT

In the early 1960s, computer use was generally restricted to groups of people in large organizations with specialized tasks to perform. For example, people in accounting used computers to prepare payrolls and bills, and aeronautical engineers used the machines to analyze aircraft designs. Computing hardware was expensive. The languages and operating-system programs of the time often seemed geared to satisfying the needs of machines rather than the needs of people. And those who could have benefited from computer usage were often denied access to the machines. But as time passed, the access problem was relieved through the use of timesharing. In the mid-1960s, as you'll recall, Dartmouth professors Kemeny and Kurtz were motivated to create a programming language (BASIC) that would make it easy for people at timesharing terminals to *interact* with computers.

It didn't take long for BASIC to become popular. Over the years, hundreds of thousands of students and customers of timesharing vendors have quickly learned to use BASIC (Figure 14-1). And BASIC is now the primary language used by the millions who own personal microcomputers. Since its inception, BASIC has been improved and its scope has been extended. We've seen that there are many different versions or dialects in existence today. Unfortunately, this means that a BASIC program prepared for use on one manufacturer's equipment may not run without modification on another system. In the pages that follow, we'll discuss certain BASIC program statements that permit the computer to perform such activities as input, data movement, and output. The use of these statements in the example programs found in the chapter follow the rules of many BASIC dialects. The differences that may exist between the BASIC version that your computer system uses and the version used in this chapter should be relatively easy to resolve.

The Equipment

Since BASIC is a language that's meant to be used for interactive computing, the user typically writes programs and enters some or all of the necessary data from the *keyboard* of a timesharing terminal or a personal computer system. Data may also be entered through paper tape readers, magnetic tape cassette units, and floppy disks drives that are attached to terminals. The *output* information used by humans is usually obtained from a visual display or character printer. Output may also be punched into paper tape or recorded on magnetic tapes or disks through the use of appropriate terminal/system attachments.

Sign-On Procedures

Let's assume that you glanced ahead in this chapter to get an idea of what's involved in preparing a BASIC program. Since we are supposing, let's also assume that at the first opportunity you then rushed to an available keyboard to try your hand at writing a program. Alas, banging on the keyboard produced no results—you neglected to turn the computer on, or you were unable to follow the proper sign-on (or "log-on") procedure required to get access to the CPU from your terminal.

In a *personal computing environment,* the sign-on "procedure" may simply involve turning on the power. The BASIC interpreter may be permanently stored in integrated circuit chips inside the CPU, instantly ready for use. In a *timesharing environment,* the terminal must be turned on first. A procedure is then required to establish communication between the terminal and the central processor. This procedure may involve typing specified words—e.g., HELLO or LOGIN—and/or pressing specified keys on the terminal. It may also involve dialing a number on a phone next to the terminal and using a communications device called a modem to make a connection with the CPU. Once hooked up, the computer may automatically send a sign-on request to the terminal in the form of a message or special character. The user must then follow a prescribed sign-on procedure. Typically this involves supplying one or more of the following: an account or project number, a user name or identification, and/or a password. After this information has been supplied, some systems that support multiple languages also require that the user indicate the programming language that will be used. Thus, it may also be necessary to type BASIC so that the computer can call up the BASIC translating software.

To illustrate these comments, in several Digital Equipment Corporation PDP-11 systems, the sign-on procedure is to turn on the terminal and type

HELLO. The computer responds with an information line and then prints #. The user types in a project number and programmer number, and the computer responds with PASSWORD. After the password is supplied, the system is ready. In a Hewlett-Packard 3000 system, the terminal is turned on, and the user presses the RETURN key and types HELLO followed by an identification number. The computer responds with an information line and then types the colon (:). The user then types BASIC, and when the system replies with the > character, the system is in BASIC and ready to be used.

Obviously, there's no standard sign-on procedure. But there are no difficult ones either. The procedures for signing on the particular system you'll be using are easy to learn and are available from local sources.

System Commands and Program Statements

System commands and program statements are both found in a BASIC programming environment, and both make use of certain designated words. Let's make sure we know the difference between these two categories. We've seen that some computer systems may require the user to type key words like HELLO or LOGIN as a part of the sign-on procedure. Such words are referred to as **system commands.** They are entered by the user into the system, and they direct the computer to take immediate action to accomplish a specific task. A number of system commands are found in every BASIC programming environment, but the words vary with the system being used. Some typical system commands found in most settings are:

▌ RUN (to execute the user's program of current interest).

▌ LIST (to list the contents of a current program).

▌ SAVE (to store a current program—which must be given a name—in online secondary storage for later access).

▌ BYE (to sign off the system).

As with sign-on procedures, the system commands for the particular equipment you'll be using are available from local sources.

Designated words such as READ, INPUT, LET, and END are also found in the sequence of numbered individual instructions or **program statements** that make up a BASIC program. We'll discuss the meanings and uses of these key words later in the chapter.

You've seen that when a system command is entered, it causes the computer to take *immediate action.* When a program statement is initially keyed in, however, the computer may take *no apparent action at all.* Of course, the machine is probably checking the statement for syntax errors and storing it with other statements, but the program instruction in the statement is not immediately executed at the time of entry. Rather, the individual statements are stored until a complete program is formed and until the user turns the control of the computer over to the program through the use of a RUN command. The statements are then executed to process the input data and produce the output results.

SOME BASIC NECESSITIES

We are about ready to write the programs needed to solve the problems discussed (and flowcharted) in Chapter 12. Only a few *program entry, arithmetic,* and *error-correcting* necessities stand in our way.

Program Entry Elements

Key words are used in constructing program statements, and statements are then put together to form a BASIC program. A BASIC statement may take the following form:

<u>line number</u>   <u>type of statement</u>   <u>value(s)</u>

Let's look at each of these statement elements.

Line numbers. Each statement in a BASIC program begins with a **line number (ln).** Depending on the equipment used, the ln can be any integer (whole number) beginning at 1 (and going to 4 or 5 digits) that *you* select. The *order* of these line numbers is used by the computer during the execution of the program. Beginning with the lowest ln, statements will be processed in ascending order until conditional or unconditional transfer statements are encountered that cause a change in the sequence. It's generally desirable to number your statements in increments of 5 or 10. That way you'll have room later to include any additional instructions or modifications that may be needed, and you won't have to renumber the lines that follow the insertion. For example, let's assume that you've written a BASIC program that looks like this:

$$10 \quad \text{LET A} = 5$$
$$20 \quad \text{LET B} = 8$$
$$30 \quad \text{LET C} = \text{A} + \text{B}$$
$$40 \quad \text{END}$$

This program will add the values of A and B, but since you've forgotten to tell the computer to print out the result of this tough computation, it will forever remain a mystery. To remedy this oversight, you can type the following statement at the bottom of the program:

35 PRINT C

The computer will then know that you want to print the value of C after line 30 has been executed. If you should later enter a system command to LIST the program, you'll see that ln 35 has been correctly positioned between statements 30 and 40.

Types of BASIC statements. Every statement in BASIC has a *statement type,* and learning the language is mainly a matter of learning the rules that apply to these statement types. As you'll recall from the last chapter, computer instructions are found in all languages to permit input/output, calculation, logic/comparison (to permit transfer of program control), and storage/retrieval and data movement operations. In the simple program we've just encountered, the LET statement was used to initially *assign* values to storage locations labeled "A" and "B" in the computer. The LET statement was also used to look up the values of the contents of A and B, calculate the sum of those values, and assign the total to a storage location labeled "C" (30 LET C = A + B). Thus, the LET, or *assignment,* type of statement can be used to assign input values to locations, perform calculations, and move processed results to other locations. The PRINT type of statement, of course, is used for *output.* An END statement is the highest-numbered statement in any program and simply indicates the completion of the program. In the pages that follow, we'll examine a number of other types of BASIC statements.

Values in BASIC. BASIC deals with values that may be constants or variables. A *constant* is a value that is provided explicitly by the program and *cannot* be changed by the computer at any time during program execution. Valid **numeric constants** include such values as 55, −16.5, 3.14159, and 1.09E + 8. The 55 could represent a constant rate of speed, that is, 55 miles per hour. The −16.5 could represent the constant amount of dollars to be deducted from paychecks for a group insurance plan. And the 3.14159 could be the approximation of pi used in calculations. The E (exponential) notation used in the constant 1.09E + 8 is needed because there's only a limited amount of space available to store a value in the computer's memory. Thus, 1.09E + 8 can be used to represent 1.09×10^8 or 109000000. Also, 1.26E − 6 can be used to represent 1.26×10^{-6} or .00000126. (Don't worry too much about this E notation shorthand for expressing very large or very small quantities. It's mentioned here so that if you should receive some output in E notation form, you'll understand what it means). Valid constants may also include strings of alphanumeric characters. **Character string constants** may be any string of characters enclosed in quotation marks, e.g., "4009 SARITA DRIVE" or "KAY OSS."

Unlike a constant, a **numeric variable** is a quantity that can be referred to by name and that *can* change values at different stages during the running of a program. Although it's true that the *location* in storage that holds the variable (and the *name* given by the programmer to that location) *doesn't change,* the *contents* of the storage location (like the contents of a post office box) may be altered many times during the program's processing of the available data. For example, you may recall from Chapter 12 that a counter can be used to record the number of times that a loop has been executed. To do this, a storage location with the **variable name** K can be established by the programmer and assigned an initial value of one. An appropriate BASIC statement to do this is

10 LET K = 1

where K names a variable. After each pass through the loop, the contents of the counter will change or be incremented by a value of 1. That is,

100 LET K = K + 1

Obviously, in this BASIC statement the equals sign (=) does not mean the same as it does in algebra. Rather, the numeric variable value stored at the location identified by "K" is retrieved from storage, a value of 1 is added to it, and the new variable quantity replaces the previous contents in the location named "K." Thus, if a loop is executed 30 times, there will be 30 different values for K.

It will be up to you to name the variables that are needed in the programs you write. The rules in BASIC that govern the naming of variables are easily remembered, but they're much more restrictive than the rules that apply to many other languages. This is a shortcoming of BASIC. For example, *a numeric variable is generally restricted to a name that consists of a single letter or a single letter followed by a single digit.* Thus, A, X, B1, and T2 are all valid numeric variable names, but 7G, AB, RATE, and B24 are not.

In addition to numeric variables, there are also **string variables**—i.e., strings of alphanumeric and special characters—that can be referred to by name and that can change during the running of a program. For example, the contents of the storage space that contains a customer's name will change constantly during the processing of a billing program. *In naming the string variable, you'll probably be restricted to using a single letter followed by a dollar sign ($).* Thus, E$, B$, and N$ are all valid, but AB$, $X, and XYZ$ are not. (Some BASIC systems also allow a string variable name to be any valid numeric variable name followed by a dollar sign. Thus, A1$ and C2$ are valid examples in such systems.)

Arithmetic Operations

You'll be concerned with five arithmetic operations in writing BASIC programs: addition, subtraction, multiplication, division, and exponentiation (raising to a power). The symbols used to indicate these operations (and examples of their use) are shown in Figure 14-2. Note that in BASIC the multiplication symbol must be present, even though it can be omitted in algebra. Failure to use the asterisk is a common error, and the computer will probably send you an error message if you forget it.

A formula in a program may include several operations. You must understand the order in which the computer handles these operations so that you may avoid errors. What value will be assigned to A, for example, when the computer encounters this statement that you've written?

$$50 \quad \text{LET A} = 4 + 6 \wedge 2/10 - 2$$

If the computer simply started at the left and performed operations in sequence, the result would be 4 plus 6 (or 10), raised to the second power (giving 100), divided by 10 (10), minus 2, giving a value of 8 to assign to A. But the computer follows a different set of rules in determining the order of operations. Moving from left to right in a formula *without parentheses:*

Figure 14-2 Arithmetic operations: Symbols and examples in the BASIC language.

Operation	BASIC Symbol	BASIC Examples	Algebraic Equivalent
Addition	+	A + B 2 + 8	A + B 2 + 8
Subtraction	−	B − C 6 − 3	B − C 6 − 3
Multiplication	* (asterisk)	D * E 4 * F	DE or D(E) or D X E 4F or 4(F) or 4 X F
Division	/ (slash)	G/H 8/2	$G \div H$ or $\frac{G}{H}$ $8 \div 2$ or $\frac{8}{2}$
Exponentiation	$\wedge$ or ↑	$J \wedge 2$ (or J ↑ 2) $3 \wedge 3$	J^2 3^3

1. All exponentiation is performed first.

2. All multiplication and division operations are then completed.

3. Finally, all addition and subtraction takes place.

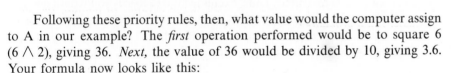

Following these priority rules, then, what value would the computer assign to A in our example? The *first* operation performed would be to square 6 ($6 \wedge 2$), giving 36. *Next*, the value of 36 would be divided by 10, giving 3.6. Your formula now looks like this:

$$4 + 3.6 - 2$$

Finally, moving from left to right, 4 is added to 3.6, giving 7.6, and 2 is then subtracted from 7.6 to give the final value of 5.6 to assign to the variable name A.

If parentheses are used, the computations within the parentheses are handled first, using the above order rules. If several sets of parentheses are nested within one another, the operations in the innermost group are performed first. For example, suppose your assignment statement had looked like this:

$$50 \quad \text{LET } A = (8 + (6 * 4)/2)/2$$

The first part of the formula evaluated is (6 * 4) in the innermost set of parentheses. The result is

$$50 \quad \text{LET } A = (8 + 24/2)/2$$

Within the remaining set of parentheses, the division operation is performed first, and the resulting value of 12 is then added to 8. This total of 20 is then divided by 2 to get a value of 10 to assign to A.

Correcting Errors

In entering your program statements at the keyboard, you'll probably make errors that will have to be corrected. A very common error, of course, is to strike the wrong key or keys during program or data entry. If, as is often the case, you immediately detect your mistake, you need correct only one or two characters and then continue on with the line you are typing. For example, let's assume that the correct entry should be

$$50 \quad \text{LET } A = (4 * G)/2$$

but you type

$$50 \quad \text{LEG } A$$

and then catch your error. How can you "erase" the G and enter the T? Different BASIC systems use different approaches, but generally a special correction key (such as RUBOUT, DELETE, or ← key) is used for this purpose. Each time you strike this **correction key** (CK), you erase one character in the typed line and move to its left. Thus, to change the G to a T, you would need to press the CK 3 times: once to erase A, once to erase the blank character, and once to erase the G. You could then enter the T and complete the line.

Suppose, however, you discover that you've typed

$$50 \quad \text{LTE A} = (4 * \text{G})/2$$

before you press the RETURN key that will cause the computer to analyze the statement. In this case you *could* backtrack with the correction, but it would probably be easier to delete the *entire line* and start over. The method to do this varies with the system being used, but on many systems the procedure is to hold down the CONTROL or CTRL key and then press either the U or the X key.

Finally, let's assume that you've typed

$$50 \quad \text{LTE A} = (4 + \text{G})/2$$

instead of

$$50 \quad \text{LET A} = (4 * \text{G})/2$$

and you *have pressed* the RETURN key. In this case, the computer will probably detect the *syntax error* in the spelling of LET, reject the statement, and send you an error message. You'll then have to reenter the statement. If in retyping the statement you repeat the mistake of *adding* 4 to the quantity stored in G rather than *multiplying* these values, the computer will accept the statement because it contains no syntax errors, but, of course, a *logical error* still remains. To correct this statement that has now been stored in the computer, you need only reenter the same line number with the correct information, and this second entry will completely erase the previous contents of the line (a very nice feature). If you should want to delete from a program a line that has already been stored, you simply type the line number and then hit the RETURN key, and the previous entry will be deleted.

Now that you have a grasp of some of the details associated with program entry, arithmetic operation, and error correction, it's time to look at some example programs that illustrate the use of various types of BASIC statements.

SIMPLE INPUT, PROCESSING AND OUTPUT PROGRAMS

Several example problems were analyzed and flowcharted in Chapter 12. As you know, all these examples apply to R-K Enterprises. Let's now see how programs for these examples can be prepared in BASIC.

Program 1: Simple Billing, Single Customer

The billing program to compute the net amount owed by a single customer, along with the output bill produced by this program, is shown in Figure 14-3. (The flowchart for this program is shown in Figure 12-3, page 326.) Some general observations about Figure 14-3 are possible. You'll notice, for example, that this program was written earlier and stored or saved under the arbitrary name of GDS1. In response to the LOAD and LIST system commands used by the R-K Enterprises computer, the machine has printed a listing of the program. In response to the RUN command, the computer has executed the program to produce the output results shown.

Before we examine the program in Figure 14-3 in more detail, we should digress briefly for a few words about **programming style.** "Style" may be defined as the way in which something is said or done, as distinguished from its

```
>LOAD GDS1
>LIST
    10 REM *BILLING PROGRAM
    20 REM *
    30 REM *VARIABLE NAMES
    40 REM * N$ NAME
    50 REM * Q   QUANTITY PURCHASED
    60 REM * P   UNIT PRICE
    70 REM * A   NET AMOUNT
    80 REM *
    90 REM *READ NAME,QUANTITY PURCHASED AND PRICE
   100      READ N$,Q,P
   110 REM *COMPUTE NET AMOUNT
   120      LET A = Q*P
   130 REM *PRINT NAME AND NET AMOUNT
   140      PRINT N$,A
   160 REM *INPUT DATA
   170      DATA "ROCKY COLLEGE STORE",3.25,25.00
   180      END
```

Computer listing of the program

```
>RUN

14:01   MAR 26  GDS1...
ROCKY COLLEGE STORE              81.2500

      180 HALT
```

Output produced by the computer in response to the system command RUN

Figure 14-3 BASIC Program 1: Simple billing, single customer.

substance. An objective of this chapter is to present the programs in a style that will make them *easier to read and understand*. For this reason, you'll see a lot of program statements in this chapter that begin with REM—a BASIC abbreviation for REMark. A **REMark statement** is used for program documentation and is provided *solely* for the benefit of people who want to read and understand the program. As far as the computer is concerned, as soon as it encounters the letters REM, it ignores the rest of the statement and moves on to the next line number! Every program in this chapter uses REM statements to (1) identify the program, (2) define the variable names used in the program, (3) place explanatory headings throughout the body of the program, and (4) add spacing within the program to aid readability. Indentation of statements is also used to aid readability. Of course, the disadvantages of these stylistic features are that they add to program length, are harder to type, and take up more storage space. After all, 12 of the 17 lines in the program in Figure 14-3 are "unnecessary" REM statements. Usually, though, the merits of REM documentation will outweigh their inconvenience in the programs you write.

The first nine lines in Figure 14-3 are self-explanatory REMark statements. The program is identified, variable names used in the program are defined, and a heading explains the purpose of line number (ln) 100. The statement in ln 100 is an input **READ statement** that *must be combined* with a **DATA statement.** The general form of these statements is

ln READ   list of variable   ln DATA   list of data
             names   values

where the values to be assigned to the variable names identified in a READ statement are found in a DATA statement. Thus, when the computer encounters

100   READ N$, Q, P

it looks for a DATA statement (which it finds at ln 170) and reads the first three data values it finds. In other words, it "uses up" the data by assigning them to the variable names, as follows:

100   READ   N$,   Q,   P
170   DATA   "ROCKY COLLEGE STORE",   3.25,   25.00

You'll notice that since the customer's name is a string variable, it's referred to as N$ in the program to conform to the rules for naming string variables discussed earlier. The numeric variable names given to quantity purchased (Q) and unit price (P) also follow these rules. These variables are named by the programmer and are arbitrary choices. The customer name variable, for example, could just as easily have been C$ (or A$, B$, . . .) as N$.

Each of our data items could have been placed in a separate DATA statement. It's common, however, to compress multiple data items into a single statement as shown here. But the data must always be typed in the DATA statement(s) in the *order indicated by the READ statement*. The computer doesn't care how many DATA statements there are because before it executes the program it will arrange in order, in a single long list, all the values contained in all the DATA statements. A *pointer* is set internally in the system at the *first* value in the list, and, as we've seen, the first variable name encountered in a READ statement during program execution is assigned the value indicated by the pointer. The pointer then shifts to the next value, which will be "used up" by the next variable name encountered in a READ statement. And so it goes throughout the entire data list. Although DATA statements may be typed anywhere in the program except after the END statement, it's common practice to locate then near the end of the program, as shown in Figure 14-3.

Once the *data-input* operation has been accomplished, the next step in the program is to compute the amount owed by the customer. This *processing* is carried out by using the **LET statement** in ln 120. The amount owed is found by multiplying the 3.25 dozen tee shirts purchased (Q) by the unit price of $25.00 per dozen (P). The net amount owed is assigned the variable name A.

The *output* bill produced by the program consists of one printed line (ln 140). **A PRINT statement** is used to display program results. (Such commands, when found at the end of very long programs, may account for the expression "Some day your PRINTs will come.") The PRINT statement in ln 140 causes the computer to produce the output line shown in Figure 14-3. You'll notice that the N$ and A variable names shown in ln 140 are not printed in the output. Rather, the contents of the storage locations given these names are printed.

Commas in PRINT statements serve a specific function. A statement that reads

015   PRINT A,B,C,D,E

will cause the values of the five variable names to be printed across the page, with A beginning at the left margin, B beginning (perhaps) 14 spaces to the right, C beginning 28 spaces to the right, etc. The width of many terminal printers is 72 characters, and the use of commas in the PRINT statement *automatically* establishes a format of five columns or zones. The automatic spacing can vary from one system to another. This implicit format-specification feature of BASIC is especially appreciated by problem-solvers who are not professional programmers. In our example, the customer name is printed beginning at the left margin. Since the customer name exceeds the spacing of the first zone and extends into the second zone, the comma causes the net amount of the bill ($81.25) to be printed beginning at the third zone.

Semicolons are also used in PRINT statements to cause items to be printed close together. Although a small amount of space may be automatically placed before and after a variable quantity in some systems, the spacing is much closer than when commas are used. Suppose, for example, the following statement is written in a program:

195   PRINT "NET = ";A

The first thing you'll notice is that quotation marks are used. Characters (including blank spaces) that are bounded by these marks in a PRINT statement are printed exactly as they appear in the statement when the program is executed. The marks themselves, however, aren't printed. Thus, NET = is printed, beginning at the left margin, when this program is run. The value of the variable name A following the semicolon is then printed with little additional spacing.

A print statement can be used to produce *vertical spacing* in the output. If, for example, you write the following statement:

25 PRINT

the computer will follow your wishes—it will fill a line with blank spaces and advance the output page to the next line. Any number of empty PRINT statements can thus be used to control output line spacing.

The last program statement in Figure 14-3 is the **END statement.** It's the last statement in a BASIC program, and it includes only a line number. Some versions of BASIC don't require an END statement. But it's a good idea to use it because you might someday want to run your programs on other systems that do require its use.

Feedback and Review 14-1

You may remember that in Feedback and Review 12-1, page 326, you were asked to modify problem 1 in that chapter by preparing a program flowchart for customer bills that included the computation of a 6 percent sales tax. It was specified that the output of the modified program should be a bill giving the customer's name, net amount owed, sales tax amount, and total amount owed. A possible flowchart of this program is shown at the end of Chapter 12. The variable names used in that flowchart are:

N$ Customer name
Q   Quantity purchased
P   Unit price
A   Net amount owed
T1   Sales tax amount
T2   Total amount of bill

Using these names (or other variable names of your own choosing), write a BASIC program to process the following input data:

Customer: WYNN D. TOOTS, INC.
Quantity purchased: 5.50 dozen tee shirts
Unit price: $25.00 per dozen

The output should be a two-line bill. The *first* line should be the customer's name. The *second* line should be in this format:

NET = (net amount)   TAX = (sales tax)   TOTAL = (total amount)

DECISIONS AND LOOPS IN BASIC PROGRAMS

As we saw in Chapter 12, Rob and Kay quickly learned that using a program that would compute one customer bill and then stop was the pits. And so, they revised it.

Program 2: Simple Billing, Multiple Customers

The program shown in Figure 14-4 was written so that bills could be processed for any number of customers. (The logic of this program was charted in Figure 12-4, page 328.) This added flexibility is achieved through the use of a loop controlled by a logic/comparison statement.

The REMark statements from ln 10 through ln 110 are similar to those in Program 1. Since Program 2 will also process a customer's local address (S$) as well as a city and state address (C$), names have been supplied for these variables. (The Zip code is included in C$.)

The READ statement in ln 120 is combined with the DATA statements in ln 270 through ln 390 to provide the program with the input data to be processed. The first time the READ statement is executed in our example, the input data in ln 270 ("PIERRE'S RECORD SHOP") are assigned to N$, the data in ln 280 ("6453 ORLEANS STREET") are assigned to S$, the data in ln 290 ("BOOGIE, LOUISIANA 54321") are assigned to C$, and the data in ln 300 (300 dozen tee shirts and $25.00 per dozen) are the quantity and price assigned to Q and P.

On ln 140 we find a new statement type—the **IF . . . THEN conditional branching statement.** IF . . . THEN statements take the following form:

ln IF (logical assertion) THEN ln

For example, in

120   IF A < 10 THEN 30

the computer is told that if the logical assertion is *true*—i.e., if A is *less* than 10—program control is transferred to line number 30. If, however, the condition expressed in the assertion isn't met, the program moves to the next statement in the line number sequence. Other examples of logical assertions are:

```
>LIST
    10 REM *BILLING PROGRAM
    20 REM *
    30 REM *VARIABLE NAMES
    40 REM * N$  NAME
    50 REM * S$  ADDRESS
    60 REM * C$  CITY AND STATE
    70 REM * Q   QUANTITY PURCHASED
    80 REM * P   UNIT PRICE
    90 REM * A   NET AMOUNT
   100 REM *
   110 REM *READ NAME,ADDRESS,QUANTITY PURCHASED AND PRICE
   120     READ N$,S$,C$,Q,P
   130 REM *TEST QUANTITY FOR LAST INPUT
   140     IF Q=-99.9 THEN 400
   150 REM *COMPUTE NET AMOUNT
   160     LET A = Q*P
   170 REM *PRINT NAME,ADDRESS AND NET AMOUNT
   180     PRINT N$
   190     PRINT S$
   200     PRINT C$
   210     PRINT TAB(3);"NET = ";A
   220     PRINT
   230     PRINT
   240     GO TO 120
   260 REM *INPUT DATA
   270     DATA "PIERRE'S RECORD SHOP"
   280     DATA "6453 ORLEANS STREET"
   290     DATA "BOOGIE,LOUISIANA 54321"
   300     DATA  300.0,25.00
   310     DATA "ROCKY COLLEGE STORE"
   320     DATA "1563 BEETHOVEN DRIVE"
   330     DATA "ROCKTOWN,MARYLAND 20765"
   340     DATA  3.25,25.00
   350     DATA "WYNN D.TOOTS,INC."
   360     DATA "120 BROWNING STREET"
   370     DATA "GONG,CALIFORNIA 98765"
   380     DATA  2.00,25.00
   390     DATA "L","L","L",-99.9,0.
   400     END
```

Computer listing of the program

```
>RUN
PIERRE'S RECORD SHOP
6453 ORLEANS STREET
BOOGIE,LOUISIANA 54321
  NET =    7500


ROCKY COLLEGE STORE
1563 BEETHOVEN DRIVE
ROCKTOWN,MARYLAND 20765
  NET =    81.2500


WYNN D.TOOTS,INC.
120 BROWNING STREET
GONG,CALIFORNIA 98765
  NET =    50


   400 HALT
```

Output produced by the computer in response to the system command RUN

Figure 14-4 BASIC Program 2: Simple billing, multiple customers.

$$A = B$$
$$B > C$$
$$D <= 0 \quad \text{(D is less than or equal to 0)}$$
$$M >= N \quad \text{(M is greater than or equal to N)}$$
$$S <> T \quad \text{(S is not equal to T)}$$
$$3 * Z > X/T$$

As you can see, a "logical assertion" consists of a first expression (a constant, a variable name, or a formula), a relational ($=$, $<$, $>$, or some combination of these), and a second expression.

In the statement on ln 140 of our example program,

140   IF Q $= -99.9$ THEN 400

the value assigned to the quantity purchased field (Q) of the input record is compared to a sentinel value of -99.9. (A *sentinel value,* you'll recall, is an arbitrary data item placed at the end of a file to indicate that all valid data have been processed.) Since the value of Q during the first pass through the loop is the 300 dozen tee shirts purchased by Pierre's Record Shop, the logical assertion is false and the program moves on to ln 160. You'll notice, however, that a last dummy record has been placed in ln 390 with a sentinel value of -99.9 for Q. When this record is finally read, the logical assertion will be true, the exit condition will be met, program control will be transferred to ln 400, and processing will END.

The statement in ln 160 computes the amount of the bill for Pierre's Record Shop. And the three PRINT statements in ln 180 through ln 200 cause the system to print the customer's name, local address, city, state, and Zip code on the bill as shown in the output section of Figure 14-4. These three lines of print begin at the left margin of the page.

The **PRINT TAB function** in ln 210 is a little different. In this statement,

210   PRINT TAB(3);"NET $=$ ";A

the TAB(3) part of the instruction controls the *spacing on the print line* much as a tabulator setting controls the spacing on a typewriter. When the computer encounters this part of the statement, it knows that it's to move three spaces *from the left margin* and then begin printing the heading enclosed in quotes. After NET $=$ is printed, the amount of Pierre's bill is also supplied, as you can see in the output of Figure 14-4. (Mosquito bird tee shirts are obviously selling well in Louisiana!) Suppose the following PRINT statement had been encountered:

180   PRINT TAB(18);M;TAB(28);N

The value of the variable name M would be printed beginning 18 spaces from the left margin, and the value of N would be printed starting at 28 spaces *from the left margin* (not from M).

The two empty PRINT statements in ln 220 and ln 230 cause the output page to advance two lines before printing the next customer's bill. On ln 240, we find another new BASIC statement type. There's nothing difficult about this **GO TO unconditional branching statement.** It simply transfers program control to the line specified in the statement. Thus,

240   GO TO 120

causes program control to branch back to the READ statement on ln 120 to begin processing the next customer's bill.

An Alternative to Program 2

Let's assume (have you noticed that we do a lot of assuming in this book?) that instead of using READ . . . DATA statements, Rob and Kay would rather *interact* with the computer and give the necessary input data in the form of responses to questions and messages supplied by the program. The program in Figure 14-5 shows us how this might be done. The first eleven line numbers in this program are about the same as those in Figure 14-4.

In the PRINT statements in ln 115 and ln 120, however, things start to change. As you know, the messages enclosed in quotes in these PRINT statements will be produced as output. In this case, the output messages are requesting input data from the program user. As you'll notice in Figure 14-5, when the program is run, these two message lines are printed immediately.

Line number 130 is

130   INPUT N$,S$,C$,Q,P

This is a new type of BASIC statement that causes the computer to (1) print a question mark (?), and (2) stop executing the program until the user supplies it with the necessary input data for the variable names listed in the **INPUT statement.** INPUT is always followed by one or more variable names separated by commas. Therefore, the *first* result of ln 130 is to cause a ? to be printed as shown in the output of Figure 14-5. The *second* result of the INPUT statement is to halt the program until Rob or Kay types in the customer's name (N$), complete address (S$ and C$), quantity purchased (Q), unit price (P), and then presses the RETURN. The first output is produced as follows:

ENTER NAME, ADDRESS, QUANTITY, AND PRICE

(ENTER −99.9 FOR QUANTITY AMOUNT TO INDICATE END OF DATA

Produced by the PRINT statements on ln 115 and ln 120

?   "PIERRE'S RECORD SHOP", "6453 ORLEANS STREET", ...

caused by   keyed in by user
INPUT statement
on ln 130

```
>LIST
    10 REM *BILLING PROGRAM
    20 REM *
    30 REM *VARIABLE NAMES
    40 REM * N$   NAME
    50 REM * S$   ADDRESS
    60 REM * C$   CITY AND STATE
    70 REM * Q    QUANTITY PURCHASED
    80 REM * P    UNIT PRICE
    90 REM * A    NET AMOUNT
   100 REM *
   110 REM *INPUT NAME,ADDRESS,QUANTITY PURCHASED AND PRICE
   115       PRINT "ENTER NAME,ADDRESS,QUANTITY AND PRICE"
   120       PRINT "(ENTER -99.9 FOR QUANTITY AMOUNT TO INDICATE END OF DATA)"
   130       INPUT N$,S$,C$,Q,P
   140       IF Q=-99.9 THEN 250
   150 REM *COMPUTE NET AMOUNT
   160       LET A = Q*P
   170 REM *PRINT NAME,ADDRESS AND NET AMOUNT
   172       PRINT
   174       PRINT
   180       PRINT N$
   190       PRINT S$
   200       PRINT C$
   210       PRINT TAB(3);"NET = ";A
   220       PRINT
   230       PRINT
   240       GO TO 115
   250       STOP
   400       END
```

> Computer listing
> of the program

```
>RUN
ENTER NAME,ADDRESS,QUANTITY AND PRICE
(ENTER -99.9 FOR QUANTITY AMOUNT TO INDICATE END OF DATA)
?"PIERRE'S RECORD SHOP","6453 ORLEANS STREET","BOOGIE,LOUISIANA 54321",300.00,25.00

PIERRE'S RECORD SHOP
6453 ORLEANS STREET
BOOGIE,LOUISIANA 54321
  NET =    7500

ENTER NAME,ADDRESS,QUANTITY AND PRICE
(ENTER -99.9 FOR QUANTITY AMOUNT TO INDICATE END OF DATA)
?"ROCKY COLLEGE STORE","1563 BEETHOVEN DRIVE","ROCKTOWN,MARYLAND 20765",3.25,25.00

ROCKY COLLEGE STORE
1563 BEETHOVEN DRIVE
ROCKTOWN,MARYLAND 20765
  NET =    81.2500

ENTER NAME,ADDRESS,QUANTITY AND PRICE
(ENTER -99.9 FOR QUANTITY AMOUNT TO INDICATE END OF DATA)
?"WYNN D. TOOTS, INC.","120 BROWNING STREET","GONG,CALIFORNIA 98765",200.0,25.00

WYNN D. TOOTS, INC.
120 BROWNING STREET
GONG,CALIFORNIA 98765
  NET =    5000

ENTER NAME,ADDRESS,QUANTITY AND PRICE
(ENTER -99.9 FOR QUANTITY AMOUNT TO INDICATE END OF DATA)
?L,L,L,-99.9,0.0

    250 HALT
```

> Output produced by the
> computer in response to
> the system command RUN

Figure 14-5 An alternative to Program 2 using the INPUT statement.

Before moving on, let's consider one other aspect of PRINT and INPUT statements. Suppose a program contains the following statements:

100   PRINT "ODOMETER READING AT START OF TRIP";

110   INPUT M

The effect of placing a semicolon *at the end of a PRINT statement* is to suppress the automatic printer carriage return that usually takes place when the computer reaches the end of a PRINT instruction. Thus, the printing (or display) mechanism does not return to the left margin. So when the computer encounters the INPUT statement in ln 110, the ? caused by this statement will be printed to the right of the message produced by ln 100. The output would then look like this:

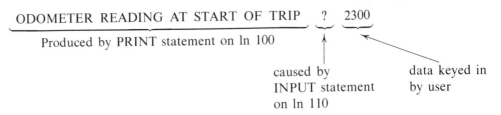

ODOMETER READING AT START OF TRIP   ?   2300

Produced by PRINT statement on ln 100

caused by
INPUT statement
on ln 110

data keyed in
by user

Once the user has supplied the input data for a customer record in our example and has pressed the RETURN key, the program takes over to print the customer's bill as shown in the output of Figure 14-5. There are only slight differences in the remainder of this program from the one shown in Figure 14-4. One difference is that a new **STOP statement** in ln 250 has been included here to halt the execution of the program. Commonly used in more complex programs that incorporate subordinate program modules or subroutines, the STOP statement works exactly like a GO TO the END statement. Thus, the statement in ln 140 could just as easily have been

140   IF Q = −99.9 THEN 400

which would have branched program control to the END statement.

Program 3: Preparing Mailing Labels

You know that R-K Enterprises mails promotional materials to the prospective customers on its mailing list. The program in Figure 14-6 is used to prepare the gummed labels for these mailings. (The logic for this program was charted in Figure 12-6, page 329.) Since there are no new types of BASIC statements used in this program, you should be able to follow most of the coding steps to see how the output labels are printed.

You'll notice that the last customer in the mailing list file is WYNN D. TOOTS, INC. If there had been no DATA statement in ln 380, the computer would first try to READ more data after processing the TOOTS record. Since no more data are present, some message such as "OUT OF DATA" would probably be printed, and the execution of the program would stop automati-

```
>LIST
    10 REM *MAILING LIST PROGRAM
    20 REM *
    30 REM *VARIABLE DEFINITIONS
    40 REM * N$ NAME
    50 REM * A$ ADDRESS
    60 REM * C$ CITY AND STATE
    70 REM *
   100 REM *READ NAME,ADDRESS,CITY AND STATE
   110      READ N$,A$,C$
   120 REM *TEST NAME FOR END OF DATA
   130      IF N$="END OF DATA" THEN 500
   140 REM *PRINT MAILING LABEL
   150      PRINT
   160      PRINT
   170      PRINT TAB(3);N$
   180      PRINT TAB(3);A$
   190      PRINT TAB(3);C$
   200      GO TO 110
   210 REM *INPUT DATA
   220      DATA "ED'S CULTURAL CENTER    "
   230      DATA "822 PHILHARMONIC AVENUE "
   240      DATA "CRAMPS, TEXAS 77786     "
   250 REM *
   260      DATA "PIERRE'S RECORD SHOP    "
   270      DATA "6453 ORLEANS STREET     "
   280      DATA "BOOGIE, LOUISIANA 54321 "
   290 REM *
   300      DATA "ROCKY COLLEGE STORE     "
   310      DATA "1563 BEETHOVEN DRIVE    "
   320      DATA "ROCKTOWN, MARYLAND 20765"
   330 REM *
   340      DATA "WYNN D. TOOTS, INC.     "
   350      DATA "120 BROWNING STREET     "
   360      DATA "GONG, CALIFORNIA 98765  "
   370 REM *
   380      DATA "END OF DATA","DUMMY","DUMMY"
   500      END
```

Computer listing of the program

```
>RUN

   ED'S CULTURAL CENTER
   822 PHILHARMONIC AVENUE
   CRAMPS, TEXAS 77786

   PIERRE'S RECORD SHOP
   6453 ORLEANS STREET
   BOOGIE, LOUISIANA 54321

   ROCKY COLLEGE STORE
   1563 BEETHOVEN DRIVE
   ROCKTOWN, MARYLAND 20765

   WYNN D. TOOTS, INC.
   120 BROWNING STREET
   GONG, CALIFORNIA 98765

      500 HALT
```

Output produced by the computer as the program is executed

Figure 14-6 BASIC Program 3: Preparing mailing labels.

cally. Perhaps terminating the program with such a message would be satisfactory in this example, but provision is made in our program to avoid that message. An exit path out of the program loop is established in ln 130. This path is followed when the prospect's name (N$) is equal to "END OF DATA." Then, as you can see in ln 380, a dummy record at the end of the prospect file gives this sentinel value to the string variable N$.

Program 4: Sales Compensation, Single Commission Rate

You'll remember from Chapter 12 that Kay and Rob receive a sales compensation report every four weeks that's used to evaluate salesperson performance and prepare paychecks. In problem 4 outlined in Chapter 12 (and charted in Figure 12-7, page 331), it was specified that a single 10 percent commission rate be used to compute the earnings for each salesperson. The BASIC program for this application is shown in Figure 14-7.

The first nine REMark statements in this program are self-explanatory. In ln 100, however, we come to a new type of **PRINT USING function** that's used here to prepare a heading for the sales compensation report. The statement

100   PRINT USING 225

is used to align the output of the computer according to a *specified format*. In ln 100, the computer is instructed to PRINT the headings found in ln 225 in the exact format shown on the *image line* in ln 225. An image line for a PRINT USING statement is identified by a colon immediately after the line number. Thus, the output headings in Figure 14-7 are reproduced exactly as specified in ln 225. Another PRINT USING statement found in this program

190   PRINT USING 230, N$,S,E

uses the format specified in image line 230 to print the values located in the variable names N$, S, and E. In the dialect of BASIC used here, the # characters can be thought of as "place holders" for the alphanumeric data contained in N$, S, and E. Thus, there are 20 spaces allocated for the salesperson's name (N$). The periods in the spaces allocated for sales amount (S) and earnings (E) figures indicate exactly where the decimal point will be printed. You can see the effect of using the format specified in ln 230 in the output report. The advantage of the PRINT USING statement is that it gives the programmer strict control over the output format. However, not all dialects of BASIC have a PRINT USING statement, and the details of usage in those which do can vary. You should check the operating manual of your particular system for possible differences.

The remaining statements in Figure 14-7 should be easy to follow. Each salesperson's name and weekly sales amounts are READ (ln 120) from the DATA statements (ln 250 through ln 310). After a test for exit condition is made (ln 140), the weekly sales amounts are added (ln 160), the 10 percent

```
>LIST
    10 REM *SALES COMPENSATION REPORT
    20 REM *
    30 REM *VARIABLE NAMES
    40 REM * N$    NAME
    50 REM * W1-W4 SALES DATA FOR WEEKS 1 TO 4
    60 REM * S     SALES AMOUNT
    70 REM * E     EARNINGS
    80 REM *
    90 REM *PRINT HEADING
   100     PRINT USING 225
   110 REM *READ NAME AND SALES
   120     READ N$,W1,W2,W3,W4
   130 REM *TEST W1 FOR END OF DATA
   140     IF W1=-99.9 THEN 320
   150 REM *COMPUTE SALES AMOUNT AND EARNINGS
   160     LET S = W1+W2+W3+W4
   170     LET E = S*.10
   180 REM *PRINT NAME,SALES AMOUNT AND EARNINGS
   190     PRINT USING 230, N$,S,E
   200     GO TO 120
   220 REM *FORMAT STATEMENTS
   225:NAME                    SALES AMOUNT        EARNINGS
   230:#################,      ######.##          ######.##
   240 REM *INPUT DATA
   250     DATA "ALFRED E. BOWMAN"
   260     DATA  50.00,80.00,33.50,680.26
   270     DATA "R. GOLDBERG"
   280     DATA  2.00,4.00,8.00,16.00
   285     DATA "C. MACARTHY"
   287     DATA  10.52,20.36,15.30,50.00
   290     DATA "C. NATION"
   300     DATA  35.26,18.50,52.30,758.50
   310     DATA "END OF DATA",-99.9,0.,0.,0.
   320     END
```

Computer listing
of the program

```
>RUN
NAME                     SALES AMOUNT        EARNINGS
ALFRED E. BOWMAN            843.76             84.38
R. GOLDBERG                 30.00              3.00
C. MACARTHY                 96.18              9.62
C. NATION                  864.56             86.46

    320 HALT
```

Output produced by the
computer as the program
is executed

Figure 14-7 BASIC Program 4: Sales compensation, single commission rate.

sales commission amount is computed (ln 170), and a line is printed on the output report (ln 190). These steps are repeated until the last dummy record in ln 310 is read and the processing stops.

Feedback and Review 14-2

Using what you've now learned of the BASIC language, update Program 2 to take into account the changes outlined in Feedback and Review 12-2, page 330, and shown in the flowchart for Feedback and Review 12-2 presented at the end of Chapter 12. These changes involve computing a 6 percent sales tax on the net amount owed by a customer, and then adding this tax amount to the customer's net amount to get the total amount owed. The same *input data* used in Program 2 should be processed, and the same variable names can be used. Additional variable names for tax amount (T) and total amount owed (S) are also needed.

The *output* of the first bill should look like this:

```
PIERRE'S RECORD SHOP
6453 ORLEANS STREET
BOOGIE, LOUISIANA 54321
     NET = 7500.00     TAX = 450.00     TOTAL = 7950.00
```

There should be two line spaces between each output record.

MULTIPLE DECISIONS IN BASIC PROGRAMS

Only a single logic/comparison statement was used in the preceding programs. But we know that many decision paths are needed to solve more complex problems. Although the following program isn't particularly complex, it does illustrate the use of multiple decisions. Later programs will also use a series of logic decisions.

Program 5: Simple Billing With Discount

Let's assume that to encourage large shipments, Rob and Kay decide to offer a 15 percent discount on purchases with a quantity greater than or equal to 100 dozen tee shirts. A 6 percent sales tax must be charged on the amount owed after any discount is deducted. The flowchart outlining in detail the logic of this program is shown in Figure 12-8, page 333.

Figure 14-8 shows the program for this billing application example. Since there are no new types of BASIC statements used in this program, you should be able to follow it without too much trouble. The first 14 lines are self-explanatory REMark statements. Input data contained in ln 460 through ln 580 are read, a record at a time, by the READ statement in ln 150. The *first* decision, found in ln 170, is an IF . . . THEN statement that controls the program loop. The exit condition is satisfied when the dummy record in ln 580 is read. The *second* decision on ln 210

$$210 \quad \text{IF Q} >= 100.0 \text{ THEN } 240$$

sets up a selection structure. If quantity purchased (Q) is greater than or equal to 100, program control goes to ln 240 and the discount amount (D) is computed. If Q is less than 100, however, control moves to ln 220 and the discount amount is set at zero.

After the appropriate 'discount path has been selected and the discount amount has been computed or assigned, the 6 percent sales tax (T) is computed on the amount owed after the discount is deducted (ln 260). The total amount of the bill (S) is then computed (ln 280), and the output results shown in Figure 14-8 are prepared using the PRINT and image line statements shown on ln 300 through ln 440. After an input record has been processed and a bill has been printed, program control branches back to read another record (ln 390).

 **Feedback and Review 14-3**

Here's your chance to update the sales compensation report shown in Figure 14-7. Let's assume that the partners decide to pay salespeople a 12 percent commission if their total sales for a period are greater than or equal to $100. If total sales are less than $100, however, the commission rate remains at the 10 percent value used in Program 4. The *input data* should be the same as in Figure 14-7. The *output report* format should also be the same as in Figure 14-7. A possible flowchart for this updated program is the one shown for Feedback and Review 12-3 at the end of Chapter 12.

THE USE OF ACCUMULATORS

Two sales analysis reports are used to help manage R-K Enterprises. An important programming technique—the use of an accumulator—is used to prepare both reports. As you saw in Chapter 12, an *accumulator* is a programmer-designated storage location that's used to accept and store a running total of individual values as they become available during processing. The contents of the accumulator location must initially be set to zero. Each successive value placed in the accumulator is then added to the value already there. Accumulators are used in the R-K sales analysis reports to accumulate total sales figures.

Program 6: Sales Report Classified By Type of Product

Figure 14-9 shows a listing of the program used to prepare this sales report along with the output produced when the program is executed. As you can see,

```
>LIST
      10 REM *BILLING PROGRAM
      20 REM *
      30 REM *VARIABLE NAMES
      40 REM * N$ NAME
      50 REM * A$ ADDRESS
      60 REM * C$ CITY AND STATE
      70 REM * Q  QUANTITY PURCHASED
      80 REM * P  UNIT PRICE
      90 REM * A  AMOUNT BEFORE DISCOUNT
      95 REM * D  DISCOUNT
     100 REM * T  SALES TAX
     120 REM * S TOTAL
     130 REM *
     140 REM *READ NAME,ADDRESS,QUANTITY AND PRICE
     150       READ N$,A$,C$,Q,P
     160 REM *TEST QUANTITY FOR END OF DATA
     170       IF Q=-99.9 THEN 590
     180 REM *COMPUTE AMOUNT BEFORE DISCOUNT
     190       LET A = Q*P
     200 REM *COMPUTE DISCOUNT
     210       IF Q>=100.0 THEN 240
     220       LET D = 0.
     230       GO TO 260
     240       LET D = A*.15
     250 REM *COMPUTE SALES TAX
     260       LET T = (A-D)*.06
     270 REM *COMPUTE TOTAL
     280       LET S = A-D+T
     290 REM *PRINT RESULTS AND RETURN
     300       PRINT N$
     310       PRINT A$
     320       PRINT C$
     330       PRINT
     340       PRINT USING 420, Q,P
     350       PRINT USING 430, A,D,T
     355       PRINT USING 440, S
     360       PRINT
     370       PRINT
     380       PRINT
     390       GO TO 150
     410 REM *FORMAT STATEMENTS
     420:QUANTITY = ######.##    PRICE    = #######.##
     430:AMT      = ######.##    DISCOUNT = #######.##    TAX = ####.##
     440:TOTAL    = ######.##
     450 REM *INPUT DATA
     460       DATA "PIERRE'S RECORD SHOP"
```

Computer listing
of the program

```
470        DATA "6453 ORLEANS STREET"
480        DATA "BOOGIE,LOUISIANA 54321"
490        DATA  300.00, 25.00
500        DATA "ROCKY COLLEGE STORE"
510        DATA "1563 BEETHOVEN DRIVE"
520        DATA "ROCKTOWN,MARYLAND 20765"
530        DATA  3.25,  25.00
540        DATA "WYNN D. TOOTS,INC."
550        DATA "120 BROWNING STREET"
560        DATA "GONG,CALIFORNIA 98765"
570        DATA  50.00 25.00
580        DATA "END OF DATA","X","X",-99.9,0.
590        END
```

Computer listing
of the program

```
>RUN
PIERRE'S RECORD SHOP
6453 ORLEANS STREET
BOOGIE,LOUISIANA 54321


QUANTITY =     300.00  PRICE   =     25.00
AMT      =    7500.00  DISCOUNT =   1125.00   TAX =  382.50
TOTAL    =    6757.50




ROCKY COLLEGE STORE
1563 BEETHOVEN DRIVE
ROCKTOWN,MARYLAND 20765


QUANTITY =       3.25  PRICE   =     25.00
AMT      =      81.25  DISCOUNT =      0.00   TAX =    4.87
TOTAL    =      86.12




WYNN D. TOOTS,INC.
120 BROWNING STREET
GONG,CALIFORNIA 98765


QUANTITY =      50.00  PRICE   =     25.00
AMT      =    1250.00  DISCOUNT =      0.00   TAX =   75.00
TOTAL    =    1325.00


    590 HALT
```

Output produced by the
computer as the program
is executed

Figure 14-8 BASIC Program 5: Simple billing with discount.

```
>LIST
 10 REM *SALES REPORT PROGRAM
 20 REM *
 30 REM *VARIABLE NAMES
 40 REM * N$ NAME
 50 REM * A$ ADDRESS
 60 REM * C$ CITY AND STATE
 70 REM * P$ PRODUCT NAME
 80 REM * Q   QUANTITY SOLD
 90 REM * P   UNIT PRICE
100 REM * A   NET SALES
110 REM * T   TAX
120 REM * S   TOTAL SALES
130 REM * G   GRAND TOTAL SALES
140 REM *
150 REM *INITIALIZE ACCUMULATOR
160     LET G = 0.
170 REM *READ PRODUCT NAME AND PRINT HEADING
180     READ P$
190     PRINT USING 490, P$
195     PRINT
200 REM *READ NAME,ADDRESS,QUANTITY AND UNIT PRICE
210     READ N$,A$,C$,Q,P
220 REM *TEST QUANTITY FOR END OF DATA
230     IF Q=-99.9 THEN 400
240 REM *CALCULATE NET AMOUNT,SALES TAX AND TOTAL
250     LET A = Q*P
260     LET T = A*.06
270     LET S = A+T
280 REM *ACCUMULATE GRAND TOTAL
290     LET G = G+S
300 REM *PRINT NAME AND ADDRESS
310     PRINT N$
320     PRINT A$
330     PRINT C$
335     PRINT
340 REM *PRINT SUBHEADING
350     PRINT USING 500
360 REM *PRINT QUANTITY,UNIT PRICE,NET AMOUNT,SALES TAX AND TOTAL
370     PRINT USING 510, Q,P,A,T,S
373     PRINT
375     PRINT
377     PRINT
380     GO TO 210
390 REM *PRINT GRAND TOTAL AND STOP
400     PRINT
410     PRINT USING 520
420     PRINT USING 530
430     PRINT USING 540, G
470     STOP
480 REM *FORMAT STATEMENTS
490:SALES REPORT FOR ##################
500:QUANTITY   UNIT PRICE   NET AMOUNT   SALES TAX      TOTAL
510:#####.##    #######.##   #######.##   ######.##   #######.##
520:                                                    GRAND
530:                                                    TOTAL
540:                                                  #######.##
550 REM *INPUT DATA
555     DATA "TEE SHIRTS(DOZ)"
560     DATA "PIERRE'S RECORD SHOP"
570     DATA "6453 ORLEANS STREET"
580     DATA "BOOGIE,LOUISIANA 54321"
590     DATA  300.00,25.00
600     DATA "ROCKY COLLEGE STORE"
610     DATA "1563 BEETHOVEN DRIVE"
620     DATA "ROCKTOWN,MARYLAND 20765"
630     DATA  3.25,25.00
640     DATA "WYNN D. TOOTS,INC."
```

Computer listing
of the program

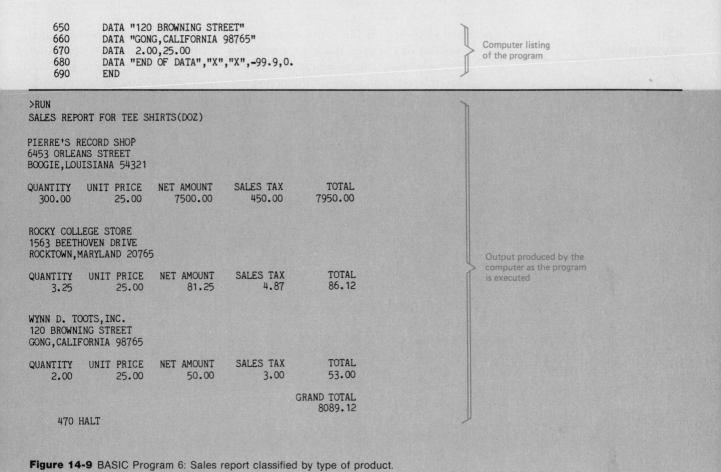

```
650      DATA "120 BROWNING STREET"
660      DATA "GONG,CALIFORNIA 98765"
670      DATA  2.00,25.00
680      DATA "END OF DATA","X","X",-99.9,0.
690      END
```
Computer listing of the program

```
>RUN
SALES REPORT FOR TEE SHIRTS(DOZ)


PIERRE'S RECORD SHOP
6453 ORLEANS STREET
BOOGIE,LOUISIANA 54321

QUANTITY   UNIT PRICE   NET AMOUNT   SALES TAX      TOTAL
  300.00        25.00      7500.00      450.00    7950.00


ROCKY COLLEGE STORE
1563 BEETHOVEN DRIVE
ROCKTOWN,MARYLAND 20765

QUANTITY   UNIT PRICE   NET AMOUNT   SALES TAX      TOTAL
    3.25        25.00        81.25        4.87      86.12


WYNN D. TOOTS,INC.
120 BROWNING STREET
GONG,CALIFORNIA 98765

QUANTITY   UNIT PRICE   NET AMOUNT   SALES TAX      TOTAL
    2.00        25.00        50.00        3.00      53.00

                                      GRAND TOTAL
                                          8089.12

   470 HALT
```
Output produced by the computer as the program is executed

Figure 14-9 BASIC Program 6: Sales report classified by type of product.

.this report classifies the purchases made during a period by a named customer according to the type of product shipped. Different reports can be prepared for each of the products sold by Kay and Rob. The logic of this program was discussed in Chapter 12, and the flowchart for the program is shown in Figure 12-9, page 336.

The first 15 lines are REMark statements. In ln 160,

$$LET \quad G = 0$$

the location that's used to accumulate the grand total sales figure (G) is set to zero. The name of the particular product being considered is READ (ln 180) from DATA line 555, and the appropriate heading is printed on the output report using the PRINT and format statements found in ln 190 and ln 490. Since we've examined similar statements in other programs, you should have no difficulty now in understanding the effects of ln 195 through ln 270.

In ln 290,

$$LET \quad G = G + S$$

the value of G is the grand total sales in the accumulator, and S is the total amount of the sales made to a customer. In processing the first record for Pierre's Record Shop, we can see from the output results in Figure 14-9 that Pierre's total purchases for the period amounted to $7,950.00. When ln 290 is executed, this amount is added to the previous amount (0) in the accumulator. The new total of $7,950.00 is then assigned to the accumulator thereby erasing the previous value of 0. When the next record for Rocky College Store is processed, the $86.12 total for this customer will be added to $7,950.00 now in the accumulator to get a new total of $8,036.12 ($7,950.00 + $86.12). And so the process of updating the accumulator continues until all records have been processed.

The name and complete address of each customer is printed on the output report by the PRINT statements in ln 310 through ln 330. After spacing a line (ln 335), a row of subheadings is printed for each customer using the statements in ln 350 and ln 500. The sales figures for each customer are then printed using the statements in ln 370 and 510. The program then loops back at ln 380 to read the next customer record. When the last valid record has been processed, the exit condition in ln 230 is satisfied, and program control branches to ln 400. The PRINT USING statements in ln 410 and 420, and the image line statements in ln 520 and 530 establish the GRAND TOTAL subheading at the bottom of the report. The statements in ln 430 and ln 540 then cause the printing of the grand total sales amount stored in the accumulator. Program control then moves to ln 470, and the STOP statement halts the processing.

Program 7: Sales Summary Report

The purpose of this report is to summarize the sales of all products sold by R-K Enterprises during a period. A listing of the program used to prepare this report, along with the output produced by the program, is shown in Figure 14-10. The flowchart outlining the specifications and logic of this program is shown in Figure 12-10, page 338.

After the headings shown on the report are printed (ln 110–115, and ln 320–325), the accumulator is set to zero (ln 130). Input data are read (ln 150), a test for exit condition is made (ln 170), the net sales for a product are computed (ln 190), and the sales amount is accumulated (ln 200). A line on the output report is printed for the product (ln 220 and ln 330), and the program loops back to read another record (ln 230). After all valid records have been processed, the exit condition in ln 170 is satisfied, and program control branches to ln 250. The same procedure discussed in the preceding program is then followed to print the TOTAL NET SALES subheading at the bottom of the report. The accumulated total net sales figure is then printed below the subheading and the processing stops.

```
>LIST
    10 REM *SALES SUMMARY REPORT
    20 REM *
    30 REM *VARIABLE NAMES
    40 REM * P$ PRODUCT NAME
    50 REM * Q   QUANTITY SOLD
    60 REM * P   UNIT PRICE
    70 REM * A   NET SALES
    80 REM * T   TOTAL NET SALES
    90 REM *
   100 REM *PRINT HEADING
   110     PRINT USING 320
   115     PRINT USING 325
   120 REM *INITIALIZE ACCUMULATOR
   130     LET T = 0.
   140 REM *READ PRODUCT,UNIT PRICE AND QUANTITY SOLD
   150     READ P$,Q,P
   160 REM *TEST QUANTITY FOR END OF DATA
   170     IF Q=-99.9 THEN 250
   180 REM *COMPUTE NET SALES AND ACCUMULATE TOTAL NET SALES
   190     LET A = Q*P
   200     LET T = A+T
   210 REM *PRINT PRODUCT,PRICE,QUANTITY AND NET SALES THEN RETURN
   220     PRINT USING 330, P$,P,Q,A
   230     GO TO 150
   240 REM *PRINT TOTAL NET SALES AND STOP
   250     PRINT
   260     PRINT
   270     PRINT USING 340
   280     PRINT USING 350
   290     PRINT USING 360, T
   300     STOP
   310 REM *FORMAT STATEMENTS
   320:              SALES SUMMARY REPORT
   325:PRODUCT            UNIT PRICE      QUANTITY      NET SALES
   330:###################   #######.##    #######.##    #######.##
   340:                                                    TOTAL
   350:                                                  NET SALES
   360:                                                  #######.##
   370 REM *INPUT DATA
   380     DATA "TEE SHIRTS(DOZ)"
   390     DATA  35.75, 25.00
   400     DATA "MOSQUITO BIRD R"
   410     DATA  300.0, 6.00
   420     DATA "MOSQUITO BIRD T"
   430     DATA  50.00, 7.00
   440     DATA "KAY OSS IN CONCERT R"
   450     DATA  200.0, 8.00
   460     DATA "KAY OSS IN CONCERT T"
   470     DATA  70.00, 8.50
   480     DATA "OH WHAT? BOOK"
   490     DATA  2.00,  9.95
   500     DATA "END OF DATA",-99.9,0.
   510     END
```

Computer listing
of the program

Figure 14-10 BASIC Program 7: Sales summary report.

```
>RUN
             SALES SUMMARY REPORT
PRODUCT               UNIT PRICE     QUANTITY     NET SALES
TEE SHIRTS(DOZ)           25.00        35.75        893.75
MOSQUITO BIRD R            6.00       300.00       1800.00
MOSQUITO BIRD T            7.00        50.00        350.00
KAY OSS IN CONCERT R       8.00       200.00       1600.00
KAY OSS IN CONCERT T       8.50        70.00        595.00
OH WHAT? BOOK              9.95         2.00         19.90


                                                    TOTAL
                                                  NET SALES
                                                   5258.65

   300 HALT
```

Output produced by the
computer as the program
is executed

**Feedback and
Review 14-4**

It's time once again for you to become a maintenance programmer! Your assignment is to update the sales compensation report program you prepared for Feedback and Review 14-3. You'll use the same *input data,* and the same general output format. However, you should modify the program so that the *output* looks like this:

NAME	SALES AMOUNT	EARNINGS
ALFRED E. BOWMAN	843.76	84.38
R. GOLDBERG	30.00	3.00
C. MACARTHY	96.18	9.62
C. NATION	864.56	86.46
	TOTAL	TOTAL
	SALES	EARNINGS
	1834.50	183.45

As you can see from the output, only a 10 percent commission rate is applied to each person's sales amount to get their earnings. Multiple commission rates aren't used for this exercise. What *is* being emphasized here, however, is the use of an accumulator to total the sales made by each salesperson. The flowchart for Feedback and Review 12-4, shown at the end of Chapter 12, should help you prepare this program.

THE USE OF COUNTERS

Another important programming technique discussed in Chapter 12 is the use of a counter. A *counter,* you'll recall, is a special type of accumulator that's often used to record the number of times a loop has been processed. The counter is incremented with each pass of the program through the loop. When the counter value reaches a predetermined number, an exit condition based on the value of the counter is satisfied, and an exit path out of the loop is followed.

Program 8: Simple Billing With a Counter

The listing in Figure 14-11 shows how a counter can be used to control a loop. The flowchart for this program is found in Figure 12-11, page 338.

The counter (K) is initialized at 1 in ln 120, and the number of records to be processed (and thus the number of passes to be made through the loop) is read in ln 130. In our example, the number of records to be processed (N) is set at 4 by the first DATA item in ln 300. After the first customer record has been processed (ln 150 through ln 210), a test for exit condition is made in ln 230. In the first pass through the program loop, this statement

230   IF K = N THEN 410

```
>LIST
    10 REM *BILLING PROGRAM
    20 REM *
    30 REM *VARIABLE NAMES
    40 REM * N$ NAME
    50 REM * Q  QUANTITY
    60 REM * P  UNIT PRICE
    70 REM * A  NET AMOUNT
    80 REM * N  NUMBER OF RECORDS TO BE PROCESSED
    90 REM * K  COUNTER
   100 REM *
   110 REM *INITIALIZE COUNTER AND READ NUMBER OF RECORDS
   120      LET K = 1
   130      READ N
   140 REM *READ NAME,QUANTITY AND PRICE
   150      READ N$,Q,P
   160 REM *COMPUTE NET AMOUNT
   170      LET A = Q*P
   180 REM *PRINT NAME AND NET AMOUNT
   190      PRINT USING 280, N$,A
   200      PRINT
   210      PRINT
   220 REM *TEST FOR END OF DATA
   230      IF K=N THEN 410
   240 REM *INCREMENT COUNTER AND RETURN
   250      LET K = K+1
   260      GO TO 150
   270 REM *FORMAT STATEMENT FOR OUTPUT
   280:###################   NET = #######.##
   290 REM *INPUT DATA
   300      DATA    4
   310      DATA "ED'S CULTURAL CENTER "
   320      DATA    3.50,     25.00
   330      DATA "PIERRE'S RECORD SHOP "
   340      DATA    5.75,     25.00
   350      DATA "ROCKY COLLEGE STORE   "
   360      DATA   10.00     25.00
   370      DATA "WYNN D. TOOTS, INC.   "
   380      DATA    6.00,     25.00
   410      END
```

Computer listing of the program

```
>RUN
ED'S CULTURAL CENTER   NET =      87.50


PIERRE'S RECORD SHOP   NET =     143.75


ROCKY COLLEGE STORE    NET =     250.00


WYNN D. TOOTS, INC.    NET =     150.00


   410 HALT
```

Output produced by the computer as the program is executed

Figure 14-11 BASIC Program 8: Simple billing with a counter.

compares the initial value of the counter (1) to the number of records to be processed (4). Since the counter value obviously doesn't equal 4, program control moves on to ln 250. In this step,

$$250 \quad \underline{\text{LET } K = K + 1}$$

the counter is incremented by a value of 1, and so its new value is 2. When the last customer record has been processed, and when K = N, the exit path out of the loop will be followed to ln 410, and processing will END without any need for a dummy record at the end of the file.

Built-In Looping With an Automatic Counter

Since using a counter to control a loop is such a useful technique, most programming languages have instructions that can be used to establish an automatic counter. The program listing in Figure 14-12 shows how an automatic counter can be set up in BASIC. This program represents an alternative to Program 4 shown in Figure 14-7. The number of input records is specified in Figure 14-12, but otherwise the input data and output results are the same for both programs.

The statements from ln 10 through ln 140 are familiar types. But this program then uses a pair of statements—the **FOR statement** on ln 150 and the **NEXT statement** on ln 230—that you're not familiar with. These FOR and NEXT statements must always be used together. The FOR statement *opens* a loop, and the loop is *closed* with the NEXT statement. That is, a FOR statement sets up a loop and is placed at the beginning of the loop, while the NEXT statement is located at the end of the loop. The program line or lines that are *between* the FOR and NEXT statements are executed repeatedly and form the *range,* or *body,* of the loop.

The general form of these statements is

```
ln   FOR v = i TO t STEP n
ln        ·
ln        ·
ln        ·
ln   NEXT v
```

where ln is a line number, v is a variable name acting as an automatic counter or index, i is the initial value or expression given to the counter, t is the terminal value or expression of the counter when the looping is completed, and n is the amount by which the counter should be stepped up or down after each pass through the loop. (If the step value is omitted in the FOR statement, the

```
>LIST
    10 REM *SALES COMPENSATION REPORT
    20 REM *
    30 REM *VARIABLE NAMES
    40 REM * N$     NAME
    50 REM * W1-W4 SALES DATA FOR WEEKS 1 TO 4
    60 REM * S      SALES AMOUNT
    70 REM * E      EARNINGS
    80 REM * N      NUMBER OF RECORDS TO BE PROCESSED
    90 REM *
   100 REM *READ NUMBER OF RECORDS TO BE PROCESSED
   110       READ N
   120 REM *PRINT HEADING
   130       PRINT USING 260
   140 REM *PROCESS DATA USING LOOP
   150       FOR K=1 TO N
   160 REM *READ NAME AND SALES DATA
   170       READ N$,W1,W2,W3,W4
   180 REM *COMPUTE SALES AMOUNT AND EARNINGS
   190       LET S = W1+W2+W3+W4
   200       LET E = S*.10
   210 REM *PRINT NAME,SALES AMOUNT AND EARNINGS THEN RETURN
   220       PRINT USING 270, N$,S,E
   230       NEXT K
   240       STOP
   250 REM *FORMAT STATEMENTS
   260:NAME                    SALES AMOUNT        EARNINGS
   270:###################     #######.##      #######.##
   280 REM *INPUT DATA
   290       DATA  4
   300       DATA "ALFRED E. BOWMAN"
   310       DATA   50.00,  80.00,  33.50, 680.26
   320       DATA "R. GOLDBERG"
   330       DATA    2.00,   4.00,   8.00,  16.00
   340       DATA "C. MACARTHY"
   350       DATA   10.52,  20.36,  15.30,  50.00
   360       DATA "C. NATION"
   370       DATA   35.26,  18.50,  52.30, 758.50
   380       END
```

> Computer listing
> of the program

```
>RUN
NAME                    SALES AMOUNT        EARNINGS
ALFRED E. BOWMAN           843.76             84.38
R. GOLDBERG                30.00               3.00
C. MACARTHY                96.18               9.62
C. NATION                 864.56             86.46

    240 HALT
```

> Output produced by the
> computer as the program
> is executed

Figure 14-12 An alternative to Program 4, Figure 14-7, showing built-in looping with an automatic counter.

computer will automatically use a step size of 1.) Some examples of valid FOR . . . NEXT statements are:

150   FOR K = 1 TO N

230   NEXT K

130   FOR J = 5 * N TO A/B STEP 2

180   NEXT J

160   FOR P = 25 TO 1 STEP − 1

260   NEXT P

The first of these FOR . . . NEXT examples is found in our program in Figure 14-12. In our example, the automatic counter (K) is initially set at 1 in the FOR statement (ln 150), a salesperson's record is read and processed (ln 170 through ln 200), an output line is printed (ln 220 and ln 270), and the end of the loop is reached at the NEXT statement (ln 230). An automatic test is made to determine if the counter value (K) is equal to or greater than N (in this case 4). Since K is now 1 and obviously doesn't equal N, the counter is automatically stepped up by 1 and the next pass through the loop occurs. When the records of the four salespeople have been processed, the value of K *will* equal N, the processing will stop, and program control will exit from the FOR . . . NEXT loop structure to the next executable line number in sequence. In our example, this is the STOP statement on ln 240. As this example illustrates, the built-in looping capability available through the use of FOR . . . NEXT statements gives the programmer a relatively simple and powerful repetitive processing tool.

ADDITIONAL BUSINESS DATA PROCESSING IN BASIC

Only two more R-K Enterprises programs remain to be considered—a final billing program and an inventory control program. The flowchart for the billing program is shown in Figure 12-13, page 342, and the inventory control flowchart is found in Figure 12-12, page 341. Since there are no new programming techniques and no new types of BASIC statements to consider in these programs, we'll move through them quickly.

Program 9: Final Billing Program

Many of the features found in the program listed in Figure 14-13 were shown earlier in Program 5, Figure 14-8. But a number of additional features have also been added. For example, this program accommodates all possible products sold by Rob and Kay rather than just the single product discussed in Program 5. In addition, accumulators are set up (ln 180 and ln 190) to total the amounts billed before and after discounts have been computed.

After the name and complete address of the first customer are read and printed (ln 210 through ln 280), a heading line for the customer's bill is printed (ln 290 and ln 590). The name, quantity, and price of the *first* product are entered next (ln 310). An end-of-record test is then made

$$330 \quad \text{IF P} = -99.9 \text{ THEN } 210$$

to see if all products in a customer's record have been processed. If they all *have* been processed, a dummy price field with a value of -99.9 at the end of a customer's record is encountered (see ln 690, 790, and 890), and program control branches back to ln 210 to read and print the name of the next customer. Since none of the products purchased by the first customer have yet been processed, however, program control moves to the next statement.

This statement

$$340 \quad \text{IF Q} = -99.9 \text{ THEN } 530$$

is an end-of-file test. When all valid data in the last customer's record have been processed, a dummy quantity field with a value of -99.9 is read (ln 940), program control moves to ln 530, accumulated totals are printed (ln 550 and 610, and ln 560 and 620), and processing stops (ln 570).

But that operation comes later. Right now, we are processing the first product item bought by Ed's Cultural Center in Cramps, Texas. The statements from ln 360 through ln 440 are identical to those explained in problem 5, so we can skip them here. You'll notice in ln 460 and ln 470, however, that the before and after discount amounts for the first product (mosquito bird record) are added to the accumulators. The totals of all successive products will also be accumulated. The name of the first product and other pertinent facts are then printed on the first customer's bill (ln 500 and ln 600). Program control then branches from ln 510 back to ln 310, and the next product is processed. This continues until the last product bought by the first customer has been accounted for. Then, as we've seen, the exit test condition for ln 330 will be met and processing will begin on the next customer's record.

Program 10: Inventory Control Report

Figure 14-14 shows a listing of the program for the inventory control report along with the output produced when the program is executed. The

```
>LIST
    10 REM *BILLING PROGRAM
    20 REM *
    30 REM *VARIABLE NAMES
    40 REM * N$ NAME
    50 REM * A$ ADDRESS
    60 REM * C$ CITY AND STATE
    70 REM * P$ PRODUCT NAME
    80 REM * Q  QUANTITY
    90 REM * P  UNIT PRICE
   100 REM * A  AMOUNT BEFORE DISCOUNT
   110 REM * D  DISCOUNT
   120 REM * T  TAX
   130 REM * S  TOTAL
   140 REM * G1 GRAND TOTAL AMOUNT BEFORE DISCOUNT
   150 REM * G2 GRAND TOTAL AMOUNT AFTER DISCOUNTS
   160 REM *
   170 REM *INITIALIZE ACCUMULATORS
   180     LET G1 = 0.
   190     LET G2 = 0.
   200 REM *READ CUSTOMER NAME AND ADDRESS AND PRINT HEADING
   210     READ N$,A$,C$
   220     PRINT
   230     PRINT
   240     PRINT
   250     PRINT N$
   260     PRINT A$
   270     PRINT C$
   280     PRINT
   290     PRINT USING 590
   300 REM *READ PRODUCT,QUANTITY AND PRICE
   310     READ P$,Q,P
   320 REM *TEST QUANTITY FOR END OF DATA AND PRICE FOR LAST PRODUCT
   330     IF P=-99.9 THEN 210
   340     IF Q=-99.9 THEN 530
   350 REM *COMPUTE AMOUNT BEFORE DISCOUNT
   360     LET A = Q*P
   370 REM *COMPUTE DISCOUNT BASED ON QUANTITY SOLD
   380     IF Q>=100. THEN 410
   390     LET D = 0.
   400     GO TO 430
   410     LET D = .15*A
   420 REM *COMPUTE TAX AND TOTAL
   430     LET T = .06*(A-D)
   440     LET S = A-D+T
   450 REM *ACCUMULATE TOTALS
   460     LET G1 = G1+A
```

Computer listing of the program

Figure 14-13 BASIC Program 9: Final billing program.

```
470        LET G2 = G2+S
480 REM *PRINT PRODUCT,QUANTITY,PRICE,AMOUNT BEFORE DISCOUNT,DISCOUNT,
490 REM *      TAX AND TOTAL THEN RETURN
500        PRINT USING 600, P$,Q,P,A,D,T,S
510        GO TO 310
520 REM *PRINT GRAND TOTALS THEN STOP
530        PRINT
540        PRINT
550        PRINT USING 610, G1
560        PRINT USING 620, G2
570        STOP
580 REM *FORMAT STATEMENTS
590:PRODUCT                  QTY  PRICE     AMT  DCOUNT   TAX    TOTAL
600:################## ####.## ###.## #####.## ####.## ###.## #####.##
610:AMT TOTAL   = ######.##
620:GRAND TOTAL = ######.##
630 REM *INPUT DATA
640        DATA "ED'S CULTURAL CENTER"
650        DATA "822 PHILHARMONIC AVENUE"
660        DATA "CRAMPS,TEXAS 77786"
670        DATA "MOSQUITO.BIRD R    ", 200.00,  6.00
680        DATA "MOSQUITO BIRD T    ", 300.00,  7.00
690        DATA "LAST PRODUCT", 0.,-99.9
695 REM *
700        DATA "PIERRE'S RECORD SHOP"
710        DATA "6453 ORLEANS STREET"
720        DATA "BOOGIE,LOUISIANA 54321"
730        DATA "TEE SHIRTS(DOZ)    ",   3.00, 25.00
740        DATA "MOSQUITO BIRD R    ",  50.00,  6.00
750        DATA "MOSQUITO BIRD T    ",  60.00,  7.00
760        DATA "KAY OSS IN CONCERT R", 110.00,  8.00
770        DATA "KAY OSS IN CONCERT T", 200.00,  8.50
780        DATA "OH WHAT? BOOK      ",  30.00,  9.95
790        DATA "LAST PRODUCT", 0.,-99.9
795 REM *
800        DATA "ROCKY COLLEGE STORE"
810        DATA "1563 BEETHOVEN DRIVE"
820        DATA "ROCKTOWN,MARYLAND 20765"
830        DATA "TEE SHIRTS(DOZ)    ",   6.25, 25.00
840        DATA "MOSQUITO BIRD R    ",   6.00,  6.00
850        DATA "MOSQUITO BIRD T    ",   5.00,  7.00
860        DATA "KAY OSS IN CONCERT R",   2.00  8.00
870        DATA "KAY OSS IN CONCERT T",   2.00  8.50
880        DATA "OH WHAT? BOOK      ",   4.00  9.95
890        DATA "LAST PRODUCT", 0.,-99.9
895 REM *
900        DATA "WYNN D. TOOTS,INC."
910        DATA "120 BROWNING STREET"
920        DATA "GONG,CALIFORNIA 98765"
930        DATA "OH WHAT? BOOK      ",   5.00, 9.95
940        DATA "END OF DATA", -99.9, 0.
950        END
```

Computer listing
of the program

```
>RUN

ED'S CULTURAL CENTER
822 PHILHARMONIC AVENUE
CRAMPS,TEXAS 77786

PRODUCT               QTY   PRICE      AMT   DCOUNT     TAX     TOTAL
MOSQUITO BIRD R    200.00    6.00  1200.00   180.00   61.20   1081.20
MOSQUITO BIRD T    300.00    7.00  2100.00   315.00  107.10   1892.10



PIERRE'S RECORD SHOP
6453 ORLEANS STREET
BOOGIE,LOUISIANA 54321

PRODUCT                  QTY   PRICE      AMT   DCOUNT     TAX     TOTAL
TEE SHIRTS(DOZ)         3.00   25.00    75.00     0.00    4.50     79.50
MOSQUITO BIRD R        50.00    6.00   300.00     0.00   18.00    318.00
MOSQUITO BIRD T        60.00    7.00   420.00     0.00   25.20    445.20
KAY OSS IN CONCERT R  110.00    8.00   880.00   132.00   44.88    792.88
KAY OSS IN CONCERT T  200.00    8.50  1700.00   255.00   86.70   1531.70
OH WHAT? BOOK          30.00    9.95   298.50     0.00   17.91    316.41



ROCKY COLLEGE STORE
1563 BEETHOVEN DRIVE
ROCKTOWN,MARYLAND 20765

PRODUCT                 QTY   PRICE      AMT   DCOUNT     TAX     TOTAL
TEE SHIRTS(DOZ)        6.25   25.00   156.25     0.00    9.37    165.62
MOSQUITO BIRD R        6.00    6.00    36.00     0.00    2.16     38.16
MOSQUITO BIRD T        5.00    7.00    35.00     0.00    2.10     37.10
KAY OSS IN CONCERT R   2.00    8.00    16.00     0.00    0.96     16.96
KAY OSS IN CONCERT T   2.00    8.50    17.00     0.00    1.02     18.02
OH WHAT? BOOK          4.00    9.95    39.80     0.00    2.39     42.19



WYNN D. TOOTS,INC.
120 BROWNING STREET
GONG,CALIFORNIA 98765

PRODUCT         QTY   PRICE     AMT   DCOUNT     TAX    TOTAL
OH WHAT? BOOK  5.00    9.95   49.75     0.00    2.98    52.73


AMT TOTAL   =    7323.30
GRAND TOTAL =    6827.78

     570 HALT
```

Figure 14-13 *continued*

Output produced by the computer as the program is executed

```
>LIST
    10 REM *INVENTORY CONTROL REPORT
    20 REM *
    30 REM *VARIABLE NAMES
    40 REM * P$ PRODUCT NAME
    50 REM * B  BEGINNING INVENTORY
    60 REM * R  QUANTITY RECEIVED
    70 REM * S  QUANTITY SOLD
    80 REM * A  AVAILABLE INVENTORY
    90 REM * E  ENDING INVENTORY
   100 REM *
   110 REM *PRINT HEADING
   115     PRINT USING 340
   118     PRINT
   122     PRINT USING 350
   126     PRINT USING 360
   130 REM *READ PRODUCT,BEGINNING INVENTORY,QUANTITY RECEIVED
   140 REM *AND QUANTITY SOLD
   150     READ P$,B,R,S
   160 REM *TEST QUANTITY RECEIVED FOR END OF DATA
   170     IF R=-99.9 THEN 320
   180 REM *COMPUTE AVAILABLE INVENTORY
   190     IF R>=0. THEN 220
   200     LET A = B
   210     GO TO 240
   220     LET A = B+R
   230 REM *COMPUTE ENDING INVENTORY
   240     IF S>=0. THEN 270
   250     LET E = A
   260     GO TO 300
   270     LET E = A-S
   280 REM *PRINT PRODUCT,BEGINNING INVENTORY,QUANTITY RECEIVED
   290 REM *QUANTITY SOLD AND ENDING INVENTORY THEN RETURN
   300     PRINT USING 370, P$,B,R,S,E
   310     GO TO 150
   320     STOP
   330 REM *FORMAT STATEMENTS
   340:                 INVENTORY CONTROL REPORT
   350:PRODUCT              BEGINNING    QUANTITY     QUANTITY    ENDING
   360:                     INVENTORY    RECEIVED     SOLD        INVENTORY
   370:################### -#######.##   #######.##   #######.## -#######.##
   380 REM *INPUT DATA
   390     DATA "TEE SHIRTS(DOZ)     ",  50.00,   10.00,    30.75
   400     DATA "MOSQUITO BIRD R     ",  30.00,   20.00,    20.00
   410     DATA "MOSQUITO BIRD T     ",  20.00,   20.00,    30.00
   420     DATA "KAY OSS IN CONCERT R",  10.00,    6.00,  5000.00
   430     DATA "KAY OSS IN CONCERT T",  10.00,    5.00,  5000.00
   440     DATA "OH WHAT? BOOK       ",   5.00, 6000.00,    00.00
   460     DATA "END OF DATA         ",   0.00,  -99.90,    00.00
   470     END
```

Figure 14-14 BASIC Program 10: An inventory control report showing the undoing of R-K Enterprises.

```
>RUN
                INVENTORY CONTROL REPORT

PRODUCT              BEGINNING    QUANTITY    QUANTITY    ENDING
                     INVENTORY    RECEIVED    SOLD        INVENTORY
TEE SHIRTS(DOZ)         50.00       10.00       30.75       29.25
MOSQUITO BIRD R         30.00       20.00       20.00       30.00
MOSQUITO BIRD T         20.00       20.00       30.00       10.00
KAY OSS IN CONCERT R    10.00        6.00     5000.00    -4984.00
KAY OSS IN CONCERT T    10.00        5.00     5000.00    -4985.00
OH WHAT? BOOK            5.00     6000.00        0.00     6005.00

    320 HALT
```

body of the program loop begins after the report headings are printed (using ln 115 through ln 126, and ln 340 through ln 360). Input data are entered (ln 150), a test is made to see if all valid records have been processed (ln 170), and the inventory available for sale is determined (ln 190 through ln 220). The ending inventory is then found (ln 240 through ln 270). An output line for a product is printed (ln 300 and ln 370), and program control then branches from ln 310 back to ln 150 to read and process another record.

A Final Sad Note

The output for the inventory control report in Figure 14-14 shows some distressing figures. For one thing, there's a great demand for "Kay Oss in Concert" records and tapes, but R-K Enterprises has none of these records and tapes to sell, and so the report shows a severe "backorder" condition for these products. Even more distressing is the fact that a huge inventory of the *Oh What?* book of poems written by Rob's English teacher, Ms. Fitt, is available, but absolutely no one is buying it. Rob cannot understand this lack of market interest. After all, Ms. Fitt is noted for her motto of "Write it right, write it good." Thus, we have this tragic situation: The R-K products in demand cannot be reordered because all the partners' capital is tied up in a bomb of a book that Rob has published. And so, like this chapter, R-K Enterprises has come to an end. We won't have Rob and Kay to kick around anymore.

1. BASIC is a popular timesharing and personal computing language that makes it easy for people to interact with computers. Sign-on procedures, the keywords used in system commands, and other details of language usage vary from one system to another.

2. Key words are used in constructing BASIC statements, and these statements are then put together to form a program. Each statement in a BASIC program begins with a line number, and each type of statement has certain rules that must be followed. A number (but certainly not all) of these rules have been discussed in the chapter for the following types of statements and functions:

REM	IF . . . THEN
READ . . . DATA	GO TO
LET	STOP
PRINT	FOR . . . NEXT
INPUT	PRINT TAB
PRINT USING	END

3. The values used in BASIC statements may be constants or variables. There are numeric constants and character string constants, and there are also numeric variables and string variables. Specific rules for naming and using these numeric and string values must be followed.

4. The computer handles arithmetic operations in a specific order. The rules used in determining the order of these operations have been spelled out in the chapter. Some common procedures for correcting errors that may occur during program and data entry have also been discussed.

5. Solutions have been written in BASIC for all the problems analyzed and flowcharted in Chapter 12. All programs have been written in a programming style that may make them easier to read and understand. Beginning with some short programs to accomplish simple input, processing, and output, we have moved on to more detailed examples that use decisions, loops, counters, and accumulators. The language rules and programming techniques that have been considered during the discussion of these programs can be used to solve very complex problems. Of course, BASIC has many additional features that were not considered in this chapter.

KEY TERMS AND CONCEPTS

You should now be able to define and use the following terms and concepts (the numbers shown indicate the pages where the terms and concepts are first mentioned):

system commands 394	line number (ln) 395	character string constants 397
program statements 394	numeric constants 397	numeric variable 397

TOPICS FOR REVIEW AND DISCUSSION

1. Explain the procedures required to sign on the system you are using.

2. (*a*) What is the difference between a system command and a program statement? (*b*) Which typically causes the computer to take immediate action?

3. Identify and discuss the elements that may be found in a BASIC statement.

4. "BASIC deals with values that may be constants or variables." Discuss this sentence.

5. Define and give examples of a (*a*) numeric constant, (*b*) character string constant, (*c*) numeric variable, (*d*) variable name, (*e*) string variable, and (*f*) string variable name.

6. (*a*) Why is it important to understand the order in which the computer handles the arithmetic operations in a formula? (*b*) What is this priority order in a formula without parentheses? (*c*) What changes are made in this order when parentheses are used?

7. Explain the procedures required by the system you are using to correct the errors that may occur in program and data entry.

8. "Diagnostic messages detect syntax errors but not logical errors." Discuss this statement.

9. What will the computer do in executing the following BASIC statements:

- **(a)** 010 READ A,B,C,D,E
  200 DATA 025,200,300
  210 DATA 060,150,175, ... , 125
- **(b)** 120 PRINT A,B,C
- **(c)** 020 PRINT TAB(10);"HELP"
- **(d)** 050 IF N <= 50 THEN 100
- **(e)** 130 FOR J = 1 to 10 STEP 2

  170 NEXT J
- **(f)** 60 INPUT S$
- **(g)** 20 REM GIVE THE USER A SHOCK
- **(h)** 40 LET A = (K*P/G)/2
- **(i)** 60 PRINT "WHAT IS YOUR AGE";
  70 INPUT A
  80 PRINT
- **(j)** 210 PRINT USING 440, A,B,C
  440:   ###.##   ####.##   ##.#
- **(k)** 150 PRINT TAB(20); "HOW DO I GET OUT?"

10. Program 9 is referred to as the "Final" Billing Program. Can you see any deficiencies in this program that might call for further modifications?

11. After reviewing Program 4 in Figure 14-7, how could you modify it so that Rob and Kay could interact with the program and supply the INPUT (hint) data at the time of processing? Let's assume that the program should print instructions on how to enter the input data, and it should print a heading line for each salesperson showing "NAME," "SALES AMOUNT," and "EARNINGS." It should also print an "END OF DATA?" message after each record has been processed to allow the partners to stop processing or to continue with another record.

12. After reviewing Program 8 in Figure 14-11, how could it be changed so that the total amount billed to each customer can be accumulated and then printed with a "TOTAL AMOUNT" subheading at the end of the billing run?

13. After reviewing Program 8 in Figure 14-11, make the following modifications so that data may be entered for each customer by the use of INPUT statements: (*a*) Print a message asking the user to enter the number of customer records to be processed. (*b*) Print a message asking for the user to supply a customer's name, quantity purchased, and unit price. The output produced for each customer should be in the same format used in Figure 14-11, but, of course, the messages instructing the user to supply the needed facts will also be printed.

14. After reviewing the possible program for Feedback and Review 14-4 shown on page 438, write a program using two accumulators to total both the SALES AMOUNT and EARN-

INGS columns in the output.. Then, instead of using TOTAL SALES and TOTAL EARNINGS subheadings at the bottom of the report, use the following format:

$$\vdots$$

C. NATION	864.56	86.46
	1834.50	183.45

Finally, process the data within the program loop using FOR . . . NEXT statements.

15. Write a program for the specifications outlined in question 18 at the end of Chapter 12 (page 351).

16. Write a program for the specifications outlined in question 19 at the end of Chapter 12 (page 351).

ANSWERS TO FEEDBACK AND REVIEW SECTIONS

Possible programs for Feedback and Review sections 14-1 through 14-4 follow. Your versions may differ in several ways and still be correct. For example, PRINT statements using various TAB functions, quotation marks, commas, and semicolons can easily be substituted for the PRINT USING statements and image lines presented in the following programs. And, of course, different REM statements and different variable names will cause a difference in appearance without any signficant difference in content.

A possible BASIC program for Feedback and Review 14-1.

```
>LIST
     10 REM *BILLING PROGRAM
     20 REM *
     30 REM *VARIABLE NAMES
     40 REM * N$ NAME
     50 REM * Q   QUANTITY PURCHASED
     60 REM * P   UNIT PRICE
     70 REM * A   NET AMOUNT
     80 REM * T1 TAX
     90 REM * T2 TOTAL AMOUNT
    100 REM *
    110 REM *READ NAME,QUANTITY PURCHASED AND PRICE
    120      READ N$,Q,P
    130 REM *COMPUTE NET AMOUNT
    140      LET A = Q*P
    150 REM *COMPUTE TAX AND TOTAL PRICE
    160      LET T1 = A*.06
    170      LET T2 = A+T1
    180 REM *PRINT NAME,NET AMOUNT,TAX AND TOTAL
    190      PRINT N$
    195      PRINT "NET = ";A;"TAX = ";T1;"TOTAL = ";T2
    210 REM *INPUT DATA
    220      DATA "WYNN D. TOOTS,INC.",5.50,25.00
    230      END
```

Computer listing of the program

```
>RUN
   WYNN D. TOOTS,INC.
   NET =    137.500  TAX =     8.25000  TOTAL =      145.750

       230 HALT
```

Output produced by the computer in response to the system command RUN

```
>LIST
   10 REM *BILLING PROGRAM
   20 REM *
   30 REM *VARIABLE NAMES
   40 REM * N$   NAME
   50 REM * S$   ADDRESS
   60 REM * C$   CITY AND STATE
   70 REM * Q    QUANTITY PURCHASED
   80 REM * P    UNIT PRICE
   90 REM * A    NET AMOUNT
  100 REM * T    TAX
  110 REM * S    TOTAL AMOUNT
  120 REM *
  130 REM *READ NAME,ADDRESS,QUANTITY AND PRICE
  140      READ N$,S$,C$,Q,P
  150 REM *TEST QUANTITY FOR LAST INPUT
  160      IF Q=-99.9 THEN 440
  170 REM *COMPUTE NET AMOUNT,TAX AND TOTAL AMOUNT
  180      LET A = Q*P
  190      LET T = A*.06
  200      LET S = A+T
  210 REM *PRINT NAME,ADDRESS,NET,TAX AND TOTAL
  220      PRINT N$
  230      PRINT S$
  240      PRINT C$
  250      PRINT USING 298, A,T,S
  260      PRINT
  270      PRINT
  280      GO TO 140
  295 REM *FORMAT STATEMENT FOR OUTPUT
  298:    NET = ####.##   TAX = ###.##   TOTAL = ####.##
  300 REM *INPUT DATA
  310      DATA "PIERRE'S RECORD SHOP"
  320      DATA "6453 ORLEANS STREET"
  330      DATA "BOOGIE,LOUISIANA 54321"
  340      DATA  300.0,25.00
  350      DATA "ROCKY COLLEGE STORE"
  360      DATA "1563 BEETHOVEN DRIVE"
  370      DATA "ROCKTOWN,MARYLAND 20765"
  380      DATA  3.25,25.00
  390      DATA "WYNN D.TOOTS,INC."
  400      DATA "120 BROWNING STREET"
  410      DATA "GONG,CALIFORNIA 98765"
  420      DATA 200.0,25.00
  430      DATA "L","L","L",-99.9,0.0
  440      END
```

250   PRINT TAB(3);''NET = '';A;''TAX = '';T;''TOTAL = '';S

then your output spacing might look slightly different, and you might have more or less digits in some of your output values, but that doesn't make your program wrong. In fact, it shows that you're learning this language!

} Computer listing of the program

```
>RUN
PIERRE'S RECORD SHOP
6453 ORLEANS STREET
BOOGIE,LOUISIANA 54321
  NET = 7500.00   TAX = 450.00   TOTAL = 7950.00


ROCKY COLLEGE STORE
1563 BEETHOVEN DRIVE
ROCKTOWN,MARYLAND 20765
  NET =   81.25   TAX =   4.87   TOTAL =   86.12


WYNN D.TOOTS,INC.
120 BROWNING STREET
GONG,CALIFORNIA 98765
  NET = 5000.00   TAX = 300.00   TOTAL = 5300.00


    440 HALT
```

} Output produced by the computer as the program is executed

```
>LIST
     10 REM *SALES COMPENSATION REPORT
     20 REM *
     30 REM *VARIABLE NAMES
     40 REM * N$    NAME
     50 REM * W1-W4 SALES DATA FOR WEEKS 1 TO 4
     60 REM * S     SALES AMOUNT
     70 REM * E     EARNINGS
     80 REM *
     90 REM *PRINT HEADING
    100       PRINT USING 280
    110 REM *READ NAME AND SALES DATA
    120       READ N$,W1,W2,W3,W4
    130 REM *TEST W1 FOR END OF DATA
    140       IF W1=-99.9 THEN 500
    150 REM *COMPUTE SALES AMOUNT
    160       LET S = W1+W2+W3+W4
    170 REM *CALCULATE EARNINGS AS 12 PCT FOR SALES GREATER THAN OR EQUAL
    180 REM *TO 100 AND AS 10 PCT FOR SALES LESS THAN 100
    190       IF S>=100. THEN 220
    200       LET E = S*.10
    210       GO TO 240
    220       LET E = S*.12
    230 REM *PRINT NAME,SALES AMOUNT AND EARNINGS THEN RETURN
    240       PRINT USING 290, N$,S,E
    250       GO TO 120
    270 REM *FORMAT STATEMENTS
    280:NAME                    SALES AMOUNT        EARNINGS
    290:################      ######.##      ######.##
    300 REM *INPUT DATA
    310       DATA "ALFRED E. BOWMAN"
    320       DATA   50.00,  80.00,  33.50, 680.26
    330       DATA "R. GOLDBERG"
    340       DATA    2.00,   4.00,   8.00,  16.00
    450       DATA "C. MACARTHY"
    460       DATA   10.52,  20.36,  15.30,  50.00
    470       DATA "C.NATION"
    480       DATA   35.26,  18.50,  52.30, 758.50
    490       DATA "END OF DATA", -99.9,0.,0.,0.
    500       END
```

Computer listing of the program

```
>RUN
NAME                  SALES AMOUNT       EARNINGS
ALFRED E. BOWMAN         843.76          101.25
R. GOLDBERG              30.00             3.00
C. MACARTHY              96.18             9.62
C.NATION                864.56          103.75

     500 HALT
```

Output produced by the computer as the program is executed

```
>LIST
     10  *SALES COMPENSATION REPORT
     20  REM *
     30  REM *VARIABLE NAMES
     40  REM * N$      NAME
     50  REM * W1-W4 SALES DATA FOR WEEKS 1 TO 4
     60  REM * S       SALES AMOUNT
     70  REM * E       EARNINGS
     80  REM * T       TOTAL SALES
     90  REM * G       TOTAL EARNINGS
    100  REM *
    110  REM *INITIALIZE ACCUMULATOR
    120        LET T = 0.
    130  REM *PRINT HEADING
    140        PRINT USING 340
    150  REM *READ NAME AND SALES DATA
    160        READ N$,W1,W2,W3,W4
    170  REM *TEST W1 FOR END OF DATA
    180        IF W1=-99.9 THEN 280
    190  REM *COMPUTE SALES AMOUNT AND EARNINGS
    200        LET S = W1+W2+W3+W4
    210        LET E = S*.10
    220  REM *ACCUMULATE TOTAL SALES
    230        LET T = T+S
    240  REM *PRINT NAME,SALES AMOUNT AND EARNINGS
    250        PRINT USING 350, N$,S,E
    260        GO TO 160
    270  REM *COMPUTE TOTAL EARNINGS AND PRINT TOTAL SALES AND EARNINGS
    280        LET G = T*.10
    290        PRINT
    300        PRINT USING 360
    310        PRINT USING 370
    320        PRINT USING 380, T,G
    330  REM *FORMAT STATEMENTS
    340:NAME                      SALES AMOUNT        EARNINGS
    350:####################      #######.##         #######.##
    360:                              TOTAL           TOTAL
    370:                              SALES           EARNINGS
    380:                          #######.##         #######.##
    390  REM *INPUT DATA
    400        DATA "ALFRED E. BOWMAN"
    410        DATA  50.00,  80.00,  33.50, 680.26
    420        DATA "R.GOLDBERG"
    430        DATA   2.00,   4.00,   8.00,  16.00
    440        DATA "C. MACARTHY"
    450        DATA  10.52,  20.36,  15.30,  50.00
    460        DATA "C. NATION"
    470        DATA  35.26,  18.50,  52.30, 758.50
    480        DATA "END OF DATA",-99.9,0.,0.,0.
    490        END
```

A possible BASIC program for Feedback and Review 14-4. (Again, remember that this is just one of many programs that will produce essentially the same results.)

Computer listing of the program

```
>RUN
NAME                    SALES AMOUNT        EARNINGS
ALFRED E. BOWMAN            843.76            84.38
R.GOLDBERG                  30.00             3.00
C. MACARTHY                 96.18             9.62
C. NATION                  864.56            86.46

                           TOTAL             TOTAL
                           SALES             EARNINGS
                          1834.50            183.45

    490 HALT
```

Output produced by the computer as the program is executed

Not So Basic Anymore

Basic started out as the "Beginner's All-Purpose Symbolic Instruction Code," but it is no longer necessarily a programming language for the neophyte.

Still simple and easy to learn, Basic has grown dramatically in breadth and depth since its mid-60s introduction as a programming tool for the noncomputer professional in the university time-sharing environment.

Actually, Basic was more of a return to an initial subset of Fortran, defined and contained in an early IBM document, the "Fortran Primer." The important distinction for Basic was not so much formal language and syntax as its introduction for operation in the emerging conversational and interactive timesharing environment. And that's really what simplicity was all about—the convenience of entering a line at a time statement under the power of an on-line edit program and the subsequent execution of that code in an interpretive environment.

Basic was fun and easy to use because of the convenient and simple language facility that operated in a substantially improved and friendlier user environment.

Obvious Choice

While Basic has evolved into many more complex forms and capabilities, these fundamental attributes are still present. That's why it became the obvious first choice in programming facility for the microcomputers entering the personal computing marketplace. Basic has kept up with the times, and the associated language statements, functions and commands not only encompass conventional data processing needs, but also provide capability to control and execute processing related to graphics, color presentation and sound. These latter features are a contribution of the microprocessing industry to the entire computing world.

We take note of how simple and elegant Basic can be. It allows for arithmetic and Boolean operations on both numeric and character strings, and a good slice of typical computing can be accomplished with only seven statement types—namely PRINT, LET, INPUT, IF . . . THEN . . . FOR . . . NEXT and, despite the prejudices of today, the GOTO. What more can the beginner need and want?

The rest of the process can all be automatically provided via easy-to-use keyboards and screen which facilitate:

(*a*) Syntax checking.
(*b*) Edit functions.
(*c*) Statement sequencing.
(*d*) Program execution.

TRS-80 Basic

The spread of Basic capability can readily be seen in one family of language offerings as, for example, the Radio Shack line for the TRS-80 computers.

There are actually four Basic programs offered by the manufacturer of the TRS-80, apart from competing compilers available from independent sources. These systems are Level I and Level II for the Model I computers, an interpretive and compiler version for the Model II line and an advanced system for the Model III.

Level I and II are resident in read-only memory (ROM) as is the Model III Basic. The system for Model II is random-access memory (RAM)-based. Level I includes 26 statements plus a few variants.

On the other hand, Level II Basic operates much faster and with additional I/O facilities to communicate with printers and disks. Level II includes more than 75

Basic programs are available for many purposes. This program is being used to prepare a financial analysis. (Courtesy Radio Shack Division, Tandy Corporation)

commands, statements and functions plus some variants, as well as a richer capability in error detection.

For Models II, III

This brings us to the Model II and Model III Basic. These Basics are further extensions of the Level II language, providing a maximum of upward compatibility from the Model I systems.

The Model II capability adds more than a dozen new commands and is an ongoing, supported system since it is RAM- and not ROM-based.

The main difference in the progression of Basic capability reflected for the TRS-80 family of computers is in the increasing complexity of the environment and, hence, the system. The language extends in order to encompass these enhancements.

Other Improved Versions

But the large market of the TRS-80 has invited competition from independent sources who bring improved Basics to that line. Thus, for example, one supplier provides a compiler version with the additional attributes of faster execution speeds and optimized and relocatable object code, but at the expense of not being interactive in the program development phase. . . .

Typical criticism of Basic has been its slow operation as an interpretive system, the paucity of business-oriented data processing language capability, its lack of file handling and poor string manipulation, absence of a screen orientation and, strangely enough, the ease with which the source code can be understood, which invites loss of code protection. But there are good responses to all of these points with the more complex versions of Basic coming to the marketplace.

There seems to be no end to the increasing power of Basic. For example, a new advanced Basic has arrived on the scene and boasts:

(*a*) Six data types.

(*b*) Local and global variables, functions and procedures.

(*c*) Complete compiler, relocatable code and automatic linking to libraries.

(*d*) Enhanced language statements supportive of nestable, structured programming.

(*e*) Recursively used functions and procedures.

(*f*) Dynamic inclusion of files and library source modules at compile time.

(*g*) Formatted printing.
(*h*) Sequential and random files.
(*i*) Efficient execution capability.
(*j*) Debugging and documentation aids.

Basic compiler building has become a big business. One vendor, Microsoft, boasts the use of its Basic on more than 300,000 microcomputers, performing in a host of operating system environments.

The popularity and ubiquity of Basic is reflected not only in the large number of executable programs, but also in the vast amount of literature. Titles such as *My Computer Likes Me When I Speak in Basic* and *Computer Programming for the Complete Idiot* are just one reflection of the impact of this language.

Basic has been popularized through catalogs such as *The Basic Cookbook* by Ken Tractor and *The Basic Handbook* by David Lien. Lien's book is further described as an encyclopedia of the Basic language covering 250 varia-

tions of statements, functions, operations and commands found in hundreds of dialects or versions of Basic existing today.

Serious texts such as *Problem Solving and Structured Programming in Basic* by Koffman and Friedman and *Foundations of Programming Through Basic* by Moulton are also available.

But most significant, the Basic source language has become the de facto standard for program publishing and exchange in the personal computer marketplace.

It is possible to get lost in the alphabet soup of various Basic implementations. We note the proliferation of everyman's Basic as reflected in such offerings as Basic-80, S-Basic, extended Basic, Business Basic, Basic-Plus, minimal Basic, Ubasic, Mbasic, Cbasic, Power Basic, Tiny Basic, Infinite Basic and on and on. . . .

—Werner L. Frank, "Not So Basic Anymore," *Computerworld,* Mar. 2, 1981, p. 37. Copyright 1981 by CW Communications, Inc., Framingham, Mass.

chapter 15

Operating Systems
Concepts and Functions

INTRODUCING THE BOSS

The mainframe computer in a large savings and loan institution can handle transactions being entered from multiple terminals in multiple branch offices while it also computes the interest rates on thousands of accounts. The computer may not actually do both these tasks at once. Rather, it may be switching from program to program—from task to task—with dazzling speed. Literally portions of seconds are devoted to different programs. The computer performs these tasks and the switching back and forth among tasks under the direction of a manager, or boss, the operating system (OS) supervisor.

Because computers are so fast and because it's inefficient to let expensive number crunchers sit idle, operating systems have been developed to allow computers to run more than one application program at a time. The OS supervisor is not a person despite the "humanness" of the title. The OS supervisor is a master program that performs the overall management tasks of a computer system. That is, the OS supervisor directs the running of all the other programs and functions as the master program of a computer system. Since the computer is so fast, it needs a fast boss.

"Every so often I unplug it just to show it who's boss."

The subject of this chapter is operating systems—a very important software category that hasn't been discussed in the other chapters of this Programming Module. In the first section of the chapter, you'll learn what an operating system is and when and why such systems were developed. You'll then study some of the control functions of an operating system. And in the last section, you'll see how the program call-up capability of an operating system can be used to simplify processing operations.

Thus, after studying this chapter, you should be able to:

- Give a definition of an operating system and tell when and why such systems were developed
- Outline the role of the operating system supervisor, and describe the functions of a job control program
- Discuss overlapped processing and explain the functions performed by channels and buffers
- Explain the difference between multiprogramming and multiprocessing
- Understand why an operating system must be able to handle processing interruptions in a multiprogramming environment
- Explain why operating systems with virtual storage capability have been developed
- Identify the types of programs that can be called up by an operating system in order to simplify processing operations
- Understand and use the key terms and concepts listed at the end of this chapter

AN ORIENTATION TO OPERATING SYSTEMS

In the last two chapters we've been concentrating on computer software that falls into translating and applications categories. In Chapter 13, we saw how *translating programs* such as assemblers, compilers, and interpreters are used to transform the instructions that people write in a convenient language into the machine-language codes required by computers. We also saw in Chapter 13 how *applications programs* written to control the processing of a particular task could either be obtained from outside vendors of applications packages or written specifically to satisfy the possible unique needs of users. Then, in Chapter 14, the focus was exclusively on writing applications programs in the BASIC language.

But if you have an exceptional memory, you'll recall from Chapter 4 that there's a third category of software that we've not yet considered. An **operating system (OS)** is an integrated set of programs that's used to manage the resources and overall operations of a computer system. The OS permits the system to supervise its own operations by automatically calling in the applications programs, translating any other special service programs, and managing the data needed to produce the output desired by users. Thus, as Figure 15-1 indicates, the OS tends to isolate the hardware from the user. The user communicates with the OS, supplies applications programs and input data, and receives output results. But the user is usually not too concerned with the hardware specifics of the system, or with how the OS will direct the hardware to handle certain tasks.

The Development of Operating Systems

The computer systems running under OS control today range in size from small personal computers to the largest mainframes and supercomputers. But it wasn't always that way. It's generally conceded that one of the first elementary operating systems was produced in the early 1950s at the General Motors Research Laboratories for use with an IBM 701 computer. Then, in 1955, programmers at GM and North American Aviation joined forces to write an OS for the IBM 704—one of the most powerful scientific processors of that time.

Many other OSs were produced during the late 1950s and early 1960s by other users, computer manufacturers, and university researchers. These OSs were rather primitive by today's standards. They were limited in use to sequential (batch) processing applications, and they were generally designed to run on only one type of machine. But from these beginnings, systems have evolved to permit direct-access processing in critical real time situations. Modern OSs are designed to operate on entire families of machines.

Beginning in the 1950s (and continuing up to the present time), the general goal of OS developers has been to devise ways to operate a computer with a minimum of idle time and in the most efficient and economical way during the execution of user programs. In pre-OS days, computer operators would go through the same ritual to process each job. The job program and input data would be loaded on input devices, the storage locations in the CPU would be cleared of any data remaining from the previous job, appropriate switches would be set, and the job would run alone in the CPU until it was completed. After completion, the job program, input data, and output results would be unloaded by the operator, and the entire ritual would begin again for the next job.

Because the computer sat idle while the operator loaded and unloaded jobs, a great deal of processing time was lost. The OSs of the late 1950s and early 1960s reduced this idle time by allowing jobs to be stacked up in a waiting line. When one job was finished, system control would branch back to OS software which would automatically perform the housekeeping duties needed to load and run the next job. This automatic job-to-job transition is still one of the major functions performed by a modern OS.

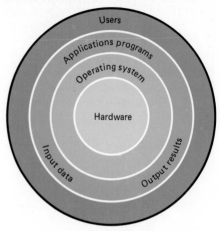

Figure 15-1 An OS is a set of programs that, in a sense, disguises the hardware being used. For example, a popular OS used with personal computers is Digital Research's CP/M. A person who knows how to communicate with CP/M can run CP/M-compatible programs on a number of microcomputers without being concerned about the hardware specifics of the various machines. Likewise, programs written for use with CP/M can usually be run on the systems produced by many different manufacturers whose machines will accept the CP/M operating system.

WHAT IS UNIX?

UNIX is an operating system developed by Dennis Ritchie and Ken Thompson of Bell Laboratories. UNIX is trademarked by Bell Labs and is available under license from Western Electric. Although UNIX is a relatively small operating system, it is quite powerful and general. It has found considerable favor among programming groups, especially in universities, where it is primarily used with DEC computers—various versions of the DEC PDP-11 and the VAX. The operating system and its software are written in a high level programming language called C, and most of the source code and documentation is available on-line. For programmers, UNIX is easy to understand and to modify.

For the nonexpert programmer, the important aspect of UNIX is that it is constructed out of a small, basic set of concepts and programming modules, with a flexible method for interconnecting existing modules to make new functions. All system objects—including all I/O channels—look like files. Thus, it is possible to cause input and output for almost any program to be taken from or to go to files, terminals, or other devices, at any time, without any particular planning on the part of the module writer. UNIX has a hierarchical file structure. Users can add and delete file directories at will and then "position" themselves at different locations in the resulting hierarchy to make it easy to manipulate the files in the neighborhood.

The command interpreter of the operating system interface (called the "shell") can take its input from a file, which means that it is possible to put frequently used sequences of commands into a file and then invoke that file (just by typing its name), thereby executing the command strings. In this way, the user can extend the range of commands that are readily available. Many users end up with a large set of specialized shell command files. Because the shell includes facilities for passing arguments, for iterations, and for conditional operations, these "shell programs" can do quite a lot, essentially calling upon all system resources (including the editors) as subroutines. Many nonprogrammers have discovered that they can write powerful shell programs, thus significantly enhancing the power of the overall system.

By means of a communication channel known as a pipe, the output from one program can easily be directed (piped) to the input of another, allowing a sequence of programming modules to be strung together to do some task that in other systems would have to be done by a special purpose program. UNIX does not provide special purpose programs. Instead, it attempts to provide a set of basic software tools that can be strung together in flexible ways using I/O redirection, pipes, and shell programs. Technically, UNIX is just the operating system. However, because of the way the system has been packaged, many people use the name to include all of the programs that come on the distribution tape. Many people have found it easy to modify the UNIX system and have done so, which has resulted in hordes of variations on various kinds of computers.

—"What Is Unix?" *Datamation*, November 1981, p. 141. Reprinted with permission of *Datamation*® magazine, © Copyright by Technical Publishing Company, a Division of Dun-Donnelley Publishing Corporation, A Dun & Bradstreet Company, 1981. All rights reserved.

A Preview of Operating System Elements

An OS is an integrated set of specialized programs. Each program performs specific tasks. Although there are numerous programs in an OS, most OS elements can be classified as either *control* or *processing* programs.

We've just seen that one of the functions of an OS is to *control input/output housekeeping operations.* By shifting the control of these operations from human operators to specially prepared programs, the earlier OSs reduced operator drudgery. They also cut down on the need for programmers to rewrite certain I/O instructions for each program, provided relatively nonstop operation (operators could load tapes and cards for the next job while the current job was being processed), and therefore speeded up the amount of processing that could be accomplished.

But a modern OS does much more than just control I/O housekeeping activities. *Other sophisticated control programs* are required to keep ever-faster and more powerful hardware occupied. In addition to running batch processing jobs, most medium-sized and larger minis, and virtually all mainframes, are able at the same time to accommodate requests for direct-access processing from a number of online terminals that are simultaneously using the resources of the system. It's up to the OS to determine when the execution of one program stops and another begins.

In addition to control routines, an OS also includes or has access to a number of programs designed to simplify *processing* operations. These programs can reduce the time and expense of program preparation.

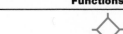

CONTROL PROGRAMS IN AN OPERATING SYSTEM

The Role of the OS Supervisor

The overall management of a computer system is under the control of an OS master program. This master program is referred to by such names as **supervisor, monitor,** or **executive routine.** The supervisor program coordinates all other parts of the OS, and it resides in the primary storage section of the CPU. Other programs in the OS are kept in an online **system residence device** (usually a magnetic disk drive) so that the supervisor can call them up and temporarily store them in the CPU when they are needed. When a specialized OS program is called up for use, the supervisor turns system control over to the specialized program. After the specialized task has been completed, system control branches back to the supervisor. The following discussion of the use of job control programs shows the supervisor's role in maintaining system control.

Job Control Programs

It was noted earlier that providing automatic job-to-job linkages during the processing of applications programs was one of the major functions performed by an OS. These linkages are handled by a job control program. When a number of jobs are to be run in a *batch processing* (or **stacked job**) environment, a deck of **job control cards** may be assembled by the computer operator and placed in a card reader. The job control cards contain statements presented in the codes of a **job control language (JCL).** These coded statements tell the OS such things as the name of the job, the user's name and account number, the I/O devices to use during processing, the assembler or compiler to use if language translation is needed, and so on.

In Figure 15-2a, let's assume that the job control cards for Job 1 have been read, the Job 1 program has been loaded into the CPU from a magnetic disk drive, and the input data stored on a reel of magnetic tape are being processed.

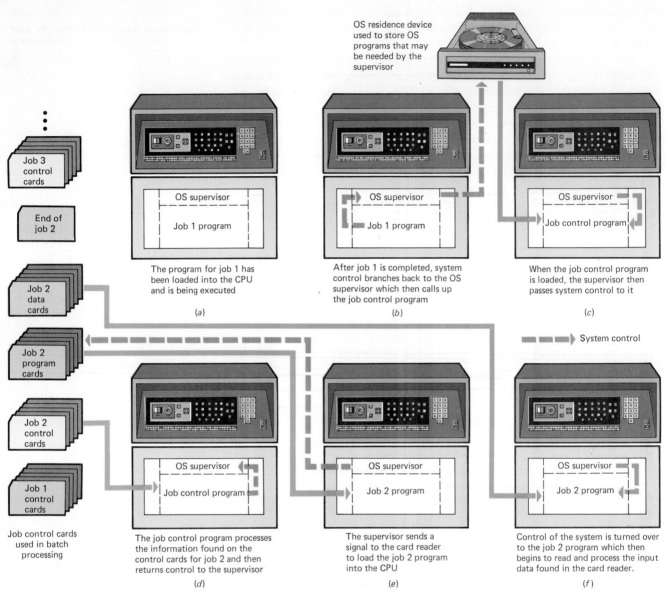

Figure 15-2 The role of the OS supervisor and the job control program in providing job-to-job linkages.

When the processing is completed, system control branches back to the OS supervisor which then sends a signal to the OS residence device to load the **job control program** into the CPU (Figure 15-2b). When this program is loaded, the supervisor branches control to it (Figure 15-2c). The *function of the job control program* is to read and process the special codes written in the JCL that are found on the Job 2 control cards. The job control program then returns control to the supervisor (Figure 15-2d). Since both the program and data for

Job 2 happen to be stacked in the same card reader as the job control cards, the supervisor sends a signal to the card reader to load the Job 2 program into the CPU (Figure 15-2e). After this operation is completed, the supervisor turns system control over to the Job 2 program which then begins to read and process the input data found in the card reader (Figure 15-2f). An end-of-job card placed at the end of the data deck returns control to the supervisor, which calls the job control program, which reads the Job 3 control cards . . . and so it goes.

Other Job/Resource Control Activities

Figure 15-2 showed the CPU processing one job at a time. But since CPUs of almost any size today can process far more data in a second than a single set of I/O devices can supply or receive, it's common to **overlap** processing jobs. When this happens, the OS must be ready to:

☑ Perform *system scheduling* tasks.

☑ Handle *system interruptions*.

☑ *Monitor system status* and supply appropriate messages to people.

System scheduling. Whenever possible, multiple jobs are scheduled to balance I/O and processing requirements. As noted above, this often involves overlapping I/O and processing operations. The channels shown in Figure 15-3 are used to facilitate overlapped processing.

A **channel** consists of hardware that, along with other associated monitoring and connecting elements, controls and provides the path for the movement of data between relatively slow I/O devices and the high-speed CPU. A channel may be a separate, small, special-purpose control computer located near the CPU, or it can be a physical part of the CPU which is accessible to both I/O devices and other CPU elements. Once a channel has received appropriate instruction signals from the OS, it can operate independently and without supervision while the CPU is engaged in performing computations. For example, Figure 15-4 shows that in **time slice** 5 when the CPU is processing the record labeled 2 for Job A, Channel 1 can be accepting another Job A input record, Channel 2 can be receiving processed information from Job A for an output device, Channel 3 can be accepting an input record for Job B, and Channel 4 can be transmitting Job B information to an output device. The OS switches control back and forth between Jobs A and B (and, perhaps, between Jobs C, D, . . .) throughout their execution. You'll notice in Figure 15-4 that the CPU would be idle in time slice 6 if it did not branch to Job B.

In addition to channels, small high-speed storage elements called **buffers** also play an important role in overlapping input, processing, and output operations. Buffers may be located in peripheral devices, or they may be reserved sections of the CPU primary storage. Data from input devices are fed under channel control into an *input buffer.* This input buffer has an important char-

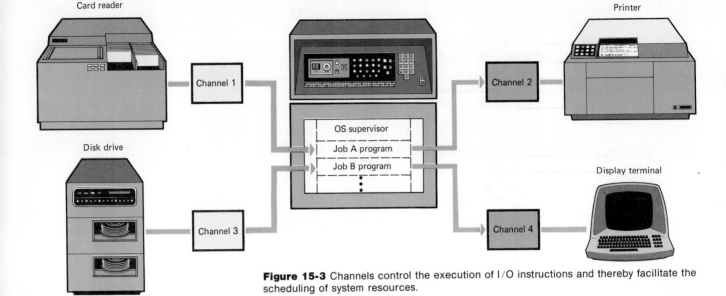

Card reader

Channel 1

Disk drive

Channel 3

OS supervisor

Job A program

Job B program

Channel 2

Printer

Channel 4

Display terminal

Figure 15-3 Channels control the execution of I/O instructions and thereby facilitate the scheduling of system resources.

acteristic: It can accept data at slow input speeds and release them at electronic CPU speeds. (The reverse is true of the *output buffer:* It accepts data from the CPU at electronic speeds and releases them at the slower operating speeds of output devices.) Thus, in Job A in Figure 15-4, the first two time slices are required to read record 1 into the input buffer. Once in the buffer, however, there is virtually *no delay* in releasing record 1 to the CPU for processing in time slice 3. While the first record is being processed, a second record starts to enter the input buffer. As soon as the first record is processed, it's *immediately* transferred under channel control to the output buffer. Two more time slices are then required before the output device can complete the writing operation.

Figure 15-4 The OS uses channels to balance system input, output, and processing capabilities.

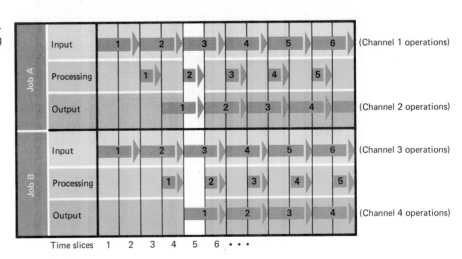

Job A
Input	1	2	3	4	5	6	(Channel 1 operations)
Processing	1	2	3	4	5		
Output	1	2	3	4		(Channel 2 operations)

Job B
Input	1	2	3	4	5	6	(Channel 3 operations)
Processing	1	2	3	4	5		
Output	1	2	3	4		(Channel 4 operations)

Time slices   1   2   3   4   5   6 • • •

450

But during this time (see slices 4 and 5), the CPU processed a Job B record and another Job A record.

Multiprogramming is the name given to what we've been examining in Figure 15-4. It is the *interleaved* execution of two or more different and independent programs by the same computer. Notice, however, that multiprogramming is *not* defined to be the execution of instructions from several programs at the *same instant* in time. Rather, it *does* mean that there are a number of programs available to the CPU and that a portion of one is executed, then a segment of another, and so on. As we've seen, the OS switches control from one program to another almost instantly. The CPU can thus keep busy while channels and buffers are occupied with the job of bringing in data and writing out information. If a number of programs are being processed, the OS may allocate only a small amount of time—say 150 milliseconds per second—to each program being executed. Fifteen-hundredths of a second may not seem like much time to you, but that's enough to calculate the amounts owed to hundreds of employees for a given pay period. The result of such speed is that those whose programs are being processed may feel that they have the undivided attention of the computer. In some multiprogramming systems, only a *fixed* number of jobs can be processed concurrently (multiprogramming with a fixed number of tasks or MFT), while in others the number of jobs can *vary* (multiprogramming with a variable number of tasks or MVT).

Multiprocessing is the term used to describe a processing approach in which two or more independent CPUs are linked together in a coordinated system. In such a system, instructions from different and independent programs can be processed at the same instant in time by different CPUs. Or the CPUs may simultaneously execute different instructions from the same program. Again, it's the job of the OS to schedule and balance the input, output, and processing capabilities of these systems. This is no easy task! In fact, in distributed data processing networks with multiple processors, small CPUs called *front-end processors* are often dedicated to the single function of scheduling and controlling all work entering the system from remote terminals and other input devices. The front-end processor(s) thus permit one or more larger *host computers* to devote their time to processing large and complex applications programs. (If you've read Chapter 9, you already know about distributed data processing networks and front-end processors.)

The larger CPUs in a multiprocessing system may have separate primary storage sections, they may share a common primary storage unit, or they may have access to both separate and common memories. A common OS may control all or part of the operations of each CPU. Each CPU may be dedicated to specific types of applications. For example, one can process direct-access jobs while another is concentrating on batch applications. However, it's common for one CPU to be able to take over the workload of another malfunctioning machine until repairs are made.

As you would expect, scheduling and coordinating the input/processing/output activities of multiple CPUs requires a very sophisticated OS. In fact, the largest OSs need a primary storage size of between 4 and 6 million bytes before they can get out of their own way and allow the system to produce useful work for users.

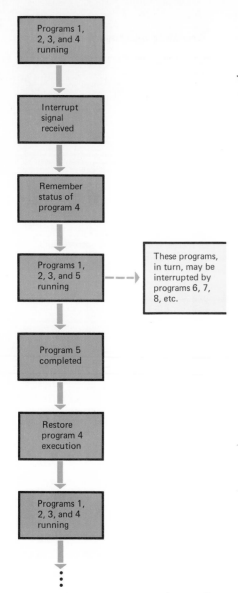

Programs 1, 2, 3, and 4 running

↓

Interrupt signal received

↓

Remember status of program 4

↓

Programs 1, 2, 3, and 5 running - - -→ These programs, in turn, may be interrupted by programs 6, 7, 8, etc.

↓

Program 5 completed

↓

Restore program 4 execution

↓

Programs 1, 2, 3, and 4 running

⋮

Figure 15-5 Handling system interruptions is a function of the OS.

Handling system interruptions. Priorities are typically assigned to the programs in a multiprogramming system. A high priority is given to the programs used in direct-access processing that manipulate data and respond to inquiries coming from people at online terminals. A lower priority is assigned to batch processing programs that don't require such quick response. Thus, it often happens that a high-priority program will interrupt the processing of a lower-priority program. When a **program interrupt** occurs, the OS must see to it that the data, instructions, and intermediate processing results of the interrupted program are kept separate from any other job. The storage *partitions* reserved for each job must be properly handled, shifted, and protected. After the higher-priority program(s) have been processed, the OS must restore the interrupted program and continue with its processing (Figure 15-5).

In addition to protecting and restoring interrupted low-priority programs, the OS in many installations is also able to partition the programs being executed into primary and online secondary storage portions. This is an important capability. For many years, the size of an application program was effectively limited by the size of the computer's primary storage section. This was because the complete program was held in primary storage during its entire execution. If the program size didn't exceed the limited primary storage capacity, then there was no problem. But if, on the other hand, the task required thousands of instructions, then the programmer might be forced to find ways to trim the program or to divide it into separate jobs. This can be a tedious and time-consuming chore.

To avoid this situation, OSs with **virtual storage** capability have been developed. The basic approach is to divide total programs into small sequences of instructions called either **pages** or **segments.** Then, only those program pages or segments that are actually required at a particular time in the processing need be in the primary (or *real*) storage. The remaining pages or segments may be kept temporarily in online (or *virtual*) storage, from where they can be rapidly retrieved as needed following a program interruption (see Figure 15-6). The OS handles the swapping of program pages or segments between primary and online secondary storage units. Thus, from the applications programmer's point of view, the effective (or "virtual") size of the available primary storage may appear to be unlimited.

Monitoring system status. The OS constantly monitors the status of the computer system during processing operations. It directs the computer to type messages on an operator's terminal when I/O devices need attention, when errors occur in the job stream, or when other abnormal conditions arise. When an error in a job is detected, however, the computer usually doesn't stop and wait for the operator to take appropriate action. Rather, the message is printed and control passes on to the next job without delay.

The OS also keeps a log of the jobs that have been run. These jobs are clocked in and out of the system. The elapsed time required to compile and/or run programs may be recorded and printed. The security of the system may also be monitored. The attempt to use unauthorized passwords from online terminals may be noted. And messages may be printed if suspicious activity is occurring at one or more terminal sites.

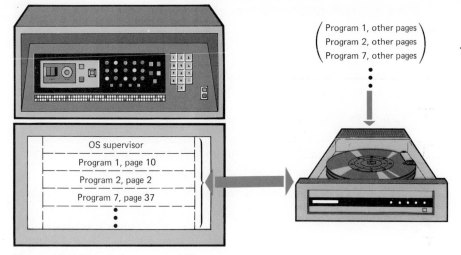

Figure 15-6 Virtual storage capability.

PROCESSING PROGRAMS IN AN OPERATING SYSTEM

The **program call-up capability** of an OS gives it access to a number of programs that can simplify processing operations. Translating programs, utility (or service) programs, and library programs are examples of OS-controlled software that can reduce the time and expense of preparing applications programs. As we saw in Chapter 13, and in Figure 13-3, page 366, translating programs such as assemblers and compilers are read into the CPU where they are used to facilitate program preparation. What wasn't mentioned in Chapter 13, however, is that the translating program (for COBOL, FORTRAN, etc.) is usually called up from a direct-access storage device only after the job control program of the OS interprets a job control statement and informs the OS supervisor of what's needed.

Utility (service) programs are generally supplied by the computer manufacturer, and are also available for call-up by the OS. These routines perform needed services such as sorting records into a particular sequence for processing, merging several sorted files into a single large updated file, or transferring data from one I/O device to another. Job control statements again tell the OS supervisor which utility programs are needed.

A library of frequently used subroutines supplied by users and computer vendors can also be stored on a direct-access device. These tested **library programs** are stored in a machine language form. They are then called up by the OS whenever they are required in the processing of other programs. This eliminates the need for a programmer to rewrite these modules every time they are used. A **librarian program** controls the storage and use of the programs in the system library. The "librarian" maintains a program directory. It also spells out the procedures used to add and delete programs from the library.

**Feedback and
Review 15-1**

The purpose and functions of computer operating systems have been discussed in this chapter. To test and reinforce your understanding of the chapter material, answer the following true-false questions by placing a T or F in the space provided.

___T___ **1.** An operating system is an integrated set of programs that's used to manage the resources and overall operations of a computer system.

___T___ **2.** An OS tends to isolate the hardware from the user.

___F___ **3.** An operating system was first developed for the ENIAC in 1945.

___F___ **4.** The first operating system was produced by IBM for multiprogramming applications.

___F___ **5.** A modern OS is restricted to running on a single machine model.

___T___ **6.** A goal of OS developers is to devise ways to operate a computer with a minimum of idle time.

___F___ **7.** Automatic job-to-job transitions were performed by early OSs, but are no longer needed in a modern system.

___T___ **8.** Most OS elements can be classified as either control or processing programs.

___F___ **9.** The overall management of a computer system is under the control of an OS master program called the Job Controller.

___T___ **10.** The OS supervisor resides in primary storage while other OS programs are kept in an online system residence device.

___T___ **11.** Job control cards contain information presented in the codes of a job control language.

___T___ **12.** The OS supervisor calls up a job control program to read and process the special codes written in a job control statement.

___T___ **13.** Whenever possible, jobs to be processed are scheduled to balance I/O and processing requirements.

___F___ **14.** A channel is always located in the CPU.

___F___ **15.** Only one channel is needed for multiprogramming systems.

___T___ **16.** Small high-speed storage elements called buffers play a role in overlapping input, processing, and output operations.

___F___ **17.** Multiprogramming is defined to mean the execution of instructions from several programs at the same instant in time.

___T___ **18.** A multiprocessing system can execute instructions from several programs at the same instant in time.

___F___ **19.** In a multiprogramming system, a higher priority is assigned to batch processing than to direct-access processing.

___F___ **20.** The OS isn't concerned with system interruptions.

___T___ **21.** The effective size of the primary storage available for programs may appear to be unlimited when virtual storage concepts are used.

___T___ **22.** The program call-up capability of an OS gives it access to programs that can simplify processing.

1. An operating system (OS) is an integrated set of programs that's used to manage the resources and overall operations of a computer system. Users communicate with an OS, supply input data and applications programs, and receive output results.

2. Operating systems were developed in the mid-1950s to reduce CPU waiting time between jobs. An automatic job-to-job transition procedure was devised then, and this is still one of the major functions performed by a modern OS. Other activities carried out by an OS can generally be placed in control or processing categories.

3. The OS supervisor controls and coordinates all other parts of the OS, and it resides in primary storage. Other programs in the OS are kept in an online system residence device so that the supervisor can retrieve them when they are needed.

4. In a batch processing (stacked job) environment, a deck of job control cards may be placed in a card reader. These cards contain statements telling the OS the name of the job, the I/O devices to use, etc. The statements are presented in the codes of a job control language. A job control program in the OS is then used to read and execute these codes.

5. Since all but the smallest of today's CPUs can usually process far more data in a second than a single set of I/O devices can supply or receive, it's a common practice now to overlap processing jobs. Whenever possible, multiple jobs are scheduled to balance I/O and processing requirements. Channels and buffers facilitate the overlapping of processing tasks.

6. Multiprogramming is the interleaved or concurrent execution of two or more different and independent programs by the same computer. Multiprocessing describes a system in which two or more CPUs are linked together in a coordinated way. Instructions from two or more programs can be processed at the same instant in time in a multiprocessing system, but not in a multiprogramming environment. Sophisticated OS software is needed to manage such systems.

7. Priorities are typically assigned to the programs in a multiprogramming system. When a high-priority program interrupts the processing of a lower-priority program, the OS must see to it that the data, instructions, and intermediate processing results of the interrupted program are kept separate from other jobs. The execution of the interrupted program must then be restored at a later time.

8. A computer with virtual storage capability keeps active program pages or segments in primary storage and assigns other program parts to an online storage device. The OS handles the swapping of program pages between primary and online secondary storage units as needed.

9. The program call-up capability of an OS gives it access to a number of translating programs, utility programs, and library programs that can be used to simplify processing operations.

KEY TERMS AND CONCEPTS

You should now be able to define and use the following terms and concepts (the numbers shown indicate the pages where the terms and concepts are first mentioned):

operating system (OS) 444
OS supervisor, monitor, or executive
 routine 447
system residence device 447
stacked job processing 447
job control cards 447
job control language (JCL) 447

job control program 448
overlapped processing 449
channel 449
time slice 449
buffers 449
multiprogramming 451
multiprocessing 451

program interrupt 452
virtual storage 452
program pages or segments 452
program call-up capability 453
utility (service) programs 453
library programs 453
librarian program 453

TOPICS FOR REVIEW AND DISCUSSION

1. (*a*) What's an operating system? (*b*) When were operating systems developed? (*c*) Why were they developed?

2. "The OS tends to isolate the hardware from the user." Discuss this comment.

3. (*a*) Into what two categories can most OS programs be classified? (*b*) Give an example of an OS program from each category.

4. Explain the role of the OS supervisor.

5. Discuss how job control cards, a job control language, and a job control program are used to provide job-to-job linkages in a batch (stacked job) environment.

6. (*a*) How are channels used to facilitate overlapped processing? (*b*) How are buffers used?

7. (*a*) What is multiprogramming? (*b*) What is multiprocessing?

8. Why must an OS be prepared to handle system interruptions in a multiprogramming environment?

9. (*a*) What is virtual storage? (*b*) Why was it developed?

10. How can the program call-up capability of an OS be used to simplify processing operations?

ANSWERS TO FEEDBACK AND REVIEW SECTION

15-1

1. T	6. T	11. T	16. T	21. T
2. T	7. F	12. T	17. F	22. T
3. F	8. T	13. T	18. T	
4. F	9. F	14. F	19. F	
5. F	10. T	15. F	20. F	

An Operating System at Work

Moving products out the plant door on time while order volume is rapidly rising poses a manufacturing challenge.

The challenge is tougher when most orders must be customized to exacting specifications and all require carefully integrated job steps performed at any of dozens of plant work centers. And the problem takes on added dimensions when the typical customer order takes months to complete using costly, sophisticated facilities that are not readily expandable.

Xtek, Inc., a Cincinnati-based manufacturer of specialized parts and equipment, faced this type of challenge and found a solution. A computerized Capacity Planning and Operations Sequencing system now enables the company to better utilize available facilities and manpower and to produce more without undue cost increases. In-process inventory levels are lower and so are lost labor and idle machine times. Production scheduling is more flexible and responsive to changing priorities. On-time percentages are higher and promised delivery dates are more realistic.

"The new system gives us a vastly improved manufacturing planning and control tool that is solving many production-related problems and bringing important advantages to virtually every aspect of our plant operation," says Sanford Brooks, Xtek's board chairman.

With an average of over 5,000 work orders out on the shop floor at any given time, and with the average order calling for 16 separate job operations, the production scheduling and control problem at Xtek is unusually severe. The Capacity Planning and Operations Sequencing System (CAPOSS) was implemented to ease the problem by balancing workloads and permitting better utilization of available plant resources.

An IBM Program Product, CAPOSS runs on Xtek's System/370 Model 125 computer. It works with open-order and work-in-process record files to schedule production against order delivery dates, load the plant's nearly 200 work centers against capacity, prevent bottlenecks stemming from materials shortages or machine breakdowns, and reduce labor lost to broken setups, lost items or idle time.

The system, company officials say, offers exceptional scheduling flexibility, something that the former manual system lacked.

This scheduling flexibility is a prime contribution of CAPOSS, in the view of John Hentz, production control supervisor. "The system takes the actual situation into account—new orders, order changes, rework buildups, machine downtimes, manpower shortages, whatever—and then reflects needed schedule changes through the entire plant operation. As a result, we can keep the work moving on a priority basis with the right jobs in process in the right sequence at the right work centers at the right times."

CAPOSS takes over after incoming customer orders are entered, needed materials are purchased and the materials arrive on the plant premises. Inputs to the system are work projects to be scheduled, including new orders, change orders and deletions, priority and due date changes, plus any short-term capacity changes, queue time or move-time alterations.

The system's short-range objective, which involves daily operations sequencing, is to meet targeted order ship dates while minimizing the duration of the work steps that are necessary to complete the order. The former keeps work centers busy and work flowing smoothly; the latter helps to reduce the capital invested in work-in-process.

—"Balancing Workloads and Resources," *Data Processor*, September 1979, pp. 12, 14. Courtesy IBM.

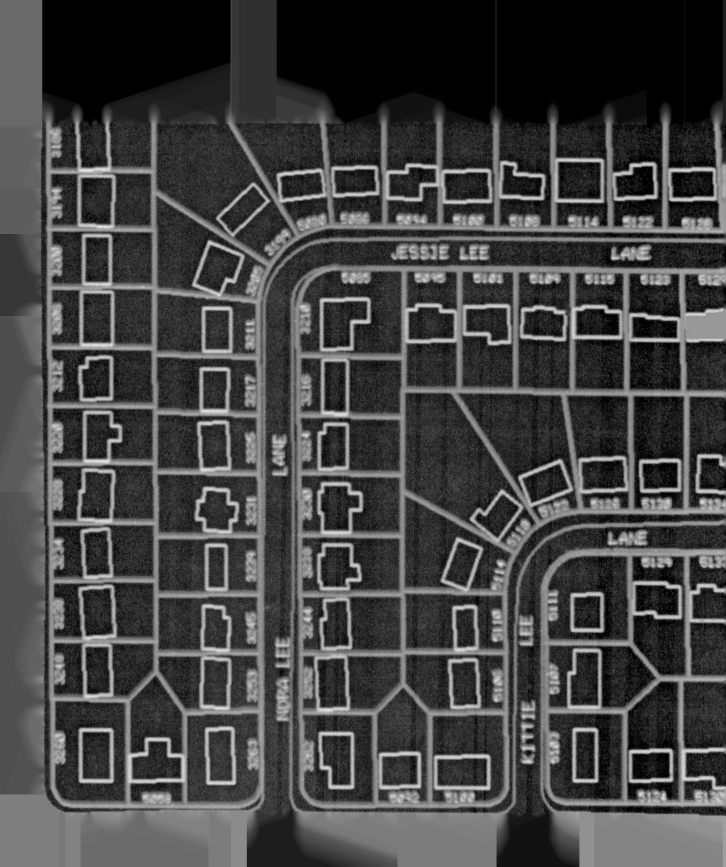

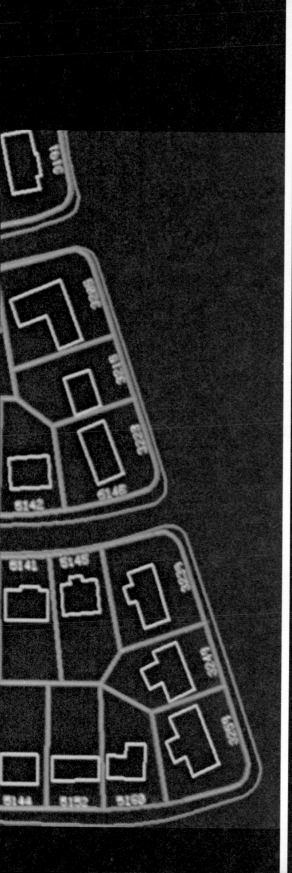

Information Systems Concepts

You saw back in Chapter 3 that before computers can do any useful work, people must complete a series of steps in a system study. Several of these steps involve the programming function and are presented in the Programming Module. The remaining steps, involving problem definition and the analysis, design, and implementation of a system, are considered in this Systems Module. Management information systems concepts are also included here. The social impact of computers at work is the focus of Module 5.

The chapters included in the Systems Module are:

16. System Analysis, Design, and Implementation Considerations
17. System File and Processing Alternatives
18. Management Information Systems

Town planning via computer graphics. This is just one facet of an information system that would be developed for successful urban planning. (Courtesy Intergraph Corporation)

chapter 16

System Analysis, Design, and Implementation Considerations

WHAT USERS WANT

In the United States there's a birth every 9 seconds. A death every 17 seconds. And every 5 minutes, the start of a crisis meeting to hash out some company's data processing problems—at least that's what Jack L. Hancock wagers.

After nearly thirty years in data processing, much of the time "darting heroically from crisis to crisis" during a twenty-six-year career with the Army, Hancock maintains that at systems implementation time, the central issue is always the same, regardless of the company or organization: "Users say the systems design people didn't program what they [the users] wanted. Data processing says, 'We've given you exactly what you wanted—but now those requirements are no longer valid.' The result: failure of data processing to meet users' needs." The reason, according to Hancock: when it comes to dp and communications systems planning, traditional business rules simply cannot work.

Currently senior vice president and head of Chemical Bank of New York's Information Services Group, Hancock, who is fifty, is responsible for programming and implementing the bank's dp and communications systems.

"Conventional wisdom makes us fool ourselves into thinking the user knows what his requirements are," he notes. "But, in fact, he can't know his requirements in detail because usually he's dealing with an area in which he's had limited experience. He knows generally what he wants; but you can't program something general—a program must be specific." Often, the upshot is a succession of post-imple-

System analysis occurs after a problem has been defined. A study team works closely together to gather and analyze data about the current system and then to design new system specifications. (Courtesy Honeywell, Inc.)

mentation enhancements and improvements requested by users. These may cost up to 80 percent of the total systems design effort.

So, Hancock ponders: "Is something inherently wrong with the design process, something that can be corrected, or are we damned to continue an almost contentious relationship between users and dp staffs?" Searching for an answer, he recognizes that a major part of the problem can be traced to a wall that divides the two groups, one which both groups have helped to build. "Dp people," he concedes, "have attempted to protect their turf with terminology and jargon that isn't understandable. They've tried to create a mystique, and users have become very disenchanted, assigning much of the blame for problems to the dp people."

Hancock, who joined Chemical Bank in 1977 after retiring from the Army with the rank of Major General, proposes two techniques for untying the dp design knot and achieving an ongoing dialogue between users and dp teams. The techniques are: (1) simulation, in which a computer estimates the impact on operations should a given series of actions be taken, and (2) software breadboarding, whereby dp and users work together to develop "quick and dirty" throwaway programs that can be used to validate the concepts on which the final system will be based—before any so-called hard programming takes place.

These methods allow users to express their views and work in cooperation with dp personnel to arrive at the optimum satisfactory system, Hancock says. "The conventional way of doing things is for data processing to complete a project and *then* find out it doesn't fit the user. But if we can get interaction between the two groups, they can work it out together from the start."

The barest outline of the material presented in this chapter was first presented in Chapter 3. Our purpose here is to flesh out that outline and give
you more information about the system study steps that people follow to put
computers to work. Before considering system study details, we'll look at the
reasons for system changes and the human resistance that such changes
may produce. We'll then look at each of the early steps in the system study
beginning with problem definition, and then moving to system analysis and
system design. Finally, we'll look at some of the considerations that may be
involved in implementing a new system.

Thus, after studying this chapter, you should be able to:

▍ Explain the reasons for change and why people are likely to resist information systems change

▍ Outline the procedures that may be followed during the problem definition step

▍ Describe how data are gathered and then analyzed during the system
analysis step

▍ Discuss some issues that may affect system design choices

▍ Summarize the types of system specifications produced during the
design step

▍ Discuss factors to be considered in acquiring new equipment

▍ Outline some of the general system implementation activities required
to replace an old system with a new one

▍ Understand and use the key terms and concepts listed at the end of
this chapter

SYSTEM CHANGES: REASONS AND RESISTANCE

People constantly face change. Opportunities come and go. Problems arise
and must be solved. In organizations in general, and in businesses in particular, people must respond daily to changing conditions.

Reasons for Change

Although there are countless specific reasons for the changes that occur in
organizations, many of these changes can be traced to the following interrelated **system change factors**:

1. *Technological factors.* The ancient Greeks had several dreams. One of
   these was the Promethean dream of stealing fire from the gods. Another was the dream of soaring away from Earth and beyond the

planets. After remaining unrealized for thousands of years, both dreams have been achieved in just the last few decades. The fires of atomic furnaces have been ignited, and people and their machines have moved out into space. People have never before lived in a time when the scope of scientific inquiry was so broad, or when the speed of applying new discoveries was so swift. The application of new technology accounts for many changes in organizations.

2. **_Social and economic factors._** A wave of social and economic changes often follows in the wake of new technology. New opportunities may arise in a business to improve on a production process or to do something that was previously not possible. Changes in the ways individuals are organized into groups may then be necessary, and new groups may compete for economic resources with established units. The effects of applying or failing to apply new technology can change the relationships that exist between a business and its competitors, customers, suppliers, and governmental regulatory agencies.

3. **_High-level decisions and operating pressures._** In response to technological, social, and economic factors, top-level managers may decide to reorganize operations, build a new plant, and introduce new products. Or they may implement new budgeting procedures to help bring operating problems under control. And lower-level managers of operating departments (e.g., accounting, inventory control, marketing, and production departments) often initiate changes in order to gain recognition and receive tangible and intangible rewards.

Regardless of the reason, however, frequent changes create conditions or problems that managers and other people must deal with.

Coping With Change

Business managers today face stiff competitive pressures. They must often respond to these pressures with decisions about: (*a*) new and existing products, (*b*) product prices and distribution channels, and (*c*) financing the necessary resources. In addition, they must consider the effects of their decisions on social groups, existing production systems, and human skills and feelings. To make the necessary decisions, managers and other decision makers need information of the highest possible quality. Thus, they are often motivated to seek new computer-based applications or to modify existing information systems in order to cope with changing conditions.

As we saw in Chapter 3, information users, systems analysts, programmers, and other data processing specialists must work together to complete a series of six steps in a system study. Only after these steps, shown in Figure 16-1, have been completed can the computer be used to produce the desired results. We'll examine the first three steps along with some system implemen-

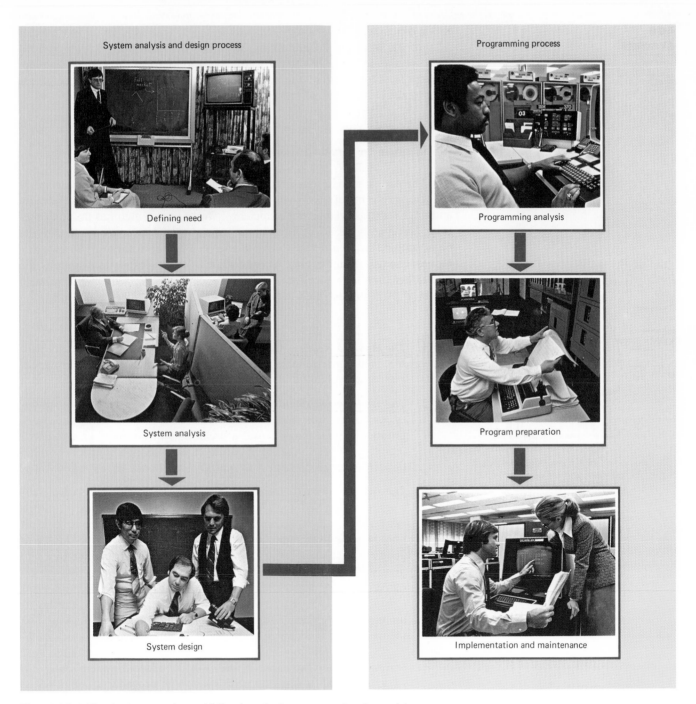

System analysis and design process

Defining need

System analysis

System design

Programming process

Programming analysis

Program preparation

Implementation and maintenance

Figure 16-1 The six steps people must follow in order to use computers for useful purposes may be classified into system analysis/design and programming stages. The chapters in this module deal with the three steps in the system analysis/design stage. Details of the programming process are presented in Module 3. (Photos courtesy Western Electric; Honeywell, Inc.; TRW, Inc.; General Electric Information Systems Company; Edith G. Haun/Stock, Boston; and Control Data Corporation)

tation concepts in this chapter. (Steps 4 and 5 are treated in detail in Chapters 12 through 14 of the Programming Module.) Before turning to step 1, however, we should consider a topic that's too important to the system development process to postpone: the natural **resistance to system change** that people often feel.

Resistance to System Change

The people who initiate information system changes often rush forward in the reasonable belief that such changes will increase employee productivity and improve the organization's efficiency. What they sometimes fail to appreciate, however, is the effects their proposed changes may have on others in the organization. In their desire to create and be a leader in the use of new techniques, change initiators may ignore the fact that resistance to change is the rule rather than the exception, and that the changes they seek may appear to others to be a threat—a threat that may take one or more of the following paths:

1. *The threat to security.* Computers have a reputation for replacing people. Thus, there's the understandable fear of loss of employment and/or of reduction in salary.

2. *The reduction in social satisfaction.* The introduction of a computer system often calls for a reorganization of departments and work groups. When change causes a breaking up of friendly groups and a realigning of personnel, it may also cause a reduction in job satisfaction. Resistance to such a proposed change may be expected.

3. *The reduction in self-esteem and reputation.* People need to feel self-confident. But self-confidence may be shaken by the lack of knowledge about and experience with a computer system. The equipment may be strange to them, and they may fear that they'll be unable to acquire the skills necessary to work with it. In short, their self-esteem may suffer as a result of the change, and so the change may be resisted. Fear of loss of status and/or prestige is also an important reason for resistance by both managers and employees. Department managers, for example, may oppose a change because to admit that the change is needed may imply that they have tolerated inefficiency—an admission that can hardly enhance their reputations. And employees knowledgeable in the ways of the old system may also suffer a loss of prestige because when new procedures are installed they may no longer be looked to for information.

People resist change in different ways. At one extreme, they may temporarily feel threatened by a change, but after a brief adjustment period they resume their previous behavior. At the other extreme, reaction may result in

"The computer says it recorded our Christmas party last week and will consider selling the tapes at very reasonable prices."

Canevari

open opposition and even destruction. Between these extremes are a number of other symptoms including:

- *Withholding facts.* People sometimes withhold facts about current operations during the system study.

- *Providing inaccurate facts.* Data containing known inaccuracies may be submitted during the system study.

- *Showing lowered morale.* Sloppy effort and an attitude of indifference may be observed.

As noted in Chapter 3, people are responsible for successfully putting the computer to work. But resistant employees and managers have also been able to scuttle a number of computer system efforts in the past. The best problem definition, and the use of the most effective analysis and design techniques may not help much if users and other interested people resist a change and don't want it to succeed. Remember as you read the following pages that managing change is a difficult task. Those who conduct the system study are inviting failure if they become so preoccupied with system problems of a technical nature that they ignore the human factors involved in the transition. To reduce their chances of failure, change initiators should:

1. ***Keep people informed.*** Information relating to the effects of the change on their jobs should be periodically presented to people at all levels. Topics discussed should include loss of jobs, transfers, the extent of necessary retraining, the reasons for (and the benefits of) the change, the effect on various departments, and what is being done to alleviate employee hardships.

2. ***Seek employee participation.*** People are more likely to support and accept changes that they've had a hand in creating. The participation of knowledgeable people yields valuable information during the system study. Participation also helps these people satisfy ego and self-fulfillment needs, gives them some degree of control over the change and thus contributes to a greater feeling of security, and removes their fear of the unknown. Of course, people asked to participate must be respected and treated with dignity, and their suggestions must be carefully considered.

PROBLEM DEFINITION

Problem definition is the first and perhaps the most important step in the system study. After all, people must recognize that a need or problem exists before they can create a solution. A clear and accurate problem definition—one that's not open to misinterpretation by people with different backgrounds—isn't easy to prepare. But since it's the foundation for all the system study steps that follow, such a definition must be created.

The Problem Definition Survey

A preliminary **problem definition survey** is often conducted to identify the problem or need. There's certainly nothing new about such surveys. In the Bible in chapter 13 of the Book of Numbers, Moses sent out a team to survey the Promised Land and report back their findings. Three important prerequisite principles were observed in this early survey:

1. *The survey had support at the highest levels.* God told Moses: "Send men to spy out the land of Canaan . . . from each tribe of their fathers shall you send a man, every one a leader among them." Moses certainly had support at the highest level! Although requests for system changes or additions may originate from many sources, top-level management support is important to the success of the change effort.

2. *The survey team consisted of highly respected people.* Only tribal leaders were sent on the mission. Members of the team seeking to define the problem should also be qualified people selected for the offsetting talents they can bring to the job. At least one member (and very possibly the leader of the survey team) represents the interests of the end users of any new system that will be developed. Another member should be familiar with system development and the technical side of data processing. An auditor may also be included to evaluate the effects of any proposed changes on existing data integrity and system security controls.

3. *The scope and objectives of the survey were clearly stated.* Moses specifically told his team to investigate the richness of the land and the strength of the occupants. In a problem definition survey, the nature of the operation(s) that is (are) to be investigated, and the objectives that are to be pursued, should be specifically stated. The organizational units that are to be included should also be identified.

The biblical survey team returned to Moses after 40 days. The team members agreed on the richness of the land, but not on the strength of the occupants. Sessions were held to present the differing viewpoints. It's also usually necessary for the problem definition team to hold preliminary sessions with those who are likely to be affected by any changes. These **requirements sessions** allow people to participate in setting or revising specific system goals. Such participation, as we've seen, allows those who are most familiar with existing methods to make suggestions for improvement and to personally benefit from the change.

A repeating (or iterative) process may be necessary before the problem definition step is completed. There's no definite procedure to be followed before detailed system analysis can begin. A top executive may believe that informational deficiencies exist. He or she may prepare a general statement of objectives and then appoint a manager to conduct a survey. A number of requirements sessions may be held to translate general desires into more specific goals. The scope of the survey may be enlarged or reduced, and objectives may also change as facts are gathered. When it appears that approval has been reached on the problem definition, the survey team should put the detailed definition *in writing* and send it to all concerned for written approval. If differences remain, they should be resolved in additional requirements sessions. There are those who may become impatient with the "delays" in system development caused by these additional sessions. But wiser heads know that the really lengthy and expensive delays occur when users discover very late in the development process that the designed system is unsatisfactory because of earlier requirements oversights (see Figure 16-2).

The System Study Charter

As a final act before the detailed system analysis step begins, the survey leader should prepare a *written charter* for approval by the executive or steering committee in charge of the overall data processing program. This **system study charter** should include:

▋ A detailed statement of the scope and objectives of the system study.

▋ A list of those who should be assigned to the system study team.

▋ A grant of authority to permit this team to use some of the working time of specified individuals.

▋ A development schedule giving a target date for the completion of the study, and interim "checkpoint" dates for the presentation of progress reports to interested parties. (These progress reports give users, managers, and auditors a chance to determine the accuracy and completeness of the study effort.)

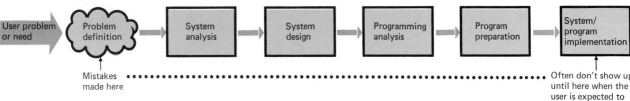

Figure 16-2 The cost of correcting an oversight in problem definition can mushroom later in the process. It's estimated that an oversight that's not detected until the implementation stage can cost 10 to 100 times more to fix than one that's found during the definition step.

SYSTEM ANALYSIS

Since most new business systems are based to some extent on existing procedures, a first step for the study team analysts is often to gather data on current operations. In short, they must find out where they are before they can figure out where they want to go.

Data Gathering

It's likely that preliminary facts were gathered during the problem definition step. But more details are now needed to determine the strengths and weaknesses of current procedures. The data to be collected will vary, of course, from one study to another. But in most cases the study team members should answer the following general questions about current operations:

1. *What output results are currently being achieved?* The content, purpose, and use of reports and other output results should be determined, and the accuracy and timeliness of the output should be checked.

2. *What processing procedures and resources are being used to produce this output?* The records and files being processed, the frequency, volume, and accuracy of this processing, the sequence of steps being followed, the people and departments doing the work, the processing and storage equipment being used, the cost of the processing—these and other matters should be checked.

3. *What input data are used to produce output results?* The source, form, and volume of input data should be understood. The frequency of input, the accuracy of the input, and the input cost should also be known.

You recognize that these questions refer to the input/processing/output components found in any data processing system. But the input to output sequence is often reversed during system analysis because the analysts need an early understanding of current output before they can properly separate and analyze the processing and input functions that are relevant to the output.

Data-Gathering Aids. The following tools and techniques are often used during data-gathering operations:

   Organization charts and organization standards. An **organization chart** indicates by position titles the formal place in the organization of each job. Such a chart can give analysts a better picture of the people and departments that may be affected by expected changes. Some organizations have developed **standards manuals** that spell out the steps to be completed during (and after) the data-gathering phase. These manuals

HIGH PRODUCTIVITY HINGES ON END-USER EDUCATION

Effective training of nontechnical end users has become indispensable to high information systems productivity, according to Vicki McConnell, head of a Palos Verdes, Calif.-based consulting firm.

A business can install the most advanced hardware and software in the world, but unless its end users know how to apply that technology effectively, the company's productivity will still lag badly, McConnell warned.

"Just because you can produce a report doesn't mean anyone will know how that report should be used," McConnell told attendees at the 1981 Data Processing Management Association (DPMA) conference [in San Francisco].

McConnell, who serves as president of The McConnell Group, characterized training as one of the computing field's most crucial but woefully neglected expense items. Of the estimated $500 billion spent each year for information processing, only about .5% is applied to the training of technically skilled personnel like programmers and systems analysts. An even smaller share of the education dollar goes to nontechnical end users.

Neglected End Users

"We really don't know how much money is spent each year to teach end users how to operate the systems we give them," McConnell said. "The amount is so small we don't even keep statistics on it."

This almost complete neglect of end-user training goes a long way toward explaining why U.S. productivity growth has steadily slowed at the same time the country's use of computing has rapidly increased, McConnell said.

Since the mid-1960s, U.S. productivity has continued to rise each year—but by progressively smaller amounts. Ironically, the start of the country's current productivity woes coincided with the advent of widespread computer use.

"High technology was originally intended to be a solution," McConnell said. "Now, it's increasingly becoming just another part of the [productivity] problem."

"Most of the people who are responsible for developing and installing new systems are so concerned with hardware and software that they often forget to ask themselves how

the technology is likely to affect its end users," McConnell said. "Systems developers frequently sell convenience without considering the consequences."

To ensure that new sytems are used as they were intended, companies should treat end-user training and support as a full-time job and create a separate department dedicated to just that one function, McConnell said.

Companies can further minimize ineffective systems use by:

• Designing applications to be compatible with the way people do their jobs.

• Persuading rather than forcing users to adopt new programs.

• Explaining a new installation's purpose at the outset and enumerating its potential benefits.

• Furnishing clear, useful documentation.

• Working to improve end-user/computing department communication, which is frequently marred by mutual misunderstandings.

—Jeffry Beeler, "Training of Non-Tech End Users Seen Vital to High Productivity," *Computerworld*, Nov. 16, 1981, p. 36. Copyright 1981 by CW Communications, Inc., Framingham, Mass.

benefit the organization by helping produce studies that are more thorough and more consistent. They also help analysts answer such questions as: What's the next step? How should this procedure be documented? When have we gathered enough data?

System flowcharts. The system flowcharts discussed in Chapter 3 are often drawn up during the data-gathering stage. They are used to record the flow of data in a current procedure from the originating source, through a number of processing operations and machines, to the output report. The flowchart may help an analyst acquire a better understanding of the procedure than would otherwise be possible. It can also help point out possible bottlenecks in the data flow of the system. In com-

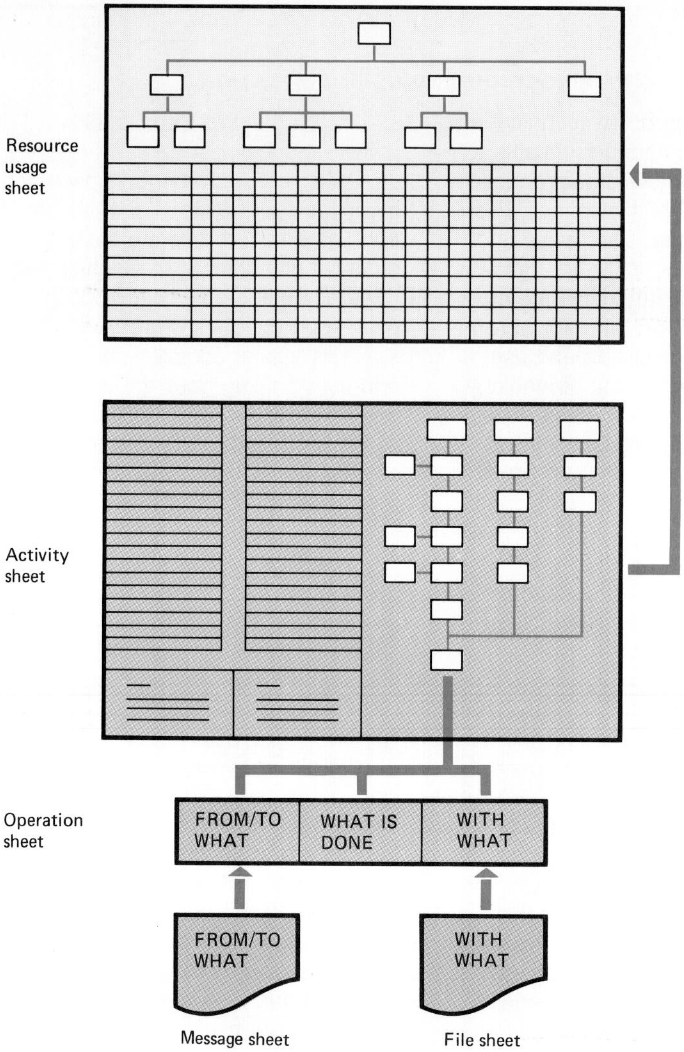

Figure 16-3 In IBM's *Study Organization Plan* (SOP), five data-gathering forms are used to describe the existing system. When completed, the *message sheets* provide detailed facts on current output and input. The *file forms* show the data stored in the system. And the *operation sheets* present the detailed processing steps performed by the system. A separate operation sheet is typically keyed to each step outlined by the system flowchart on the *activity sheet*. Finally, the organizational environment of the current system and the costs of the system are presented on the *resource usage sheet*. (Courtesy IBM Corporation)

plex systems, there's likely to be an overall "macro chart" that describes the general input/processing/output components of the system. There may then be a hierarchy of more detailed "micro charts," each of which describes a module in a higher-level chart. This decomposition of a system into a series of detailed input/processing/output graphics is a frequently used analysis technique. For example, SofTech's SADT (Structured Analysis and Design Technique), and IBM's HIPO (Hierarchy plus Input-Process-Output) are both techniques that follow this approach.

Questionnaires and special-purpose forms. A printed form can be used by analysts to obtain answers to commonly asked questions. These questionnaires and other specialized data-gathering forms are often keyed to the activities presented in a system flowchart. They supply the details about processing frequencies, I/O volumes and materials, and the time needed to perform each activity. One forms-driven approach to data gathering is shown in Figure 16-3.

■ *Interviews and observations.* Interviews are needed to gather data, prepare charts, and fill in questionnaires and forms. Analysts can watch as people perform the tasks required by the system being studied. An analyst can also take an input document and "walk it through" the processing procedure. Such a walkthrough gives the analyst a chance to obtain suggestions from people about ways in which a procedure can be improved.

You can observe a lot just by watching.
Yogi Berra

Analysis of the Problem

After the necessary data have been gathered, the analysts must study their findings to determine the strengths and weaknesses of the existing procedures. During data gathering, the emphasis was on learning *what* was being done. Now, the focus is on learning *why* the system operates as it does. The purpose of this analysis is to develop suggestions on how the study goals may best be achieved.

Analysis Aids. The following tools and techniques may be used to analyze the current system and develop suggestions for improvement:

■ *Checklist of questions.* Questions dealing with procedural, personnel, organizational, and economic considerations should be answered. A few representative questions are shown in Figure 16-4.

■ *System flowchart analysis.* Charts can be examined to help locate essential data and files. And they can also be used to identify bottlenecks

Figure 16-4 Questions for analysis.

Procedural considerations

- Is faster reporting desired? Is faster reporting necessary? Can the processing sequence be improved? What would happen if any documents were eliminated?
- Is greater accuracy needed?
- What monetary value do users place on the output? Are they willing to have their budgets charged with all or part of the cost of preparation?
- Is the output in a useful form? Has writing been minimized?
- Does an output document cause action when it's sent to a manager? If not, why is it sent?
- Is the output stored? If so, for how long? How often is it referred to?
- Can documents be combined? Is the same information duplicated on other reports? In other departments? If so, can procedures be integrated?
- Is unnecessary output generated? Do current reports clearly point out exceptions?

- Is system capacity adequate? Do bottlenecks exist? Is customer service adequate?

Personnel and organizational considerations

- Is the output being prepared in the proper departments? By the right people? Could departments be combined? What effects would organizational change have on people?
- What effect would any procedural changes have on people? What would have to be done to reduce resistance to change? What would be done with those whose jobs would be eliminated or changed? If new jobs were created, what consideration would have to be given to selecting and training workers to staff these vacancies?

Economic considerations

- What is the cost of the present system? What would be the cost of processing with revised current procedures? Approximately what would it cost to satisfy needs using other alternatives?

and unnecessary files. For example, a chart may show a file where information is being stored, but from which little or nothing is being retrieved.

▌ *Forms analysis.* The input/processing/output forms such as those shown in Figure 16-3 that describe I/O documents and processing logic are also helpful both in identifying key data items and in uncovering those items that are processed and stored but are seldom used.

▌ *Grid charts.* Special **grid** (or **input/output**) **charts** may be used to show the relationship that exists between system inputs and outputs. Input documents are listed in rows on the left of the chart (see Figure 16-5), while the output reports produced by the system are identified in the chart columns. An "x" is placed at the intersection of a row and column when a particular document is used to prepare a specific report. For example, in Figure 16-5 form A is used to prepare reports 1 and 4. The chart enables the analyst to identify independent subsystems for further study. This is done by (*a*) drawing a vertical line down any single report column and then (*b*) drawing a horizontal line across any row with a covered x, etc., until further vertical and horizontal lines are impossible. For example, if we draw a line down column 1, we cover only one x—the one indicating that form A is used in preparing report 1. If we then draw a horizontal line along the form A row, we cover the x in column 4. We then draw a vertical line down column 4 and a horizontal line along any row with a covered x. The result of this procedure is that forms A, B, and E and reports 1, 2, and 4 combine to form an independent subsystem.

▌ *The top-down analysis methodology.* If the system being analyzed is complex, a "divide and conquer" methodology is often used to break the system down into smaller components. A top-level function is identified, analyzed, and then broken down into a series of second-level components. Each of these components, in turn, may be further reduced into still lower-level elements. A hierarchy of understandable subfunctions may be the result of this **top-down analysis methodology.**

Figure 16-5 An example of a grid chart.

Input source documents	Output reports							
	1	2	3	4	5	6	7	8
Form A	x			x				
Form B		x		x				
Form C			x					
Form D						x		
Form E		x		x				
Form F			x					x
Form G				x		x		

The Analysis Report

Regardless of the aids used, the final product of the system analysis step should be a *documentation package* and a report of the analysts' findings. The documentation package should include copies of all forms, charts, questionnaires, I/O documents, and written procedural descriptions that have been gathered and analyzed. The **analysis report** should include:

▎ A restatement of the problem.

▎ A summary of current procedures and a statement of present problems or opportunities.

▎ A listing of the general specifications needed to solve the problem along with some preliminary suggestions for solution alternatives that could be considered.

▎ An evaluation of the operational feasibility of the project from a personnel and organizational standpoint.

▎ An estimate of the economic feasibility of the project.

After evaluating the analysis report, responsible managers may decide to revise the study goals, cancel the project, postpone development until later, or proceed to the system design phase.

SYSTEM DESIGN

During the system design phase, designers must decide *how* to produce an efficient (economical) and effective (relevant and useful) system. To do this, they must first *determine feasible alternatives* and then settle on a single set of *detailed specifications* for the problem solution. This isn't easy! As Figure 16-6 shows, there are many factors that have a bearing on the design task. These factors present practical limits to the number of system alternatives that can actually be evaluated.

Determining Alternatives: Some Design Issues

A number of issues involving methodology and the use of resources usually have a bearing on the alternatives that are finally selected. Included in these issues are questions about:

1. *The long-range design plans that are followed.* Many organizations have developed conceptual models or long-range plans for the evolution of their information systems. These models or plans usually allow

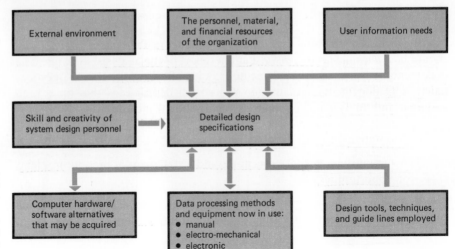

Figure 16-6 Some factors having a bearing on the design process. The detailed design specifications depend on such input factors as user needs, the skill of system designers and the tools they use, the external environment, and the organization's resources. Design specifications may also depend on existing methods and equipment and on the hardware/software alternatives that may be obtained.

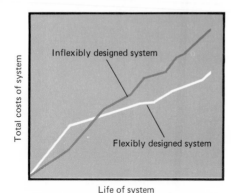

Figure 16-7 The total system cost over the life of the system may be less when flexibility is a design goal.

for the gradual integration of the information-producing systems in the organization. The alternatives that designers can consider in implementing specific projects must conform to the overall design plan that has been adopted.

2. *The flexibility that should be designed into the system.* Designers must decide how adaptable the new system should be to changing circumstances. An organization in a stable industry that sells only a few staple products to a reliable group of customers need not be as concerned with **system flexibility** as one in a dynamic industry that sells many products that are vulnerable to changing demand and competitive pressures. In most cases, systems will need to be changed several times during their useful life. And these changes are often unpredictable. Designers may thus face a dilemma: They can produce a relatively inflexible system that has (perhaps) lower design costs, and then incur the high costs required to periodically rebuild the system. Or, they can initially spend the extra time (and money) to produce a flexible design that may require fewer future changes. As Figure 16-7 shows, the *total cost* over the life of the system may well turn out to be less when flexibility is a design goal.

3. *The control provisions that should be included.* Designers must make sure that procedures and controls are built into any alternative to ensure that the integrity of the data and the security of the system are not impaired. An "audit trail" that permits the tracing of transactions through the system from input to output must be included in the design. A basic issue facing designers is how to balance the control need against the possibility of creating an "overcontrolled" system that's expensive to operate and that produces delays in getting information into the hands of users.

4. *The advisability of "making" the system in-house or of "buying" it from an outside supplier.* Designers must often choose between creating a new in-house design or buying an existing applications package or custom-built system from an outside supplier. The pros and cons of this choice are discussed in Chapter 13, page 357.

5. *The attention that should be given to human factors.* Will the proposed alternatives be easy for people to understand and use? Will the alternatives give prompt response, relieve people of unnecessary chores, and be pleasant to use? These and many other questions bearing on the operational feasibility of a system must be considered. A nonresponsive design that harasses users and wastes their time will be resisted.

6. *The economic tradeoffs that should be made.* The question of economic feasibility underlies the whole system development effort. The decisions made by designers in considering all the above issues can be reached only after a careful study has been made of the available economic resources. A very flexible real time system that can immediately update and retrieve all records might be nice to have, but the designers may elect to settle for a less expensive online system that gives immediate access to records that are only periodically updated using batch processing techniques.

There are so many variables bearing on the design process that it's impossible to establish exact rules to follow in selecting alternatives. The issues we've now examined are resolved in different ways by different designers using different resources in different environments. Different design tools and techniques are also used.

Design Tools and Techniques

The following tools and techniques are among those used during system design:

▌ *Organization standards.* Some organizations have standards manuals that specify a consistent design approach. The procedures to follow in designing output reports, input forms, and processing logic may also be spelled out.

▌ *Top-down design methodology.* The **top-down design** technique requires the early identification of the top-level functions in the proposed system. Each function is then broken down into a hierarchy of understandable lower-level modules and components as shown in the **hierarchical charts** in Figure 16-8. After a top-level chart showing the total structure of the system is prepared, lower-level diagrams are created to show the input/processing/output details of each function, module, and component. Several iterations will usually occur in this design and

An old-fashioned programmer named Dunn
who worked on the UNIVAC-One
Proclaimed that it's fine
to have top-down design,
"But mostly, the program should run."
Skip Jordan

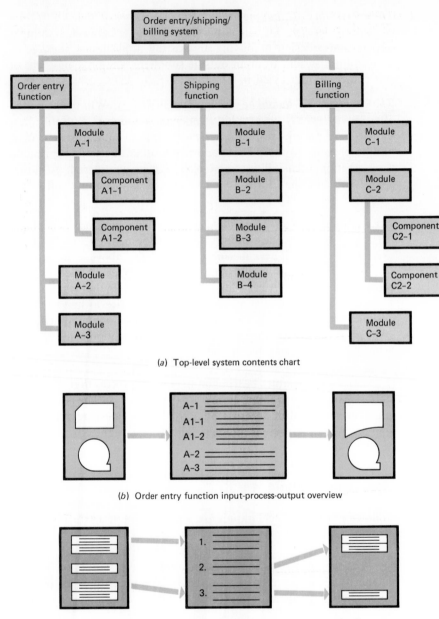

(a) Top-level system contents chart

(b) Order entry function input-process-output overview

(c) Order entry module/component input-process-output detail

Figure 16-8 Hierarchical charts used in top-down design.

charting process. Designers may start with simple diagrams showing general solutions. This first effort is then refined to produce more complete charts as the design requirements become clearer.

Design reviews and walkthroughs. Periodic sessions may be held so that interested users can review the design progress. Designers can present sample outputs and "walk through" the input and processing operations to describe the handling of data. Users can be encouraged to look for errors and to make comments during this **design walkthrough.**

▍ *Special charts and forms.* The charts and forms prepared during the system analysis phase are very helpful in the design stage. Weaknesses spotted during analysis can now be corrected. And the existing input/processing/output relationships may now be used to design a more integrated system.

▍ *Automated design approaches.* The computer itself may also be used in the system development process. The ISDOS (<u>I</u>nformation <u>S</u>ystems <u>D</u>esign and <u>O</u>ptimization <u>S</u>ystem) project at the University of Michigan is working on a software package that will design systems in accordance with stated criteria. Special computer programs can be used to evaluate various hardware/software alternatives during the design stage. Processing requirements can be supplied, and a computer program can then determine how efficiently these requirements can be processed using different equipment alternatives.

Choosing an Alternative

It's assumed at this point that the designers have prepared a detailed set of written and documented system specifications to achieve the system study goals. These specifications should include:

1. *Output requirements.* The form, content, and frequency of output is needed.

2. *Input requirements.* The necessary new input data should be identified along with the stored file data that are required.

3. *File and storage requirements.* The size, contents, storage media, record formats, access restrictions, and degree of permanency of any affected files should be known.

4. *Processing specifications.* The procedures needed for the computer to convert input data into desired output results should be indicated. Manual processing procedures should also be noted.

5. *Control provisions.* The steps required to achieve system control should be specified, and the later system testing and implementation procedures should be outlined.

6. *Cost estimates.* Preliminary estimates of the costs of different alternatives should be made.

We've seen that there are no exact rules to follow in selecting alternatives. Likewise, there aren't any precise guidelines to follow in choosing from among the alternatives selected. In some situations, study results may indicate that the use of a **remote computing service** (or *service bureau*) is the best choice. Such outside firms can do the programming and processing that's required. In other situations, the system can be implemented using existing equipment. And in some system development projects, implementation may call for the acquisition of new hardware.

Hardware Evaluation, Selection, and Acquisition Factors. If new hardware is needed to implement the selected alternative (and it *is* often needed), the study team must then consider a whole new set of questions:

- Which computer and/or peripheral device, when combined with its supporting software, is best suited for our needs?

- Which hardware/software package is the most economical?

- How should we acquire the equipment?

In answering the first question, teams have often considered the **equipment selection factors** listed in Figure 16-9 to limit the choices, and have then followed one of the **equipment selection approaches** listed in Figure 16-10. In answering the second question, the costs associated with each option are compared with the benefits produced. Both costs and benefits must be quantified. Since many benefits tend to be *intangible,* however, it's often hard to assign a value to them. (Machine A costs more than machine B, but it's also faster so it will reduce the time needed to process customer orders. What value is then assigned to the benefit of better customer service?)

The answer to the third question depends on the type of equipment being acquired. Most micro- and minicomputers are purchased. Mainframe systems, however, are obtained in the following ways:

1. *Renting.* Mainframes are often rented from the manufacturer. This is a flexible method that doesn't require a large initial investment. It's also the most expensive method if the equipment meets company needs for 4 or 5 years or longer.

2. *Purchasing.* Many mainframes are purchased because it's the least expensive acquisition method when hardware is kept for several years. But there's also the risk of technological obsolescence—of being "locked-in" to a system that doesn't meet changing needs.

3. *Leasing.* Under one leasing arrangement (many others are possible), the mainframe user tells the leasing company what equipment is needed. This company arranges for the purchase of the equipment and then leases it to the user for a period (usually 3 to 5 years). This method eliminates the large purchase price and is less expensive than renting over the life of the lease. But, of course, the user has contracted to keep the machine for a relatively long period.

Economic factor

1. Cost comparisons

Hardware factors

1. Hardware performance, reliability, capacity, and price
2. Number and accessibility of backup facilities
3. Firmness of delivery date
4. Effective remaining life of proposed hardware
5. Compatibility with existing systems

Software factors

1. Software performance and price
2. Efficiency and reliability of available software
3. Programming languages available (not promised)

4. Availability of useful and well-documented packaged programs, program libraries, and user groups
5. Firmness of delivery date on promised software
6. Ease of use and modification

Service factors

1. Facilities provided by manufacturer for checking new programs
2. Training facilities offered and the quality of training provided
3. Programming assistance and conversion assistance offered
4. Maintenance terms and quality

Reputation of manufacturer

1. Financial stability
2. Record of keeping promises

Figure 16-9 Equipment selection factors.

1. **Single-source approach.** This noncompetitive approach merely consists of choosing the hardware/software package from among those available from a selected vendor. There's a lack of objectivity in this approach, and poor results have been produced. But it's often used.

2. **Competitive-bidding approach.** System specifications are submitted to vendors with a request that they prepare bids. Included in the bid request may be a requirement that cost and performance figures be prepared for a specified *benchmark* processing run. The vendors select what they believe to be the most appropriate hardware/software packages from their lines and submit proposals.

3. **Consultant-evaluation approach.** Qualified data processing consultants can assist businesses in selecting the hardware/software package. Consultants can bring specialized knowledge and experience and an objective point of view to bear on the evaluation and selection problem.

4. **Simulation approach.** As we've seen, specialized computer programs are available from a number of organizations to simulate the performance of selected hardware/software alternatives. Simulation programs are capable of comparing the input, output, and computing times required by each alternative to process specific applications.

Figure 16-10 Equipment selection approaches.

The Design Report

Guided by a written charter which defined the problem, people have analyzed relevant facts. The design of a detailed set of system specifications has evolved from this analysis, and the team has settled on the alternative that it thinks will result in the "best" problem solution. The team has made many decisions. But the final decisions are made by top-level managers. It's now the team's job to prepare a system **design report** and make recommendations. It's the responsibility of top executives to decide on system implementation.

The report of the study team should include the following points:

▌ A restatement of study scope and objectives.

▌ The design specifications for procedures and operations that will be changed.

▌ The anticipated effects of such changes on organizational structure, physical facilities, and company information.

▌ The anticipated effects on people, and the personnel resources available to implement the change.

▌ The hardware/software package chosen (if needed), the reasons for the choice, and the alternatives considered.

▌ The economic effects of the change, including a cost/benefit analysis and an analysis of acquisition methods (if needed).

▌ A summary of the expected problems and benefits arising from the change.

SYSTEM IMPLEMENTATION

Figure 16-11 shows that after top executives have evaluated the design report and have decided to implement the design specifications, the next steps in the system project are programming analysis and program preparation. Since these steps are discussed in detail in Chapters 12 through 14 of the Programming Module, we'll not consider them here. We'll also not repeat the *program* implementation procedures presented in Chapter 13. But there are some general **system implementation** concepts associated with the task of replacing an old system with a new one, and we'll examine those.

The Consequences of Earlier Decisions

The time and effort required to implement a system depends largely on the quality of the work that's done earlier in the system study. We've seen in Figure 16-2, for example, that oversights during problem definition are difficult to correct at the time of implementation. On the other hand, the implementation phase is often simplified as a result of the following preinstallation decisions:

▌ *Decision to follow standard rules and procedures.* The job of testing systems is made easier when procedures are consistently applied, when data items are consistently defined, and when documentation rules are consistently followed.

▌ *Decision to use a modular design approach.* Dividing complex systems and programs into smaller modules simplifies testing and implementation efforts.

▌ *Decision to use tested applications packages.* Buying proven software, where appropriate, may make it possible to bypass many implementation problems.

Equipment Implementation

We've seen that it's sometimes necessary to acquire new hardware or upgrade existing equipment in order to implement a new system. If only a few new I/O devices are added, then little time or effort may be needed. But if a completely new computer system must be installed, then a great deal of plan-

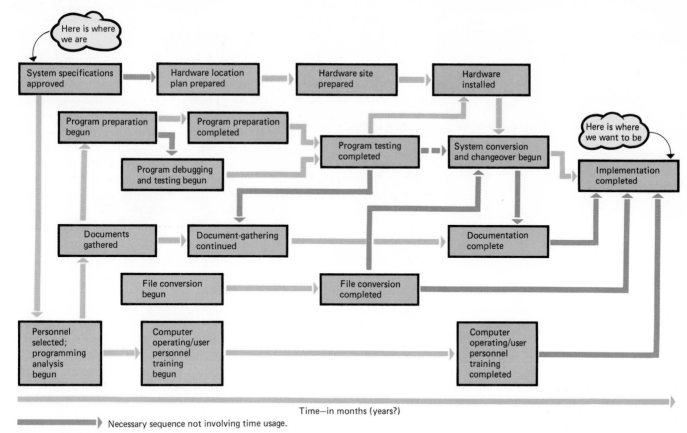

Figure 16-11 System/program implementation considerations.

ning may be required in preparing a suitable site to receive the new hardware. Some of the factors that are considered during site planning for larger installations are:

- *Location.* The physical security of the site and its access to users must be evaluated.

- *Space and layout.* The size of the equipment, the location and length of power and connecting cables, the room needed to service the equipment and store I/O media and supplies, the room needed for offices—these and other factors must be evaluated in determining the space requirements and site layout.

- *Site utilities.* Provisions must be made for air conditioning, electrical power, and site illumination. A fire protection system using heat and smoke detectors, emergency power cutoffs, and appropriate Halon gas and other fire prevention devices may be needed.

System Conversion and Changeover

After programs appear to be producing correct results, the system conversion and changeover may begin. This conversion period is almost always a period of personnel and organizational strain. Data processing people may work long hours and be subjected to pressure to complete the conversion. Unforeseen problems, last-minute corrections, and the disruption of data processing services to using departments, customers, suppliers, etc., may contribute to these pressures. It's at this time that cooperation is badly needed between data processing specialists and the people in affected departments. Yet it's precisely at this time that cooperation frequently breaks down because of preoccupation with technical conversion matters at the expense of good human relations.

Everyone who will be affected by the new system should receive some training prior to the conversion period to become familiar with the changes. This training is likely to become more intense now, however, as new procedures are phased into operation, as old forms are replaced by new ones, as old input devices are retired in favor of new hardware, and as last-minute changes are made in manual methods and personnel assignments.

During system conversion, current files must be changed into a form acceptable to the processor. This can be a tremendous task, and it's one that's often underestimated. Files should be consolidated and duplicate records eliminated. Errors in current files must be detected and removed. And file inconsistencies must be found *before* the changeover rather than later when they can cause system malfunctions.

There's frequently a transitional changeover or shakedown period during which applications are processed by both currently used and new procedures as a final check before the cutover to the new system occurs. A **parallel running** conversion involves the processing of *current* input data by old and new methods. If a significant difference appears, the cause must be located. Various **pilot testing** approaches may also be used during conversion. For example, input data for a *previous* month's operations may be processed using new methods, and the results may be compared with the results obtained from existing operations. If new hardware is being acquired, preliminary pilot tests can be run on the vendor's equipment prior to delivery of the user's hardware. Thus, testing may be facilitated through the use of actual input data, and it may be possible to reduce the time (and costs) associated with maintaining two different systems at a later data. Also, a pilot conversion approach is often used when a system is to be installed in a number of different locations over a period of time. One location—say a regional warehouse—may be selected for the initial conversion effort. Once the start-up problems have been solved and the system has been proven under actual operation conditions, the organization can then convert other warehouses to the new procedures.

Regardless of the conversion approach, final changeover to computer production runs comes from satisfactory performance during this shakedown period.

Once the system is implemented and in operation, a thorough audit or post-implementation review should be made. This follow-up is commonly conducted by people who have an independent viewpoint and are not responsible for the development and maintenance of the system. Some of the questions that should be considered in the audit are:

▌ How useful is the system to decision makers? How enthusiastic are they about the service they receive? Do they receive output in time to take action?

▌ Are planned processing procedures being followed? Are all new procedures being processed on the computer? Have old procedures been eliminated? If not, why not?

▌ Are responsibilities of data processing people defined and understood? Are training programs of acceptable quality?

▌ Are system controls being observed? Is documentation complete? Have procedures to control program changes been established? Are any modifications or refinements indicated as a result of operating experience? If so, are they being made?

▌ How do operating results compare with original goals and expectations? Are economic benefits being obtained? If variations exist, what's the cause? What can be done to achieve expected results?

Feedback and Review 16-1

This chapter has introduced you to a number of concepts associated with the analysis, design, and implementation of an information system. To test and reinforce your understanding of these concepts, answer the following multiple-choice questions by placing the letter of the most nearly correct answer in the space provided.

_D_ **1.** The changes that occur in organizations are due to

    a) technological factors.
    b) social and economic factors.
    c) operating problems.
    d) all the above reasons.

_D_ **2.** The sequence of steps followed in a system study is

    a) problem definition, system design, system analysis, programming, and implementation.
    b) problem definition, system analysis, programming, and implementation.

c) system analysis, system design, and system implementation.

d) problem definition, system analysis, system design, programming analysis, program preparation, and implementation.

_B_ **3.** Information system changes

a) are usually appreciated by everyone in an organization.

b) can reduce the job satisfaction of some people.

c) invariably increase the self-confidence of department supervisors.

d) are usually easy to implement because design techniques have become standardized.

_A_ **4.** Which of the following activities don't usually belong in the problem definition step:

a) a preliminary survey is conducted by unbiased people who have no interest in the problem.

b) a series of requirements sessions may be held.

c) the problem definition is put in writing and approved by system users.

d) all the above activities belong in the problem definition step.

_C_ **5.** During the data-gathering phase of the system analysis step,

a) program flowcharts are often prepared.

b) the system design specifications are outlined.

c) a number of specialized forms may be prepared.

d) a standards manual is of little use.

_D_ **6.** Which of the following tools is *not* normally used during system analysis:

a) system flowchart.

b) question checklist.

c) grid chart.

d) program flowchart.

_B_ **7.** The approach used in top-down analysis and design is to

a) identify the top-level functions by combining many smaller components into a single entity.

b) identify a top-level function, and then create a hierarchy of lower-level modules and components.

c) prepare flowcharts after programming has been completed.

d) none of the above.

_A_ **8.** Which of the following tools is *not* normally used during system design:

a) program reviews and walkthroughs.

b) hierarchical charts.

c) standards manual.

d) all the above are used.

_D___ **9.** Design specifications *don't* normally include

    a) output requirements.
    b) input and storage requirements.
    c) control provisions.
    d) blueprints showing the layout of hardware.

_C___ **10.** In acquiring new hardware, an organization

    a) may choose to rent a machine since this is the least expensive acquisition method.
    b) may buy the equipment to reduce the risk of technological obsolescence.
    c) may lease a machine in order to avoid a large purchase price.
    d) may choose to build its own system from bins of integrated circuits.

_C___ **11.** Which of the following is *not* likely to be a system implementation consideration:

    a) preparing a site plan for new equipment.
    b) using parallel running or pilot testing conversion techniques.
    c) having enough work to keep data processing people busy.
    d) training those who will use the new system.

Looking Back

1. The initiative for many changes in the information systems of an organization may be traced to the technical, social, and economic changes occurring in society. Executives, information users, and data processing specialists in an organization may respond to these external forces, and to other internal factors, by seeking to develop better computer-based applications. The six steps followed in the system development process are: (a) problem definition, (b) system analysis, (c) system design, (d) programming analysis, (e) program preparation, and (f) system/program implementation and maintenance.

2. Individual resistance frequently accompanies system change. This resistance to change may take many forms, and it may come from all levels in an organization. The level of opposition can be reduced if change initiators are aware of the problem and follow certain guidelines.

3. A preliminary system survey is often conducted during the problem definition stage to identify the need. This survey should have high-level support and should be conducted by qualified people. A number of requirements sessions are often held to allow people to participate in setting or revising system goals. At the conclusion of the problem definition step, the team should prepare a detailed written statement of the scope and objectives of the study.

4. Analysts gather data on current operations during the system analysis stage. Some of the tools they use during data gathering are organization charts, standards manuals, system flowcharts, questionnaires, special-purpose forms, and interviews. After data have been gathered, analysts study these facts to develop suggestions on how the study goals may be achieved. The analysis tools they may use include checklists of questions, a hierarchy of system flowcharts, and grid charts. An analysis report is written at the end of this step.

5. During the system design phase, designers decide how to produce an efficient and effective system. Feasible alternatives are identified, and a set of detailed specifications for the problem solution are prepared. Issues involving methodology and the use of resources surface at this time. Six of these issues are discussed in the chapter. Design tools such as organization standards, the top-down design approach, special charts and forms, and design walkthroughs are used. Since there are so many variables bearing on the design process, however, it's impossible to establish exact rules to follow in selecting alternatives or in choosing from among the alternatives selected. If new equipment is needed to implement a system design, the study team recommends a hardware/software package, and the acquisition approach to use in obtaining this package.

6. After considering the design report prepared by the study team, top executives decide on system implementation. If the design specifications are implemented, programs are prepared and tested. After programs appear to be running properly and producing correct results, the system conversion and changeover may begin. There's frequently a transition period during which applications are processed by both the old and new procedures before the cutover to a new system occurs. After the new system is implemented, a thorough follow-up appraisal or audit is often conducted.

You should now be able to define and use the following terms and concepts (the numbers shown indicate the pages where the terms and concepts are first mentioned):

system change factors 463

resistance to system change 466

problem definition 467

problem definition survey 468

requirements sessions 468

system study charter 469

organization chart 470

standards manuals 470

grid (input/output) chart 474

top-down analysis methodology 474

analysis report 475

system flexibility 476

top-down design 477

hierarchical charts 477

design walkthrough 479

remote computing service 480

equipment selection factors 480

equipment selection approaches 480

design report 481

system implementation 482

parallel running 484

pilot testing 484

post-implementation review 485

TOPICS FOR REVIEW AND DISCUSSION

1. (*a*) How may pressures from sources external to a business create the need for changes in the firm's information systems? (*b*) How can decisions made by top executives, department managers, and information system specialists lead to changes in the firm's information systems?

2. (*a*) What are the steps in the system development process? (*b*) Which step do you think is most important?

3. (*a*) Why is resistance to information system change the rule rather than the exception? (*b*) What can be done to reduce this resistance?

4. What principles should be observed in conducting a problem definition survey?

5. Why is it important to not become impatient with "delays" that occur during problem definition?

6. (*a*) What tools and techniques may be used to gather data about current operations? (*b*) To analyze the current system and develop suggestions for improvement?

7. "There are a number of issues that have a bearing on the design alternatives that are finally selected." What are five of these issues?

8. What tools and techniques are used during system design?

9. What should be included in the written design specifications?

10. (*a*) What factors should be considered in selecting equipment? (*b*) What selection approaches may be used?

11. Discuss the methods that are often used to acquire mainframe computers.

12. "The conversion from an old system to a new one is almost always a time of personnel and organizational strain." Discuss this comment.

13. (*a*) What's a parallel running conversion? (*b*) What's meant by the pilot testing approach to system conversion?

ANSWERS TO FEEDBACK AND REVIEW SECTION

16-1

1. D	4. A	7. B	10. C
2. D	5. C	8. A	11. C
3. B	6. D	9. D	

System Design Errors Impact My Existence

I used to laugh at the preposterous plots for many TV detective shows. Our heroes, even when on vacation, seemed always to be on the scene when some criminal act took place.

When a drugged jockey fell from his horse, for example, they just happened to be spending their day off at the racetrack. When a visitor to Sea World who couldn't swim was nudged into the whales' pool, our heroes were there entertaining a visiting relative.

Now, however, I don't laugh anymore. The number of DP system design errors that have impacted my existence recently must certainly not be typical of the average American's encounters, but they have happened nonetheless. Is it a conspiracy? Or do such problems seek out those people most likely to be upset by them?

For example, I recently received my monthly bill for gas and electricity from the Philadelphia Electric Co. [Peco]. The electric bill was its usual absurdly high figure, but it was dwarfed by the gas bill: more than $800 for one month.

This from a house where the gas bill has been a constant zero for the last year or so. The only gas appliance in the house—which for the last year has served as my office—is a stove that is used to make an occasional cup of tea or hot chocolate (the coffee maker is electric).

Surely a "reasonability" check could be inserted in the billing algorithm to unearth such absurdities or, even more importantly, to identify potential sites of gas leaks. In my case, the gas meter reading of 6,506 was either misread, misinterpreted or misentered as 8,506. Because the 6,506 is unchanged from January of 1979—and since 2,000 units would be close to a yearly figure for a house with gas heating and all gas appliances—a flag should have gone up somewhere to trigger a rereading of the gas meter and/or a check of the gas line.

Instead, I will probably be subjected to a now-familiar fight to "get even." I expect a reply shortly. It will probably be a form letter telling me my account is overdue, with no acknowledgment of my letter. If things hold true to form, I will probably have to make several telephone calls and write one or two more letters to straighten out things.

A Duplicate Case

A similar situation has been going on for three months now with my leased copier. Every month I send the company a card indicating the present meter reading. The company subtracts the previous month's reading and bills me a fixed fee for 6,200 copies or less per month and charges a per-copy for each copy in excess of 6,200.

In November, I filled out the card and placed it in the "to be filed" pile rather than the "to be mailed" pile. This came to light when I received the bill for the month. In the absence of an input card, the company had assumed a usage of some 12,000 copies, somewhat more than double my usual monthly total of 6,000.

There was no indication on the invoice that the usage was an estimate, nor did the absence of input for the month produce a follow-up request for a correct meter reading.

Searching through the piles of paper that typically obscure the surface of my desk, I located the missing meter reading and forwarded it to the company along with a note of apology. Here things got truly interesting.

A real human being took over the disposition of the problem. I assume this to be the case since the amended bill I received had a rather flagrant arithmetic mistake.

My actual number of monthly copies was 7,520. After the "free" 6,200 were subtracted, I should have been billed for 1,320. However, the invoice showed 1,720 copies. Hopefully this was a human error, not the computer program's goof.

The computer system, unfortunately, soon demonstrated that it did not know about the amended bill. About two weeks after I sent the company a check for the correct number of copies, I received another dunning notice for the 1,200 copies. Again, a long frustrating struggle is clearly under way, just to "get even."

The solutions to these two situations are quite simple. Some reasonability checks could certainly be built into Peco's billing algorithms, especially important because major departures from the norm could be indicative of dangerous gas leaks.

As for the copier company's system, usage estimates should be flagged as estimates (Peco does this when the meter reader cannot gain admittance to read the meter), and estimates should be somewhat close to actual usage.

Poor Systems Design

Computers are supposed to improve the quality of life, not complicate it. Instead, more and more systems are being designed to minimize human involvement. If the systems were designed better, such a change could be beneficial; instead, it seems the design of many such systems does not deal even with likely anomalies.

The blame for the resultant complications is usually placed on the poor computer. Those of us in the industry, however, know the error is almost invariably poor systems design.

With the advent of large data base systems in the offing—not to mention electronic funds transfer, office automation and a host of yet-to-come microcomputer applications—we must do something about improving systems design.

The popularizations of structured walkthroughs is a step in the right direction, as long as the technique is properly employed. Don't just step through the logic represented on the system flowcharts. Ask "what if" questions, with no bounds on the rest of the questions.

Several design groups I have worked with have gotten quite upset by such questions as invalid data input values (that can't happen), missing values (the system will catch it before here) and invalid fields.

Ask these questions. You may not be popular at first, but the systems that result will be the better for such analyses.

—Stephen L. Robinson, "System Design Errors Impact My Existence," *Computerworld,* Mar. 24, 1980, pp. 31 and 34. Copyright 1980 Stephen L. Robinson.

chapter 17

System File and Processing Alternatives

HARNESSING INFORMATION: DATA BASE MANAGEMENT SYSTEMS

The amount of information being stored in computers is soaring. In the United States today, more than 1.7 trillion characters are stored online—a number just about equal to two full-size novels for every person in the country. And according to predictions by IBM, by 1985 the amount of electronically stored data is expected to multiply seven times.

To avoid being buried under all this information, many organizations are moving into data base management systems (DBMS). Such systems are special software packages—somewhat akin to electronic librarians—that standardize the ways in which data are entered and stored in computer systems. This standardization eliminates unnecessary duplication of data, such as separate departmental files containing the same information.

In 1981, less than 10 percent of companies using computers had data base management systems, but by 1990 over 90 percent of computer users are expected to have them. By that time, the market for such systems will top $4 billion annually, according to Strategic Inc., a California market research firm.

—Source of data: "Opening Up Data Files To Laymen," *Business Week*, Aug. 10, 1981, p. 64.

The data base is a vital component of today's emerging electronic office environment. (Courtesy Burroughs Corporation)

Looking Ahead

This chapter outlines some of the system file and processing alternatives available to system designers. In fact, the material presented here is often considered during the system design phase of a system study.

A review of data organization concepts is followed in this chapter by a section that outlines the different approaches that may be used to organize, access, and process three different types of files. The problems that can surface in an organization when each department independently develops its own applications and files are presented. And the use and management of data base systems (see opening vignette) to reduce these difficulties is explained.

Thus, after studying this chapter you should be able to:

▌ Explain how data are organized in business data processing systems

▌ Discuss how records are stored, accessed, and processed in sequential, direct, and indexed sequential files

▌ Outline the advantages and limitations of the sequential, direct, and indexed sequential file alternatives

▌ Identify the problems that are often created when different departments independently develop their own applications and files, and describe how the data base concept alleviates these problems

▌ Explain how a data management system can be used

▌ Outline the benefits and limitations of data base systems

▌ Understand and use the key terms listed at the end of this chapter

DATA ORGANIZATION AND FILE ALTERNATIVES: REVIEW AND PREVIEW

You'll recall from Chapter 16 that it's the job of system designers to create a system solution that will satisfy the information needs of users. To do this job, designers determine feasible alternatives and then settle on a single set of detailed specifications for the new application or system. Before detailed input, processing, and output specifications can be prepared, however, the data to be processed must first be organized or grouped in some logical arrangement. Before moving any further into this chapter, let's review some of the terminology and data organization concepts that were first presented in Chapter 2.

Organizing Data: A Review

In business information systems, data are organized into different levels ranging upward from data fields to records, files, and data bases. Let's briefly look at these levels or groupings of data in the context of the billing and accounts-receivable (A/R) applications outlined in Chapter 2.

The objects of billing-A/R processing are to:

1. Send bills or invoices to credit customers as purchases are made during a period.

2. Keep track of all purchases made during the period.

3. Send periodic summary statements to customers to remind them of their debts.

4. Stay abreast of credit purchase trends, delinquent accounts, and other relevant information.

Each bill will contain *several* data items or fields. The customer's name and account number will be two fields. Other fields will include the customer's address, the date of purchase, and item(s) purchased. A *field*, then, is a group of related characters that are treated as a single unit.

Related fields are grouped to form a single entity called a *record*. This record contains all the necessary data about some object. An A/R record, for example, pertains to a credit customer and includes such data as the customer's name, account number, address, and credit limit.

A *file* is a collection of related records that are treated as a unit. Each record in a file is identified by a *record key*. This key is a value found in every record in the file, and this value must be *unique* for each record. In a simple, *manually processed* A/R file, for example, the key could be the last name of customers, and record folders could be organized and filed in alphabetical sequence in a file cabinet. Between statement preparation dates, copies of customer bills can be used to update record folders in a **transaction file** drawer as shown in Figure 17-1. When statements are prepared, the copies of the bills are removed from the transaction file drawer. Calculations are made to determine total purchase amounts, the transaction file data are transferred to the **master file** in the bottom drawers of the cabinet, and statements are sent to customers.

In a *computer-processed* A/R application, on the other hand, the primary key used to organize records in the file is likely to be the customer account number. Transaction and master file records will be stored on computer-readable media, and these records will be processed in a numerical sequence during statement preparation (see Figure 17-2). Files may also be restructured around "secondary keys" for different retrieval and processing uses. The customer account number key used for statement preparation might be replaced by a customer name key in a second file of the same data when the file is to be used by employees responding to customer complaints and inquiries.

Finally, a *data base* is a collection of logically related data elements that are structured in various ways today to reduce such duplication of data items and to provide improved access to the needed facts. Records in an A/R file, for example, could be linked with sales, shipping, contract pricing, and payment records that might be located in other files. Figure 17-3 summarizes the data organization hierarchy used in business data processing systems.

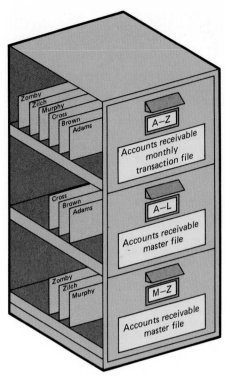

Figure 17-1 Transaction and master files in a simple manual accounts receivable system.

Figure 17-2 These accounts receivable master file records are organized on magnetic tape by using an ascending sequence of customer account numbers.

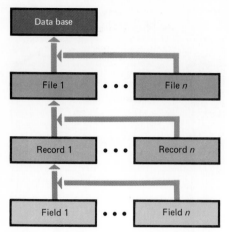

Figure 17-3 Data are normally organized into a hierarchy for computer processing. The field is the smallest entity to be processed as a single unit. Related fields are grouped to form records, and related records are combined to form files. The highest level in the data organization hierarchy is the data base which is a collection of logically related data elements that may be structured in various ways and used for multiple purposes.

File Alternatives Open to System Designers: A Preview

You saw in Chapter 16 that there are many variables affecting the ways that designers choose to deal with the records and files that will be used in a new system. One such variable, you'll recall, concerns the amount of flexibility to build into a system. Different degrees of flexibility *can* be created by using different approaches to *organize, access,* and *process* files. For example, designers can elect to:

▎ Use a direct or indexed sequential file organization for some applications.

▎ Employ the latest online hardware and data base management software so that users can have immediate access to records in one or more data bases.

Such a system can be more flexible (and initially more expensive) than one that uses sequentially organized files and batch processing techniques.

But wait a minute! What do some of these terms mean? What's an indexed sequential file organization? What's data base management software? These are terms that refer to some of the file and processing alternatives available to system designers as they consider how to meet the needs of users. As Figure 17-4 indicates, some of these file alternatives can be classified into sequential, direct, and indexed sequential categories. We'll look at these options in the next section. We'll then briefly examine ways that data can be integrated and used in a data base environment.

SEQUENTIAL, DIRECT, AND INDEXED SEQUENTIAL FILES

Sequential Files

As you read in Chapter 2, **sequential files** may be *organized* so that records are stored one after another in an ascending or descending order determined by the record key. There are likely to be tens of thousands of these records in customer account number sequence in the A/R files of electric, telephone, and oil companies. Once a file is sequenced according to a designated key field, however, it's almost certain to be out of any sequence in every other field. An

Figure 17-4 System designers can choose to organize, access, and process records and files in different ways depending on the type of application and the needs of users.

File organization	Record access method	Processing approach
1. Sequential 2. Direct (or random) 3. Sequential (but with an index)	1. Sequential 2. Direct 3. Indexed sequential	1. Sequential 2. Direct (or online) 3. Indexed sequential

A/R file sequenced by customer account number, for example, will not be in a Zip code sequence or an alphabetical sequence. We've seen that other files could be sequenced on these record keys, but maintaining multiple files of duplicate data can be expensive.

When computer processing is used, the stored records in a sequential file are usually kept on magnetic tape, magnetic disk, or punched paper media. To

Figure 17-5 The sequential file processing approach. Transactions affecting file records must be identified by a record key, and these transactions must be arranged into the same ascending or descending sequence as the master file before processing can begin. Transaction data and old master file records are then read into the CPU. The record key is used to match a new transaction with the appropriate old file record. The old record is then updated by program instructions and a new file record is created and written on an output medium. Various documents such as checks, bills, and reports may also be prepared during the processing.

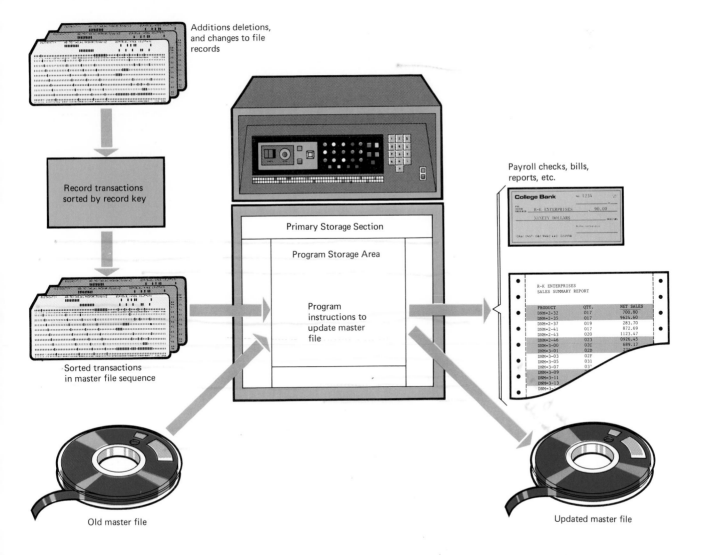

access these records, the computer must read the file in sequence from the beginning. To locate a particular record, the computer program must read in each record in sequence and compare its record key to the one that's needed. Only when the record keys match will the retrieval search end and processing begin. If only a single record in a sequential file is needed, the computer would read, on the average, about half the file before it found the one it wanted.

Since an entire sequential file may need to be read just to retrieve and update a few records, it's desirable to accumulate transactions of a similar type into batches, sort these batches into the record key sequence used in the file, and then *process* the entire batch in a single pass through the file (see Figure 17-5). Designers have found that this is a very efficient processing approach to use when a high proportion of the file records in an application need to be updated at regularly scheduled intervals. Applications such as payroll processing, billing and statement preparation, and bank check processing meet these conditions.

Direct Files

There are many other applications, however, that don't meet these conditions. In these applications, the proportion of file records to be processed is often low, the timing of record transactions and/or inquiries is often unpredictable, and the processing delays caused by accumulating transactions into batches is often unacceptable. One such application illustrated in Chapter 2 was the updating of Rob Brooks' savings account record from an online teller terminal. Another application illustrated in Chapter 6 was the updating of production records by factory workers using data collection stations located on the plant floor.

When a **direct file** (also called a **random** or **relative** file) organization approach is used, the computer can directly locate the key of the needed record without having to search through a sequence of other records. This means that the time required for online inquiry and updating of a few records is much faster than when batch techniques are used. Of course, this also means that direct file records must be kept in a direct-access storage device (DASD). A record is stored in a direct file by its key field. Although it might be possible to use the storage location numbers in a DASD as the keys for the records stored in those locations, this is seldom done. Instead, an arithmetic procedure called a **transform** is frequently used to convert the record key number into a DASD storage location number. For example, the record key number might be divided by a value determined by the transform. The record could then be stored in the DASD location that corresponds to a value calculated by the division operation. Sometimes a transform produces **synonyms**—i.e., two or more records whose keys generate the same DASD location number. Several methods are followed to overcome this difficulty when it occurs. One approach is to include a **pointer** field at the location calculated by the transform. This field points to the DASD location of another record that has the same calculated transform value.

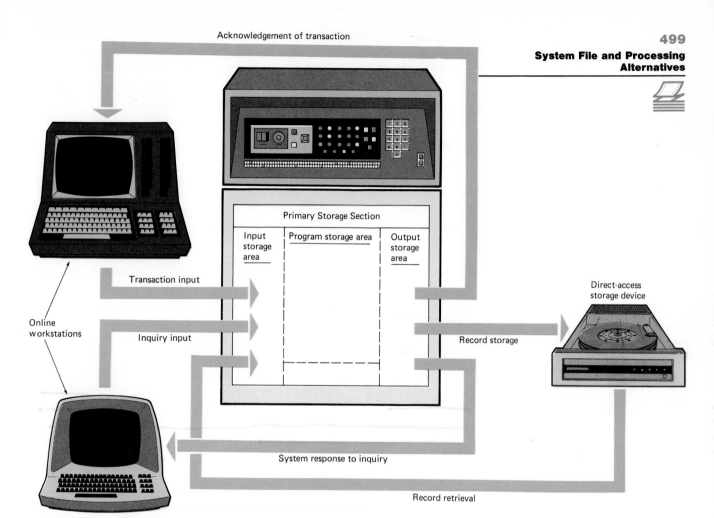

Figure 17-6 The direct-access processing approach. Transactions and inquiries about the current status of records are entered into the CPU from online workstations. Sorting of transactions is not required. The access to, and retrieval of, a file record stored in an online secondary storage device is accomplished through the use of a record key in a fraction of a second and without the need for a sequential search of the file. Once the record has been updated or has provided up-to-the-minute information about its contents to the inquiry station, it is returned directly to a designated location in the direct-access storage device.

When the computer is given the key of a record to be processed at a later date, it reuses the transform to locate the stored record. If the record is at the location calculated by the transform, the search is over and the record is *directly accessed* for processing. If the record at the calculated location does not have the correct key, the computer looks at the pointer field to continue the search. Thus, as Figure 17-6 indicates, direct files are direct accessed and *directly processed.* It's also possible to process direct file records in a record key sequence. But if a large number of file records need to be processed in sequence, the computer may have to repeatedly use the transform algorithm and constantly reposition the reading mechanism of the DASD to retrieve and process these records. When compared to batch processing procedures, this would be an inefficient and expensive approach to use.

Indexed Sequential Files

You've now seen that there are some processing situations that are best suited to the use of sequential files, and there are others that need the benefits to be obtained from a direct file organization. To further complicate the lot of system designers, there are also some files that are commonly used to support both batch and online processing operations. An inventory file, for example, may be updated each week. Transactions involving quantities of parts received and quantities sold may be batched, sorted by part number, and used to produce a new report each week of the inventory available for sale. The purchasing department may use this report for reordering purposes. However, the same inventory file may also be used to provide availability data in response to inquiries coming from online terminals in the sales department. Similarly, a business may want to use batch techniques to update an A/R file and at the same time use that file to give quick answers to customer inquiries.

When both batch and online processing must be supported, an **indexed sequential file** may be used. The records in this type of file are *organized in sequence* for the efficient processing of large batch jobs, but an **index** is also used to speed up access to the records. This file organization is thus a compromise approach that combines some of the advantages (and avoids some of the limitations) of both the sequential and direct approaches. Records are stored sequentially by a record key in a DASD. When these records are periodically updated during a batch run, the direct-access capability of the DASD really isn't used. The *first* record may be directly *accessed,* but all others are then read in sequence as if they were stored on a magnetic tape.

Indexes are used to permit access to selected records without requiring a search of the *entire* file. The use of an index is already familiar to you. If you wanted to find information on one or a few topics in this book, you would not begin on page 1 and read every page until you came across the topic(s) of interest. Rather, you would find the subject by turning to the index at the back of the book to locate the page number, and then by turning directly to that page to begin reading. In the same way, a computer can use an **indexed sequential access method (ISAM)** to locate a record by using an index rather than by starting every search at the beginning of the file. In an A/R file, for example, customer records may be sequentially organized by account number. One or more indexes of these account numbers can then be stored in the DASD as shown in Figure 17-7. The account number key represents the *highest* customer account number in the storage area. Thus, to locate customer number 1932, the computer is instructed to access storage area 12. Another index for storage area 12 would probably then be used to further pinpoint the location of

Figure 17-7

Account number key	Storage area for customer data
1492	10
1776	11
1945	12
2232	13
2565	14
•	•
•	•
•	•

the record. A sequential search, involving only a tiny fraction of the entire file may then be made to retrieve the desired record. In summary, then, <u>records in indexed sequential files can be batch processed or accessed quickly through the use of indexes.</u>

Advantages and Limitations of These File Approaches

Which of the above file organization approaches should system designers use? There's no single answer to this question, of course, unless the answer is "all of them." The best approach to use in a given application is the one that happens to meet the user's needs in the most effective and economical manner. In making the choice for an application, designers must evaluate the distinct strengths and weaknesses of each approach. These advantages and limitations are summarized in Figure 17-8.

DATA BASE SYSTEMS

Data processing activities in businesses have traditionally been grouped by departments and by applications. Most of the early computers used in business were installed to process a few large-volume jobs in a small number of departments. Preparing customer bills and maintaining an A/R file was one of these early applications. Other applications, treated independently, were added over the years. Each separate application had its own master file organized in a sequential, direct, or indexed sequential fashion. The records in each file were

Figure 17-8 Factors to consider in evaluating file alternatives.

SEQUENTIAL FILES

Advantages
- Simple-to-understand approach
- Locating a record requires only the record key
- Efficient and economical if the *activity rate* — i.e., the proportion of file records to be processed — is high
- Relatively inexpensive I/O media and devices may be used
- Files may be relatively easy to reconstruct since a good measure of built-in backup is usually available

Disadvantages
- Entire file must be processed even when the activity rate is very low
- Transactions must be sorted and placed in sequence prior to processing
- Timeliness of data in the file deteriorates while batches are being accumulated
- Data redundancy is typically high since the same data may be stored in several files sequenced on different keys

DIRECT FILES

Advantages
- Immediate access to records for inquiry and updating purposes is possible

Disadvantages
- Records in the online file may be exposed to the risks of a loss of accuracy and a breach of security;

- Immediate updating of several files as a result of a single transaction is possible
- Transactions need not be sorted

special backup and reconstruction procedures must be established
- May be less efficient in the use of storage space than sequentially organized files
- More difficult to add and delete records than with sequential files
- Relatively expensive hardware and software resources are required

INDEXED SEQUENTIAL FILES

Advantages
- Permits the efficient and economical use of sequential processing techniques when the activity rate is high
- Permits quick access to records in a relatively efficient way when this activity is a small fraction of the total workload

Disadvantages
- Less efficient in the use of storage space than some other alternatives
- Access to records may be slower using indexes than when transform algorithms are used
- Relatively expensive hardware and software resources are required

BUSINESS LEADS THE WAY IN ELECTRONIC DATA RETRIEVAL

While the market for videotex services is only emerging, U.S. businesses have been spending at an accelerating rate over the past decade to obtain electronically stored information. They have accounted for most of the growth so far of the computerized information services—in essence commercial videotex systems—that are now available. With 800 of these online services already accounting for 10% of the $10 billion business information market, revenues from these business data bases are growing at a 30% annual clip, nearly double the 16% gain for such conventional print products as magazines and newspapers.

The business market for online information began to take off when publishers realized that corporate readers would pay a premium to get information on a more timely basis. Some of the best-known data bases such as the New York Times Information Bank, Mead Data Central, and Dow Jones News Retrieval Service largely repackage and index what is already widely available in printed form. Now, however, dozens of data bases have cropped up for such specialized markets as the economic forecasts of the Data Resources Inc.

subsidiary of McGraw-Hill Inc.

New ones are being added every day. In March, for instance, Pergamon International Information Corp. rolled out Patsearch, which enables a user to call up the text of any patent. The terminal, which includes a videodisc player used to display the patent drawings, is far from cheap at $6,000. But, says Peter F. Urbach, PII's president, "I've got people beating down my door."

To cope with such rapidly growing interest, the data base companies are looking into ways to make their systems easier to use. "Normally, training to use our data base requires a day and a half," says George Plosker, marketing representative of Dialog Information Retrieval Service, a subsidiary of Lockheed Missiles & Space Co., which sells bibliographic data. But interest in Dialog has become so great that the company may not be able to train its new users quickly enough, so it is investigating a shift to self-training software.

Both CompuServ Inc. and Source Telecomputing Inc., which originally had put together data bases for personal-computer hobbyists, are now adding data bases and other services that are aimed at the businessman.

"Right now the market that will accept our services is the up-scale professional," says Marshall Graham, president of Source Telecomputing.

Checking Stock Prices

This business trend has certainly been the case in Britain. Prestel introduced a videotex service for residential customers then discovered that those signing up were businessmen. "It's probably closer to 100%," adds Richard Hooper, Prestel's director, because many of his terminals are owned by businessmen who check closing prices on the New York markets—information not available until 10 p.m. in London.

Like other suppliers of online business information, Prestel's Hooper hopes that once his terminals are in the home, they will also be used to access nonbusiness information. "We're looking for applications that bring [terminals] in the home," he says, "and tax-deductible business use is a way to get our foot in the door."

organized according to a single key field. Each application also had its own input data, and its own processing program to update the file and supply information.

When the key field of the file wasn't relevant to the information that was needed, the entire file would have to be searched. For example, to get the names of employees with a certain educational background from a personnel file organized by employee number would require a search of all file records. If the personnel department's need for such "exception" information became routine, a new file structured on an educational background key would be created and a new program would be written to process this file. Of course, this second file would duplicate much of the data stored in the first personnel file.

At the same time that new files were being created and data were being duplicated *within* a department, the same duplication of related data was occurring *between different departments*. This comes as no surprise to you. After all, you've seen in Chapters 2 and 3 that many of the same data items are often kept in different files and used in different ways by people in sales, shipping, billing, A/R, and inventory control departments. Each department's applications and files were often created as the need arose without any serious thought given to the total information needs of the organization. Several problems were also created by this departmental file-oriented approach:

1. *Data redundancy.* The same basic data fields are included in many different files. For example, a great deal of redundant data on a bank customer (e.g., home address, age, and credit rating) might be contained in separate checking account, savings account, automobile loan, and personal loan files. The cost of entering and storing the same data in many files can be quite expensive.

2. *File updating problems.* When changes occur in a data item, every file which contains that field should be updated to reflect the change. Confusion can result when one file is updated while another isn't (an all too common occurrence). For instance, the credit rating of Charlie Brown, account number 1234 in the auto loan department, may be changed to reflect the fact that Charlie's car had to be repossessed. But this change in credit status may not be carried over to the file in the personal loan department that contains the record of Charles M. Brown, account number 5678. And, of course, the cost of running different updating programs can be high.

3. *Lack of program/data independence.* The programs used with file-oriented applications usually contain "picture," "format," or "data" statements that precisely define each data field to be processed. A brief survey at one university showed that the data element "student name" was stored in 13 different files and in five different formats. Anytime there's a need to add, delete, or change data formats, the application program must also be changed. Likewise, a significant revision in a program may require a restructuring of the data file processed by the program. Changing programs to accommodate data format changes is a major maintenance activity in many data processing installations today.

The Data Base Concept

Dissatisfied with the problems caused by the departmental file-oriented approach, some system designers began looking in the late 1960s for ways to consolidate activities by using a data base approach. Although there are differences of opinion about what constitutes a data base system, the most prevalent view is that such systems are designed around a centralized and integrated shared data file (or data base) that emphasizes the independence of programs and data. This data base is located in a DASD. Data transactions are introduced into the system only once. These data are now a neutral resource with respect to any particular program, and specific data elements are readily available as needed to all authorized applications and users of the data base. All data base records that transactions affect may be updated at the time of input.

The data base concept requires that input data be commonly defined and consistently organized and presented throughout the organization. And this requirement, in turn, calls for rigid input discipline. A **data base administrator (DBA)** has the overall authority to establish and control data definitions and standards. A **data dictionary** is used to document and maintain the data definitions. The DBA is also responsible for determining the relationships among data elements, and for designing the data base security system to guard against unauthorized use.

Data Base Management Systems

Computer programs are required to store and retrieve data from a data base. Since, as we'll see in the next section, complex data relationships and linkages may be found in data bases, the programs that manage a data base are usually quite sophisticated. A collection of these storage/retrieval programs is called a **data base management system (DBMS).** Most DBMSs are purchased from computer manufacturers and independent software vendors. The market for them is expanding rapidly. They are available for machines of all sizes, and some of those used on large mainframe models cost tens of thousands of dollars.

A DBMS can organize, process, and present selected data elements from the data base. This capability enables decision makers to search, probe, and query data base contents in order to extract answers to nonrecurring and unplanned questions that aren't available in regular reports. These questions might initially be vague and/or poorly defined, but people can "browse" through the data base until they have the needed information. In short, the DBMS will "manage" the stored data items and assemble the needed items from the common data base in response to the queries of those who aren't programmers. In a file-oriented system, users needing special information may communicate their needs to a programmer, who, when time permits, will write one or more programs to extract the data and prepare the information. The availability of a DBMS, however, offers users a much faster alternative communications path (see Figure 17-9).

To illustrate the flexibility of a DBMS, let's assume that a personnel manager of a large multinational corporation has just received an urgent request to send an employee to a foreign country to effect an emergency repair of a hydraulic pump that the company stopped making 6 years ago. The employee needed must be a mechanical engineer, must have knowledge of the particular pump (and therefore, let's assume, must have been with the corporation for at least 8 years), must be able to speak French, and must be willing to accept an overseas assignment. Obviously, there's not likely to be a report available that

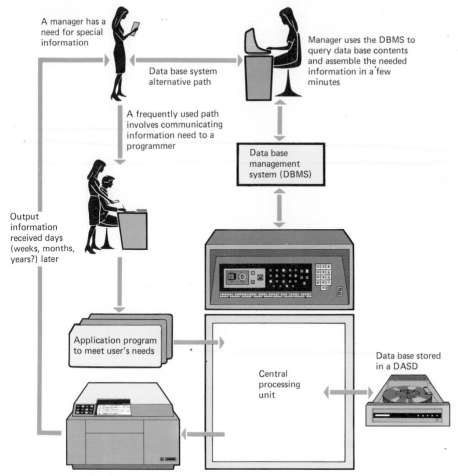

A manager has a need for special information

Data base system alternative path

Manager uses the DBMS to query data base contents and assemble the needed information in a few minutes

A frequently used path involves communicating information need to a programmer

Data base management system (DBMS)

Output information received days (weeks, months, years?) later

Application program to meet user's needs

Central processing unit

Data base stored in a DASD

Figure 17-9 A data base management system can give fast response to users with special information needs.

will have the names of engineers with just these characteristics. But the records on each employee stored in the data base do contain information on educational background, date of employment, work experience, and language capability. It might have been necessary in the past for the personnel manager to spend hours going through a lengthy printout of the entire personnel file in order to locate employees who match the requirements. With a DBMS, however, it's now possible for the manager to use an online terminal to request that personnel records be searched for the names and locations of French-speaking engineers with 8 or more years of company experience. Armed with such information obtained by the DBMS in a few minutes, the manager can then contact the named employees to fill the overseas assignment. You can take a closer look at the time-saving advantages of the DBMS in the reading that follows this chapter.

In addition to having direct access to data generated *within* the organization, a decision maker may also have *externally produced* data in his or her data base that can be readily accessible by the DBMS. Data suppliers may make external data available to users in several ways. In the least restrictive form, data may be *sold outright* by vendors on some medium such as magnetic tape, and buyers may then store these facts in their data bases in almost any way they choose. Economic statistics and United States census data, for example, may be purchased on tapes from government agencies for use in this way. Some organizations offer data on a *rental basis* to subscribers. Users then access these facts from terminals and pay for the resources used according to the pricing scheme employed by the supplier. A somewhat similar service is offered by firms that maintain *information retrieval data bases.* Many libraries, for example, use retrieval services that can access tens of millions of worldwide document references to quickly supply their users with sources of information on practically any subject. Finally, a user may buy special reports prepared from a data base owned by an outside supplier.

Figure 17-10 List structure.

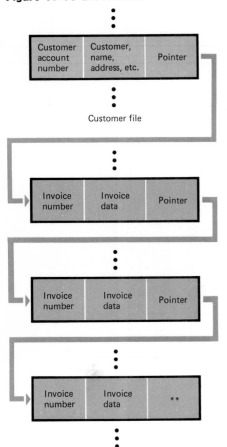

Data Base Structuring Techniques

We've seen how sequential, direct, and indexed sequential approaches are used to organize and structure the data in single files. But a DBMS is able to integrate data elements from several files to answer specific user inquiries for information. This means that the DBMS is able to access and retrieve data from nonkey record fields. That is, the DBMS is able to structure and tie together the logically related data from several large files.

Logical Structures. Identifying these logical relationships is a job of the data administrator. A **data definition language** is used for this purpose. The DBMS may then employ one of the following logical structuring techniques during storage, access, and retrieval operations:

1. *List structures.* In this logical approach, records are linked together by the use of pointers. We've seen that a pointer is a data item in one record that identifies the storage location of another logically related record. Records in a customer master file, for example, will contain the name and address of each customer, and each record in this file is identified by an account number. During an accounting period, a customer may buy a number of items on different days. Thus, the company may maintain an invoice file to reflect these transactions. A **list structure** could be used in this situation to show the unpaid invoices at any given time. Each record in the customer file would contain a field that would point to the record location of the first invoice for that customer in the invoice file (Figure 17-10). This invoice record, in turn, would be linked to later invoices for the customer. The last invoice in the chain would be identified by the use of a special character as a pointer.

2. *Hierarchical (tree) structures.* In this logical approach, data units are structured in multiple levels that graphically resemble an "upside down" tree with the root at the top and the branches formed below. There's a superior-subordinate relationship in a hierarchical (tree) structure. Below the single-root data component are subordinate elements or nodes, each of which, in turn, "own" one or more other elements (or none). Each element or branch in this structure below the root has only a single owner. Thus, as we see in Figure 17-11, a customer owns an invoice, and the invoice has subordinate items. The branches in a tree structure are not connected.

3. *Network structures.* Unlike the tree approach, which does not permit the connection of branches, the **network structure** permits the connection of the nodes in a multidirectional manner (see Figure 17-12). Thus, each node may have several owners and may, in turn, own any number of other data units. Data management software permits the extraction of the needed information from such a structure by beginning with any record in a file.

4. *Relational structures.* A relational structure is made up of many tables. The data are stored in the form of "relations" in these tables. For example, relation tables could be established to link a college course with the instructor of the course, and with the location of the class (see Figure 17-13). To find the name of the instructor and the location of the English class, the course/instructor relation is searched

Figure 17-11 Hierarchical (tree) structure.

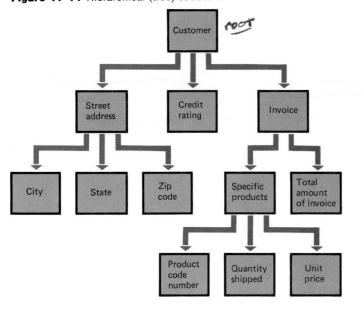

Figure 17-12 Network structure.

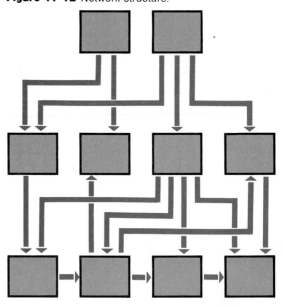

Course/instructor relation		Course/location relation		Other relations
COURSE	INSTRUCTOR	COURSE	LOCATION	For example, course related to time of meeting, days of meeting, hours of credit, etc.
ENGLISH 103 SCIENCE 116 MATH 101 • • •	FITT GOMEZ PIRELLI • • •	ENGLISH 103 MATH 101 SCIENCE 116 • •	MAIN 142 SCIENCE 125 SCIENCE 111 • •	

Figure 17-13 Relational structure.

to get the name ("Fitt"), and the course/location relation is searched to get the class location ("Main 142"). Many other relations are, of course, possible. This is a relatively new data base structuring approach that's expected to be widely implemented in the future.

Physical Structures. People visualize or structure data in logical ways for their own purposes. Thus, records R_1 and R_2 may always be logically linked and processed in sequence in one particular application. However, in a computer system it's quite possible that these records that are logically contiguous in one application are not physically stored together. Rather, the physical structure of the records in media and hardware may depend not only on the I/O and storage devices and techniques used, but also on the different logical relationships that users may assign to the data found in R_1 and R_2. For example, R_1 and R_2 may be records of credit customers who have shipments sent to the same block in the same city every 2 weeks. From the shipping department manager's perspective, then, R_1 and R_2 are sequential entries on a geographically organized shipping report. But in the A/R application, the customers represented by R_1 and R_2 may be identified, and their accounts may be processed, according to their account numbers which are widely separated. In short, then, the physical location of the stored records in many computer-based information systems is invisible to users.

Of course, the extent to which the logical structure of the most frequently processed applications corresponds to the physical storage techniques used may determine the amount of processing the system software must perform to reassemble the data to meet user requests. As you might expect, trying to design systems to efficiently serve many users while minimizing the use of computing resources is a difficult task that involves complex tradeoffs.

Advantages and Limitations of Data Base Systems

The advantages and disadvantages to be considered by the designers of data base systems are summarized in the following list:

Advantages	Limitations
Fewer applications programs and lengthy regular reports containing reference data may be needed when users can directly access the data base.	More complex and expensive hardware and software are needed.
Better integration (and less duplication) of data originating at different points is feasible.	A lengthy conversion period may be needed, higher personnel training costs may be incurred, and more sophisticated skills are needed by those responsible for the data base system.
Faster preparation of information to support nonrecurring tasks and changing conditions is possible.	People may be reluctant to adapt to significant changes in data processing procedures.
Savings in the cost of developing new applications, and in data entry and data storage costs, may be possible.	Sensitive data in online storage might find its way into unauthorized hands.
Fewer errors (and thus an increase in data integrity) may result when several records may be updated simultaneously.	Hardware or software failures might result in the destruction of vital data base contents.

Feedback and Review 17-1

A number of the file organization and processing alternatives available to system designers have been presented in this chapter. To test and reinforce your understanding of this material, rearrange the scrambled words to spell out the correct word indicated in the following sentences:

1. A _Field_ is a group of related characters that are treated as a single unit. Ⓓ Ⓔ Ⓕ Ⓘ Ⓛ

2. Related fields are grouped to form a record, and a collection of related records that are treated as a unit is a _FILE_. Ⓛ Ⓘ Ⓕ Ⓔ

3. Each record in a file is identified by a record key that must be _uNique_. Ⓔ Ⓤ Ⓝ Ⓤ Ⓘ Ⓠ

4. A data _BASE_ is a collection of logically related data elements that are structured in various ways to reduce data redundancy and improve access to needed facts. Ⓔ Ⓑ Ⓢ Ⓐ

5. Records in a sequential file are stored one after another in an ascending or descending order determined by the record _KEY_. Ⓔ Ⓨ Ⓚ

6. _Batch_ processing is very efficient when a high percentage of the file records in an application need to be periodically updated. Ⓐ Ⓣ Ⓗ Ⓒ Ⓑ

7. In storing records in a direct file, an arithmetic procedure called a _transform_ is often used to convert the record key into a DASD storage location number. Ⓜ Ⓣ Ⓡ Ⓐ Ⓡ Ⓞ Ⓝ Ⓢ Ⓕ

(E) (N) (X) (I) (D)

8. When both batch and online processing must be supported by the same file, the records may be organized in sequence and an ___index___ may also be used to speed up record access time.

(P) (R) (S) (R) (A) (O) (M) (G)

9. Problems created when each department develops its own applications and files include data redundancy, file updating difficulties, and a lack of independence between data and ___programs___

(A) (S) (D) (D)

10. A data base is located in a ___DASD___.

(A) (A) (D) (T)

11. A ___Data___ dictionary is used by a data base administrator to document and maintain the definitions of the input data used in an organization.

(M) (S) (B) (D)

12. A collection of programs used to manage a data base is identified by the initials ___DBMS___.

(R) (K) (O) (N) (W) (E) (T)

13. Logical structuring techniques used by data base management systems include list, hierarchical, ___network___, and relational approaches.

510

1. Data may be organized into fields, records, files, and data bases. Different degrees of flexibility can be built into a system by using different approaches to organize, access, and process files.

2. A sequential file is one in which records are stored in an ascending or descending order determined by the record key. To access a sequential file record, the computer program must start at the beginning of the file, read in each record in sequence, and compare its key to the one that's needed. Transactions are typically accumulated, sorted into file key sequence, and processed in a single pass through the file. This is an efficient processing approach for many types of applications.

3. When a direct file organization is used, the computer can directly locate the key of the needed record without having to search through a sequence of records. A record may be stored in a direct file when its key number is converted by a transform algorithm into a DASD storage location number. When the computer is given the key of a record to be processed at a later time, it reuses the transform to go directly to the stored record.

4. When both batch and online processing must be supported by a single file, an indexed sequential file approach is often used. File records are organized in sequence for efficient batch processing, but an index is also used to speed up access to the records for online processing purposes. The advantages and limitations of the sequential, direct, and indexed sequential file approaches are summed up in Figure 17-8, page 501.

5. Problems are often created in an organization when each department independently develops its own applications and files. There's considerable duplication of data, all this redundant data may not be updated to accurately reflect the changes that occur, and the programs that process the data must usually be revised anytime there's a change in data format.

6. The data base concept was developed to reduce these difficulties. A data base system is designed around an integrated data file that emphasizes the independence of data and programs. Data transactions are introduced into the system only once. These data are then available as needed to all authorized applications and users of the data base. A data base administrator is responsible for establishing and controlling the data definitions and standards used by the organization. He or she is also responsible for determining the relationships among data elements.

7. A data base management system (DBMS) is a collection of storage and retrieval programs used to manage the data base. A DBMS can organize, process, and present selected data elements from the data base in response to queries from users. This permits users to "browse" through the data base until they have answers to nonrecurring questions. It also adds a great deal of flexibility to the information resources of an organization.

8. A DBMS may employ list, hierarchical, network, or relational structuring techniques to perform its functions. Each of these techniques is briefly summarized in the chapter. Some of the advantages and disadvantages of data base systems are also summarized at the end of the chapter.

KEY TERMS AND CONCEPTS

You should now be able to define and use the following terms and concepts (the numbers shown indicate the pages where the terms and concepts are first mentioned):

transaction file 495

master file 495

sequential files 496

direct (random or relative) file 498

transform 498

synonyms 498

pointer 498

indexed sequential file 500

index 500

indexed sequential access method (ISAM) 500

data base administrator (DBA) 504

data dictionary 504

data base management system (DBMS) 504

data definition language 506

list structure 506

hierarchical (tree) structure 507

network structure 507

relational structure 507

physical structure 508

TOPICS FOR REVIEW AND DISCUSSION

1. (*a*) How are data organized in business data processing systems? (*b*) What role does a record key play in file creation?

2. (*a*) How is a sequential file organized? (*b*) How are records in a sequential file accessed? (*c*) How are these records processed?

3. What conditions support the use of sequential files and batch processing?

4. What conditions support the use of direct files and direct-access processing?

5. (*a*) How is a record stored in a direct file? (*b*) How is it retrieved and processed?

6. (*a*) How are records stored in an indexed sequential file? (*b*) How are they retrieved and processed?

7. Discuss the advantages and limitations of the sequential, direct, and indexed sequential file approaches.

8. "If the key field in a sequential, direct, or indexed sequential file isn't relevant to the information that's needed, the entire file will likely need to be searched." Discuss this statement.

9. "Several problems are often created when different departments independently develop their own applications and files." Identify and discuss three of these problems.

10. How does the data base concept alleviate the problems identified in the previous question?

11. Why is the job of a data base administrator important?

12. (*a*) What's a data base management system? (*b*) Discuss how this DBMS can be used.

13. Identify and discuss the logical structuring techniques used by DBMSs.

14. (*a*) What are the advantages of data base systems? (*b*) The limitations?

17-1

1. field	6. batch	11. data
2. file	7. transform	12. DBMS
3. unique	8. index	13. network
4. base	9. programs	
5. key	10. DASD	

Making Decisions Faster with Data Base Management Systems

During a typical day in 1985, the manufacturing manager of a small, independent manufacturing company will employ sophisticated data base management systems utilizing computers to an extent presently affordable only by large firms. This significant change, which began in the late seventies, centers around a reinterpretation of the entire philosophy of information management.

Instead of "data processing" departments, with their technical jargon, there are "information management" departments. No longer do departments control "their" files; rather a system of organized collection and storage of basic transactions keeps track of operations such as production, material received, and shipment of finished goods, while the data base management system allows a reordering or manipulation of information to suit the needs or desires of each using department. Arthur E. Hutt describes the concept in the *Computer Handbook for Senior Management:* "An information system must be systematic and regular, like the bloodstream, and it must respond to fluctuations in need without depriving or drowning any of the organizations it serves." [1]

Computer Decisions magazine says, "Data base management systems are the hallmark of advanced computer use today. Enlightened organizations are spending hundreds of thousands of dollars to convert to this mode of information handling. Data base management systems change the way data is stored, organized and thought about." [2]

What does all of this mean to the manufacturing manager of the small manufacturing company in the year 1985? Let's consider the typical day of the manager of a

molded parts company which employs three hundred hourly workers.

7:30 a.m.—Foreman Jones is waiting to see the manufacturing manager when he arrives. Jones has a serious problem with employee Smith who recently transferred from another department. Smith's efficiency performance has been only 50 percent since joining the new department.

The manager submits an inquiry on the CRT to data files and determines the composite efficiency percentage for Smith since date of hire and from the department prior to transfer. He also calls up attendance history and records of previous disciplinary action. Based upon the composite information, the manager advises Jones to initiate discharge action. The manager will support discharge based upon data available.

8:00 a.m.—Personnel Manager Jackson stops by the manufacturing manager's office to get his signature on papers for Smith's discharge and also informs the manufacturing manager that he is concerned about safety conditions in Department 20.

The manager submits an inquiry on the CRT to data files of reported accidents in Department 20 including frequency and severity rates compared with all other departments. He agrees with Jackson that a worrisome trend is developing and agrees to initiate special housekeeping and safety efforts in that department.

9:30 a.m.—Materials Manager Clark calls a meeting to review scheduling in the machining department which is presently a bottleneck because of the breakdown of a major machine.

The manager submits an inquiry on the CRT terminal to determine all orders in the house routed to the work center involved, as well as orders presently in queue directly in front of the bottleneck center. He considers the

---

[1] *Computer Handbook for Senior Management,* chap. 10 (New York: Macmillan, 1978).

[2] "Consolidating the Data Base Successfully," *Computer Decisions,* March 1979, p. 34.

displayed critical ratio (that is, combination of promised ship data and time required for remaining operations) and advises the materials manager as to which orders are to be given priority.

10:30 a.m.—Manufacturing Engineering Manager Newell comes to the manufacturing manager's office to discuss a number of projects.

First, an engineering change is being considered on a manufactured component.

The manager submits an inquiry on the CRT terminal to determine available inventory and cost at each stage of production for the part to be changed. With the aid of the engineer, estimates are made of material and labor costs under the new method and this information is input to data file and a projected new manufacturing cost is displayed. A decision is made as to the effective date of the change and the disposition of inventories.

Second, the Engineer indicates that Foreman Rose is complaining that standards can not be met on part number 98765.

The manager submits an inquiry on his terminal for part number 98765 for the same operation being performed on all shifts. He determines that the rate is being met by other shifts. Foreman Rose is notified.

Third, there is some indication of an error in yield assumptions on the bill of material for part number 56789.

The manager submits an inquiry on his terminal to determine actual versus standard yield for part number 56789 for the year to date. Indications are that an error must exist in the bill of material for part number 56789, and the engineer is asked to investigate.

1:15 p.m.—The quality manager complains that part number 23456 is being scrapped at a very high rate in the molding operation.

The manager submits an inquiry on his terminal to the tool history record of the mold used for part number 23456 and determines the last time the mold was cleaned and sharpened and the number of pieces made since the last repair. He determines that the mold should be removed from service and suggests that the manufacturing engineer and materials manager take appropriate action.

2:00 p.m.—A meeting is held with Controller Dewey to discuss a number of problems.

First, a question of actual performance versus projected performance of a new piece of equipment—a capital project follow-up—is undertaken.

The manager inquires on his terminal to determine actual production rates and cost for the work center of the new machine. Comparison with the plan shows the project to be on target.

Second, a concern is expressed about inventory turnover in product line X.

The manager inquires on his terminal to determine inventories of items in product line X and the months of supply on hand. The controller and the manager agree that a reduction in schedule is necessary.

Third, a concern is expressed about the profitability of product line Y.

The manager inquires on his terminal to determine current actual versus standard cost of product line Y. They agree that a special program must be initiated to improve performance on that product line.

4:00 p.m.—Before leaving the plant for the day, the manufacturing manager submits an inquiry on his terminal to determine first shift production in units and dollars in comparison with plan. Total shipments are determined and specific inquiries are made regarding "hot list" items scheduled for shipment.

In the past, the primary limitation of information management from the user's point of view has been the slow, laborious task of programming to meet each user's need, one at a time. If in the eighties, managers can create an atmosphere within their organizations which gives proper recognition to the value of the information resource and *the quality of input data,* they can take advantage of the major breakthrough which data base management offers: "When a nonprogrammer manager can explore the database and produce reports himself, executive questions can be answered in minutes, not weeks." [3]

[3]"Data Base System Helps Management Help Itself," *Computer Decisions,* October 1979, p. 86.

—Robert L. French, *Business Horizons,* October 1980, pp. 33–36. Reprinted with permission.

chapter 18

Management Information Systems

MANAGEMENT INFORMATION: BLESSING OR CURSE?

At a recent regional meeting of the Independent Computer Consultants Association, one of the members was telling his table partners about a system he'd run across in which an order triggered an *addition* to the inventory count.

Less serious are systems that trigger useless reports. One of my clients, soon after he took over an MIS department, rode the circuit of his outlying user sites. He wanted to get acquainted with them, find out what services he might be able to provide to them.

The manager of one plant was eager to let him know. "Yeah sure," he said, "you can be a lot of help to me." The MIS director was equally eager to know how. "Could you *please* stop sending me that report every month," he added.

At one of my former jobs, I was the mystified recipient of a monthly report for which I had no earthly use. The first few months after it started to appear on my desk, I studied it, seriously. I figured it had to tell me something. It never did. I knew it came from the DP department, but I couldn't figure out why.

Finally, I checked with the DP manager—a friendly, accommodating fellow—who told me he'd be damned if he knew. He'd inherited it, and its origin and purpose were lost forever. But the computer continued to churn it out every month. I shudder to think how many unread, unused reports are being distributed every day.

—Robert B. Forest, "Blessings/Curses on Thee, Designer," *Infosystems*, May 1980, p. 98. Reprinted with permission.

Any system—and the MIS is no exception—requires the cooperative efforts of those served by the system and those who develop and maintain it. (Photo courtesy Control Data Corporation)

Looking Ahead

This chapter introduces you to some general management information concepts and shows you why management information systems (MIS) are needed. You'll then consider some of the issues involved in planning for an MIS and in using an MIS for decision making. The next section presents some of the organizing issues that must be faced when an MIS is implemented. And the last section in the chapter discusses some of the control issues that arise when an MIS is installed.

Thus, after studying this chapter, you should be able to:

▌ Explain why different types of information are needed by managers at different levels in a business

▌ Define the MIS concept and discuss the issues that must be considered during the planning for an MIS

▌ Describe how an MIS can help improve managerial planning and decision making

▌ Identify and discuss a number of organizing issues that must be considered when an MIS is installed

▌ Outline the managerial control implications and the internal control issues that arise from the use of an MIS

▌ Understand and use the key terms and concepts listed at the end of this chapter

MANAGEMENT INFORMATION CONCEPTS

As long as an important resource is supplied to us when and where we need it, in the right quantity and quality, and at a reasonable cost, we tend to take it for granted. It's only when the cost increases and/or the supply and quality of the resource seems to deteriorate that we recognize its importance. So it has been with management information. Previously acceptable information systems have seemed to deteriorate in recent years. In simpler times, many of the systems that have been discarded in the last decade were considered models of efficiency. But times are not simple today for managers. The growing size of many organizations, and the speed with which new technological discoveries are now being applied for competitive purposes combine to produce a complex and challenging management environment. At the beginning of this century, for example, there was an average wait of 33 years between an invention and its application. But the laser was invented in 1958 and was being used just 7 years later for manufacturing and surgical purposes. And as this application rate continues to accelerate, less reaction time is available to managers (see Figure 18-1). Thus, as pressures increase from domestic and foreign competitors, managers have found that previously acceptable systems are no longer adequate to meet their information needs.

Information Needs of Managers

What information does a manager need to manage effectively? A common need basic to all managers is an understanding of the purpose of the organization i.e., its policies, its programs, its plans, and its goals. But beyond these basic informational requirements, the question of what information is needed can be answered only in broad general terms because individual managers differ in the ways in which they view information, in their analytical approaches to using it, and in their conceptual organization of relevant facts.

An additional factor that complicates the subject of the information needed by managers is the *organizational level* of the managerial job. In the smallest businesses, there are few managerial levels, and the managers tend to be generalists. That is, they are knowledgeable about most (if not all) of the firm's activities. But as firms grow in size, people with specialized knowledge are hired and additional managerial levels are created. Information that's satisfactory for generalists (who can often use their overall knowledge of the business to fill in the missing gaps) is often not acceptable when supplied to specialists. It thus becomes necessary to supply different types of information to people at different levels.

Top-level managers still must have a general understanding of the firm's activities. Since they are charged with weighing risks and making major policy decisions on such matters as new product development, new plant authorizations, and so on, they need the type of information that will support these long-range **strategic plans and decisions.** *Middle-level managers* are responsible for making the **tactical decisions** that will allocate the resources and establish the controls needed to implement the top-level plans. And *lower-level managers* make the day-to-day **operational decisions** to schedule and control specific tasks. The actual results of an operation may be checked daily against planned expectations, and corrective actions may be taken as needed. In short, as Figure 18-2 shows, managers use their time differently, need internal information with varying degrees of detail, and need different mixes of internal and external information in order to make their decisions.

Properties of the Needed Management Information

As a general rule, the more information serves to reduce the element of uncertainty in the decisions made by managers at all levels, the greater is its value. But like other basic resources available to managers, information is usually not free. The cost of acquiring information must usually be compared with the benefits to be obtained from its use. Just as it's economically foolish to spend $100 to mine $75 worth of coal, so, too, is it unsound to produce information costing $100 if this information doesn't lead to actions that yield a greater return. Generally speaking, information that possesses the properties of *accuracy, timeliness, completeness,* and *conciseness,* will be more valuable than information lacking one or more of these characteristics. However, compromises are often made in one or more of these properties for economic reasons.

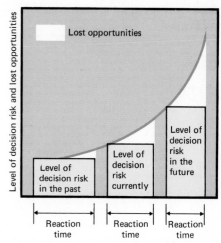

Figure 18-1 A major business decision that might have taken several years to implement 10 years ago must now be carried out in a shorter period if the business is to remain competitive. But while the available management reaction time is shrinking, each decision may carry a greater risk and be valid for a shorter time period. Furthermore, as reaction time shrinks, profitable opportunities are lost because preoccupied managers fail to recognize them.

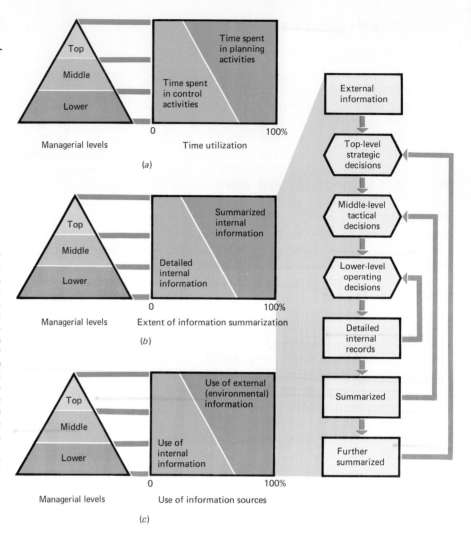

Figure 18-2 (*a*) More time is generally spent at the lower managerial levels performing control activities (e.g., checking to make sure that production schedules are being met), while at the upper levels more time is spent on planning (e.g., determining the location and specifications of a new production plant). (*b*) Lower-level managers need detailed information relating to daily operations of specific departments, but top executives are best served with information that summarizes trends and indicates exceptions to what was expected. (*c*) The higher a manager is in an organization, the more likely it is that he or she will use information obtained from external sources. A supervisor uses internally generated feedback information to control production processes, but a president studying the feasibility of a new plant needs external information about customer product acceptance, pollution control, local tax structures, and labor availability.

Accuracy. **Accuracy** is the ratio of correct information to the total amount of information produced over a period. If 1,000 items of information are produced and 950 of these items give a correct report of the actual situation, then the accuracy level is 0.95. Whether this level is high enough depends on the information being produced. Fifty incorrect bank balances in a mailing of 1,000 bank statements are intolerable. But if physical inventory records kept on large quantities of inexpensive parts achieve an accuracy level of 0.95, this might be acceptable. In the case of bank statements, greater accuracy *must* be obtained. In the case of the parts inventory, greater accuracy *could* be achieved, but the additional value to managers of having a more accurate inventory might be less than the additional costs required.

Timeliness. <u>Timeliness</u> is another important information characteristic. It's of little consolation to a manager to know that information that arrived too late to be of use was accurate. Accuracy alone isn't enough. How fast must be the response time of the information system? Unfortunately, it's once again impossible to give an answer which will satisfy all situations. In the case of regular reports, an immediate response time following each transaction would involve a steady outpouring of documents. The result would be a costly avalanche of paper that would bury managers. Thus, a compromise is often required. The response time should be short enough so that the information does not lose its freshness and value, but it should be long enough to reduce volume (and costs) and reveal important trends that signal the need for action. Of course, when instant access to "time critical" information is needed, quick-response online systems must be used.

Completeness. Most managers faced with a decision to make have been frustrated at some time by having supporting information that's accurate, timely—and incomplete. An example of the consequences of failure to consolidate related pieces of information occurred at Pearl Harbor in 1941. Historians tell us that data available, in bits and pieces and at scattered points, if integrated, would have signaled the danger of a Japanese attack. Better integration of the facts available at scattered points in a business for the purpose of furnishing managers with more **complete information** is a goal of information systems designers.

Conciseness. Many traditional information systems have been designed on the assumption that lack of completeness is the most critical problem facing managers. This assumption has often led designers to employ an ineffective shotgun approach, peppering managers with more information than they can possibly use. Important information, along with relatively useless data, is often buried in stacks of detailed reports. Managers are then faced with the problem of extracting those items of information that they need. **Concise information** that summarizes the relevant data and points out areas of exception to normal or planned activities is what is often needed by—but less often supplied to— today's managers.

An MIS Orientation — *structure data so is readily available to all levels in the form they need.*

In the late 1960s and early 1970s, many managers began to realize that they weren't able to cope with rapidly changing conditions merely by using the routine reports that their traditional systems were producing. Their information didn't possess the properties mentioned above, and it was no longer adequate to meet their needs. Responding to these management needs, system designers began to develop new computer-oriented management information systems that were more responsive and more comprehensive than those that had existed just a few years earlier. There was initially talk of designing a

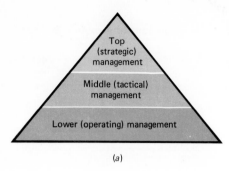

(a)

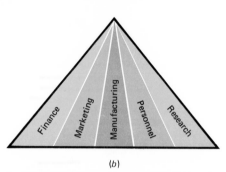

(b)

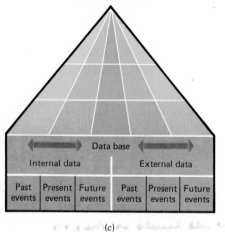

(c)

Figure 18-3 MIS design considerations.

completely integrated "total system" built around a single online data base that would instantly give managers all the information they needed to make their decisions. As you might expect, this proved to be an unrealistic goal that failed to recognize the complexities of operating a modern business. Few, if any, total system designs were actually attempted. Instead, the system designers in an organization developed a long-range conceptual model of a management information system for their organization and then gradually began to integrate the existing information-producing systems in the organization into their long-range plan. This integration continues today.

The **management information system (MIS)** concept has been defined in dozens of ways. Since one organization's model of an MIS is likely to differ from that of another, its not surprising that their MIS definitions would also vary in scope and breadth. For our purposes, an MIS can be defined as a network of computer-based data processing procedures developed in an organization and integrated as necessary with manual and other procedures for the purpose of providing timely and effective information to support decision making and other necessary management functions.

Although MIS models differ, most of them recognize the concepts shown in Figure 18-3. In addition to what might be termed the *horizontal* management structure shown in Figure 18-3*a*, an organization is also divided *vertically* into different business specialties and functions which require separate information flows (see Figure 18-3*b*). Combining the horizontal managerial levels with the vertical business specialties produces the complex organizational structure shown in Figure 18-3*c*. Underlying this structure is a data base consisting, ideally, of internally and externally produced data relating to past, present, and predicted future events.

The formidable task of the MIS designer is to develop the information flow needed to support decision making. This flow is illustrated in Figure 18-4. Generally speaking, much of the information needed by managers who occupy different levels and who have different responsibilities is obtained from a collection of existing information systems (or subsystems). These systems may be tied together very closely in an MIS. More often, however, they are more loosely coupled.

PLANNING ISSUES AND THE MIS

To "plan" is to decide in advance on a future course of action. Thus, *planning* involves making decisions about long-term goals, and about the procedures and controls needed to achieve these goals. An MIS affects the planning function in at least two ways. *First,* MIS designers must consider a number of issues as they make plans to create and implement an MIS in an organization. And *second,* the use of an evolving MIS is likely to have an impact on the quality of the business plans being made by managers.

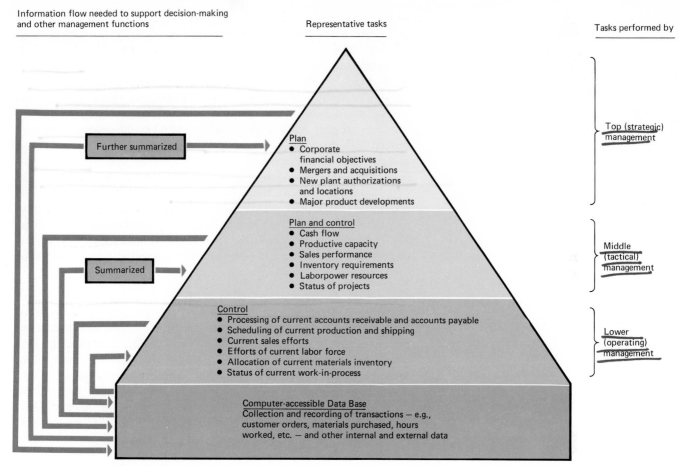

Information flow needed to support decision-making and other management functions	Representative tasks	Tasks performed by

Plan
- Corporate financial objectives
- Mergers and acquisitions
- New plant authorizations and locations
- Major product developments

Plan and control
- Cash flow
- Productive capacity
- Sales performance
- Inventory requirements
- Laborpower resources
- Status of projects

Control
- Processing of current accounts receivable and accounts payable
- Scheduling of current production and shipping
- Current sales efforts
- Efforts of current labor force
- Allocation of current materials inventory
- Status of current work-in-process

Computer-accessible Data Base
Collection and recording of transactions — e.g., customer orders, materials purchased, hours worked, etc. — and other internal and external data

Further summarized

Summarized

Top (strategic) management

Middle (tactical) management

Lower (operating) management

Figure 18-4 The task of MIS designers is to develop the information flow needed to support decision making.

Issues Involved in Planning for an MIS

Figures 18-3 and 18-4 may have given you a *general* idea of the problems and challenges MIS designers face as they draw up long-range plans for an organization's MIS. But some of the more *specific* questions that may be considered during the planning for an MIS are:

▌ *Should a "top-down" or "bottom-up" approach to MIS development be followed?* The *top-down approach* begins with studies of organizational goals and the types of decisions made by managers. From these studies comes a model of the information flow in the organization and the design requirements for the system. The *advantage* of this approach is that it's a logical and sensible way to attack a problem (buildings and airplanes are essentially designed in this way), and it can make it easier

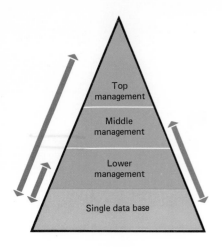

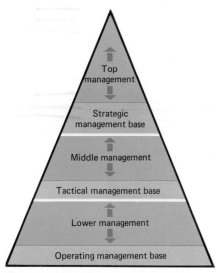

Figure 18-5 MIS design alternatives.

to integrate system elements. The *disadvantage* is that it's difficult to define organizational goals and the decision-making activities of managers in the precise terms required for MIS design. There's a risk of building a large and expensive system that's not effective. The **bottom-up approach,** on the other hand, begins at the operating level with the existing procedures for processing transactions and updating files. The add-on modules to support planning, controlling, and decision-making activities are then built as they are needed. The *advantage* of this approach is that smaller "bites" of work are tackled, and the danger of building a complex and ineffective MIS is minimized. The *disadvantage* is that this approach may not lead to the development of high-potential systems above the operating level. And if such higher-level systems are attempted, it's then often necessary to redesign the existing programs and procedures to provide the integration of information that higher-level managers require. Given these considerations, it's not surprising that MIS designers often attempt to use the best attributes of each of these approaches.

Can a single data base be created to satisfy the differing information needs of the three managerial levels? Most information systems today serve the needs of operating managers and, to a lesser extent, middle managers. They provide internally produced data dealing with past and current activities. However, a growing number of MISs are now using internal data and carefully developed planning models incorporating assumptions about external conditions to simulate responses to the "what if?" questions of top executives. A problem facing MIS planners is whether to attempt to organize and structure a *single* data base to meet varying needs or to create *different* bases for different *horizontal* levels. Figure 18-5 shows the alternatives.

Can different business specialties share the same data base? Can the MIS supply from a single data base the information needed by marketing, production, finance, and personnel managers at different levels, or must separate *vertically* oriented data bases be designed for each specialty? Different business functions have traditionally had their own information systems. Attempting to integrate these separate systems into one or more corporate data bases that will serve the broader needs of many managers is a formidable challenge, but the effort is being made.

Can externally produced data be incorporated into a data base? To be of value to higher-level managers, an MIS must supply information about the external world. The growing availability of external data in machine-sensible form and/or the use of external data banks makes more data available to the firm's MIS. It's the designer's responsibility to see that these new facts are incorporated into an MIS in meaningful ways.

To what extent should an attempt be made to "solve the triangle"? That is, to what extent should designers attempt to create an overall MIS that would simultaneously satisfy the information needs of most or all the segments shown in Figure 18-3c? The complexity of the problems involved usually dictates that designers take a gradual and conservative approach.

Managerial Planning With an MIS

When compared with earlier information systems, an MIS can have an impact on the quality of a manager's plans by:

▎ *Causing faster awareness of problems and opportunities.* An MIS can quickly signal out-of-control conditions requiring corrective action when actual performance deviates from what was originally planned. New plans can then be implemented to correct the situation(s). Masses of current and historical internal and external data can be analyzed by the use of statistical methods in order to detect opportunities. And data stored online may permit managers to probe and query a data base to receive quick replies to their planning questions (Figure 18-6).

Figure 18-6 Access to an effective MIS can aid managers in making decisions in all phases of their jobs: organizing, planning, staffing, and controlling. (Courtesy IBM)

Figure 18-7 Graphics generated by the computer and developed with information supplied by the MIS can contribute to well informed management decisions. (Courtesy Radio Shack Division, Tandy Corporation)

■ *Enabling managers to devote more time to planning.* Use of an MIS can reduce the need to wade through mounds of routine reports. More attention may then be given to analytical and intellectual matters associated with planning.

■ *Permitting managers to give timely consideration to more complex relationships.* An MIS gives the manager the ability to evaluate more possible alternatives. More of the internal and external variables that may have a bearing on the outcome of these alternatives can also be considered. And managers can do a better job of identifying and assessing the probable economic and social effects of different courses of action. The awareness of such effects, of course, influences the ultimate decision. In the past, oversimplified assumptions had to be made if resulting decisions were to be timely. More complex relationships can now be considered and scheduled. These relationships are increasingly being highlighted through the use of charts, maps, and other visual presentations displayed on the screens of the *graphic terminals* discussed in Chapters 6 and 8 (Figure 18-7). In short, an MIS can furnish managers with planning information that couldn't have been produced at all a few years ago or that couldn't have been produced in time to be of any value.

■ *Assisting in decision implementation.* When decisions have been made, an MIS can assist in the development of subordinate plans that will be needed to implement these decisions. Computer-based techniques to schedule project activities have been developed and are now widely used. Through the use of such techniques, business resources can be utilized and controlled effectively.

Computer-based MISs now regularly support the planning and decision-making activities of managers in a number of business areas (see Figure 18-8). The components of an MIS that assist managers in these activities are often called **decision support systems (DSS).** One important planning and decision-making tool is simulation.

The Use of Simulation. As Figure 18-9 shows, the simulation concept rests on reality or fact. In complex situations few people (if any) fully understand all aspects of the situation. Theories are thus developed which may focus attention on only part of the complex whole. In some situations models may then be built in order to test or represent a theory. Finally, **simulation** is the use of a model in the attempt to identify and/or reflect the behavior of a real person, process, or system. In business, for example, managers may evaluate proposed projects or strategies by constructing theoretical models. They can then determine what happens to these models when certain conditions are given or when certain assumptions are tested. Simulation is thus a trial-and-error problem-solving approach that's very useful in planning.

Simulation models have helped *top executives* decide, for example, whether or not to acquire a new plant. Among the dozens of complicating variables that would have to be incorporated into such models are facts and assumptions about the present and potential size of the total market, and the

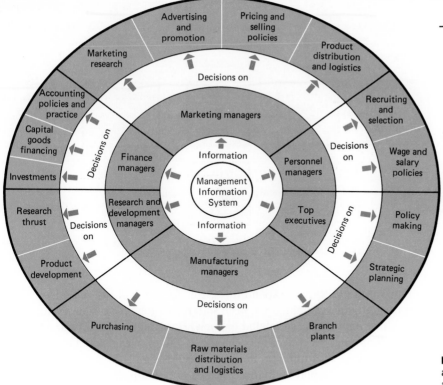

Figure 18-8 An MIS supports the planning and decision-making activities of many managers.

present and potential company share of this total market. Simulation is also helpful to *middle-level managers.* For example, simulation models are used to improve inventory management. The problem of managing inventories is complicated because there are conflicting desires among organizational units. To illustrate, the purchasing department may prefer to buy large quantities of materials in order to get lower prices. The production department also likes to have large inventories on hand to eliminate shortages and make possible long—and efficient—production runs. And the sales department prefers large finished-goods inventories so that sales will not be lost because of out-of-stock conditions. But the finance department is opposed to large inventory levels because storage expense is increased and funds are tied up for longer periods of time. Through the use of simulated inventory amounts and simulated assumptions about such factors as reorder lead times and cost of being out of stock, managers can experiment with various approaches to arrive at more profitable inventory levels.

Simulation models serving managers at different levels may also be integrated into an overall **corporate modeling** approach to planning and decision making. For example, Potlatch Forests, Inc., a producer of lumber and wood pulp products, has a corporate planning staff that has developed an overall corporate financial model. Given assumptions from top executives about eco-

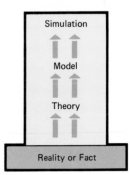

Figure 18-9 The simulation concept.

Figure 18-10 The strategies, goals, and economic assumptions of managers serve as the basis for *market forecasts*. This expectation of how many items can be sold then becomes the basis for determining (1) how and when to acquire materials and make the items (the *production plans*), (2) how and when to have the money on hand to pay for the acquired materials and produced items (the *financial plans*), and (3) how and when to promote and distribute the items (the *marketing plans*). And these plans are then used in simulations to estimate such variables as profit and return on investment. Of course, the results of these simulations may bring about changes in established plans and/or the results may cause changes in strategies and assumptions. Once initial simulations have been concluded and high-level plans have been made, operational plans at lower levels are often needed to implement the decisions.

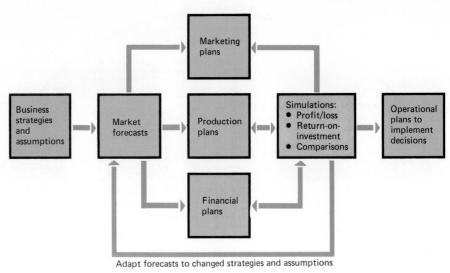

Adapt forecasts to changed strategies and assumptions

nomic conditions, capital expenditures, etc., for a 5-year future period, simulation runs produce estimated financial statements for each of the 5 years. Executives then analyze the simulated financial statements. If results are judged to be disappointing, executives may change variables in the model that are under their control—e.g., future capital expenditures—and the simulations are repeated. When acceptable financial results are obtained, they become the targets for planning at lower levels in the company. When feasible, lower-level plans are formulated (again, simulation models are used), and they are assembled into an overall corporate plan. In summary, then, the planning and decision process followed by many business managers may resemble the one shown in Figure 18-10. Of course, the output of simulation models is only as good as the facts and assumptions that people feed into the computer.

ORGANIZING ISSUES AND THE MIS

The **organizing** function involves the grouping of people and other resources into logical and efficient units in order to carry out plans and achieve goals. In a manufacturing company, for example, people may be grouped by *type of work* (production, marketing), by *geographic area* (district sales offices), and by *product line* produced or sold. As MISs are designed and implemented, there's often a need to reconsider the answers to several important and interrelated organizing questions. Included in these questions are:

▌ Will decision making be centralized or decentralized?

▌ Will data processing be centrally located or dispersed?

▌ Will the data itself be centrally stored or dispersed?

- Where will computing resources be located?

- How will the MIS function be organized?

As is often the case, the "right" answers to these questions for one firm may be very wrong for another. We can, however, look at some of the general implications of these MIS issues.

The Centralization/Decentralization of Authority

"Authority" is the right to give orders and the power to see that they're carried out. **Centralization of authority** in a business refers to a concentration of the important decision-making powers in the hands of a relatively few executives. **Decentralization of authority,** on the other hand, refers to the extent to which significant decisions are made at lower levels. In very small businesses, *all* decision-making power is likely to be centralized in the hands of the owner. In larger firms, the amount of authority that's held at different levels can vary.

When an MIS is used, a greater degree of centralized control *can* be supported in a business because top executives can be given information from dispersed departments in time to decide on appropriate action. Without an MIS, such action must often be determined at lower levels because of time, distance, and familiarity factors. An MIS may thus permit top executives to exercise decision-making options that were previously not feasible. Note, though, that the fact that an MIS reduces the necessity for decentralization of authority doesn't mean that authority should now be centralized. What it does mean is that the degree to which authority is centralized or decentralized in an organization is now often determined more by managerial philosophy and judgment than by necessity.

The Centralization/Dispersal of Data Processing Activities

In precomputer days, data processing activities were handled by each department on a separate and thus decentralized basis. When computers first appeared, however, the tendency was to maximize the use of expensive hardware by establishing one or more central processing centers to serve the organization's needs. Today, the rapid reduction in hardware costs and the improvements being made in data communications services make it possible for organizations to structure their MIS around either a centralized or a more dispersed approach to data processing. They can still use a **centralized data processing** approach to process data originating at all using points. They can decide to use **decentralized data processing** by placing small and inexpensive computers in the hands of every using group. Or they can choose to follow some alternative *distributed data processing* (*DDP*) approach between these centralized and decentralized extremes. As Figure 18-11 indicates, there are a countless number of alternative DDP possibilities available today along the

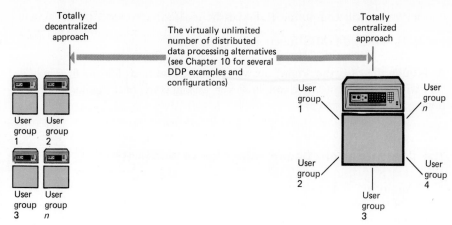

Figure 18-11 Data processing activities can be totally centralized, totally decentralized, or distributed in different degrees and in countless ways to meet the needs of the organizations they serve. Chapter 10, "Data Communication and Distributed Data Processing Networks," discusses and illustrates some of the distributed alternatives. The number of DDP installations is growing rapidly today.

continuum between centralization and decentralization. If you've read Chapter 10, you're already familiar with some of the *star, hierarchical,* and *ring* variations that are possible when DDP approaches are used. If you've not yet read Chapter 10, a quick glance now through the illustrations in that chapter will give you a general idea of some of the possibilities.

The closer an organization positions its data processing activities to the *centralized approach* on the continuum shown in Figure 18-11, the more likely it is to achieve the following *benefits:*

> *Economies of scale.* With adequate processing volume, the use of larger and more powerful computers may result in lower record processing costs. Duplications in record storage and program preparation may be reduced.

> *Better systems integration.* Developing common customer account numbers is necessary to integrate the various files in which customers may be included. Such development may be easier when all customer-related files are processed at a central site. Standards and security provisions may also be easier to implement and enforce.

> *Certain personnel advantages.* It may be possible to concentrate fewer skilled programmers at a central site and make better use of their talents. A larger computer center that utilizes the latest data base management system and sophisticated MIS concepts may also be more challenging and appealing to computer professionals.

And as an organization moves on the continuum shown in Figure 18-11 toward the *decentralized approach,* it's more likely to receive the following *benefits:*

> *Greater interest and motivation at user levels.* Users in control of their own computers and MIS programs may be more likely to maintain the accuracy of input data and use the equipment in ways that best meet

their particular needs. (Of course, if a totally decentralized approach is used, it's unlikely that much progress can be achieved in developing an integrated MIS.)

▮ _Better response to user needs._ The standardization that's typically required for a centralized MIS may not be equally suitable for all users. With a more dispersed approach, special programs may be written to meet exact user needs. In addition, although small hardware will probably be slower than centralized equipment, it doesn't have to be allocated to the needs of several user groups. Information considered important to one group doesn't have to be delayed because higher priority is given to the jobs of others. Thus, prompt processing of a job by a small machine may provide users with faster _turnaround_ time.

▮ _Less downtime risk._ A breakdown in centralized equipment or communications links may leave the entire MIS inoperative. A similar breakdown in one user group, however, doesn't affect other operations.

There's no general answer to the question of where data _should_ be processed. Some small organizations have centralized data processing because their departments lack the volume to justify separate systems. Some businesses made up of autonomous "companies within a company" follow a decentralized approach. But most larger organizations today are following some type of DDP approach that disperses some processing capability to user groups to achieve the benefits just outlined. However, the overall coordination and control of the processing network, and the development of companywide MIS plans, are generally handled at one or a few central sites.

The Centralization/Dispersal of Stored Data

In precomputer days, detailed data were typically stored in using departments, and summarized facts needed to prepare companywide reports were sent to central offices. When the first centralized computer centers were established to maximize the use of expensive hardware, the tendency was then to transfer much of the storage of the detailed data to magnetic tapes and other media kept at a central computer site.

Data with companywide significance continue to be stored at a central site. But hardware cost reductions, data communications improvements, and DDP network designs now make it possible to return files with local significance to user departments for storage and maintenance. Thus, many organizations are now in the process of deciding to what extent (if any) they will relocate previously centralized computer-based data to user groups. Questions involving such factors as data redundancy, file security, file updating problems, and data communications costs must be considered in these data storage decisions.

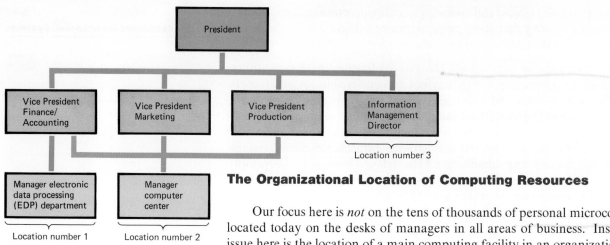

Figure 18-12 Alternative locations for computing resources.

The Organizational Location of Computing Resources

Our focus here is *not* on the tens of thousands of personal microcomputers located today on the desks of managers in all areas of business. Instead, the issue here is the location of a main computing facility in an organization. Let's look at three possibilities for a typical manufacturing firm as shown in Figure 18-12.

Location Number One. Historically, people in finance and accounting departments were often the first to see that a computer could be used to process large-volume applications such as customer billing. Thus, the computer was most often placed under the control of financial managers. It still remains in this traditional location in many organizations in spite of the following possible drawbacks:

▌ Computer center people are likely to give a higher priority to accounting applications at the expense of important nonfinancial jobs.

▌ Buried several management levels down in one functional area of the business, computer people lack organizational status and have a limited view of how to develop an overall MIS.

Location Number Two. An approach that can avoid the lack of objectivity in setting job priorities is to establish a company "service center" to handle applications. The computer center manager may report to a neutral top-level executive or an executive committee. The center basically occupies a position that's outside the mainstream of the organization. The center manager thus has limited influence. Little attempt is usually made to initiate system improvements or develop an integrated MIS plan.

Location Number Three. Overcoming the limitations of the other alternatives, location three:

▌ *Confers organizational status.* A high-level location is needed to give impartial service to all groups that receive processed information. The top computer executive (holding such titles as "Information Management Director," "Director, MIS," "Vice President, Information Management" and so on) has a strong voice in determining suitable new applications. He or she is also responsible for studying existing corporatewide systems and for developing the MIS model that will permit better integration of information resources.

▎ *Encourages innovation.* People in an independent department can be encouraged to recommend improvement and change whenever and wherever the opportunity arises.

Organizing the MIS Department

The organization of the MIS department itself can take many forms depending on how an organization responds to the issues presented earlier in this section. Recognizing, then, that other logical arrangements are possible, Figure 18-13 gives us a framework from which combinations or further subdivisions may be made as needed.

The *data base administrator* function discussed in the last chapter is usually found in an MIS department. The activities of the DBA include establishing and controlling data definitions, defining the relationships between data items, and designing the data base security system to guard against unauthorized use. The *system analysis/design* section acts as the vital interface between user groups and the other sections in the MIS department. The *program preparation* function is often subdivided into new applications and maintenance groups. The function of the *computer-operations* section is to prepare input data and produce output information on a continuing basis. The control of equipment time and the scheduling of processing activities are duties of the

Figure 18-13 Possible functional organization of MIS department.   **Figure 18-14** Possible project organization of MIS department.

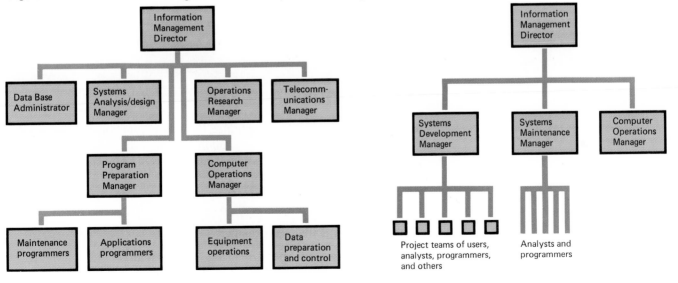

operations supervisor. Controls are also needed to ensure that input data are accurate. Computer operators, operators of input devices, and media librarians are found in this section. **Operations research (OR)** is the name given to the quantitative methodology and knowledge that's used to help managers make decisions. Those in the operations research section may logically be assigned to some other corporate planning element. But since the use of computers and data bases is required to support many of the planning and decision support systems that OR people often help design, there are good reasons to include them in an MIS department.

The *telecommunications* function can also logically be placed elsewhere. However, there's a growing tendency to place the responsibility for both computing and telecommunications services under a single information management executive. In smaller firms, an analyst or programmer might be able to make the necessary telecommunications decisions. But as the knowledge needed to manage the complex data communications networks discussed in Chapter 10 becomes more specialized, the need for a separate telecommunications function becomes more acute.

The term **information resource management (IRM)** is now being used to emphasize the belief that all the fragmented and overlapping information functions in an organization should be combined and placed under the control of a senior information executive. An IRM emphasis would thus also likely include in Figure 18-13 the *word processing and electronic mail/message office system functions* discussed in Chapter 11. Few businesses have taken this step beyond the MIS organization presented in Figure 18-13, but there's little doubt that many organizational changes will be made in the next decade as the distinctions between data processing, telecommunications, and office technologies become more blurred.

Figure 18-14 shows an alternative to the **functional organization** of the MIS department presented in Figure 18-13. Special system study teams of users, analysts, programmers, and others are often assigned the responsibility for designing and implementing a new system. Under this type of **project organization,** a project leader might report to a systems development manager. When tasks are completed, team members are reassigned to different projects.

CONTROL ISSUES AND THE MIS

Unlike planning which looks to the future, the *control* function looks at the past and the present. It's a follow-up to planning and a check on past and current performance to see if planned goals are being achieved. The **control process** is thus based on the following steps:

1. Establishing predetermined goals or standards.

2. Measuring actual performance.

3. Comparing actual performance to the standards.

4. Making appropriate control decisions.

There are numerous control implications and issues associated with the use of an MIS. A primary concern of managers is that the MIS supply them with the **managerial control** information they need to monitor the operations for which they're responsible. A second area of vital concern to managers is to ensure that the **internal control** over the MIS itself is adequate so that it operates efficiently and maintains the integrity and security of data, records, and other assets.

Mangerial Control Implications

The output of an MIS can help a manager carry out the control steps in many ways. For example, better information can lead to better planning and the creation of *more realistic standards.* We've seen that simulation can help managers set goals by showing them the effects of alternative decisions when certain conditions are assumed. An MIS can also help managers control by gathering and summarizing *actual performance data* promptly and accurately. Once performance data are read into the computer, it's possible for the machine to *compare* the actual performance with the established standards. Periodic reports showing this comparison can be prepared. And triggered exception reports may be furnished to managers only when variations are outside certain programmed limits.

It's also possible for an MIS to signal when *predetermined decisions* should be carried out. For example, a program may specify that when the inventory of a basic part falls below a given level, an output message signals the need to reorder and indicates the reorder quantity. By thus relieving managers of many of the routine control tasks, the MIS frees them to devote more time to planning and leading the all-important human resources of the organization. Figure 18-15 shows the place of an MIS in the overall managerial control process.

Figure 18-15 Managerial control and the MIS.

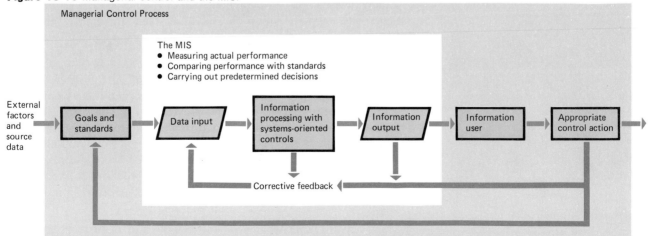

Internal Control Issues

In noncomputer systems, data processing is typically separated into several departments, with a number of employees being responsible for some portion of the total activity. For example, in the processing of a customer order, credit approval may come from one location, control of the inventory of ordered items may reside in another department, customer billing may be handled by a third group, and receipt of payment for items shipped may be in a fourth location. Thus, the organizational structure separates those who initiate the order from those who record and carry out the transaction. And both of these groups are separated from those who receive payment. Such a division of activities makes it difficult for fraud to go undetected since several people from different groups would have to be a party to any deception. Also, people in each department can check on the accuracy of others in the course of their routine activities. Thus, internal control has been achieved by departmental reviews and cross-checks.

But the use of an MIS makes it possible for processing steps to be integrated so that they may all be performed by only one or two groups. With fewer departments involved, however, it may appear that the use of an MIS reduces internal control. Managers have sometimes been distressed to learn that such a reduction can occur in a poorly controlled MIS. The issues and risks involved in controlling an MIS can be expressed in the following series of questions. The threats and problems that MIS designers must counter are suggested in the discussion of each question.

How can we safeguard assets? In the absence of proper internal controls, knowledgeable employees (or a skilled outsider) can steal data and/or programs and sell them. They can add, delete, or change transactions in the data for fraud or embezzlement purposes. And they can do these things at the computer site or at a remote terminal. Thieves are interested in computerized records today because the job of accounting for the assets of many firms has now been entrusted to computer systems. When paper money was introduced, thieves used presses. Now plastic money (credit cards) and magnetic money (money cards with magnetic strips, and magnetic tapes and disks) are used, and thieves are using computers. Measures must be taken to protect the system against the theft of assets.

How can we prevent MIS attack and penetration? As Figure 18-16 indicates, an MIS is vulnerable to attack and penetration from many sources if adequate controls aren't provided. The motivation for such penetration sometimes comes from simple curiosity and the challenge of solving a puzzle or playing a joke. (This type of thinking may be a carryover from a penetrator's school days when he or she played the disturbing "game" of penetrating the control programs of the school's computer.) Or the purpose may be to steal the secrets of an individual or competitor, or to cause a competitor's MIS to "crash"—i.e., become

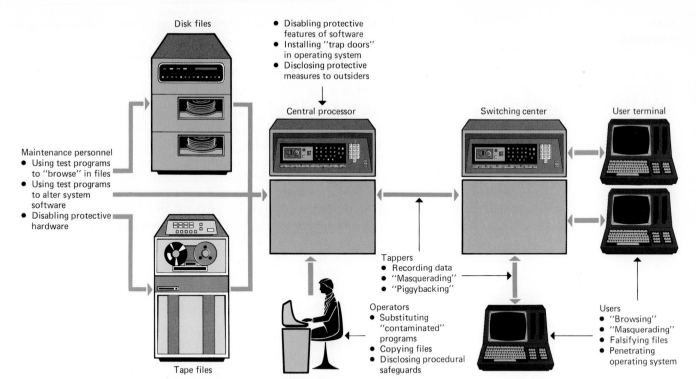

Disk files

- Disabling protective features of software
- Installing "trap doors" in operating system
- Disclosing protective measures to outsiders

Central processor

Switching center

User terminal

Maintenance personnel
- Using test programs to "browse" in files
- Using test programs to alter system software
- Disabling protective hardware

Tappers
- Recording data
- "Masquerading"
- "Piggybacking"

Operators
- Substituting "contaminated" programs
- Copying files
- Disclosing procedural safeguards

Users
- "Browsing"
- "Masquerading"
- Falsifying files
- Penetrating operating system

Tape files

Figure 18-16 Programmers, operators, and maintenance people often have the opportunity to penetrate system security. Programmers, for example, may insert instructions into operating system programs in such a way that they provide a "trap door" for penetration at any convenient future date. Unscrupulous outsiders may also attack online systems by using the techniques of "masquerading" or "piggybacking." Penetrators can obtain the passwords of legitimate users by wiretapping or other means, and can then use these passwords to *masquerade* as authorized users to browse in a data base. In one case, for example, a minicomputer was hooked to a wiretapped line and was used to "impersonate" a central computer. The mini intercepted user calls to the legitimate processor, obtained a record of user passwords, and then informed users that the system was overloaded and requested that they call back in an hour. The identification of many users was thus obtained. The *piggybacking* approach is similar in that a small "bootleg" processor or terminal is attached to a tapped line to intercept and modify legitimate messages. Transmissions between branch banks could be intercepted, for example, and additional credits to the tapper's account could be added to the message. Numerous other techniques that don't require wiretapping are also available to the penetrator.

inoperable. Regardless of the motivation, one authority has observed that penetrating today's MIS is about as difficult as solving the crossword puzzle in a Sunday paper. Obviously, controls must be designed to make attack and penetration more difficult than that.

How can we protect privacy rights of people? Businesses keep records on those with whom they come in contact. In contrast to the personal records stored in older systems, however, records maintained in large, integrated data bases may be more accurate and more complete. They may thus be more worthy targets for those seeking to ferret out private and confidential facts. Seemingly innocent data recorded at one time can be correlated with other data collected from different sources to reveal potentially damaging information about people. Thus, an MIS must be designed to safeguard the privacy rights of those whose records are stored in it.

▎ *How can we maintain the physical security of the computer site?* The preceding internal control questions dealt with the general subject of **data integrity** and **data security.** Another internal control issue involves **physical security.** That is, it concerns the issue of how to *physically protect* the MIS hardware and software against damage or destruction from such hazards as *fire, flood,* and *sabotage.* Thousands of military records were destroyed in a fire at the Army Records Center in St. Louis. Rains accompanying tropical storm Agnes flooded numerous computer centers in the Eastern United States. And computers have been bombed, shot, knifed, and bathed with milk shakes by radical students, disgruntled employees, and frustrated programmers. Provisions must be made to store important programs and data at a backup site, and to protect the computer site against disasters of this type.

▎ *How can we maintain the audit trail?* Periodic examinations or *audits* of an MIS are conducted by company auditors and by independent certified public accountants to evaluate internal control arrangements. As they examine the safeguards created to maintain data integrity and security, auditors check to see if there's a proper separation of duties within the MIS department between those who prepare the programs and those who run them. They also trace processed transactions through the audit trail to monitor systems activity and to determine if integrity/security controls are effective. An **audit trail** begins with the recording of all transactions, winds through all the processing steps, and ends with the production of output results and updated records. By selecting sample transactions and following the audit trail, the auditor traces the transactions effects to their final destinations as a means of testing MIS controls. A readily traceable paper trail is found in a manual system. In an MIS, however, the form of the trail has changed. (It can't be eliminated since it's required by the Internal Revenue Service.) No paper source documents may be prepared when input data are entered through online terminals. And intermediate steps that were previously visible have *seemed to vanish* into magnetizeable and erasable media. It's the job of the MIS designers to satisfy auditors that adequate controls are built into the MIS to prevent unintentional or deliberate damage to "invisible" files and records stored in an erasable data base.

In spite of the threats and problems that we've now considered, *there's no reason why a company should have less internal control because of computer usage.* On the contrary, there's no reason why *system-oriented controls,* in the form of computer programs, can't be substituted for the employee-oriented controls of manual systems. Also, there's no reason why the separation of duties and responsibilities can't be maintained *within* the MIS department to safeguard the integrity of the system-oriented controls. In fact, there's no reason why a firm can't achieve better control because of:

- The computer's ability to execute processing procedures uniformly.
- The difficulty of changing and manipulating, without detection, properly programmed MIS controls.
- The computer's accuracy advantage when given correct input data.

Controlling the MIS Department

An MIS manager is responsible for safeguarding data integrity and system security, and for controlling the operating efficiency of his or her department.

Data Integrity Controls. The purpose of these controls is to see that all input data are correctly recorded, all authorized transactions are processed without additions or omissions, and all output is accurate, timely, and distributed only to those authorized to receive it. A number of *input controls* are identified and discussed in Chapter 6, page 149. Programmed *processing controls* are established to determine when valid data are lost, or when invalid or unauthorized data are entered for processing. Techniques involving the use of record counts, sequence checks, reasonableness checks, and so on are used. The number of possible processing controls is limited only by the programmer's imagination. *Output controls* are established as final checks on the accuracy and propriety of the processed information. Feedback from users and a variety of techniques are used.

System Security Controls. Easy access to the computer(s) by people with the skills needed to manipulate or destroy the system is a primary reason for the difficulty in maintaining data security and physical security. Thus, an important step in achieving a more secure system is to limit access to the computer site. Analysts and programmers shouldn't be involved with day-to-day production runs, and computer operators shouldn't participate in the preparation of data or programs. Included in the controls designed to achieve system security are:

- *Control over console intervention.* It's possible for computer operators to bypass program controls. They have the ability to interrupt a program run and introduce data manually into the processor through the console keyboard. With organizational separation of program preparation and computer operation, it's unlikely that an operator will have enough knowledge of a program's details to manipulate it successfully for improper purposes. However, the possibility of unauthorized intervention can be reduced in a number of ways. For example, a micro-

THREE DRAMATIC BANK CRIMES

The Wells Fargo Heist

An operations officer at a Wells Fargo branch bank in California allegedly created bogus deposits at one branch office by using an interbranch account settlement process to withdraw funds from a different branch. To keep the system from catching the manipulations, new fradulent credits were created to cover the withdrawals. The take over a 2 year period exceeded $21 million!

The Security Pacific Caper

Stanley Mark Rifkin, a former computer consultant for this Los Angeles bank, obtained the electronic funds transfer code from the bank's wire transfer room. He then used a public telephone and the code to send over $10 million to a Swiss account. By the time the fraud was detected by the bank's computer, Rifkin had flown to Switzerland and had converted the money into diamonds. Only after bragging about his feat was he identified and convicted of his crime.

The Union Dime Case

The chief teller at a Union Dime Savings Bank branch in New York City embezzled about $1.5 million from the bank's accounts. Hundreds of legitimate accounts were manipulated; money was transferred to fradulent accounts and then withdrawn; and false information was fed into the bank's computer so that when quarterly interest payments were due the legitimate accounts appeared intact. And all this was done by a person who didn't have direct access to the computer. He was caught when police investigated a gambling parlor and found that he was in the habit of placing large bets.

According to the Federal Bureau of Investigation (FBI), the average *reported* computer crime loss suffered by organizations is about $500,000 (compared to an average bank robbery loss of $3,200). The FBI also estimates that only *1* percent of computer crimes are detected, and of those discovered, only one in eight is reported to the police! Given these statistics, it's little wonder that some computer security experts believe that organized crime will soon be sponsoring computer attacks. In addition to the techniques described here, other techniques used by computer-wise thieves include (*a*) deducting a few cents in excess service charges, interest, taxes, or dividends from thousands of accounts and writing themselves a check for the total amount of the excess deductions; and (*b*) reporting inventory items as broken or lost and then transferring the items to accomplices. In short, it's been estimated that losses suffered by organizations as a result of fraud and embezzlement now exceed those caused by robbery, loss, and shoplifting—and the MIS is the target in an increasing number of theft cases.

computer can be used to record and analyze the processing actions performed by the host computer as well as any interventions in the host's operation. That is, the micro can be used like a flight recorder in an airplane. The recorder monitors the performance of the plane and its crew, but it's not accessible to the crew. Additional control techniques include rotating the duties of computer operators (or others in sensitive positions) and having them account for computer operating time. Manual intervention is slow, and manipulation can thus result in processing times that are longer than necessary for affected runs.

■ *Control over the use of online terminals.* Control procedures to identify authorized users of the system should obviously be given special attention. Such identification is typically based on something that users *know* (e.g., a password), something they *have* (e.g., a card with a magnetically coded identification number), some *personal quality* they possess (e.g., fingerprint or "voice print" characteristics that can be stored by the computer system and used for identification purposes), or some combination of these elements. Passwords are most commonly used, but when used frequently (and carelessly) these words lose their security value. Once an authorized user has been identified and has gained access to the system, various techniques employing **cryptography**—that is, "hidden writing"—are available to thwart those who would intercept the messages traveling between the computer and the remote terminal. For example, data encryption techniques for coding and decoding messages can be implemented on silicon chips located in the terminals and host computers. If an authorized user wants to access or send sensitive data, the host computer may generate a random **session key**—a key to be used only for that exchange. This session key is sent to the terminal encrypt/decrypt circuitry and a copy is retained at the host. Any data passing from a host program to the terminal are automatically encrypted by the host, transmitted, and then decrypted by the terminal. (Of course, the reverse occurs when the message originates at the terminal.) This coding/decoding process is invisible to the user. At the end of the session, the session key disappears. The data that have been transmitted would be unintelligible to anyone without the one-time session key.

■ *The creation of a physical security program.* Definite controls should be established to safeguard programs and data from fire and water damage or destruction. Duplicate programs and master files may have to be kept at a location away from the computer site. A fireproof storage vault at the computer site is a wise precaution. Control over library tapes, cards, disks, and blank forms is necessary. Adequate insurance protection should be provided. And a waste-disposal procedure to destroy carbon papers and other media containing sensitive information should be followed.

Control of Operating Efficiency. The same steps used to control any activity are used to control the efficiency of the MIS function. Departmental standards should be established for people and machines. Actual performance should then be measured. Measuring the performance of creative people is more an art than a science, and the approaches vary from one MIS facility to another. It's easier to measure hardware performance because special monitors are available for this purpose. Overworked (or underutilized) components and bottleneck situations can be identified through the use of these evaluation tools. Once performance measurements are available, they are compared to the standards, and appropriate control decisions are made as needed.

**Feedback and
Review 18-1**

You've covered a lot of material in this chapter on management information, the systems that produce it, and the issues associated with the use of MIS. To test and reinforce your understanding of MIS concepts, place a T or F in the space provided in the following true-false questions:

_____ **1.** Managers at different organizational levels need the same kinds of information since they do the same kinds of planning.

_____ **2.** Lower-level managers need information to support strategic planning.

_____ **3.** Accuracy is the ratio of incorrect information to the total amount of information produced.

_____ **4.** Regular reports should be prepared on a regular hourly basis.

_____ **5.** Traditional information systems seem to have been designed on the assumption that lack of completeness is the most critical problem facing managers.

_____ **6.** Numerous ''total systems'' were designed in the late 1960s.

_____ **7.** An MIS is a network of computer-based data processing procedures developed in an organization and integrated as necessary to provide timely and effective information to support decision making.

_____ **8.** In planning for an MIS, designers are in agreement that the ''bottom-up'' approach is best.

_____ **9.** Most MISs today serve the needs of top-level managers and, to a lesser extent, the needs of operating managers.

_____ **10.** An MIS can give managers more time to devote to planning.

_____ **11.** Simulation models can be used to improve inventory planning.

_____ **12.** An MIS requires a greater degree of centralized decision making.

_____ **13.** A centralized data processing approach may provide for better systems integration.

_____ **14.** A decentralized data processing approach results in reduced interest and motivation at user levels.

_____ **15.** There are only two distributed data processing alternatives available today.

_____ **16.** The main computing facility in an organization must be headed by an MIS director.

_____ **17.** An MIS department is likely to be the organizational home of a data base administrator.

X T **18.** ''Information resource management'' is a term used by those who want to place all the overlapping information functions in an organization under the control of a senior information executive.

_____ **19.** The control process is based on establishing standards, measuring performance, comparing performance against standards, and then taking appropriate action.

20. An MIS is of little help to a production manager in controlling production activities.

21. Internal control in noncomputer systems is employee-oriented.

22. An MIS is invulnerable to attack and penetration by outsiders.

23. Privacy rights of people are of no concern to MIS designers.

24. An audit trail can be eliminated only in the interests of improving efficiency.

25. Authorized users of online systems may be identified by what they know, by what they have, or by a personal quality they possess.

26. Cryptography can be used to improve the security of messages traveling between CPUs and terminals, but users have to enter data in complex codes.

"I brought this computer in to do an efficiency study, and the first thing it suggested was to get rid of *me*!"

Looking Back

1. Different types of information are needed by people at different levels in a business. Top-level managers need information to support long-range strategic planning, middle-level managers need information for tactical decisions, and lower-level supervisors need information to support their day-to-day operational functions. Regardless of the level, however, the information provided should be accurate, timely, complete, and concise.

2. An MIS is a network of computer-based data processing procedures developed in an organization and integrated as necessary with manual and other procedures for the purpose of providing timely and effective information to support decision making and other necessary management functions. The formidable task of the MIS designer is to develop the information flow needed to support decision making. This isn't an easy task since there are a number of unresolved issues to consider during the planning for an MIS. These issues are outlined in the chapter.

3. An MIS can help improve managerial planning by giving managers (*a*) faster signals of problems, (*b*) more time to devote to planning, and (*c*) the ability to evaluate more alternatives. The components of an MIS that help improve planning are often called decision support systems. Simulation is a trial-and-error problem-solving technique that's also very useful in planning. Simulation models can be used by managers to evaluate proposed projects or strategies. Managers can see what happens to these models when certain conditions are given or when certain assumptions are tested.

4. There are generally a number of organizing issues that must be considered when an MIS is installed. These issues involve questions about the degree of centralization or decentralization of authority, data processing activities, and data storage. Questions about the organizational location of computing resources and the composition of the MIS department are also raised. Each of these issues is outlined and discussed in the chapter.

5. The control process involves establishing standards, measuring actual performance, comparing performance to standards, and taking appropriate action. A primary concern of managers is that the MIS supply them with the managerial control information they need to monitor their activities. A second area of vital concern is that the internal control over the MIS itself is adequate to maintain the integrity and security of data, software, and hardware. Managerial control implications and internal control issues are outlined in the chapter.

KEY TERMS AND CONCEPTS

You should now be able to define and use the following terms and concepts (the numbers shown indicate the pages where the terms and concepts are first mentioned):

TOPICS FOR REVIEW AND DISCUSSION

1. Why have traditional information systems failed to meet the needs of managers?

2. "A factor that complicates the subject of the information needed by managers is the organizational level of the managerial job." Discuss this statement.

3. Identify and discuss the properties that management information should possess.

4. (*a*) What is an MIS? (*b*) Identify and discuss four issues involved in planning for an MIS.

5. How can an MIS affect the quality of a manager's plans?

6. (*a*) What is simulation? (*b*) How can it be used in planning and decision making?

7. Identify and discuss four organizing issues that need to be considered when MISs are designed and implemented.

8. (*a*) Discuss the benefits that may be obtained from a centralized approach to data processing. (*b*) From a decentralized approach.

9. (*a*) Identify three locations for a main computing facility in a business. (*b*) Which is likely to best support an integrated MIS?

10. (*a*) Identify and discuss the functions that may be included in an MIS department. (*b*) How can an MIS department be organized along project lines?

11. (*a*) What are the steps in the control process? (*b*) What are the managerial control implications of an MIS?

12. Identify and discuss four internal control issues arising out of the use of a computer-based MIS.

13. Identify and give examples of the types of controls needed within an MIS department.

ANSWERS TO FEEDBACK AND REVIEW SECTION

18-1

1. F	10. T	19. T
2. F	11. T	20. F
3. F	12. F	21. T
4. F	13. T	22. F
5. T	14. F	23. F
6. F	15. F	24. F
7. T	16. F	25. T
8. F	17. T	26. F
9. F	18. T	

Are Personal Computers a Threat to Management Information Systems?

"Leave work early tomorrow," read the ad in the business section of the Sunday *Dallas Morning News*. "Managers, put a TRS-80 on your desk to improve your personal productivity. Use it with our ready-to-run software for financial planning, electronic filing and even word processing."

They arrived only a half-dozen years ago disguised as toys. The first programs on these dirt-cheap micro-based machines were whiz-bang graphics battles between robots and spacecraft.

But it was the managers and professionals—not the kids—who were quick to discover the real value of these information machines. At first, like the radio HAMS of the 1930s, they installed them in spare closets and whiled away evenings and weekends learning BASIC. And they wrote software that was personal, to use in their jobs—software that would give them a competitive edge in their career.

Tandy Corp.'s Radio Shack led the way, selling their TRS-80s like hamburgers. "Over 100,000 sold," boast the banners in more than 8,000 company-owned retail stores. They've done everything but erect golden arches to create awareness of their "personal computer."

And it didn't take too long for the DP professionals to look under the covers of these cheap devices—the TRS-80s, the Apples, the Commodore PETs and a swarm of others on the market today—and discover that they are indeed well-built microcomputers.

Overnight, the personal computer came out of the closet and began appearing in large numbers on desks and executive credenzas. Companies began buying microcomputers like they buy typewriters to supplement the large CPUs. And when the DP department wouldn't buy them, middle managers became quite innovative in bury-ing the cost of a contraband computer by spreading it throughout the budget or having it billed as "spare parts."

Dr. Hal Kinne, who teaches at the University of Texas at Dallas, said at least a half-million and probably closer to a million of the personal type machines are in use in corporations today because managers want more control over processing the data they use to do their jobs. Why this proliferation of "personal" computers in business use? Is it good? Or bad? What's the effect on the bottom line?

Much has been written in the DP publications about it. There have been mutterings about "loss of control" by the MIS director. But a sampling of MIS manager attitudes by *Infosystems* uncovered little more than an occasional "not-invented-here" problem.

"It's got to help the MIS people with their user relations just through the learning process and understanding of DP services," said Nat Turner, of the Dallas-based Turner and Paul management consulting firm. "My former employer (a bank) was considering bringing in some minicomputers for a distributed network setup and I was against it at first but simply because I was afraid we'd never get rid of them when the project ended.

"But immediate access to computing is important," Turner said. "You wouldn't have thought anything about somebody going out and buying a slide rule, or a pocket calculator a few years back. The issue is about the same. So why not a personal computer?

"No, if there's anything negative, it's just got to be a political issue," he said.

Donald F. Hamilton, Systems Software Manager at Lockheed Missiles and Space Corp., Sunnyvale, CA, was perhaps typical of the managers *Infosystems* talked with. Hamilton, who is a member of the *Infosystems* User

Council, said there are "literally hundreds" of microcomputers being used by the 23,000 employees there. Mostly Apple, TRS-80 and Hewlett-Packard HP-85.

"No, I don't feel threatened," Hamilton said. "It's going to happen. It needs to happen in order to improve productivity. As long as we in MIS maintain configuration of data, and data access, then why should we really care whether that's a dumb or intelligent terminal out there? People are authorized access to certain data and they're going to do something with it."

Hamilton pointed out that all the subsystems in the big computers have protection software requiring IDs and passwords. And they get systems logs revealing who used the data base at a particular time.

Why this urge to have a "personal computer at the office? Isn't EDP doing its job well enough?

An extensive study last year by INPUT, a Palo Alto market research firm, concluded that there is indeed widespread dissatisfaction with the DP department. More than 25 percent of the respondents told INPUT that was why they wanted their own system. DP just wasn't responsive enough to the needs of end users, they said. Users of data were fed up with the long delays in getting new applications on stream, or with waiting for one-time reports or analyses.

But most likely, the dissatisfied user, the manager who is already swamped with more large CPU data than he wants, complains that the DP department is solving *company* problems such as accounting and budgeting but is ignoring what he perceives that he needs most to accomplish his *own* particular job.

Quite simply, the big mainframe DP department cannot compete with the flexibility and individuality of the personal computer, especially in the area of software. A lot of good—and bad—micro software is available today.

Dick Brown, president of The Computer Store, says that about the only things holding back even more widespread use of executive desk-top computers is physical design (portable would be better), lack of communications software (it's just around the corner) and entrenched DP departments.

The use of personal computers in corporations can unload the MIS computer and they can unload the MIS staff from an increasing demand for services. The effect on the bottom line is greater productivity.

"I don't feel threatened," says Steward Plock, Information Systems Manager at Hewlett-Packard, Palo Alto, CA. "My philosophy is the smarter our users are, the better they're going to be to work with. They usually come back when it gets too big. They may screw around for six months developing programs that may be helpful to them but all of a sudden they realize they need a bigger disk drive or they need to communicate with some other system and they come right back into the fold. I think it's a good thing. It'll happen whether we allow it or not so we better get on the bandwagon."

—Steve Stibbins, "Personal Computers Come Out of the Closet," *Infosystems*, September 1981, pp. 86–88. Reprinted with permission.

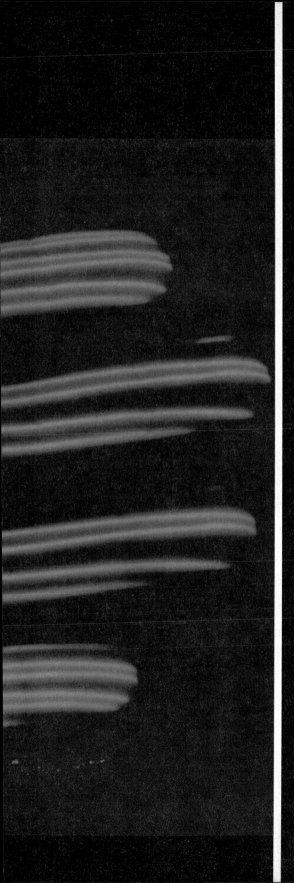

Computers and Society

Computers have become highly visible tools in our modern society. And people relate to these tools with an extraordinary range of views and emotions.

Of course, computers aren't the only machines capable of evoking strong feelings, for people also develop positive or negative attachments to cars, stereos, and recreational vehicles. But computers touch on a sphere that people have always regarded as uniquely human: That sphere is intelligence. Thus, peoples' feelings about computers involve a higher order of hopes and fears. Throughout this module we'll look closely at some of the benefits and potential dangers of computer usage that prompt these hopes and fears.

The chapters included in this Social Impact Module are:

19. The Impact of Computers on People
20. The Impact of Computers on Organizations
21. Computers Tomorrow

A laser-driven robot eye scans a human hand. (Dan McCoy from Rainbow)

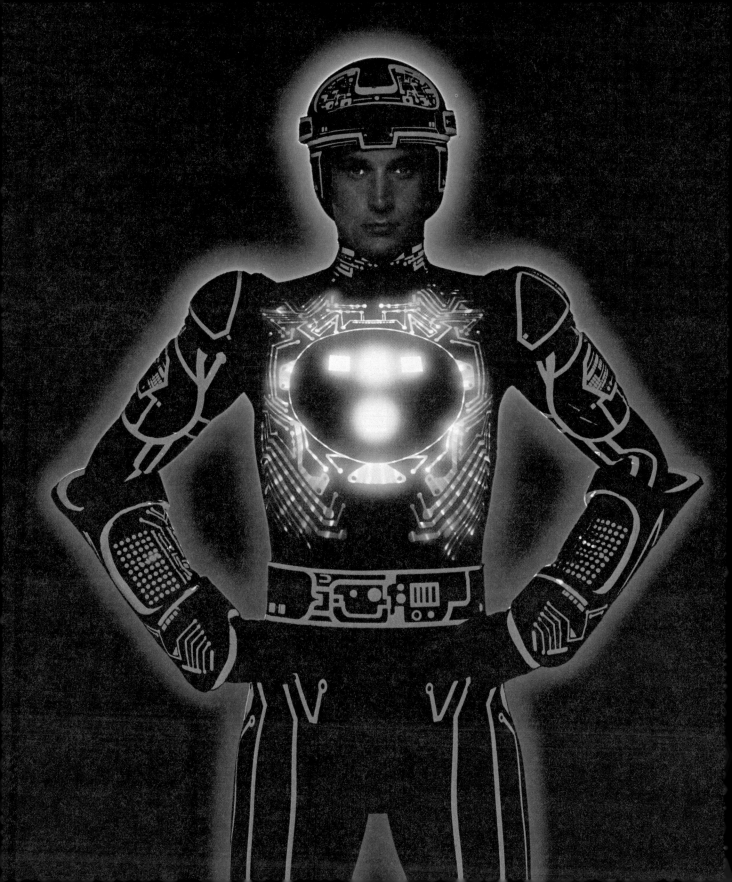

chapter 19

The Impact of Computers on People

"I HAVE SEEN THE FUTURE, AND IT GLOWS"

Author and Sesame Street consultant Christopher Cerf uses a word processor to store notes, to create new text, to edit, and to organize. According to Cerf, "It's the most important tool writers have been given since Gutenberg created movable type. I have seen the future, and it glows."

Cerf is referring to the glow from his CRT screen, but he is implying something more. He is suggesting a world where daily life without "computer contact" is the exception rather than the rule. The world he imagines is portrayed in brief by Alvin Toffler in his book *The Third Wave*—a world of electronic cottages. And that world, filled with the presence of computers, is not far away.

It may not be an exaggeration to say that in the industrialized nations, every person's life will be touched in some way, each day, by computers. In the United States, each birth is noted by a computer— as is each death. When you register for your social security number, you have registered for the rest of your life in one of the world's largest data banks.

We trust that most of the results of computer operations will be positive—that we will live longer, be healthier, learn more, and enjoy both our work and our leisure time more than we might have without computers. To ensure that computers work for us, we all need to be knowledgeable about what those machines can and cannot do. We need to follow the advice of an old Japanese proverb: "Exploit the Inevitable."

A rebellious video warrior from a computer world controlled by an evil master program in the movie *TRON*. (© MCMLXXXII Walt Disney Productions. Buena Vista Releases)

Looking Ahead

In this chapter, you'll see how people react to and may be affected by computer usage. You may find reinforcement for your own ideas on the subject, and you may as likely be forced to rethink your opinions and perhaps to form new ones. We'll begin by considering the subject of artificial intelligence and the controversy about whether computers can be programmed to think and learn. Next, you'll see how our lives may be improved by the ways organizations use computers and by the ways we can use our own personal systems. (You'll also see in the "Closer Look" section at the end of the chapter that excellent career opportunities exist for those working in the data processing field.)

Since it's also possible for computer systems to have a negative impact on some people, the focus of the chapter next turns to some of the potential dangers associated with computer usage. As you read about these problem areas, however, you should keep two thoughts clearly in mind. *First,* some adverse effects that are often attributed to the computer systems in our society—e.g., the loss of individual privacy—may often be the subtle consequences of complex and interrelated technological forces operating in a society with a growing population density. And *second,* computers, being inanimate objects, do no wrong—but the people who use them sometimes do. Fallible humans who design computer systems have sometimes overlooked these negative aspects, and the computer—rather than the poorly designed system—has received the blame.

After you've studied this chapter, you should be able to:

▐ Comment on some of the developments that have taken place in the field of artificial intelligence

▐ Explain how people may benefit from their organizations' use of computers

▐ Identify and discuss a number of possible benefits that people may receive as a result of the use of computers by profit-oriented and not-for-profit organizations

▐ Outline how people can benefit from the use of personal computers

▐ Summarize the employment problems that computer usage may create

▐ Describe some questionable data processing practices that affect peoples' private lives, and discuss the possible problems associated with the issues of system security and personal privacy

▐ Understand and use the key terms and concepts listed at the end of this chapter

HUMAN THINKING AND ARTIFICIAL INTELLIGENCE

The superhuman computers found in science fiction don't exist. But science fiction often has a way of becoming science fact. Experimenters are now studying the ways in which computers may be used to solve unstructured problems—the types of problems that we take for granted would require human intelligence to solve. These research efforts are usually classified under the heading of **artificial intelligence (AI).** They combine concepts found in disciplines such as psychology, linguistics, and computer science, and are aimed at learning how to prepare programs (or construct systems) that can do tasks that have never been done automatically by machines before.

For example, computers have been programmed to play checkers and to modify their programs on the basis of success and failure with moves used in the past against human opponents. In one such program, the computer has continually improved its game to the point where it easily defeats the author of the program. Thus, the machine has "learned" what not to do through trial and error.

Dozens of chess-playing programs have been written that can run on machines ranging from micro-sized personal computers to very large supercomputers (see Figure 19-1). As you learned in Chapter 1, the possible number of moves in a chess game is so large that all the moves could not possibly be stored or analyzed by any computer. Thus, the only feasible approach is to program the computer to play the game by evaluating possible moves and formulating a playing strategy.

At the *beginning* of a chess game, proven approaches to minimize losses and, perhaps, to create openings are often followed for the first seven to 10 moves. Much less predictable is the *middle part* of the game. Good chess players must adopt a strategy and "look ahead" to determine the future consequences of a move. (Chess masters can accurately foresee the consequences 12 to 15 moves later; the author's vision is good for about $1\frac{1}{2}$ moves.) If the middle game is complicated, the *end game* is absolutely mind-blowing. Each

Figure 19-1 A robot hand machine connected to a special-purpose computer plays chess with a human. (Dan McCoy from Rainbow)

player may have six or seven pieces left. The sides of the board have generally lost their meaning, and the pieces may be positioned in ways that have *never occurred before* in the history of the game. In a few moves, a strong attack can result in an impossible defense. People may develop new strategies at this time. A computer program, of course, must also try to adapt to end-game situations.

Given this brief summary of chess, a natural question is: How have computer programs fared against humans in this very intellectual game? This question can be answered by looking at the "Levy challenge." In 1968, David Levy, a Scottish chess champion with an international master ranking (that's one rank below the top grandmaster rank), beat John McCarthy, a Stanford University professor of AI in a chess game. McCarthy remarked that although he couldn't beat Levy, there would be within 10 years a computer program that could. A bet of 250 British pounds ($625) was made between Levy and McCarthy. Levy would win the bet unless a computer program won a match against him before the end of August 1978.

During the next few years, other AI professors and computer programmers joined McCarthy in betting against Levy. In 1977, Levy played a match against a Northwestern University program named Chess 4.5 that had just won the Minnesota Open championship against human opponents. Levy won the match and later in the year beat Kaissa, a Russian program. As the 1978 deadline approached, a final six-game match was arranged between Levy and Northwestern's Chess 4.7 (a successor to Chess 4.5). The first game was a draw (each side received $\frac{1}{2}$ point). Levy won the second and third games, the computer won the fourth game, and Levy won the fifth game. (A sixth game was unnecessary since Levy had scored $3\frac{1}{2}$ points out of a possible 6.) Although the human won this round, the Levy challenge continues, with a new bet totaling $10,000 to be decided by January 1984. There's also a prize of $100,000 being offered through Carnegie-Mellon University to the creator of the first computer program to wrest the world chess champion title from a human. Carnegie-Mellon professor Hans Berliner recently wrote a program that defeated the world backgammon champion. Berliner believes there's a 50-50 chance that a program will be the chess champion by 1990. By the year 2000, he says, a program is almost sure to win.

In the past few years, much has been written pro and con about whether computers can be programmed to "think" and "learn." Most of the controversy probably stems from (1) a lack of understanding about the processes involved in human thinking and learning, and (2) the absence of acceptable definitions of such words as *think* and *learn*.

One test—a game—to find out if a computer might be considered to possess intelligence and the ability to think was proposed by Alan Turing, a British mathematician. Participants in the game would be two respondents—a machine and a human—and a human interrogator who tries to determine which of the unseen respondents is the human. Communications terminals are used to answer questions posed by the interrogator. The machine tries to deceive while the human tries to convince the interrogator of his or her true identity.

Intelligence and the ability to think would, according to **Turing's test,** be demonstrated by the machine's success in fooling the interrogator.

Have machines passed Turing's test? Not yet, but the machines *have* passed incomplete versions of the test. For example, several years ago Joseph Weizenbaum, an MIT professor, wrote a program with which one could "converse" in English. The program plays the role of a psychotherapist engaged in an interview with a patient. A hypothetical conversation between patient and "doctor" might go like this (computer entries are in capital letters):

DO YOU HAVE ANY PROBLEMS?
Yes, I am depressed

I AM SORRY TO HEAR YOU ARE DEPRESSED
My boyfriend makes me unhappy
TELL ME ABOUT YOUR BOYFRIEND

In a variation of Turing's test (people tested didn't know it was a test, and the program wasn't competing with a human), staff members at Massachusetts General Hospital let a number of people "talk" to Weizenbaum's program for a time. When they were asked if they had been talking with a human or a machine, a majority thought they had been in contact with a human. David Levy, the chess master, believes that since the Chess 4.7 program he competed against is stronger than 99.5 percent of all human chess players, it has already reached and passed the stage where he could correctly identify it as a human or computer opponent under Turing-test conditions.

Where's the current research in AI likely to lead us? No one knows. **Heuristic** (pronounced hew-ris'-tik) is a word that means "serving to discover." It's used to describe the judgmental, or *commonsense,* part of problem-solving. That is, it describes that part of problem-solving which deals with the definition of the problem, the selection of reasonable strategies to be followed, and the formulation of hypotheses and hunches. Human beings are now *far superior* to the computer in the heuristic area of intellectual work. As people's thinking and learning processes become better understood, however, it may be possible to develop new programs and machines with improved heuristic abilities. Certainly, some very able researchers are working toward this end. However, for the foreseeable future, the role of the computer should continue to be that of an intelligence amplifier in an alliance with humanity. This alliance would combine the current superiority of the human brain in matters involving creativity, judgment, and intuition with the computer's superiority in matters involving processing speed, accuracy, and tireless attention to detail. The word **synergy** refers to the ability of two entities to achieve together what each is incapable of achieving alone. As Figure 19-2 indicates, the alliance between humans and computers could produce a synergistic effect. While the potential achievements of such an alliance are not unlimited, they also cannot be restricted in any way we can now anticipate.

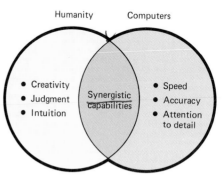

Figure 19-2 The strengths of humans and computers differ.

PEOPLE AND COMPUTERS: SOME POTENTIAL BENEFITS

As you'll see in "A Closer Look" at the end of this chapter, many people are needed to manage and operate the computer systems used in profit-oriented and not-for-profit organizations. These people enjoy challenging careers in the computing field. But each of us is a beneficiary of the use of computers in organizations. We benefit *on the job* even though we aren't computer specialists. We benefit as the *consumers* of the goods and services provided by these computer-using organizations. And we benefit *at home* by using personal computers to entertain and serve us.

Employment Benefits

Managers and other noncomputer specialists are receiving employment benefits from computer usage.

Managerial Benefits. The primary role of *top managers* lies in formulating policies and planning and guiding overall organizational strategy. As noted in Chapter 18, computer-based systems (MISs) have, through the use of improved simulation techniques, online data bases, and computer graphics terminals, helped remove some of the uncertainties from the usually unique and ill-structured problems that top executives face. And Chapter 11 describes how executives may use electronic mail/message systems to reduce telephone interruptions, improve the dissemination of messages to subordinates, and reduce the time required for scheduled meetings through the use of computerized conferencing techniques.

An important role of *lower-level supervisors* is to provide face-to-face communication, direction, and leadership to operating employees. By permitting supervisors to (1) schedule operations more efficiently, (2) maintain better control over economic resources, and (3) cope with a generally increasing level of paperwork, computers have made it possible for them to give more attention to this important personnel administration aspect of their work.

Some *middle-level managers* no longer need to spend as much time in controlling because the computer can be programmed to take over many clerical control activities. For example, it can signal with a triggered report whenever actual performance varies from what was planned. Time saved in controlling has enabled some middle managers to devote more attention to planning and directing the work of subordinates. More accurate and timely organizationwide information supplied by an MIS has also given them the opportunity to spend more time identifying problems, recognizing opportunities, and planning alternate courses of action. In this respect, then, their jobs have become more challenging and more nearly resemble those of chief executives. With managers having more time to devote to departmental employee matters, improved morale may be expected. And the more timely information that's now available to some middle managers puts them in a position to be able to react more rapidly to external changes.

Benefits to Other Personnel. *Scientists* are now able to use computers to conduct research into complex problem areas that could not otherwise be considered. *Design engineers* and *architects* are now using computers to simplify design work and increase the alternatives that can be studied. *Structural engineers* are using computer models to predict the effect of stresses on different structural configurations. *Lawyers* are using legal data banks to locate precedent cases in order to serve clients better. *Sales personnel* can now receive more timely information about customers and product inventories, can promise more efficient handling of sales orders in order to serve their customers better, and can thus improve their sales performance because of computer systems. And the job duties of some *clerical employees* have changed from routine, repetitive operations to more varied and appealing tasks through computer usage.

Benefits from Profit-Oriented Organizations

We all know that the federal government provides to individuals many services that require the use of computers. Without computers, for example, the Social Security Administration could not keep up with the payment of benefits to widows, orphans, and retired persons. But we sometimes fail to realize the extent to which we benefit as consumers from the use of computers by businesses. Some (but certainly not all) of the possible benefits that people may receive from their dealings with computer-using businesses are discussed below.

Benefits of Greater Efficiency. Most of us have been upset by the way prices have increased for much of what we buy. But what we may fail to realize is that to the extent that businesses have avoided waste and improved efficiency through the use of computers, the *prices we now pay may be less than they would otherwise have been.* Edmund Berkeley, editor of *Computers and People,* has estimated that the use of computers has reduced prices by 10 to 30 percent and often much more, than they would be without computers. For example, about one-third of all the dairy cows in the nation are now bred, fed, milked, and monitored for productivity with the help of computers. The average "computerized" cow will produce 30 percent more milk than a typical cow that's not subject to computer analysis. By applying the latest knowledge, the dairy industry today can produce all the milk that was supplied 15 years ago with only half as many cows. If computer use can significantly improve **productivity**— i.e., the amount of goods or services possessing economic value that people and machines can produce in a given time period—then these productivity gains may lead to higher levels of real income for an increased number of people.

Figure 19-3 Computer applications used by businesses can improve service to customers. (Courtesy NCR, Dayton, Ohio)

Benefits of Higher-Quality Products. Computers may also help improve the quality of the products we receive from businesses. For example, microcomputers are now installed in cars to provide a more efficient means of controlling the engine's fuel mixture, ignition timing, and exhaust emissions. If you're late for an appointment and low on gas, and if there's a deserted stretch of highway ahead, an on-board micro can monitor the gas consumption, rate of speed, and miles to destination to tell you if you should take the time tò look for an open service station. The microcomputer can also perform engine diagnostic functions and pinpoint problems.

In other areas, computer-controlled tools can produce machined parts with closer tolerances than were feasible with previously used equipment. Computer-controlled manipulators or *robots* can be used to assemble products or components in a precise way. And process-control computers can be used to carefully monitor the flow of chemical raw materials into a blending tank so that the finished product is of a more uniform quality.

Benefits of Better Service. Businesses also use computers to improve the services they provide to customers. Computer processing techniques, for example, make possible:

▌ Shorter waiting lines at airline ticket offices and at the reservation desks of hotels, motels, and car-rental agencies.

▌ Faster and more accurate answers to the inquiries of people served by the business (Figure 19-3).

▌ More efficient control of inventory in retail outlets so that popular items are reordered in time to avoid frustrating out-of-stock situations.

Possible Benefits of EFTS. Financial and retailing firms are interested in the use of electronic funds transfer systems (EFTS). Although EFTS are still in the formative stages, their general shape is clear enough for us to identify certain advantages for people. In a **checkless payment system,** for example, authorized credits to specified individuals from an employer, pension fund, etc., are recorded on magnetic tape along with the name of the recipient's bank and his or her bank account number. The tape is delivered to the paying organizations' bank. This bank sorts out its own customers, deposits the payment amounts to their accounts, and then transfers the remaining names to an **automated clearing house (ACH) facility.** An ACH computer sorts the remaining names according to their banks and then notifies these banks of the amounts to be deposited in the specified accounts. A benefit of this approach is that it eliminates the fear of theft of checks. Millions of people are now receiving direct-deposit social security payments in lieu of mailed checks.

Another way in which EFTS may benefit people involves the use of terminals conveniently located anywhere that substantial numbers of financial transactions occur. EFTS terminals owned by financial institutions and connected to their computers may be located in such public places as shopping centers and supermarkets. As discussed in Chapter 6, a person can insert his or her "money" card into an *automated teller machine* (ATM), key in appropriate data in response to instructions given on a terminal display, and make deposits or withdraw cash. Other terminals connected to bank computers may be located at the point-of-sale (POS) counters of retail outlets and may be used along with store-owned *POS stations.* After a person has supplied a money card, these EFTS stations can be used to:

- Identify the individual, authorize credit, and/or authorize money card cash advances.

- Guarantee the availability of funds to cover the individual's checks.

- Transfer funds between accounts, e.g., from the individual's account to the merchant's account.

People may also be able to use EFTS to *automatically pay their bills* from their homes. Those with dial phones can call a bank operator seated in front of a visual display terminal to handle the transaction. People with Touch-Tone phones or personal computers can communicate directly with the bank's computer.

Possible Benefits of UPC. Merchants selling products coded with the Universal Product Code (UPC) discussed in Chapter 6 expect to receive the benefits of greater efficiency and reduced costs. But their customers may also find that a UPC system

- Reduces their waiting time and gives them faster service at checkout counters.

Reduces the chances for human error.

Provides them with an itemized sales receipt rather than just a tape with a column of numbers.

Possible Recreational Benefits. Some businesses are using computers solely to amuse and entertain people. In one application, image enhancement technology developed for the Mariner spacecraft project has been used to convert a small customer photograph into a mosaic of computer printer characters (Figure 19-4). In addition to image enhancement, **computer photography** (also developed for the space program) is also being used to amuse people. A TV camera captures the desired image from a photograph or a live subject. The image is frozen and is then transferred by computer to a tee-shirt, handbag, etc. **Computer animation** (Figure 19-4) is being used to give the illusion of movement to inanimate objects. The results of computer animation are now seen in movies and on TV. For example, a briefing-room scene in the movie *Star Wars* that showed how a rebel pilot could maneuver down a trench on the surface of the battle station "Death Star" was accomplished by means of computer animation. And entertaining games containing microcomputers are being built by dozens of businesses.

Figure 19-4 (*left*) Computer-produced mosaic from a customer photograph. (Recreational Computer Systems, Inc.). (*below*) The "electronic warrior" on the left sits at the controls of a video game tank in the movie *TRON*. The interior as well as the exterior of the tank (shown on the *right*) is a computer simulation. (© MCMLXXXII Walt Disney Productions. Buena Vista Releases)

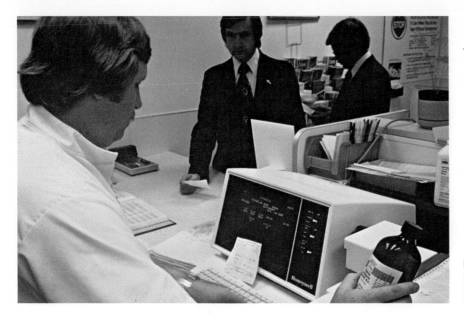

Figure 19-5 This pharmacist is using Honeywell's COMPASS system to improve his services. (Courtesy Honeywell Information Systems)

Possible Aid to the Handicapped. As pictured in Chapter 1, Kurzweil Computer Products builds the Kurzweil Reading Machine—a desk-top device that accepts written material printed in most common typefaces and converts the print into a synthetic voice output. Printed material is placed face down on a glass plate, where it's scanned by an electronic camera. The camera transmits its image to a microcomputer which is programmed to separate the image into character forms, recognize the letters, group the letters into words, compute the pronunciation of words, and produce the necessary speech sounds. Microcomputers can also be used to control devices that permit severely handicapped persons to feed themselves even though they have no upper limb responses. And computer-based man-machine analyses are making it possible for businesses to develop more effective artificial limbs for amputees.

Benefits of Improved Safety. Computer usage can contribute to personal safety in a number of ways. Computer-controlled braking systems in aircraft and in future cars may help prevent dangerous skids and produce the optimum stopping distance in all weather conditions. Minicomputer systems in pharmacies can be used to check a patient's medical profile against possible reactions to any ingredients in a new prescription or to determine the possibility of dangerous interactions between the ingredients in old prescriptions and those in the new prescription (Figure 19-5). And computers permit gas utility companies to do a better job of managing and controlling the pipeline leaks that can seriously jeopardize public safety. Dispatchers can provide work crews with information about an area, including work-history details of prior gas leaks. New leaks can be identified and old leaks analyzed through online terminals.

Benefits of Better Information Retrieval. A New York surgeon contacted a medical library when a near-term pregnant woman lapsed into a hepatic coma. He needed immediate information on exchange blood transfusions for the woman. Using a computer terminal and an information retrieval program, the librarian was able to search more than a half-million medical documents in a few minutes to get the information needed by the surgeon to perform an emergency blood transfusion. The patient recovered fully from the hepatitis. Although most information retrieval projects obviously don't involve life-or-death situations, quick computer-assisted retrieval can save time and aggravation for many individuals. People whose interests range from the hobbyist looking for information on a particular coin to the citizen seeking information on congressional hearings can locate sources quickly by using the on-line information services offered by many businesses. A number of these retrieval organizations are identified, and their services are discussed, in Chapter 10. The use by individuals of *videotex systems* for information retrieval is also discussed in that chapter.

Benefits from Not-for-Profit Organizations

We all receive benefits from the ways in which public organizations such as those in government, health care, and education use computers. Some (but again certainly not all) of these benefits are outlined below.

Benefits from Computers in Government. One obvious benefit of government computer usage is that to the extent that this usage results in *greater efficiency,* the taxes we now pay (high as they are) may be less than they would otherwise have been. Los Angeles County, for example, expects to save $10 million annually through the use of its Welfare Case Management Information System. And Philadelphia is saving $350,000 annually merely by using optical character recognition technology to capture payment data from a variety of tax revenue documents.

Another benefit is that individuals may now receive *better service* from government agencies. The Los Angeles County welfare system mentioned above can process new applicants quickly and keep records updated on a daily basis so that recipients can receive their checks on time and at the right address. In contrast to the bureaucratic runaround that often accompanies a call to city hall, a Long Beach, California, system enables citizens calling city hall with an inquiry or complaint to dial a single number, get the right department, and be guaranteed a response. The computer creates a record of each call, prints a letter to the caller, and sends a copy to the appropriate city council representative. If a final disposition on a call is not received within a given period of time, a follow-up procedure is initiated.

Figure 19-6 Examples of local government computer installations. (*left*) The Fire Department computer center in Brooklyn, New York. (Edith G. Haun/Stock, Boston) (*right*) The control center for the Bay Area Rapid Transit (BART) system in Oakland, California. (Peter Menzel/Stock, Boston)

State and local governments (Figure 19-6) are also using computers to:

▎ Match people looking for work with available jobs.

▎ Gather data for the purpose of controlling air and water pollution.

▎ Design safer roads.

▎ Study the incidence of fires and crimes in various locations in order to improve public safety.

▎ Coordinate traffic signals to improve traffic flow, reduce transportation delays and costs, and allow emergency vehicles such as ambulances to have priority at an intersection.

▎ Locate and recover stolen cars (and apprehend those who may be driving them).

▎ Store the names and addresses of invalids online so that when a fire alarm is received, a dispatcher can determine if an invalid lives at the address and then notify firefighters of the invalid's location in order to save precious time.

The *federal government*—the world's largest computer user—is employing computers in thousands of ways ranging from:

▎ Processing satellite data in order to prepare more accurate weather forecasts and make better predictions of future water supplies for farmers, to

▎ Developing wheelchairs that respond to voice directions so that quadriplegics will enjoy greater mobility and freedom, to

563

▌ Installing systems that enable any of the nearly 40 million Americans eligible for veteran's benefits to walk into any Veterans Administration office in the country and within seconds begin the filing process for compensation, pension, and education benefits.

Countless other examples could be cited.

Benefits from Computers in Health Care. One interesting application is the use of computer-generated maps of a geographic area to show the possible diffusion of an epidemic as well as to search for possible correlations between environmental factors in the area and the area's incidence of cancer. Other applications use computers to provide:

▌ Faster and more thorough approaches to the preparation and analysis of medical histories (Figure 19-7).

▌ Faster and more thorough testing to detect and identify disease.

▌ More accurate methods of physiological monitoring.

▌ Better control of lab test results (Figure 19-7).

▌ Better control of pharmacy services at public hospitals.

Still other computers are used to train doctors and other health care personnel by simulating a patient with an emergency condition. The student is given the symptoms and is challenged to save the patient before time runs out by using a logical progression of diagnostic tests and treatments. Student errors are pointed out immediately by the computer.

Figure 19-7 (*left*) People benefit when health-care organizations use computers to aid in the preparation and analysis of medical histories. (Russ Kinne/Photo Researchers) (*right*) A computerized blood analyzer that automatically tests for 25 separate factors in a blood sample. (Russ Kinne/Photo Researchers)

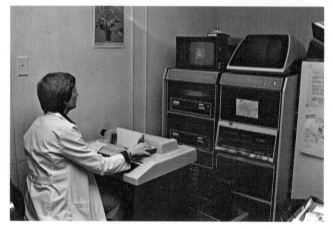

Benefits from Computers in Education. We've just seen one example of how computers may be used to benefit students. Another example is provided at San Antonio College in Texas. Students with writing handicaps gain needed skills in a remedial English laboratory by practicing the basic concepts of sentence structure and usage. At Louisiana State University, a chemical engineering professor has constructed a computer simulation model that helps explain how solid particles move in fluids. For those who like oysters, one benefit of this model is that ship channels can be dredged periodically, and the sediments can be deposited elsewhere, without endangering the oyster beds or those who work them. And researchers at the University of Wisconsin are working on a tiny computer that can be carried around by heart patients to continuously monitor the heart's rhythm and sound a warning in case of trouble. Benefits too numerous to mention are being produced at many other educational institutions around the world.

Benefits from Personal Computing

If you've read Chapter 9, you know that personal microcomputers can be used in the home for entertainment and other personal computing applications. Since the uses of personal computers are as numerous and varied as human ingenuity and imagination will permit, the benefits of personal computing are also limited only by ingenuity and imagination. The following examples indicate just a few of the possibilities.

Entertainment and Hobby Benefits. A personal computer is a general-purpose machine that may be programmed to play chess one minute and football or "Star Trek" the next. In fact, a personal computer can entertain you with hundreds of challenging games. Many game-playing programs are packaged on tape cassettes or floppy disks and are available from computer stores and other retail and mail-order outlets. *CLOAD* magazine is "printed" monthly on a tape cassette and sent to subscribers. Each cassette contains "programs of the month" ranging from games to programs of a practical nature. Of course, only a computer can read this "magazine."

Storehouses of information for the personal computer owner are available from the videotex systems discussed in Chapter 10. One such service is called *The Source*. To tap the data base and the more than 2,000 programs in The Source, the user pays a hookup fee, dials a toll-free number, and then pays an hourly service charge. In return, The Source allows the user access to the latest news, energy-saving suggestions and automotive news, the data banks of *The New York Times* and United Press International, theater and sports attractions, foreign-language tutorials and physics lessons, recipes and personal finance information, backgammon and Monopoly games—the list goes on and on!

Educational Benefits. Games can be educational as well as entertaining. For example, children can learn to identify the letters of the alphabet and match these letters to the appropriate keys on the keyboard by "shooting"

Figure 19-8 Home use of personal computers is growing as fast as people can think of more ways to use them. (Courtesy of Apple Computer, Inc.; Dan McCoy from Rainbow)

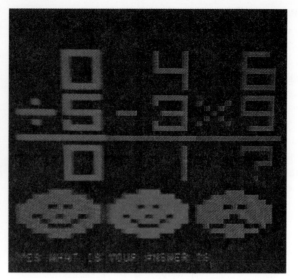

letters as they bounce around on the screen. The key corresponding to the target letter is "fired." If the ricochet angle and lead time are correct, the target letter will be hit. Educators agree that the home computer can be a powerful motivating and learning tool (Figure 19-8). When children (and adults) use personal computers, they have some real control over what they learn, how they learn, and how fast they learn. Making a sophisticated machine do one's bidding is fun for many people, and writing a computer program requires a person to analyze and understand the subject being studied. In addition, using word processing software with a personal computer encourages people to polish their writing skills because changes and corrections are made easily.

Personal Finance Benefits. A personal computer could help you:

- Prepare your budget and balance your checkbook.
- Control your installment purchases.
- Control your home's energy use.
- Analyze your investments and prepare your tax returns.

If you wanted information on current prices, you could call the toll-free number of one videotex service, obtain access to the data base of Dow-Jones & Company, and use the service's programs to obtain quotes and other information on any stock listed on any of the six major exchanges in the United States. If you were trying to decide whether to buy a home, you could load an available program into your computer, supply the necessary input data (e.g., purchase price, down payment, loan term, taxes, utility costs, mortgage interest rate, etc.), and find out exactly what the costs and financial benefits are.

Benefits of Greater Personal Efficiency. People can use personal computers to save time and/or use time more efficiently. To cite just one example, WHATSIT is a personal information retrieval program that enables a user to store up to 25,000 entries on a single online disk. The data are loaded onto the disk according to the subject keys that the user selects. Additional entries can be entered and indexed in any approprite sequence at any time, and old entries can be deleted at any time. Instead of spending a lot of time looking in a desk or file cabinet for information such as names, telephone numbers, addresses, birthdays, warranty expiration dates, hobby inventory items, and countless other things worthy of retrieval, the user can simply enter the appropriate subject key or keys at the keyboard, and the information is retrieved in a second or two.

PEOPLE AND COMPUTERS: SOME POTENTIAL DANGERS

We've just seen how people may benefit on the job by their organization's use of computers. But some people have also seen their jobs disappear in the past when new computer systems were installed. And today others are being threatened with obsolescence and loss of jobs because of computer-based changes. The possible negative impact isn't limited to people on the job. Many in private life have also had unfavorable experience with computerized systems.

Employment Problems: Displacement and Unemployment

Displacement and unemployment aren't the same. **Unemployment** refers to the total number of people involuntarily out of work. **Displacement** occurs when jobs are eliminated as a result of technological change. *If* displaced workers can't find similar jobs elsewhere and *if* they can't find work in other occupations, then there is, indeed, an increase in the unemployment figures. Optimists and pessimists disagree on the long-range effects of computers and automated tools on total employment. But both groups agree that to the employee being displaced, the future consequences are of secondary importance.

Some middle-level managers whose decisions were structured and repetitive have found that those decisions were programmable on a computer. The information systems have therefore taken over those duties, and the need for as many administrators to perform the remainder of the job duties has been reduced. In some organizations, those who were not displaced found their jobs less challenging because, although they retained the duties that required less judgment, their other tasks that called for the skilled interpretation of systems information were moved upward in the organization. And some lower-level supervisors have suffered because their departments have been eliminated or reduced in scope and status as a result of the installation of computer information systems. Of course, when computers displace employees, the supervisors of those employees may no longer be needed.

COMPUTERIZING COMPANIES SHOULD WATCH EMPLOYEE MORALE

Businesses are computerizing with long-awaited glee. After all, computers are heralded as growth hormones for the marketplace, swords that knife through red tape and payroll complications, and the ultimate service department manager. But firms that are cheerily plopping computer terminals on employees' desks should keep an eye on morale, according to MIT's Shoshanah Zuboff, in a study entitled "Psychological and Organizational Work."

While business computers may be intended to raise productivity on all levels, says Zuboff, the electronic wunder-kind may actually be increasing stress, creating job boredom, undermining loyalty to the firm, and lowering production. When workers feel that their skills and worth to the company are being undercut by a computer, they begin to feel "insignificant and overwhelmed . . . this situation can exacerbate the issues of power and powerlessness that haunt all levels of organizational life."

Zuboff contends that when employees believe that they have lost control over work environs, the result may be computer or system sabotage as well as sharp increases in sick leave and related problems. Also, employees may try to prove the system ineffective or simply not use it at all. Most managers, she adds, do not take such trends into account when computerizing their firm. Zuboff warns that greater attention should be paid to the psychological impacts of the new technology on employees to avoid these problems.

Wilbert Galitz, a consultant for CNA Insurance, agrees. Speaking at a recent National Institute for Occupational Safety and Health conference, Galitz said computer systems flop because upper-level managers fail to deal with the issue of change.

Managers should plan for change, says Galitz. They should determine the best time to carry out office automation and take slow steps so that employees can adjust.

Management goals for computerization should be made clear as well, Galitz says. System design is also critical, he added. The computer sys-

"Last week it told me if I didn't come in on Sunday not to bother coming in on Monday."

tem should be easy to use, within current employee capabilities, and thorough documentation and training should be available.

Clerical employees have often been displaced by computers. Much of the $10 million annual savings expected from the Los Angeles County Welfare Case System mentioned earlier will come from the elimination of 900 jobs over a 3-year period. The extent to which clerical displacement actually occurs and the significance of the problem in particular cases may depend in large measure on the following factors:

▪ *The rate of growth of the organization and the economy.* If the organization is growing rapidly so that more work must be done to handle the expanding volume, there may be little or no effect on the number of workers employed.

▪ *The objectives sought.* Is the organization introducing a computer system for processing purposes that couldn't otherwise be considered? Or is it to save money by eliminating existing jobs?

■ *The types of occupations threatened.* In the past, few clerical workers were laid off in larger organizations when job reductions occurred. This was possible because workers in affected departments who quit during the many months required to implement a system were simply not replaced.

When the affected jobs are not of the clerical type, the displacement problem may be more severe. The affected workers may be older employees whose skills are no longer needed. They're not as likely to quit, and so attrition may not be of much help.

Displacement is occurring in some skilled production-oriented occupations, such as those which involve the operation of certain metal-working tools and typesetting devices, as a result of the installation of computer-controlled machines. A more serious displacement problem, however, is likely to result from the increased use of computer-controlled robots in assembly operations (Figure 19-9). The automobile industry is a leading user of robots that for several years have performed such production tasks as stamping, heat-treating, welding, and spray painting. Robots perform these dreary, dirty, and/or dangerous tasks without complaint, and "first-generation" robots have usually been applied in such areas of worker discontent. But production techniques are now changing rapidly in the automobile industry. In the $80 billion retooling program required to build smaller cars that will meet foreign competition and the mileage and emission standards of the late 1980s, auto manufacturers are replacing old machines with a new generation of robots. According to the Society of Manufacturing Engineers, 20 percent of the direct labor in automobile final assembly will be replaced by programmable robots by 1985

Figure 19-9 Unimate robots at work on a Chrysler assembly line. If you look very closely, you can also see a few humans at work. (Courtesy Chrysler Corporation)

and 50 percent by 1995. By 1988, half of the direct labor needed to assemble small components such as starters will also be replaced. And according to Robert Lund, a researcher at MIT's Center for Policy Alternatives, the result of this creation of robotized plants will be a substantial permanent sector of unemployment. The forthcoming changes, Lund believes, will divide workers into high-skilled and low-skilled categories, wiping out the intermediate skill range vital for a sense of upward mobility.

Nor are employees in the professions immune from the effects of computer usage. The advancement in scientific and engineering knowledge (which may be attributed in part to the expanding use of computers) makes it increasingly difficult for scientists and engineers to keep abreast of their fields. They must have the ability and willingness to learn about computers, adopt new techniques, and, perhaps, go through several "retreading" periods in their careers simply to retain marketable skills. Otherwise, as one expert has observed, they may become, over time, uneducated and therefore incompetent at a level at which they once performed quite adequately. The possible suffering and anxiety associated with the conviction that technical obsolescence is likely in a relatively short time is thus something that certain professionals may have to learn to live with.

Questionable Practices Affecting Private Lives

Since computer systems are now performing vital functions in society, it's essential that the data affecting people aren't lost or stolen, errors aren't introduced, and facts aren't originated, stored, retrieved, or communicated without proper justification. Unfortunately, questionable data processing practices have caused some computer systems to fall short of these standards.

Data Originating/Recording: A Lack of Control? A staggering volume of information of a highly personal nature has been collected by government agencies and private organizations. In the government sector, for example, a study conducted a few years ago by the Senate Subcommittee on Constitutional Rights found that 858 data banks in 54 federal agencies contained a total of more than 1.25 *billion* records and dossiers on individuals—and these figures understated the actual situation at the time. These hundreds of federal data banks, when combined with more than 600 others operated by the states and more than 1,700 others operated by cities and counties, provide governments with specific information on virtually every citizen. And in addition, there are hundreds of private organizations—e.g., credit bureaus—that engage in investigative reporting for a fee.

Several problems associated with all this data gathering have been identified. These problems are:

▌ *Gathering data without a valid need to know.* For years, the Justice Department maintained a computer-based Inter-Divisional Information System (IDIS) to gather data about the "agitational activities" of political dissidents. In the early 1970s, at Senate hearings on federal data banks, an assistant attorney general defended the IDIS and gave assurances that it was used only on a "need to know" basis. However, after examining IDIS files, Senate investigators concluded that "massive amounts of irrelevant information had been compiled on innocent individuals." Another example of questionable data-gathering activities involves the private firms that collect personal data about people for insurance companies, employers, and credit grantors. It's common practice for insurance companies to ask a private agency to investigate a policy applicant's background to help determine the sort of underwriting risk he or she would be. This is understandable since certain personal habits—e.g., heavy drinking or participation in a hazardous sport—may involve obvious health risks. The problem is that the data gathered may go beyond those which have probable risk value to an insurance company. These data are frequently gathered by an interviewer from two or three of the applicant's neighbors or acquaintances. In about 20 minutes, the interviewer will ask a respondent questions about the applicant's use of alcohol or narcotics, whether there's anything adverse about his or her reputation, life-style, and home environment, and if there's any news of domestic troubles or reports of dubious business practices. Questions calling for such detailed and impressionistic responses in such a short time are an open invitation to gossip and faulty moral assessments. Furthermore, some of these questions may have little bearing on the applicant's insurability. But this is the data-gathering method used by Equifax, Inc., the nation's largest consumer reporting service. The applicant's file is added to the millions of other similar files in the Equifax data bank. Once stored, the contents of the file are then available to others, such as credit grantors and potential employers, for a small fee.

Gathering inaccurate and incomplete data. We've just seen that Equifax methods can permit inaccuracies to be introduced into a computer data bank. (Each year about 200,000 people lodge complaints against the firm.) Unintentional mistakes in filling out input forms and keying records are common enough in any record-keeping system. But the consequences may be more serious in a computer-based system because there may be fewer people to catch errors and because the speed with which inaccurate information is made available to system users may be much faster than the speed with which errors are detected and corrected. For example, in converting data on a questionnaire into machine-readable form, a data entry operator may hit the 1 key instead of the 2 key (where the 1 is the code for "yes" and the 2 is the code for "no") on a question concerning a felony conviction, a prior bankruptcy, or a history of mental disorder or venereal disease. You can appreciate the possible consequences of this simple unintentional mistake! Deliberate errors have also been introduced into data banks which are so important to people. For example, a former Equifax interviewer told a Senate banking committee that he had completely invented 25 percent of his reports, and that he was far from alone in doing so. Finally, input data are also subject to serious errors of omission. If, for example, an individual is arrested and accused of, say, auto theft, this fact will probably be entered into several law enforcement data banks. But if the person is found to be innocent of the charges, this very important fact that's needed to complete the record may not be entered into the data banks. It's estimated that 70 percent of the arrest records stored in the FBI's National Crime Information Center (NCIC) contain no information about the final outcome of the cases.

Problems of confusion and bewilderment associated with data gathering. People are often confused and bewildered by computer data-input procedures. A significant cause of this confusion is that people aren't told what the system does or how it works. The result may be the belief on the part of people that they have been tricked or deceived by the system. For example, in signing application forms for insurance policies, individuals may not know that a fine-print statement at the bottom of a form authorizes a firm representing an insurance company to quiz neighbors and acquaintances for "any and all information" about them. People also may not realize that the supplied data may be entered into third-party data banks and used in rather secretive ways. Individuals may also find it confusing to operate the computer input devices that are replacing more familiar forms and procedures. Automated voting systems, for example, have confused voters and have produced questionable tallys.

Standardization and Depersonalization. A standard defines or specifies something so that people and machines that must use it and/or produce it do so in a uniform and efficient way. Entering input data according to some standard coding scheme can contribute to an economical and efficient system. But **standardization** may also lead to unwanted depersonalization. As we come in contact with a growing number of computer systems, the use of numerical codes for identification purposes may be expected to increase. We may understand that being treated as numbers can lead to standardized and efficient computer usage by organizations, but we may wish that it were not so. Instead of being numerically coded and molded to meet the computer's needs, we might prefer that computer systems be designed so that we will be treated as persons rather than numbers. *This isn't likely to happen.* The social security number is now being used as the personal identifier in numerous large data systems. The Internal Revenue Service, The U.S. Army, colleges and universities, state driver's license departments, insurance companies, banks—these and many other organizations may know you as 353-27-2345. The threat of an eventual "universal identifier," of course, is that the separate data records you've established for particular purposes can more easily be consolidated through the use of the common number, and the combined data can be merged into a large personal dossier.

In addition to treating people as numbers, standardized procedures, once established, may tend to become inflexible. Thus, if a person's needs don't conform to the "norms" of the system, there may be difficulty in getting the system to deal properly with the exception. This tendency to try to force everyone into the same mold may naturally give the individual a feeling of helplessness in trying to cope with a cold, impersonal, and remote organization.

System Mistakes. System mistakes are primarily due to human errors in preparing input data and in designing and preparing programs. Thus, when the computer itself is blamed for some foul-up, it's frequently being used as a convenient "scapegoat" to cover up human error, carelessness, or indifference. Of course, the unfortunate fact remains that numerous "computer" foul-ups *have occurred.* We can conclude this section with a few pitiful examples of computer-system atrocities that have had a negative impact on people.

- Some voters in areas using computerized vote-counting systems may have been disenfranchised. For example, the validity of the count of the computer-processed ballots in Washington, D.C., and Austin, Texas, in past elections is subject to question.

- A New York City employee failed to get his check for three pay periods after a computer payroll system was installed. Finally, after the employee had initiated legal action against the city, a program bug was discovered and removed, and Mr. Void was at last paid.

- People have been arrested for "stealing" their own cars. The sequence of events goes something like this: The car is stolen, the theft is reported to a law enforcement data bank, and the car is recovered (perhaps in another jurisdiction) and returned to its owner. The recovery is not entered into the data bank, and the owner is then picked up while driving his or her recovered property. Since the arrest may also be entered into the data bank, but the final disposition may not be, the owner may wind up with an arrest record for "grand theft—auto." If you don't think this can be serious, you should consider the plight of the ex-Marine from Illinois who has been jailed several times for desertion because of incorrect information stored in the FBI's computerized National Crime Information Center.

The System Security Issue

If input data important to people are accurate and complete when they enter a computer system, are processed correctly, don't become inaccurate through subsequent errors, and aren't distorted or lost through system mistakes, we could be confident about the integrity of the data. But even if we were successful in controlling **data integrity,** this wouldn't be enough to eliminate all the adverse effects that computer systems may have on the private lives of people. It doesn't help much for a person to know that the information

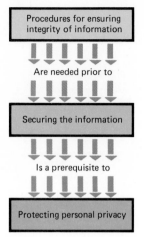

Figure 19-10 The relationship among data integrity, systems security, and personal privacy.

relevant to him or her that's stored in a data bank is accurate and complete if he or she also knows that the information isn't *secured and protected* against theft, fraud, or malicious scrutiny and manipulation.

Both information *integrity and security* are needed to protect a person's right to privacy—i.e., to protect the legitimate right of an individual to limit access to personal and often sensitive information to persons authorized to use it in the individual's best interest. If a lack of integrity in a law enforcement data bank permits the arrest of an individual for driving his or her own car and then results in the creation of an arrest record that may not be purged from the system, and if a lack of systems security subsequently permits the circulation of this arrest record to prospective employers and credit agencies, these deficiencies have certainly contributed to an invasion of the individual's privacy. In short, data integrity, information security, and personal privacy are interrelated, as shown in Figure 19-10.

For our purposes, **systems security** involves:

- The protection of stored *data* against accidental or malicious disclosure.

- The *physical* protection of hardware and software against damage or destruction.

The consequences that an organization may face when it fails to maintain system security were outlined in Chapter 18. It's equally important from an individual's point of view that confidential records be preserved and used only for approved purposes, and that the equipment and programs needed to store and retrieve them be protected against damage or penetration.

The vulnerability of computer systems has increased in recent years, and so the security issue has become more important. Early computers were located in self-contained installations, were accessible to a relatively small number of specialists, and were used to process batches of data in a single stream. As computer systems increased in number and became more sophisticated, however, many more people had access to them, the use of shared resources and jointly used data became common, and direct interaction with a computer became a routine activity for even casual users. Such an environment has obviously increased the difficulty of maintaining security. The vulnerability of systems has also increased because:

- The information to be found in a relatively complete and up-to-date data bank may be of sufficient value to provide the incentive for outsiders to seek access to it.

- More people have now been trained in the skills required to program, penetrate, and manipulate computer systems.

Lack of Control Over Security. The computer hardware in general use today was not designed with security provisions in mind. Thus, the provisions that do exist are found in the software and in the organizational policies and data processing controls that may exist in the particular system.

When it comes to security, existing software is indeed soft. Clever individuals have had no difficulty in breaking through the security provisions of those computer operating-system programs that they've sought to penetrate. Today's computer operating systems aren't completely predictable, and so there's no analytical method for proving that an operating system *isn't* performing unauthorized acts. Thus, there's no guaranteed defense against several known techniques by which a programmer can corrupt a system.

Impact on People. The lack of control over computer system security has resulted in undesirable consequences for people. *Economic loss, inconvenience, loss of privacy*—these are just a few of the aggravations people have suffered because computer systems weren't secure.

Individuals as well as organizations lose money to the computer thief. In one instance, a computer was used to send out phony invoices to people. The thief knew that some people pay authentic-looking bills automatically, without questioning their validity. When a phony bill was questioned, however, the thief would merely send back a form letter saying "Sorry. Our computer made an error." A person's finances can also become fouled up as a result of the penetration of an EFTS. For example, a Chicago woman was mailed a bank money card and a personal identification number without having requested them. Both were intercepted by a thief and used to empty a $600 account of hers and run up an additional overdraft of $1,200. The bank then froze the woman's other account because she was overdrawn. It took an attorney and 2 months of wrangling with the bank to get her money released.

A lack of control in handling input media can result in inconvenience. Suppose a shift supervisor at a computer center servicing dozens of banks processes a tape containing a day's checks and deposits but fails to properly record this processing run. The next shift supervisor may then rerun the tape with the result being that double deposits and double withdrawals may appear in customer accounts. You're delighted with your double credit, but I am really chapped by my double withdrawal. And we are both inconvenienced by the later attempts to straighten out this mess.

Finally, as noted earlier, a lack of control over systems security can lead to the invasion of an individual's legitimate right to privacy.

The Privacy Issue

We know that for years private and public organizations have been building separate files containing "threads" of information about those with whom they come in contact. But many of these older files are incomplete and poorly maintained. Thus, the value of their contents may be such that unauthorized persons have little incentive to snoop. *The development of computer data banks, however, has changed the situation.*

Dossiers and the Invasion of Privacy. Files maintained in large, integrated computer data banks are more complete. Seemingly innocent data recorded and stored at one time may be retrieved and correlated quickly and

As every man goes through life, he fills in a number of forms for the record, each containing a number of questions. There are thus hundreds of little threads radiating from each man, millions of threads in all. If these threads were suddenly to become visible, people would lose all ability to move.
Alexander Solzhenitsyn

inexpensively by the computer with other data collected from different sources and at different times to reveal potentially damaging information about individuals. It might then be possible to bring pressure to bear on people to make them do things they might otherwise not have done.

Thoughtful opponents of consolidated data banks acknowledge that such banks can help public and private organizations provide individuals with many of the benefits discussed earlier in the chapter—e.g., better and more efficient service and greater safety. But they are concerned about the threat that these banks might eventually present to an individual. This concern is perhaps summarized in a *Saturday Review* cartoon which shows a distressed executive listening to a telephone message. The message is: "This is the Computer Data Bank. Leave $100,000 in small bills in Locker 287 at the Port Authority Bus Terminal or I'll print out your complete dossier and send it to your wife."

Automated tellers are intended for convenience, but the EFTS system can also be viewed as a potential threat to the right of privacy. (Courtesy NCR, Dayton, Ohio)

Impact on People. A few examples and speculations here should be sufficient to demonstrate how a computer system or network may be used for surveillance, for the creation of a climate that restricts individual freedom, and for other abuses.

EFTS Surveillance Possibilities. Although the electronic funds transfer systems being implemented by banks and other financial institutions aren't intended for *surveillance,* they could be easily adapted to this purpose in the future. The use of *cash* in a transaction reveals little or no information about the parties to the transaction. When a *check* is written, a record is created of the payer, the payee, and the transaction amount. And when a *money card* is used, all this information, along with the transaction time, location, and nature of the transaction, is recorded. Thus, if all your transactions were normally to be processed through EFTS computers, a *daily record* of much of *what* you do and *where* you do it could be prepared. A few years ago, a group of computer, communications, and surveillance experts was gathered and given the following hypothetical problem: As advisers to the head of the KGB (the Russian secret police), they were to design an *unobtrusive* surveillance system to monitor the activities of all citizens and visitors inside the U.S.S.R. As one of these experts testified in Congressional hearings:

> That exercise . . . was only a two-day effort. I am sure we could add some bells and whistles to increase its effectiveness somewhat. But the fact remains that this group decided that if you wanted to build an unobtrusive system for surveillance, you couldn't do much better than an EFTS.

Of course, EFTS proponents maintain that adequate laws can be passed to prevent surveillance abuse. But critics aren't so sure. They point out that existing check authorization systems can "flag" accounts so that if a "flagged" individual tries to cash a check someone (police perhaps?) can be notified of the individual's exact location. They are fearful that future operators of EFTS networks would be unable to resist the pressures from governments to allow the EFTS to be used for surveillance purposes.

List-Compiling Abuses. Mailing lists giving details about people are regularly compiled and sold by both private and public organizations. State auto licensing agencies, for example, sell lists to auto equipment suppliers. There's probably not much harm in this if it results only in your receiving literature that tries to persuade you to buy seat covers a few weeks after you've registered your new car. But what about the case of the computer dating service that sold its list of female clients to a publishing organization that printed and sold through local newsstands lists of "Girls Who Want Dates?" Try to tell one of those women that her privacy hasn't been invaded!

Freedom Restrictions. Consider the following facts:
(*a*) Thousands of law enforcement officers and bank, employment agency, and credit company clerks have easy access to networks containing information on millions of people. Many of these officers and clerks without any real "need to know" may while away the time browsing through the records of friends and acquaintances just to see what they can uncover.
(*b*) Most categories of personal information gathered for legitimate research purposes by reputable social, political, and behavioral scientists don't enjoy any statutory protection. Thus, sensitive personal information gathered by these researchers may be obtained through a subpoena issued by a court or other government body and put into data banks for future use. If the researchers, who may have assured the respondents that their replies would be kept in strictest confidence, refuse to honor the subpoena and turn over the data, they may be cited for contempt and be made to suffer the consequences. Given that alternative, they generally surrender the data.

Being aware of such facts and of the possible uses of large computerized data banks may have a sobering effect on people. It may restrict their actions even when the data are accurate, the use of the data is authorized by law, and controls on the use of the data are imposed. You may be in favor of the use of computers to curtail crime, but you may also resent being listed with felons in an unsecured data bank. And you may believe that a university professor should conduct a study that requires the gathering and analyzing of personal data, but you may not feel free to personally participate in that study. In short, you may now tend to behave differently (and less freely) than you once would have because of your increasing awareness that what you say and do may become part of some computer record.

Privacy Controls. We've been discussing an individual's "right" to privacy, but the word *privacy* doesn't appear anywhere in the Constitution. What, then, is the legal status of privacy? An early consideration of privacy as a legal concept was presented in 1890 by Louis Brandeis and Samuel Warren in an article entitled "The Right to Privacy." In 1928, after being appointed to the Supreme Court, Justice Brandeis again took up the concept when he wrote in a minority opinion: "The right to be let alone is the most comprehensive of rights and the right most valued by civilized men."

Of course, what one person may consider to be a privacy right may be judged by others to be an item of genuine public concern. For example, if a newspaper reporter unearths the fact that a member of Congress has put a number of relatives on the government payroll for no good purpose, and if the reporter then reveals this fact and prints the names and salaries of the relatives, she has undoubtedly infringed on their privacy. But she has also used rights guaranteed to her in the Bill of Rights (the First Amendment's freedom of speech and freedom of the press) to perform a public service. Thus, there may be legitimate rights operating against privacy in some situations. In short, since privacy is not one of the specific constitutional rights, and since a balance has to be struck between the need for privacy on the one hand and society's need for legitimate information on the other, *the extent to which individuals are given privacy protection must depend on judicial and legislative decisions.* That is, the *continuous* task of balancing human rights against basic freedoms in order to establish privacy controls is the responsibility of the judicial and legislative branches of government.

Lawmakers have been busy in recent years in an effort to restore some balance in favor of privacy. The result has been that numerous federal statutes and about 150 state bills have been passed over a brief time span to control the invasion of privacy. Some *examples of existing* **privacy laws are:**

✓ *Fair Credit Reporting Act of 1970.* This federal law gives people the right to know what information is kept on them by credit bureaus and other credit investigation agencies. People also have the right to challenge information they consider to be inaccurate.

✓ *State "Fair Information Practice" Laws.* The California Fair Information Practice Act of 1974 (and similar laws in many other states) spells out the rights of people when dealing with state government data banks. Individuals have the right to know what information is kept on them in the various data banks, and to contest the "accuracy, completeness, pertinence, and timeliness" of the stored data.

✓ *Privacy Act of 1974.* This federal law became effective late in September 1975. It's aimed at some of the uses and abuses of federal data banks. Some of its provisions are:
(*a*) With the exception of classified files, civil service records, and law enforcement agency investigative files, people have the right to see their records in federal data banks.
(*b*) They may point out errors in their records, and if these errors aren't removed, they may ask a federal judge to order the correction.
(*c*) Unless specifically authorized by law, federal agencies cannot sell or rent personal data bank information, nor can they monitor a person's religious or political activities.

Feedback and Review 19-1

The subject of artificial intelligence has been discussed in this chapter. And some of the benefits available to people from computer usage, along with some of the possible dangers associated with the use of computer systems have also been outlined. To test and reinforce your understanding of these subjects, match the letter of the appropriate term to the definition or concept to which it belongs. (Place the correct letter in the space provided.)

_l_ **1.** The amount of goods or services possessing economic value that people and machines can produce in a given time period is their _____.

_i_ **2.** Computers can help businesses provide higher-quality products and better _____.

_f_ **3.** People may benefit from the use of EFTS and _____.

_m_ **4.** Computer _____ is being used to give the illusion of movement to inanimate objects.

_n_ **5.** A _____ system can be used by individuals to retrieve information from dozens of data banks.

_g_ **6.** People may benefit from the use of computers by governments, educational institutions, and _____ organizations.

_b_ **7.** Personal _____ benefits are one of many categories of benefits that can be obtained through the use of personal computers.

_o_ **8.** An acronym for the use of computers to solve relatively unstructured problems such as programming computers to play chess is _____.

_p_ **9.** The author of a test to determine if a computer program might be considered to possess intelligence.

_c_ **10.** A word used to describe the judgmental part of problem-solving.

_j_ **11.** Studies have shown that computers can _____ large numbers of clerical workers.

_k_ **12.** A serious displacement problem is likely to result from the use of _____ in assembly operations.

_a_ **13.** Data have been gathered about people in the past when there was no valid "need to _____" basis for doing so.

_d_ **14.** The social security number is being used as the personal _____ in numerous large data systems.

_h_ **15.** Both data integrity and system security are needed to protect a person's right to _____.

_e_ **16.** It would be possible to use an _____ as an unobtrusive surveillance system.

_q_ **17.** Privacy protection depends on _____ and legislative decisions.

a) know
b) finance
c) heuristic
d) identifier
e) EFTS
f) UPC
g) health-care
h) privacy
i) service
j) displace
k) robots
l) productivity
m) animation
n) videotex
o) AI
p) Turing
q) judicial

Looking Back

1. Computer chess programs can now defeat 99.5 percent of all human chess players. Experiments are being conducted by researchers in the field of artificial intelligence to improve the machines' heuristic capabilities. But humans still remain far superior to computers in this area of intellectual work. The potential of an alliance between humans and computers, however, cannot be restricted in any way we can now anticipate.

2. Some managers and employees in organizations have found their jobs more rewarding because of computer systems, and consumers have received benefits from the ways in which both businesses and not-for-profit organizations use computers. For example, the prices we now pay to businesses for some goods and services may be less because of computer usage than they would otherwise have been, and the quality of these goods and services has often been improved. Also, without computers the possible benefits of EFTS and UPC wouldn't be feasible, handicapped persons would be denied tools that make their lives more meaningful, and retrieving needed information would be a more tedious task.

3. Greater efficiency and better service are also benefits that people receive from the use of computers by federal, state, and local governments. Many beneficial applications of computers exist in the areas of public health care and education. And personal computers can be used by people for entertainment and educational purposes.

4. Although some managers and employees have benefited by the use of computers on the job, others haven't been so fortunate. Some have lost their jobs or have suffered a loss of status and prestige when computer systems were installed. Clerical employees, for example, have often been displaced by computers, and production employees are being threatened by the rapidly growing use of computer-controlled robots.

5. In private life some people (who may have been helped on the job by computers) have been inconvenienced and confused by computer information systems employing questionable data processing practices. In some systems there seems to be a lack of control over the data originating/recording step. Data are sometimes gathered without a valid reason; when a valid reason does exist, gathered facts are sometimes used in ways that were not originally intended. A number of people have also been the casualties of systems errors of commission and omission and/or the victims of a cold, impersonal, and remote computer system that classifies, sorts, and treats them as depersonalized numbers.

6. Information integrity and security are needed to protect a person's legitimate right to privacy. Systems security involves the protection of both the data and the hardware and software used to process the data. Computer security difficulties are caused by the fact that many skilled people may have access to the system, and by the fact that the value of the sorted data may warrant the attempt to penetrate the system. Although there are hardware and software security provisions in a typical system, these provisions are seldom capable of blocking the attempts of a skilled penetrator. The lack of control over computer systems security has resulted in economic loss, inconvenience, and a loss of privacy for people.

7. There are many benefits to be obtained from the creation of data banks, but there's also a concern about the threat these data banks might present to an individual. Ways in which computers are used (or could be used) for surveillance, for the creation of a climate that restricts individual freedom, and for other abuses are presented in the chapter. Several laws passed to restore some balance in the favor of privacy are also mentioned.

KEY TERMS AND CONCEPTS

You should now be able to define and use the following terms and concepts (the numbers shown indicate the pages where the terms and concepts are first mentioned):

artificial intelligence (AI) 553	automated clearing house 559	standardization 572
Turing's test 555	computer photography 560	data integrity 573
heuristic 555	computer animation 560	right to privacy 574
synergy 555	unemployment 567	systems security 574
productivity 557	displacement 567	privacy laws 578
checkless payment system 559	standard 572	

TOPICS FOR REVIEW AND DISCUSSION

1. Why does controversy surround the question of whether computers can be programmed to "think"?

2. Robert Jastrow, Director of NASA's Goddard Institute for Space Studies, has written that the alliance between humans and computers will not last very long. He states that: "Computer intelligence is growing by leaps and bounds, with no natural limit in sight. But human evolution is a nearly finished chapter in the history of life." Jastrow believes that a new kind of intelligent life will probably emerge on the earth, and this life "is more likely to be made of silicon." (*a*) What's your reaction to this opinion? (*b*) Are your views changed by the fact that Jastrow believes the evolution of the new silicon species will take about a million years?

3. (*a*) How have managers of organizations benefited from computer usage? (*b*) Identify employees of organizations who have benefited, and explain how they've been helped.

4. Discuss how the following individuals in organizations may benefit from computer usage: (*a*) law enforcement officers, (*b*) members of Congress, (*c*) school teachers, (*d*) nurses, and (*e*) district office managers.

5. Identify and discuss four ways in which consumers may benefit from the use of computers (*a*) by businesses, and (*b*) by public organizations.

6. How may people benefit from the use of personal computers?

7. (*a*) How have managers been the victims of computer usage? (*b*) How have employees been victimized?

8. Westinghouse Electric Corporation has a grant from the National Science Foundation to experiment with the use of robots to replace people in low-volume or batch-manufacturing operations—the types of operations that account for about 75 percent of all U.S. manufacturing. According to a Westinghouse spokesperson, "complex assembly tasks will continue to be performed by people, but many repetitive, boring tasks, and those performed in an unpleasant environment can and should be automated." Discuss this statement.

9. How may a lack of control over data originating/recording lead to undesirable results for people?

10. "Data integrity, information security, and personal privacy are interrelated." Define these terms and discuss this statement.

11. Explain how a lack of data security and physical security can lead to undesirable consequences for people.

12. (a) Discuss the EFTS surveillance possibilities. (b) How may questionable activities by government organizations create a climate that restricts personal freedom?

13. In George Orwell's *1984,* Big Brother controls individuals through sensors housed in the two-way (send-receive) TV screens located in all homes, offices, and public squares. The sensors tune in on people and monitor their heartbeats. Recently, a young physiologist, seeking to measure the physiological activities of salamanders, created a delicate instrument that can detect and record from a distance an animal's heartbeat, respiration, and muscle tension. In all, Orwell described 137 "futuristic" devices in *1984* (which was published over 30 years ago). About 100 of these devices are now practical. Do you think that a democratic society has anything to fear from such technology?

14. "What one person may consider to be a privacy right may be judged by others to be an item of public concern." Discuss this statement.

15. Identify and discuss some of the legal controls that are available to restore some balance in favor of privacy.

ANSWERS TO FEEDBACK AND REVIEW SECTION

19-1

1. l	7. b	13. a
2. i	8. o	14. d
3. f	9. p	15. h
4. m	10. c	16. e
5. n	11. j	17. q
6. g	12. k	

Career Opportunities

In considering the impact of computers on people in Chapter 19, we've considered both the benefits and potential dangers of computer usage. One group that should obviously benefit are those hundreds of thousands of people who are working in computer installations. For these people, the career opportunities have never been better. In fact, for the past 4 years computer specialists have been classified by personnel recruiting firms as the most sought-after employees in the United States. Demand for computer people far exceeds the supply, salaries in the field are rising so fast that published figures become outdated in just a few months, and qualified new entrants into the job market can usually choose from several good offers. Every issue of *Computerworld,* a weekly newspaper for the computer industry, contains dozens of pages of "help wanted" ads with enticing captions (see Figure 19-A). These ads are aimed at finding people to fill the occupational categories presented in the following sections. As you read these sections, perhaps you'll find a path that will lead to future opportunities.

Information System Managers

Like all managers, a *manager of a department* such as system analysis/design or program preparation must perform the functions of planning, organizing, staffing, and controlling. To be able to plan effectively and then control his or her department activities, such a manager must possess technical know-how in addition to managerial ability. But too much emphasis on technical competence at the expense of management skills should be avoided. Too often in the past, the most skilled technician was promoted to group manager only to demonstrate, very soon, a lack of competence in management techniques. It's likely that the larger the department, the more important

Figure 19-A A small sampling of ads from an issue of *Computerworld.* Scores of ads covering dozens of pages were included in this issue.

managerial skills become in the total mix of skills required by a manager (Figure 19-B).

The *management information system (MIS) director* must also possess technical knowledge, for he or she is responsible for planning and controlling the information resources of an organization. In addition, however, the MIS director must:

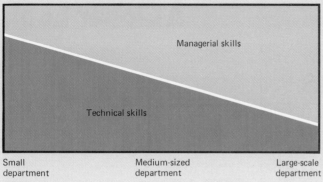

Small department   Medium-sized department   Large-scale department

Figure 19-B Total mix of skills required by an information systems manager.

- Clearly understand the firm's business, its purpose and goals, and its unique data processing needs.

- Be able to communicate with, motivate, and lead a number of highly skilled people.

- Possess the poise and stature to command the respect of other company executives as well as data processing employees.

People planning to seek a career in information system management should acquire a college degree. Courses in business administration, economics, personnel management, data processing, and statistics are desirable. And practical experience is also required to attain the maturity that's needed.

Data Base Administrators

The data base in an organization and some of the functions of those who administer it are discussed in Chapter 17. The role of a *data base administrator* (*DBA*) is to:

- Establish a data dictionary that records company-wide data definitions and standards.

- Coordinate the data collection and storage needs of users.

- Act as a file design and data base consultant to others in the organization.

- Design the data base security system to guard against unauthorized use.

To perform these duties, a DBA must have a high degree of technical knowledge. He or she must also have the political skills needed to balance conflicting user needs, and the ability to communicate effectively with users who have dissimilar backgrounds.

Given this job description, it's not surprising that the DBA has sometimes been called the "superperson" of the data processing installation. Educational backgrounds vary, but a college degree that emphasizes data processing, management, and communications skills is appropriate. In large organizations, there can be several DBAs working under the direction of a manager of data base administration.

Systems Analysts

The title of *systems analyst* is given to those who are responsible for analyzing how computer data processing can be applied to specific user problems, and for designing effective data processing solutions. Although there are often several grades of systems analyst (lead, senior, junior), the job consists of:

- Helping users determine information needs.

- Gathering facts about, and analyzing the basic methods and procedures of, current information systems.

- Designing new systems, integrating existing procedures into new system specifications as required, and assisting in the implementation of new designs.

Senior systems analysts are often chosen to act as leaders of system study teams (discussed in Chapter 16) and systems development project teams (mentioned in Chapter 18).

Analysts must usually be very familiar with the objectives, personnel, products and services, industry, and special problems of the firms that employ them. They must also know the uses and limitations of computers as well as other types of data processing equipment, for they are the interpreters between users and other data processing specialists. They must understand programming basics and be able to determine which jobs are candidates for computer processing. In addition to logical reasoning ability, they must also have initiative and the ability to plan and organize their work since they will frequently be working on their own without much direct supervision. And they must be able to communicate with and secure the cooperation of operating employees and supervisors. Educational backgrounds vary, but a college degree or the equivalent is generally needed. Courses that have proven valuable to the types of system analysts described above are the same ones mentioned for data processing managers.

Programmers and Programmer Team Personnel

Programmers may be classified here into two categories: applications programmers and systems programmers. The job of an *applications programmer* is often to take the systems specifications of analysts and transform them into effective, efficient, and well-documented programs of instructions for computers. However, there are different applications programmer categories, and their duties can vary in different organizations. In some companies, for example, the duties of system analyst and applications programmer are combined into an *analyst/programmer* job. In other organizations, some applications programmers work primarily on new program development while others devote their time almost exclusively to maintaining existing programs. A single programmer may be assigned to develop a new program, or a team of programmers may be given the task. As Figure 19-C shows, job opportunities for programmers will continue to grow throughout the 1980s.

The organizing of programmers into *chief programmer teams* and *"egoless" programming teams* is discussed in Chapter 13. When chief programmer teams are used, a highly skilled *lead* or *"chief" progammer* is in charge of the team, another senior programmer acts as the chief's *backup programmer,* and a *team librarian* is assigned to gather and organize the records and documents associated with the project. Other applications programmers are assigned to the project team as needed.

The job of a *systems programmer* is to select, modify, and maintain the complex operating system software described in Chapter 15. Systems programmers thus perform a support function by maintaining the operating system software environment in which applications programmers and computer operators work. They also participate in decisions involving hardware/software additions or deletions.

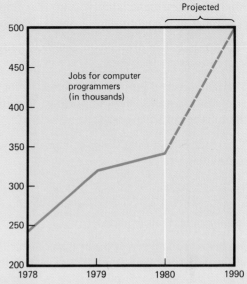

Figure 19-C Jobs for trained programmers are expected to double from their 1978 level of a quarter million to over half a million. The 1981 demand for programmers was some 36 percent higher than in 1980. In other words, job positions are opening up at a fast pace. Others in high demand will be software engineers, systems analysts, and management-level personnel with computer knowledge, including data base managers and managers of information service systems. (Source: Bureau of Labor Statistics)

Since programmer job descriptions vary, the educational requirements for these jobs also vary. A systems programmer is likely to need the courses offered in a computer science degree program or the equivalent in professional training. The educational background needed by applications programmers depends on such factors as:

- The degree of separation between the systems analysis and programming functions.

- The complexity of the data processing systems in the organization.

- The industry in which the business operates.

Completion of a 4-year college program isn't an absolute condition for employment in most applications programming groups, but the skills acquired from a 2-year college program are often needed.

Regardless of the educational background requirements, however, all programmers need the following basic skills:

- Analytical reasoning ability, and the ability to remember and concentrate on small details.

- The drive and motivation to complete programs without direct supervision.

- The patience and perseverance to search for small errors in programs, and the accuracy to minimize the number of such errors.

- The creativeness to develop new problem-solving techniques.

Telecommunications Personnel

Telecommunications specialists are responsible for the design of the data communications networks described in Chapter 10. They work with others such as systems programmers to evaluate and select the communications processors to be used in the network. The analysis of network traffic and the preparation of data communications software are included in their duties. They may also establish the standards for network operation. Nondata communications links used for voice and picture transmission are also likely to be included in their responsibilities. Like systems programmers, telecommunications specialists perform a support function. And also like systems programmers, they need a strong technical background.

Computer Operations Personnel

As Figure 19-D shows, about 40 percent of the people in a typical MIS division in a large company perform computer operations functions. The duties of *computer operators* include setting up the processor and related tape and disk drives, starting the program run, checking to ensure proper operation, and unloading equipment at the end of a run. Some knowledge of programming is needed. Programs at some 2-year colleges are designed to train computer operators. But on-the-job training and experience are often all that's required to hold operating jobs.

Data entry operators transcribe data from source doc-

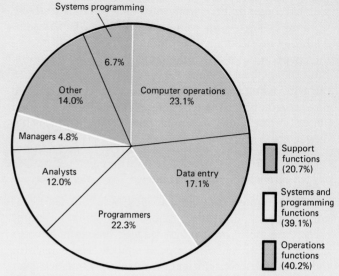

Figure 19-D How people are classified in a typical MIS division in a larger company. (Source: International Data Corporation)

uments into a punched paper or magnetic media form that's suitable for input into a computer system. Skill at a keyboard is usually needed, and intelligence and alertness is required to recognize and correct errors. A formal educational background is usually not necessary, but careful on-the-job training is needed to minimize data entry errors. Data entry operators may be grouped together at a centralized site or dispersed at remote terminal locations.

Program and media librarians are often found in the computer operations section. They have the very important task of maintaining and protecting the installation's programs and data. The documentation of programs and procedures is controlled by a librarian. Magnetic tapes, disks, and punched cards are catalogued, stored, and supplied to authorized people by a librarian. Computer operators and programmers must get a librarian's approval to check out programs and data, and charge-out records are kept. Media cleaning and inspection are also a librarian's responsibility. Clerical record-keeping skills are needed. On-the-job training is generally used to prepare people for librarian jobs.

Figure 19-E summarizes some of the possible career paths for those who choose opportunities in data processing.

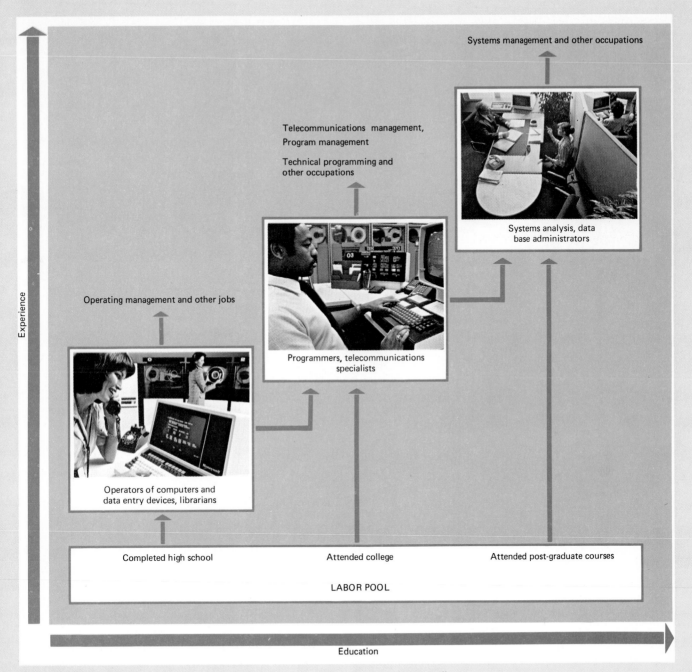

Systems management and other occupations

Telecommunications management,
Program management

Technical programming and
other occupations

Systems analysis, data
base administrators

Operating management and other jobs

Programmers, telecommunications
specialists

Operators of computers and
data entry devices, librarians

Experience

Completed high school   Attended college   Attended post-graduate courses

LABOR POOL

Education

Figure 19-E Some of the possible career paths in data processing. (Courtesy Honeywell, Inc., and General Electric Information Systems Company)

chapter 20

The Impact of Computers on Organizations

FEAR OF AUTOMATION

"I went to the Exposition; I noticed that fountain which spouts gigantic artificial flowers. The sight of all those machines makes me feel bad. I don't like the stuff which, all alone and left to itself, seems to be producing things worthy of admiration."—*the painter Eugene Delacroix, writing in his diary on August 3, 1855, after visiting the Paris International Exposition, a seven-month celebration of scientific and technological progress*

Women call a press conference to announce their intention to slow or even prevent the introduction of automation technology into the office. French computer workers join an underground that smashes computer installations and computer sales offices in Toulouse and Paris. Employees at *The New York Times*, anxious about radiation from the video display screens at which they work, leak rumors of tragic eye disease to medical and press reporters. And, as automation begins to affect white-collar as well as blue-collar workers, gloomy warnings about its impact on what work will be like in the next couple of decades start to come from allies of business as well as from its predictable enemies.

What gives? Has automation, for years touted as mankind's willing and efficient slave, finally been revealed to be a cruel and mindless master? Well, not exactly, but people *are* afraid of the changes that technology will make in their workplaces, and successful managers in the late twentieth century will have to deal with this fear if technology is to give their businesses the leg up they will need to compete with increasingly automated competitors both here and abroad.

—Parker Hodges, "Fear of Automation," *output*, August 1980, p. 34. Reprinted with Permission of Output magazine. Copyright by Technical Publishing Company, A Dun & Bradstreet Company, 1980. All rights reserved.

Left Computer-controlled robots can sense the need for a task and can then take the actions necessary to perform the task. The increasing use of such automated tools promises both positive and negative effects for society. (Courtesy of Unimation)

Looking Ahead

In this chapter you'll see how organizations react to and may be affected by computer usage. In the first section we'll discuss the impact on businesses in the information processing industry itself. Some of the effects of computer systems on other types of businesses are considered in the second section. The focus of attention then switches to not-for-profit organizations, and you'll see a few of the ways that computers are being applied in government, health-care, and educational organizations.

Thus, after studying this chapter you should be able to:

▌ Discuss the rapid changes taking place in the information processing industry

▌ Explain how computers can be used to plan and control various business operations

▌ Outline how computer systems can affect the productivity and security of businesses

▌ Discuss and give examples of how computers are used in federal, state, and local governments for planning, control, and law enforcement purposes

▌ Identify some planning/decision making and control applications that are having an impact on health-care organizations

▌ Describe applications in the areas of planning/decision making, control, computer-assisted instruction, and simulation that are affecting educational organizations

▌ Understand and use the key terms listed at the end of this chapter.

THE INFORMATION PROCESSING INDUSTRY

Computers have created a dynamic industry which produces and maintains the machines and supplies much of their software. The growth curve has been climbing so rapidly in the information industry that sales statistics and other measuring data become outdated almost as soon as they are gathered and published. Even during economic recessions, information industry sales have continued to expand. This is because computer systems can boost productivity in offices and factories and so customers of these systems continue to buy them to reduce their costs.

The latest figures available at this writing show that industry sales had grown over 20 percent from the preceding year, and total revenues for just the top 100 U.S.-based firms exceeded $60 *billion.* (The revenues of Japanese and European businesses added additional billions to these figures.) Industry spending for new plants and equipment had increased 37 percent in a year's time, and the spending for research and for the development of new products had grown 22 percent. The industry leader is IBM with revenues of over $20 billion.

Since it is technology-driven and subject to short product cycles and rapid obsolescence, the information processing industry is one in which *rapid change is the rule.* The following points illustrate this fact:

- Company rankings in the top-100 group can change dramatically in a single year. In one recent year, a large mainframe manufacturer had sales of over $2 billion and still dropped from second to sixth place, while a microcomputer vendor jumped past 27 other top-100 companies.

- Tiny companies producing micro- and minicomputers have grown almost overnight into large $100 + million operations. These vendors (and those who supply software for their machines) have created new types of retail establishments—the computer retail store and the software outlet, as shown in Figure 20-1.

- Mainframe builders such as IBM have felt it necessary to establish their own retail stores and move into the production and sale of small personal-sized microcomputers as mainframes continue to lose a percentage of their total market to minicomputer, microcomputer, and word processing systems. Large department store chains are now selling products made by leading mainframe suppliers—a development that would have been considered most unlikely just a few years ago.

- Large and well-financed companies such as General Electric, RCA, and Xerox have tried to compete in the mainframe market sector and have

Figure 20-1 These days, buying a computer can be easier than buying a car. All the models are under one roof at your local computer store. (Neal Slavin)

failed while much smaller "plug-compatible" vendors of mainframes that run IBM software have been successful.

▌ Entrepreneurs with technical and managerial skills have started many small companies with money supplied by venture capitalists, have nursed these start-up operations into thriving businesses, have sold out to larger organizations at attractive prices, and have then started a second, third, or even fourth high-technology company. For example, Gene Amdahl left IBM to form Amdahl Corporation, and his son Carlton was a founder of Magnuson Computer Systems. Father and son are now working together at Trilogy Systems Corporation—the second plug-compatible mainframe start-up venture for both of them. Numerous other similar examples could be given.

▌ Several companies that buy computers to meet the specifications of users and then lease these systems to the users have gone bankrupt because technological change drastically reduced the value of the used computers they owned.

▌ Makers of integrated circuits are putting the mainframes of a few years ago on one or a few silicon chips. New semiconductor companies are regularly formed, and a premium is placed on innovation and being the first to reach the market with a new device. A "long" lead over the competition is often measured in a few months. And "silicon spies" quickly obtain new chips and analyze them for the competition.

▌ Barely in existence a decade ago, the independent software sector of the industry is now experiencing explosive growth. Software houses are selling off-the-shelf applications packages and operating system programs.

▌ The merging of data processing, word processing, and data communications technologies has made competitors out of those firms that a few years ago were not considered to be included in the "computer industry." For example, the American Telephone and Telegraph Company has agreed to split off its Bell Telephone operating companies in response to a federal government antitrust action. Thus, AT&T and other previously regulated telecommunications organizations are now moving into the unregulated and competitive information processing industry.

▌ Competition from Japanese and European companies is growing. The Japanese are aggressively promoting their microcomputers and small peripheral devices.

The Effects of Change

As you can see from the above examples, competition is strong in the information processing industry. Some small firms have become overnight successes in one sector of the industry. Some large businesses such as RCA have retreated almost totally from the industry. And some businesses such as Xerox have failed in one sector and have come back strong in others.

The speed with which new technology is being applied produces a complex and challenging competitive environment. The reaction time available to a firm to take advantage of new discoveries is constantly shrinking. The rewards are great for those that respond quickly and accurately to the information needs of users, but the penalties are also severe for those who fall behind. (One company in the top-100 firms in the industry was passed by 15 others in just one year.)

SOME EFFECTS OF COMPUTERS ON OTHER PROFIT-ORIENTED ORGANIZATIONS

Computers are used in business to improve the quality of, and accelerate the flow of, information, and to thus speed up and improve the performance of planning, decision making, and control activities.

Some Examples of Business Computer Usage

In many businesses, the planning and decision process begins with the setting of business strategies and long-term goals based on product and economic assumptions. These strategies and goals are then tested through the use of *market forecasting* techniques. The expectation of how many goods or services can be sold then becomes the basis for *production plans* (how and when to acquire materials and make the items) and *financial plans* (how and when to have the money on hand to pay for the items produced). This overall business planning and decision process is discussed in more detail in Chapter 18.

Market Forecasting and Planning. Managers must plan and make decisions about marketing new and existing products and/or services, changing existing products, and promoting new and existing products. In making their market plans and decisions, managers are increasingly relying on the results of market research efforts. The American Marketing Association defines **market research** as "a systematic gathering, recording and analyzing of data about problems relating to the marketing of goods and services." Since we know that a computer is especially suited for recording and analyzing data, it stands to reason that computers can make a valuable contribution in market research and thus in market forecasting and planning.

Market researchers gather statistical data on consumer preferences from consumer surveys and from the results of market testing in limited geographic areas. Past sales data on similar products in an industry may be obtained from the company's own past sales records and through the facilities provided by online information retrieval services. For example, the Cybernet Division of

Control Data Corporation has combined resources with Economic Information Systems, Inc., to produce an online retrieval system that offers market researchers share-of-market data for all major firms in all the geographic, industrial, and business markets of the United States. Other online retrieval services— e.g., Lockheed's *Dialog*—supply market research users with a wealth of population and economic data. The data gathered from these sources may be processed by a computer to produce summary statistical measures (market percentages, product rankings, etc.). These summary measures may then be analyzed by managers or by computer programs. These analyses, in turn, can be used as input to computerized statistical forecasting procedures that may be used to project sales volume into the future, given assumptions about pricing, economic trends, promotional effort, competitive reactions, and so on. Armed with this information, managers may be able to do a better job of planning marketing strategies. And as we've seen, market plans become the basis for production plans and financial plans.

Computer technology is changing the face of industries such as printing. (Courtesy IBM)

Production Planning and Scheduling. Computers are used extensively for **production planning** and scheduling purposes. The amount of planning and scheduling required varies from one production process to another. An **assembly production line** which produces a standard item with little or no variation requires less in the way of planning and scheduling than does the operation of a machine shop where nonstandard items are produced every day and where different jobs require different raw materials and different machine operations.

This doesn't mean that assembly operations are simple to plan and schedule. On a farm-tractor assembly line, for example, thousands of component parts must come together at the right time, at the right place, and in the right sequence. Manually planning and scheduling such an assembly process can take weeks. The use of computers can slash the time dramatically, and the computer can print out the parts requirements and schedules for use by assembly personnel. When automobiles rather than tractors are being assembled, the job naturally becomes more complex because of the numerous color combinations that must be matched correctly and the modifications that must be made whenever certain options are installed (e.g., whenever air-conditioning is installed on a car at the factory, that car is usually equipped with a heavier-duty cooling and electrical system).

Unlike an assembly line, however, a **job shop** doesn't produce the same general product every day. Rather, a wide variety of products are produced, and the shop is typically organized by types of machines used (i.e., lathes may be at one location, stamping machines at another, etc.). Also unlike an assembly line, the *sequence* of operations *varies* in a job shop from one product to another. Not surprisingly, the planning and scheduling is more difficult because each job may require completely different raw materials and a completely different production sequence. In one job, for example, drill presses may be required near the end of the project, and in another job the same machinery may be needed at an early stage. Managers must attempt to plan and schedule operations to minimize bottlenecks at one location and slack periods at another. In short, planners must seek to minimize waiting times for raw materials, maximize the use of expensive machinery, and complete jobs on the dates promised the customers. Computers are used in this complex environment to help planners obtain maximum total performance at the lowest possible cost.

Financial Planning. Provisions must be made to have adequate financial resources available to carry out marketing and production plans. The costs and revenues associated with alternative estimates of promotion plans and prices, and sales and production volumes must be analyzed to determine the **financial planning** implications. To evaluate these implications (and to determine the expected profitability of various alternatives), financial managers frequently use computer programs to make cash flow analyses, time-series financial forecasts, and loan and interest rate projections. Decisions about the advisability of making investments in new plants and equipment are often made with the help of a computer.

Operational Planning. Lower-level **operational plans** are designed to achieve efficiency of performance in the short term once market forecasts, sales quotas, advertising programs, production schedules, and financial and personnel resources are known. For example, in their operational planning activities, trucking companies use computers to plan daily pickup and delivery routes. And airlines use computers to select flight plans. Given data on wind velocity and air turbulence from scores of geographic locations, a computer program can consider these factors in arriving at an optimum flight plan. For example, when a flight plan is needed, the computer is given the final destination, locations of any intermediate stops, expected payload, type of aircraft, and published schedule times. One or more plans are then computed, taking wind and turbulence factors, along with these other variables, into account. The pilot then chooses from among the alternatives prepared. Generally the preferred plan is the one which gets the plane to its destination(s) on time and with minimum fuel consumption. However, another alternative is likely to be selected if turbulence conditions on the "least-cost" route would result in passenger discomfort.

Operational Control. If you've read Chapter 18, you know that control is a follow-up to planning. It's the check on performance to see if planned goals or standards are being achieved. Computers are regularly used to control *continuous processes, production operations,* and *inventories.*

Process Control. Computerized **process-control systems** are being used to monitor *continuously operating* facilities such as oil refineries, chemical plants, steel and paper mills, and electric power generating stations. These processes are similar in that they convert input materials and energy into output materials, products, converted energy, and waste. During the process, instruments measure variables such as pressure, temperature flow, and so on. If the process is deviating from an acceptable standard, regulating devices are adjusted to bring the process back into control. In an **open-loop process control** operation, the computer records instrument readings, compares the readings against standards, and notifies process control personnel of needed manual adjustments in regulating devices. In a more complex **closed-loop process control operation** (Figure 20-2), the computer receives measurements, makes comparisons, and, *in addition,* sends signals to the regulatory devices to make the necessary changes. Of course, human operators may monitor the overall process and instruct the computer to make occasional changes in control parameters in particular situations, but the control operation is essentially automatic. Use of the computer in this way permits quicker-responding and more accurate control than would otherwise be possible. The use of minicomputers for process control applications is expanding rapidly.

__Production Control.__ During the actual production on an assembly line or in a job shop, data entry stations may be used to transmit such facts as the time spent on an operation, the status of a machine tool, the size of a queue requiring work, or the need for machine setup or repair. The computer may then be used to compare the actual conditions against the production plan in order to determine if appropriate control action is required. A **production control** example from Chapter 6 is illustrated in Figure 20-3. In addition to controlling the overall production process, computers may also be used to control individual production tools such as shapers, milling machines, and drill presses.

Figure 20-2 A computerized process control system. (Photo: Dan McCoy from Rainbow)

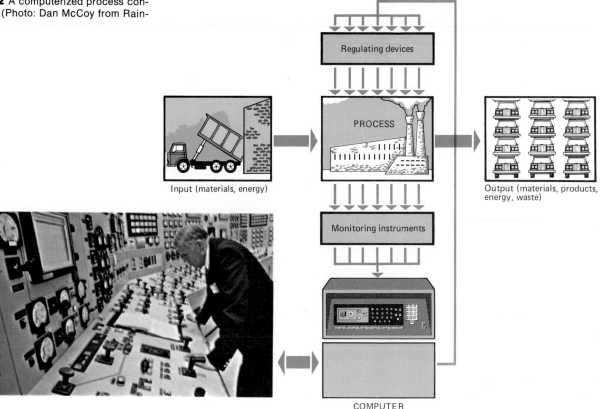

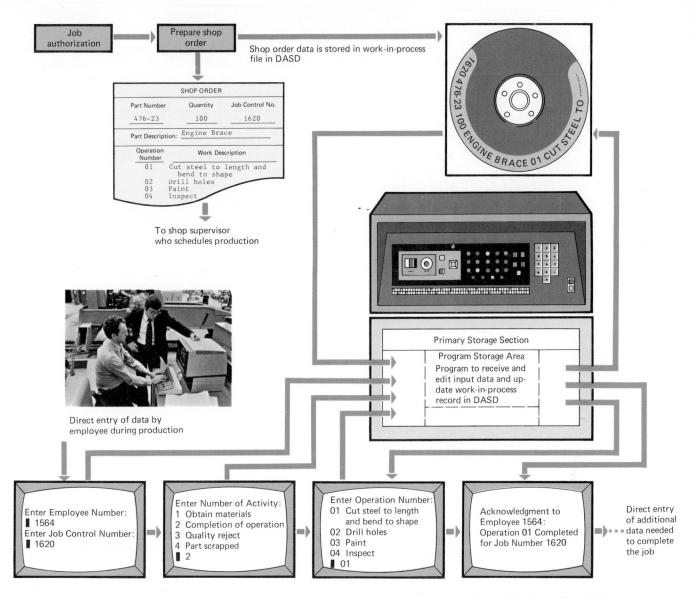

Figure 20-3 A computerized production control system. (Photo courtesy Raytheon Corporation)

Numerically controlled machine tools, directed by computer-produced tapes, can be used to automatically produce precision parts meeting blueprint specifications. An early use of **numerical control (NC) machines** was in the aircraft industry to cut airplane sections from solid metal. But NC machines are now employed for such dissimilar tasks as constructing prefabricated house walls and producing hydraulic presses. Rapid operation and low scrap losses are two advantages of these automatic machines. Finally, as we saw in the last chapter, programmable **robots** are machines controlled by built-in computers that can sense the need for, and then take the actions necessary to perform, various assembly tasks. The use of robots rather than humans may result in improved quality control. A human welder on an automobile assembly line may leave out a couple of welds so that a consumer gets a car with rattles. A robot programmed to do the same welding operation may produce more consistent quality.

Inventory Control. Transaction recorders are often used to keep **control of the inventory** of parts and materials used in production. Let's assume, for example, that an employee needs a dozen hinges to complete a job. The employee gets the hinges and an identification card from a supply station. The card identifies the hinges by part number and contains any other *fixed* information (such as unit price) that's necessary. The worker inserts the card into a transaction recorder and then keys or moves levers to indicate the *variable* part of the transaction—the number of hinges taken, the job number, etc. The worker than pushes a TRANSMIT button to send the data to the computer, where they are checked for accuracy and then accepted to update the proper record in the inventory file. If an error is detected, a signal may be relayed back to the recording station. Numerous other inventory control systems are used in nonproduction areas. For example, a computerized inventory control system is used by Martin-Brower Corporation, a Chicago-based distributor of paper products, nonperishable food products, and service supplies to drive-in restaurants specializing in fast service. Martin-Brower has 10 warehouses and a 5,000-item inventory to control. The system estimates future demand by computing current market trends and seasonal fluctuations for items like bags and cups. A forecast is prepared for each warehouse. The system also reports two or three times a week on the demand rate for each item in the inventory. Items that appear to be in short supply are flagged by the system, and recommended reorder quantities are computed. Managers then make the reorder decision based on their knowledge of the situation.

Effects on Productivity

Economists tell us that the amount of goods or services possessing economic value that individuals can produce in a given time period—i.e., their *productivity*—is dependent on such factors as:

- The attitudes, health, and training of people.
- The abundance of natural resources.
- The amount of capital equipment available and the technological sophistication of this equipment.

Computers, we've seen, are sophisticated tools that can significantly improve productivity. And productivity gains, in turn, can lead to a stronger competitive position in the world. During the 1970s and early 1980s, the overall increases in productivity in U.S. businesses trailed the gains made in many other industrial nations. Thus, a concerted effort is now under way to apply computers in design and production processes in order to improve productivity. The use of robots to improve productivity in production processes has been mentioned several times. Let's consider here how **computer-aided design (CAD)** can also improve productivity.

Computer-Aided Design. Certain steps are generally required in the development of a wide range of items. These steps are (1) preliminary design, (2) advanced design, (3) model development, (4) model testing, (5) final testing, and (6) production and construction. All these steps are being facilitated by the use of computers. In the past, preliminary sketches, design drawings, and engineering drawings were usually prepared early in the design and development of new products and projects. When designers or engineers had a new thought, they would make some preliminary sketches to get the idea down on paper so that it could be analyzed more thoroughly. As the design was modified, additional drawings would be required. When the design was finally approved, further detailed production drawings were prepared. Thus, the preparation of drawings could occupy a substantial portion of the designers' time. And time spent at the drafting board was time that couldn't be devoted to considering other (perhaps better) alternative designs.

If you've read Chapter 6, you know that special electronic pens and graphic display devices now make it possible for the computer to receive human sketching directly. Changes and modifications in the sketches of an engineer can be made quickly. Once the initial drawings are finished and displayed to the engineer's satisfaction, the computer may then be instructed to analyze the displayed design and report on certain characteristics. Interactive communication between designer and computer may continue until a design with a desirable set of characteristics is produced. Such interaction between designer and machine is now relatively common (Figure 20-4). In addition, it may be common in the near future to have the computer prepare (1) detailed engineering blueprints from the stored design, and (2) control tapes that program automatic machine tools and robots to precisely produce component parts of new products according to the blueprint specifications. In other words, in such a **computer-aided design/computer-aided manufacturing (CAD/CAM)** environment, it may be common for the computer to interact with the engineer from the time of the initial idea until the final production step is completed.

Some current applications of CAD are in:

Electronic circuit design. Computers are now being used to assist engineers in designing circuits for other computers. Several hundred programs are available to help electronic engineers in their circuit design work. An engineer may define the circuit requirements, and then the computer develops, analyzes, and evaluates trial designs that may meet the requirements. A trial design may be modified by the engineer as required. The computer then analyzes and evaluates the modification. Computer-aided design is also used to plan the layout of integrated circuits, the location of circuit boards in the computer, and the ways in which these boards will be interconnected.

Figure 20-4 Computer-aided design is a fast-growing application of new technology. (Courtesy Computervision Corporation)

▌*Ship design*. Computers may do much of the detailed design work such as determining the positioning of hull reinforcing members, determining welding requirements, and generating numerical control programs to control the flame cutting machines that are used to shape steel plates.

▌*Aircraft design*. Aircraft designers working at a display can draw the shape of a fuselage and have the computer analyze the physical characteristics of the shape. They can also vary the position, angle, and length of the wings and have the computer report on structural strength and life characteristics.

▌*Highway design*. The Ohio Highway Department has a computer system that enables design engineers to quickly determine the social and economic impact of proposed road construction. The system permits engineers to consider factors such as alternate routes, amount of earth to be moved or added, number of citizens that will be forced to relocate, and construction costs of alternate routes. Aerial photographs are converted by computer into three-dimensional topographical maps. Proposed routes are then plotted on these maps, and a computer is used to evaluate the alternatives.

▌*Automobile design*. Automobile manufacturers are using computers to evaluate the structural characteristics of alternative designs. Engineers can "assemble" models of the components in a car and then "road test" the proposed car design on a simulated drive route. A chassis cross-member, for example, can be redesigned to reduce weight, and the effects of the change can be determined by a computer program. This design approach significantly reduces the costly and time-consuming process of making and testing a series of prototype parts until the desired results are obtained.

Threats to Security

If you've read Chapter 18, you know that businesses can be vulnerable to computer systems that aren't adequately controlled. In fact, there are organizations whose very existence has been threatened by computer-system control problems. They have failed to design adequate controls to prevent theft, fraud, espionage, sabotage, accidental erasure of vital records, and/or physical destruction of important files. In one reported case, for example, an organization received a long-distance call from a computer operator who had failed to report for work. The operator was calling from a European city with disturbing news: He claimed to have the only tape of a vital master file and announced that he would return it only when the organization had deposited a large amount in a numbered Swiss bank account. His claim was quickly checked and found to be correct, and the ransom was reluctantly paid. Other organizations have been equally vulnerable, as you can verify in Chapter 18.

CAD/CAM: BIG MARKETS FOR FACTORY SYSTEMS

Computer-aided design and computer-aided manufacturing (CAD/CAM) is one of the most exciting applications of data processing. Made possible by high-density, low-cost computer chips—needed for the large amount of computer processing and storage capacity used in generating graphics—and advanced computer graphics software, CAD/CAM is booming. It should be among the fastest-growing high technology markets of the eighties.

With CAD/CAM systems, drawings can be produced by sketching a new design directly on a tablet with an electronic pen or by tracing existing drawings on an electronic drafting table. The operator can view, modify, or update a stored design with a video display, zooming into one section of the drawing, rotating the object represented in three dimensions, and erasing or editing sections of the drawing at will. A completed design can be stored, reproduced in hard copy on a plotter, or converted into tape for use by numerically controlled machine tools.

Typical CAD/CAM systems are expensive—costs range from $150,000 to $600,000. But because they provide increased productivity, payback is often less than two years.

The major application for CAD/CAM systems is mechanical engineering, including the generation of mechanical drawings. Others are electrical engineering, specifically in the design of integrated circuits and printed circuit boards; architecture, engineering, and construction; and mapping and earth sciences.

In order of market share, the top manufacturers that currently enjoy over 70 percent of the specialized CAD/CAM market are: Computervision, Applicon (recently acquired by Schlumberger Ltd.), Calma (recently purchased by General Electric), Intergraph, and Auto-Trol Technology Corp. Each of these companies' revenues exceeded $50 million in their latest fiscal year. . . . International Data Corp. expects the CAD/CAM market to grow from $480 million in 1980 to $1.8 billion by 1984, an average annual growth of 40 percent.

Two attractive and representative investments in the CAD/CAM market are Intergraph Corp. and Computervision.

Intergraph (originally M&S Computing, Inc.) was founded in 1969 by a group of former IBM employees. The Huntsville, Alabama firm manufactures and markets complete turnkey computer-aided design systems selling for an average of $400,000. These systems consist of modular computer and graphics hardware, peripherals, and custom-designed software.

Intergraph has concentrated on two major market areas: architectural layout and design, plant design, and finite modeling; and mapping, including map generation for land-use studies, resource management, oil exploration, site planning, and highway design.

Computervision, located in Bedford, Mass., is the world's leading manufacturer of CAD/CAM equipment with 35–40 percent of the market. It markets equipment for all areas of CAD/CAM.

Unlike many other suppliers, Computervision uses its own computer design for all of its systems. Although this requires a large R&D investment—in 1980, 10 percent of its revenues went for R&D—the company feels this policy gives it an edge in product distinction and manufacturing efficiencies.

—Bud Anderson, ''CAD/CAM: Big Markets for Factory Systems,'' *High Technology*, January/February 1982, p. 99. Reprinted with permission.

Actual screen image showing a model of a cold box for cryogenic air processing. (Courtesy Intergraph Corporation)

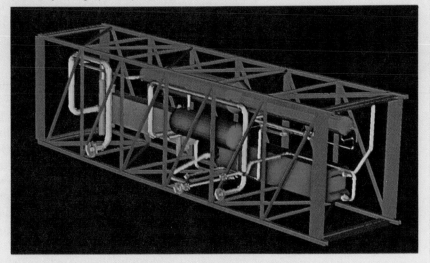

"There's never a computer around when you need one."

Computer Systems and National Borders

International airlines have reservation systems that cross many national boundaries, and international news agencies have worldwide information and retrieval networks. Stock quotation services have expanded to provide their customers with up-to-the-minute quotations from the major securities exchanges in the free world. And engineering, extracting, and manufacturing companies link multinational facilities by computer-communications networks for planning and control purposes. Such broad networks may be expected to improve decision making and efficiency for the multinational businesses, but they may also increase the tension among nations and the companies that operate within their boundaries.

Nations claim sovereignty over the types of changes that occur within their borders, but rapid cultural, social, and economic changes may result from the operations within their jurisdictions of powerful multinational corporations using global technology. These organizations have found that computer usage has brought them into greater conflict with national governments. In the mid-1970s, for example, *The Reader's Digest* was denied permission by the Swedish government to process a large file containing information on Swedish households at a data center located in another country. Invoking their Data Act of 1973, which restricts the creation and use of data files on their citizens, the Swedes reasoned that permitting *The Reader's Digest* to export a large amount of information about Swedish citizens might invade their personal privacy and might also compromise Swedish national security.

At this writing, **transborder data flow** is a hot issue in Europe. Austria, Denmark, West Germany, and Norway have followed the Swedish example by passing their own data protection laws, and most other European countries are working on similar legislation. Many multinational businesses and many other organizations in the United States feel that these barriers to international data transmission are a form of trade restriction and an obstacle to the free exchange of scientific and cultural information.

SOME EFFECTS OF COMPUTERS ON NOT-FOR-PROFIT ORGANIZATIONS

Many of the public concerns of modern nations have become so intertwined with computer technology that they are virtually inseparable. For example, government agencies such as the Internal Revenue Service and the Social Security Administration have such large volumes of data to process in repetitive fashion that they *must* use computers. Law enforcement agencies, public hospitals, and government space and missile laboratories need the quick-responding and accurate information systems made possible by computers. And the large size of many public organizations encourages computer usage as a means of dealing with complexities brought about by their size. In the remaining pages of this chapter, we'll look at a few of the effects that computer systems are having on government, health-care, and educational organizations.

Computers in Government Organizations

Computers are used in federal, state, and local governments for *planning/decision-making, control,* and *law enforcement* purposes. Let's look at how a few applications in each of these areas are having an impact on government organizations.

Planning and Decision Making. Government planners have a mandate to effectively use public funds and resources in ways that best serve the needs of society. Unfortunately, policy makers have often been required to function in settings where the data available for planning are inadequate and/or inaccurate. They have thus turned to computer usage in the hope that higher quality information will enable them to make better plans and decisions. Some examples of how computers are now being used for planning and decision-making purposes are discussed below.

Environmental Planning. **Technology assessment** is a phrase used in the federal government to refer to the evaluation of the consequences of technological change beyond short-term economic costs and benefits. Because many of the problems of environmental quality are the result of changes in technology, use of the technology-assessment concept has become increasingly important in **environmental planning** and in the protection of our natural resources. The

National Environmental Policy Act requires federal agencies to include a detailed statement in every proposal for legislation or other action that significantly affects the quality of the environment. As a result of this act, greater emphasis has been given to the use of computers for ecological and environmental research and planning. To cite just two examples:

1. The Department of Health, Education, and Welfare has sponsored the development and use of a highly sophisticated computer simulation to predict the life-sustaining ability of rivers. In addition to analyzing existing river conditions, the model can also be used by planners to gain insights into the cause-and-effect relationships of water pollution so that preventive action can be taken to protect a river.

2. The Soil Conservation Service of the Department of Agriculture uses radio signals reflected from ionized meteor trails in the earth's atmosphere to relay data on snowfall and rainfall from sensors located at 160 remote stations in 10 Western states to central data-collection sites in Boise, Idaho, and Ogden, Utah. The data are processed by minicomputers at these sites, forwarded to the Conservation Service's Portland, Oregon center, and then distributed to farmers, ranchers, and government irrigation agencies in the 10-state area. The data on the amount of snowfall in the mountains are particularly important to these agricultural planners because about 85 percent of the annual water supply in the 10-state area comes from melting snow.

Military Planning. Computers are being used increasingly by military planners. For example, they are used to *simulate wars*—i.e, to sharpen analytical skills and gain experience in decision making through the use of "war games." They are also used by military leaders for planning and controlling logistics—i.e., for managing the procurement, storage, and transportation of needed supplies and equipment.

Planning Research Examples. Computers are used by the federal government for research purposes in many agencies and for many types of applications. The Federal Reserve System is the nation's central banker. A member of its board of governors may use a computer in researching the tradeoffs between inflation and unemployment at given times prior to making monetary policy judgments. Or the governor may use the computer to research the concentration of banks in a particular market area prior to making a decision on a merger application.

By classifying, sorting, and manipulating census data, the Census Bureau can assist planners in weighing the needs and problems of whole groups or any segment of the population. For example, information about families living in poverty areas can be analyzed. Also, the computers can pigeonhole the massive national census data by state, county, or even city block if research and planning needs are served by such information.

The Department of Agriculture, in a joint effort with the National Oceanic and Atmospheric Administration (NOAA), and the National Aeronautics and

Figure 20-5 Data from satellite photos are fed into computers and analyzed for planning and research purposes. (*left*) Two Landsat satellite photos are combined to show the ice patterns that have formed along the western shore of the Delmarva Peninsula. Factory smoke from the northeastern shore of the peninsula is also visible as the winds drive the pollution eastward. (*above*) An infrared photo of the Finger Lakes region of New York was taken from an altitude of over 500 miles by NASA's Earth Resources Technology Satellite. Healthy crops and vegetation show up bright red. Areas with sparse vegetation appear light pink. Clear water is black. Lake Ontario is at the top left of the picture, and the Finger Lakes appear at the bottom of the image. (Courtesy National Aeronautics and Space Administration)

Space Administration (NASA), is using the *Landsat* earth-orbiting satellite to view the croplands planted in wheat and other grains in such important growing regions as the United States, the Soviet Union, Canada, Australia, and India. The satellite photos (Figure 20-5) allow planners to estimate the acreage under cultivation, and the worldwide weather data supplied by NOAA during the growing season permit them to develop computer-based crop yield models and make harvest predictions. A better foreign crop assessment capability is important to those who must make decisions about domestic agricultural policy.

At NASA's Goddard Space Flight Center at Greenbelt, Maryland, the Telemetry Data Processing Facility reduces telemetry data from over a dozen orbiting scientific satellites into proper form for study and analysis by scientists. Instruments in satellites perform experiments and transmit the results to earth. The data are received from worldwide tracking stations, are processed, and the information is forwarded to scientists located throughout the United

States, Canada, and Europe. This information, in turn, adds to the storehouse of scientific knowledge, leads to plans for additional space experiments, and serves to reinforce or change existing scientific theories.

And scientists at the Laboratory for Applications of Remote Sensing at Purdue University have used a computer to analyze the multispectral scanner data obtained by *Landsat* satellites while passing over the Great Lakes region of the United States and Canada. Maps produced as a result of the analysis pinpoint industrial and agricultural areas that may be dumping pollutants into the lakes. Of course, once pollution sources are identified, plans can be made to minimize further environmental damage.

Congressional and Legislative Data Systems. Members of Congress and the state legislatures are expected to perform in at least three capacities: As *lawmakers* deciding on important legislation; as *responsible representatives* of their states or districts; and as *public servants* who will try to assist their constituents on both important and trivial matters. To perform these roles, they need accurate and timely information. Even though much substantive work is performed by working committees, each lawmaker must still do research, form opinions, and make decisions on scores of bills each session. It's not surprising, then, that representatives have voted on bills in the past without understanding all the implications of the legislation. In fact, it's a difficult task for lawmakers and their staff aides to maintain even the most rudimentary knowledge of the content and status of "major" legislation.

In Congress, a system called LEGIS records, stores, and provides prompt computer response to inquiries about the current status of all bills and resolutions. A SOPAD system provides members with an up-to-the-minute "summary of proceedings and debates" taking place on the floors of the House and Senate, and FAPRS (Federal Assistance Program Retrieval System) helps members determine what federal loans and grants can be used by their constituents.

And a number of state legislatures—New York, Washington, Florida, Pennsylvania, Hawaii, and North Carolina, to name just a few—make effective use of computers to index, store, process, and retrieve statutory material; draft bills; prepare roll-call vote reports; provide census population data for planning purposes; address mailing labels; and provide other information and services to legislators and their staffs.

Social Welfare Planning. In social welfare agencies, as in other organizations, computer usage can be of value in administrative planning. For example, in the administration of one social welfare agency—Family Service of Metropolitan Detroit—computer-processed data have speeded up administrative analysis and improved program planning. Caseloads of social workers, median income of the families served, size and composition of families (presence of young children, aged dependents, etc.), family stress caused by such factors as divorces and unemployment—all this information is used by Detroit administrators to analyze the effects of possible changes in agency policies and services.

Urban Planning. It's no secret that many urban planners are currently facing an explosion of problems. Traffic congestion, pollution, tensions within and between racial, ethnic, and economic groups, deteriorating public housing and other facilities—all these problems are facing many areas. Attempts have thus been made to develop more comprehensive urban information systems that would provide planners with the information needed to cope with these difficulties. For example, _traffic congestion_ problems have been tackled by planners using computers to simulate traffic flow patterns. Variables such as the expected distribution of trips, the type of travel modes used, and the routes traveled are used to estimate the flow of persons and vehicles on transit facilities and roads. Various alternative transportation systems can be evaluated through computer simulation. In evaluating alternative traffic systems, however, the planner must take into consideration the interactions which exist between transportation systems and other aspects of urban life. All too often in the past, traffic planners have begun road construction without considering recreational, housing, and other alternative land-use needs.

The need to consider alternative uses of land as a vital input of detailed traffic models has, in fact, resulted in the development of local and regional **land-use models.** Included in land-use simulation equations are future expectations as to population, employment, number of households, income, and distribution of available land for commercial and residential purposes. These data, in turn, can be used as input into traffic planning simulations. In the Washington metropolitan area, a computer land-use data system is used for planning. This system receives data from continuously updated files and is of value to satellite governments as well as Washington planners.

Control Applications. Computers are used by many government agencies for control purposes. The Internal Revenue Service, for example, uses computers to monitor the returns of individual and corporate taxpayers. Filed reports of interest paid to individuals by banks may be compared against interest income reported by the taxpayer. Without computers, such comparisons would probably not be possible. Computers may also be used by the IRS in randomly selecting and making preliminary audits of tax returns.

Computers are used for **environmental control** purposes. Federal agencies processing environmental data with the help of computers include the Air Pollution Control Office and the Water Quality Office of the Environmental Protection Agency, the National Center for Health Statistics, the U.S. Geological Survey, and the Department of Agriculture. States and cities are also using computers to evaluate and control the levels of pollution. To cite just one example from the many that exist, the Empire State System of New York collects water and air data from monitoring stations located at critical sites around the state. Data from the stations are automatically forwarded to a central computer. Each air-monitoring station reports every 15 minutes, and each water station transmits once every hour. Upon receiving transmitted data, the computer edits the message, sends any necessary operating instructions to the station, compares edited information to acceptable environmental standards, and, if standards are not met, sends an appropriate alarm message to either the Air Resources or Pure Waters Division of the Department of Environmental Conservation. Corrective action may then be taken.

Computers are also helping to *conserve* natural resources. California's State Water Project, for example, is designed to conserve water by moving it from surplus areas in northern California to needy areas in the south and west. Water is moved hundreds of miles through a network of canals, tunnels, gates, pipelines, pumping stations, and power plants. All these facilities are monitored by computers located at five remote control centers. In the event of emergency, a control center will quickly shut down the affected part of the system. For example, should a canal be broken by an earthquake, check gates in the affected section would be closed immediately to prevent serious loss of water.

Computers in Law Enforcement. The Federal Bureau of Investigation makes extensive use of computers. The FBI's computerized National Crime Information Center (NCIC) is an automated nationwide **police information network.** Online terminals installed at local police stations are connected to central police computers in the states and to the NCIC computers in Washington. The central state computers are, of course, also connected to the NCIC network. Electronic direct access to the arrest records of people is thus possible in a short period of time. Obtaining such information can help federal, state, and local law enforcement officers make decisions about detaining, interrogating, and arresting those suspected of having committed crimes (Figure 20-6). The NCIC computers also store information on stolen property and wanted persons. More than 260,000 transactions involving fugitives, stolen property, and criminal history records are handled daily, and an average of over 1,000 positive responses ("hits") involving wanted persons and stolen property are

Figure 20-6 A computerized system called CATCH helps local police at the 48th precinct in the Bronx, New York, to identify crime suspects. (Dan McCoy from Rainbow)

produced daily. Of course, as we saw in the last chapter, some concerned citizens question whether the issues of *individual freedom* and the *right to privacy* are being given proper consideration in the use of systems such as NCIC.

Three examples of the many law enforcement computer systems located at the state and local levels are:

1. Los Angeles County's Automated Want and Warrant System keeps track of those wanted by the police. In one case, a University of Southern California student was stopped for making an illegal left turn. Upon inquiry, the police officer found that 48 traffic violations covering a 3-year period were charged against the student and fines totaling $555 were unpaid.

2. The Law Enforcement Information Network (LEIN) at Michigan State Police headquarters contains online information about wanted persons, stolen cars and other property, and revoked or suspended drivers' licenses. A patrol officer can radio the license number of a car he or she has stopped or is chasing and can be warned to exercise extra caution if the car is stolen or if the occupant is believed to be dangerous. Police in Michigan cities are using terminals connected to the state system to see if arrested individuals are also wanted elsewhere. In one 24-hour period, Detroit police found that 17 persons they were holding were wanted in other jurisdictions. Of course, LEIN is tied into NCIC.

3. The New York Statewide Police Information Network (NYSPIN) has a central computer complex that serves hundreds of online terminals located in state and municipal agencies, criminal justice departments, the FBI, the National Auto Theft Bureau, and the Federal Bureaus of Narcotics and Customs. NYSPIN is also linked with a number of other computers including those at the NCIC, the National Law Enforcement Telecommunications System in Phoenix, Arizona, and the Department of Motor Vehicles in Albany. Most of the functions performed in the systems described above are available with NYSPIN.

Computers in Health-Care Organizations

You don't have to look far to discover reasons for the accelerating use of computers in health fields:

▍ There's a serious shortage of doctors, nurses, and medical technicians. By relieving scarce people of routine tasks, computers can help increase their effectiveness.

▍ Computers may make it possible for physicians and health scientists to conduct research that will extend the frontiers of medical knowledge. Without computers, some promising research couldn't be explored.

▎ Computers can help improve the quality of a physician's diagnoses on the one hand, and can help improve the control of important medical processes on the other.

▎ Medical knowledge is advancing rapidly. The ability to acquire and quickly apply new information may mean the difference between life and death. Computers are needed to retrieve relevant information rapidly.

Let's look now at a few *planning/decision-making* and *control* applications that are having an impact on health-care professionals and organizations.

Computers in Medical Planning/Decision Making. Applications of computers which have medical planning and decision-making implications include *computer-assisted diagnosis and research,* and *medical history preparation and retrieval.*

Computer-Assisted Diagnosis and Research. Some doctors are using the computer as a **diagnostic tool** in hospitals and clinics. At a number of "multiphasic" screening centers around the country, for example, patients are given physical exams consisting of a series of basic tests. Data from the tests may be fed into a computer in a separate operation, or the testing equipment may be linked directly to a computer for an automatic transfer of results. Once the data are received, the computer can compare test measurements against the standards established in the program. Within a few minutes after the examination procedures are completed, the computer output is ready. The test results are reported, and if they fall outside prescribed limits, procedures that should be repeated and/or additional tests that should be conducted may be indicated. The computer may also be programmed to suggest tentative diagnoses to explain abnormal test results. The patient's physician, of course, is responsible for the final diagnosis. The Kaiser Foundation Hospital in Oakland, California, is processing about 4,000 people per month through its 19-step physical exam, and Good Samaritan Hospital in Cincinnati has a successful multiphasic testing program.

Statistical techniques can also be used for diagnostic purposes. For example, at the University of Pittsburgh, Drs. Jack Myers and Harry Pople have developed a diagnostic system they call INTERNIST. The system includes about 350 diseases and 2,800 disease manifestations. There's a listing of the associated manifestations that are known to occur with each disease, along with a statistical estimate of the frequency of occurrence. Using INTERNIST, a doctor can sit at a terminal and provide data on a patient. After considering the initial data, the program begins asking questions about the patient. During this questioning, INTERNIST tells the doctor what diagnoses it's considering and what data it's temporarily disregarding. The program may provide its diagnosis for the doctor in a few minutes. In order to save the patient money by avoiding unnecessary lab tests, INTERNIST is programmed to consider the least costly diseases first.

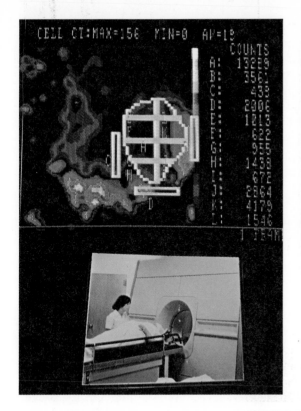

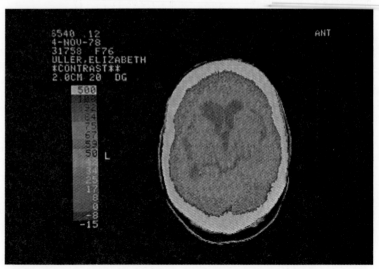

Figure 20-7 (*left*) Use of the CAT scanner isn't limited to the brain. The scanner shown at the bottom of this photo is used to zero in on cells in the heart. The scan display shown at the top of the photo indicates that the heart is diseased and that the patient requires corrective surgery. (*above*) Graphic display of a brain scan produced by a CAT scanner. (Dan McCoy from Rainbow)

Computers are also being used for such diagnostic purposes as (1) displaying heart function on a terminal screen from motion-picture x-rays and calculating the volume and width of the patient's left ventricle—the heart's pump, and (2) determining by means of a **computer-aided tomography (CAT) scanner**—a device that x-rays tiny slices of body structures and then combines the thousands of shots into a single picture—the area in the brain that has been damaged by a stroke so that the proper medication can be given right away (Figure 20-7).

In addition to being a diagnostic tool, the computer is also a *research tool* that's providing insights into:

1. *Causes and prevention of stroke.* A stroke usually occurs suddenly and is due to a disruption in the normal flow of blood in the brain. Statistical research to correlate many of the factors suspected of causing stroke is being conducted by the Iowa Heart Association. By isolating the most important causes of stroke, the researchers plan to educate the public on possible preventive measures and contribute information of value in stroke diagnosis and treatment.

2. *Patterns of drug addiction.* There's currently no agreement on the causes of drug addiction, nor is there any consensus on what consti-

tutes a cure. However, the National Institute of Mental Health has a research program under way at 16 treatment agencies that will, it's hoped, shed new light on the causes of addiction and its treatment. Each of the 16 agencies assesses the effectiveness of its own efforts, and each agency supplies information to a data bank established at Texas Christian University. Data on addicts are obtained when they are initially admitted for treatment and at 2-month intervals thereafter. Computer analyses of the data gathered on several thousand addicts and their responses to different treatment approaches may lead to future plans for combatting the addiction problem.

Medical History Preparation and Retrieval. In developing a record of a patient's medical history, a usual practice is for the doctor or nurse to ask the patient a series of questions about past illnesses or health problems. This history-taking is a time-consuming aspect of the patient-physician relationship. Computers can be used to reduce the time involved and to tailor the questions to the patient's situation.

At the Mayo Clinic in Minnesota, Dr. John Mayne has developed a system that displays medical history questions and multiple-response choices on the screen of a terminal. The patient answers the questions by pointing to the appropriate response with a light pen—a device attached to the terminal that permits the computer to detect the response selected. Medidata Sciences, Inc., in Massachusetts also uses a display terminal to project questions for patient response. The patient answers by pressing one of the five buttons opposite the most appropriate answer to the question. The computer is programmed to follow certain question paths depending on the answers received. For example, if the question is "Do you smoke?" and the answer is yes, several additional questions will be asked. If the answer is no, these questions will be omitted. After the patient has answered all relevant questions, the medical history can be printed out for the doctor's use, or it may be stored on magnetizeable or microfilm media.

Once the patient's history and medical records are available in machine-accessible form, they may be retrieved by the doctor as necessary for review and updating. Although the records of most people are currently maintained in file cabinets in doctors' offices, it's possible that in the future this record-keeping function will increasingly be handled by a computer data bank. With available technology, this data bank need not be located in a large computer complex. Any doctor could enter patient data into an office microcomputer system for rapid online retrieval. These data could include type of ailment, level of severity, results of most recent examination, etc. When a patient moves, personal health records may be transferred to a new data bank, alleviating the need for completing a new medical history. Since the patient is often a poor transmitter of personal health data, the new doctor would probably have a more complete and accurate record available than would otherwise be possible.

Health Control. Control of the *physiological status of patients* and *laboratory tests* are among the many applications of computers in medicine.

Physiological Monitoring. Several real time computer systems are being used for patient monitoring. For example, patients who have just had major surgery, and those who have recently suffered heart attacks are connected to computer-monitored sensing devices capable of immediately detecting dangerously abnormal conditions (Figure 20-8). If necessary, the system flashes a warning signal to doctors and nurses. At the Pacific Medical Center in San Francisco, the body functions of patients in the cardiopulmonary intensive care unit are *continuously* checked. At Los Angeles County Hospital, patients suffering from circulatory shock are monitored about once every 5 minutes.

Control of Laboratory Tests. Some of the more successful applications of computers in hospitals are found in the laboratory. From the doctor's initial request for a test to the printing of test results, a computer may be used to monitor each step in the process. Automated testing may lead to greater accuracy and faster reporting of findings. Also, the information reported may be in a more useful format—e.g., abnormal results may be emphasized for special attention and compared with normally expected readings for those in the patient's age and sex category.

One example of a computer-controlled laboratory program is IBM's Clinical Laboratory Data Acquisition System, which enables hospitals to link dozens of lab instruments directly to a computer for automatic monitoring and reporting of test results. The system may, for example, collect, analyze, and verify data extracted from blood specimens by an automatic blood-testing device. At the same time, it can monitor the operation of the device to make sure that it's calibrated correctly. At the end of each test run, the computer prints the results for the patient's physician, for lab records, for administrative reports, and for patient-billing purposes. In addition to providing information that's accurate and timely, the system also reduces the time that technicians must spend on paperwork and instrument checking.

Figure 20-8 A nurse is reading computer-monitored heartbeat information in this intensive care unit. (Bruce Roberts/Photo Researchers)

Computers in Educational Organizations

It's possible to consider the subject of computers in education in at least two ways. From the contents of much of this book, it's obvious that computer hardware and software can first be considered as *subjects for study*. Colleges have offered computer courses for many years. And the introduction of hundreds of thousands (millions?) of microcomputers into elementary and high schools in recent years has enabled those schools to also offer computer courses. In fact, responsible public and private schools below the college level are hard pressed now to come up with excuses for not giving their students courses in computer literacy. Those organizations that fail to offer such courses will be placing their students at a disadvantage in future years. The second way to view the computer in education is as a *tool to be used in the educational process.* The objective of this section is to consider this second view.

Computers can bring to the educational process such attributes as untiring patience, around-the-clock availability, and individualized and student-paced instruction programs. And their use *can* lead to improved student performance in thinking logically, formulating problem solution procedures, and understanding relationships. A look at a few applications in the areas of planning/decision making, control, computer-assisted instruction, and simulation can show us how computers are affecting educational organizations.

Planning and Decision Making in Education. Operating on the reasonable assumptions that differences exist between students, and programs tailored to the needs of individuals are educationally more effective than those aimed at "average" groups, some schools are seeking to plan and implement more individualized programs of instruction. Up to now, individualized instruction programs have been used primarily with gifted or handicapped students, and separate facilities and special teachers have often been employed. But the computer is a tool that may now permit teachers in conventional classroom settings to manage individual instruction programs. **Computer-managed instruction (CMI)** is a name sometimes given to this use of the machines. A properly programmed computer may help teachers manage a student's schedule of activities as the student progresses through a program of instruction. Educational research centers at such schools as the University of Pittsburgh and Florida State University are working on CMI projects.

At one elementary school participating in a University of Pittsburgh project, a computer is being used to make required day-to-day instructional plans and decisions. In the science curriculum, for example, a student may specify a particular subject he or she wishes to study. The computer may then be used to evaluate the student's background in order to determine any needed prerequisite lessons prior to beginning the study of the specified topic. Control Data Corporation's PLATO system (Figure 20-9) has extensive capabilities for implementing CMI in an industrial training setting as well as in public and private academic institutions. Sales training courses, for example, may be offered to salespersons through the use of PLATO.

Computers are also speeding up the scheduling of classes every term in hundreds of schools. Improved class scheduling procedures make it possible for school administrators to make better plans and decisions about the use of such resources as teachers, textbooks, and classroom space.

Control in Education. Two control applications of computers in education are found in the areas of testing and error analysis. In one area of *testing*—interactive **computer-assisted testing**—student progress can be determined quickly, students can get immediate feedback of their successes and mistakes, and instructors can be relieved from having to grade the tests. To illustrate, at Dartmouth College randomized vocabulary tests in Latin may be taken by students. Sitting at an online terminal, students select the Latin lesson or lessons they wish to be checked on. The computer program may randomly select Latin words from the indicated lesson, and the students must then respond with the English meanings. If the students miss on the first try, they are given one more chance before the correct response is supplied. If they have no idea what the correct response should be, they can type a question mark and the proper word will be presented. Of course, the computer is keeping track of the students' success (or lack of success) during the exercise. The stored results of computer-assisted testing may also be used for *error-analysis* purposes. The types of errors being made by students during testing can be analyzed, and suggestions for eliminating detected deficiencies may be supplied to the student and/or the teacher at the end of the session.

Computer-Assisted Instruction. Computer-assisted instruction (CAI) is a term that refers to a learning situation in which the student interacts with, and is guided by, a computer through a course of study aimed at achieving certain instructional goals. In a typical CAI setting, the student sits at a microcomputer or an online terminal and communicates with the program in the CPU. Interaction may take place in the following way: (1) The computer presents instructional information and questions; (2) the student studies the information or instructions presented, answers the questions, and, perhaps, asks questions of his or her own; and (3) the computer then accepts, analyzes, and provides immediate feedback to the student's responses, and it maintains records of the student's performance for evaluation purposes.

The simplest and most-used form of CAI is the **drill-and-practice approach** that's designed to complement instruction received from teachers, printed materials, and other noncomputer sources. Student responses are given to factual questions presented by the computer (Figure 20-10). Learning is facilitated because the computer can quickly supply correct answers as feedback to stu-

Figure 20-9 The PLATO system pioneered the use of computers in education. (Courtesy Control Data Corporation)

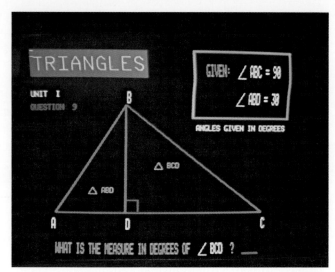

Figure 20-10 (*left*) These fourth-grade students are learning by working with a computer in their school. (Camilla Smith from Rainbow). (*right*) A CAI program may be used to drill students on the concepts presented in a geometry course. (Dan McCoy from Rainbow)

dent mistakes. However, new material is generally not introduced, and the student-computer interaction is highly structured so that little or no deviation from a programmed sequence of steps is allowed. The drill-and-practice approach has been found useful in learning areas such as mathematics, statistics, languages, reading, spelling, etc., where substantial memory work is required.

A second and more complex level of interaction between a student and a CAI computer program is found in the **tutorial approach.** With this approach, the program assists in presenting new material to the student. The intent of the tutorial approach, of course, is to have the computer program approximate the actions of a private and very patient tutor working with an individual student. Numerous branching opportunities in the CAI program permit a choice of materials to be presented, depending on how a student responded to the previous question. However, the student-computer interaction is still structured. The sequence in which information is presented is prescribed, and the expected student responses must all be anticipated by the program author. Tutorial CAI programs have been developed by Stanford University researchers for reading and elementary mathematics courses.

Two interesting applications of the CAI concept are:

1. The University of Illinois's use of the PLATO system at its Champaign-Urbana campus to help teach 150 subjects ranging from physics to Swahili. The PLATO system was developed at Illinois with the help of Control Data Corporation, and it's now being marketed by Control Data Education Corporation. PLATO delivers instructional materials in the form of text, drawings, and animated graphics. Users communicate with the lesson materials through the keyboard or by touching the screen. PLATO terminals are available on a number of other campuses.

2. The University of California at Irvine's Physics Computer Development Project, which enables students to control the timing of their progress through the introductory physics course. Different CAI modes are selected by students, and a management system keeps a record of student progress.

Some of the advantages of CAI are:

▌ Individual help is available to a student who might otherwise be ignored in a classroom.

▌ By being able to privately move at their own pace, gifted children are not bound, slower students are not rushed, and shy students are not embarrassed by incorrect answers given in public.

▌ The computer is impartial, patient, and objective, and the student gets immediate feedback to answers given.

However, some CAI problems remain to be overcome before its promise can be fully realized. Included among these problems are:

▌ There's a lack of good, inexpensive CAI software, and some school systems still feel that they can't afford the hardware.

▌ The incentive and people to develop appropriate CAI programs may not be present in many school systems.

▌ The resistance to change of a number of educators is caused, in part, by the fact that CAI is new to them, and the extent of its effectiveness has not yet been demonstrated to them.

Simulation as a Teaching Aid. Computers are being used for educational simulation in various fields.

Physics. High school physics students in Lexington, Massachusetts, have written a program that simulates an Apollo moon landing. The object of the program is to have a physics student land the spacecraft safely—an operation requiring the student to apply information that she or he has learned about gravitational effects and Newton's laws of motion. The simulation begins with the spacecraft traveling at a velocity of 3,600 miles per hour and at an altitude of 120 miles above the moon. Every 10 seconds a "radar" check is made and measurements are taken of velocity and remaining fuel. At this time, the student must tell the computer the amount of fuel to use during each of the following 10 seconds. A safe landing requires a touchdown at a speed of a tenth of a mile per hour or less, with an exhausted fuel supply. Most students "crash" on their first landing attempt and must go back and make calculations to support the decisions they will make on the next attempt. These calculations, of course, reinforce the physics concepts being taught. Similar lunar lander simulation programs are now available for microcomputers at most computer retail stores. In addition to its ASTRO lunar lander simulation, the Talcott Mountain Science Center in Connecticut has programs named POL-

LUTE (a water pollution simulation) and WEATHERWISE (a simulation to help students learn how to interpret weather data so that they can pilot a ship safely across the Atlantic Ocean from New York to Iceland).

History. History students may be paired up (one representing the North, the other the South) to make decisions about tactics, troops, supplies, etc., prior to the beginning of a specific Civil War battle. The object of the simulation is to win the battle. Since the simulation program is based on actual Civil War conflicts, the history student is motivated to learn about the clashes because he or she will be "participating" in them. It's possible for an informed "Southern General" to defeat an uninformed Northern opponent at the Battle of Gettysburg. Elementary students in Yorktown Heights, New York, are also encouraged to take a greater interest in history by being placed in the role of the king of ancient Sumer. The "king" makes decisions about ruling the kingdom, and the computer acts as the king's prime minister and chief adviser.

Forestry. The School of Forestry at the University of Georgia uses a program to simulate a forest and the effects on the forest of various cutting practices. Students make decisions about tree harvesting and are thus able to test and put into practice concepts in forestry management that they've been taught.

Feedback and Review 20-1

To test and reinforce your understanding of the impact that computer systems may have on organizations in society, place a T or F in the space provided in the following true-false questions:

___F___ **1.** Sales in the information processing industry are growing at a rate that exceeds 100 percent per year.

___T___ **2.** The information processing industry is technology-driven and is subject to short product cycles and rapid product obsolescence.

___T___ **3.** In recent years, mainframe computers have lost a percentage of their total market to mini- and microcomputers.

___F___ **4.** Competition is weak in the information processing industry because of the dominance of a few large firms.

___F___ **5.** Computers are of little use in market research.

___T___ **6.** Market research results can be used in developing production plans and financial plans.

___F___ **7.** A job shop requires much less in the way of production planning and scheduling than does an assembly line that produces standard items.

___F___ **8.** Operational planning must precede the development of market forecasts.

___F___ **9.** Computers are used in open-loop process control facilities, but not in those facilities that use closed-loop control techniques.

F **10.** Computers can be used to control individual machines, but aren't of much use in controlling the overall production process.

T **11.** Productivity is dependent, in part, on the amount of sophisticated capital equipment that's available for use.

T **12.** Computer-aided design can speed up the product development process and thus improve productivity.

T **13.** Computers can be used to help engineers design circuits for newer computers.

T **14.** An organization's existence can be threatened by the inadequate control of its information systems.

F **15.** Transborder data flow is a strong issue in the United States, but is of little concern to other nations.

T **16.** Computers are commonly used for ecological research and environmental planning and control.

F **17.** Computers are seldom used by the federal government for research purposes.

F **18.** Congressional and legislative data systems are designed primarily to print mailing labels for lawmakers.

F **19.** Land-use models are used by the National Park Service, but are of little use in urban areas.

T **20.** Law enforcement computer systems are located at federal, state, and local levels and are tied together by telecommunications networks.

T **21.** Computers are used to help doctors diagnose human disease.

F **22.** A CAT scanner is used primarily in research on the cause of strokes in animals.

T **23.** Computers are commonly used to monitor patients in critical condition and to control laboratory tests.

T **24.** CMI permits teachers to manage individual instruction programs.

F **25.** The simplest and most-used form of CAI is the tutorial approach.

F **26.** An advantage of CAI is that there's an abundance of inexpensive CAI software.

T **27.** Simulations can be used to put students into challenging and entertaining learning situations.

Looking Back

1. Computer systems are obviously having a profound impact on the dynamic information processing industry that produces them. This industry is technology-driven, and its products are subject to rapid obsolescence. The competition can be fierce, and company positions in the industry can change dramatically in a year's time.

2. In other business organizations, computers can make a valuable contribution in market research and thus in market planning. Once market plans have been established, computers can then be used for production planning and scheduling and for financial planning purposes. Computer systems are also regularly used to control continuous processes, production operations, and inventories.

3. A concerted effort is now under way in industrial nations to apply computers in design and production processes in order to improve productivity. Computer-aided design techniques are used to speed up product development, and robots and numerical control machines are used during production. Several applications of computer-aided design are discussed in the chapter.

4. In addition to productivity and other benefits, however, the use of computer systems can also lead to difficulties. Organizations can be vulnerable to computer systems that aren't adequately controlled. And multinational corporations have found that computer usage has brought them into conflict with governments in some of the nations where they operate.

5. Government planners at all levels have a mandate to efficiently use public funds and resources in ways that best serve the needs of society. High-quality information is needed by planners to achieve their objectives, and hundreds of computer applications have been developed to supply planners with better information. Federal government decision makers are actively using computers in such areas as environmental planning, military planning, and research. State and municipal planners are concerned with such areas as social welfare planning and urban planning. Members of Congress and legislators are finding legislative data systems to be of value. The control function is being performed at all levels of government by computer systems. Conservation and environmental control applications by federal, state, and municipal agencies are discussed in the chapter. Millions of dollars have been channeled into the development and use of law enforcement computer systems. Many of these systems are tied together at the state levels, and the state systems are, in turn, linked to the FBI's NCIC system. Thus, a nationwide network of police data banks is now operational.

6. Computers are being used to assist doctors in diagnosing illnesses, and computer-assisted research is providing new insights into the way the body functions and into the causes and cures of disease. By placing the medical history of a patient in a data bank, one or more doctors can retrieve and update it as needed. Better information about a patient's medical background should enable doctors to do a more effective job of preventing potential health problems and detecting illnesses. Control of the physiological status of patients, and control of laboratory tests are also important applications of computers.

7. Computers can bring to the educational process such attributes as patience, around-the-clock availability, and individualized and student-paced instruction programs. Computer-managed instruction is the name given to the use of computers to assist teachers in the administration of individual instruction programs. Computer-assisted instruction refers to situations where students themselves interact with computers and where instruction is presented or reinforced. Control applications of computers in education are found in the areas of testing and error analysis. In some subjects, CAI methods are well suited for testing student progress. The simplest and most-used form of CAI is the drill-and-practice approach. The advantages and problems of CAI are discussed in the chapter. Computer simulations may be used as teaching aids. Students learn by making decisions and by learning of the consequences of those decisions. Theories can be put into practice, and valuable experience can be gained in a safe and inexpensive way.

KEY TERMS AND CONCEPTS

You should now be able to define and use the following terms and concepts (the numbers shown indicate the pages where the terms and concepts are first mentioned):

market research 593
production planning 594
assembly production line 594
job shop 594
financial planning 595
operational plans 595
process control systems 595
open-loop process control 595
closed-loop process control 596
production control 596
numerical control (NC) machines 597

robots 597
control of the inventory 598
computer-aided design (CAD) 599
computer-aided design/computer-aided manufacturing (CAD/CAM) 599
transborder data flow 603
technology assessment 603
environmental planning 603
land-use models 607
environmental control 607
police information network 608

diagnostic tool 610
computer-aided tomography (CAT) scanner 611
computer-managed instruction (CMI) 614
computer-assisted testing 614
computer-assisted instruction (CAI) 615
drill-and-practice approach 615
tutorial approach 616
educational simulation 617

TOPICS FOR REVIEW AND DISCUSSION

1. "The information processing industry is one in which rapid change is the rule." Explain why this statement is true and give examples to illustrate your points.

2. (*a*) How may computers be used in market forecasting and planning? (*b*) In production planning and scheduling?

3. (*a*) What's a job shop? (*b*) How does a job shop differ from an assembly line?

4. (*a*) What are the characteristics of an open-loop process-control operation? (*b*) Distinguish between an open-loop and a closed-loop process-control system.

5. (*a*) What are numerical control machines? (*b*) How are they controlled?

6. (*a*) Identify three factors that help determine productivity. (*b*) How can computer-aided design (CAD) improve productivity? (*c*) Identify and discuss four CAD applications.

7. Why do multinational corporations object to transborder data flow legislation?

8. (*a*) Discuss and give examples of how computers have been used for planning and decision making at the federal government level. (*b*) At state and local levels.

9. (*a*) What's a legislative data system? (*b*) For what purposes are such systems used?

10. (*a*) Give examples of ways in which computers are used by the federal government to perform the control function. (*b*) Give examples of state and local government control activities.

11. (*a*) What's the NCIC? (*b*) What functions does it perform? (*c*) Identify two other systems that are tied into NCIC.

12. Consider the following case: A Decision Information Distribution System (DIDS)—a low-frequency radio network to warn people quickly of impending attack—has been under development in the Pentagon. If this system ever materializes, all citizens would be expected to buy a specially designed unit capable of receiving DIDS warning broadcasts. The DIDS would also warn listeners of impending floods, hurricanes, and similar emergencies, and would provide other services. Because of the warning functions of DIDS, the receiving units in the homes could be turned on *automatically* by the message-sending agency (the circuitry to do this has already been developed). Under questioning by a congressional subcommittee member, a Pentagon delegate admitted that the DIDS receiver could also be converted into a *transmitter*. A subcommittee staff member has commented: "They'll ultimately decide to go ahead with DIDS because they'll be evaluating only its *technical* peformance, not its *political* possibilities." Plans have been made to seek funds to install DIDS units on new radio and TV sets. A coast-to-coast network could be in operation in a few years. *Question:* On balance, is DIDS a good idea?

13. Why is there an accelerating use of computers in health fields?

14. "Some doctors are now using the computer as a diagnostic tool in hospitals and clinics." Discuss this statement.

15. How can a computer be of value in physical examinations?

16. (*a*) How can a computer be used to take a medical history? (*b*) Would there be any advantages to a medical record data bank? (*c*) Would there be any possible disadvantages to such a data bank?

17. (*a*) How can a computer be used for physiological monitoring? (*b*) Discuss the use of computers in controlling laboratory tests.

18. In the 1970s, doctors found that the radiation therapy used to treat certain thyroid diseases in the 1950s actually caused thyroid tumors to occur at a later time in a patient's life. Similarly, high doses of diethylstibestrol were later found to produce uterine tumors. (*a*) How could a computerized medical record retrieval system be of help in these cases? (*b*) Do the possible advantages of such a retrieval system outweigh the potential dangers?

19. (*a*) What is meant by computer-managed instruction? (*b*) What is meant by computer-assisted instruction?

20. Identify and discuss the two CAI approaches.

21. (*a*) What are the advantages of CAI? (*b*) What are the problems to be solved before CAI achieves its potential?

22. Discuss ways in which computer simulation can be used for instructional purposes.

ANSWERS TO FEEDBACK AND REVIEW SECTION

20-1

1. F	10. F	19. F
2. T	11. T	20. T
3. T	12. T	21. T
4. F	13. T	22. F
5. F	14. T	23. T
6. T	15. F	24. T
7. F	16. T	25. F
8. F	17. F	26. F
9. F	18. F	27. T

Experiments in Telecommuting

'Mid pleasures and palaces though we may roam,
Be it ever so humble, there's no place like home.
— *John Howard Payne, 1823*

The sentiment of Payne's couplet seems particularly appropriate today when, thanks to computer technology, more and more people are managing to combine their work and home lives and avoid a long commute.

Written in the heyday of the Industrial Revolution when workers were leaving home in droves to work in factories, the poem could be seen as a nostalgic glance backward at the first 10,000 years of human existence, during which people worked at home as a matter of course.

Recognizing that it is only in the last 300 years that out-of-home work has predominated, author Alvin Toffler in *The Third Wave* went so far as to predict that the office work place eventually may cease to exist or at least dwindle in importance.

Toffler claimed that the work place as we know it will be replaced by home and neighborhood work centers, comprising an "electronic cottage" in which families will live and work together on home computers linked to employers' computers.

Indeed, the electronic cottage is already a reality for an estimated 20,000 to 30,000 workers "mostly in the U.S., to a lesser degree in Europe and to an unknown degree in Japan, where they're very interested in it," according to Jack Nilles, director of the Center for Future Research at the University of Southern California.

Originator of the term "telecommuting," the ramifications of which he has studied since 1975, Nilles projects there may be as many as 10 million telecommuters by 1990.

Support for Toffler's and Nilles' predictions lies in the several corporate experiments now going on in the U.S. Control Data Corp., as part of its Alternate Work Site project, has enrolled 60 professional and managerial employees in a voluntary work-at-home pilot project.

CDC has also opened neighborhood offices in a nationwide experiment that has been, "for the most part," very popular and successful, according to Ronald A. Manning, general manager for office technologies. In addition, the firm plans to install word processing equipment in the homes of clerical employees who might otherwise drop out of the work force.

Besides CDC's effort, Walgreen, McDonald's and Mountain States Telephone & Telegraph have installed terminals in homes of the handicapped for programming jobs. The handicapped, in fact, may be the greatest benefactors of the concept of telecommuting, since it offers them a chance at employment they often would not otherwise have. . . .

Then there's the bad news. The bad news in telecommuting stems from the very freedom and independence that home workers cherish. "People get tired of working by themselves," Nilles observed.

In addition to feelings of loneliness, those who work for one employer "may worry about getting promoted because they're not in the situation to see the 'Big Boss'," Nilles said. "They feel they could lose chances for upward mobility."

"The impersonal personal computer is not felt to be a suitable surrogate for the 'pressing of the flesh' involved in high-level management conferences and casual meetings in the corridor," he noted.

Furthermore, there are not "the same kinds of fringe benefits; some perquisites disappear, such as niftier quarters, wider hallways, things you don't think about. . . ."

Besides removing workers from the social life of the office, working at home can breed mistrust in the minds of fellow workers. "I still think there's a mentality around here that people who work at home are not working," theorized the telecommuting vice-president of a management consulting firm.

— Marguerite Zientara, "Companies Experiment with Telecommuting," *Computerworld*, Nov. 30, 1981, p. 23. Copyright 1981 by CW Communications, Inc., Framingham, Mass.

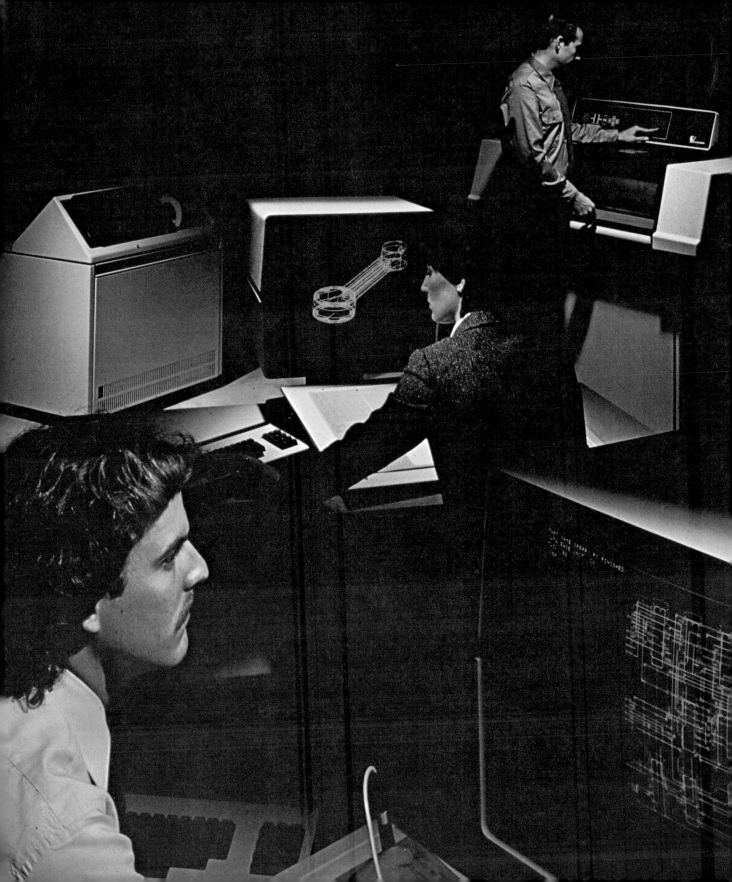

chapter 21

Computers Tomorrow

THE THREE LAWS OF ROBOTICS

Mars. The Second Expedition. The First Expedition, for unknown reasons, failed. And the Second is about to. Speedy (SPD 13), an electronic whiz of a computer, "extremely specialized, and as expensive as a battleship," is out on the planet surface, refusing to respond to orders and return with the precious selenium that is vital to Powell and Donovan's survival. The only way to recover Speedy is to somehow circumvent—or manipulate—the Three Laws of Robotics.

Powell's radio voice was tense in Donovan's ear: "Now, look, let's start with the three fundamental Rules of Robotics—the three rules that are built most deeply into a robot's positronic brain." In the darkness, his gloved fingers ticked off each point.

"We have: One, a robot may not injure a human being, or, through inaction, allow a human being to come to harm."

"Right!"

"Two," continued Powell, "a robot must obey the orders given it by a human being except where such orders would conflict with the First Law."

"Right!"

"And three, a robot must protect its own existence as long as such protection does not conflict with the First or Second Laws."

"Right! Now where are we?"

Where indeed? Firmly in the grip of "Runaround," an early Asimov short story that first appeared in *Astounding Science Fiction* (March 1942). This, and eight other classic Asimov stories, are collected in a book entitled *i, robot*.

—From Isaac Asimov, *i, robot*. Reprinted in Isaac Asimov, "I Am a Signpost," *Popular Computing*, November 1981, p. 32. © 1981 Popular Computing, Inc. Used with permission.

Left CAD/CAM systems such as the one shown here are among the computer applications that mark the continuing evolution of our industrial society toward an information society. (Courtesy Computervision Corporation)

Looking Ahead

The purpose of this chapter is to speculate briefly on some of the computer—and computer-driven—developments that may be possible through the 1980s. We'll survey some possible applications of future computer systems first. Next, we examine the technological outlook for computer hardware and software. As we move from an industrial society that emphasizes standardized mass production to a new information/communications society that will produce customized and individualized configurations of products and services, it will be necessary to develop future information systems that are quicker-responding and broader in scope. The outlook for such information systems is the subject of the third section in the chapter. And in the last section we'll take a look at the future outlook for individuals.

Thus, after studying this chapter, you should be able to:

▌ Identify some of the possible applications of future computer systems

▌ Discuss some of the possible developments in hardware, software, and information systems that you expect in the 1980s

▌ Present the optimistic and pessimistic views about the future impact of computer systems on people

▌ Form some opinions of your own on the future impact that computer systems are likely to have on society

TOMORROW'S APPLICATIONS

Imagine this: Most families own computers, most doctors have installed computer-assisted diagnostic systems in their offices, and microelectronic implants have restored the sight and hearing of many handicapped persons. As Figure 21-1 shows, these are just a few of the technological developments and applications effects of computer systems that are expected before the turn of the century. We'll highlight some of these applications areas in this section. The applications presented here seem to be *technically* possible during the 1980s; whether they are all *socially desirable*, however, is another matter. Most of the applications that we've speculated on in earlier chapters aren't repeated here. The applications we will consider have been arbitrarily classified into those which may affect people in *private life* and those which may have an impact on people in *organizations*. (Of course, the development, for the home, of new computer-controlled products that would affect the private lives of some people would also have an impact on people in the organizations that developed the products.)

Applications That Will Affect People

Some of the computer-related applications that could affect our lives at home and at play during the 1980s are outlined in the following section.

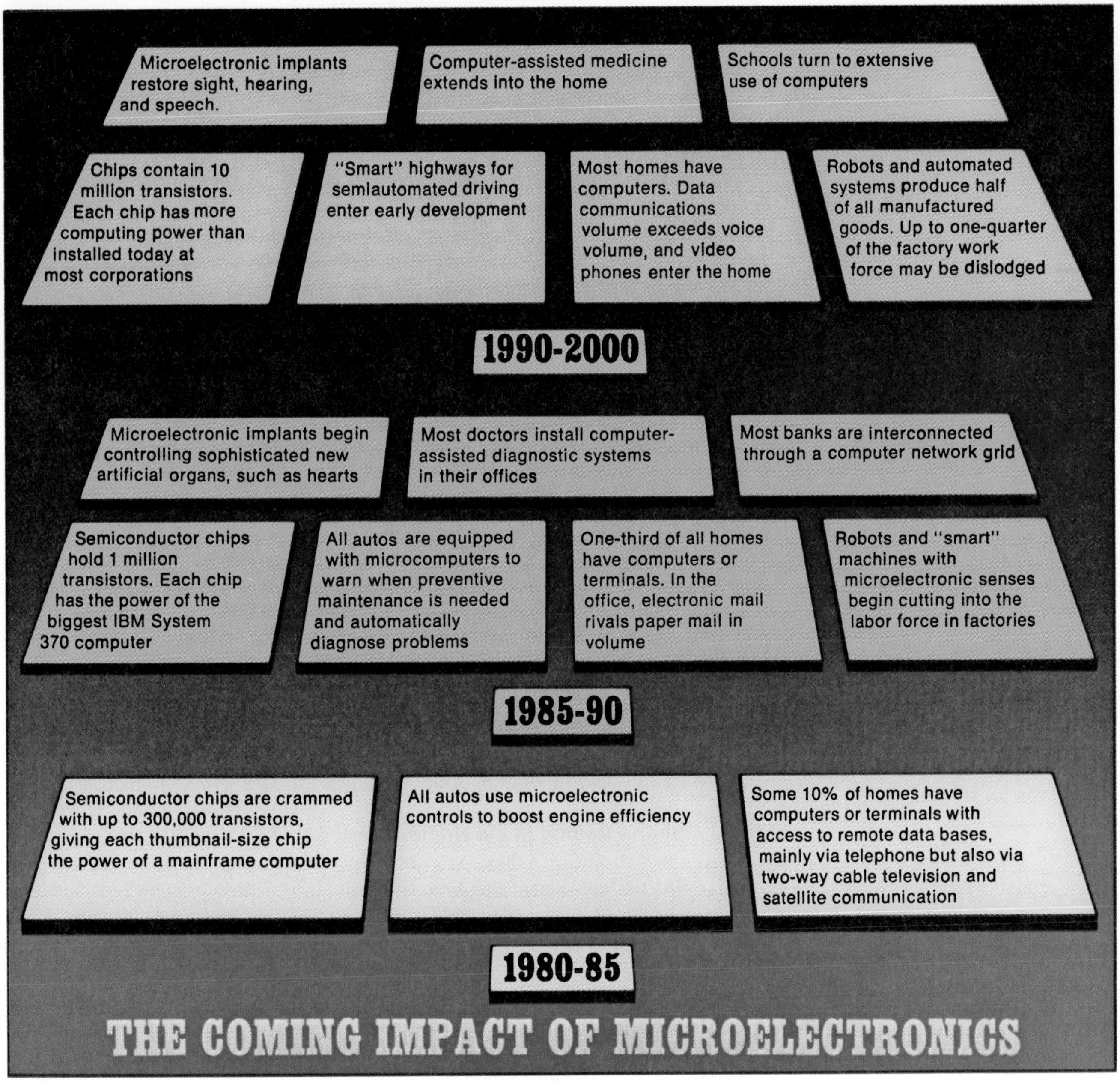

Microelectronic implants restore sight, hearing, and speech.

Computer-assisted medicine extends into the home

Schools turn to extensive use of computers

Chips contain 10 million transistors. Each chip has more computing power than installed today at most corporations

"Smart" highways for semiautomated driving enter early development

Most homes have computers. Data communications volume exceeds voice volume, and video phones enter the home

Robots and automated systems produce half of all manufactured goods. Up to one-quarter of the factory work force may be dislodged

1990-2000

Microelectronic implants begin controlling sophisticated new artificial organs, such as hearts

Most doctors install computer-assisted diagnostic systems in their offices

Most banks are interconnected through a computer network grid

Semiconductor chips hold 1 million transistors. Each chip has the power of the biggest IBM System 370 computer

All autos are equipped with microcomputers to warn when preventive maintenance is needed and automatically diagnose problems

One-third of all homes have computers or terminals. In the office, electronic mail rivals paper mail in volume

Robots and "smart" machines with microelectronic senses begin cutting into the labor force in factories

1985-90

Semiconductor chips are crammed with up to 300,000 transistors, giving each thumbnail-size chip the power of a mainframe computer

All autos use microelectronic controls to boost engine efficiency

Some 10% of homes have computers or terminals with access to remote data bases, mainly via telephone but also via two-way cable television and satellite communication

1980-85

THE COMING IMPACT OF MICROELECTRONICS

Figure 21-1 Technological developments and applications effects: A 20-year forecast. (Source: "The Microchip Revolution: Piecing Together a New Society," *Business Week*, Nov. 10, 1980, p. 96. Reprinted by special permission, © 1980 by McGraw-Hill, Inc., New York, NY. All rights reserved.)

Home and Hobby Possibilities. There will be a flood of microprocessors on small chips into the home in the 1980s. They will be used to control most home appliances. Television sets will use them to perform automatic fine tuning and color-regulating operations. And typewriters will become similar to some of today's stand-alone word processors by incorporating them for control, storage, and duplication purposes. Millions of people will buy inexpensive personal computers with considerable power and use them for home recreation and education purposes.

We've seen that videodisk players attached to television sets currently use optical disks to provide viewers with up to an hour's worth of television programming for approximately the price of a phonograph record. Future home systems will *merge* videodisk players and personal computers into a combination that can either include a television screen or be attached to a TV set. Videodisks for this "visual computer" will be sold in stores and may contain complete interactive entertainment, hobby, and educational sequences including computer programs, audio segments, and video materials. In short, an exciting environment designed to simultaneously stimulate the user's senses will be created. Home-delivered videodisks could someday supplement or replace newspapers and magazines with a more versatile product.

A more immediate impact on the print media, however, may come from the *videotex home systems* that will emerge in the 1980s. Massive data bases including the latest news and weather information, airline schedules, tax information, etc., will be stored in central computer systems. A page of this information will be requested from a home microcomputer connected to a telephone or cable television line, and the requested page will be returned over the line to a receiving screen. If the viewer wants a permanent copy, the page can be printed by the home computer system. In short, users can browse through the electronic newspaper/magazine/encyclopedia, select the sections that interest them, and thus tailor the information to their individual needs.

Opinion Polling in the Home. Subscribers to the QUBE cable television system in Columbus, Ohio can choose incoming programs from many channels. But the cable can also be used to communicate *outgoing* messages. In other words, subscribers can talk back to the tube (Figure 21-2). By pressing a button, a viewer can respond to a politician, evaluate the features in a local newspaper, and give an opinion on a contestant in a talent program (an electronic "gonging"?). Responses can be recorded and tabulated by a computer. As similar systems spread throughout the nation, national "town meetings" could be called to provide political leaders with the instant electronic "votes" of citizens on important issues.

Telemedicine Applications. Satellite communications between ill or injured persons in remote areas and specialists in urban areas should be in widespread use in the late 1980s. Medical aides in remote areas can administer the emergency treatment recommended by a specialist backed up by diagnostic computing resources. Instrumented hospital beds in remote clinics may regularly be linked with computers and/or intensive-care monitors at an urban hospital.

Figure 21-2 QUBE cable television transforms TV sets into interactive message systems. (Courtesy Warner Amex/QUBE)

Applications That Will Affect Organizations

A few of the computer-related applications that may have an impact on organizations in the late 1980s follow.

Computer-Assisted Manufacturing. As we saw in Chapter 20, micro- and mini-sized computers are now routinely used to control individual production tools such as milling machines and shapers. As we've also seen, computer-controlled robots are being developed rapidly, and tens of thousands of them will be installed in assembly operations during the 1980s. Automobile workers will soon be working alongside robots capable of assembling components such as carburetors and alternators. In fact, in studies conducted jointly by the University of Michigan and the Society of Manufacturing Engineers, it's predicted that by 1988:

✓ Half the human labor in such small-component assembly will be replaced.

✓ The production control function will be automated to the point that 80 percent of all in-process technology will be computer-controlled.

✓ Fifty percent of the work force remaining on the production floor will be the highly skilled and trained engineers and technicians needed to keep the automated plants operating.

Since many of the robots installed during the 1980s can be switched from the production of one item to another simply by changing the program, it will be feasible to keep equipment busy by having it produce small quantities of a number of different customized and individualized items. Thus, small-lot manufacturing may become nearly as economical as mass production is today. In fact, computers and robots may reduce overall costs in small-lot manufacturing by more than 50 percent during the 1980s. Since the machines that will be used in future mass production operations will themselves be produced in small lots, the net effect is that they will be relatively less expensive, and so may be the prices of the items they produce.

Automatic Meter Reading. At this writing, many telephone companies have installed computer-controlled testing equipment to check on the condition of telephone lines. In the 1980s, gas, electric, and water meters may be connected to these telephone lines so that as the system automatically tests line condition, it will also read the meters for the utility companies.

Attending Meetings Electronically. The material presented in Chapter 11 showed how an *electronic mail/message system* (EMMS) can now be used to permit "conferences" to be held at the convenience of the participants (Figure 21-3). Telephone and/or cable TV lines may be combined with computers in a future extension of this EMMS concept to provide an integrated voice-data-picture communication system for some organizations. By the late 1980s, it may be possible for some employees such as managers, teachers, engineers, typists, etc., to perform some of their job duties in offices located in the home. Typists, for example, could receive dictation by phone and handwritten drafts by facsimile, and they could return finished copy via communicating word processors. Thus, the transmission of information may be substituted for the transportation and concentration of humans. Technology can be substituted

Figure 21-3 The use of teleconferencing services promises to grow steadily during the 1980s. (Courtesy AT&T)

for energy. To some extent, communications can replace commuting. Organizations may find it less costly to furnish certain employees with the necessary terminals and communications lines so that they can work at home much of the time, rather than establishing offices for them in expensive buildings.

Witnesses could testify at government hearings without leaving their hometowns. They could go to a local courthouse and be sworn in, and their testimony could be recorded and transmitted to the hearings room at the state or national capital. The need to crowd together into cities may be reduced. Communities of interest and interaction may be linked electronically rather than by geographic boundaries.

Educational Applications. The same low-cost computer/television systems that will entertain and educate in the home in the 1980s will also be used in schools. More importantly, perhaps, these low-cost systems will lead to the development of innovative and much-needed educational software. Bright students will learn the subject matter and will help teach other students by writing educational programs at home and at school. Hobbyists (including teachers) with home computers will write programs with high educational value for their own children and will then share these programs with others. And clubs of computer hobbyists may make the preparation of good educational programs a club project. Future homework may consist of a student taking a computer tape cassette or videodisk home and playing it on the family system.

TOMORROW'S TECHNOLOGY

Although the explosion in electronics technology is having a profound effect on such things as the way time and other variables are measured (with digital display devices), food is cooked (with microwave devices), and people are entertained (with home videotape recorders), we'll limit our discussion in this section to the outlook for computer hardware and software. Throughout this chapter, there may be terms that are unfamiliar to you that have been introduced and discussed in earlier chapters. You can locate unfamiliar terms by using the glossary and index at the back of the book.

Computer Hardware

Numerous changes may be expected in the next few years in *I/O devices* and *central processors.*

I/O Equipment. In the *data entry* field, there will be little change in the performance of *punched card* equipment. Although punched cards are still an important I/O medium, their use peaked in 1969, and the total demand for punched card devices will continue to decline in the future. By the late 1980s,

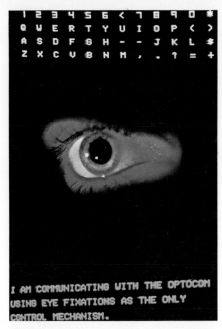

Figure 21-4 Handicapped persons will be able to supply input data via systems such as OPTOCOM, which produces characters in response to eye movements. (Dan McCoy from Rainbow)

many existing keypunches and stand-alone data systems will have been replaced by *multifunction online terminals* that capture data at the point of transaction. Many of these terminals will perform *both* word processing and data processing functions. Of course, many organizations cannot convert overnight to online terminals for transaction-oriented processing. Thus, *optical character recognition* (OCR) equipment will often be used to avoid the need to rekey data captured by nonelectronic data entry devices such as typewriters. The use of offline multistation *keyboard-to-disk* storage devices for data entry purposes is therefore likely to decline gradually over the next decade. *Speech recognition* will become the preferred means of supplying input data to future computers in a growing number of applications. And Figure 21-4 shows a system which permits severely handicapped people to control data entry solely by eye movements.

The speed of *impact printers* will not change much in the next few years. A booming market for the low-speed line and character impact printers used with micro- and minicomputers is assured. Improvements in dot-matrix character printers will result in output that's of full-strike typewriter quality, and prices of these and other low-speed printers are likely to drop substantially. New *nonimpact printers* in the 1,000-line-per-minute speed range will appear to challenge chain, drum, and band-type impact machines. Since these new printers will be much less expensive, they'll succeed in replacing many of the older "workhorses." New systems requiring a great deal of archival storage will bypass printing altogether and make greater use of lower-cost *computer-output-to-microfilm* (COM) equipment. There should also be some cost reduction in *magnetic tape drives* in the next few years, and there should be a doubling in transfer speeds as the amount of data packed in an inch of tape doubles. Overall, however, the life cycle of magnetic tape may have peaked.

Direct-access storage devices will continue to be a hotbed of research activity for years to come. Such devices will be developed to provide virtually unlimited online secondary storage at a very modest cost. *Storage hierarchies* will continue—i.e., the fastest auxiliary storage utilizing the latest technology will be more expensive and may have less storage capacity than slower and less expensive alternatives. Mass storage approaches being considered by equipment designers include:

> *Higher-density magnetic direct-access systems.* Recording techniques using magnetic disk surfaces that will significantly increase the density of data storage on a given surface are expected to be developed in the near future. It will not be long before the contents of over 600 books of this size can be stored in a disk device occupying the space of two small present-day floppy-disk drives. About 10 million bits of data are currently being stored on a square inch of disk surface. In the next 6 or 7 years, there will be a tenfold improvement—to 100 million bits or more. The costs of disk storage will also drop dramatically. A 20-million-character disk drive for personal microcomputers will soon be available for less than $1,000.

Figure 21-5 A beam of laser light converts the information stored on a videodisk to audiovisual signals. (Courtesy Xerox Corporation)

▌ *Optical direct-access systems.* Information may be stored on a special optical disk. A beam of laser light is used to burn tiny holes or pits into a thin coating of metal or other material deposited on a spinning disk. Visible only under a powerful microscope, these holes are used in commercial television *videodisk systems* to represent images and sounds. A less powerful laser light beam (Figure 21-5) in a *videodisk player* is used to read the hole patterns and convert these patterns into audio/visual signals that can be fed to a television set. The same technology that's used to record and play back sound and images can also be used to store and retrieve data. The storage density of optical disks is enormous, and the storage cost is extremely low. Laboratory systems with the potential to store on a single disk the contents of a library of several thousand volumes have already been demonstrated. In the next decade, it's likely that many permanent archives now stored on microfilm and magnetic tape will be placed on optical disks. One small inexpensive disk will be able to replace 25 reels of magnetic tape.

The *dollar amount* of sales of *online terminals* is expected to increase by at least 50 percent during the 1980s. In terms of the *number of terminals sold each*

Figure 21-6 Electronic point-of-sale terminals have replaced manual cash registers in many businesses. (Courtesy NCR, Dayton, Ohio)

year, the market is likely to double in size in this same period. Much of this growth is expected to be in the categories of *typewriterlike terminals* (or *Teleprinters*), *intelligent visual display terminals* with graphics capabilities, and *specialty terminals* (see Figure 21-6).

Many of the teleprinters of the late 1980s, however, will have undergone considerable change. They'll be "intelligent" devices containing microprocessors and memory chips, and they'll be used in organizations to meet both word and data processing needs. As data entry stations, they'll be used to capture and relay facts to a distributed or host computer; as *communicating word processors,* they'll be used to distribute (and receive) electronic mail and messages. And they'll also be used by participants in the computerized conferences described in Chapter 11.

Intelligent visual display terminals will also be used for word processing and data entry applications. Sales of such specialized data stations as *POS terminals* and *teller terminals* will grow rapidly in the early 1980s, but by 1988 market saturation may cause a tapering off of sales to replacement levels. However, other specialized terminals such as those used in (1) security systems to read industrial and office badges, (2) manufacturing data entry systems, and (3) executive suites are poised for rapid growth. Hand-held portable terminals that will be linked to a computer by radio transmission will also probably experience enormous growth.

The proliferation in the number of intelligent terminals installed during the 1980s will, of course, be accompanied by the creation of new *distributed processing networks* in many more organizations. These organizations will be (1) using the intelligent terminals to carry out autonomous word and data processing operations, and (2) utilizing a host and/or node computer(s) to serve the terminals by managing data bases and by executing those jobs which require extensive computations.

Central Processors. There will continue to be substantial reductions in the *size* of electronic circuits. The average number of components packed on advanced integrated circuit chips has about doubled every year since 1965, and this trend is likely to continue through the 1980s (Figure 21-7). By the end of the 1980s, tiny memory chips capable of storing 64K bits will give way to chips of about the same size that may have up to 200 times the storage capacity. Processors with more computing power than large machines of just a few years ago are already dwarfed by their peripherals. Before the end of the 1980s, 32-bit *microcomputers* with 1 million bits of random access memory (RAM) storage will be fabricated on a single chip. These single-chip microcomputers will:

✓ Employ the same instruction sets as present-day mainframe models.

✓ Execute up to 1 million instructions per second.

✓ Accept without modification the large libraries of software written for such mainframe families as the IBM System/370.

Figure 21-7 Processor size shrinks as capacity grows: a single chip smaller than a dime (*above*) may contain the comparable capacity of one of today's mainframe processors (*right*). (Courtesy Motorola, Inc.; IBM Corporation)

By way of comparison, the largest System/370 model of the early 1980s occupies several cubic yards of space and can execute 5 million instructions per second. Of course, by 1990 a mainframe model may execute 70 million instructions per second and have 16 million bytes of primary storage and a large cache memory section. Such a model could be packaged in a 6-inch cube!

As the above paragraph indicates, *greater speed* will accompany further size reductions. Future supercomputers will be able to execute thousands of millions of instructions per second by harnessing many powerful micro-sized computers in a parallel assembly. *Superconductive cryogenic circuits* employing the *Josephson junction*—named for British Nobel Prize winner Brian Josephson—will be in use by the end of the 1980s. These circuits operate in a liquid helium bath at close to absolute zero temperature (more than 400 degrees below zero on the Fahrenheit scale). At that temperature, barriers that would ordinarily restrain the flow of electricity lose their resistive ability. The switching speeds of the Josephson junction circuit are up to 100 times faster than those of the circuits used in large present-day mainframes.

What about the *cost* of future central processors? You already know the answer to this question: For a given level of computing power, cost will continue to drop like a brick. The cost of primary storage in a CPU represents a significant part of the total cost. Figure 21-8 shows the cost trends for 1 million bytes (a *megabyte*) of primary storage. As you can see, the retail price per megabyte was about $95,000 in 1975, but it's expected to be $80 by 1991! We're likely to see similar trends for other components in the CPU.

Figure 21-8 Cost trends for 1 million characters of primary storage capacity in the central processor. (Source: Adapted from Portia Isaacson, "1984's Information Appliances," *Datamation,* February 1979, p. 216)

Year	Bits/Chip	Retail Price/MB
1975	1K	$95,528.
1977	4K	37,196.
1979	16K	14,924.
1981	64K	6,108.
1983	256K	2,532.
1985	1M	1,058.
1987	4M	444.4
1989	16M	185.12
1991	64M	80.28

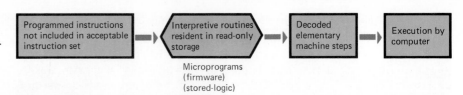

Figure 21-9 A use of microprograms, or firmware, which is software substituted for hardware and stored in read-only memory.

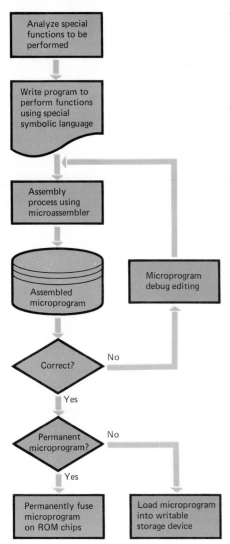

Figure 21-10 Procedure for customizing a computer with microprograms.

The subject of *microprograms* was introduced in Chapter 5. Such microprograms stored in *read-only memory* (ROM) devices may be used to interpret the problem-solving instructions written by a programmer and to translate these instructions into steps that the hardware can accept. For years, microprograms have also been used to permit one computer to interpret and execute instructions written for a different machine. In other words, the microprograms (also called *stored logic* and *firmware*) would analyze and decode foreign instructions into the elementary operations that the particular CPU was designed to execute (Figure 21-9).

In addition to permitting one computer to *emulate* another, it's also feasible to use various combinations of plug-in microprograms with *generalized* central processors to create custom-built systems for specific users. This "computer within a computer" approach can facilitate standardized CPU manufacturing and maintenance operations. It also makes it possible to convert software routines into microprograms that can be executed in a fraction of the time previously required. Furthermore, it's possible for vendors and users to *permanently* fuse important microprograms into ROM chips and thus, in effect, convert important software into hardware. Figure 21-10 illustrates how a computer manufacturer or user can create a customized computer system. Unlike the special-purpose computers of earlier years, however, the same processor can now be adapted to different functions by a simple change of microprograms. As Figure 21-10 indicates, if nonpermanent microprograms are desired, they may be loaded into a writable storage device that can be plugged into the CPU, and if permanent firmware is needed, it may be fused onto ROM chips by a special writing device. You saw in Chapter 19 that persons subscribing to *CLOAD* magazine can now get a tape cassette each month that's filled with game and educational programs for their personal computers. It's likely that "ROM of the Month" clubs will also spring up in the 1980s to send subscribers new applications programs written in ROM chips that can be plugged into personal micros.

Computer technology will probably make much greater use of firmware in the future. By converting functions currently being performed with software into circuit elements (which are becoming less expensive), the need for some of the detailed programming currently being done may be reduced. For example, in performing its functions of scheduling, control, etc., the *operating system* (OS) software discussed in Chapter 15 uses storage space in, and the time of, the CPU—space and time resources that might otherwise have been used for data processing tasks. To reduce this OS overhead, resident microprograms operating at hardware speeds may be substituted for some of the tasks currently being accomplished at relatively slow speeds with a series of OS program instructions. Also, specialized microprocessors and microprograms are likely to be used frequently in the future in place of software for language translation, data security, and data manipulation and control. Chapter 10 shows how "front-end" processors are used to relieve a host CPU of data communications functions. In the future, "back-end" processors may also be commonly used to handle *data-base management functions* (Chapter 17), and to control the movement of data between various storage elements in a storage hierarchy. Thus, the traditional and still very popular *uniprocessor* computer system that features single control, storage, and arithmetic-logic units will give way in the future to *multiprocessor* systems in all but the smallest installations. Of course, the component micro- and mini-sized processors dedicated to performing the specialized functions such as data-base management and security are likely to be smaller than those reserved to process user jobs in multiple and simultaneous streams. But future users—connected to such a multiprocessor system, perhaps, by intelligent terminals that further distribute and decentralize the computing power of the network—may expect faster, more reliable, and more secure service.

Computer Software

There are numerous technical articles being published that predict with confidence the course of hardware development over the next decade. But you won't find this confident tone in the few articles dealing with the future of software development. Perhaps this is due to the fact that the development of software will continue to be slower, much more expensive, and more painful than hardware development because the functions performed by software are now (and will continue to be) more complex than the operations performed by hardware. Of course, as we saw in the preceding section, many of the functions now being performed by OS and system software may be taken over by future hardware elements. And the future use of multiprocessor systems may *reduce* the need for complex *multiprogramming* software (Chapter 15) that permits instructions from several programs to be interleaved and executed on a single processor. In short, the cost trends for information systems will encourage the replacement of expensive software with cheap hardware whenever possible.

The comments just made should not be interpreted to mean that there will be no progress in software development. On the contrary, existing *languages* such as BASIC, COBOL, FORTRAN, Pascal, etc., will be enhanced and improved to accommodate the *structured programming* approach discussed in Chapters 12 and 13. Furthermore, new very high level languages will be developed to solve particular types of problems so that nonprogrammer users can conveniently make use of computing capabilities. From the users' standpoint, such languages will be more like their native English (or German, French, Spanish, etc.), and they will be *conversational*—i.e., the computer itself will keep track of the acceptable vocabulary of the language, and it may display permissible alternate terms and statements to users in a "question and answer" format until the problem is satisfactorily formulated. The machine will then compute the answer to the problem. Thus, the users' major skill will be in their ability to state problems, and they will be assisted by a "dialogue" with a "user-friendly" computer system as it seeks to find out what they want to say.

Conversational programming is likely to be a feature of the *data-base management software* described in Chapter 17. In 1974, there were only about 1,500 true data base management systems in worldwide use. By 1988, however, there will be tens of thousands of these software systems in operation. They will be more comprehensive, they will be large and may require a million characters or more of storage to operate effectively, and they will enable the end user of the information to frequently bypass the services of applications programmers. Additional provisions to ensure the *integrity* and *security* of stored information will be incorporated into future data base software as well as future hardware.

Finally, *program development aids* such as structured programming will result in higher programmer productivity, shorter program development times, and more understandable and error-free program modules. And the trend toward the greater use of packaged programs will have to accelerate rapidly because of the continued shortage of in-house programmers available to develop custom systems.

TOMORROW'S INFORMATION SYSTEMS

We're now in a period of transition between an existing industrial society that emphasizes standardized mass production and distribution and an emerging information/communications society that will carefully fit standard components together to produce highly customized and individualized configurations of products and services. The traditional batch processing computer installations used to good advantage in a standardized setting are economical, are well suited to many types of routine applications, and are going to continue to be used to process large volumes of information. But the trend toward a customized and individualized society will require future systems that will be *quicker responding* and *broader in scope* than these traditional installations.

Quick-Response Systems

We've seen that emphasis is currently being given to the development of:

✓ Distributed computer systems with logic and storage capability moved to the point of origin of transactions.

✓ User-oriented interactive programming languages designed to enable operating personnel to get information quickly without having to wait for the help of an applications programmer.

New direct-access storage devices, online terminals, and multiprocessor computer configurations.

These developments, in turn, signal a definite trend in the direction of quick-response systems that will give remote users immediate access to very powerful computing facilities (Figure 21-11). *Real time processing* will become increasingly common in those applications where immediate updating of records is justifiable. When the time limitations are not so severe, *online processing,* with periodic updating of those records which affect other users of a distributed network, will often replace traditional batch processing methods. Source data will frequently be keyed directly into the computer system, thus eliminating the need for cards and/or tapes in many applications. As we've seen, the same

Figure 21-11 Ground microwave stations are one method used in data communications networks to send and collect information from remote locations. (Courtesy Raytheon)

Figure 21-12 Fiber optics: voices carried on a beam of light. (Fred Ward/Black Star)

terminals used to enter data will also be used as communicating word processors to distribute (and receive) electronic mail and messages.

With increased emphasis being placed on quick-response systems, there will obviously be greater use of *data communications* facilities. In fact, the transmission of data is expected to continue to increase by at least 35 percent *each year* between now and the late 1980s. New data communications services will be established, and the current services offered by data carrier organizations will be expanded to meet this demand. Satellites will be used more extensively in space, and the *fiber optic* and *laser* technology discussed in Chapter 10 will be used in land-based transmission channels. When compared to costs at the beginning of this decade, telecommunications costs will be reduced by up to 50 percent by the mid-1980s. When the use of fiber optic/laser channels becomes widespread, this technology will reduce enormously the cost of communications (Figure 21-12). At that point, an individual will be able to utilize transmission resources that only the largest organizations can now afford.

Broader Systems

Many of the quick-response systems that will be developed in the next few years will take a broader data base approach (Chapter 17) to the needs of the organization. Given the rapid growth expected in data base management software, this isn't a surprising prediction. The data base approach can be flexible: It may be used by organizations combining large centralized computers and a centralized data base with nonintelligent terminals located at the operating level; it may be used by organizations with a smaller central processor to maintain a centralized data base for a network of distributed minicomputers and outlying intelligent terminals; or it may be used by organizations adopting some other alternative.

Regardless of the technical approach used, the trend in many organizations will be to define, classify, and store certain types of basic data commonly so that better integration will be possible. The development efforts to produce data banks that will replace a multitude of the independent files maintained at the present time will probably continue at a more rapid pace in spite of the potential dangers to individual privacy. Why will this happen? It will probably happen because managers will have to respond to future changes that may occur at a much faster rate than in the past. Therefore, decision makers forced to make quicker choices involving greater risks will press for relatively complete information rather than settle for information in bits and pieces located in scattered files.

TOMORROW'S OUTLOOK

The Optimistic View

Optimistic forecasters believe that computer usage will result in greater freedom and individuality and a more human and personalized society. They point to many of the computer applications we've described here and in earlier chapters to prove their contention that the benefits to be obtained far outweigh any temporary difficulties and inconveniences.

For example, the computer-assisted manufacturing trends described in this chapter and elsewhere, and the resulting outlook for productivity gains, they are convinced, will lead to a higher standard of living, a shorter work week, and increased leisure time. And home computers may be used to stimulate the analytical and intellectual abilities of people and add to their enjoyment of this increased leisure time. Furthermore, optimists foresee a time when opinion polling in the home will bring about a higher level of democracy because citizens will take a greater interest in important local and national issues when their opinions are sought on a frequent and regular basis. Of course, these optimistic views don't go unchallenged.

The Pessimistic View

The pessimistic view of the future is that the effects of computer usage will not lead to greater freedom and individuality. On the contrary, pessimists can examine many of the same applications as optimists and come to the opposite conclusion that computer usage will:

▌ Dominate our lives as a society and as individuals.

▌ Sweep us along in a tide over which we—the harassed and exposed victims of a depersonalized and dehumanized process that places greater value on efficiency than on the more noble qualities of life— shall have little control.

Pessimists do agree with optimists, however, that computer-assisted manufacturing techniques will result in enormous gains in productivity. But the pessimists argue that when humans must compete with robots the humans will lose—they'll lose their jobs, they'll lose their security, and they'll lose their personal dignity. The pessimists look at the possibility of opinion polling in the home with alarm. What's to prevent the system from monitoring the individual? How do people know that the information they reveal about themselves in responding to questions is kept private? Furthermore, is it really a good idea, the pessimists ask, to have instant polls of public opinion on controversial issues? Many times in our past history, they point out, sober minority opinion has been found to be preferable to the "lynch mob" mentality of the majority. Finally, pessimists can also see dangers in educational applications. For example, research has been conducted on the feasibility of installing voice-print analyzers into future computerized teaching systems. These analyzers would be able to determine the student's identity and also his or her mental stability and emotional state. Optimists say that this voice analysis will enable the system to determine if a student is unhappy, angry, nervous, or cheerful so that a teaching program may be selected automatically to respond in a more personal way to the student's mood. But pessimists are convinced that such monitoring of individuals, with the concomitant danger to privacy, is truly an Orwellian prophecy come true.

A Final Note

Is it possible in this last section to draw any conclusions from the many different viewpoints that have so often been presented in the pages of this social impact module? Perhaps. We can conclude, for example, that there are at least three different contemporary views of computers and technological change:

1. *Computers and technology are an unblemished blessing.* This uncritical, optimistic view holds that technology is the source of all progress for the individual and society, that social problems will inevitably be solved through the application of technology, and that every new technological possibility will automatically be beneficial.

2. *Computers and technology are an unbridled curse.* This pessimistic view holds that technology increases unemployment, leads to depersonalization and bewilderment, threatens an individual's right to dignity and privacy, and threatens to pollute and/or blow up the world.

3. *Computers and technology are undeserving of special attention.* This unconcerned view holds that technology has been with us forever, and we are now better educated and more able than ever before to adapt to the new ideas and changes which it has brought and will bring.

Each of these views is deficient, although each probably contains an element of truth. The optimists are correct when they conclude that new technology often creates new opportunities for society. The pessimists are correct when they conclude that new problems are often created by new tools. And the unconcerned are correct when they conclude that social institutions (e.g., schools) can, and often do, play an important role in tempering the effects of technology.

No one is sure about the future effects on employment of technology advances. Computers have caused displacement. But has the development of the computer caused a larger number of people to be unemployed than would otherwise have been the case? In other words, have computers reduced the total number of jobs available in the total labor market? Professor Yale Brozen, University of Chicago economist, expressed the views of many authorities a few years ago when he wrote:[1]

> The reigning economic myth is that automation causes unemployment. It has only a slight element of truth—just enough to make the proposition plausible. Automation does cause displacement. A few become unemployed because of it. However, it does not create unemployment in the sense that a larger number are unemployed than would have been if no automation had occurred. . . . Many persons point to specific persons unemployed as a result of automation. What they fail to do is point to the unemployed who found jobs because of automation or to those who would have joined the jobless if new technology had not appeared.

[1]Yale Brozen, "Putting Economics and Automation in Perspective," reprinted from *Automation* (now *Production Engineering*), April 1964, p. 30.

CIRCUITS BRED LIKE CATTLE?

By the end of this century, computer circuitry may be grown and bred like Hereford cattle or American Beauty roses.

Computer technology is helping to establish genetic engineering as an industry, which may in turn allow computer manufacturers to fashion processors from organic material. So said Sperry Univac staff futurist Earl Joseph at the Data Processing Management Association's (DPMA) annual convention.

According to Joseph, scientists have begun devising methods to express in molecules of deoxyribonucleic acid (DNA) the information presently storable in bits that comprise semiconductor chips. In animals, DNA is known to direct the process by which cells replicate, ultimately determining the composition of living tissue.

If this line of research delivers a good harvest, the chip makers of Silicon Valley will go the way of most village blacksmiths unless they join or emulate the recombinant DNA laboratories presently concentrated near Boston's Charles River.

Genetic scientists have turned into genetic engineers at Harvard University and MIT, Joseph told a DPMA session concerned with artificial intelligence (AI). The fledgling industry of genetic engineering—which promises to allow fast breeding of animals and plants, as well as organic substances with medicinal properties—may spring up as large as the computer industry in the next decade or two, he asserted.

"Recombinant DNA" is a phrase that indicates what generic engineering comes down to: deliberate recombination of DNA molecules. The ob-

jective might be control over the gender of a human fetus, the meatiness of a prospective steer, the nutritional value of a wheat sheaf or the composition of a substance believed capable of thwarting disease.

According to Joseph, recombinant DNA techniques may allow computer manufacturers to turn out computer components with unprecedented power in much shorter time frames and with less risk of production flaws. Computer technology, for its part, allows genetic engineers to estimate what may happen when they start growing something.

—Brad Schultz, "Circuits Bred Like Cattle?" *Computerworld,* Nov. 9, 1981, p. 25. Copyright 1981 by CW Communications, Inc., Framingham, Mass.

A majority of economists today probably believe that (1) displacement must not be prevented, and (2) unemployment is best avoided by high levels of capital investment, unhampered mobility of capital and labor, and a continuing high level of technological progress. Since other nations are strongly committed to the concept of factory automation and the goal of higher productivity, our alternative to technological progress is apt to be economic stagnation and a declining standard of living.

Pessimists have definitely pointed out influences and possibilities that the concerned citizen should keep in mind. Many pessimists *don't* disagree with the optimistic position that computer technology *could* increase freedom, individuality, social justice, and well-being. But the pessimists doubt that the effort to increase social awareness and give adequate attention to necessary safeguards will be made.

The predictions of optimists or pessimists will become facts or fables if people make them so. We cannot know what people will do in the future. They *could* achieve the optimistic vision. But if in using computers they choose procedures that are impersonal and coldly efficient, they should not be surprised if the results are inhumane and inflexible. Thus, in the years ahead, it will be up to concerned and informed citizens who have an awareness of the potential dangers to see that the optimistic view prevails. Of course, developing such citizens has been a primary purpose of *Computers Today*.

Feedback and Review 21-1

In spite of the profound warning contained in an old proverb—"Prediction is difficult, particularly when it pertains to the future"—we've attempted in this final chapter to briefly summarize some of the computer—and computer-related—developments that you may expect in the next few years. Topics relating to applications, hardware/software, systems, and social impact have all been considered. These topics, of course, represent the main themes of *Computers Today*.

Charles McCabe of the San Francisco *Chronicle* has noted that "Any clod can have the facts, but having opinions is an art." Since this chapter deals primarily with opinions rather than certain facts, there are no objective questions for you to answer here. After all, is the statement "Josephson junction technology will be a regular feature of mainframes in 1990" true or false?

1. Dramatic developments are expected in the next few years in computer hardware. Some of the likely changes have been outlined in this chapter. For example, it's expected that central processors will become much smaller, faster, and cheaper; the number of online terminals sold each year will have doubled by 1988; and microprograms will be used extensively to permit the substitution of hardware for expensive software. Distributed processing networks using intelligent terminals and other small processors will gain rapidly in popularity. And millions of personal-sized microcomputers will be sold this decade.

2. In the software area, new conversational languages and data base management software will receive greater emphasis. Much of the new software will be developed using structured programming concepts. And the sale of packaged software will grow at a rapid rate.

3. Future information systems will be quicker responding and broader in scope than the average installation in operation today. Data communications services will have to be expanded to handle the rapid increase in data transmission. A network of distributed processors and a broader data base approach will be frequently used to respond to the needs of organizations and decision makers.

4. The future uses of computers are viewed by some people with optimism, while others believe that computers and technology are likely to be the curse of humanity. Which view—optimism or pessimism—will prevail? No one knows. Predictions of each group will become facts or fables only if people make them so. An enlightened citizenry, aware of the dangers, can help bring about the optimistic version.

Looking Back

KEY TERMS AND CONCEPTS

Most of the terms and concepts presented in Chapter 21 have appeared earlier. You can refer to the glossary and index at the end of the book for the definitions of unfamiliar terms.

TOPICS FOR REVIEW AND DISCUSSION

1. Discuss the changes that may be expected in the next decade in I/O equipment.

2. What changes may be expected in future central processors?

3. How will future hardware developments support (*a*) distributed processing networks? (*b*) Quick-response systems? And (*c*) data base systems?

4. Discuss how microprograms may be used in the future.

5. What changes may be expected in software in the next decade?

6. "We are now in a transition between an old industrial society and a new information/communications society." Discuss this statement.

7. (*a*) Are you an optimist or a pessimist about the future impact of computer systems on people? (*b*) Defend your answer.

What's Past Is Prologue
A Glimpse into the Future

In walking the thin line between innovation and hubris, I will man overstep his bounds in an attempt to create a machine too like the human brain? Will we try to manufacture an amoeba, or an "emotional" robot or an android superior to us in every way? And will we succeed?

Such questions plague the minds of those who perhaps know "too much and yet not enough," according to the scientists. "There's nothing in principle that I would seriously believe we can't do," said Roger Schank, director of Yale University's Artificial Intelligence Laboratory.

"The only one is this emotions issue," he noted, explaining, "We probably won't be able to give these things emotions, though we'll be able to have them act as if they have emotions."

Now the question is, do we want something around "acting as if" it has emotions? Isn't that the worst kind of chicanery? Or would it be a real comfort to the growing numbers of people who will spend their days working with machines? Would it break up the tedium or would it be an insult to human intelligence?

Humans being what they are, the answers to such queries undoubtedly will depend on the human and machine involved in any one situation. In any event, it would be wise to examine just how far we've gone in developing artificial intelligence and what we may expect in the future.

Artificial intelligence (AI) is an examination of the way humans perceive and assimilate data, reason abstractly, adapt and communicate in an effort to produce such behavior in computers. Although the formal discipline is a new one, questions regarding the nature of intelligence were being asked 50 years ago by such computing pioneers as Alan Turing, Norbert Wiener and John Von Neumann.

As of now, the useful development of AI centers almost exclusively around computer-controlled industrial robots, and the acknowledged worldwide leader in the field is Japan.

Typical of the Japanese robotic environment is an engine factory in a suburb north of Tokyo that employs a small crew of human workers during the day, at the end of which robots take over the work and toil tirelessly throughout the night under the supervision of a lone human overseer. . . .

The Japanese reportedly are also developing a new generation of robots expected to be able to handle objects with great precision. Nippon Electric has an in-house robot named Arms-D, said to operate at micrometer-level tolerances.

Nippon Electric claims that the Arms-D technology could ultimately cut the electronics factory work force in half, because it would be more economical to produce many kinds of products in small amounts. Arms-D reportedly will be commercially available in several years.

In the U.S., car and farm- and truck-equipment manufacturers have pushed hard in the last year to make some progress in robotics. Rising labor costs and foreign competition convinced these manufacturers to pour millions into retooling factories and installing robots on assembly lines for welding and parts selection.

"A robot can perform the functions of two people," according to Mark Cocroft of General Motors Corp., which expects to have 14,000 to 15,000 robots by 1990. GM's current robot population, including those on order, stands at 1,000.

Chrysler Corp. spent $75 million retooling for robots in its K-Car plants last summer, and now has about 220 robots in three plants. Ford Motor Co., now with 246 robots, expects to double that population by 1984. Ford and GM both use robots for numerically controlled painting projects, as well as for emission checking and the thankless tasks of loading/unloading and stacking/unstacking goods and pallets.

At the Springfield, Ill., body plant of International Harvester, 52 robots spotweld tractors and truck bodies. Two robots perform heavy press loading at the firm's Louisville, Ky., plant and in Cincinnati, axles are forged by robots.

While microprocessors control smaller robotic movements, most of the robots used by the auto and farm equipment manufacturers are run by minicomputers and even mainframes. John Deere uses a Digital Equipment Corp. PDP-11/44 and an IBM 370 for nearly all its factory operations, including bookkeeping and payroll.

A significant breakthrough in robotics recently came from Machine Intelligence Corp. (MIC) in a development that promises to revolutionize the manufacturing process. The breakthrough is a first step toward the solution of what AI researchers call "the vision problem."

After years of research at such academic institutions as Stanford University, Carnegie Mellon Institute and SRI International, a nonprofit research institute, MIC has made commercially available a so-called "hand-eye system," allowing robots to "see" and differentiate objects from one another.

The vision system looks at black-and-white images on a high-contrast scene. By analyzing them in two dimensions, the system can reportedly identify and sort objects of mixed types. The system is said to be usable for materials handling as well as assembly tasks.

Teaching the system, which is controlled by a DEC LSI-11, is simple. "You show it that this is a widget and this is a gadget," explained Earl Sacerdoti, MIC's director of research. "You show it to it five or six times in different positions with different fields of view and then it 'knows' it.

"The underlying techniques that it uses to do object recognition," he explained, "are very standard artificial intelligence pattern recognition techniques."

Whatever the uses or users, the benefits of robotics are uniform and clear: Improved quality, efficiency, precision and consistency are cited again and again by those who have taken the plunge.

That, of course, is the view from the top of the corporate ladder. What about the thousands of workers whose jobs will necessarily be eliminated by robots? GM's plans to acquire as many as 15,000 robots by 1990 will eliminate an estimated 28,000 to 30,000 jobs now performed by humans.

The issue has not been totally ignored, according to GM's Cocroft, who predicted that attrition would take care of some of the job loss, while some workers will be retrained to perform robot and computer maintenance.

No one can promise that displaced workers will be taken care of—one way or another—but history has shown that a new technology somehow eventually manages to blend into the fabric of existence, resulting in irrevocable changes, both good and bad, that are impossible to stop. The attempt would be foolhardy.

Of no consolation at all to victims of technological progress will be the fact the machines over which they watch, or which have replaced them, are actually extremely stupid. AI researchers and potential users now realize that it is not necessary to have human-level intelligence in a machine to create a useful product.

However, at least that knowledge may help dispel the image of the superior robot in human form, ready to control the controller and perhaps even the entire world. As Sacerdoti is fond of telling his lecture audiences, "Look—computers are really stupid. If we can make a computer as smart as a chicken, it will be much more useful than what we have today."

—Marguerite Zientara, "What's Past Is Prologue: A Glimpse into the Future," *Computerworld*, Nov. 30, 1981, pp. 31ff. Copyright 1981 by CW Communications, Inc., Framingham, Mass.

The communication of facts and ideas in any field is dependent on a mutual understanding of the words used. The purpose of this section, then, is to present definitions for some of the terms that are often used in the field of computers and data processing.

access To locate the desired data. See *direct-access, random access, remote-access, serial-access.*

access time The elapsed time between the instant when data are called for from a storage device and the instant when the delivery operation is completed.

accumulator A register or storage location that forms the result of an arithmetic or logic operation.

ACM Acronym for Association for Computing Machinery, a professional group dedicated to advancing the design, development, and application of information processing.

acoustic coupler A type of modem which permits data communication over regular telephone lines by means of sound signals.

acronym A word formed from the first letter(s) of the words contained in a phrase or name.

Ada A high-level programming language developed by the Department of Defense for use in military systems.

address An identification (e.g., a label, name, or number) that designates a particular location in storage or any other data destination or source.

ADP Automatic Data Processing.

ALGOL (ALGOrithmic Language) An algebraic, high-level language similar to FORTRAN that is widely used in Europe.

algorithm A set of well-defined rules for solving a problem in a finite number of operations.

alphanumeric Pertaining to a character set that includes letters, digits, and, usually, other special punctuation character marks.

analog computer A device that operates on data in the form of continuously variable physical quantities.

analyst See *system analyst.*

annotation symbol A symbol used to add messages or notes to a flowchart.

ANSI (American National Standards Institute) An organization that develops and approves standards in many fields.

APL (A Programming Language) A mathematically oriented high-level language frequently used in timesharing.

application program Software designed for a specific purpose (such as accounts receivable, billing, or inventory control).

architecture The organization and interconnection of computer system components.

arithmetic-logic unit The part of a computing system containing the circuitry that does the adding, subtracting, multiplying, dividing, and comparing.

artificial intelligence (AI) A computer science branch that's involved with using computers to solve problems that appear to require human imagination or intelligence.

ASCII (American National Standard Code for Information Interchange) A standard code used to exchange information among data processing and communications systems.

assembler program A computer program that takes nonmachine-language instructions prepared by a programmer and converts them into a form that may be used by the computer.

assembly language A means of communicating with a computer at a low level. This language lies between high-level languages (such as BASIC and COBOL) and machine language (the 1s and 0s the computer understands).

automated office A general term that refers to the merger of computers, office electronic devices, and telecommunications technology in an office environment.

auxiliary storage A storage that supplements the primary internal storage of a computer. Often referred to as *secondary storage.*

back-end processor A computer that serves as an interface between a larger CPU and data bases stored on direct-access storage devices.

background processing The automatic execution of lower-priority (background) computer programs during periods when the system resources are not required to process higher-priority (foreground) programs.

backup Alternate programs or equipment used in case the original is incapacitated.

BASIC (Beginners All-Purpose Symbolic Instruction Code) A high-level interactive programming language frequently used with personal computers and in timesharing environments.

batch processing A technique in which a number of similar items or transactions to be processed are grouped (batched) and processed in a designated sequence during a machine run. Often referred to as *sequential processing.*

baud A unit for measuring data transmission speed.

BCD (Binary-Coded Decimal) A method of representing the decimal digits zero through nine by a pattern of binary ones and zeros (e.g., the decimal number 25 is represented by 0010 0101 in 8-4-2-1 BCD notation).

binary digit Either of the characters 0 or 1. Abbreviated "bit."

binary number system A number system with a base or radix of two.

bit See *binary digit.*

block Related records, characters, or digits that are grouped and handled as a unit during input and output. A section of program coding treated as a unit.

branch An instruction that transfers program control to one or more possible paths.

broadband channels Communications channels such as those made possible by the use of laser beams and microwaves that can transmit data at high speed.

buffer A storage device used to compensate for the difference in rates of flow of data from one device to another—e.g., from an I/O device to the CPU.

bus Circuits that provide a communication path between two or more devices, such as between a CPU, storage, and peripherals.

byte A group of adjacent bits, usually eight, operated on as a unit.

cache A very high speed storage device.

CAD/CAM (Computer-Aided Design/ Computer-Aided Manufacturing) A general term applied to the efforts being made to automate design and manufacturing operations.

CAI (Computer-Assisted Instruction) A general term that refers to a learning situation in which the student interacts with (and is guided by) a computer through a course of study aimed at achieving certain instructional goals.

call A transfer of program control to a subroutine.

canned programs Programs prepared by an outside supplier and provided to a user in a machine-readable form.

cathode ray tube (CRT) An electronic tube with a screen upon which information may be displayed.

central processing unit (CPU) The component of a computer system with the circuitry to control the interpretation and execution of instructions. The CPU includes primary storage, arithmetic-logic, and control sections.

channel (1) A path for carrying signals between a source and a destination. (2) A track on a magnetic tape or a band on a magnetic drum.

character string A string of alphanumeric characters.

chip A thin wafer of silicon on which integrated electronic components are deposited.

clock A device that generates the periodic signals used to control the timing of all CPU operations.

COBOL (COmmon Business-Oriented Language) A high-level language developed for business data processing applications.

code A set of rules outlining the way in which data may be represented; also, rules used to convert data from one representation to another. To write a program or routine.

collate To combine items from two or more sequenced files into a single one.

COM (Computer Output Microfilm) A technology that permits the output information produced by computers to be stored on microfilm.

communications channel A medium for transferring data from one location to another.

compiler A computer program that produces a machine-language program from a source program that's usually written in a high-level language by a programmer. The compiler is capable of replacing single source program statements with a series of machine-language instructions or with a subroutine.

computer An electronic symbol manipulating system that's designed and organized to automatically accept and store input data, process them, and produce output results under the direction of a detailed step-by-step stored program of instructions.

computer network A processing complex consisting of two or more interconnected computers.

computer operator One whose duties include setting up the processor and peripheral equipment, starting the program run, checking on processor operation, and unloading equipment at the end of a run.

conditional transfer An instruction that may cause a departure from the sequence of instructions being followed, depending upon the result of an operation, the contents of a register, or the setting of an indicator.

connector symbol Used in a flowchart to represent a junction in a flow line, this symbol is often used to transfer flow between pages of a lengthy chart.

console The part of a computer system that enables human operators to communicate with the computer.

constant A value that doesn't change during program execution.

control program Generally part of an operating system, this program helps control the operations and management of a computer system.

control unit The section of the CPU that selects, interprets, and sees to the execution of program instructions.

counter A device (e.g., a register) used to represent the number of occurrences of an event.

CPU See *central processing unit.*

crash A hardware or software failure that leads to an abnormal cessation of processing.

CRT See *cathode ray tube.*

cybernetics The branch of learning which seeks to integrate the theories and studies of communication and control in machines and living organisms.

cylinder All tracks on magnetic disks that are accessible by a single movement of the access mechanism.

DASD Acronym for Direct-Access Storage Device.

data Facts; the raw material of information.

data bank See *data base.*

data base A stored collection of the libraries of data that are needed by organizations and individuals to meet their information processing and retrieval requirements.

data base administrator The one responsible for defining, updating, and controlling access to a data base.

data base management system (DBMS) The comprehensive software system that builds, maintains, and provides access to a data base.

data communications The means and methods whereby data are transferred between processing sites.

data entry operator One who transcribes

data into a form suitable for computer processing.

data processing One or more operations performed on data to achieve a desired objective.

debug To detect, locate, and remove errors in programs and/or malfunctions in equipment.

decision symbol This diamond-shaped symbol is used in flowcharts to indicate a choice or branch in the processing path.

diagnostics Error messages printed by a computer to indicate system problems and improper program instructions.

digital computer A device that manipulates discrete data and performs arithmetic and logic operations on these data. Contrast with analog computer.

disk A revolving platter upon which data and programs are stored.

disk pack A removable direct-access storage medium containing multiple magnetic disks mounted vertically on a single shaft.

diskette A floppy disk. A low-cost magnetic medium used for I/O and secondary storage purposes.

direct-access Pertaining to storage devices where the time required to retrieve data is independent of the physical location of the data.

distributed data processing (DDP) A general term describing the processing of a logically related set of information processing functions through the use of multiple, geographically separated, computing and communications devices.

documentation The preparation of documents, during system analysis and subsequent programming, that describe such things as the system, the programs prepared, and the changes made at later dates.

downtime The length of time a computer system is inoperative due to a malfunction.

EBCDIC (Extended Binary Coded Decimal Interchange Code) An 8-bit code used to represent data in modern computers.

edit To correct, rearrange, and validate input data. To modify the form of output information by inserting blank spaces, special characters where needed, etc.

editor A program used to interactively review and alter text materials and other program instructions.

EDP Acronym for Electronic Data Processing.

electronic funds transfer (EFT) A general term referring to a cashless approach used to pay for goods and services. Electronic signals between computers are often used to adjust the accounts of the parties involved in a transaction.

electronic mail A general term to describe the transmission of messages by the use of computing systems and telecommunications facilities.

emulator A stored logic device or program that permits one computer to execute the machine-language instructions of another computer of different design.

executive routine A master program in an operating system that controls the execution of other programs. Often referred to as the executive, monitor, or supervisor.

facsimile system A system used to transmit pictures, text, maps, etc., between geographically separated points. An image is scanned at a transmitting point and duplicated at a receiving point.

fiber optic cable A data transmission medium made of tiny threads of glass or plastic that is able to transmit huge amounts of information at the speed of light.

field A group of related characters treated as a unit—e.g., a group of adjacent card columns used to represent an hourly wage rate. An item in a record.

file A collection of related records treated as a unit.

file processing The updating of master files to reflect the effects of current transactions.

floppy disk See *diskette*.

flowchart A diagram that uses symbols and interconnecting lines to show (1) a system of processing to achieve objectives (system flowchart), or (2) the logic and sequence of specific program operations (program flowchart).

FORTRAN (FORmula TRANslator) A high-level language used to perform mathematical computations.

front-end processor A CPU programmed to function as an interface between a larger CPU and assorted peripheral devices.

generator A computer program that constructs other programs to perform a particular type of operation—e.g., a report program generator.

graphic display A visual device that is used to project graphic images.

hard copy Printed or filmed output in humanly readable form.

hardware Physical equipment such as electronic, magnetic, and mechanical devices. Contrast with *software*.

heuristic A problem-solving method in which solutions are discovered by evaluating the progress made toward the end result. A directed trial-and-error approach. Contrast with *algorithm*.

HIPO charts (Hierarchy plus Input-Process-Output charts) Charts used in the analysis, design, and programming of computer applications.

high-level language A programming language oriented toward the problem to be solved or the procedures to be used. Instructions are given to a computer by using convenient letters, symbols, or English-like text, rather than by using the 1s and 0s code that the computer understands.

Hollerith Code A particular type of code used to represent alphanumeric data on 80-column punched cards.

host computer A main control computer in a network of distributed processors and terminals.

hybrid computer A data processing device using both analog and discrete data representation.

information Meaning assigned to data by humans.

information retrieval The methods used to recover specific information from stored data.

input/output (I/O) Pertaining to the techniques, media, and devices used to achieve human/machine communication.

input/output symbol A figure in the shape of a parallelogram that's used to indicate both input and output operations in a flowchart.

instruction A set of characters used to direct a data processing system in the performance of an operation—i.e., an operation is signaled and the values or locations of the instruction operands are specified.

intelligent terminal A terminal with a built-in CPU that can be programmed to perform specific functions such as editing data, controlling other terminals, etc.

interactive system One that permits direct communication and dialog between system users and the operating program in the CPU.

interface A shared boundary—e.g., the boundary between two systems or devices.

internal storage The addressable storage in a digital computer directly under the control of the CPU.

interpreter A computer program that translates each source language statement into a sequence of machine instructions and then executes these machine instructions before translating the next source language statement. A device that prints on a punched card the data already punched in the card.

I/O See *input/output*.

ISAM (Index Sequential Access Method) A method whereby records organized in a sequential order can be referenced directly through the use of an index based on some key or characteristic.

item A group of related characters treated as a unit. (A record is a group of related items, and a file is a group of related records.)

job A collection of specific tasks constituting a unit of work for a computer.

job-control language (JCL) A language that permits communication between programmers and an operating system. A job-control program written in this language can be translated into requests for action that can be executed by the computer.

jump A departure from sequence in executing instructions in a computer. See *conditional transfer*.

K An abbreviation for a value equal to 2^{10} or 1,024.

key A unique item that's used to identify a record.

label One or more characters used to identify a program statement or a data item.

language A set of rules and conventions used to convey information.

library routine A tested routine maintained in a library of programs.

light pen An electrical device that permits people to provide input to computers by writing or sketching on the screen of a cathode ray tube.

logic diagram See *flowchart*.

LSI (Large Scale Integration) The process of integrating a large number of electronic circuits on a single small chip of silicon or other material.

machine language A language used directly by a computer.

macro instruction A source language instruction that's equivalent to a specified number of machine-language instructions.

magnetic ink character recognition (MICR) The recognition of characters printed with a special magnetic ink by machines.

magnetic storage Utilizing the magnetic properties of materials to store data on such devices and media as disks, drums, cards, cores, tapes, chips, and films.

main control module The highest level in a hierarchy of program modules. This module controls others below it.

maintenance programming The act of changing and modifying existing programs to meet changing conditions.

management information system (MIS) A computer-based information system designed to supply organizational managers with the necessary information needed to plan, organize, staff, direct, and control the operations of the organization.

master file A file containing relatively permanent data. This file is often updated by records in a transaction file.

memory Same as *storage*.

message switcher A communications processor that receives messages and forwards them to appropriate locations.

MICR See *magnetic ink character recognition*.

microcomputer The smallest category of computer, consisting of a microprocessor and associated storage and input/output elements.

microprocessor The basic arithmetic, logic, and storage elements required for processing (generally on one or a few integrated circuit chips).

microprogram A sequence of elementary instructions that is translated by a micrologic subsystem residing in the CPU.

microsecond One-millionth of a second.

millisecond One-thousandth of a second.

minicomputer A relatively fast but small and inexpensive computer with somewhat limited input/output capabilities.

MIS See *management information system*.

mnemonic Pertaining to a technique used to aid human memory.

modem A device that modulates and demodulates signals transmitted over voice-grade communication facilities.

modular approach Dividing a project into segments and smaller units in order to simplify analysis, design, and programming efforts.

monitor routine See *executive routine*.

multiplex To simultaneously transmit messages over a single channel or other communications facility.

multiprocessing The simultaneous execution of two or more sequences of instructions by a single computer network.

multiprocessor A computer network consisting of two or more central processors under a common control.

multiprogramming The simultaneous handling of multiple independent programs by interleaving or overlapping their execution.

nanosecond One-billionth of a second.

narrow bandwidth channels Communications channels that can only transmit data at slow speeds—e.g., telegraph channels.

natural language A human language such as English, French, German, etc.

network An interconnection of computer systems and/or peripheral devices at dispersed locations that exchange data as necessary to perform the functions of the network.

node An end point of a branch in a network, or a common junction of two or more network branches.

nonvolatile storage A storage medium that retains its contents in the absence of power.

object language The output of a translation process. Contrast with source language.

object program A fully compiled or assembled program that's ready to be loaded into the computer. Contrast with source program.

OCR (Optical Character Recognition) The recognition of printed characters through the use of light-sensitive optical machines.

octal Pertaining to a number system with a base of eight.

offline A term describing persons, equipment, or devices not in direct communication with the CPU.

online A term describing persons, equipment, or devices that are in direct communication with the CPU.

operand The data unit or equipment item that's operated upon. An operand is usually identified by an address in an instruction.

operating system An organized collection of software that controls the overall operations of a computer.

operation code The instruction code used to specify the operations a computer is to perform.

overlapped processing An approach that permits the computer to work on several programs instead of one.

parity check A method of checking the accuracy of binary data after those data have been transferred to or from storage. The number of 1 bits in a binary character is controlled by the addition or deletion of a parity bit.

Pascal A popular high-level programming language that facilitates the use of structured programming techniques.

patch The modification of a program in an expedient way.

peripherals The input/output devices and auxiliary storage units of a computer system.

picosecond One-thousandth of a nanosecond.

PL/I (Programming Language I) A high-level language designed to process both scientific and file processing applications.

plotter A device that converts computer output into a graphic, hard-copy form.

pointer A data item in one record that contains the location address of another logically related record.

point-of-sale (POS) terminal An I/O device capable of: (1) immediately updating sales and inventory records at a central CPU, and (2) producing a printed sales transaction receipt.

primary storage section Also known as *internal storage* and *main memory,* this section of the CPU holds program instructions, input data, intermediate results, and the output information produced during processing.

printer A device used to produce humanly readable computer output. A wide range of impact and nonimpact printers are currently available.

processing symbol A rectangular figure used in flowcharts to indicate a processing operation—e.g., a calculation.

program (1) A plan to achieve a problem solution; (2) to design, write, and test one or more routines; (3) a set of sequenced instructions to cause a computer to perform particular operations.

program flowchart See *flowchart.*

program library A collection of programs and routines.

programmer One who designs, writes, tests, and maintains computer programs.

programming language A language used to express programs.

PROM (Programmable Read-Only Memory) A read-only storage device that can be programmed after manufacture by external equipment. PROMs are usually integrated circuit chips.

pseudocode A programming analysis tool. Counterfeit and abbreviated versions of actual computer instructions that are written in ordinary natural language.

radix The base number in a number system—e.g., the radix in the decimal system is 10. Synonymous with base.

RAM (Random-Access Memory) A storage device structured so that the time required to retrieve data is not significantly affected by the physical location of the data.

random access See *direct-access.*

real time Descriptive of online computer processing systems which receive and process data quickly enough to produce output to control, direct, or affect the outcome of an ongoing activity or process.

record A collection of related items of data treated as a unit.

register A device capable of storing a specific amount of data.

relational symbols Symbols such as > ("greater than"), < ("less than"), or = ("equal to") that are used to compare two values in a conditional branching situation.

remote access Relating to the communication with a computer facility by a station (or stations) that is distant from the computer.

report program generator (RPG) Software designed to construct programs that perform predictable report-writing operations.

ROM (Read-Only Memory) Generally a solid-state storage chip that's programmed at the time of its manufacture and may not be reprogrammed by the computer user.

routine An ordered set of general-use instructions. See *program.*

run time The time required to complete a single, continuous, execution of an object program.

scratchpad storage A memory space used for the temporary storage of data. Typically, scratchpad memories are high-speed integrated circuits. See *cache.*

semiconductor storage A memory device whose storage elements are formed as solid-state electronic components on an integrated circuit chip.

sequential processing See *batch processing.*

serial access Descriptive of a storage device or medium where there is a sequential relationship between access time and data location in storage—i.e., the access time is dependent upon the location of the data. Contrast with *direct access* and *random access.*

simulation To represent and analyze properties or behavior of a physical or hypothetical system by the behavior of a system model. (This model is often manipulated by means of computer operations.)

software A set of programs, documents, procedures, and routines associated with the operation of a computer system. Contrast with *hardware.*

solid state Descriptive of electronic components whose operation depends on the control of electric or magnetic phenomena in solids, such as transistors and diodes.

sort   To arrange data into a predetermined sequence.

source language   The language that is an input for statement translation.

source program   A computer program written in a source language such as BASIC, FORTRAN, COBOL, etc.

statement   In programming, an expression or generalized instruction in a source language.

storage   Descriptive of a device or medium that can accept data, hold them, and deliver them on demand at a later time. Synonymous with *memory*.

structured programming   An approach or discipline used in the design and coding of computer programs. The approach generally assumes the disciplined use of a few basic coding structures and the use of top-down concepts to decompose main functions into lower-level components for modular coding purposes.

supercomputer   Computer systems characterized by their very large size and very high processing speeds. Generally used for complex scientific applications.

supervisor   See *executive routine*.

system   (1) A grouping of integrated methods and procedures united to form an organized entity; (2) an organized grouping of people, methods, machines, and materials collected together to accomplish a set of specific objectives.

system analysis   A detailed step-by-step investigation of related procedures to see what must be done and the best way of doing it.

system analyst   One who studies the activities, methods, procedures, and techniques of organizational systems in order to determine what actions need to be taken and how these actions can best be accomplished.

system commands   The means by which programmers communicate with the operating system of the computer.

system design   The creation of alternative solutions to the problems uncovered in system analysis. The final design recommendation is based on cost effectiveness and other factors.

system flowchart   See *flowchart*.

systems programming   The development and maintainance of operating system software.

telecommunications   Transmission of data between computer systems and/or terminals in different locations.

terminal   A device that performs I/O operations in a computer system.

terminal symbol   An oval-shaped figure used in a flowchart to indicate starting and termination points.

throughput   The total amount of useful work performed by a computer system during a given time period.

timesharing   The use of specific hardware by a number of other devices, programs, or people simultaneously in such a way as to provide quick response to each of the users. The interleaved use of the time of a device.

top-down methodology   A disciplined approach to organizing complexity by identifying the top-level functions in a system and then decomposing these functions into a hierarchy of understandable lower-level modules.

unconditional transfer   An instruction that always causes a branch in program control away from the normal sequence of executing instructions.

UPC (Universal Product Code)   A machine-readable code of parallel bars used for labeling products found in supermarkets.

utility routine   Software used to perform some frequently required process in the operation of a computer system—e.g., sorting, merging, etc.

videotex systems   A general term used to describe personal computing/communications networks that permit interaction between people and stored data bases.

virtual storage   Descriptive of the capability to use online secondary storage devices and specialized software to divide programs into smaller segments for transmission to and from internal storage in order to significantly increase the effective size of the available internal storage.

visual display terminal   A device capable of displaying keyed input and CPU output on a cathode ray tube.

VLSI (Very Large Scale Integration)   The packing of hundreds of thousands of electronic components on a single semiconductor chip.

voice-grade channels   Medium-speed data transmission channels that use telephone communications facilities.

volatile storage   A storage medium that loses its contents in the event of a power interruption.

word   A group of bits or characters considered as an entity and capable of being stored in one storage location.

word length   The number of characters or bits in a word.

word processing   The use of computers to create, view, edit, store, retrieve, and print text material.

zone bits   Used in different combinations with numeric bits to represent alphanumeric characters.

Index

Job opportunities, computer-created, 92

Job satisfaction, computer-created, 93

Job shops, effects of computers on, 594

Josephson junction, 124
  future outlook for, 635

K (storage symbol), 123

Kemeny, John, 10, 371

Key-to-disk-to-tape systems, 160

Key-to-diskette data entry, 165

Keypunches, 155

Kilobytes, 197

Kurtz, Thomas, 371

Land-use models, effects of computers on, 607

Languages (see Programming languages)

Large-scale integration, 87

Lasers:
  data transmission with, 271
  future outlook for, 640
  recording systems using, 203
  storage using, 203
  transmission rate of, 269–270

Latency time (magnetic disks), 199

Law enforcement, effects of computers on, 608–609

Leased lines, 268

Legislative activities, effects of computers on, 606

Leibniz, Gottfried, 34

LET statements in BASIC, 403

LEXIS, 280

Librarian programs for operating systems, 453

Librarians for programming teams, 358

Library programs for operating systems, 453

Light pens, 175, 176

Limit checks in error detection, 150

Limitations of computers, 29–30

Line numbers for BASIC, 395

Line printers, 218

LISt Processing Language (LISP), 380

List structures for data basis, 506

Local networks, 274

Lockheed Information Systems, 280

Logic/comparison operations, 14
  applications of, 53–59

Logic patterns, summary of, 343–344

Logical errors, 383

Loop structures, 344

Loops (computer programs), 327

Lower-level managers, informational needs of, 519

Machine languages, 363

Machine-readable data, 571

Macro flowcharts, 322

Macro instructions, 365

Magnavision, 203

Magnetic bubble storage, 201–202

Magnetic core storage, 121–122

Magnetic direct-access storage systems, future outlook for, 632

Magnetic disks:
  accessing data on, 198–200
  advantages and disadvantages of, 200
  for direct-access storage, 194–200
  for sequential-access secondary storage, 192–194
  storing data on, process for, 196–198

Magnetic drums, 200

Magnetic ink character recognition (MICR), 166

Magnetic reader-sorter units, 166

Magnetic tape, 158–164
  data representation on, 160–162
  input using, advantages of, 163–164
    limitations of, 164

Magnetic tape (Cont.):
  for sequential-access secondary storage, 190, 192

Magnetic tape equipment, 163

Magnetic Tape Selectric Typewriters, 299–300

Mailing lists, preparation of, 44–45

Maiman, Theodore, 203

Main-control flowcharts, 322

Main memory section, 17

Mainframe computers, 26, 247, 250–254
  characteristics of, 254
  commercial models of, 251–253
  uses of, 250, 254

"Make or buy" decisions:
  computer programs for, 357
  for software, 389
  in system design, 477

Management information:
  concepts of, 518–522
  properties of, 519–521

Management of information, reasons for, 83

Management information systems, 517–547
  careers of directors of, 583–584
  development of, 521–522
  organization of, 533–534
  personal computers as a threat to, 546–547
  planning of, 523–528
  security of, 536–541

Managerial benefits from computers, 556–557

Managerial control, relation to management information systems, 535

Managerial planning, relation to management information systems, 525–528

Managers, informational needs of different levels of, 519

Manipulation of symbols, 11–15

Mark I computer, 36

Market forecasting, effects of computers on, 593–594